The Book of Welsh Pirates and Buccaneers

Terry Breverton

Wales Books
Glyndŵr Publishing
2003
ISBN 1-903529-093

Terry Breverton is a Fellow of the Chartered Institute of Marketing, and a Fellow of the Institute of Management Consultants. He studied in the universities of Manchester, Birmingham and Lancaster, has had a career in international management consultancy, and has been a board level director of multinational companies. Returning with his family to live in Wales, he is a Senior Lecturer in Marketing and International Business Management at UWIC Business School, Cardiff. He founded Wales Books (Glyndwr Publishing), to counter-balance existing material upon Wales, and to promote Welsh heritage and culture to the Welsh people and potential tourists. Wales Book's website, walesbooks.com   is developing a unique listing of Welsh societies across the globe; to encourage further research and publications upon 'forgotten' Welshmen such as Dr Richard Price and Owain Llawgoch. It is hoped that such work will also rehabilitate Iolo Morganwg in the eyes of academics and force them to reassess history from original sources, rather than from the opinion of their teachers' teachers.

Breverton has in the past published research papers upon multinational tax avoidance, children's books and is the author of the acclaimed 'An A-Z of Wales and the Welsh', 'The Secret Vale of Glamorgan', 'The Book of Welsh Saints', '100 Great Welsh Men' , 'The Path to Inexperience', '100 Great Welsh Women' and 'The Welsh Almanac.' This book has, like all other Wales Books publications, been priced to break even and to cover the costs of publishing more books upon Wales. Forthcoming publications are detailed in the back of this book. We welcome submissions of manuscripts, by which method we will soon be publishing a rational reassessment of Prince Madoc, a life of the great warrior Owain Llawgoch, Princesses of Wales and Glamorganshire Castles (Volume I of Castles of Wales).

Also by Terry Breverton:

An A-Z of Wales and the Welsh (publisher Christopher Davies 2000)
300pp ISBN 0 715407 341

The Secret Vale of Glamorgan (publisher Wales Books 2000)
228pp, illustrated 1 903529 00X

The Book of Welsh Saints (publisher Wales Books 2000)
614pp hardback, illustrated ISBN 1 903529 018

100 Great Welshmen (published Wales Books 2000)
366pp, illustrated ISBN 1 903529 034

100 Great Welsh Women (published Wales Books 2001)
304pp, illustrated ISBN 1 903529 042

'The Path to Inexperience' (published Wales Books 2002)
160pp, illustrated ISBN 1903529077

'The Welsh Almanac' (published Wales Books 2003)
320pp hardback, illustrated ISBN 1903529107

'Glamorgan Seascape Pathways' (published Wales Books 2002)
– 52 walks in the southern Vale of Glamorgan, ISBN 1903529115

Also published by Wales Books (Glyndŵr Publishing):

The Dragon Entertains - 100 Welsh Stars, by Alan Roderick 2000 220pp ISBN 1
903529 026

A Rhondda Boy, by Ivor Howells 144pp, illustrated, ISBN 1 903529050

David Thomas - From Wales to Pennsylvania, by Dr Peter Williams 2002
112pp illus. ISBN 1903529085

Glyn Dwr's War - The Campaigns of the Last Prince of Wales, by G.J. Brough 2002
240pp illus. ISBN 1903529069

For my late father-in-law
Captain John Alfred Lewis
The South American Saints Line

Copyright 2003 Terry Breverton

Published in 2003 by Wales Books (Glyndŵr Publishing),
Porth Glyndŵr, Sain Tathan, Bro Morgannwg CF62 4LW
www.walesbooks.com

A CIP catalogue record for this book is available from the British Library.

ISBN 1 903529 093

Printed and bound in Wales by
J&P Davison, 3 James Place,
Trefforest, Pontypridd

List of Contents

Introduction viii

Chapter I
PIRATE AND PRIVATEERING TERMS 1

Chapter II
WELSH PIRATES AND BUCCANEERS 13th - 18th centuries 90

13TH CENTURY
William Marsh fl. 1231-1242 90

FIFTEENTH CENTURY
Colyn Dolphyn fl. 1470 91

SIXTEENTH CENTURY
William Hughes fl. 1529 93
Thomas Carter fl. 1535 93
Walter Herbert fl. 1537 94
Captain Griffith fl. 1540 94
John Phillips fl. 1540 94
Captain Owen fl. 1540 95
Walter Vaughan of Dunraven fl. 1542 95
Sir John Wogan fl. 1542 - 1555 96
Michael James fl. 1546 96
Richard Vaughan fl. 1546 96
Morgan Matthew fl. 1548 96
Griffiths of Cefnamlwch fl. 1563 97
Welsh Buccaneers on the Pelican 1570-72 (1595) 97
John Salisbury fl. 1570-1591 100
The Legend of Captain Jones 101
Miles Phillips fl.1574-1582 101
Captain Henry Roberts fl. 1576-1595 105
David Gwynne fl. 1588 105
Welsh Buccaneers under Francis Drake 1585-1595 108
JOHN CALLICE f. 1571-1587 *The Most Dangerous Pyrate in the Realm* 109
Tom Clarke fl. 1577 - 1578 116
SIR JOHN PERROT 1550-1600 *The Son of Henry VIII* 117
John Wyn ap Hugh d. 1576 122
Pirs Griffith 1568-1628 122
William Vaughan fl. 1582 123
Thomas Beavin d. 1583 124
Sir Richard Bulkely fl. 1591 124
Captain William Myddleton c.1550 - c.1600 124
David Myddelton d. 1615 125
John Myddleton fl. 1563 - 1595 126

SEVENTEENTH CENTURY

Tomas Prys 1564-1634 … … … … … … … … … … … … … … … … … … 126
William Hughs fl. 1611 … … … … … … … … … … … … … … … … … … 128
John Norman fl. 1631 … … … … … … … … … … … … … … … … … … 128
Sir Sackville Trevor d.1634 … … … … … … … … … … … … … … … … 129
Admiral Sir Thomas Button d. 1634 … … … … … … … … … … … … … 129
Davy Jones fl. 1636 … … … … … … … … … … … … … … … … … … 130
Nicolas Hookes d. 1637 … … … … … … … … … … … … … … … … … 130
Admiral Sir Robert Mansell 1573-1653 … … … … … … … … … … … … 130
HENRY MAINWARING 1587-1653 *The Most Famous Sea-Rover of his Day* … … 132
Morris Willams fl. 1659-64 … … … … … … … … … … … … … … … … 135
Bledri Morgan fl. 1660 … … … … … … … … … … … … … … … … … 135
Lt-Colonel Edward Morgan d.1664 … … … … … … … … … … … … … 135
Lt-Colonel Thomas Morgan fl. 1665 - 1685 … … … … … … … … … … 136
William James fl. 1660-1663 … … … … … … … … … … … … … … … 136
Captain James … … … … … … … … … … … … … … … … … … … 137
Captain Lewis 1687 - 1726 … … … … … … … … … … … … … … … … 137
Captain John James fl. 1699 … … … … … … … … … … … … … … … 139
Captain Evan Jones fl. 1699 … … … … … … … … … … … … … … … 140

EIGHTEENTH CENTURY

Tom Collins fl. 1695 - 1715 … … … … … … … … … … … … … … … … 140
Samuel Hopkins d.1709 … … … … … … … … … … … … … … … … … 140
Henry Jennings fl. 1714 … … … … … … … … … … … … … … … … … 142
William Lewis d. 1718 … … … … … … … … … … … … … … … … … 143
James Williams d. 1725 … … … … … … … … … … … … … … … … … 144
Captain Robert Jenkins fl. 1731-1738 … … … … … … … … … … … … 145
Christopher Bassett d.1760 … … … … … … … … … … … … … … … 146
Lt. Paul Lewis fl. 1763 … … … … … … … … … … … … … … … … … 146
Thomas Knight fl.1783 … … … … … … … … … … … … … … … … … 147
O'Neill … 148

Chapter III
ADMIRAL SIR HENRY MORGAN … … … … … … … … … … … … … 149
'THE GREATEST OF ALL THE BRETHREN
OF THE COAST', 'THE SWORD OF ENGLAND' 1635-1688
Footnote on the Recovery of the Jamaica Merchant … … … … … … … … 193
Footnote on Captain Kidd, Henry Morgan and the … … … … … … … … 193
Oak Island Money Pit

Chapter IV
David Williams fl. 1698 - 1708 … … … … … … … … … … … … … … … 195

Chapter V
John Bowen d. 1704 … … … … … … … … … … … … … … … … … … 198
Note on Thomas Howard … … … … … … … … … … … … … … … … 201
Footnote on Captain Richard Bowen … … … … … … … … … … … … … 201

Chapter VI
Paulsgrave Williams and 'Black Sam' Bellamy fl. 1715 - 1717 … … … … … … 203
Postscript on the Maria Hallett Legend … … … … … … … … … … … … … 212

Chapter VII
HOWELL DAVIS 'THE CAVALIER PRINCE OF PYRATES' d.1719 … … … … 213
Book III of 'A New Account of Some Parts of Guinea … … … … … … … … … 227
and the Slave Trade' - Capt. William Snelgrave 1734
Footnote on Edward England … … … … … … … … … … … … … … … … 254
Footnote on John Taylor … … … … … … … … … … … … … … … … … 255
Footnote on Olivier Levasseur … … … … … … … … … … … … … … … 256
Seychelle News report of Levasseur's treasure … … … … … … … … … … 257
Treasure Islands of the Indian Ocean … … … … … … … … … … … … … 257

Chapter VIII
BLACK BART ROBERTS 'THE BLACK CAPTAIN',' … … … … … … … … … 261
THE MOST LETHAL PYRATE OF THEM ALL' 1682 - 1722
Footnote on Chaloner Ogle … … … … … … … … … … … … … … … … 315
Fotnote on Walter Kennedy … … … … … … … … … … … … … … … … 316
Footnote on Thomas Anstis … … … … … … … … … … … … … … … … 316
The Trial and Verdicts
The Kru Tribe
Black Bart, 'Boulevardier Bandit'

Chapter IX
John Phillips d. 1724 … … … … … … … … … … … … … … … … … … … 329

Chapter X
John Evans d. 1723 … … … … … … … … … … … … … … … … … … … 334

Chapter XI
WILLIAM WILLIAMS - LLEWELLIN PENROSE 1727 - 1791 … … … … … 336

APPENDICES
A. A Proclamation for the Suppressing of Pyrates … … … … … … … … … 340
B. The White Women of Lundy … … … … … … … … … … … … … … … 341
C. The Legend of Thomas Lacy and the Pirate … … … … … … … … … … 346
D. The Robert Edwards Heirs' Claim to Manhattan … … … … … … … … 348
E. Dick Hughes (from the Newgate Calendar) … … … … … … … … … … 352
F. William Davis, 'The Golden Farmer' (from the Newgate Calendar) … … … 353
G. Thomas Stradling, Alexander Selkirk and Robinson Crusoe … … … … … 356
Miles Phillips' deposition (7 chapters) … … … … … … … … … … … … 358

Booklist
Other Books from Glyndŵr Publishing, and Forthcoming … … … … … … … 380
Publications.

INTRODUCTION -
THE BOOK OF WELSH PIRATES

The genesis for this book came from a notice in a sea-life centre in Pembrokeshire. Above the children's stationary play-boat was a short notice about Black Bart, *'the most famous pirate in history'*. I had never heard of him, but research showed that he had been the most successful pirate on record, and he came from a little village in Wales. More information on *Black Bart* Roberts was accumulated for my recent books, *'The A-Z of Wales and the Welsh'* and *'100 Great Welshmen'*.

Visiting Tredegar House near Newport, the ancestral home of the Morgans, a few weeks later, I mused upon the fact that a relative of its former owners, Captain Henry Morgan, had been the most successful buccaneer in history. Thus two Welshmen were the foremost pirate and buccaneer respectively. Any other country would have theme parks and tourist destinations dedicated to them, but Wales seems to have swept its past into a Black Hole. Even Wales' Arthur, that most fabled legend in history, has been physically moved out of the country and publicised as being from other areas. A further lucky occurrence was that Hywel (Howell) Davis, also from *Black Bart's* Pembrokeshire, was the pirate captain who turned Roberts to piracy. Further research showed Davis to be perhaps the most cunning of all the sea-rovers, a duplicitous yet brave rogue, *'The Cavalier Prince of Pirates'*, whose story deserves a film by Spielberg. We can also add *'the most dangerous Pyrate in the realm'*, Tintern's John Callice of the 16th century, Henry VIII's son Sir John Perrot, and Sir Henry Mainwaring, the 17th century *'most famous sea-rover of his day'* to the list of great pirates and buccaneers who are hardly known to history.

While working on a book on Welsh saints in the so-called *Dark Ages*, I carried on with writing this book on pirates and buccaneers. Hardly anything is known of the *'Age of the Saints'* in Wales, when the Brythonic Welsh kept Christianity alight in pagan Europe. If tradition is correct, a Welsh woman, Elen, may have even converted Constantine and the Roman Empire to Christianity. The very first Bishop of Rome, Linus, had a Welsh mother. Also, Wales may have had the first university in Europe, not Bologna. And the fabled King Arthur was definitely associated with some of these early Celtic saints, in tales and traditions which predate the medieval romances. The Archbishop of Canterbury commented that *'The Book of Welsh Saints'*, detailing over 900 Welsh saints from the 1st century onwards, *'is a really extraordinary achievement: a compilation of tradition, topography and literary detective work that can have few rivals. I have enjoyed browsing it enormously.'* However, its tangled sources and complexities meant that I had to put this pirates volume in the background, while I then became engrossed with writing books on great Welsh women and men, and editing and publishing other books upon Welsh culture and heritage.

The differences between our Welsh *'Age of the Saints'* in Europe's Dark Ages, with its garbled genealogies and semi-mythical characters, could not contrast more with the *'Age of the Brethren of the Coast'*. One moves from a paucity of information, as much Welsh literature such as land deeds were deliberately destroyed by incoming armies and those who took possession of Welsh lands. (When one studies Wales, one really does learn that *'all property is theft'*.) However, for certain periods such as *'The Golden Age of Piracy'* in the early 18th century, there is almost too much information. Much documentation still exists in the form of court records, trial proceedings, shipping movements etc., and is corroborated. Esquemeling, a prime source, fought with the buccaneers under Admiral Morgan. Daniel Defoe, under the pseudonym Charles Johnson, talked to ex-pirates who knew Black Bart and Hywel Davis. Snelgrave and Atkins wrote at first-hand about the great days of piracy. Defoe's account of the Caribbean pirates is a brilliant evocation of the times as well as the facts. Another Welsh buccaneer, Llewellin (William) Williams, was captured by the Spanish, marooned, wrote America's first novel (*The Journal of Llewellin Penrose - Seaman*), and taught America's most famous artist, Benjamin West, to paint! His life is so fascinating that the author had to truncate his description in this book, to begin a book upon Williams.

Just as unknown saints and associations surfaced in one set of research, so did once-famous pirates for this book. An American website on Pirates and Pirate Ships states that *'in the 1700's about half of the pirates were of Welsh descent'*. This is an over-exaggeration, but certainly the rosters, of those where we know their origins, show a disproportionate amount of men from Wales and the West Country, the poorer regions of Britain, where the only escape was the sea. Another website makes an analysis of pirates as 35% English, 25% colonial Americans, 20% based out of the Caribbean, 10% Scottish, 7% Welsh, and 2-3% Spanish, French, Dutch or Danish.

This book is meant to be entertaining rather than academically turgid. These are fabulous stories which need to be researched further by experts. My small publishing company's mission is to publicise the Welsh and their achievements. It is independent and receives no external funding. For any mistakes of fact or fiction, I must apologise. Unlike many books published in Wales, our publications receive no subsidies. We cannot afford outside proof-readers, company cars, salesmen or colour illustrations. My particular books are written on a four-year-old computer shared with my wife and teenage children. They are proof-read several times by myself. They are then taken to a small family firm of Welsh printers in Trefforest to be typeset, then proof-read again because of the problems associated with using Windows documents in an Apple-based printing world. They are then bound in Ystradgynlais or Trefforest, and stored above my garage. The invoicing, administration, packaging and posting are all done by this author outside the hours of his full-time job as a business lecturer.

For books by other people, I proof-read and edit, and the same process is undergone. The whole cost is borne by a remortgage of my home, not by the taxpayer. For this reason, there are no extensive footnotes, references or indices to this book. The only criticism of the 606-page *'The Book of Welsh Saints'* came from an academic review bemoaning the lack of referencing and indexing. The book was sold at cost -price, and to fully reference and index it would have made the printing costs prohibitive and the book twice as long. It may have sold 30 copies to libraries, instead of 600 to people who wish to learn about Wales and its heritage. For this book on pirates to be 'perfect' , fully referenced and annotated and indexed, there would be the same problems as with the Welsh saints book. *The Book of Welsh Pirates and Buccaneers* has taken around six years to write, during which time the author has written seven other books and held down a full-time job in an unrelated

*The author at Black Bart's monument on
Little Newcastle Green*

area. I hope that the reader enjoys this book - although it has involved hard work in the research, it has been tremendous fun to write. The section on *Pirate Terms* alone is not only educative and informative, but an enjoyable read.

WHY DID SO MANY SEAMEN BECOME PIRATES ?

It seems that then, as now, managers preferred to rule by fear rather than co-operation. The author's own quotation contribution to his *The Welsh Almanac* was *'arrogance is the façade of the charlatan'*. Then, as now, managers were untrained and unwilling to learn. Any fraternisation would expose their weaknesses and lack of common sense. Seamen, whether from the Royal Navy or merchant fleets, were mainly forcibly *pressed* men, not volunteers, who were treated abominably and not allowed to go on to dry land for fear of desertion. The ships were under-manned, so they were overworked, and also fed disgusting rations in disease-ridden conditions. There were not many 'old' sea-dogs. The opportunity to join what pirates called their 'Commonwealth,' where there were neither masters nor beatings, was a welcome one. Everyone had equal shares, and the captain was only *'captain'* in times of battle or chase. The section in the book entitled *'Pirate Terms'* demonstrates the cruelty of these times.

The author had the good fortune to read the brilliant *'Longitude'* by Dava Sobel in 1995, before it was published in Britain. The following superb description from the start of Chapter 2, *'The Sea Before Time'*, will suffice to explain both why men turned to piracy, and also why *Black Bart* Roberts became lost crossing the Atlantic Ocean:

"Dirty weather," Admiral Sir Clowdisley Shovell called the fog that had dogged him twelve days at sea. Returning home victorious from Gibraltar after skirmishes with the French Mediterranean forces, Sir Clowdisley could not beat the heavy autumn overcast. Fearing the

ships might founder on coastal rocks, the admiral summoned all his navigators to put their heads together.

The consensus opinion placed the English fleet safely west of Ile d'Ouessant, an island outpost of the Brittany peninsula. But as the sailors continued north, they discovered to their horror that they had misgauged their longitude near the Scilly Isles. These tiny islands, about twenty miles from the Southwest tip of England, point to Land's End like a path of stepping-stones. And on that foggy night of October 22, 1707, the Scillies became unmarked tombstones for two thousand of Sir Clowdisley's troops.

The flagship, the 'Association', struck first. She sank within minutes, drowning all hands. Before the rest of the vessels could react to the obvious danger, two more ships, the 'Eagle' and the 'Romney', pricked themselves on the rocks and went down like stones. In all, four of the five warships were lost.

Only two men washed ashore alive. One of them was Sir Clowdisley himself, who may have watched the fifty-seven years of his life flash before his eyes as the waves carried him home. He had been approached by a sailor, a member of the Association's crew, who claimed to have kept his own reckoning of the fleet's location during the whole cloudy passage. Such subversive navigation by an inferior was forbidden in the Royal Navy, as the unnamed seaman well knew. However, the danger appeared so enormous, by his calculations, that he risked his neck to make his concerns known to the officers. **Admiral Shovell had the man hanged for mutiny on the spot.**

No one was around to spit "I told you so !" into Sir Clowdisley's face as he nearly drowned. But as soon as the admiral collapsed on dry sand, a local woman combing the beach purportedly found his body and fell in love with the emerald ring on his finger. Between her desire and his depletion, she handily murdered him for it. Three decades later, on her deathbed, this same woman confessed the crime to her clergyman, producing the ring as proof of her guilt and contrition.

The demise of Sir Clowdisley's fleet capped a long saga of seafaring in the days before sailors could find their longitude. Page after page from this miserable history relates quintessential horror stories of death by scurvy and thirst, of ghosts in the rigging, and of landfalls in the form of shipwrecks, with hulls dashed on rocks and heaps of drowned corpses fouling the beaches. In literally hundreds of instances, a vessel's ignorance of her longitude swiftly led to her destruction.'

This, then, is the background of 'The Book of Welsh Pirates and Buccaneers'.

CHAPTER I

PIRATE TERMS AND PLACES

It may seem strange to begin a book with definitions, but this book is written to be entertaining and informative, and this will help understand words used in the rest of the book. Just in the A-B section following, the reader will find the origin of country *'bumpkin'*, a *'brace of shakes'*, *'born with a silver spoon'*, *'booby prize'*, *'to take on board'*, *'above board'*, *'bombed'* (in the sense of being drunk), the *'blues'*, *'blind-side'*, *'blind drunk'*, *'the pot calling the kettle black'*, *'reach the bitter end'*, *'wasters'* (in the sense of people being useless), *'ahoy'*, *'all at sea'*, *'to keep aloof'*, *'piss-artist'*, *'taken aback'*, *'barbecue"* and *'bamboozle'*. Other colourful terms which have passed out of common usage, such a *'bring one's arse to anchor'* (sit down), *'belly timber'* (food) and *'bog orange'* (potato) are also included, as well as important pirate haunts and technical terms.

ABACK
When sails face into a head-on wind, the ship stops going forwards. Today's phrase *'taken aback'* comes from this nautical term.

ACT OF GRACE, or ACT OF PARDON
General amnesty given to a pirate who promised to reform his ways. The November 1698 proclamation offered a free pardon to all pirates operating east of the Cape of Good Hope, except for Captain Kidd. However, nine of his crew that surrendered under this Act of Grace were hung with him, in Execution Dock, off Wapping Old Stairs. Captain John Bowen and his crew would not surrender because they did not trust the authorities.

ADAM'S WILL
The nickname given to the Treaty of Tordesillas, when Pope Alexander VI confirmed Spanish *'ownership'* of the New World.

AHOY
This naval term seems, to this author, to stem from the *'hoy'*, a common 16th century coastal vessel (q.v.), although no dictionary attributes this derivation.

ALBATROSS
It was unlucky to kill one, as they were supposed to carry the souls of dead sailors. Coleridge's *'The Rime of the Ancient Mariner'* was inspired by the shooting of a black albatross, described in Captain Shelvocke's *'A Voyage Round the World.'*

ALCATRICE
The offspring of an African slave and a native Indian.

ALL AT SEA

The Viking term was *'all at sea'* when they could not see land. If absolutely unsure of their whereabouts, they released a raven (which came to be their emblem), which soared into the sky until it could see land. The Vikings then followed its direction. See *'straight as the crow flies'*.

ALOOF

On a lee shore, the order *'keep aloof'* meant to keep the ship's head nearer to the wind to prevent the vessel being driven to the shore. Hence the modern expression to *'keep aloof'*, means to 'keep away *from*', or *'keep your distance'*. Sir Henry Mainwaring wrote *'If the ship go by a wind, or quarter winds, they say aloof, or keep your loof, or fall not off, wear no more, keep to her, touch the wind, have a care of the lee-latch; all these do imply the same in manner, and are to bid him at the helm to keep her near to the wind.'* (quoted in John Harland, 'Seamanship in the Age of Sail', 1984)

ANCHOR, TO BRING ONE'S ARSE TO AN

To sit down

ANTILLES

The larger Antilles islands in the Caribbean, Cuba, Hispaniola, Porto Rico and Jamaica were those first taken by the Spanish from before 1500. From there, they moved on to Mexico and the rest of South America. This left the chain of *'Lesser Antilles'*, that is the Leeward and Windward Isles, open to other European powers to colonise. The Dutch were trading in the West Indies from 1542, and had a toehold in mainland Guiana by 1580. Between 1609 and 1619, various French, English and Dutch missions moved onto islands in between the mouth of the Orinoco river and that of the Amazon. The English settled in St Kitts from 1623, and Barbados in 1624-25. In 1628, St Kitts settlers moved on to Nevis and Barbuda, then in 1632 to Antigua and Montserrat. In 1625 the Dutch and English jointly took possession of Santa Cruz. The French took Guadeloupe, Martinique and other Windward Islands from 1635 onwards. Between 1632 and 1634 the Dutch established trading stations on St Eustatius, Tobago and Curacao.

APOSTLES

17th century term for the charges carried in a bandolier, slung across a pirate's chest when operating on land, because there were usually about a dozen cartridges.

ARQUEBUS

An early handgun, called by Esquemiling in 1684 a *'harquebus'*, and also spelt in early sources as: arkbusshe, hacquebute, hargubush, harquebuz, herquebuze and hagabus.

ARMADA

Spanish for a fleet of warships. *'The Armada of the Ocean Sea'* was organised in 1522 to protect the West Indies trade, and a tax called the *'averia'* was levied to pay for the fleet. It originally escorted the merchant fleet to the Azores, and met the homecoming fleet also at the Azores, to protect it from privateers. Later, protection had to be extended across the Atlantic. *'The Armada of the South Seas'* escorted loot from Peru to the Pacific coast at Panama.

ARMADILLO

A Spanish term for a smaller fleet, or flotilla of warships. The term could apply to just two Spanish men-of-war.

ARRACK
Very potent liquor brewed from rice, sugar and coconuts juice. The home-made hooch made from coconuts in the West Indies was particularly strong. In modern Lebanon, the strong alcohol Arak has an aniseed taste.

ARTICLES
The rules of the ship, that every pirate had to sign, or put his thumb-print to. These simple rules helped stop arguments and fights developing. There had to be a form of discipline upon ship, and they were arrived at by a democratic process of agreement of the ship's crew. The Welsh Captains Black Bart Roberts and John Phillips had their articles transcribed by Defoe after speaking to captured and forced men, and condemned pirates, and they are included in the entries upon those two captains.

ARTIST
A skilled man such as a surgeon, carpenter or navigator. Sometimes these, like musicians, were 'forced' to join the pirates to cover gaps in the crew. Pirate captains then issued them with a notification that they had been 'forced', in order to use at any possible trial by the Crown. While most pirates at trial would say that they had been 'forced', usually only skilled men, 'artists', would be acquitted. All of Black Bart's surgeons were acquitted, except Scudamore who seemed to revel in telling the truth of the matter, that he joined up voluntarily. The term 'piss-artist' , meaning someone whose trade is drinking, comes from the use of 'artists' as a skilled tradesmen.

ASIENTO, TREATY OF
A part of the peace settlement when Britain defeated Spain in the War of Spanish Succession (1702-1713). Britain was given the monopoly on supplying negro slaves to the Spanish West Indies for thirty years, at 4,800 slaves a year. Many more slaves than this were smuggled into the Spanish colonies, along with smuggled English goods. By 1739 continued conflict between British merchant ships and the Spanish 'garda costa' led to another war, The War of Jenkins' Ear, in 1739. An 'asiento' meant any contract to supply Spain and its dependencies, although by the 17th century the British came to understand it to refer exclusively to the provision of African slaves to Spanish-America.

AS RICH AS A WEST INDIAN PLANTER
With sugar and rum coming from the plantations to supply an insatiable European demand, this phrase supplanted 'as rich as Croesus' from the 1660's onwards. The more successful buccaneers like Captain Morgan (after whom the best-selling rum is named) bought plantations to retire.

ATTACK
Buccaneers were superb marksmen, and their favoured method of attack was to sail in fast sloops into musket range of heavy, home-ward bound merchant ships. Most of the crew lay prone on the deck to avoid terrible injuries caused by grapeshot, while the musketeers picked off the helmsman and any sailors in the ship's rigging. As soon as the merchant was unable to manoeuvre, the pirates made for the stern, often in a pinnace, to jam the rudder and swarm up the side of the boat. Homebound ships were preferred as they carried silver, jewels and easily traded loot, rather than slaves, wine and wheat. Night attacks were also popular, especially off Tortuga.

AVAST
Be quiet, or stop! Possibly from the Italian 'basta'! (enough!).

BAMBOOZLE
Dating from the 17th century, this was the Spanish custom of flying false flags to disguise your nationality.

BANK
A rising ground in the sea, differing from a shoal, because it was not rocky but formed from sand, mud or gravel.

BARBADOS
Until the taking of Jamaica in 1655, this tiny island and St Kitts were England's only possessions in the West Indies. It was a lawless, brawling place, and used by Cromwell to send defeated Irish and Welsh prisoners in the Civil War as indentured servants (slaves). Henry Whistler described it thus: *'This island is the Dunghill whereine England doth cast forth its rubidge (rubbish): Rodgs (rogues) and hors (whores) and such like people are those who are generally Broght (brought) heare. A rodge in England will hardly make a cheatere here; a Baud (bawd, harlot) broght over puts on a demuor (demure) comportment, a whore if hansum makes a wife for sume rich planter.'* It was full of deported Irish and Welsh, Royalist prisoners, beggars, exiled Huguenots, Quakers and political dissidents such as *'Perrot, the bearded ranter who refused to doff his hat to the Almighty, ended up in Barbadoes'*. A description of Barabados' inhabitants in 1665 is *'convict gaol birds or riotous persons, rotten before they are sent forth, and at best idle and only fit for the mines.'* Its escaped bondsmen, transported criminals and unemployed seamen made a happy breeding-ground for piracy, especially at the end of Queen Anne's War in 1713.

BARBARY COAST
From the 14th century, this was the name for the coastal regions ruled from Tripoli, Tunis and Algers. These were the Barbary States, city-states on the edge of desert. Later, Morocco was included, although its rulers did not live by piracy. It was a pirate haven from around 1520-1830, *'barbary'* being derived from the original Berber inhabitants. In 1538, Andrea Doria led a combined Christian fleet against Barbarossa, off the Albanian coast, and was defeated by a smaller force, despite leading 80 Venetian, 30 Spanish and 36 papal galleys with 60,000 men and 2,500 guns. In 1541, the Islamic corsairs won a great battle off Algiers, against the 500 ships of a Christian Europeans fleet, led again by the Italian Andrea Doria. Thousands were taken as slaves, and 8,300 men were killed or drowned. In the late 16th century, Elizabethan pirates and captains such as Callice began joining up with the Barbary pirates, teaching them sailing skills. In 1622, English towns raised £70,000 to ransom English captives held on the Barbary Coast.

BARBECU
The Carib Indian term for a wooden grate or hurdle (*grille de bois*), placed at a distance from a slow fire. The meat cured this way was called *'boucan'* as was the place where it was cooked. The flesh of cattle was usually dried in the smoke rather than salted first, and it dried a red colour. Wild hogs were salted first. *'Barbacoa'* or *'arjoupa'* was the Indian name given to the rough house of leaves and skins used by the *'boucaniers'*.

BARCO DE AVIFO
A Spanish *'packet-boat'*, or mail-ship, sent every year between the King of Spain and his *'flota'* or *'treasure fleet'* captains. It usually held vital intelligence upon the movements and timings of the treasure galleons. The captains of these packet boats *'navios de avifo'* swore to the King to destroy or sink any letters rather than let them fall into pirate hands.

BARNACLE
These stuck in huge numbers to the hull of wooden sailing ships, slowing them down and attracting weed. Until around 1800, they were generally thought to turn into Barnacle Geese.

BARQUE or BARK
A smallish ship with three or four masts. The foremast and following one or two masts are rigged square and the aftermast (mizzen mast) is rigged fore and aft.

BARQUENTINE
A small three-masted ship, square-rigged forwards, and fore-and-aft rigged on the other two masts.

BAWDY HOUSE BOTTLE
A term for a very small sized bottle of alcohol. This probably derives from the brothels making excessive money on selling alcohol, similar to modern strip-joints and sleaze-parlours.

BAYAMO
A violent storm of heavy rain and lightning that occurs around southern Cuba, especially in the Bight of Bayamo.

BEAM ENDS
'Nearly on one's beam ends' means that the ship is lying over and about to sink.

BEAT
Sail against the wind, usually on alternate tacks.

BELAY
Similar to 'avast', belay meant stop doing something, or else something nasty would happen to you. In knotting, belaying is looping the line around the base, under the arms of a cleat, bringing it up and over diagonally, around and over one arm, then over, around and under the other, in a continuous figure eight, securing the 'bitter end' by tucking it under the last crossover.

BELAYING PINS
These thick wooden movable posts held ropes in place, and were also useful in an emergency for hitting someone, if a pirate was 'out of arms' (his pistols had fired) or his sabre was stuck between someone's ribs.

BELLY TIMBER
Food, especially meat. 'There can be no adventure without belly timber' was a saying of the 18th century. The ready availability of green turtles in the West Indies in effect helped the spread of piracy, and they were kept for weeks on deck until ready to be eaten. The leatherback turtle was inedible, and the hawksbill, or tortoise-shell, turtle unpleasant to taste. Green turtles were the only vegetarian turtle, and made superb soup when laced with sherry.

BIGHT OF BENIN
A bight is a usually a narrow inlet of the sea. It was said that the Royal Africa Company had three governors for each of its Guinea Coast trading forts. There was one who had just died, one in post, and one on his way to replace him.
'Beware and take care of the Bight o' Benin
For one that comes out there were forty went in'

BILBOES
Long iron bars fastened onto prisoners' legs stretching them apart and making it difficult to escape. The sliding shackles meant that usually prisoners could only sit and not stand. Bilboes were also humorously known as 'garters'. They were almost equivalent to the village stocks, and the word derives from Bilboa, which was supposed to make the best steel for fine swords in Europe. A 'bilbo' was a rapier bought from the Bilboa region.

BILGE RAT
Common term of abuse, as in 'you scurvy bilge rat!'. The bilge was the filthy, dirty, stagnant lowest part of the ship, where rats could always be found. Rats were despised both for their urine smell, and for fouling precious food. However, in bad times, they were the only source of fresh meat on a vessel. Bilge-water stank as it lay on the floor of the flat bottom of the ship, so could not be pumped out. Rubbish and waste gathered in it, in the 'waist' or centre of the bottom of the boat, creating difficulties in steering. 'Waisters' were older, unfit or forced seamen who were given the unpleasant job of trying to clear up the mess, and prevent the bilge-water becoming too much of a problem. They were useless sailors who could not be trusted in the rigging, and were given other menial tasks like 'swinging the lead', casting around to sound out the depth. Spelling over time changed to today's 'wasters', people who are a target for derision.

BILLIARDS
Several taverns such as the George and the Feathers in 17th century Port Royal had billiard rooms, which were usually situated in the yard, or away from the main bars, to prevent fights occurring.

BITTER END
The last part of the anchor cable that remains within the ship when the ship is at anchor. Thus to let a chain or rope out 'to reach the bitter end' means that has all been paid out and there is nothing left to be let go.

BLACKAMOOR'S TEETH
Cowrie shells.

BLACK ARSE
A kettle, this was the origin of the more polite term used today, 'the pot calling the kettle black (arse)'.

BLACK BART
This most famous pirate in history was born John Roberts, and was a lifelong teetotaller. It is interesting that in the 19th century, doing 'a John Roberts' in Wales, was to drink enough to keep drunk from Saturday morning until Sunday night.

BLACK BOY
A vicar, or man of God, from his clothing. Also called a 'black coat'. Later in the 18th century, a 'black fly' came to mean a clergyman, because farmers had to pay church tithes and looked upon the clergy as the worst of land pests. A 'black box' was a lawyer, from the colour of the case where he kept his papers. A 'black gown' was a learned gentleman.

BLACK BIRDERS
Slave ships. Crews were difficult to get for these, as the mortality amongst them probably rivalled that amongst the 'blackbirds' or slaves. This evil trade was known as 'blackbirding', and many merchants made fortunes from it after the Treaty of Asiento.

BLACKBEARD
Edward Teach, also known as Thatch Drummond, was a giant of a man from Bristol. First sailing under the pirate captain Hornigold, by 1718 he was in charge of the forty-gun Queen Ann's Revenge. He dressed all in black, had a beard to his waist, and tied coloured ribbons in his pigtails. One of the more foul-mouthed of the pirate captains, he set fire to slow-burning fuses on his hat in battle, to make himself appear more frightening. For a joke, he shot Israel Hands under his captain's table, crippling him for life. Blackbeard blockaded Charleston, South Carolina, and a reward of £100 was on offer from the Governor of North Carolina. It took twenty-five separate wounds to kill him in a fierce battle with the Royal Navy. Israel Hands appears in R.L. Stevenson's 'Treasure Island'. The sailing master Israel Hands was also known as 'Basilica' Hands, and was sentenced for piracy in Virginia, September 1718, but pardoned. He was last heard of begging in London. The Welshman Owen Roberts was Blackbeard's ship's carpenter, and was killed with Edward Teach in Queen Ann's Revenge off North Carolina on November 22nd, 1718. Blackbeard took 23 ships in 7 months, all in the West Indies, which puts Black Bart Roberts' total of over 400 in two years, on both sides of the Atlantic, into perspective.

BLACK DOG
Between 1705 and 1730, a counterfeit silver coin. The bad mood associated with this term became a colloquialism in the 19th century. To 'blush like a black dog', or a 'blue dog' meant that a pirate never blushed at all, i.e. he was absolutely shameless.

BLACK GENTLEMAN
The devil. The term 'blackguard', meaning scoundrel, comes from someone evil who guards the devil. 'Black Spy' also meant the devil.

BLACK IVORY
Dealing in 'black ivory' was a euphemism for the slave trade. Pope Alexander VI gave Spain all new lands west of Brazil in 1494, and gave Portugal all new lands east of it. Spain was therefore unable to get slaves from the Guinea Coast of Africa. The English merchant marine (and the reigning sovereign) found great profits here, especially the Royal Africa Company (see Asiento Treaty, Black Birders, Middle Passage and the chapters on Howell Davis and Black Bart).

BLACK JACK
Another name for the pirate flag, The Jolly Roger. Also the slang given to a sailor who suffered from the bubonic plague, as he was supposed to turn black. A 'black jack' was also a leathern drinking-jug.

BLACK-MOUTHING
Slandering.

BLACK RENT
Herring had to be salted within 24 hours to retain its flavour, so lords who owned ports in Ireland grew rich on the dues (black rent) paid to them by fishermen for the use of their harbours for refitting, re-victualling and landing a catch. Because of its quickness in going 'off', herring was the only fish allowed to be sold on a Sunday.

BLACK SHIP
An East-India Company trading ship, built from teak.

BLACK SQUALL
A sudden and violent storm in the West Indies, responsible for the unexplained loss of many a privateer and pirate. The differential between very warm air near land and the onset of colder air off the sea sometimes generates spectacular electrical storms.

BLACK'S THE WHITE OF MY EYE
A sailor's way of vehemently protesting that he has told the truth, when accused of wrongdoing.

BLACK STRAP
A lethal combination of rum, molasses and chowder beer, the favourite tipple of Black Bart's crew. Later in the 18th century it was the pejorative term for thick, sweet port, also known as 'black stripe'.

BLACK VELVET
The term given by Black Bart Roberts' and Howell Davis' pirate crews to the accommodating native women in the Gambia and Sierra Leone. It seems that a child who was a 'picanniny' (little one, from the Spanish picayune) with a paler skin was a mark of prestige with some women.

BLADDER
A chattering, talkative fellow who irritates.

BLIND
Extremely drunk. 'Liquored' had the same meaning. A 'blind man's holiday' was the night-time. The 'blind-side' was the weakest part to attack, the origin of the rugby union position 'blind-side wing forward'. 'When the devil is blind' meant 'never', as in 'I'll win the National Lottery when the devil is blind'.

BLOODY FLAG
Naval warships used to raise this large red flag upon going into battle. When pirates hoisted it, it meant that they would give no quarter, after exhausting negotiations to take a ship peaceably.

BLOWING MARLINSPIKES
Marlinspikes (marlingspikes) were metal spikes used for repairing and joining ropes. If there was a heavy storm where the skin was made to sting, the weather was 'blowing marlinspikes'.

(TO COME OFF) BLUELY
To have bad luck, to miss a prize.

BLUE MONDAY
Traditionally the day for handing out the brutal punishments of the Royal Navy. There was a superstition that evil would befall the ship if the treatment was not delivered on Mondays - see 'gunner's daughter'. One might dread 'the blues', and slave music on plantations evolved into 'blues' music.

BLUE-SKIN
The offspring of a white man and black woman in the West Indies. Also the term for a Presbyterian.

BLUNDERBUSS
This long hand-gun was so powerful that it had to be held away from the body - the recoil would knock a pirate over.

BOARD
If anything at sea went overboard it was 'by the board', with no chance of being recovered. To 'take aboard' was to put all useful things on the deck, ready for immediate use. 'All above board' meant that the planks, or boards which make up the deck are visible to everyone, nothing can be hidden. Above board meant having one's hands above the card table when gambling. Similarly, 'under board' meant acting deviously. Thus today, when we take instructions 'on board', we will not forget anything.

BOARDING
When pirates 'boarded' or went aboard a victim's ship, the 'boarding party' was usually chosen by ballot. Everyone had an equal share of the booty, but being on the 'boarding party' against a boat which had not struck its colours was obviously dangerous. 'Sea-artists' like carpenters and surgeons were never risked. Some pirates volunteered to board, and made up for those on the list who did not wish to board.

BOAT (TO HAVE AN OAR IN EVERY BOAT)
To meddle in other people's business.

BOATSWAIN
The bo'sun was in charge of the rigging, sails, cables and anchors, making sure they all worked efficiently. He was also usually in charge of stores, and replacement of provisions. In charge of all the work on deck, he translated the captain's orders into operations by the crew. Interestingly, the lower ranks on board, boatswain, coxswain and seaman are all derived from the people's language, Anglo-Saxon. The names of the officers, admiral, captain and lieutenant are all derived from the language of the court in medieval times, French. Incidentally, so many West Countrymen went to sea that they influenced our pronunciation of words like boatswain, which became 'bo'sun'. Similarly, bowline is pronounced 'bo'lin'; gunwale is pronounced 'gunnel'; leeward is 'loo-wud'; forward is 'forrud', forecastle is 'focs'l', foresail is 'fors'l' and main sail is 'mains'l.

BOG-ORANGE
Potato – so many came from Ireland. A 'Bog-lander', later 'bog-trotter', was an Irishman, the nationality despised by Black Bart because of the supposed desertion of the Ulsterman, Walter Kennedy.

BOMBED
This used to be a fashionable slang for being drunk. A 'bombard' was a leather jug which held 8 pints of ale. We must remember that ale was far stronger in past centuries, until beer was taxed on its strength in the First World War to stop munitions workers becoming slapdash. Thus anyone who drank a full container was definitely 'bombarded' or 'bombed'. The phrase 'tanked up' has a similar derivation, from tankard.

BOOBY
The brown gannet, 'sula cyanops', eaten when no other meat at all was available. 'Booby prize' came to mean something that no-one particularly wanted but had to have.

BOOMS
Fenders to which sails are fixed to control its position.

BOOT-TOPPING
For pirates, this was a hurried and partial cleaning of the ship's hull. Only the upper part of the ship's bottom was cleaned. It was also the name for a resinous mixture of tallow and sulphur or lime used to coat the bottoms of ships, to deter barnacles and weeds, and reduce friction when sailing.

BORN UNDER A THREEPENNY-HALFPENNY BLANKET
That is, not even 'worth a groat', a pirate or buccaneer who was thought to be very unsuccessful, and therefore unlucky to sail with.

BORN WITH A SILVER SPOON
This term was applied to those officers in the Royal Navy who entered the service without examinations and because of family connections. They were said to have joined the navy 'through the cabin windows'. Those 'born with a wooden ladle' were officers who attained their posts by merit, and entered the navy 'through the hawseholes', the holes through which the anchor passes.

BOTTLE-HEAD
Idiot or fool.

BOWSPRIT
The spar sticking forward over the bows of the ship, above any figurehead, carrying the headstay as far forward as possible.

BRACE OF SHAKES
A phrase still used today – brace means a pair, as in 'bagging a brace of pheasant'. 'I'll be with you in a brace of shakes' literally means 'I'll be with you before the sail has time to shake twice,' that is 'straight away'.

BRETHREN OF THE COAST, LES FÈRES DE LA CÔTE
From the 1530's onwards, Europeans had formed small settlements on the coasts of Jamaica, Cuba and especially Hispaniola. The surviving Indians, those not wiped out by the Spanish, showed them how to cure long strips of meat on a barbecue over a slow fire, in a hut called a 'boucan'. They caught wild cattle and pigs, and exchanged the hides, meat and tallow for guns, clothes, provisions and alcohol. These butchers evolved a system of living where the past was not mentioned, and were only known to each other by Christian names. Excellent sharpshooters, their favourite food was the warm marrow from the bones of newly slaughtered animals. In retaliation against Spanish attacks on their settlements, they attacked Spanish shipping in 'pirogues' or 'piraguas', hollowed-out tree-trunks that served as canoes. The Spanish tried to massacre their herds, and this turned the 'Brethren of the Coast' even more to piracy and buccaneering, and from 1630 the island of Tortuga became their unofficial headquarters.

They evolved a strict code, the 'Custom of the Coast' whereby they shared booty on an even basis, and did not know each other's pasts or surnames. Crossing the Tropic of Cancer 'drowned' their former lives, according to their superstition. A 'buccaneer council' of equals decided where they would get provisions, and where they would attack under an elected captain. Esquemeling records these negotiations from the point of view of a former buccaneer: 'In the first place, *therefore, they mention how much the Captain ought to have for his ship. Next the salary of the carpenter, or shipwright, who careened, mended and rigged the vessel.... Afterwards for provisions and victualling they draw out of the same common stock....Also a competent salary for the surgeon and his chest of medicaments.... Lastly, they stipulate in writing what recompense or reward each one ought to have, that is either wounded or maimed in his body, suffering the loss of any limb, by that voyage. Thus they order for the loss of a right arm 600 pieces of eight, or six slaves; for the loss of a left arm 500 pieces of eight, or five slaves; for a right leg 500 pieces of eight, or five slaves; for the left leg 400 pieces of eight, or four slaves; for an eye 100 pieces of eight, or one slave; for a finger of the hand, the same reward as for the eye.'*

The above was paid out before any booty was shared, with the captain receiving five or six times the reward of an ordinary sailor, and officers three or four times. Stealing or hiding of plunder was forbidden. Anyone stealing from a brother had his nose sliced off, and a second offence led to marooning with just a jug of water, a musket and some shot.

BRIGANTINE, or BRIG
A twin-masted workhorse of a ship, favoured by pirates for its manoeuvrability. Both masts are fully square rigged, with a fore and aft sail on the lower part of the mainmast. The choice of many pirates, they could hold 100 crew and many cannon.

BROACH
To spike or pierce a cask of rum, brandy or wine for drinking. Also to incline suddenly to windward of the ship's course against the helm, so as to present her side to the wind, and to endanger her losing her masts.

BROACH THE ADMIRAL
An old story tells of an admiral dying in the West Indies, and his body being put in a coffin filled with rum to preserve it on the way home. A sailor left to guard the coffin was often seen to be drunk. *'To broach the admiral'* came to mean stealing drink from a cask.

BROADSIDE
Firing a broadside meant that every cannon on one side of the ship could be fired at once. Some would aim for the waterline, others for the men on decks, others for the gundecks and others for the rigging, depending upon their purpose and how they were loaded. A standard *culverin* could fire one cannon ball a minute, but soon became too hot too operate. The powder charge and its wad were rammed firmly home and set under the touch-hole, the 18-pound cannon ball tamped hard, right down the barrel, the priming powder was ignited by a slow-burning match, and everyone stood clear. The 3-ton culverin would recoil, held fast by its breech-rope, and the ship would shake.

BRULOT
French for fireship, a ship loaded with explosives and set alight to drift into the enemy's fleet, especially successful if the fleet was anchored in port.

BUCCANEERS
These *'boucaniers'* attacked ships, but not usually those of their own homeland. They were named after a French term *'boucan'* (from the Indian *'bukan'*) – a hut in which there was a slow grill of animal dung and green twigs over which meat was smoked or cooked. See *'Brethren of the Coast.'* Their favoured form of attack was in long canoes or small single-masted barques. They packed the boat with sharpshooters to fire at anyone trying to fire a cannon at them, and came from astern of the prize ship, giving a minimal target to aim at. They then jammed the

rudder and climbed up the stern of the ship, under cover of a fusillade of musket-fire. Although they called themselves '*privateers*', they rarely had letters of commission or marque. Sometimes they carried expired commissions, and sometimes forgeries.

A Hispaniola Buccaneer

BULLY BEEF
Meat such as pork and beef was packed into barrels and covered with salt to preserve it at sea. Salt beef was sometimes boiled to make it edible, and the French '*boeuf bouille*' became '*bully beef*'. Sometimes the meat was too tough to eat, and the pirates made snuff boxes or ornaments out of it to pass the time. It was in the interest of the ship's cook to boil meat extremely well, as all the fat and grease could be used by the cook to make tallow or candles, a perk of the job.

BUM BOAT
Derived from the Dutch boom-boat, a broad-beamed small boat which carried provisions to ships, and also to remove their rubbish.

BUMBOO, BOMBO
Along with *rumfustian*, the favoured alcoholic beverage on New Providence, a mix of rum, water, nutmeg and sugar. Because all the ingredients were readily available, it was quick to make, and undeniably effective, so it was the common drink of sailors

BUMPKIN
A nautical terms for wooden vessel for carrying water. The term '*country bumpkin*' came to refer to a non-seafarer, with only water in his '*wooden*' head, i.e. an idiot.

BURGOO
Oatmeal, boiled and seasoned with butter, sugar and salt – a gruel similar to Welsh porridge. It was easy for anyone to prepare this in the ship's galley, even in the roughest seas, and it had enough sustenance to help with the hard work aboard ship. Pirates uniformly hated it.

BURIED TREASURE
Very few buccaneers or pirates ever buried plunder. They shared it out and usually spent it within days on women, gambling and alcohol. One buccaneer, John Morris is known to have paid a hundred guineas just for the sight of a naked prostitute. The Dutchman Roche Brasiliano was known to the English as '*Rock the Brasilian*', and was noted for his extreme cruelty, roasting Spanish prisoners on wooded spits until they told him where they had hidden their valuables. Captured by the Spanish, he was tortured by the Inquisition at Campeche, and told them of his treasure buried on the Isla de Pinos, off Cuba. Spanish soldiers retrieved over a hundred thousand pieces of eight, upon which the Spanish put '*Rock*' out of his misery. Legend persists that Black Bart hid treasure inside a cave on Little Cayman Island, after his pillaging of the Portuguese fleet at Bahia.

BURTHEN
A ship's tonnage or carrying capacity, based on the number of tuns of wine that could be carried in the holds, the total number giving the burthen (burden).

BUTCHER'S BILL
Slang for the dead and wounded littering the deck after a battle.

CACAFUEGO
A bully, braggart or '*spitfire*', meaning literally to defecate fire. *Nuestra Senora de la Concepcion* was pursued by Francis Drake for several days before he took it on March 1st, St David's Day, 1579. She was the greatest prize in history, being valued at around 1.5 million ducats at the time, or around half a billion pounds in today's money. She had been given the vulgar name of the *Cacfuego* by the chasing privateers, '*shitfire*', because she was one of the few Spanish ships of the time to have cannon on the Pacific Coast of South America. Queen Elizabeth took most of the booty. A Spanish youth on the captured vessel said that his ship '*shall no longer be called the Cacafuego, but the Cacaplata (shit-silver)*', and that Drake's Hind should be renamed the Cacafuego.

CACKLING FART
An egg. A '*cackling cheat*' was any type of fowl. A '*cackler*' was a blabber who gave away secrets.

CANKY
A standard native meal for the men serving on the Guinea Coast. Indian meal and water or palm-wine, baked to make bread and cakes, or boiled to make cakes.

CANVAS
All sails and hammocks were made from strong-fibred hemp, the Greek '*kannabis*'. Although modern sails are made of oil-derived materials, they are still named after a semi-legal drug.

CAPITANA
Flag-ship of a Spanish fleet, '*almiranta*' being a vice-flagship, the inverse of the British admiral - captain relationship.

CAPSTAN
'*The capstan*' was a punishment whereby the arms were outstretched on a capstan bar and a heavy weight suspended from the neck, popular in the navy through the 17th century until the early 18th century.

CAPTAIN
A pirate captain had remarkably few rights or benefits, only being in charge when the crew was fighting, chasing or being pursued. In such action, he was allowed to strike, stab or shoot any man who disobeyed his orders. He also had power over prisoners and whether they were ill-used or freed, but no power over the captured vessel or its cargo. He was usually chosen for being '*pistol-proof*', having a dominating and daring character. He had the right to sole use of the great cabin, but no privacy there. Any man could enter his cabin, drink from his punch bowl, swear at him and take his food with little come-back. He was usually deposed by popular vote, just as he was elected.

THE CAPTAIN IS NOT AT HOME
To have run out of money. ('*The captain is at home*' came to mean menstruation in the late 18th century, perhaps a pun on *catamenia*.)

CAPTAIN GRAND
A haughty, or *'hoity-toity'* individual.

CAPTAIN SHARP
Bartholomew Sharp was a famous pirate, but possibly not the origin of this term from the late 17th to early 19th centuries. It means that someone is a cheating, sneaking, cowardly bully. In the same period, *'captain Tom'* was the leader of a mob.

CARAVEL
Portuguese and Spanish ships used for ocean voyages as well as coastal trade, with two or three masts.

CARDS
With dice, the most important way of passing the time when pirates were on board ship, or holed up hiding somewhere. Many men lost all their booty this way, and were thus condemned to a life of perpetual piracy. Arguments were very common, and arguments were settled by a duel or by the ship's quartermaster. The most popular games of Black Bart's time were the following:

'All Fours', a game popular in the late 17th century, which in America later was called High-Low Jack, Old Sledge and Seven-Up.

'Brag' evolved from *'Primero'*, mentioned by Shakespeare, and from *'Post and Pair'*, and *'Commerce'* and in its own turn evolved *'Poker'*. Still an extremely popular form of gambling, as it is so simple, the odds of a *'Prial'* (three suits of the same rank in a hand of three) are 425:1, so the odds of the best hand, three threes, are around 5,100:1. The odds of the next best *'hand'*, a *'running flush'*, are slightly worse at 464:1. The odds for a *'run'* are 31:1, for a *'flush'* are 20:1 and for a pair only 6:1.

'Cribbage', still popular in pubs and clubs, used a marker-board which has a two-peg scoring system to prevent cheating. The poet-soldier Sir John Suckling (1609-1642) is credited with its invention, but it seems to be based on three earlier games, the most noted of which was *'Noddy'*. There are terms such as *'two for his heels'*, *'one for his nob'*, and if a player miscounts his score his opponent may shout *'Muggins!'* and *'peg'* the score for himself.

'Euchre', still played in some Welsh and West Country ports, which became the most popular game in America before being replaced by bridge and poker in the early 19th century. The *'joker'* was invented for this game.

'Piquet', played by Charles II, and mentioned by Rabelais in the 16th century. Piquet *'markers'*, for recording scores, can still be found in antique shops. It is the most skilful and interesting of all the two-player card games.

'Farmer' is an old European game, still played in rural America, where the object is to get as near to 16 points as possible. It is probably the ancestor of the games of *'Pontoon'* and *'Blackjack'*.

'Ombre' was an old Spanish game, which became popular in Stuart England with the marriage of Catherine of Braganza to Charles II in 1662. Still very popular in Denmark, and known as *'Tresillo'* in Spain and as *'Rocamber'* in Latin America. By Thackeray's time it had lost its popularity. In *'The Virginians'* in 1858 he wrote that *'very likely there are not six ladies of fashion in London who know the difference between Spadille and Manille'*, terms used in the game. The game swept Europe in the late 17th century, with terms like *'The Vole'* (winning all nine tricks), *'matadors'* (the three top trumps), *'estuches'* (honours), *'voltereta'* (a bid to win). Interestingly, our term for the suit *'Spades'* comes from *'espadas'*, the suit of *'Swords'* in this game.

'Primero' was the most popular card game in Tudor England, originally Spanish or Italian, which was replaced by *'Brag'* in the early 18th century. Both Henry VIII and Elizabeth I played it.

'Whist', or 'Whisk', developed from either the 16th century French game of 'Triomphe', or the English game of the same century called 'Trump' and also known as 'Ruff and Honours'. It was already a popular lower-class game when taken up by Lord Folkestone and Edmond Hoyle at London's Crown Coffee House. In 1674, Charles Cotton wrote 'every Child almost of Eight years old hath a competent knowledge in that recreation.' In the 18th and 19th centuries it was the most popular card game in the English-speaking nations, being overtaken by Bridge at the end of the 19th century. Hoyle wrote his 'Short Treatise' on it in 1742.

The playing of the above games is described fully in 'The Penguin Book of Card Games' by David Bartlett, and in 'The Complete Book of Card Games' edited by Peter Arnold and published by Octopus. 'The Compleat Gamester' of 1674, by Charles Cotton, is excellent reading for those who wish to study the games further.

CAREEN

A ship was taken to a quiet and isolated place ('careenage') and hauled over ('heaved to') on its side to clean or repair the wooden hull. It was a time when the pirate was most vulnerable, for example Bannister's 36-gun Golden Fleece was destroyed by the Royal Navy when he was careening in Hispaniola in 1686. The masts had to be pulled to the ground, in order to present the ship's bottom for inspection. Marine borers and weed made vessels not only slow, but awkward to steer, fatal for a pirate ship. The worst borer was a mollusc known as the teredos, with saw-shaped teeth. (See Teredos) Careening had to take place in the warm waters at least every two or three months. Guns were set up to guard the bay, and provisions taken off the boat. The hull was scraped of barnacles, patched, and if time allowed coated with tallow and pitch to try and keep out the teredos worm. Incidentally, late in the 18th century it was noted that copper sheathing upon hulls deterred the barnacles and seaweed which clung to ships, necessitating their 'careening' every six months or so. The Royal Navy 'copper-bottomed' its extensive fleet, at huge expense to the public purse, and consequently out-sailed Napoleon's fleet at the Battle of the Nile and elsewhere. The term 'a copper-bottomed guarantee' stems from this time.

CARPENTERS

These were vital for not only ship repairs and careening, but for stripping prizes to be used as pirate ships. Also, because of their great saws, they used to amputate limbs, rather than the ship's surgeon.

CARTAGENA

This was the treasure port between Panama and Venezuela, now part of Colombia. It was one of only three treasure ports visited by the annual Spanish flota. Pearls were shipped from Margarita Island, as well as precious woods, gold, silver and emeralds.

CAST AWAY

To be forced away from a ship by disaster - The Mariner's Dictionary

CATGUT SCRAPER

Any of the ship's band's fiddlers.

THE CAT HAS KITTENED IN MY MOUTH

I have a foul taste after drinking too much.

CAT O' NINE TAILS

A short stick with nine knotted ropes used to flog seamen. One lash could take the skin off the back, and six would make the back raw. Punishments of over a hundred lashes meant that the miscreant died in agony. From this implement of torture, we get today's phrase *'there's no room to swing a cat'* – the deck was sometimes too full of on-lookers and cannons etc. to draw back the arm properly to inflict the *'cat o' nine tails'* (see *'gunner's daughter'*). As the gun decks had only 4 feet 6 inches headroom, the punishment had to be carried out on the main deck, where there was hopefully plenty of room to use the *'cat'*.

The punisher *'combed the cat'* after each lash, drawing each of the bloody 18 inch ropes apart. If this was not done, the coagulated tails would stick together, and give permanent damage to the victim. In the Royal Navy, the prisoner was forced to make the *'cat'*, and tie knots in the each of the nine tails. It largely replaced keel-hauling as a method of punishment in the Royal Navy, where there was a theoretical maximum of 12 lashes that could be given. Vicious captains ignored this, and it was only ended as a form of punishment in 1879. For theft in the army and navy, a special *'thieves' cat'* was used, which had three knots in each of the nine tails. Originally made by the victim, they were later standard ready-made issue at military stores. (See *'let the cat out of the bag'*).

Intriguingly, the former ship's surgeon, Tobias Smollett, who was the first to note *'Davy Jones' Locker'* in print, was also the first to mention the cat, in *'Humphrey Clinker'* (1771), where his character compares the *'clear, elastic, salutary air'* of Brambleton-hall to that of London: *'I am pent up in frowzy lodgings, where there is not enough room to swing a cat; and I breathe the streams of endless putrefaction; and these would, undoubtedly, produce a pestilence, if they were not qualified by the gross acid of sea-coal.'* The *'Questions Answered'* column in The Times, May 28th, 2002 included a wonderful answer to the question of the origin of *'not enough room to swing a cat'* from Ronald Turner of Southampton: *'This questioner is quite capable of answering this himself. I am afraid that this epitomises the sad lack of interest in the experimental sciences that is found all too often in today's young people.'* (Incidentally, another newspaper around the same time featured my favourite answer to a question as to the location of the longest and deepest cave system in the world. The simple answer from a reader was *'Not telling you'*, and signed O.B. Laden.)

In the Newgate Calendar, we see the former Governor of Goree (Senegambia) being hung, after being convicted of ordering a soldier to be flogged to death nearly twenty years previously. Benjamin Armstrong had been sentenced to 800 lashes by Governor Wall, and died 5 days later, on July 15th, 1782. The blameless Armstrong, who had not been tried on any offence, had been strapped to a gun-carriage, and whipped by black men brought in for the purpose, instead of the drummers, as was usual. 32 men each gave Armstrong 25 lashes, not with the normal cat o' nine tails, but with a thicker rope, which inflicted more punishment. Wall encourage the men to whip harder, urging 'Cut him to the heart and the liver.' The Board of the Admiralty put out a reward for Wall's arrest, but he lived on the Continent and under assumed names. Wall was hung on January 28th, 1802, and the calendar states: *'Without waiting for any signal, the platform dropped, and he was launched into eternity. From the knot of the rope turning round to the back of his neck, and his legs not being pulled, at his particular request, he was suspended in convulsive agony for more than a quarter of an hour.'* His body was taken for dissection.

CATTING

Chasing harlots.

CAYMAN ISLANDS

Grand Cayman and Little Cayman were discovered by Columbus in 1503, and he named them Las Tortugas, because they resembled turtles. Francis Drake in 1585 noted that there were *'great serpents, large like lizards, which are edible'*, as well as turtles there, and their existence was doubted until archaeological digs in 1993 and 1996 proved that they had been native to the islands. The islands came under Britain's control when captured from Spain, along with Jamaica, by Cromwell's expeditionary force. They were officially ceded to England in 1670 by the Treaty of Madrid. They were a popular stop-over for Sir Henry Morgan, and the Owen Roberts Airfield was opened in 1935.

CAULK
An unpleasant job, often given as a punishment, driving strands of old rope or oakum, into the ship's seams (between planking), then sealing with pitch or resin to prevent leaking, or the oakum rotting from contact with salt-water. Before this a shipwright used a *'beetle'* (heavy mallet) to drive *'reeming-irons'* (iron wedges) into the sides and decks, to open a gap between the planks. The oakum was *'chinched'* in by pressing it with a knife or chisel into the seam, as a temporary measure if there was no time for proper caulking. The narrow seam between planks, which is sealed with oakum and pitch, is necessary as wood expands in water. As the planks *'take up'* the water, they compress the oakum and make the boat more water-tight.

CAY, KEY
Small islands, often coral formations, in the West Indies, with sparse vegetation and usually no water. From the word *'cayos'* (Spanish for rocks), the Florida Keys are examples. In these hundreds of islets, e.g. off Florida (the Florida Keys), pirates could lay low, carouse or clean (careen) their ships. Sometimes men were marooned on them.

CHASE GUNS
Cannons in the bows of the ship, used when *'chasing'* another ship.

CHEW THE FAT
Meat was preserved in brine in wooden casks, and a chemical reaction meant that salt-hardened fat became attached to the walls of the barrel. The cook might scrape this and give it to the crew while they were waiting to eat - they would *'chew the fat'* and make small talk before their meal. However, the cook generally tried to secrete some of this fat in his *'slush fund'*. The fat was used for greasing masts, preserving leather, cooking and making candles, and he could sell it when he reached port. Pirate cooks generally shared their slush fund with the crew.

CHOCK-A-BLOCK
When two tackle blocks are so close that no movement is possible. The sails could be pulled in tight so that the ship sailed *'as close to the wind'* as possible. To *'chock'* is to secure goods tightly on deck, when the vessel is rolling in high seas.

CHOCOLATE GALE
A brisk North-Westerly wind common in the Spanish Main and West Indies.

CLAP IN IRONS
To chain up a prisoner.

CLEAN BILL OF HEALTH
Merchant ships were issued with a *'Bill of Health'* document to notify that it had suffered from no epidemic or infection at time of departure.

CLEAN SLATE
Courses, distances and tacks were recorded on a log slate. If there had been no problems, the new watch would disregard the old record and *'start a clean slate'*.

CLEAR THE DECK
Get ready for battle by getting rid of all coils or rope etc., which might hinder movement.

CLOSE QUARTERS
A small wooden fortress or barricade erected on the deck of a merchant when attacks by pirates were expected. Small openings, loop-holes, enabled sailors to fire weapons with some protection. Wooden partitions in the quarters below decks also had loopholes pierced in them to allow defenders to thrust pikes and cutlasses through, and fight off boarders.

COCK UP
In port, the merchant ship's *'cock up crew'* had to slew the yard arms inboard, and neatly brace them so that they did not interfere with another ship's rigging or any dock equipment, before the crew was allowed ashore. Today, *'cock up'* has come to mean making a mess of something, the opposite of its original meaning.

COLOURS 'TIED TO THE MAST'
This meant that a ship would not surrender, and that a fight could be expected - there was no going-back.

CONFEDERACY OF THE BUCCANEERS OF AMERICA
The grandiose name the *'Brethren of the Coast'* gave themselves when they banded in their ships under Henry Morgan to go privateering.

CORSAIRES
French for pirates, like the Spanish *'corsarios'*, and associated with the Mediterranean.

COSTA GARDA see Garda Costa

CRACKING A BOTTLE
This familiar modern slang, as in *'let's crack a bottle of wine'* stems from the days when pirates captured ships containing alcohol. In their eagerness to drink, corkscrews were not necessary as the heads of the bottles were cracked off against the nearest hard surface.

CRANK
A ship that was difficult to sail, and unstable. The modern adjective *'cranky'*, meaning eccentric, awkward or difficult to understand, comes from the saying that *'this ship's too cranky'*. Possibly from the Dutch *'krengd'*, a sailing vessel which was quite unstable.

CROMSTER, CROMPSTER, CRUMSTER
Most of Harry Morgan's buccaneering fleets were *cromsters*, a merchant ship which looked like a small galleon, quite fast, but not as manoeuvrable as a sloop. It had a foremast, a mainmast and also a third mast to the rear supporting a lateen (triangular) sail (or sometimes a gaff sail). Its advantages over the sloop was that it could carry more treasure, place more cannons and hold three or four times as many crew. Perhaps 16 guns could be carried on a gun deck, with more guns lashed to the top deck.

CROW'S NEST
A resting platform on a mast for sailors working the yard-arms. Also used as a look-out point. (see 'straight as the crow flies')

CRUELTY
Captain Edward Low was a byword in evil. A Portuguese captain dropped a large bag of gold *moidores* overboard rather than let the pirates take it. Low had the poor man's lips cut off and boiled in front of him, forced the mate to eat them and then slaughtered the whole crew. He also strapped a French cook to a mast of a ship, which he then set on fire as he would fry well *'being a greasy fellow.'* Captain Lowther, who sailed with Low, used to put slow-burning fuses between a captive's fingers, letting them burn through to the bone to find out where valuables had been hidden. He cut off a New England whaling captain's ears and made him eat them with pepper and salt.

The sadism of some pirates had been embedded in them in their days in the merchant and royal navies. William Richardson served under a slave-ship captain and recorded in his diary that he *'would flog a man as soon as look at him'* The same captain *'flogged a good seaman for only losing an oar out of the boat, and the poor fellow soon after died.'* One officer forced his men to swallow live cockroaches and others took delight in rubbing beef-brine onto the wounds of flogged sailors. An old tar complained about water rations and had his front teeth knocked out and an iron pump-bolt fixed into his mouth.

His Majesty's Royal Navy was even worse. In 1704 Captain Staines of the Rochester used a tarred one-inch diameter rope to give six hundred lashes to one of his crew. Any sailor caught swearing or blaspheming was forced to hold a heavy marlin-spike in his mouth until his tongue was bloody, then the tongue was often scrubbed with sand and canvas. If a man drew a weapon his right hand was cut off.

CULVERIN
A standard 3-ton cannon, taking 18-pound cannon balls.

CUT AND RUN
This term comes to us from the days of sail. A hemp cable was cut with an axe, leaving the anchor embedded, to make an emergency getaway. It was also applied to the fact that square rigged ships were sometimes anchored in an open 'road', with the sails furled and held by ropeyarns. Again, in an emergency, the ropeyarns would be slashed and the sails dropped ready for action.

CUT OF HIS JIB
French and Spanish ships which frequented the notoriously stormy Bay of Biscay, had their foresails cut thin, so that they could not be blown off the wind when pointing. A British ship might see a large three-decker, and if it had a thin foresail, *'not like the cut of his jib'*, knowing it to be an enemy ship. The British ship might decide to *'cut and run'*, cutting the lashings on all sails to run off before the wind at speed. The crew would then *'look around for loose ends'* or rope and lash the sails when the enemy had been *'left in its wake.'*

CUT YOUR LEG
To become drunk. Billy Connolly does an excellent impression of a drunk trying to walk when one leg stays rooted to the ground, so any progress is circular.

CUTLASS, CUTLASH
A short curved sword, ideal for close range fighting on deck. One lashes out to cut the opponent, hence the name. Rapiers and *'small swords'* had long thin blades to slide between an opponent's ribs to puncture the heart of lungs. The cutlass was shorter, thicker and wider, used like a machete for hacking at limbs.

CUTTER
A one-masted ship favoured by smugglers. Galleons were too slow, and were useless after they had been ransacked. They kept any gaff cutters, fast sloops, and often redesigned the sails to get a better airflow and increase speed.

DAVY JONES'S LOCKER
The first clear reference is in Tobias Smollet's *'The Adventures of Peregrine Pickle'* in 1751: *'This same Davy Jones, according to the mythology of sailors, is the fiend that presides over all the evil spirits of the deep, and is often seen in various shapes, perching among the rigging on the eve of hurricanes, ship-wrecks, and other disasters to which sea-faring life is exposed, warning the devoted wretch of death and woe.'* Davy Jones was a spirit, or sea-devil who lived on the ocean floor. Sending someone to Davy Jones's Locker meant despatching them to the ocean's depths. The *'locker'* was the bottom of the sea, the last resting place for sunken ships and bones. How this Welsh name is attached to a sea-devil is unknown in dictionaries, but the author believes that it probably refers to a Welsh pirate in the Indian Ocean called David Jones. Serving under Captain William Cobb, then under Captain William Ayres, Jones was in charge of a lightly manned, recently taken prize ship, filled with loot, accompanying Ayres in the *'Roebuck'*. The East India Company ship *'Swan'* under Captain John Proud took Ayres' ship in 1636 off the Comoros Islands. Jones knew he could not escape with his heavily laden ship, so he scuttled it with all its incriminating evidence. *'Old Davy'* was also known as the devil from the 18th century. Another source tells us that David Jones ran a London tavern, with his own press gang who drugged his unwary patrons and stored them in the ale lockers at the back of the inn, until they could be taken aboard some departing ship.

DEAD AS BILGE WATER
The current phrase *'dead as dish water'* comes from this expression. The foul, stinking water in the bilges in the bottom of the ship gave out noxious gases, and could asphyxiate pirates.

DEADMAN
'Deadman - an "Irish Pennant" - a loose end hanging about the sails or rigging' - 'The Mariner's Dictionary

DEAD MAN'S CHEST
Edward Teach, *'Blackbeard'* (died November 22, 1718), marooned some of his crew that he considered *'mutinous'* upon a tiny island off Tortola in the Virgin Islands. It is now called Dead Chest Island. The rock was known to sailors as *'The Dead Man's Chest'* as nothing could live there except lizards, snakes and mosquitoes. Each mutineer was handed a cutlass and a bottle of rum, in the hope that they would kill each other, but a month later when he visited, fifteen were all still alive. The incident sparked the verse in Stevenson's *'Treasure Island'*:
Fifteen men on the dead man's chest,
Yo ho ho and a bottle of rum!
Drink and the Devil had done for the rest,
Yo ho ho and a bottle of rum!

Alison and Waller wrote a *'capstan shanty'* for the musical version of Treasure Island, which continues the bloodthirsty verse:

The mate was fixed by the boatswain's pike
The boatswain brained with a marlinspike
And cooky's throat was marked belike
It had been gripped by fingers ten:
And there they lay, all good dead men
Like break of day in a boozing den
Yo ho ho and a bottle of rum!

Fifteen men of the whole ship's list
Yo ho ho and a bottle of rum!
Dead and be damned and the rest gone whist!
Yo ho ho and a bottle of rum!
The skipper lay with his nob (head) *in gore*
Where the scullion's axe his cheek had shore
And the scullion he was stabbed times four
And there they lay, and the soggy skies
Dripped all day long in up-staring eyes
In murk sunset and foul sunrise
Yo ho ho and a bottle of rum!

Fifteen men lying stiff and stark
Yo ho ho and a bottle or rum!
Ten of the crew had the murder mark
Yo ho ho and a bottle of rum!
'Twas a cutlass swipe or an ounce of lead
Or a yawning hole in a battered head
And the scuppers' glut with a rotting red
And there they lay, aye, damn my eyes
All lookouts clamped on Paradise
All souls bound just contrary-wise
Yo ho ho and a bottle of rum!

Fifteen men of 'em good and true
Yo ho ho and a bottle of rum!
Ev'ry man Jack could ha' sailed with Ol' Pew,
Yo ho ho and a bottle of rum!
There was a chest on chest of Spanish gold
With a ton of plate in the middle hold
And the cabins riot of loot untold,
And there they lay that took the plum
With sightless glare and their lips struck dumb
While we shared all by the rule of thumb
Yo ho ho and a bottle of rum!

More was seen through the sternlight screed
Yo ho ho and a bottle of rum!
Chartings no doubt where a woman had been

Yo ho ho and a bottle of rum!
'Twas a flimsy shift on a bunker cot
With a thin dirk slot through the bosom spot
And the lace stiff dry in a purplish blot
Oh was she wench or some shudder' maid
That dared the knife and took the blade?
By God! She had stuff for a plucky jade
Yo ho ho and a bottle of rum!

Fifteen men on a dead man's chest
Yo ho ho and a bottle of rum!
Drink and the devil had done for the rest
Yo ho ho and a bottle of rum!
We wrapped 'em all in a mains'l tight
With twice ten turns of a hawser's bight
And we heaved 'em over and out of sight,
With a 'Yo-heave-ho!' and a 'fare-you-well'
And a sudden plunge in a sullen swell
Ten fathoms deep on the road to Hell,
Yo ho ho and a bottle of rum!

DEAD RECKONING
Until the 18th century, captains relied on a system of '*dead reckoning*' to gauge their distance east or west of a home port. Dead seems to be an abbreviation, like many sailing terms, of which the origin was '*deduced*'. The captain or navigator threw a log overboard and observed how quickly it moved away from the ship. This crude speedometer reading was noted in the log-book, along with the direction of travel, taken from the stars or a compass, plus the length of time on this particular course, reckoned by a sand-glass or pocket-watch. Intuitively reckoning the effects of currents, winds and errors of judgement, the captain could guess his longitude. Sometimes he missed his destination altogether, as did Black Bart. Other times not enough food and drink was aboard, as the voyage lengthened through navigational errors, and the crew contracted scurvy or dehydrated to death.

DEADWOOD
Heavy longitudinal timbers fastened over the keelson, to which are attached the timbers of the bow and stern. The term now is used for people who are '*along for the ride*' in the terms of being a waste of space, and dragging everyone else down.

DEFOE, DANIEL (c.1660-1731)
Captain Charles Johnson, the most reliable authority on pirates (much like Esquemeling on buccaneers) wrote '*A General History of the Robberies and Murders of the Most Notorious Pyrates*', which was first published in 1724. Many editions followed, and much information came from the transcripts of pirate trials of the time and accounts published in the Daily Post and London Gazette. In 1732 it was claimed that this was none other than Daniel Defoe, who had also published pirate fiction (*Robinson Crusoe* and *Captain Singleton*) and pirate non-fiction (on Captain Avery and John Gow). P. Furbank and W. Owens rebutted this argument in 1988 ('*The Canonisation of Daniel Defoe*'), and David Cordingley at least among pirate experts, believes that the book can no longer be attributed to Defoe.

DERROTERRO

Sailing directions used by the Spanish. The equivalent Portuguese 'roteiro' became the French 'routier', and the English 'rutter'. These were of incomparable value in the New World and East Indies. A captain could see views of the coast taken from seaward, with instructions added. Captain Bartholomew Sharp captured one in the South Pacific from the Spanish ship Rosario in 1680. This was most unusual, because they were usually thrown weighted overboard in the face of pirate attack. When Sharp was tried for piracy, he gave Charles II the translation of the priceless derroterro he had captured from the Rosario. He was acquitted, and made a captain in the Royal Navy. English rutters held details of anchorages, harbours, courses etc., and were continually updated by their owners, often being passed down from father to son.

A GENERAL

HISTORY

OF THE

Robberies and Murders

Of the most notorious

PYRATES,

AND ALSO

Their *Policies, Discipline* and *Government*,

From their first RISE and SETTLEMENT in the Island of *Providence*, in 1717, to the present Year 1724.

WITH

The remarkable ACTIONS and ADVENTURES of the two Female Pyrates, *Mary Read* and *Anne Bonny*.

To which is prefix'd

An ACCOUNT of the famous Captain *Avery* and his Companions; with the Manner of his Death in *England*.

The Whole digested into the following CHAPTERS;

Chap. I. Of Captain *Avery*.   VIII. Of Captain *England*.
II. The Rise of Pyrates.   IX. Of Captain *Davis*.
III. Of Captain *Martel*.   X. Of Captain *Roberts*.
IV. Of Captain *Bonnet*.   XI. Of Captain *Worley*.
V. Of Captain *Thatch*.   XII. Of Captain *Lowther*.
VI. Of Captain *Vane*.   XIII. Of Captain *Low*.
VII. Of Captain *Rackam*.   XIV. Of Captain *Evans*.
And their several Crews.

To which is added,

A short ABSTRACT of the Statute and Civil Law, in Relation to PYRACY.

By Captain CHARLES JOHNSON.

LONDON, Printed for *Ch. Rivington* at the *Bible* and *Crown* in St. *Paul's Church-Yard*, *J. Lacy* at the *Ship* near the *Temple-Gate*, and *J. Stone* next the *Crown* Coffee-house the back of *Grey's-Inn*, 1724.

Frontispiece of the General History

DEVIL TO PAY (also see Caulk)

The first plank on the outer keel of a wooden ship was called the *garboard*, but known universally by seamen as the '*devil*', because it was the most awkward to get at during careening. It was the longest seam in the vessel. It was almost impossible to keep the devil above water, to '*pay*' oakum into its seam, hammer home and cover with hot pitch to seal it. '**The devil to pay**, *and no pitch hot*' was a desperate situation where seamen could see no means of solving a problem. '**Between the Devil and the deep blue sea**' also comes from a ship's devil, meaning that there was only the thickness of the ship's hull plank between the garboard seam and the ocean depths. The use of '*devil bolts*' was a corrupt practice used by ship-builders to save money. The 64-gun warship York foundered in the North Sea because copper bolts were not used to hold the ship's timbers together at key points. Instead, the bolts had been faked by inserting copper heads and tails in appropriate positions, connected only by hidden wooden dowels.

DINGHY

A small ship's boat with no sail.

THE DOCTOR

The name given by West Indians to the cooling trade wind. The '*Harmattan*', a cooling easterly wind from December to February (the dry season) on the west coast of Africa, is also known as the '*doctor*'. Perhaps slavers or slaves took the terminology across the Atlantic with them.

DON'T SPOIL THE SHIP FOR A HA'PORTH OF TAR

Leaving a job half-done by not properly using hot tar to fill in the planks when careening.

DOUBLOONS
The largest of Spanish gold coins, derived from '*doblon*'. The '*ducado*' was worth less, about 10 '*reales*', and known to the British seaman as a ducat. The '*escudo*' was worth 10 reales. Silver pesos were known as '*pieces of eight*' (q.v.)

DOUGHBOYS
Hard dumplings made of a quarter pound of flour and boiled in sea-water, described in Dampier's '*Voyages*' of 1697. They were still standard fare in the Royal Navy in 1897. The use of the word in the early twentieth century, describing an American private in the army, was because the shape of the buttons on his tunic resembles '*doughboys*'.

DRESSING DOWN
Canvas sails could easily become waterlogged, which made the ship hard to handle and caused rot and tears. Thus they had to be treated with preservatives and oils to repel water. This could only be done when the sails were rigged, rather than rolled up. Thus to '*dress down*' both sides of a sail, hanging off ropes, while the sail was flapping and snapping in one's face, was an unpleasant but necessary experience, the origin of today's term.

DRINK LIKE A FISH
A term from the 1640's on, meaning to constantly drink alcohol. Pirates drank to while away the boredom between prizes.

DRINK TILL YOU GIVE UP YOUR HALFPENNY
To drink until one vomits.

DROGER
A coastal trade ship in the West Indies.

DROPSY
Old naval term for Oedema, internally swelling with water retention. The following definition comes from the Welsh-American Ambrose Gwinnett Bierce's '*The Devil's Dictionary*' of 1911.
'*Dropsy, n. A disease which makes the patient's lease of life a kind of naval engagement.*
Dick, through all his life, had cherished
An ambition when he perished
To be drowned in the deep ocean, -
Not from any foolish notion,
That so damp a death was cheerful,
But because the wretch was fearful
That he some day would exhibit
On the tight-rope of a gibbet;
Or, escaping that curtailment,
Die of some distressing ailment,
Giving up the ghost by inches
With contortions, twinges, flinches.
Death at last one day assailed him,
And with agonies impaled him -
Pegged him firmly for the slaughter
Fifteen hundred miles from water !
Now, his bowels all were topsy
Turvy with a case of dropsy,
And his abdomen was bloating,

And his vitals were a-floating,
When, between the paroxysmal
Rush of tides along the dismal
Channels of his ventilating
Apparatus - when his lungs were
Full as barrels, and no bungs were
Hand to reduce the billow,
Richard, strangling on his pillow,
Turned his body, spouted finely
Like a whale, and smiled divinely,
Saying "twixt convulsions frantic:
"Every man his own Atlantic".'

DRY GRIPES
Pirates referred to this as a peculiarly West Indian disease. It was poisoning caused by drinking large quantities of rum, which had been distilled in lead pipes as glass was not readily available.

DRY TORTUGAS
A shoal of islands used by British pirates, at the western end of the Florida Keys. Turtling was important to pirate diets, and they were possibly called this to distinguish them from Tortuga (Ile de la Tortue) off Hispaniola, and Salt Tortuga off Venzuela. Turtles caught at Sale Tortuga were cured using salt from the nearby salt-pans of the Araya Peninsula. Perhaps turtles caught at the Dry Tortugas were dry-cured.

DUCKING AT THE YARD ARM
For a punishment in the Royal Navy, a seaman was tied under his arms, around his waist and under his groin, hauled up on a rope to a spar and dropped violently into the sea several times. (See *Keel-Hauling*). Some pirates amended the ducking so that the victim was dropped onto the deck, to encourage others to divulge the whereabouts of loot, before it was their turn for a 'ducking'. Other punishments favoured at sea were being forced to eat live cockroaches, filling up someone's mouth with iron bolts, and knocking out teeth with metal bolts.

DRUNK WITH A CONTINUANDO
Plastered, in a drunken condition for days at a time.

DUTCH
Slang for good beer. A '*Dutch bargain*' was a one-sided transaction. A '*Dutch caper*' was a small privateering ship. The '*Dutch pump*' was a punishment involving vigorous exercise pumping out bilge-water. A '*Dutch widow*' was another term for a prostitute, or bawd.

DUTCH COURAGE
There seem to have been few Dutch pirates, although it was a great seafaring nation, because Holland had fisheries where men could find work, whereas in England and Wales men had to beg for a living. Pirates were also wary about attacking Dutch ships because of their reputation for bravery and prolonged resistance. Thus the alliance of 'Dutch courage' with the effects of alcohol giving bravado seems to be a demeaning, and later use of the phrase. In the 17th century the Dutch were hated commercial and military enemies, and other derogatory meanings of Dutch are '*Dutch auction*' (where everything is backwards); '*double Dutch*' (gibberish); '*to go Dutch*' (to pay for yourself, a variation of '*Dutch treat*', and '*I'm a Dutchman*'.) It seems to have

stemmed from the Anglo-Dutch Wars in the 1660's, when British captains propagandised their crews by saying that the Dutch could only fight when fortified with schnapps. A historical account of the time reads *'the (Dutch) captain of the Hollander man-of-war, when about to engage with our ships, usually set a hogshead of brandy before the mast, and bid the men drink ... and our men felt the force of the brandy to their cost.'* However, it may be that the origin was the ability of Dutch gin to give an Englishman courage. Until its sale was restricted to licensed premises, Dutch gin was the cheapest and most powerful alcohol freely available in Britain, as Hogarth's brilliant *'Gin Street'* etchings show its effect upon the general population. One last possible origin of the term is when Dutch traders sailed up the Thames in the time of the Great Plague to carry on business, although all other commerce had stopped.

EARRINGS
These were extremely popular in pirate companies as some believed that they improved eyesight. Early blindness was common for lookout men, perhaps squinting into the sun for hours at a time. However, it seems that the real reason for the wearing of an earring by nautical men was that it would pay for their funeral if they died on land.

THE HONOURABLE EAST INDIA COMPANY
One of 8 companies set up in the late 16th century to exploit trade in India, the East Indies and the Far East. Others were set up by Scotland, Holland, France, Denmark, Spain, Austria and Sweden, but only the Dutch company was significant competition. It was given a charter by Elizabeth 1 on December 31, 1600, with 215 shareholders, and by 1612 friendly relations were established with the Shogun of Japan, thanks to John Adams. By 1630, it had a practical monopoly of the India trade. There is a remarkable description of torture carried out on East India Company men by Dutch officials, relating to the *'Amboyna Massacre'* in the wonderful *'Nathaniel's Nutmeg'* by Giles Milton. To relate these practices, carried out to protect the spice monopoly, would sicken the reader.

EAST INDIAMAN
A magnificent armed merchant ship, owned and operated by the East India companies for trading with India and the East. A *'Guineaman'* traded with the Guinea coast of Africa. These were the largest ships built, and the captain, passengers and officers had relatively excellent accommodation.

EGAD, MATELOT!
According to W. Adolphe Roberts, a traditional buccaneer greeting, but far more likely, fiction.

ESQUEMELING, JOHN (c.1645-c.1707)
This French Huguenot, often described as a *'Dutchman'*, wrote the definitive history of the buccaneers, *'The Bucaniers of America'*. He tells us that he went voluntarily to the West Indies, to Tortuga, in the service of the French West India Company. They sold him on to a cruel landowner, who fell ill, and sold Esquemeling to a surgeon for seventy pieces of eight. The surgeon treated him humanely, supplying reasonable food and decent clothes, and after a year offered Esquemeling his freedom for indenture, for just one hundred pieces of eight, that should be repaid when the Dutchman was *'in a capacity to do so.'* Being an honourable man, he resolved to repay this debt and joined the buccaneers as the quickest way of doing so. He voyaged during these years in the fleet under Henry Morgan. As he had assisted a surgeon, he travelled as a ship's surgeon until he returned home in 1674, some time after the great assault on Panama. (See Sea Rovers). The 1684 English version was translated from the anti-English Spanish

Buccaneers taking a Spanish ship, from Juhn Exquemelin's *Bucaniers of America*, Amsterdam, 1700.

version and was therefore libellous to Sir Henry Morgan. The first edition of the book was principally entitled 'De Americaensche Zee-Roovers' and published in 1678 in Amsterdam. It was followed by a 1679 Nuremburg edition called '*Americanische Seerauber*' and the 1681 Spanish edition 'Piratas de la America.' The 1684 '*Bucaniers of America; or a true account of the ....assaults committed...upon the coasts of the West Indies, by the Bucaniers of Jamaica...especially the...exploits of Sir Henry Morgan....written originally in Dutch by J. Esquemeling... now rendered into English, London 1684*'. A second edition followed within three months, followed shortly by a different English version in 1684 vindicating Morgan and absolving him of the cruelties and lusts so obvious in the first two editions – the new book was entitled '*The History of the Bucaniers; being an impartial account of all the battels, sieges, and other most eminent assaults committed for several years upon the coasts of the West Indies by the pirates of Jamaica and Tortuga. More especially the unparalleled achievements of Sir Henry Morgan.... Very much corrected from the errors of the original, by the relations of some English gentlemen, that then resided in those parts*'

EXECUTION DOCK
This is still pointed out by the guides on river trips on the Thames in London. Pirates were executed here at Wapping Old Stairs, usually by hanging, but in former years by tying them to poles in the mud, and waiting for the tide to come in and cover them. Usually the pirates were left on tall gallows, hung in chains as an example to others.

EYE-PATCH
The most common cause for this amongst '*sea-dogs*' was not sword-play but staring into the sun. Before John Davis invented the '*backstaff*' in 1595, navigators had to use '*sighting-sticks*' to measure the sun's height above the horizon by looking directly into its glare to find latitude. In a few years, the sight of the eye was ruined.

FACE (OR BRAG) IT OUT WITH A CARD OF TEN
To set upon the enemy with none too sure an opinion of the outcome. In a card game, a card of ten spots is useful, but not sure to win. This assumption of a bold front would be better with a '*sure card*', another saying of the time.

FATHOM
A depth of six feet.

FEELING BLUE
This may refer to the dread of '*Blue Monday*' with its harsh punishments. It is more likely to

have come from the fact that any sailing ship that lost its captain or any officer at sea, flew a blue flag, or painted a blue band across the hull, when returning to port.

FELONY
In these times, all felonies were capital offences (see Punishment and Pillory). However, for very minor offences, if a thief could prove he could read he might plead *'benefit of clergy'* and escape with being branded *'T'* for thief on his cheek. This punishment lasted until 1829. Some pirates managed to get away with the brand of *'P'*.

FIGHTS
In Mainwaring's 'Seaman's Dictionary' of 1644, these are *'the waist cloths which hang around the ship to hide men from being seen in fight. Also any bulkhead or small shot (compartment) wherein men may cover themselves and yet use their arms are called close fights.' 'Top armours are the cloths which are tied around the top of the masts for show, and also for men to hide in fight which lie there and throw firepots, use small shot, or the like.'*

FILIBUSTIERS
Another French term for buccaneer, in Spanish *'filibusteros'* and in English it became *'filibusterers'* and freebooters. The origin is the Dutch *'vrijbuiter'*. Other sources say that the French could not pronounce vrijbuiter or freebooter, and their attempt, *'filibustier'* returned into the English language as filibuster in the nineteenth century. A more recent theory is that the origin was the Dutch *'vliebooter'*, the small flyboat used so successfully in the fight for independence from Spain in the 16th century. By the end of that century, the term had come to mean a fast sailing vessel used for piracy or discovery, and by the late 17th century had come to mean seaborne raiders.

FIRESHIP
As used against the Spanish Armada, and by Henry Morgan. The preferred option was to use grappling irons to attach the fireship against an enemy vessel, whereupon the attacking crew would light a slow match and escape in a small boat.

FIREWORKS
Devices used to set alight enemy ships, such as fire-balls, which were cannon balls heated red-hot in a brazier before being fired. Fire-pikes were boarding pikes with burning twine or cloth attached, thrown like javelins at the sails and decks.

FISH
A large piece of wood attached to the mast to strengthen it.

FISH BROTH
Salt water, the sea.

FISHMONGER
'Fishmonger' meant whore, probably derived from *'fleshmonger'*, and *'fishmonger's daughter'* also came to mean a harlot, from the late 16th century.

FLAKE OUT
It was important to keep the anchor chain in good condition, and it was regularly laid out along the deck - *'flaked'* - to check for weak links. The anchor was also often *'flaked out'* on deck in preparation for anchoring, laid out in such a way so that it does not *'foul up'* when the anchor is dropped. Lying down in the sun on deck became known as *'flaking out'*.

FLAW

A sudden and unexpected gust of wind. The modern word flaw, in the sense of an unexpected defect, may have the same origin.

FLIP

A strong, and favourite pirate 'cocktail' of 'small beer', brandy and sugar, heated with a red-hot iron, popular from the 17th century onwards. 'Small beer' was a light or watered beer, and flip seems to have been derived from the name Philip. The pirate captain, Henry Every, was described as 'lolling at Madagascar with some drunken sunburnt whore, over a can of flip.' This sounds a very appealing description of piracy to those tolling under the most onerous taxation burden in Europe in the present day.

FLOGGING THE MONKEY

Small casks of rum were known as monkeys, and a thirsty sailor would obtain an illicit drink by rinsing it out with water to get some alcohol into his system.

FLOGGING ROUND THE FLEET

Yet another device used by the Royal Navy to encourage men to desert or become pirates. A court-martialled man was strapped across a grating on a boat and rowed alongside the ships of the fleet lying in harbour. He was given 12 strokes of the cat o' nine tails at the first ship by the boatswain's mate, twelve at the second and so on. The crew of each ship was paraded on deck to watch the punishment.

FLORIDA STRAITS

Probably the best place for pirates and privateers to wait for Spanish treasure fleets leaving America. Passing through these, the Spanish could then pick up strong Westerly winds to get back to Spain.

FLOTA

The Spanish treasure fleet that usually made its way once a year towards Spain from the gold and silver mines of South and Central America. Its captains took an oath to burn, sink or destroy their ships rather than let them fall into enemy hands and enrich their resources. Thus pirates tried to take such ships by stealth, or extremely quickly. Swinburne, in 'Travels in Spain', 1779, wrote 'The flota is a fleet of large ships which carry the goods of Europe to the ports of America, and bring back the produce of Mexico, Peru, and other kingdoms of the New World.' A flotilla was a small fleet.

The convoy of treasure ships would use the strongest ships to carry the most treasure. The flota would shun contact and run rather than fight, but could be caught by sloops. However, the galleons' tremendous firepower deterred most pirates and buccaneers. If a ship came in close enough to attempt to board a Spanish galleon, there were razor-sharp crescent blades attached to the edges of its outermost masts, which would cut the boarder's sails to shreds. The galleons also had fighting platforms halfway up the mainmast and foremast, from where archers would release showers of arrows and crossbow bolts. They could not use firearms for fear of sparks setting the oiled sails on fire. The annual fleets heading for Veracruz in Mexico were known as flotas, and to avoid confusion, the fleets sailing to Cartagena (Colombia) and Panama were known as 'Galeones'.

FLOTSAM AND JETSAM

Flotsam is lost off a ship by accident and found floating. Jetsam is a ship's goods and equipment that has been jettisoned (thrown overboard) to make the ship more stable in heavy seas, or to lighten it if being chased.

(DUTCH) FLUTE
Early 17th century ship, cheap to build, with a large hold, and easy prey for pirates.

FLY BY NIGHT
When sailing downwind at night, a large, single, *'fly-by-night'* sail was used to do the job of several smaller sails. Requiring less attention, it could only be used downwind, usually at night, so was very rarely seen by sailors.

FOG
The greatest hindrance to pirates who drifted up the American coast from the West Indies when they reached Newfoundland, even great storms will not clear it, as Bellamy and Williams discovered. The Mariner's Dictionary tells us *'the warm water of the Gulf Stream penetrating high latitudes is productive of fog, especially in the vicinity of the Grand Banks where the cold waters of the Labrador Current makes the contrast in the temperatures of the adjacent waters most striking.'* This was the setting for the book and film *'The Perfect Storm'*.

FOOTLOOSE
The bottom of the sail is its foot, and when it is not tied to a boom, it is loose-footed, dancing freely in the wind with no restrictions, with a mind of its own, from which we get the saying *'footloose and fancy-free'*.

FORE-AND-AFT-RIGGED
The inside (*luff*) edge of a sail is attached to a mast, and the lower edge to a boom. The boom can then be moved from one side of the ship to another to direct the ship or react to winds.

FORECASTLE
Formerly a raised deck at the front of the ship, from where arrows were directed at the enemy – it served the function of a castle tower. Over the years its height was lowered and lowered to make boats more manoeuvrable, and to enable the captain on the poop deck to see what was happening. So the forecastle (pronounced *'folksle'*) just came to mean the front decking. In medieval ships there were also *'aftercastles'* for the knights and soldiers on board fighting ships, making them very unwieldy and unseaworthy.

FORLORN
17th century term for the vanguard of a military expedition such as Morgan's march on Panama. The French equivalent of a 'forlorn' was *'les enfants perdus'* - the lost children.

FOUL UP
If an anchor is entangled with its cable, it is *'fouled up'*. A *'foul berth'* is caused by another vessel anchoring too closely, where there could be a collision. A *'foul bottom'* means that it is difficult to secure anchors. *'Fall foul of'* is a nautical term for becoming impeded.

FREEBOOTER
From the Dutch *'Friebuiter'* or pirate.

FRENCH GOODS, or GOUT
Syphilis. To be *'Frenchified'* was to suffer from venereal disease. *'Frenchman'* was applied to any

foreigner, and was also a synonym for syphilis. The prevalence of venereal diseases was often the main reason for wanting a doctor on board, and sometimes ships were taken just for the contents of their medical chests to treat the illness.

FRENCH KING, TO HAVE SEEN THE
To have been blind-drunk.

FRIGATE
With upwards of twenty guns, this fast warship was not big enough to be a '*ship of the line*' for the '*line of battle*' of the Navy, but often used for independent action such as against pirates. 'A *well-dressed frigate*' could also mean a woman.

FROM THE SEAS
If a pirate ship was hailed and asked her home port, this could be the answer given. By their articles, pirates forsook their homelands, and thereupon belonged only '*to the seas*'.

FUDGE
'*Fudging the books*' comes from a Captain Fudge, known as '*Lying Fudge*'. He was the captain of the 'Black Eagle' which was to transport 55 Quakers in August 1655 from the Newgate to the Colonies, for offences against the Conventicle Act. Delayed at Gravesend, by October, 19 prisoners and some crew had died of the plague. He was arrested for debt and his remaining crew mutinied. In February 1666 the ship left for the West Indies, but was seized by a Dutch privateer and the Quakers freed.

GALE
A wind of 34-40 knots, force 8 on the Beaufort Scale. A strong gale is 41-47 knots, force 9. A storm is classified as over 49-55knots, force 10, and a violent storm is 55-63 knots, force 11. Hurricanes are over 63 knots. The violent storms and hurricanes in the Caribbean wreaked havoc with the little privateers and pirate ships. One of Morgan's flagships was only 120 tons, so would disappear from view in a stormy sea.

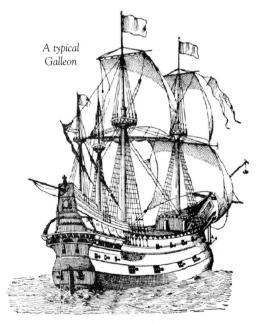

A typical Galleon

GALIZABRA
A fast Spanish frigate, heavily armed, used in the 17th and 18th centuries. These could bring treasure back to Seville from the Spanish Main by themselves, rather than wait for the escorted convoy of treasure galleons known as the '*flota*'.

GALLEON
Either used for trade or war, these huge ships had three or four masts, square rigged on the foremast and mainmast, and *latine*-rigged on the after-mast(s).

A galleon on the transatlantic route might vary between 400 and 1000 tons, with 500 being an average ship. Sailing qualities varied, with speeds of 4-8 knots, and they could carry 20-76 guns of varying calibre. If used as a man-of-war, there were 36 guns mounted on each side of her, with two remaining guns mounted aft, making 74 cannon, plus numerous swing guns mounted along the rail used to repel boarders. They were usually terribly overcrowded, often carrying an infantry company of at least 100 troops under an army captain. There was a 'split command', whereas on Dutch and English ships the naval captain also commanded the soldiers. Because of its high sides and even higher poop deck, the galleon was easily rocked by the sea, and it pitched and rolled more than other ships.

GALLEY
Formerly a ship that could be rowed, the term came to mean, in late seventeenth century England, an armed merchantman with one or more flush decks. The slave ship *Princess*, upon which Bartholomew Roberts served, was a galley of this type.

GALLEYPEPPER
The soot and ashes that fell into pirates' meals from the cook's open fire in his galley, or kitchen.

THE GALLOWS DANCE
The jiggling of feet of a man being hanged

GAMMY
Lame, as in having a '*gammy leg*'. Some ships were '*gammy*' if they were difficult to steer, especially if cargo had shifted. From the Welsh mutation of '*cam*' meaning crooked, awry or wrong, as in Dafydd Gam (David who is lame, or has a squint). In E. Annie Proulx's '*The Shipping News*' we learn that '*The common eider is called a "gammy bird" in Newfoundland for its habit of gathering in flocks for sociable quacking sessions. The name is related to the days of sail, when two ships falling in with each other at sea would back their yards and shout the news. The ship to windward would back her main yards and the one to leeward her foreyards. For close manoeuvring. This was known as gamming*' This author believes that 'gammy' is the only word of the ancient Welsh language used commonly in English, along with 'mom' or 'mum' from the Welsh 'mam' meaning mother, and 'dad' from the mutation of the Welsh 'tad', or father.

GEORGES
English gold coins

GET SPLICED
To '*get hitched*' or married, when two ropes are joined together.

GIBBET
A wooden structure for exhibiting hanged pirates over a length of time.

GILT - KNOCK THE GILT OFF THE GINGERBREAD
This means to spoil the best part of a thing or story. In German fairs, gingerbread was always on sale, and splashed with gilt to make its appearance more attractive. From this custom, the gilding and painted carvings at the bows, stern and entrance ports of sailing ships of war came to be known as '*gingerbread work*'. To '*knock the gilt off the gingerbread*' was therefore to incur the wrath of a captain by damaging the appearance of the vessel.

GIVE A WIDE BERTH
Avoid a dangerous-looking ship, or give lots of room to manoeuvring vessels. It has come to mean to 'steer clear of' any person in a foul mood.

GOING TO POT
The large kettles or cauldrons used for cooking were never cleaned out. Whatever was available was added to the existing contents, even leftovers were added. Table scraps were not wasted, but thrown into the ever-cooking stew-pot. The term referred to things that no-one wanted any more, thus we now say that a High Street is going to pot, with the advent of out-of-town shopping malls.

GO ON THE ACCOUNT
Undertake a buccaneer or pirate voyage. The term stems from the fact that if their actions were illegal, the person would have to account for his actions as within the law.

GRAPNEL, or GRAPPLE
A light anchor with very sharp flukes, which could be thrown at the ship to be boarded. The barbed flukes hooked into the ship, were difficult to extract, and pirates would climb the attached ropes.

GREEK FIRE
Fire bombs aimed at sails and rigging from cannon, to disable a ship's movement.

GRENADE
A square bottle filled with pistol shot, bits of iron and gunpowder, it was a favourite assault weapon of pirates and buccaneers. Used between 1650 and 1750, Johnston wrongly attributes their invention to Blackbeard - 'a new fashioned Sort of Grenadoes, viz. Case bottles filled with Powder, and small Shot, Slugs, and Pieces of Lead or Iron, with a quick Match in the Mouth of it.' 'Granado Shells', or 'granadoes' were in common use from about 1700, the name derived from the Spanish 'granada' meaning pomegranate. They were also sometimes also called 'powder flasks', hollow balls made of iron or wood and filled with gunpowder. With a touch hole and a fuse, it was thrown at the men on the opposite deck before boarding. No less than 15 grenades have been found on the wreck of the Whydah.

GROG
Alcohol, usually Jamaica rum. We still say we are 'feeling groggy' today if we are not very well – this refers to the frequency of pirate hangovers in the seventeenth and eighteenth centuries when pirates used to carouse between and during voyages 'on the account.' In the Royal Navy, rum replaced brandy as the daily ration because of its cheap availability from newly conquered Jamaica. However, in 1740 Admiral Vernon ensured that the rum was diluted with water, because of drunkenness in the fleet. The daily pint of rum was replaced by adding two pints of water (a quart), and dispensed upon two occasions during the day instead of at one time. As the rum in those days could easily be 60% proof and above, it is no wonder that some crews were incapable of action if they drank a pint quickly. Drunken sailors were punished until the early twentieth century by having 'six water grog', their allowance diluted with six parts water instead of three parts. Grog (in decreasing proportions) was served in the Royal Navy until 1970. Sadly, the last 'grog ration' - one part rum to three parts water -issued twice a day to sailors in half-pint measures, was drunk on July 30th, 1970.

GROG BLOSSOM

Either an inflammation on the face, or the 'purple' nose associated with heavy drinkers – often a form of Acne Rosacea rather than by over-imbibing. W.C. Fields suffered from this, as did John Pierpoint Morgan, the great American financier of Welsh descent. The author suffers from this annoying complaint, which is often triggered by alcohol and spicy food. Sometimes, life is not fair.

GROG SHOP

Tavern or pub.

GUARDACOSTA - COSTA GARDA

Private revenue cutters used by the Spanish to enforce their Caribbean trading monopoly. They were commissioned by local governors and earned their money by the prizes that they took. An account by Defoe in his General History tells us: 'A Guarda del Costa, of Porto Rico, commanded by one Matthew Luke, an Italian, took four English vessels, and murdered all the crews. He was taken by the Lanceston Man of War, in May 1722, and brought to Jamaica, where they were all but seven deservedly hanged. It is likely the man-of-war might not have meddled with her, but she blindly laid the Lanceston on board*, thinking that she had been a Merchant Ship, who thereupon catched a Tartar. Afterwards, in rummaging, there was found a Cartridge of Powder which was made up of an English journal, belonging, I believe, to the Crean snow; and upon this examination, at last, it was discovered that they had taken this vessel and murdered the crew; and one of the Spaniards, when he came to die, confessed that he had killed twenty Englishmen with his own hands.' (* to lay aboard is to draw alongside a ship to board it)

These 17th century 'Spanish' coastguard boats tried to stop all foreign trade to the West Indies. They regularly tortured English, Dutch and French merchant seamen and handed them over to the Inquisition. They were privateers, including Irish and English captains, commissioned by Spanish crown officials, and were restricted in peacetime, but from the 1670's had almost free rein to protect the Spanish West Indies and mainland from pirate, smuggling and logwood raids. They complemented the activities of the Armada de Barlovento, the Spanish royal squadron which patrolled the Caribbean. Guardacostas were given authority to patrol a particular stretch of coastline, and based in a specific port. Their crews were therefore fresh and ready for action, and had to be successful, for they were mercenaries who lived off the prizes they took. Acting Governor Molesworth of Jamaica, complained in 1684 that 'these galleys and piraguas are mostly manned by Greeks, but they are of all nations, rogues culled out for the villainies they commit. They never hail a ship; and so they can but master her, she is a certain prize. They lurk in the bushes by the shore, so that they can see every passing vessel without being seen. When our sloops are at anchor they set them by their compasses in the daytime, and steal on them at night with so little noise that they are aboard before they are discovered.' The previous year, Governor Lynch had written to London that the Spanish had armed some small craft and 'ordered them to take all ships that have on board any "frutos de esas Indias" (fruits of these Indies), whereby they make all fish that come to net. They have committed barbarous cruelties and injustices, and better cannot be expected, for they are Corsicans, Slavonians, Greeks, mulattoes, a mongrel parcel of thieves and rogues that rob and murder all that come into their power without the least respect to humanity or common justice.'

GUINEAMAN

A slave ship operating off the Guinea Coast of West Africa.

GUINEAS

English coins made from gold from Guinea.

GULF STREAM
The huge, warm 'North Equatorial Current' which moves from the Caribbean to the Gulf of Mexico, through the Florida Straits, up across the Grand Banks of Newfoundland and across the Atlantic at 80 miles per day, to warm the seas of the west coast of Britain. and Europe.

GUN, SURE AS A
To be positive, or 'true' as a gun. Not until the late 17th century did 'sure' detach itself from 'as a gun' and become a word in its own right in any context.

GUNNER'S DAUGHTER
The gun to which boys serving in the Royal Navy were tied or 'married' when being whipped. On some ships it was superstition that if the boys were not whipped on a Monday, there would be no good winds for the following week. To 'hug' or 'kiss the gunner's daughter' thus meant a whipping. When 'married to the gunner's daughter' for a flogging, the miscreant was tied to the four deck rings which held each cannon in place. As the sailor was tied to the gun barrel, the saying 'you've got me over a barrel' comes from this time. Sailors were whacked with a rope's end on the gun deck, where the ceilings were only a maximum of four feet six inches. For more serious offences, requiring enough room to 'swing a cat' of nine tails, the punishment was carried out on the main deck.

GUN WALLS, GUN WALES, GUNNELS
In the 15th century, these were called 'gonne walles', the upper edge of a ship's side, that prevented guns and other deck items from falling over the side. They had openings, to let sea water wash from the deck, and to let guns fire. The saying 'awash to the gunnels' means that the sea is coming over the deck. Derived from the same source is 'packed' or 'full to the gun wales' that is that the lower decks are crammed full of cargo and men, and so is the top deck, so that the ship can take no more plunder. A 'wale' was any of the strakes on the side of a vessel, from the Old English 'walen', or ridge.

HAG-BOAT
Also referred to as a hog-boat. In the chapter on Black Bart Roberts, we find that his Royal Rover is classified as a hog-boat: The Weekly Journal reported in 1720 on the action 'The Lisbon Fleet from the Bay of All Saints, Brazil, has arrived. But one vessel of 36 guns was taken by a pyrate ship (formerly an English hog-boat) and two others plundered.'

HAND OVER FIST
Seamen used to climb the rigging 'hand over hand', but someone who accumulated yardage quickly was said to be climbing 'hand over fist'.

HALF-MUSKET SHOT
The preferred 'killing range' for maximum effect of a broadside of cannon. At 100 yards, this was point-blank range, and the Royal Navy generally aimed at the hull to sink the ship. Other navies used different types of cannon to fire at longer range at the masts and yards of British ships to prevent them from closing in.

HALF-SEAS OVER
A term meaning half-way across the sea, or nearly finished, which came to mean 'pretty well gone' or drunk.

HALF-SLEWED

When the yards which carry the sails are not properly braced to deflect the wind, they are said to be half-slewed, faltering and swaying ineffectively - hence the synonym for affected by alcohol.

HALYARDS

The ropes by which sails are hoisted, e.g. the jib halyards, top sail halyards, etc.

HAMMOCK

Columbus noted that the Carib Indians slung a 'hamorca' between trees, and he then introduced it into European ships. Their swinging action counteracted the swell of the waves and made for a more comfortable sleep than in a bunk or on deck. Hammocks on Royal Naval vessels were first authorised in 1597.

HANGING, DRAWING AND QUARTERING

This barbarous practice was brought by the Normans to England, and practised upon various Welsh princes and their followers up until the fifteenth century. It is said that it was personally devised by King Edward for the ritual slaughter of Prince Dafydd, the brother of the murdered Llywelyn, at Shrewsbury in 1282. It stayed as the official sentence for treason, forgery, the murder of a master by a servant and (sometimes) piracy until 1814 in Britain. King Charles II watched the regicides who signed his father's death warrant suffer this sentence in 1660. The condemned man was dragged on a sledge and hanged, but not until he was dead. He would be cut down within a few minutes, then fastened to a stone block, when the executioner cut off his penis and testicles, cut open his stomach and pulled out his intestines, which had to be burnt before the prisoner's eyes. English law insisted that the prisoner be disembowelled while still alive. The body was then cut into quarters, which were displayed in various public places. These executions drew huge crowds. Women who forged or committed treason were not to be 'mangled publicly' but burnt alive. It was treason for a woman to murder her husband but not for a man to kill his wife. A woman was slowly burnt for 'coining' in 1789 in front of huge crowds in London.

HANGMAN'S KNOT

From the inestimable 'The Ashley Book of Knots', 1944, which lists and illustrates 3854* different kinds of knots: 'There are several knots recommended for this purpose, and there are several variations of the one given here that may be found in the chapter on NOOSES. But this knot of eight turns appears to be the standard one, and it may be counted upon to draw up smoothly and snugly when it fulfils its office. The noose is always adjusted with the knot slightly below and immediately in back of the left ear. This is to provide the sideways jerk, which is one of the refinements of a successful hanging. Hangings at sea were infrequent. Such an occasion furnished a bit of extra-routine labour, in which the boatswain took especial pride, and in which no bungling was tolerated. A boatswain's reputation would be forever ruined if there were any hitch on such an occasion… certain well-established conventions had to be observed… A fall was led through a single block at the fore yardarm and thence to a second single block under the fore cap. Between the two blocks was a yardarm knot, the upper bight of which was not half-hitched, as is customary, but was merely stopped with light twine. This stopping would carry away the instant the knot was hauled against the block, so spilling the sheepshank. The weight at the noose end at once dropped to take up the slack given by the spilled sheepshank, and it was brought up with a jerk by a toggle which fetched against the yardarm block. The toggle was marlingspike hitched and seized to the rope at a point which allowed for an exact six-foot drop outside the rail. In preparation for this the fall was laid at a length along the deck 'ready to be hurried aft' when twenty stout fellows seized the rope.'

*Of course, Ashley includes as knot 491, the *'double bastard weaver's knot'*. The author has had the opportunity to know some of the species known as *'double bastards'*, always in the top management layers of organisations.

HAZARD
The most common card game in Black Bart's time, to while away the hours. However, dice games were the most popular pursuit and the quarrels caused by gambling on his ship forced Black Bart to get his pirates to abandon them except on land.

HARD AS BRAZIL
A term dating from the mid-17th century, meaning extremely tough, stemming from the shipping of Brazilian hardwoods.

HARD TACK
A term for ship's biscuits, made of flour and water, which could last for months if stored correctly.

HAVEN'T A CLEW (CLUE)
The sails are attached at their corners by brass rings (*cringles*) sewn into the clews. If the clew should become undone, and the vessel *'has no clew'*, it will not sail anywhere until it is *'clewed up'* again.

HEAVE TO, or LIE TO
Sails were set to counteract each other, so the ship stayed almost motionless.

HELM
From 'The Gentleman's Dictionary', 1705, we read: *'HELM, or Tiller, of a Ship; is that Piece of timber which is fastened into the Rudder, and so comes forward into the Steerage, or Place where he at the Helm Steers the Ship, by holding the Whipstaff in his Hand. Some Ships have a Wheel, like those in Cranes, placed between the Quarter-Deck and Coach; which has several Advantages, to what the Common Methods have.'*

HEMPEN FEVER
The pirate joke was that one would rather die by this, i.e. by hanging, than suffering in the merchant or Royal Navy.

HIDE A LOUSE FOR THE SAKE OF ITS SKIN
To be thrifty or try to save something, a habit despised by most pirates, who lived their short lives by the day.
HIGH AND DRY
A ship that has been run aground so far as to be seen dry on the strand.

HISPANIOLA
Columbus called the island today shared by Haiti and the Dominican Republic 'Isla Espanola' (Island of Little Spain) in 1492, and Hispaniola is the Anglicised version of it. Under Oliver Cromwell's grandiose *'Western Design'*, he discussed a possible alliance with Spain, while sending out a force to seize Hispaniola from them. The 1654-55 expedition was a shambles, and rather than return home to his wrath, the leaders decided to take Jamaica instead, at the heart of the Spanish Caribbean possessions. In 1665, the island was taken despite the inadequacies of the campaign, simply because there were very few Spanish settlers or defences. Many of Captain

Morgan's buccaneer's were Cromwell's soldiers who stayed on in Jamaica, and fought wearing their old army 'redcoats'. The name Saint Dominic was afterwards applied to the island by the French, who were anxious to rid the island of Spanish connections as they vied with Spain for its possession.

TO HITCH
'is to catch-hold of Anything with a Roape, to hold it fast' - Sir Henry Mainwaring, 'The Seaman's Dictionary' 1644

HOLDING ITS OWN
The situation when neither ship can advance on each other. Also used to describe a ship trying to approach a port but not making any headway.

HOLY MACKEREL
Mackerel is caught in huge quantities, but 'goes off' very quickly, especially in its summer 'runs'. Thus it was the only fish that merchants were allowed to sell in the 17th century on the Holy Day, Sunday.

HONESTY AMONGST THIEVES
The sea thieves, pirates, had such severe punishments for stealing from the 'commonwealth' booty, or each other, that there was very little theft amongst them, the origin of this saying.

HOT PRESS
When it was absolutely vital for the Royal Navy to impress men in time of war, press gangs were given permission to take any men, notwithstanding that they might carry 'protections' against impressment (-certificates granted to ships masters, mates lighthouse keepers, Customs Officers, harpooners, etc., etc.) In times of 'hot press', men hid for their lives.

HOY
A small, heavy coasting-vessel for goods and passengers, keeping near to the coast, from the Dutch 'heude' and 'heu'. The English hoy, or work-sloop, dated from around the end of the 17th to the start of the 18th century, being square-rigged with a gaff sail. They were used for smuggling and piracy, taking 6-10 cannons on the top deck, with swivel guns fore and aft, and a crew of 30 men. They were hit-and-run ships, used in night attacks near the coast, not for long voyages.

HUMBLE PIE
The origin of this term is that 'umble' was the intestines of deer. The master ate pie made with venison - muscle meat - while the servants ate 'umble pie'.
IDLER
Because they worked in the day, ships' artists such as the carpenter, sailmakers and cooks were excused night watches. They were thus 'idle' and off-duty at night, and called 'idlers'.

ILE-A-VACHE
Also called Ile-de-Vache (Cow Island), this favourite pirate location off the south-west of Haiti was mispronounced by the British as Isle of Ash.

IMPRESSMENT
The official act of taking men for the service of their country, for the army or navy, usually

against their will. It is not generally known that many of Oliver Cromwell's '*New Model Army*' were impressed men. (Many of these '*redcoats*' ended up as buccaneers in the West Indies, serving in their faded red jackets under Captain Morgan). Service in the navy was hated, so there was always a shortage of seamen, and thus '*press gangs*', to press unwilling men into the service are part of British history. In 1536 Mary Tudor's government disallowed Thames watermen from exemption to from being '*pressed*'. Thus all London's taverns were a fruitful source of recruitment. Elizabeth I gave '*protection*' (exemption) to mariners from being pressed for army service in 1563, and allowed any itinerant vagrant to be pressed in 1597. Queen Anne gave protection to apprentices under 18 years old in 1703. George II exempted men over 55, Thames watermen employed by fire insurance companies, and masters and mates of merchant ships in 1740. A proportion of seamen in colliers (coal ships) were given protection in 1774. (See Hot Press, Press Pangs).

INCH OF CANDLE
The fixing of a time limit by marking a line on a lit candle, it was commonly used at auctions of prize vessels at Port Royal. The Welshman Maurice Williams, one Morgan's captains, bought the Spanish ship 'Abispa' (Wasp) for £120 in May 1659, '*by inch of candle*'. He had made the highest offer, then waited for the candle to burn the required inch. There being no other bids in the time, the ship was his.

INDENTURED SERVANTS
These were a source of manpower for the pirate captains – Esquemeling makes reference to their treatment by slave owners: '*The planters that inhabit the Caribbee Islands are rather worse and more cruel unto their servants than the preceding. In the Isle of Saint Christopher dwells one, whose name is Bettesa, very well known among the Dutch merchants, who has killed above a hundred of his servants with blows and stripes. The English do the same with their servants. And the mildest cruelty they exercise towards them is that, when they have served six years of their time (the years they are bound for among the English being seven to complete), they use them with such cruel hardship as forces them to beg of their masters to sell them unto others, although it be to begin another servitude of seven years, or at least three or four. I have known many who after this manner served fifteen or twenty years before they could obtain their freedom. Another thing very rigorous among that nation is a law in those islands, whereby if any man owes to another above five and twenty shillings, English money, in case he cannot pay, he is liable to be sold for the space of six to eight months.*' Black slaves were treated even worse than English servants, and many became pirates. The great chronicler of the buccaneers, Esquemeling, also turned to buccaneering from being an indentured servant, after he was bought and sold. The Welsh Royalist prisoners from the Civil War Battle of Saint Ffagans were sent to the West Indies as indentured servants, never to return. Cromwell also sent 7,000 Scottish prisoners, and any Irishmen he could lay his hands on. Landless paupers from France, Britain and Holland were attracted, by the promise of free land after seven years, with free passage and board, to go to the West Indies. The ruthless cruelty of employers ensured that many of them escaped into a better life of buccaneering and piracy.

On that note, Esquemeling recorded how a planter treated a bondsman who ran away and was recaptured: '*No sooner had he got him, but he commanded him to be tied to a tree; here he gave him so many lashes on his naked back, as made his body run with an entire stream of blood; then, to make the smart of his wounds the greater, he anointed him with lemon juice, mixed with salt and pepper. In this miserable posture he left him tied to the tree for 24 hours, which being past, he began his punishment again, lashing him, as before, so cruelly, that the miserable wretch gave up the ghost.*'

Known as '*engagees*' in the French colonies, Bretons and Normans were decoyed into the West

Indies by promises of a better life, not realising that they were needed to cultivate sugar-cane and tobacco as there were not enough negro slaves there. *Engagees* in the French Antilles usually gained their freedom in 18 months or three years, compared to the standard English term of seven years.

INDIGO
The genus Indigofera was harvested and refined in the West Indies and Spanish America, to make a purple-blue powder of huge value as a commercial dye in Europe. In November 1664, the Welsh Captain Maurice Williams took a Spanish prize full of logwood, chests of indigo and silver into Port Royal.

IN HIS BOOTS
Dead-drunk, also '*topsy-boosy*' meant drunk. Today, '*wellied*' means drunk, derived from '*welly*', the slang for a wellington-boot. To '*fill one's boots*' is still common slang today for getting extremely drunk.

IRISH APRICOT
A potato, also known as an Irish apple, or Irish lemon.

IRISH ARMS
Thick legs.

IRISH BEAUTY
A woman with two black eyes.

IRISH EVIDENCE
False evidence or a perjurer.

IRISH HORSE
The '*Irish Joke*' has a long history. Most Irish jokes start off as jokes told by the Irish about men from Kerry, the most south-west, rural and unsophisticated part of the island. '*Irish horse*' was the seaman's term for extremely tough salt beef (-later, corned beef earned the epithet). It was thought that the poor Irish worked their horses longer and harder than the English, which made them tough to eat. A part of an 18th century sailor's song runs:
'*Salt horse, salt horse, what brought you here ?*
You've carried turf for many a year.
From Dublin quay to Ballyack
You've carried turf upon your back.'

IRISH HURRICANE
Also called '*Paddy's hurricane*', dead calm at sea.

IRISH PENNANTS
Loose ends of rope hanging from the rigging or side of ships, noting lazy work by the crew. Also the reef sail ends left flapping when the sails were furled on a square rigged ship. These reef ends, and gasket ends (the strip of canvas or rope holding the furled sail) were also known as '*dead men*'.

IRONS
Bilboes were carried on all the Armada ships, and were soon taken up by British ships as a form of punishment. To '*iron*' a man, or '*clap him in irons*' was to put him in bilboes (see bilboes).

IRON-SICK
From Sir Henry Maiwaring's 'The Seaman's Dictionary', printed in 1644: '*A ship or boat is said to be iron-sick when the bolts, spikes, or nails are so eaten away with the rust of the salt water that they stand hollow in the planks, and so the ship doth receive in water by them; and this is the reason why they put lead over all the bolt heads under water.*'

ITCHLAND
Wales in the late 17th century, until Scotland took over the nomenclature in the early 18th century, and an '*Itchlander*' came to mean a Scot until the mid-19th century

JAMAICA
The expedition sent by Cromwell to take possessions in the West Indies was an absolute disaster. In its attack on Hispaniola, its commander, General Venables, was so frightened that he hid behind a tree '*soe possessed with terror that he could hardly spake*'. Captain Butler, sent to recruit Frenchmen on their island of St Kitts, was so drunk that he fell off his horse and spewed over the feet of the delegation of French officers sent to meet him. Jamaica was taken more by accident than design, and Venables spent some time in the Tower of London on his return to England. After the taking of Jamaica by the English in 1655, French, Dutch and English buccaneers flocked to its capital, Port Royal. The French had forced them out of their Tortuga stronghold, and the English authorities saw them as a source of considerable trading wealth, and a first line of defence against the Spanish in the West Indies. By 1662, there was so much looted silver and gold in Port Royal that the government thought about establishing a mint there.

JAMAICA DISCIPLE, or the LAW OF THE PRIVATEERS
Customs passed down from the '*boucaniers*' of the 1630's onwards in the Caribbean. There were democratic controls on any type of authority in the '*pirate code*', or '*code of the coast*'. Under the code, any '*prize*' was divided up evenly, with two shares to the captain and one each to all men. Other rules covered the presence of women on board, hours of drinking, the settlement of disputes, and the apportionment of prize money to those maimed and injured. By Henry Morgan's day, his last expedition gave the captains eight shares each, and Admiral Morgan took 1%. This was agreed before the venture.

JERKY
What Americans call today '*beef jerky*' were strips of meat called '*viande boucanee*' and what English buccaneers called '*jerked meat*' after the American-Spanish '*charqui*'. Hard and dry as a board after being slowly smoked in the '*boucanes*', they were sold by the Tortuga boucaniers in bundles of a hundred for six pieces of eight. They were essential for crew in the tropics.

JIB
A triangular sail set on the boom which runs out from the bowsprit.

JIBES, GYBES
Swinging a boom (*gybing*) when changing course can lead to someone being hurt, or damage to sail or rigging. *Gybes* came to mean unwelcome actions, and are the origin of today's *jibes*.

JIGGER
This was a light tackle consisting of a single and double block, that increased pulling power by a factor of four. It is included in this glossary because of the following delightfully explicit instruction from R. Dana's 1844 '*The Seaman's Manual*' - '*Lift the skin up, and put into the bunt the slack of the clews (not too taut), the leech and foot-rope, and body of the sail; being careful not to*

let it get forward under or hang down abaft. Then haul your bunt well up on the yard, smoothing the skin and bringing it down well abaft, and make fast the bunt gasket round the mast, and the jigger, if there be one, to the tie.'

JOLLY ROGER

An adaptation of the *'black flag'*, commonly a black flag with a skull and crossbones, flown towards the end of the Golden Age of piracy. Other versions showed a whole skeleton with a sword on one hand and an hourglass in the other. Most probably named after Black Bart Roberts, from his habit of dressing up in red silks before battle. He was known as *'le jolie rouge'*, the *'pretty man in red'*. In 1700 was the first recorded use of the black flag, used by the Breton pirate, Emanuel Wynne fighting HMS Poole off Santiago. It has a skull and crossbones and an hourglass. If an intended victim refused to surrender on the sight of the black flag being raised, a red flag was hoisted, signifying that no quarter would be given. The death's head, and skull and crossbones, were worn as a cap badge in some European regiments in the 17th century.

CADWALLADER JONES

This Welsh Governor of the Bahamas gave protection to the *'Arch-Pirate'*, *'Long Ben'* Every. Jones was said to have *'highly caressed those Pirates that came to Providence'* and *'gave Commissions to pirates without and contrary to the advice of the Council'*. Jones was said to have kept the inhabitants of New Providence in *'abominable slavery'*. He disagreed with the lawful advice of his Council so violently that on one occasion he even ordered his son to train the guns of a ship on the Council Chamber. At some point the Council had managed to imprison him, but in February 1692 he was taken from prison and restored to power as Governor by *'some desperate Rogues, Pirates and others..... a seditious rabble.'*

JUAN FERNANDEZ ISLANDS

This small group of islands was a pirate have about 400 miles west of Valparaiso in Chile. An American, Bernard Keiser, is convinced that *'the lost treasure of the Incas'*, worth over $10 billion, were hidden in a cave there, about 6 metres deep, by English corsairs in the 18th century.

KEEL

The first step in constructing a ship such as a galleon was to lay the keel (from the Spanish *quilla*) - the ship's backbone.

KEEL-HAUL, KEEL-RAKE

Possibly a Dutch invention, this soon caught on amongst other navies in the fifteenth and sixteenth centuries, as a means of discipline. A rope was attached to a high yardarm on the starboard, passed under the ship, and up to a port yardarm. A seaman, sometimes with lead weights on his legs, was dropped from the yard-arm, dragged under the keel of the boat and hauled up on the other side. Apart from the 'near-drowning' effect, the victim was banged against the keel, and lacerated by encrusted barnacles and keel splinters. Sometimes this was done several times until the man died from drowning, a broken neck or shock. Often, when under water, a great gun was fired, causing more pain in his ears. It was the standard Royal Navy punishment of the times, until flogging with a *'cat 'o nine tails'* took over around 1700. Punishment for drawing a weapon in a quarrel was usually the loss of the right hand.

A Dutch expedition to find the North-East Passage in 1595 keel-hauled two men when they were discovered stealing furs off the natives. Being keel-hauled three times in a row in the frozen waters, the first man had his head ripped off when he was pulled under the ship. The second survived, only to be cast ashore to freeze to death. Some of the crew complained, so five were hung as an example. Piracy was an attractive alternative to being a merchant seaman.

KEEP A WEATHER EYE OPEN
This is an old sailing term - trouble will always come from the side of the ship where weather is developing. If a sailor is stationed at the weather bow, he will become tired of the constant pitching of the bow and the spray and wind in his face - he will feel *under the weather*. The weather is the wind, and to *make heavy weather* is to make unnecessary work.

(A FINE) KETTLE OF FISH (see Black Arse)
Fish were boiled in huge pots or kettles. When the results sometimes went wrong and tasted foul, the contents were referred to, sarcastically, as a *fine kettle of fish* which no man would eat. The term has come to mean a messy situation which is difficult to solve.

KEYS, see CAY

KILL-CALF
A murderous ruffian, a butcher. Also *kill-cow*.

KILL-COBBLER
Gin.

KILL-DEVIL
The most popular drink in the pirate haven of Port Royal. Governor Modyford (see Captain Henry Morgan) describes this strong rum punch ……….. *the Spaniards wondered much about the sickness of our people, until they knew the strength of their drinks, but then wondered more that they were not all dead.* The Dutch equivalent, *kilduijvel*, seems to be the forerunner of kill-devil. Also a type of gun.

KILL GRIEF
Strong drink, usually rum.

KING OF SPAIN'S DAUGHTER
Pirate term for looted wine. A tun of wine was 252 gallons, so a 72-tun ship could carry 72 x 252 gallons of wine. 126 gallons was called a *pipe* of wine. Wine was stored in lead *pipes* in the West Indies, giving the seasoned alcoholic illnesses such as the *dry gripes* (q.v.)

KNOCK DOWN
Not an IKEA or MFI term. Ships had to carry a cooper, as all food and drink at sea was carried in wooden casks. Space was at such a premium in the cramped quarters and store-rooms, that the casks were usually disassembled and the staves stacked and stored neatly, when the contents were disposed of. The casks would then be made up again when new provisions were taken on.

KNOT
Nautical term of speed, one knot is 6080 feet, about 1.2 miles per hour. Knots were recorded on a stick and entered in a 'log'.

KNOTS
In his *Sea Grammar* of 1627, Captain John Smith stated that there were only three knots (of

thousands) which were needed by the sailor, the last of which was the *'shepshanke'*. The sheepshank *'is a knot they caste upon a Runner, or a Tackle, when it is too long to take in the Goods, and by this knot they can shorten a Rope without cutting it, as much as they list (wish), and presently undo it again, and never the worse.'* There are literally thousands of knots described in 'Ashley's Book of Knots'. A love knot was sent by a sailor tied loosely. If it came back tightened up, the feeling was reciprocated. A *'slippery hitch'* was used *'in small boats, especially open boats that are easily capsized, the necessity frequently being for instant casting off, and the slippery hitch is found indispensable.'*

KNOW THE ROPES
If pirates did not know all the functions of the hundred of ropes, and were not experts at the dozens of knots, their ship could neither catch another ship nor escape from superior forces. Someone who *'knows the ropes'* now means a person who is expert from both knowledge and experience. There are only three ropes aboard a sailing vessel - the bolt rope, the boat rope and the manrope. (Manropes are made of four-strand rope, canvas-covered. Bolt ropes are three-stranded and 'soft-laid', used for splicing.) However, the rigging could comprise upwards of ten miles of cordage in the largest vessels, with hundreds of different names and functions. The ropes were usually the same thickness and colour, and could only be told apart from the precise position in which they were secured.

LACED MUTTON
A wanton woman.

LADDER, CLIMB THE
To be hanged, as in *'Walter Kennedy climbed the ladder to bed.'*

LAND LUBBER
'Lubber's holes' were holes in the platforms surrounding the mast. They enabled poor sailors to clamber through them to go up and down the mast, rather than quickly climb up the *'rat lines'* (or *'futtock shrouds'* and *'topmast shrouds'*) of the rigging around the platforms. A *lubber* was someone who was very clumsy, so a *land lubber* was known to sailors as someone awkward from the land who knew nothing about sailing and rigging.

LANGRACE, LANGREL (see SHOT)
For privateers, this was possibly their favourite type of cannon shot in the 18th and 19th centuries. Also known as case shot, the case was filled with bits of iron, ostensibly to cut through the rigging of a ship and make it inoperable. Buccaneers and pirates, however, preferred to use it as an anti-personnel device. The wide scatter of the shot ripped holes out of defending seamen, while preserving the nautical integrity of the *'prize'* ship.

LANYARD
Many pirates wore crossed sashes, to hold pistols, daggers, knives and so on, to prevent these being lost overboard. Other items were fastened by lanyards to their belts and boots. From the Ashley Book of Knots: *'A sailor has little opportunity at sea to replace an article lost overboard, so knotted lanyards are attached to everything moveable that is carried aloft: marlingspikes and fids, paint cans and slush buckets, pencils, eyeglasses, hats, snuffboxes, jackknives, tobacco and money pouches, amulets, bonus's whistles, watches , binoculars, pipes and keys are all made fast around the neck, shoulder, or wrist, or else are attached in a buttonhole, belt or suspender.'*

LAP-CLAP
A copulation. To '*get a lap-clap*' was to become pregnant.

LEAGUE
About three miles. English nautical leagues in the 17th century were measured at 20 to a degree of latitude, or around 6000 yards. Each league was divided into three nautical miles. The Spanish used an identical measurement at sea, the '*legua*' being 5.57 kilometres.

LEE
The side of a ship or promontory away from the wind; the side sheltered from the wind. Leeward, with the wind, towards the point to which the wind blows, is opposite to windward. A lee shore is a dangerous coastline to which the wind blows directly, forcing the ship towards it. It is important to *allow a little leeway*, i.e. margin for error when operating off a lee shore.

LET THE CAT OUT OF THE BAG
A sailor found drunk on board was ordered to fashion a cat o' nine tails or '*make a rod for his own back*', which would then be kept in a leather bag. When sailors '*let the cat out of the bag*' they were in for misfortune, usually on *Blue Monday*. The Royal Navy's cat-o-nine-tails was kept in a red baize bag, and not removed until the offender was safely secured to the gratings and there was no possibility of reprieve, so '*the secret was out*'. Authority to use the cat was not removed from the Naval Discipline Act until an Order-in-Council of March 29th, 1949. The only form of corporal punishment which still remains is a maximum of 12 cuts with a cane for boy ratings. The French name for a cat-o-nine-tails was '*martinet*', from the 17th century disciplinarian colonel the Marquis de Martinet.

LET PASS
This was a simple licence issued usually by the Governor of Jamaica, identifying the bearer as an English vessel and requesting that it be allowed to reach its destination. Captain William James (q.v.) and Edward Mansveldt used them as a sort of licence to be a privateer. However, they were thrown overboard by the guardacostas so that ships could become prizes.

LETTERS OF MARQUE, MARK, MART (or LETTERS OF REPRISAL)
Documents, commissions or licences given to privateers by their governments, giving permission for privately owned ships to attack enemy merchant vessels. Sometimes a commission given to a commander could be used to '*cover*' ships from other nationalities. For instance Henry Morgan used to take French pirate ships from Tortuga under his 'commission' when attacking the Spanish. Other times privateers attacked anyone, as when Mansvelt and Morgan attacked the Spanish although their letter of marque was to attack the Dutch. One captain in the Caribbean justified his plundering because of a letter of marque from the Danish West Indies, written in Danish – it actually only gave permission to hunt goats and pigs, but no-one could read Danish.
The minutes of the Council of Jamaica, February 22, 1666, explain why letters of marque were needed. There were no naval frigates posted to protect this British outpost surrounded by Spanish colonies, so Jamaica needed defence, as well as the easy supply of cheap goods that privateers brought in to trade. Currencies, gold and silver, wood, cocoa, hides, dyes, wheat and tallow were all traded at Port Royal, giving its merchants a living. Poorer planters sold the privateers provisions and needed the slaves that they brought in. The first mention is in 1293, and the Convention of Paris outlawed them in 1856. The very last letters of mark and reprisal were issued by the Welsh President Jefferson Davis of the Confederate States of America, in 1861, on the outbreak of the American Civil War. President Lincoln reacted by proclaiming

that such acts would be considered piracy. W. M. Robinson's book '*The Confederate Privateers*', Yale University Press, 1928 explored the fighting further.

LETTER OF REPRISAL

A fairly rare privateering commission allowing the holder to redress a wrong which could not be satisfactorily resolved in the courts. For instance, any English ship seized by the guardacostas could be claimed as a prize, even if it was on legitimate business, with the countries at peace, if a single piece-of-eight was found on board. For the guardacosta who lived on commission, it was fairly easy to '*find*' such a coin. The aggrieved owners, who had lost their shop and cargo, were given permission to seek compensation by whatever means they thought necessary, i.e. by taking a Spanish ship in retaliation.

LIGHT MONEY

Coins which had been '*clipped*' to be worth less than their face value. In 1683, it was reported in London that the colonists in Jamaica would refuse payment in '*light money*' for their crops.

LIQUOR

'*Good liquor is to sailors preferable to warm clothing*' - Woodes Rogers, c.1718. Wearing damp clothing in the Atlantic day and night, subsisting on small portions of awful food, alcohol provided much-needed calories to keep the body temperature up. A daily liquor ration was a contractual obligation in both the merchant and Royal navies. Until the 19th century, water was a carrier of all types of illnesses, so everyone drank cider, beer or wine for preference, on land or at sea. From the 17th century, Caribbean rum became more popular than beer at sea, because beer went sour quickly.

LOBLOLLY

Porridge or gruel.

LOBSCOUSE, 'SCOUSE

A stew of small bits of salt meat, broken ship's biscuits, potatoes, onions and spices. Because of the poverty of Liverpool, something similar was a common dish at home, and the modern slang for a Liverpudlian, '*scouser*', comes from this dish. The origin of the word is the Welsh '*lobscaws*', and many poor Welsh families settled there, looking for work.

LOBSTER

18th century seaman's slang for a soldier or marine, who wore red coats. Many former '*lobsters*' turned to buccaneering and piracy.

LODEMAN

This predates the pirates, and used to mean a ship's pilot. The reason it is included is that *The Black Book of the Admiralty*, the list of maritime law, custom and usage, was codified from *The Laws of Oleron* in 1336. *The Laws of Oleron* were introduced into England by Richard the Lionheart in 1189, copied from his mother Eleanor's legislation in 1152 in Aquitaine. The tenor of these laws survived through the years in the Royal Navy. The following quote from *The Laws of Oleron* is priceless '*If a ship is lost by default of the lodeman, the maryners may bring the lodeman to the windlass or any other place and cut off his head.*'
Richard I's instructions to his 1189 and 1190 fleets, to go to the Crusades, have been preserved as the earliest naval laws, which persisted in this draconian form for over six hundred years. For murder on land, to be tied to the corpse and buried alive. For murder at sea, the offender was

tied to the victim and thrown into the ocean. For threatening with a knife, to have the hand cut off. For striking any person without drawing blood, to be plunged three times into the sea. For cursing or reviling anyone, to pay an ounce of silver for each offence. For theft to have the head shorn, and boiling pitch and feathers poured over the offender.

LOG-BOOK
The author believes that the name, for this record of a ship's progress, comes form the practice of daily throwing a log overboard, to estimate the speed of a ship.

LOGGERHEADS
These were large iron heads on long handles which were heated until they were red-hot. A sailor then wrapped cloths around the handle and took the loggerhead to insert into a bucket of pitch to make hot tar for caulking the ship. This way there was little risk of the pitch catching fire as it melted. Sailors sometimes used to spar with the cold loggerheads, during horseplay on the beach when careening. Thus the phrase 'at loggerheads' with each other came into being.

LOGWOOD or DYEWOOD
Of huge commercial value in Europe, this grew in great quantities in the Bay of Campeachy, the Bay of Honduras (modern Belize) and across the West Indies. This dark-red tree, *Haematoxylum Campechanium L.* produced a black or brown dye which did not fade in cloth like existing dyes. Around 1700 it was worth £20 a ton in the West Indies, and up to 20 times as much in London, making it a valuable target for piracy and smuggling.

L'OLONNAIS (d.1668)
Perhaps the most horrible of all buccaneers, Jean David Nau came from Les Sables-d'Olonne in France, hence his nickname. He seems to have never taken prisoners, often cutting heads off and licking the blade. On the Central American coast, he cut open the heart of a prisoner and gnawed at it before throwing it on the ground. Captured by native Indians shortly after this, they slowly cut him up into little pieces.

LONGBOAT
Towed behind a ship, this could hold up to 60 or 70 men, and was normally propelled by oars, but also a movable mast and sail might be used. These were needed in the days before quays to get stores and go ashore.

LONGITUDE
Because of the lack of knowledge of longitude until the invention of Harrison's Chronometer in the 18th century (see Sobel's book), merchant ships were forced to cluster upon well-known routes, where they were more at threat from pirate or buccaneer attack. (*See Dead Reckoning* and *Derroterro* in these Pirate Terms). Dava Sobel's exposition in his book '*Longitude*' is excellent. Suitable chronometers were not widely used until the late 18th century, so the navigational feats of pirates and circumnavigators like Woodes Rogers are truly remarkable.

LONG SHOT
Cannon had no sights, and could not be traversed right and left, and there was only small up-down adjustment, which could be negated by the movement of waves. Also each ball was slightly different and the gunpowder charges varied. Cannon balls were most likely to hit and cause real damage with a maximum effective range of 200-500 feet. Thus very few '*long shots*' were effective, and the term came to be used by gamblers.

LOOSE CANNON
An unsecured cannon in a storm could do untold damage to men and the ship as it rolled about. The term now means an unorthodox person who can cause potential damage.

LOUIS D'OR
French coin.

LOUSE-TRAP
A fine comb. A '*louse-walk*' was a hair-parting. A '*prick-louse*' was a tailor, so '*louse-pricking*' was mending clothes. '*Louse-land*' was Scotland. A saying of the times was '*if a louse misses a footing on his coat, it will break its neck*', meaning that the coat in question was thread-bare. '*Lousy*' meant either contemptible or filthy.

LUGGER
A small and fast three-masted ship, favoured by pirates.

LUTERANOS
'*Lutherans*', a common name the Spanish used for Dutch and British buccaneers, whom they turned over to the Inquisition for extremely slow torture to death.

MADAGASCAR
The most important pirate haunt outside the West Indies, French and English freebooters congregated here, 250 miles off the east coast of Africa. The natives were tolerant, there was abundant fresh water and food, citrus fruits prevented scurvy and there were hundreds of hidden harbours on Madagascar and its nearby islets. There were rich pickings on the nearby Indian Ocean and Red Sea. Each year, a fleet carrying Indian pilgrims with gold and silver to Mecca and Jeddah gathered at Mocha. Also Portuguese carracks carried precious goods from Goa to Europe. The French, British and Dutch East India Companies had ships loaded with silks, spices and jewels. The French attempt to colonise it ended with the abandonment of Fort Dauphin in 1674. As it had the first usable harbours after passing the Cape, many ships stopped there for fruit, water and provisions. It was a magnet for piracy. However, with the ending of the French wars in 1697, British men-of-war started patrolling Madagascar and St Mary's Island, capturing David Williams (q.v.) in November 1703.

MANATEE
Esquemeling describes these….. '*Thence we directed our course for a place called Boca del Dragon, there to make provisions of flesh, especially of a certain animal which the Spaniards call manentines, and the Dutch sea-cows, because the head, nose and teeth of this beast are very much like those of a cow ………Nigh unto the neck they have two wings, under which are seated two udders or breasts, much like unto the breasts of a woman*'. These poor manatees, or dugongs, seems to have been an origin of the legends of mermaids.

MANILA GALLEONS
For over two-hundred years, huge heavily-armed Spanish treasure ships passed from Manila to Acapulco, Mexico and back.

MAKE FAST
'*Instead of tying, Seamen always say, " Make Fast!"* ' (Captain John Smith, 'A Sea Grammar', 1627)

MAKE HEAVY WEATHER
To sail closer to the wind, or weather, than is really necessary, thus slowing the boat up, and making more work than is necessary.

MAN-O'-WAR
A naval warship – see rate.

MARINATED
Term for being transported as a convict, probably from pickling of fish in salt.

MAROON
To abandon a sailor or prisoner on a desolate, deserted cay or uninhabited island. He was usually given a musket, a few shot, a little gunpowder and a bottle of water. It was a rare punishment, leaving the seaman the option of killing himself if he could not survive or no rescuers arrived. A *'maroon island'* was an uninhabited island. From the Spanish *'cimarron'*, wild. Cimaroons, abbreviated to 'Maroons' were a West Indian community founded by escaped negro slaves who cohabited with Amerindian women. Maroon is thus a corruption of cimaroon, *'dweller in the mountains'* – a fugitive or lost person.

MATCH
The slow-burning rope-end used to ignite cannons.

MATELOTAGE
From this French term we have today's *'mate'*, meaning close friend/bosom buddy. The *'cow-killers'* or first *'boucaniers'* had no wives or children, but usually lived with another male who inherited from him. This custom was called *'matelotage'*. Any arguments between these *'mates'* were settled by a duel, *'la coutume de la côte'*.

MESSING ABOUT
This term seems to have originated in the *'mess-deck'*, the crowded quarter which was the only part of a ship where the crew could mingle off-duty.

MESTIZOS
The offspring of a European settler and a native Indian, called by the Spanish *'mestisas'*.

MAN-OF-WAR FOWL
The Frigate Bird, also called the sea-hawk by pirates.

MERCHANT
The commercial vessel of the late 17th and early 18th centuries was not as big as an East Indiaman, but could mount up to 30 cannon.

MERCHANT SEAMEN
Just like the Royal Navy, many of these had been forcibly *'impressed'* into service, with disgusting food, disease, dysentery, minimal wages, cramped conditions and cruel masters. Dr. Samuel Johnson said *'no man will be a sailor who has contrivance enough to get himself into jail; for being in a ship is being in jail with the chance of being drowned ...... A man in jail has more room, better food, and commonly better company.'* It is little wonder that they were unwilling to fight pirates and that former merchant seamen formed the vast bulk of the pirate brethren. Punishment was so harsh for trivial offences, as in the Royal Navy, that the popular saying *'You*

might as well be hung for a sheep as for a lamb' comes from this time. The punishment was still the same for great offences as for small, and many willing merchant seamen became pirates.

In times of peace, seamen's wages remained unchanged between 1700 and 1750. A merchant captain took about £5-£6 per month, and his first mate and surgeon around £3-£4. Cooks, carpenters and boatswains received around £2, and ordinary crew members around £1-50p. They were often not allowed to leave the ship in port, especially at home, in case they might desert, and were often unpaid if a ship was in port or at anchor. Long stays in port, seeking a cargo, could sometimes lead to mutiny by the unpaid crews.

MIDDLE PASSAGE

From the 16th to 18th centuries, slave ships from England sailed to Africa's west coast with rum, firearms and brass goods. These were bartered for slaves, who were then shipped (the middle passage) to the Spanish West Indies, then the southern states of the USA. Slaves were then exchanged for rum and sugar in the Caribbean, and tobacco and cotton in America. Each of the three passages was fantastically profitable, bringing great wealth to Liverpool and Bristol.

For the Middle Passage, the naked male slaves were pulled out of their dungeons and chained together herded onto ships. They were prodded down a ladder to the upper hold, then pushed onto a long shelf and chained by the ankle and wrist to the board. Many slaves passed out in the stench and the suffocating heat. Up to 400 slaves could be pushed into the belly of the ship, each with a space 5-6 feet long, 16 inches wide and 3-4 feet high. A little air came in through the overhead gratings, and the only place for bodily wastes was to seep between the planks they were chained to, dripping onto those on the lower shelves. They might wait in port for up to 10 months in these conditions before sailing. Women and children were taken aboard separately to the men, and were at the mercy of the whims of the captain and crew. Apart from measles, gonorrhoea, syphilis and smallpox contracted from the Europeans, the prisoners suffered from malaria, yellow fever and amoebic dysentery. The worst disease was *'the bloody flux'*, with fever and a bloody running discharge of the bowels. It stunk so much that barrels of vinegar could not remove the stench. *'Blackbirders'* could be smelt up to a mile away. The only time that the prisoners could move was when they were taken to the deck to eat. If they refused to eat, they were whipped. If they continued to refuse, iron bars were lodged into their jaws and food jammed down their throats. One captain cut off the arms and legs on *'the most wilful'* protesters to *'terrify the rest'* into obeying his orders.

Casualties were appalling, and up to 55% of the slaves could die on the Middle Passage. Captain Thomas Phillips lost 318 of his 700 cargo in the *Hannibal* in 1693. The Royal Africa Company's records show an average loss of 23% of the slaves.

MIND YOUR P's and Q's

Sailors received credit at quayside taverns until they were paid. In these blissful pre-metrification days, beer was sold in pints and quarts. The innkeeper kept a record of p's and q's for each debtor, and ensured that they were entered on his account.

MIZZEN MAST

The rear mast on a ship. The 3rd, aftermost mast of a square-rigged sailing ship.

MOIDORES

Portuguese gold coins.

MONKEY

A small wooden cask to hold rum, or a small cannon (also known as a *dog*). A monkey-jacket was the short red jacket worn by midshipmen. Jackets were cut short for sailors to enable them to climb in the rigging. A monkey poop was a short poop deck. Monkey was the generic term for anything small, such as the smallest casks, pumps or sailing-blocks. Incidentally, the phrase 'to freeze the balls off a brass monkey' has a naval origin. This monkey was a small brass tray which held a pile of iron cannon balls next to the guns. In extreme cold, the different coefficients of expansion of brass and iron meant that sometimes the neatly piled cannon would roll out of the tray.

MONMOUTH CAP
A popular pirate hat, a sort of big woollen beret with a bobble on top, made in Monmouth, Gwent, and worn on the back of the head.

MONTBARS THE EXTERMINATOR
This buccaneer surpassed Rock the Brazilian, who entertained his company by roasting Spanish captives alive on spits. Montbars' favourite torture was to slit a man's stomach open, take out his intestines and nail them to a post. Then he pressed burning wood into the victim's buttocks to force him to dance to the furthest extent of his intestines. The Spanish Inquisition practised similar tortures and possibly worse upon their European prisoners, so the Spanish were 'fair game' for such horrors.

MOR-LEIDR (LLADRON)
Welsh for Sea Robber (Lleidr = Thief or Robber. Ladron is also Spanish for thief)

MORRO
Large castle or fortification protecting a port, such as San Felipe at Porto Bello.

MORTAR
Very short cannon with a wide mouth, filled with a number of fused bombs, which exploded after hitting the target.

MOSES' LAW
A punishment on some pirate ships, which could only be carried out by the quartermaster, where an offender received 39 lashes on his bare back.

MOSQUITO COAST
Eastern coast of Nicaragua. Because of its dense mangrove swamps, hundreds of inlets and lack of arable land, it was never settled by the Spanish, and became a sanctuary for runaway slaves and a pirate hideout.

MOTHER CAREY'S CHICKENS
The storm petrel can run lightly over the sea's surface. The name comes from 'Petrello' (little Peter in Italian – St Peter could walk on water). When seamen saw them near a ship, they expected a storm to be in the offing. Storm petrels are called 'les oiseaux de Notre Dame' in French, the birds of Our Lady. In Latin, these 'Aves Sanctae Mariae' belonged to 'Mater Cara', which the British corrupted to Mother Carey. Where 'chickens' comes from is beyond the author's skills as a researcher or etymologist.

MULATTO
The offspring of a European and an African slave.

MUM
17th century strong ale made from wheat and oats, and flavoured with herbs. From the German 'mumme' in Brunswick, where it originated, the Dutch equivalent is 'mom'.

MURDERER, MURDERING PIECE
A swivel gun with a long barrel and a wide mouth for firing nails, spikes, stones and glass. They were known as 'pedreros' by the Spanish, Anglicised as 'patareros' or 'perriers'. The iron pin in the stock was fitted into a socket, and there were sockets at several places on a ship, so the gun could be quickly taken to wherever it was needed most. They were used in nearly all merchant ships to repel boarders, up to the early 19th century. In warships they were supplanted by marines, who acted as marksmen, in the early 18th century. In 1644, Mainwaring wrote: 'Murderers are small iron or brass pieces with chambers. In merchant-men they are most used at the bulkheads of the forecastle, half-deck or steerage (steer-reach), and they have a pintle which is put into a stock (socket), and so they stand and are traversed; out of which they use murdering shot to scour the decks when men enter; but iron murderers are dangerous for them which discharge them, for they will scale extremely and endanger their eyes much with them. I have known divers (many) hurt with shooting them off.'

MUSICIANS
Their prime function was to play extremely loudly, if pirates were forced to attack. They preferred to take ships peacefully, but in an attack the black or red flag was raised and as much noise was made as possible, a cacophony to frighten the victim's crew.

MUSKET
The general term for a single shot rifle of the times, and the model for the more accurate rifle to follow, the musket was only slightly more accurate than a blunderbuss. The musket ball was smaller and designed to shoot straighter, but was less likely to cause the kind of damage that a blunderbuss could inflict. The blunderbuss was a close range, devastating weapon, a large shot rifle, superseded by the musketoon of 1758. Early muskets were 5-6 feet long, using a double iron bullet, and had to be supported and fired with the aid of fork rest. For short-range work, barrels were sawn off, (like today's sawn-off shotguns), and an effective load of one musket ball and three heavy buckshot pellets was inserted. The handle, or stock, was also sawn off, to make it easier to handle and attach to a sash across the pirate's chest.

MUTINY
Some merchant ships got rid of their captains because of various reasons. If they did not shoot the captain, they usually set him and his followers adrift in a pinnace or small boat with water and biscuits. They usually then turned to piracy. More unusually, Royal Navy ships did the same, as with Fletcher Christian and Captain Bligh. Even pirate ships often mutinied if they were not successful, and elected another captain. The definition of a mutiny was refusing to obey the legal order of a superior. Mutineers were hanged at the yard-arm. If a whole ship's company mutinied, only the ringleaders were executed. Seamen in both the merchant and Royal Navy were treated abominably. The following is a partial list of naval mutinies:
1747 HMS Namur, Portsmouth. 3 hung, 12 men received 50-100 lashes.
1748 HMS Chesterfield, West Africa. 2 shot, 5 hung.
1779 HMS Defiance, North America. 1 hung, others 'severely flogged'.
1779 HMS Jackal, France. Several men hung.
1780 HMS Prothee, home station. 1 hung, 3 men 400-600 lashes.
1781 HMS Sylph, Leeward Islands. 6 hung.

1781 HMS *Namur*, Plymouth. 5 men 200-600 lashes.
1782 HMS *Narcissus*, North America. 6 hung, 2 flogged.
1783 HMS *Camilla*, Jamaica. 5 men 800 lashes.
1783 HMS *Adamant*, home station. 2 men 600 lashes.
1793 HMS *Winchelsea*, home station. 2 men 200 lashes.
1795 HMS *Defiance*, home station. 5 men hung, 6 men 300-600 lashes.
1797 HMS *Beaulieu*, home station. 4 men hung.
1797 HMS *Pompee*, home station. 5 men hung.
1797 HMS *St. George*, Mediterranean. 4 men hung.
1797 HMS *Powerful*, home station. 1 man 300 lashes, 1 man 200 lashes.
1797 HMS *Hermione*, Jamaica. Over the next few years, over 12 men hung.
1798 HMS *Amelia*, home station. 2 men hung.
1798 HMS *Renominee*, Jamaica. 4 men hung.
1798 HMS *Marlborough*, Berehaven. 1 man hung.
1798 HMS *Princess Royal*, Mediterranean. 4 men hung.
1798 HMS *Adamant*, home station. 2 men hung.
1798 HMS *Defiance*, home station. 11 men hung, 13 flogged and/or transported.
1798 HMS *Queen Charlotte*, home station. 2 men 300 lashes.
1798 HMS *Glory*, home station. 8 men hung, 3 men flogged.
1798 HMS *Captain*, home station. 10 men 100-400 lashes.
1798 HMS *Diomede*, home station. 1 hung, 1 man 500 lashes.
1798 HMS *Haughty*, home station. 2 men hung.
1800 HMS *Albanaise*. 2 men hung.
In the 19th century, men were still receiving up to 500 lashes. In 1809, on the HMS *Nereide*, there occurred flogging with a special kind of cat-o-nine-tails, and also *'the most unmerciful starting with sticks of a severer kind than is ever used in the Royal Navy'* on ten men.

MYNGS, SIR CHRISTOPHER (1625-1666)
Myngs is an absolutely intriguing character, who led Henry Morgan on his first privateering adventures, but is hardly known today. As a result, this potted history is included on a man that Samuel Pepys called *'a man of great parts and most excellent tongue among ordinary men.'* For a Royal Naval officer to be actually liked by his men was unheard of for centuries.
He was known as a *'tarpaulin captain'*, the captain of a naval ship in Tudor or Stuart times who had risen by promotion through service, as opposed to those *'appointed'* into post because of royal or political favour. The *'tarpaulin captains'* despised the *'gentleman captains'* for their rough use of crews and general incapacity to handle a ship. Myngs was notable for bringing home less than he was reputed to have plundered. He first comes to our attention in 1653, when as a privateer commanding the Elizabeth, he captured and brought in a Dutch convoy of merchant ships and its escort of two warships. He was appointed to the *Marston Moor* in 1655 to suppress a mutiny, and brought the men back to a state of discipline.
In Jamaica, Governor D'Oyley sent Captain Myngs, with a buccaneer force of 300 to terrorise the southern Caribbean, and they devastated Cumana, Puerto Caballo and Coro. He took the first major buccaneering booty back to Port Royal after his raid on Coro, the major Spanish city on Venzuela's Lake Maracaibo. Chasing the inhabitants into the forests, the small force of three hundred men found a cache of pearls, cocoa and gold plate, and twenty-four royal treasure chests. They were each filled with 180kg (400 lbs) of silver coins, worth around a million pounds. The Jamaican authorities found out that he had taken 12,000 pieces of eight, and that the expedition had also plundered six Dutch ships, and Myngs was sent back to England to explain himself. He was soon back in the West Indies, attracting buccaneers to his next two

trips, including Henry Morgan. With the restoration of Charles II in 1660, Myngs remained in favour, and was vice-admiral of the White at the 1665 Battle of Lowestoft. Admiral Myngs was killed in the '*Four Days Battle*' in 1666, during the Second Anglo-Dutch War (1665-67). His crew respected him so much that a dozen sailors formed a deputation and asked to be given a fireship, and extremely dangerous task, so that they could '*do that that shall show our memory of our dead commander and our revenge*'.

NAVAL SLOOP
Bigger and more heavily-armed than a standard sloop, a superior ship to the normal pirate sloop.

NAVAL SNOW
Comparable to a brigantine, with a crew of 80 and 8 mounted cannon.

NEGRO
The author is aware of the pejorative nature of this description, but is merely using the terms of the day. In the author's '*100 Great Welsh Women*', Nell Gwynne and Lucy Walters are described as the '*mistresses*' of Charles II rather than the modern term of '*partner*'. It is sometimes difficult to modify history in line with modern-day correctness. Up to a third of some pirate crews were black, and had the same right as white pirates to booty, and the same voting rights. Some were captured slaves and some were fugitive slaves. The deck of a pirate ship was the most empowering place in the New World for a black to be in the 18th century. Bart Roberts had at least 40 black men serving as '*free*' pirates with him, and around half of the crews of Paulsgrave Williams and Black Sam Bellamy were black. There are records of blacks being elected captains and quartermasters of pirate vessels.

NEGRO'S HOLIDAY
Sunday. Just as slaves worked seven days a week, so sailors still had to run the ship at sea on a Sunday.

NEW PROVIDENCE
This small Bahaman island was used by pirates since the 1680's, until by 1716 Governor Spotswood of Virginia called it the '*Nest of Pyrates*'. From 1716 - 1718 it was the most important pirate haven in the Caribbean. The settlement took over after the destruction of Jamaica's Port Royal, as the '*Sodom of the New World.*' Nassau was a prominent pirate port, and was important for careening in safety. Near all the trade routes, there was abundant water, meat, wood and fruit. The port of Nassau was too shallow for warships to attack, but held up to 500 smaller vessels, and was divided at its entrance by Hog Island. Thus to be effectively blockaded, two men-of-war were needed. Woodes Rogers arrived in 1718, and its pirate haven days were effectively ended. The exodus of pirates in 1718 included Howell Davis, Thomas Anstis, Olivier Levasseur (La Buze), Blackbeard, Paul Williams, Samuel Bellamy, Thomas Cocklyn, Jack Rackham, Christopher Winter, Christopher Condent and others. In 1717, Stede Bonnet, Benjamin Horniglod, Charles Vane and John Martel had also used New Providence.

NIPPERS
The anchor cable in large sailing ships was too large to bend around a capstan on the quayside. Smaller lines were used to heave the cables, and these were 'nipped' to the cable by dextrous small boys, who became known as '*nippers*'. Mainwaring in 1644 wrote that '*nippers are small ropes …, the use thereof is to hold off the cable from the main capstan, when the cable is either so slippy or so great that they cannot strain it, or hold it off, with their hands only.*'

NODDY
The tern 'sterna stolida', sometimes eaten by buccaneers when meat was in short supply.

NO PREY NO PAY, or NO PURCHASE NO PAY
Pirate motto, referring to the fact that without capturing other ships, there was no money to be made – see 'purchase'.

OAKUM
Strands of old hemp rope or manila fibres were soaked in tar, and stuffed in between the planks of a hull to stop leaks. Unpicking old rope into strands was a slow, tedious job which hurt the fingers and thumbs, and this 'picking oakum' was a regular punishment for minor misdemeanours. In the Royal Navy, each man in a ship's cells had to unpick a pound of oakum every day. The word comes from the Anglo-Saxon 'acumba', the coarse part of flax.

OCTANT
A navigational instrument, not particularly accurate, but vital before the introduction of sextants in the late 18th century. Chronometers were of no real use until the 19th century. The wonderful best-selling book 'Longitude' describes some of the problems of sailing the oceans without accurate instruments.

ON THE ACCOUNT
Being involved in piracy or buccaneering.

OUT OF TRIM
A ship that is unbalanced for sailing because its cargo, loot or ballast is not allocated correctly.

OVER HAUL
The crew went aloft to 'overhaul' buntlines to stop sails chaffing, when rigged over long periods on a downwind course. The term has gradually come to mean maintaining something in perfect condition.

PANAMA
One of the three ports used by the Spanish treasure fleets, on the Pacific coast. Every year, silver was taken from Panama on mule trains across the Panama Isthmus to Nombre de Dios, and then Portobelo on the Caribbean coast. If the Chagres River was full, small boats were used instead of mules. Panama City was sacked by Henry Morgan.

PAPAGAYO
A north-east gale off the Central American coast, which springs up without warning.

PARROT
Most of us remember Captain Flint, the rascally Long John Silver's parrot in Treasure Island, with its incessant 'Pieces of Eight ! Pieces of Eight !' Parrots were very popular on sailing ships, and William Dampier in his second voyage tells us that those near Vera Cruz in the Bay of Campeche were the biggest in the West Indies 'Their colour was yellow and red, very coarsely mixed; and they would prate very prettily and there was scarce a man but what sent aboard one or two of them. So that with provision, chests, hen-coops and parrot-cages, our ships were full of lumber, with which we intended to sail.'
They were easier to keep on ship than monkeys, and were sold everywhere. A 1717

advertisement in London's 'Post-Man' reads: '*Parrotkeets with red heads from Guinea, and two fine talking Parrotkeets from Buenos Aires, and several young talking Parrots*' were being sold at the 'Leopard and Tiger' tavern at Tower Dock. Another 1717 issue offered '*Parrotkeets which talk English, Dutch, French and Spanish, Whistle at command, small parrotkeets with red heads, very tame and pretty*', at the Porter's Lodge, Charing Cross.

THE PARROT MUST HAVE A NUT
From the Shakespearian saying, '*the parrot must have an almond*', referring to the need to bribe certain officials and governors to turn a blind eye to pirates trading on their territories. Kurt Cobhain's '*Polly wants a cracker*' , part of a splendid Nirvana song, seems to have evolved from this saying. However, the best use of slang in a modern record still remains the opening line of '*Reward*' by the Welshman Julian Cope's old group '*The Teardrop Explodes*'. It is '*Bless my cotton socks, I'm in the news.*'

PASSED WITH FLYING COLOURS
The present term comes from the fact that ships who wished to be identified would fly their pennants when passing others.

PETER PEPPER (Pierre Poivre)
Of '*picked a peck of pickled peppers*' fame, he was an East India Company administrator in Mauritius in the 1770's who introduced plant varieties from South America, including pepper, and gave incentives to grow them. Not much to do with pirates, but a fascinating gobbet, or snippet, of information with which to annoy one's friends and colleagues.

PETTICOAT BREECHES
These baggy trousers, widening out and ending at mid-calf, were ideal for barefoot pirates scrambling up the rigging.

PICAROON, PICKAROON
17th century term for a pirate, from the Spanish '*picaro*', meaning rogue or rascal.

PICKLE
The salt brine in casks, in which beef and pork was immersed to preserve it in the tropics.

PIECES OF EIGHT
Silver Spanish coins, or dollars, marked with an 8, and worth four pesetas or eight '*reales*'. In the 17th and 18th centuries, so many were in circulation that they were accepted almost anywhere in the world. The American dollar sign $ was derived from 8 stamped on the side of the '*piece of eight*', the silver peso (or *piaster*). Two pieces, or bits, made a quarter, and this is the origin of the American '*two-bit*' or quarter dollar coin. They were minted at Mexico City and Lima in Peru, and were common currency in all of England's colonies, being valued at 4 shillings and sixpence. Often they were cut into 8 pieces for ease of transaction, so that '*two bits*' made a quarter. The origin of the modern American term, '*not worth two bits*' is from the days when the English colonies around Massachusetts used this Spanish money. Gold was used for escudos and doubloons. Before the Spanish started exploiting Potosi in Peru (in today's Bolivia), silver was almost as valuable as gold in the Old World. Such were the quantities taken from the New World, that silver dropped to about a fifteenth of the value of gold. (4 billion pesos of silver and gold were taken from the New World between 1492 and 1830 by the Spanish - when one sees some of the remarkable religious architecture in Spain, remember the misery that was the source

of the resources, much like the buildings of Bristol and Bath originating from the slave trade. Cardiff was also built upon *'black gold'*, the product of the inhuman conditions and child labour in the coal mines).

PIGTAILS
Even more popular in the 17th and 18th century than today amongst art teachers, advertising executives and balding rock stars, pigtails were *'tarred'* at sea, which may be the origin of *'Jack Tar'*, the popular name for a seaman. However, it is more likely that seamen were called *'tars'* because their hands were always covered with tar off the ropes and ship's timbers. In 'The Shipping News' we read: *'Sailors once wore their hair in queues worked two ways, laid up into rattails, or plaited in four-strand square sinnets. The final touch called for a pickled eelskin chosen from the brine cask. The sailor carefully rolled the eelskin back (as a condom is rolled), then worked it up over his queue and seized it. For dress occasions he finished it off with a red ribbon tied in a bow.'* It is unknown at present whether the eelskin had a complementary usage as a condom.

PILLORY
For minor offences ashore, many pirates had suffered from the pillory before they escaped to sea. A frame held a standing man, with his head and two arms protruding through three holes. The prisoner's ears were then nailed to the wooden frame, so he could not avert his head from missiles hurled at him by the crowd. Men and women died from this punishment, and blinding was common. The last occurrence was in 1814.

PINK (Dutch *pincke*)
Any vessel with a very narrow stern, usually flat-bottomed. In the 17th and 18th centuries, large square-rigged pinks were used as merchantmen and warships

PINNACE
In the 18th century, a small, fast boat that could be rowed or sailed. Also used to describe the ship's longboat that ferried men to the shore. In the 16th and 17th centuries, pinnaces were much larger, from 20-60 tons.

PIPE DOWN
Sailors said this to someone who was talking too much. Its derivation is that the last noise at night was the boatswain's pipe, the signal for silence on the mess-decks and lights out.

PIRACY ACT 1721
Pirates were tried in civil courts until 1340, when Edward III destroyed the French fleet at Sluys, and claimed thereafter to be *'Sovereign of the Seas'*. From now on Admiralty Courts were empowered to try piracy cases. Henry VIII passed the first Piracy Act in 1536, creating a Vice-Admiral of the Coast to hold trials and sentence pirates. In 1611 another act authorised Courts of the Admiralty to try cases in the colonies and plantations of North America and the West Indies. The 1721 Act stated that anyone who traded with a pirate, if found guilty, would be treated as a pirate and charged accordingly. Until then, it was fairly easy to dispose of stolen goods. Also, anyone who provided a pirate with ammunition, stores or provisions, or who fitted out a ship for piracy, or corresponded with a pirate, was deemed to be a pirate, felon and robber.

PIRAGUA, PIROGUE, PIRAGAYA
Native dugout, a sea-going canoe used by natives in Central and South America. The term comes from the Carib language. Also sometimes in the West Indies it referred to a plank-built

boat with one sail and a flat bottom. Many pirates started their careers with a pirogue, which could not be chased around the shallow waters of the cays, and could land on any beach.

PIRATE COUNCIL
Each crew-man was a member, unlike the officers' councils of war in the Royal Navy. The council decided where to go, what to do, what punishments to make, who should be captain, whether the captain should be deposed and so on.

PIRATES
These attacked any ships, including those from their own countries.

PIRATE HAVENS
Medieval pirates favoured Wales and the West Country, with many harbours protected by hills and difficult to reach by road. They were usually welcomed by local inhabitants. In the 16th century, the buccaneers favoured Tortuga in the Caribbean, being hilly and difficult to attack and also near shipping lanes. However, as the French and English presence grew, they moved on to New Providence in the Bahamas and Madagascar in the Indian Ocean, neither under control of any government. One of the major problems was in selling contraband, as there were few traders in these havens, who took a vast profit. As a result, pirates often tried to cut a deal with corrupt governors of settlements and colonies, where there were better prices available from a multitude of traders. Jamaica's Port Royal was a haven in the mid to late 17th century, because of its distance from London.

PIRATE SHIPS
These had to be fast, and easy and quick to careen, so small boats of 30-50 tons were favoured in the Caribbean. If a large boat was taken, it was usually used to store plunder, before being destroyed, sold or set adrift. A shallow draught was essential to operate around the cays of the West Indies, and allow escape from larger vessels. All deckhouses were cut down to streamline the ship and leave the deck easy to shift cannon and resources from one side to the other in a fight. The gunwales were raised to give the crew extra protection.

A typical pirate ship

PISS IN A QUILL
16th-19th century slang for making and agreeing a plan.

PISS MONEY AGAINST A WALL
To waste money on alcohol, a favourite pirate pastime when in a safe harbour.

HE PISSES MORE THAN HE DRINKS
A pirate who boasts.

PISS-POT
A '*saw-bones*', or ship's doctor.

PISTOL
The pistol was a pirate's best friend, not a rifle. Blackbeard used to carry six in his sash, loaded and ready for action. Howell Davis carried four, and Black Bart two. It had a flintlock (presentation) mechanism, with a single shot loaded via the barrel. The *powderbox* or *powder horn* kept powder dry, and ready for action - damp powder was useless. A pirate probably did not carry his powder horn with him during combat, but used a smaller container preparatory to action. After loading his pistols and perhaps musket, he would move into action. In prolonged battles, men were probably designated to loading small arms, ready for the pirates to discharge them.

PISTOL PROOF
The description applied to Black Bart by his crew – a pirate who knows what he's doing and cannot therefore be hurt.

PISTOLE
Any foreign gold coin, especially French of Spanish.

PITCHER-BAWD
A worn-out prostitute, only good enough to take pitchers of beer to a tavern's customers. Pitchers were leather jugs, treated with tar pitch to help them hold their shape. Glass was too expensive and fragile.

PLATE
Silver, usually in bars, but sometimes in coins.

PLATE FLEET
One royal convoy, the *flota* (q.v.) left Seville every year, stopping at the Canary and Leeward Islands for water and provisions, across the Caribbean to Veracruz in Mexico. Later in the year, the '*galeones*' left Cadiz for Cartagena, then on to Portobelo in Panama to meet the merchants who brought treasure across the Isthmus from Peru. They carried expensive European manufactured goods, and each fleet usually was of over a dozen large galleons and smaller ships, accompanied by two men-of-war, the *Capitana* (q.v.) and *Almirante*. They returned to Spain with silver, gold, logwood, indigo, hides and cacao.

PLUMB THE DEPTHS
To fully investigate, by '*plumbing*' or sounding the depths in shallow waters. Perhaps the current meaning shows us that this was a really boring job, the lowest of the low, unskilled and repetitive.

POINT-BLANK
The direction of a gun when levelled horizontally.

POLEAXE
Short-handled axe or hatchet with a spike or hammer opposite the blade, used for slaughtering cattle. The *boucaniers*, or cattle-killers, began using the variety with the pike, to drive a series of them into the side or rear of a ship. They could then swarm up this '*ladder*' of axes and take their prize.

POOP DECK
The raised rear deck, above the quarter deck, where the ship was steered, and from where the captain usually directed battles. To be '*pooped*' is to be swamped by a high following sea.

POOR JOHN
Salted and dried fish, usually hake and cod. Seamen far preferred meat to fish.

PORT
When standing at the back (*aft*) of a vessel looking forward (*for'ud*), the left side of the vessel is the port (*larboard*) side. To port weapons is to carry them in your left hand. Port may be an abbreviation of '*porta il timone*' - carry the helm. Port Holes comes from the French '*porte*' or door, which opened to allow cannon to be stationed within the ship, not just on deck, whereby a ship could become top-heavy.

PORTOBELO
Because Francis Drake had sacked Cartagena and Santo Domingo, and Nombre de Dios had a worse natural harbour, the Spanish developed Portobelo as the their main Caribbean treasure port from 1595. In the 18th century, at terrible cost, a road linked it to Panama City on the other side of the Isthmus. Henry Morgan sacked it in 1668.

PORT ROYAL
Known as Cagway to Christopher Myngs, in Henry Morgan's early days on the island, the original Carib-Spanish name for Port Royal was '*cayagua*' (literally, island of water). When Cromwell's force under Penn and Venables took Jamaica in 1655, they thought the name '*cayagua*' was that of the entire cay, not just the tip of Palisadoes Point. The new port of Cagway was renamed Port Royal in 1660, on the restoration of Charles II, but was still called Cagway by Morgan and his cronies for some time after.

'*Pirate heaven*' with a huge harbour that could take up to five hundred ships, and at the heart of all the West Indies shipping routes, this was an easy market for pirate plunder. It was a series of sandbars and cays, which formed a peninsula off modern Kingston. The waters were 30 feet deep, just a few yards offshore, allowing for easy anchorage. Buccaneering was unofficially sanctioned by the governors of Jamaica, and the lawyer Francis Hanson of Port Royal wrote in 1683 '*The town of Port Royal, being as it were the Store House or Treasury of the West Indies, is always like a continual Mart or fair where all sorts of choice merchandises are daily imported, not only to furnish the island, but vast quantities are thence again transported to supply the Spaniards, Indians and other Nations, who in exchange return us bars and cakes of gold, wedges and pigs of silver, Pistoles, Pieces of Eight and several other coins of both metals, with store of wrought Plate, jewels, rich pearl necklaces, and of Pearl unsorted or undrilled several bushels.....almost every House hath a rich cupboard of Plate, which they carelessly expose, scarce shutting their doors in the night.... In Port Royal there is more plenty of running Cash (proportionately to the number of its inhabitants) than is in London.*'

Port Royal was also known for its '*grog shops*', gaming houses and brothels, earning it the nickname of '*the Sodom of the New World*'. In July 1661 alone the Council issued licences for forty new grog shops, taverns and punch houses. Amongst them were the Black Dog, Blue Anchor, Cat and Fiddle, Cheshire Cheese, Cat and Fiddle, Feathers, Jamaica Arms, Three Crowns, Windmill, Three Tunns, Three Mariners, Sugar Loaf, Sign of the George, Sign of Bacchus, Sign of the Mermaid, The Ship, The Salutation, King's Arms, Jamaica Arms and Green Dragon. Around this time Governor Modyford was making a fortune in bribes from Henry Morgan and other buccaneers. In 1680, there were over 100 licensed taverns for a population of 3000. John Starr operated its largest whorehouse, in the official 1680 census maintaining an establishment with 21 '*white women*' and 2 '*black women*'. Port Royal was the largest English or French settlement in the New World outside Boston. By 1690, one in four of its buildings were '*brothels, gaming houses, taverns and grog shops*'. A seventeenth century clergyman returned to England on the same ship as he sailed out on, writing '*This town is the Sodom of the New World and since the majority of its population consists of pirates, cut-throats, whores and some of the vilest persons in the whole of the world, I felt my permanence there was of no use.*' It was heaven for traders, who cheaply bought pirate loot, sold it in London at huge profits, and also profiteered by selling expensive supplies to pirates.

Charles Leslie, in his 1740 '*History of Jamaica*' recorded of pirates, that in Port Royal, '*wine and women drained their wealth to such a degree that in a little time some of them were reduced to beggary. They have been known to spend 2000 - 3000 pieces of eight in one night; and one gave a strumpet 500 to see her naked. They used to buy a pipe of wine, place it in the street, and oblige everyone that passed to drink.*' A pipe is a cask of 105 gallons, or 840 pints of wine. Barre's Tavern was one of the more high-class establishments in the town, frequented by Henry Morgan, and perhaps operated by the family of Charles de la Barre, secretary to Governor Lynch. It offered light refreshments including '*syllabub (q.v.), cream tarts and other quelque choses.*'

Port Royal lay on a small cay and the tip of the long sandspit called the Palisadoes, which forms Kingston Harbour. On June 7th, 1692, a combined earthquake and tidal wave destroyed this buccaneer capital, probably killing two-thirds of its 3000 population, sweeping Captain Morgan's grave into the sea. The tremors had rocked the sandy peninsula on which Port Royal was built, and caused buildings to slide and slip into the sea. Apart from the 2000 that died on that day, another 2000 died later from wounds, disease and fever. In the tidal wave that followed the earthquake, '*nothing else was seen but the dead and dying, and heard but shrieks and cries.*' So few people were left alive that the bodies just floated in and out with the tide, and rolled along the beaches. A joiner, John Pike, wrote to his brother and told him that his house was lost beneath the waves: '*I lost my wife, my son, an apprentice, a white-maid and 6 slaves and all that I ever had in the world. My land where I was ready to raise 5 houses, and had room to raise 10 more, is all sunk, a good sloop may sail over it as well as over the Point.*'

The capital of St Jago de la Vega, corrupted to Santiago, now resumed its authority over Jamaica's affairs. Port Royal was rebuilt after the earthquake, only to suffer a great fire in 1703. In 1712 Governor Hamilton reported that a hurricane had destroyed 38 ships at Port Royal and 9 at Kingston. Storms, hurricanes and two more earthquakes in 1722 and 1744 meant that the town was reduced to a British naval station with a dockyard, which closed in 1905. Chaloner Ogle (see the chapter on Black Bart Roberts) was anchored on HMS Swallow, off Port Royal on August 28th, 1722, and reported '*there was as much wind in my opinion as could possibly blow out of the heavens … all the merchantmen in the harbour foundered or drove ashore excepting one sloop.*' It is the only sunken town in the New World, and efforts are being made to have it declared a World Heritage Site, '*an underwater Pompeii*'. Underwater excavation has enabled us to 'rewalk' the narrow street of Port Royal today, and perhaps even Henry Morgan's grave may be found. Texas A&M University's Nautical Archaeology Programme has reconstructed the life of the town's main pewterer, Simon Benning, from the silver cutlery and pewter plates found on the site.

POWDER
Gunpowder - the saying *'to keep one's powder dry'* stems from the need to ensure that gunpowder was not opened and exposed to the damp in the air until the time it was needed, otherwise it might not ignite.

PRESS
To forcibly recruit men for the Royal Navy by the *'press gang'*, often from taverns in British docklands. Most pirates were former Royal Navy or merchant seamen, attracted by a far better life. Estimates are that 50% of men taken by *'press gangs'* (which preferred to take seamen rather than 'land-lubbers') died at sea between 1600 and 1800. When Captain Lowther led a mutiny on the *'Gambia Castle'*, a Royal Africa Company ship, records show that 72% of the 110 crew who refused to join him were dead within a year. Another telling statistic is that in the Seven Years War, 1522 men were killed in action, but over 150,000 were lost through disease or desertion.

PRESSING
In 1657 a sentence for refusing to plead was *'You shall go to the place from whence you came, and there being stripped naked and laid flat upon your back on the floor, with a napkin about your middle to hide your privy members, and a cloth on your face, then the Press is to be laid upon you, with as much weight as, or rather more than, you can bear. You are to have three morsels of barley-bread in twenty-four hours; a draught of water from the next puddle near the gaol, but not running water. The second day two morsels and the same water, with an increase of weight, and so to the third day until you expire.'* The last pressing took place in 1726, and it was replaced with screwing the thumbs with whipcord in front of the open court until the victim pleaded guilty or not guilty. The most famous pressing was that of Saint Margaret Clitherow in 1586 in York. She was sentenced to the *'peine forte at dure'* for refusing to plead, saying *'having made no offence, I need no trial'*. She died within fifteen minutes. The pirate Captain Gow was sentenced to pressing.
A Welsh *'pressing'* is noted in the Glamorgan Plea Rolls on 1574, for a man who murdered his wife, Matilda ferch Henry, with a towel. He refused to plead, so the sentence was *'That David ap Hopkyn is to be put naked on the ground except his breeches and a hole made under his head and his head put into it and as much stone and iron put upon his body as it will carry and more and he is to be fed on bread and water of the worst kind, bread one day and water another day, and so kept alive until he dies.'*

PRIMING-IRON
The iron rod forced down the touch-hole of a cannon. It pierced the bag of gunpowder ready for firing the cannon by applying the match. A *'rammer'* was a wooden cylinder that pushed the powder bag down the barrel of the cannon.

PRIVATEERS
Semi-official pirates, who supplemented a country's navy with *'private'* ships of war. Given *'letters of marque'*, they were allowed to attack the enemy in times of war, and keep a large percentage of any plunder. They cost nothing, and their only reward was what they could take, or *'purchase'*, as in the term *'no purchase, no pay'*. With the end of the War of Spanish Succession in 1713, there were literally thousands of privateers in the Caribbean and European ports, but the *'letters of marque'* had been withdrawn because of the peace. Thus many turned to piracy,

culminating with almost complete pirate domination of the West Indies and American coasts between 1718 and 1722. Francis Drake and John Hawkins were noted privateers. It was also the name given to the privately-owned armed vessel with a letter of marque, which enabled it to take 'prizes' in wartime. From 1589, 10% of the prize value went to the Crown, and 90% to the owner. Privateering was abolished by the Treaty of Paris in 1856.

PRIZE
A ship and its booty captured by a naval ship or privateer.

PROVIDENCE ISLAND - ISLA DE PROVIDENCIA, SANTA CATALINA
A large island and pirate haven 250 miles off Portobelo, it lay between the Cuba to Venezuela trading route. Its pirates successfully beat off a Spanish attack in 1635, but it was taken in 1640. Henry Morgan used it for his attack on Panama in 1670-71.

PROSTITUTES
Visitors complained that Port Royal's punch-houses were swarming with 'vile strumpets and common prostitutes'. John Starr's brothel there contained 21 white and 2 black women. The most famous was the 'German Princess', Mary Carleton, who had been convicted of theft and bigamy and transported to Jamaica in 1671. She was returned to London in 1673 to be hanged at Tyburn. Born in Canterbury around 1634, she was a teenage criminal before appearing on the London stage, where a play, 'The German Princess' was written especially for her. Her two years as a prostitute in Port Royal made some impact - she was described as being 'as common as a barber's chair: no sooner was one out, but another was in. Cunning, crafty, subtle, and hot in the pursuit of her intended designs.'

PUNCH
To distilled alcohol or wine, various elements were added, such as tea, fruit juice, sugar, spices and lime juice. Pirates drank from a ladle out of the bowl. Taverns were often referred to as punch-houses.

PUNCH HOUSE
Common term for a brothel, where alcohol was sold - a visitor to Port Royal wrote that its punch houses contained 'such a crew of vile strumpets and common prostitutes that 'tis almost impossible to civilise' the town.

PURCHASE
The plunder or bounty taken by pirates and buccaneers – the old meaning of 'purchase' was 'the action of hunting, the chase, the catching and seizing of prey'. Also any sort of mechanical power employed in raising or removing heavy bodies. The masts had to be 'purchased' to careen a ship's bottom. To purchase the anchor is to loosen it out of the ground.

'PUTTING A MAN TO DRY'
This phrase was an English torture practised on slaves or indentured servants in the West Indies as a punishment for rebelling on the plantations, or trying to escape. In 1700 the French priest Pere Labat recorded in Barbados that 'the slaves who are captured are sent to prison and condemned to be passed through a cane mill, or be burnt alive, or be put into iron cages that prevent any movement and in which they are hung up to branches of trees and left to die of hunger and despair.'

QUARTER
Mercy given to a surrendering or defeated crew. Pirates preferred not to fight, as did the merchant sailors who usually faced them.

QUARTERMASTER
The representative of the *'Interest of the Crew'* to the captain, and democratically elected by pirates, he was literally in charge of the operations of the ship when not in action. He judged disputes and disbursed food and cash. He often was given a prize vessel when it was taken and became captain himself. Usually, only the quartermaster could flog a seaman, and then only after a vote by the crew. Walter Kennedy explained in his trial that the role of the quartermaster prevented the captain having too much power. Pirates hated authority.

QUEUE
A *'tail'* from the French, or pigtail, affected by most pirates, who stiffened it with a mixture of flour and water, and tied the end with a ribbon.

RACK AND RUIN
The origin of the term *'ship-wrecked'* was *'ship-racked'*, and a *'racked'* ship meant that the insurers suffered from *'rack and ruin'*.

RAKING FIRE
Directing musket and cannon fire down a ship's length, from bow or from stern. The balls score the whole length of the decks.

RATCASTLE
Prison.

RATLINES
The small ropes fastened to the shrouds, by which men go aloft to trim the sails.

RAT'S TAIL
A pig-tail.

RATTLE THE BONES
Play dice.

RATE
The classification of naval warship according to how many guns it possessed. This is the origin of the term **'first rate'**, **'second rate'**, et al. In 1610, the HMS Resolution was described as a first rate of 80 guns, but with better technology, bigger ships with more guns came to be called first rates. In the 1700's, a first rate man-of-war carried over 100 guns, a second rate 84-100, a third rate 70-84, a fourth rate 50-70, a fifth rate 32-50, and sixth rate ships carried up to 32 guns. (In 1810, there was another change, with first rates having over 110 guns, second over 90, third over 80, fourth over 60 and fifth rates over 50 guns.) Only the first three rates were used in the *'line of battle'* in a main battle fleet. There were few fourth rates, and were only used in the *'line of battle'* in smaller fleets. Fifth and sixth rates were usually known as *frigates*. The sixth rates were known as *sloops*, if commanded by a commander rather than a captain. *'Feeling first-rate'* has its origins here, as has *'that was a third-rate performance'*.

READY TO FIRE
Pirate captains ensured that their gunners were always ready for action - they never knew when a prize might appear from around a headland, or if they might be surprised by a naval frigate.

Cannons were kept loaded, with wooden plugs, *'tompions'* on their muzzles to keep salt spray from spoiling the powder charge. Again to keep the powder dry, a sheepskin was laid over the touch-hole at the breech, with a lead apron holding it in place.

RED CROSS
An English ship. *'Red'* also meant anything made of gold. A *'red one'* or *'red rogue'* was a gold coin. *'Red fustian'* was port or claret.

RED FLAG
The red flag as a symbol of socialism was first used in the Merthyr Riots in Wales, when Dic Penderyn was wrongly executed. However, until around 1700 it was the emblem of a pirate ship, around when it was replaced by the black flag, and various derivations of the black flag to denote different captains. It then seems to have been run up only if the merchant crew refused to surrender at the sight of the black flag, and meant that there would be no mercy, *no quarter* given to her crew.

RED FUSTIAN
Port or claret.

RIDE A PORPOISE
To steer a ship with a yard-arm struck down to the deck

RIGGING
The two basic ways to rig sails are: Square Rigged, in which the sails are bent to the yards carried athwart the mast and trimmed with braces. Square-rigged sails are sturdy and catch a lot of wind; Fore and Aft Rigged, in which the sails are not attached to the yards but are bent to gaffs and set on the mast or on stays in the midship line of the ship, giving increased manoeuvrability.

ROAD, ROADSTEAD
A place to anchor with some shelter for all but heavy weather, but easy to escape from.

ROBINSON CRUSOE
His prototype was Alexander Selkirk (1676-1721), who volunteered as a privateer for a voyage to the South Seas in 1703. The navigator was William Dampier and the Captain Stradling, commanding the *'Cinque Ports'*. After a violent disagreement with Stradling in 1705, he asked to be marooned on the island of Juan Fernandez. He lived alone, sustained by abundant vegetables and fruit, and wild goats. In 1709 an expedition led by Woodes Rogers stopped at the island, during his circumnavigation of the world. When Selkirk saw that Dampier was navigator, he asked to be put back ashore but was dissuaded.

ROCK THE BRAZILIAN
From Groningen, Holland, he was called Roche Brasiliano from the long time he spent in Brazil, corrupted to *Rock the Brazilian* by the English buccaneers. He had a pathological hatred of the Spanish, and his practice of roasting them alive on spits is well-documented.

ROYAL AFRICA COMPANY
Charles II signed the Royal Charter for this company at Westminster on September 20th, 1672: *'We hereby for us, our heirs and successors, grant unto the same Royal African Company of England... that it shall and may be lawful to... set to sea such as many ships, pinnaces and barks as*

shall be thought fitting… for the buying, selling, bartering and exchange of, for or with any gold, silver, Negroes, Slaves, goods, wares and manufactures.' The venture was a considerable source of income for the Stuart monarchy.

RUB SALT INTO THE WOUND
After a flaying with the *'cat 'o nine tails'*, vindictive officers would order salt to be rubbed into the offender's raw flesh to make the punishment even more painful. However, it served to help the healing process if the victim lived long enough. Also, Roman sailors were paid a quantity of salt as part of their *'salarium'* (salary, from the Roman *'sal'* for salt). The sailors thought that they were being doubly punished at losing part of their salary if they had to rub salt into their wounds after battle.

RUM, KILL-DEVIL
This seems to have been dished out regularly every day upon pirate ships, following the Royal Navy tradition. Rum (sometimes known as *grog*) was plentiful in the Caribbean because it was easily made from sugar cane. It was distilled from the 1640's onwards. Sugar growers cured sugar in clay pots, and as it crystallised, a brown liquid called molasses drained out of the remaining sucrose. This was recycled by natural fermentation, and then distillation to give a clear liquid, which darkened in wooden casks. The French called it *'tafia'*, and the English *rum-bullion*, shortened to rum. Later, *rumbullion* was transferred to another drink. It was also known as *'kill-devil'*. Perhaps the term originated because it was 'rum' (odd) to get precious booty (bullion, or alcohol) out of waste products. Brandy was also easy to get hold of, and beer was carried on boats because it lasted a month or so before it turned vinegary. On the other hand, water was usually taken from a river near a port, or from a polluted river, and was only of any use in cooking. Barrels of water quickly became slimy, and was simply not potable. Pirates were often drunk because there was little alternative liquid. Fruit juices were added to prevent scurvy.
'Rum', in the sense of *'odd'*, or *'different'* was used as a prefix in much 17th and 18th century slang. A *'rum beak'* was a justice of the peace, a *'rum bite'* a swindle, a *'rum blower'* was a pretty woman, a *'rum bluffer'* or *'rum dropper'* was an inn-keeper, a *'rum bob'* was an apprentice, *'rum booze'* was good wine (later an egg 'flip' containing port, egg yolks, sugar and nutmeg), a *'rum bubber'* stole tankards from taverns, a *'rum buffer'* was a good-looking dog, a *'rum chunk'* was a gold or silver tankard, a *'rum clout'* or *'rum wiper'* was a silk handkerchief, a *'rum cod'* was a full purse of money, *'rum cole'* was newly minted money, a *'rum cove'* was a clever rogue, a *'rum cull'* was a rich fool, a *'rum doxy'* was a beautiful woman, or a pretty whore, and so on and so on. Other terms pirates would have used are *'rum slum'* for punch, and *'rum quids'* for a great share of booty or captured goods. Those interested in pursuing the meanings attached to 'rum' should consult *'The Penguin Dictionary of Historical Slang'* by Eric Partridge, 1972. Of particular interest in this fascinating book is the term *'It's naughty but it's nice'*, the phrase that an extremely popular author claims credit for when working in advertising, for a cream cake campaign. It was a song of Minnie Schult's, popular in the USA in the 1890's, which came to mean the *pleasures of copulation*. The book states that it has been a catch-phrase since the early 1900's.

RUMBULLION
This is the demon offspring of Rumfustian, described by Burl when Black Bart Robert's crew distilled it at Damana Bay, Hispaniola, in February 1721: *'For that catastrophic brew two huge vats were rowed ashore and filled with molasses, skimmings of overripe fruit, a minimum of water and a liberal splashing of sulphuric acid. The liquid fermented for 8 days while a still was constructed. A complicated system of pipes arranged vertically in a trough of water led from a capacious copper vessel over a fire to a spiral tube under a cooling waterfall that continually dribbled over it. A pewter tankard*

was set under the spiral and drop by paralytic drop the rumbullion filled it. Only the most foolhardy drank more than one mug.'

RUMFUSTIAN
A popular hot pirate drink blended from raw eggs, sugar, sherry, beer and gin. (This reminds the author of a disgusting drink called '*diesel*' that a Welsh friend Derek Rhys Williams insists that I always drink at his Breton farmhouse. It is half a pint of lager mixed with half a pint of banana liqueur. After several years of idly quaffing it for supper and breakfast, I queried why we have to drink the concoction. He replied '*I read a magazine article. It's what East German skinheads drink if they want to get pissed quickly*'. This passes for Cwmbran logic).

RUMMER
A glass for drinking rum cocktails. Pirates usually used pewter mugs or coconut shells as rummers. The '*Rummer Tavern*' in Cardiff referred to the days of piracy in the Bristol Channel.

RUTTER see DERROTERRO

SAINTE BARBE (French), SANTA BARBARA ((Spanish)
Term used in the 17th century for a powder room or magazine. St Barbara was tortured and killed by her heathen father for being a Christian, and he met divine retribution in being disintegrated by a thunder-flash. She thus became the patron saint of those working with explosives, and her image was often hung up outside a powder room on ships.

SAILING ON ANOTHER BOARD
Behaving differently.

SALAMAGUNDY or SALMAGUNDI
A Crash Test Dummies record refers to Solomon Grundy, who in the old nursery rhyme was '*born on Monday, christened on Tuesday* etc. to *died on Sunday, That was the end of Solomon Grundy*'. The obscure origin of the name was salamagundy, for which there are many recipes. This was the last dish Black Bart ate before the Royal Navy attacked him. The basic variety was '*Poor John*' (salt fish) boiled with onions. It could also include chopped meat, eggs and anchovies – whatever was available, in fact. The most luxurious version had meat, turtle, fish and shellfish marinated in spices, herbs, garlic, palm hearts, spiced wine and oil, and served with cabbage, grapes, olives, pickled onions and hard-boiled eggs. The term seems to have come from the French '*salmigondis*', a communal meat stew to which any available vegetables were added. The dish appealed to the 'Brethren of the Coast' with its shared contribution to the communal cauldron, and Botting described it as having meats that were '*roasted, chopped into chunks and marinated in spiced wine, then combined with cabbage, anchovies, pickled herring, mangoes, hard-boiled eggs, palm hearts, onions, olives, grapes and any other pickled vegetables which were available. The whole would then be highly seasoned with garlic, salt, pepper and mustard seed, and doused with oil and vinegar - and served with drafts of beer and rum.'*

SALT HORSE, SALT JUNK
Slang for the salt beef carried in casks of brine water. The meat was usually too tough to recognise as beef, so sailors believed that anything had been thrown in the casks.

SALT TORTUGAS
Name for the Isla la Tortuga off Venzuela (see Dry Totugas, Tortuga)

SAND-GLASS
The only way that pirates and buccaneers could tell the time. Like egg-timers, they consisted of two glass globes with a narrow neck, and were turned when the sand ran out of the top globe. They were usually in half-minute, half-hours, hour and four hour sizes. The half-minute was used to judge a ship's speed, by how much line would run out from a ship in a half-minute. The half-hour glass measured time, with a bell or drum being sounded at every turn of the sand-glass.

SAN JUAN DE ULUA
An island off the Mexican coast, and the port for Vera Cruz, one of the three treasure ports of the Spanish flota. Silver from Mexico was shipped from here, as well as the contents of the Manila galleons which sailed from the Phillippines to the Pacific coast and were transported across Mexico for shipping to Spain.

SARGASSO SEA
East of the Bahamas, the piece of ocean where an extremely strong eddy causes the Sargasso Weed (*Fucus Natans*) to collect in vast quantities on the surface. Columbus mentioned the difficulty of sailing through the waters as the weeds fouled ships.

SAWBONES
The ship's surgeon, who was usually not much more knowledgeable than the barber from which his profession stemmed. He was used for bone-setting, dressing wounds and amputation.

SAWDUST
This was kept on board and liberally sprinkled around the gundeck, so that men would not slip on blood in battle.

SCHOONER
An easily-handled, fast, two-masted ship, with all lower sails rigged fore and aft. With a shallow draft, it could carry up to 75 crew, mounting 8 cannon and 4 swivel guns. Less than 100 tons, it was popular with pirates in the Caribbean and Atlantic in the 18th century, and could reach up to 11 knots.

A Schooner

SCOTCH COFFEE
Also known as '*lobscouse*', this was the ubiquitous salt beef, boiled up with ship's biscuits, potatoes, onions and some vinegar.

SCRAPING THE BOTTOM OF THE BARREL
Removing the last of the hardened pork fat to put towards a slush fund.

SCRATCH
'*You scratch my back and I'll scratch yours*' - means '*do me a favour and you'll receive one in return*'. This refers to someone who was going to be punished by the '*cat 'o nine tails*'. The victim desperately tried to get a friend to carry out the punishment, or one who might receive the

whipping in future. The difference between a '*light*' scratching across the back and a flaying often meant life or death.

SCRUB AROUND IT
When sailors scrubbed the deck, they would 'scrub around' any obstacle.

SCUPPERED
A term still in use, meaning '*knackered*' or '*finished*'. The '*scuppers*' were the drainage holes in the side of the ship that let sea and rain-water drain off the deck. To '*scupper*' a ship meant that your cannons blew holes in it below its water-line, so that the new '*scuppers*' served exactly their opposite purpose and let water in, sinking the ship. A sailor knocked over by a wave, who fell near the scuppers (waterways or gutters), was said to be '*scuppered*'.

SCURVY
In 1593, Captain Richard Hawkins noted that sour oranges and lemons were the best treatment for scurvy, but not until 1795 did Royal Navy vessels carry lemon juice to combat this disease. Later the far cheaper lime juice replaced lemon, from which the American slang '*limey*' for British immigrants or visitors derived. With no fresh fruit or vegetables, this had been endemic on long voyages, for instance when Black Bart was two months at sea. It also caused shipwrecks, and crews were made so weak by lack of Vitamin C, that they sank into a dull lethargy from which they could not be shaken. Symptoms began with swollen gums, then loss of teeth, a weakened heart and black blotches beneath the skin, before a sailor sank into a final exhausted torpor with glazed eyes and swollen bodies and legs. Wounds could not heal. There was the pain of spontaneous haemorrhaging into muscles and joints. Gasping for breath like floundered fish, the blood vessels around the brain eventually ruptured and they died. In 1636, John Woodall wrote in '*The Surgeon's Mate*' that daily orange juice was the antidote. Upon Admiral Anson's round-the-world expedition of 1740-1744, 1051 of his 1955 men died of scurvy. In 1747 Dr James Lind re-established the fact that Vitamin C prevented scurvy. In 1779 2,400 seamen were put into shore hospitals after the Channel fleet had been on a ten-week cruise. Not until 1795 did the Admiralty prescribe citrus juice on all its vessels. This was after an estimated 800,000 British seamen had needlessly died. Merchant vessels only followed the practice from 1854.

SCUTTLEBUTT
This word means gossip. The butt was the cask of fresh drinking water on a ship. The scuttle was the hatch or hole on the deck of the ship near where the butt was placed. Sailors coming over for a drink used to linger for a short while to exchange the latest news with whoever else was drinking. The term in the USA has been replaced by gossiping '*around the water cooler*'.

SEA ARTIST
An excellent navigator, boatswain or respected sailing master. See Artist.

SEA-CARD
A 17th century term for a chart.

SEA LEGS
Both the ability to resist sea-sickness and to walk steadily on the deck of a pitching ship. Sailors in port took some time to recover their '*land legs*', and were easily recognisable as seamen by the '*rolling gait*' they had adopted at sea.

(IF A) SEAMAN CARRIES A MILLSTONE HE'LL HAVE A QUAIL OUT OF IT

A saying referring to the ingenuity of ships' cooks in providing food and drink out of meagre resources.

SEA PIE

Ship's biscuits between layers of meat or fish.

SEA ROVERS

Pirates, buccaneers and 'sea-robbers.' The term was used in Alexander Esquemeling's 'De Americaensche Zee-Roovers', published in 1678, and published as 'The Buccaneers of America' in London in 1684. Esquemeling went to Tortuga in 1666 as an indentured servant, but joined Morgan's buccaneers as a 'barber-surgeon' in 1669, sailing for five years until he settled in Holland. The book was amazingly popular, no doubt because it was rewritten to suit nationalities. In the Spanish version, Henry Morgan was a torturing ogre, but the English and Dutch editions ask the reader to consider how 'God permitted the unrighteousness of the buccaneers to flourish, for the chastisement of the Spaniards.' Germans referred to a pirate as a Seerauber, sea robber.

SEA SHANTY

A song with a definite rhythm, a working song to help men pull ropes together or the like. Often merchantmen were under-manned, and singing shanties helped efficiency. Many have been recorded, including 'Mrs McGraw':

'Mrs McGraw', the Captain said,
'Would ye like to make a pirate of your son Ted?
With a scarlet coat and a fine cocked hat,
Mrs McGraw wouldn't ye like that?

CHORUS
Singing to-ri-yah, fa-la-la-la. To-ri oori orri yah,
With a to-ri-yah, fa-la-la-la, to-ri oori oori yah.

Now Mrs McGraw lived on the sea shore,
For the space of seven long years or more.
She spied a ship comin' into the bay,
'This is my son Teddy, won't you clear the way?'
Chorus
'Oh My dear Captain, where hae ye been?
Have ye been out sailing on the Med'ter'ean?
Have ye any news of my son, Ted?
Is the poor boy livin' or is he dead?
Chorus
And up steps Ted, without any legs,
And in their place, there were two wooden pegs.
She kissed him a dozen times or two
Crying 'Holy b'goes, what's become of you?'
Chorus
'Now was ye drunk was ye blind,
When ye left yer two fine legs behind?

Or was ye walkin' out on the seas
That tore yer legs away from yer knees?'
Chorus
'No I wasn't drunk, nor I wasn't blind
When I left my two fine legs behind,
'Twas a big cannonball on the fifth of May
That tore my legs from my knees away!'
Chorus
'Now Teddy, me boy', the old widow cried,
'Your two fine legs were your mummy's pride.
The stumps of a tree won't do at all.
Why didn't ye run from the big cannonball?'
Chorus
'Now foreign wars I do profane
Against Don Juan and the King of Spain.
I'd rather have my Teddy the way he used to be
Than the King of France and the whole Navy.'

SEA TURTLES
These were captured and kept on deck in the Caribbean as a useful source of fresh meat.

SEE HOW THE LAND LIES
To ask for the bill in a tavern.

SELKIRK, ALEXANDER (1676-1721)
The probable prototype for *'Robinson Crusoe'*, marooned at his own request by the Welsh privateer captain Thomas Stradling, on Juan Fernandez Island in 1705. He was rescued by Woodes Rogers, another privateer, in 1709.

SEQUINS, CHEQUEENS
Italian or Venetian gold coins.

SEVEN SEAS
The Arctic, Antarctic, North Atlantic, South Atlantic, North Pacific, South Pacific and Indian Oceans.

SEWN UP
To be *'all sewn up'* means that everything is finished. A sailor who died at sea was sewn inside his hammock with a cannon ball at his feet, before being despatched to the deep. Traditionally, the last stitch was placed through the nose to ensure that the man was dead. The custom is said to have come from a sailmaker accidentally putting his needle through the nose of a *'corpse'*, the shock making the cataleptic victim revive and sit up.

SHAKE A CLOTH IN THE WIND
To be slightly drunk or tipsy, but not helpless.

SHAKES
If a ship altered course to head into the wind, the sails would *'shake'*. After a long watch, the helmsman might inadvertently *'nod off'* and the ship would naturally start heading into the

wind. The head sails would then 'shake' or luff. Sailors came to measure a short period of time before the watch changed as 'a couple of shakes'. Sometimes a sleeping helmsman could lead to the ship being 'taken aback' with the wind on the wrong side of the sails.

SHIP SHAPE AND BRISTOL FASHION
Bristol was the great port for the slave trade, also importing vast quantities of tobacco, sherry and chocolate. Slave ships not only stank, but also could carry disease, so the citizens of the prosperous port would not allow ships to dock until they were cleaned and 'made tidy' in the way that the Bristol Channel tides are predictable and orderly. Before entering the harbour, the ships were inspected to ensure that they were *ship shape and Bristol fashion*. Even when the ship moored, its sailors were not allowed ashore until they had *slewed* the yards, swinging them inboard so as not to obstruct other ships or quayside traffic or buildings. Because of the extreme differences between high and low tide in the Bristol Channel (up to 40 feet at Cardiff), ships entering Bristol had to be of an especially stout construction, as they were left 'high and dry' at low tide. Docks were not constructed until 1804.

SHIP'S BISCUITS
Bread would not keep on long voyages, so biscuits were made with flour and the minimum of water, moulded into flat cakes and packed tightly into canvas bags. The biscuits quickly became infested with a type of black-headed weevil (called 'bargemen' for some reason). As a result, before any pirate ate a biscuit, he tapped it on the table to knock the weevils out of it.
This also became a seaman's expression of apology when he burped in public – any belch could be blamed on the poor quality of 'ship's biscuits'. My father-in-law always used this expression from his merchant navy days before the war. (Dried peas also kept for a long time at sea, and so were sometimes the only other source of food when boiled.)

SHIP'S COUSIN
A favoured person aboard ship.

SHIVER ME TIMBERS !
An exclamation of surprise, probably coming from the feeling when a wooden ship hit any rocks and the ship vibrated and creaked. Possibly only used in books and articles rather than by seafarers.

SHOAL
A bank or reef, an area of shallow water dangerous for navigation.

SHOT
Round shot, or cannon balls were used to destroy masts and rigging, and splinters of timber could incapacitate crew members. However, they were not as destructive to humans as a 'whiff of grapeshot', or 'bar and chain shot', which maximised the maiming capacity of cannons.
'Case shot' was a cylindrical tin full of small shot, stones, musket bullets and small pieces of iron to scatter destruction in as wide an area as possible on the crowded decks. The bits of metal were usually enclosed in a wooden case. Sometimes canvas bags were used, but there was a danger that the canvas might snag inside the gun barrel and damage the bore.
'Angel shot' was slang for chain shot, when two halves of a cannon ball were joined by a short length of chain. It rotated, cutting a swathe through a ship's rigging, so it was also used to clear a deck of sailors, sending many to join the angels in heaven with one discharge.
Mainwaring wrote in 1644: 'There are many kinds of shot. That which flies farthest and pierces most

is called round shot; the next is cross bar, which is good for (shredding) ropes and sails and masts; the other langrel, which will not fly so far but is very good for the rigging, and the like, and for men; so is chain shot and case shot, or burr shot, which is good to ply against men which stand naked, plying of their small shot.'

SHOT-PLUG
Cone-shaped piece of wood, that was hammered into holes made by enemy cannon fire in the side of the ship.

SHOW A LEG
Not strictly a pirate term, but the origin of this term, meaning 'get out of bed', or 'move yourself', is intriguing. In the Royal Navy, the crew were forbidden to leave the ship when in home port, for fear they would desert the stinking conditions. As a result their women or 'wives', were allowed to come on board in the port, and slept with the men in their hammocks. The boatswain's mates called the men on deck every morning, and if they saw a hammock with a body still in it, shouted 'show a leg!' If the leg was hairy, the offending crewman was chased to his duties. If it was relatively hairless, the mates allowed the 'wife' to sleep on. Not until 1840 were women prohibited from sleeping when His Majesty's ships were in their home harbours.

SHOW YOUR TRUE COLOURS
A pirate ship might hoist its pirate flag when in firing distance.

SHROUDS
The horizontal ropes fixed to the masts, that latticed with vertical 'rat lines' that sailors scrambled up to furl and unfurl sails.

SIR CLOUDESLEY
Drink of small beer and brandy, with spices, sweeteners and lemon juice, named after Sir Cloudesley Shovell (1650-1707, see Introduction)

SKILLYGOLEE, SKILLY
When salt meat was boiled to make it edible, the water was then mixed with oatmeal to make a savoury broth or thick soup. It was served to naval prisoners, and prisoners-of-war kept in hulks. Skillygolee, or Skillygallee, later became an oatmeal drink sweetened with sugar (in place of cocoa) for seamen during the Napoleonic Wars (1803-1815).

SKY SCRAPER
The origin of this building term was a small, triangular sail set above the main sail on the old square-riggers, to try and catch more wind in areas of calm air - to 'scrape the sky'.

SLANT
All ships have an optimum angle of heel, the angle at which it is better to reduce sail, rather than have too much power in the rigging, pulling the boat over. This critical angle is known as the 'slant' and a good sailor will always know when 'to put a new slant on things' as sea and wind conditions change.

SLAVE PROFITS
Around the time that Howell Davis was trading with 'Old Crackers' we have a merchant captain's bill for dealing with him. In 1721. The price for a male slave was 8 guns, a wicker

bottle, 2 cases of spirits and 28 sheets of cloth. A woman cost 9 gallons of brandy, 6 iron bars, 2 pistols, a bag of powder and 2 strings of beads. A boy cost 7 large kettles, an iron bar, a length of cotton and 5 lengths of blue and white cloth. The merchant at the same time would have to pay the Royal Africa Company £15 for a man, and £12 for a woman, so their forts were always potentially full of money to attract pirates. The price was £60 for a man and £48 for a woman in the West Indies, partially because a 25% death rate on the Atlantic crossing was factored in. From this coast, the Royal Africa Company sold around 18000 slaves a year, and the private traders around 75000, but still could not meet demand. By 1820, Guinea slaves could be bought for a few beads, or $30 at the most, and sold in the Americas for $700, and American captains were said to make a million dollars from each voyage.

The hold on slave ships was usually 6-7 feet high, and was divided half-way up by a platform to double the number of slaves that could be transported. Slaves were chained in pairs at the ankle, and allowed a space of around 6 feet in length, 1 foot 6 inches wide and 3 foot six inches high. They could not stand up in the dark, and lay in their own excrement and vomit. They were daily taken to the open air so that the slave decks could be hosed down. The stench was so bad that the ships could be smelled a mile away, and candles could not be lit in the foetid air on the slave decks. Only the strongest Africans survived the Atlantic Crossing.

Note: Much of the investment capital of the wonderful buildings in Bath came from the Bristol slave trade. The town, possibly the first in the world built solely for pleasure, relied on the arms and cloth sent to Africa, the slaves sent from Africa to the colonies, and the tobacco, rum, sugar and raw cotton that came from the colonies. As a result, Nash himself noted *'Bath is become a mere sink of profligacy and extortion. Every article of house-keeping is raised to an enormous price…I have known a negro-driver, from Jamaica, pay overnight, to the master of one of the rooms, 65 guineas for tea and coffee to the company, and leave Bath the next morning, in such obscurity, that not one of the guests had the slightest idea of his person, or even made the least enquiry about his name.'* (From the entry upon Beau Nash in '100 Great Welshmen' by T.D. Breverton). Spanish cathedrals likewise were financed by genocide and the rape of the Spanish Main.

SLAVE TRADE

In 1562, John Hawkins removed 300 slaves from a Portuguese vessel, marking the beginning of the English slave trade. It was difficult to get crew for the *'blackbirders'* – their life was short and disease-ridden, and they were often treated worse than the slaves they were transporting to the Indies for work on the sugar plantations, and America for the tobacco crops. The Royal African Company, with its monopoly on the slave trade and royal patron, wished to transport healthy slaves who would achieve top prices on the market. However, merchant captains had their profit assessed on the number that arrived alive, and therefore overcrowded their ships, unknown to the Company. Any numbers left over from the official cargo made the captains extra money. Thus the mortality rate on these voyages, often accelerated by disease such as smallpox, made the mortality rate for the Atlantic crossing at least 25% in 1679. This was a Royal Africa Company estimate, but it was not in possession of the full facts.

Robert Falconbridge wrote (*An Account of the Slave Trade, 1788*) that between half and two-thirds perished each year, and around 40,000 a year were being transported in the late eighteenth century. Falconbridge describes the disgusting conditions where the slaves were packed on the decks and held in irons by the wrists and legs, lying in their own filth and urine: *'They are frequently stowed so close as to admit of no other disposition than lying on their sides, nor will the height between decks, unless directly under the grating, allow them to stand'.* Brief daily exercise was allowed to keep them mobile, and each morning they were hosed with salt water and the dead thrown overboard. If they did not eat, they were tortured. A Captain Williams used the cat-of-nine tails to keep the slaves fit by making them dance, and *'seemed to find a pleasant sensation in the sight of blood and the sound of their moans.'* His surgeon, James Arnold, gave further evidence to a Parliamentary Committee in 1789 that some of his slaves tried to revolt, and one that could not be removed from the hold had boiling fat poured over him. Two corpses were beheaded, and *'the two gory heads were successively handed to the slaves chained on the deck, and they were obliged to kiss the lips of the bloody heads. Some who refused to obey were unmercifully flogged by the captain and had the bloody part of a head rubbed against their faces.'* Williams also threw a live slave overboard, and had intercourse with the prettiest of the female slaves. If they refused him, they were flogged until they submitted. Williams also flogged his own crew until they were a *'gory mass of raw flesh'*, according to surgeon Arnold. Another captain in 1783 threw 130 sick slaves overboard on the pretext that there was no water for them. This way the underwriters had to pay for the value of the cargo, rather than the owners of the ship lose their profits by the death of the slaves.

Even in the West Indies, the life of a good, strong slave, was reckoned to be no more than 10 years in the brutal conditions of the sugar plantations. Thus, apart from new slaves for new plantations where the land had been cleared by the slaves, and for the tobacco plantations in America, there was also a 10% attrition and replacement rate each year to satisfy. Just to replace dead slaves created a demand in Jamaica for 10,000 slaves a year, and in the Leeward Islands for 6000, and for Barbados 4000 slaves.

The surgeon John Atkins, on board the HMS *Swallow's* expedition to destroy the *'murderous Captain Bart Roberts'*, interestingly noted the differences in the sales of manufactured goods along the slave coast of north-east Africa: *'The windward and leeward parts of the coast are as opposite in their demands as is their distance. Iron bars which are not asked for to leeward are a substantial part of windward cargoes. Crystals, oranges, corals and brass-mounted cutlasses are almost peculiar to the Windward coast; as are brass pans from the Rio Sethos to Applollonia (the Gold Coast) and cowries… at Whydah, copper sheets and iron bars at Calabar; but arms, gunpowder, tallow, old sheets, Indian cottons … and English spirits (whisky) are everywhere called for. Sealing wax and pipes are necessary in small quantities…'*

SLING YOUR HOOK
Unpopular ship mates were told to go and sling their hammocks elsewhere. Space was at a premium on ships, and places to sleep difficult to find.

SLUSH FUND
The grease, or *slush*, from frying salt pork on a long voyage, or from *'scraping the sides of the barrel'* was saved by the cook and sold to tanneries and candle makers. Thus the term *'scraping the barrel'* also comes from the days of sailing ships.

SLOOP
A single-masted boat up to 100 tons with a long bowsprit, almost as long as the hull, it was rigged fore and aft. The fastest boat of its day, it was liked by pirates because it was easy to handle and had a shallow draught, so could escape in shallow waters. From the eighteenth century the term was used for a small vessel with one to three masts carrying four to twelve guns on the upper deck. Capable of around 11 knots, it could take up to 75 crew and mounted 14 cannon. In general, the one-masted sloop was smaller than a 2-masted schooner, then proportionately bigger were a two—masted corvette, a three-masted snow, a three-masted frigate and a three-masted ship of the line. *'A rapier-like bowsprit almost as long as her hull enabled her to mount a parade of canvas that made her even more nimble than the schooner or brigantine.'*

SMACK
A small sloop-rigged boat used for fishing and small coastal trading.

SMALLPOX

This disease exterminated tribes of African, American Indians, and South American Indians when introduced by the white man. A terrible epidemic in Boston in 1721 affected half of its 10,000 population, and the preacher Cotton Mather recounted how the Africans dealt with the disease in their homelands. They said that they cut open a healthy person's skin and put some of the pus from the disease into the wound. On June 26th, 1721, Dr Zabadiel Boylston inoculated his small son and two of his slaves with smallpox, but the city elders were horrified. Around the same time the disease hit London and Lady Mary Wortley Montague convinced the Princess of Wales to support inoculation experiments. She asked the king to pardon six convicts if they would submit to inoculation, and they were treated on August 9th by Dr Charles Maitland. The treatment worked.

SNAP ARMS !

Fire! – to fire a pistol was to snap an arm, or firearms.

SNAP DRAGON

An alcoholic punch with raisins that had been soaked in brandy or rum. The raisins were then set alight and floated on the top of the alcohol. Sometimes, for even greater effect, the tops of lighted candles were also included.

SNOTTY

Midshipmen were young lads, little more than boys, who carried orders to the guns in the 'midships' from the officers on deck. Their dream was to become officers and gentlemen. However, being poorly fed and young, they were constantly wiping their noses with the sleeves of their jackets, and became known as 'snotties'. One admiral decided to put three buttons on their sleeves to prevent this habit. The term 'snotty' for someone thinking that they are a gentleman and acting accordingly dates from the midshipmen's running noses.

SNOW

Like a brigantine, but smaller, with a main and foremast, and a supplementary sail close behind the mainmast.

SON OF A GUN

Not a Wild West term used by John Wayne, but a Royal Navy phrase from the days of sail. In the days when the wives and mistresses of sailors were allowed to stay aboard in harbour (and sometimes go to sea), sometimes they gave birth on board ship. Both for procreating and for giving birth, hammocks were useless. There was little room, except the gangways, which had to be kept clear at all time. The only space available was between the guns on the gun decks, and the child was called a 'son of a gun', as often no-one knew its father.
'Begotten in the galley
And born under a gun,
Every hair a rope yarn,
Every tooth a marlin spike,
Every finger a fishhook,
And in his blood right good Stockholm tar'.

SOUTH SEA BUBBLE

This scandal coincided with Black Bart's years on the high seas. The South Sea Company was founded in 1711, to prosper on the vast trade that could open up with the Spanish New World.

In 1713, the Treaty of Utrecht* followed the War of Spanish Succession (1702-1713). The ending of the war gave the Asiento Treaty, whereby Britain held a monopoly on the slave trade, but all other trade was restricted to just one ship a year. Despite this, the king became governor of the company in 1718, and confidence then drove £100 shares to over a £1000 in 1719, before crashing.

*British manufacturers were terrified that the ending of the war would put an end to their lucrative trade into Africa in exchange for Spanish goods, and lobbied hard for the asiento for the slave trade. Alongside the obvious petition from the Birmingham gun makers, we can see one from the makers of Welsh flannel.

SOUTH SEAS
Generally the area around the Caribbean, including the Gulf of Mexico, the Florida Coast, Cuba, Jamaica and Hispaniola.

SPAIN AND SLAVERY
The precious-ore and jewel deposits in Mexico, Peru and Colombia needed slaves to work in the mines. However, war, disease, overwork and suicide caused the native Indian population to plummet, in one of the worst genocides in history. In the Antilles alone the native population dropped from 300,000 in 1492 to 14,000 in 1514, and millions died on the South American mainland. To save the Indians from extinction, a former explorer, Bartolome de Las Casa, proposed that the King of Spain introduced negroes to save them from extinction, as 'the labour of one Negro is more valuable than that of four Indians'. Thus in 1517, the first 'asiento' was agreed, enabling 4000 negroes to be imported into the West Indies over the following 8 years. By 1540, an estimated 30,000 men, women and children had been transplanted from Africa to Hispaniola alone. From the 1560's, Hawkins, Drake and others were trafficking slaves to Spanish America.

SPANISH
Sack, or Canary wine. Also Spanish gold or coins.

SPANISH FAGGOT
The sun.

SPANISH GOUT, POX or NEEDLE
Syphilis – sometimes Italian or French were the pejorative adjectives. It was fashionable for derogatory terms to be prefaced with the nationality of the enemy of the day - to the French, homosexuality is to this day 'the English disease' or 'English sickness'.

SPANISH MAIN
The South American mainland, from Columbia and Venezuela up to the Isthmus of Panama. From the 17th and 18th centuries, the term came to be associated with the buccaneers sailing the Spanish Main, and was more associated with the Caribbean Sea than the mainland.

SPANISH PADLOCK
A kind of chastity belt, Spanish women sometimes were forced to wear when away from their husbands. Pirates, who captured Spanish women en route to or from the Spanish Main, probably invented the term.

SPANISH WALK
To run away.

SPIKE
To prevent a gun or cannon being fired by knocking a soft nail into the touch-hole with a spike. Therefore the gunpowder could not be ignited.

SPITHEAD PHEASANT
The naval seaman's name for a kipper.

SPLICE THE MAINBRACE
The mainbrace is the rope or brace controlling the movement of the ship's mainsail. Hauling on the mainbrace required a great effort from the crew, after which possibly some reward was in order. To splice is to join two strands of rope together. To *'splice the mainbrace'* means to start a drinking session, or give out an extra portion of rum or grog. The term may come from the Dutch *'splissen'*. *Splissen* means to drink, and Dutch sailors may have confused the terms and other pirates agreed with their more agreeable interpretation of the order.

SPLICED, TO GET
A seaman's term for getting married, referring to the permanent nature of splicing two pieces of rope together.

SQUARE MEAL
Meals were served on square wooden platters, which could be easily stowed in a rack. When weather conditions were poor, sailors were constantly working, and ate food from their pockets, having to be *'lucky to get a square meal'*.

STARBOARD
Until the 13th century in Northern Europe, steering a ship was carried out by means of a huge oar, lashed to the right (*steer-board*) side of a ship. The boat had always then to be berthed on the left-hand side, i.e. it was secured to the harbour walls of the port. So the left of a boat became known as the port side, and the right as the starboard. The great problem was that a wind blowing on the starboard beam might push the ship away from the vertical, lifting the steer-board out of the water – steering was then impossible. A violent wind on the port side could roll the ship so badly that the steer-board could be broken off. Only the innovation of the centre-line rudder, brought back by Crusaders, solved the problem and made the steer-board obsolete.

STEM THE TIDE
When a ship is sailing against the tide at such a rate that she overcomes its power.

STERN CHASER
A gun fitted on the stern, often a nine-pounder, to deter chasing ships, and aimed at their rigging and masts. From the 19th century it came to mean either a penis, or a homosexual.

STEWS
The raucous area of narrow alleyways, gambling dens, taverns and brothels frequented by sailors in port.

STINKPOTS
Crockery jars filled with sulphur, gunpowder and other combustibles, with a fuse, used to help board ships. A popular method was for the pirates to suspend them from their yardarms, and when the ships closed together, light and cut them so they dropped onto the deck of the

intended prize. From Falconer's *'Marine Dictionary'* of 1771 we have the following description: *'The fuses of the stinkpot being lighted, they are immediately thrown on the deck of the enemy, where they burst and catch fire, producing an intolerable stench and smoke, and filling the air with tumult and distraction. Amidst the confusion occasioned by this infernal apparatus the (boarding) detachment rush aboard sword in hand, under cover of smoke, on their antagonist.'*

(AS) STRAIGHT AS THE CROW FLIES
British coastal vessels often carried a cage of crows. They hate large expanses of water, and head straight towards land when released at sea, useful in fogs, or when unsure of one's bearings. The lookout perch on sailing vessels thus became known as the *crow's nest*.

STRIKE COLOURS
Haul down a ship's flag as a mark of surrender. The present term *'to strike'*, i.e. refusing to work for masters (management) in order to look after one's own interests, comes from this nautical expression.

STRUMPET
Harlot, prostitute, bawd, trollop.

SUCKING THE MONKEY
Not a pirate term, but a tribute to the ingenuity of the poor sailor suffering a disgusting experience in the Royal Navy. In the War of American Independence (1775-1782), England was blockading the United States, and a large fleet was stationed in the West Indies. For years the officers could not understand why their crews of impressed men were often too drunk to stand up. They even stopped the grog supplies for a time, with no change in their condition.

Native women boarded the warships, to sell fruit and coconuts. Many men had persuaded the women to replace the coconut milk with rum, and stored and hid up to a dozen coconuts, wherever they could. When *'sucking the monkey'* they were secretly drinking rum.

SUCKY
Drunk, a *'suck-bottle'* was a drunkard. *'Suck'* was strong alcohol, and *'rum suck'* was very good quality rum. To *'suck one's face'* was to drink heavily.

SUN-DRIED
Left hanging in an iron gibbet, after execution, as an example to other pirates. Sometimes the body was tarred to preserve it from falling to pieces, or being pecked to bits by birds, and the grisly remains could be seen at prominent view-points for months or even years.

SUPERSTITIONS
No other calling has so many superstitions as seafaring. We still see a bottle of wine being cracked across the bows of a boat to be launched, which comes down to us from the libation to the gods of the sea by the

Captain Kidd hanging in chains

ancient Greeks and other cultures. Flowers on board have always been unlucky, as they can be made into a wreath for someone who dies on board. Good Friday, the first Monday in April, the second Monday in August and December 31st are unlucky days to start a voyage (being respectively Crucifixion Day, the day Cain killed Abel, the destruction of Sodom and Gomorrah and the hanging of Judas Iscariot). Priests and women are unlucky. The feather of a wren killed on New Year's Day was lucky for a year. Passing a flag between the rungs of a ladder was unlucky. There are hundreds and hundreds of superstitions, which deserve a book to themselves.

SURGEON
These were formerly known as *'barber-surgeons'* - barbers became surgeons because they had the sharpest implements for cutting. Surgeons (*'sawbones'*) were in huge demand upon pirate ships, although it was rare for them to be trained as doctors. They were bone-setters, who could extract bullets, treat venereal disease, staunch wounds and amputate to prevent gangrene.

Surgeon's at work

SWAB
From the Dutch *'zwabberen'*, *'to mop'*. The swab was a kind of large mop used to clean the ship's decks. Someone who was told to clean the decks was referred to as a *'swab'*. As it was the lowest form of duty on a ship, to call someone a *'scurvy swab'* was to call him a diseased, worthless person.

SWEAR THROUGH A DOUBLE DEAL-BOARD, or TWO-INCH BOARD, or NINE INCH PLANK
Be extremely good at lying. Also to use extremely vigorous foul language.

SWEATING
The ship's band played while one prisoner after another was forced to run between a circle of lighted candles and the mast, while being prodded with knives and swords. It ended when the prisoner collapsed, died or gave information on the whereabouts of treasure.

SWEEP THE BOARD
Win all the money from a gambling table.

SWEET TRADE
Piracy or buccaneering.

SWING THE LEAD
Slang for *'taking it easy'*. Near land, one job was to lower a lead weight on a line to find the depth near shore, to avoid shallows. It was the easiest and simplest job on ship, so anyone *'swinging the lead'* was said to be a slacker, not carrying out the normal arduous duties of his shipmates. Also, sometimes the person *'swinging the lead'* was pretending to measure the depth, out of sight of officers, especially if he knew the area.

SWUNG OFF
Hanged on a gallows.

SYLLABUBS
These were drinks or dishes sold in Port Royal taverns, made by curdling cream or milk with a mixture of wine, cider or anything alcoholic, producing a soft curd which was then whipped with gelatine, then sweetened or flavoured - the forerunner of today's alcopops.

TACK
The nautical manoeuvre of bringing a sailing vessel on to another bearing by bringing the wind around the bow, during which the ship is said to be *'coming about'*. If a ship sails too *close to the wind*, it will sail slower, and risk being put about (turned) *on the wrong tack* (in the wrong direction) by a small wind shift. The term *'on the same tack'* has the same nautical origin, with two ships heading the same way.

TAKING A CAULK
This means having a short sleep, or nap, on the deck of a ship. The spaces between the deck planks were sealed, or *'caulked'* with tar to help prevent heavy seas penetrating the lower decks. In hot climates like the Caribbean, any sailor lying down usually had stripes of tar along his clothes – he had *'taken a caulk'*.

TARPAULIN, TARPAWLING
Seamen wore canvas hats that had been coated with tar to waterproof them, known as 'tarpaulins'. They also had capes of tarpaulin to cover them in bad weather. Many sailors painted their clothes with tar to keep out the wind and rain, and were known in the North of England as *'tarry-breeks'* (tar covered trousers, or britches).

TATTOOS
Like hooped earrings, these were not affected by pirates. The first record of a sailor being tattooed is one of Captain Cook's men in Tahiti in 1764.

TELL IT TO THE PARROT
Tell everyone, spread gossip. Many ships had parrots as tokens of luck.

TEREDOS WORM
Not a worm, but a soft-shelled mollusc, and the most common and dreaded attacker of ships'

hulls in warm water. It could enter planks through tiny holes, and lay a million eggs a year. The young molluscs bored parallel to the surface, honeycombing planks with no outward signs. Ships were double-planked, with a layer of felt and pitch between them, to try to keep the teredos out, as well as other molluscs which attached themselves to the hull and proceeded to devour it layer by layer. If possible, pirates tried to capture brigs and barquentines made from cedar-wood from the Bahamas, which was more resistant to the teredos worm.

THREE SHEETS TO THE WIND
Almost totally drunk. A sheet is a line used for trimming a sail to the wind. There is only one sheet on fore-and aft sails, and there are just two on a square sail set on a yardarm. On a Bermuda-rigged vessel there are two sheets for the jib-foresail and one for the main sail. Thus a drunken man, even if he had three sheets to trim his sails and steer his course, would still be too unsteady to steer a straight course. If the boat is 'three sheets to the wind' the sails are not drawing wind and the ship will not make progress, but drift downwind.

THREE SISTERS
Three rattans bound together with waxed twine, used to hit the backs of seamen to make them 'start' or move more quickly when working. Used by the boatswain's mate in the 17th and 18th centuries, it was used at random, although totally illegal. It was not prohibited until 1809, but still in use long after that in the Royal Navy. The emblem is still seen, as the badge of office on today's master-at-arms.

THROUGH THE HOOP
In the Royal Navy, hammocks were rolled tightly every morning and lashed against the ship's rails to protect against cannon-shot, wood splinters or musket fire. The bosun's mates checked the tightness of each rolled hammock every morning with a regulation sized hoop. If a hammock could not be 'put through the hoop', the seaman was disciplined.

TIMBER
A wooden leg worn by amputees, or 'peg-legs'.

TOBACCO
This was the 'cocaine of the 17th century'. Columbus had noted in 1493 the habit of the (now extinct) Taino Indians of lighting rolls of dried leaves and inhaling the smoke through their nostrils. In the early 17th century, smoking had become so popular that 'many a young nobleman's estate is altogether spent and scattered to nothing in smoke (and) a man's estate runs out through his nose, and he wastes whole days, even years, in smoking of tobacco; men smoke even in bed.' The leaf's value equalled that of silver. Formerly growing wild in Virginia, it was cultivated by the Virginia Company, which desperately needed people to gather the lucrative crops. After 3 to 4 crops the land was exhausted, and more ground had to be cleared and planted by workers with a short life expectancy.
There were two ways to get labour from Britain - transportation (q.v.) and indentures such as Henry Morgan was supposed to have signed. A new life in the New World, where one could easily get ownership of one's own land, was an attractive and well-marketed proposition, but people could not afford the crossing. Thus a modified version of apprenticeship, the indenture was devised. Named from the Latin indentare or indentura (to give a jagged edge, to cut with teeth), it was a contract signed by two or more parties. It was a legal covenant, drawn on parchment and cut into pieces. The fit between the parts signified the agreement between the party of the first part, the master, and the party of the second part, the servant. Typically the

indenture bound a person as a servant for a period of 4-7 years, or for a minor until he or she reached 21.

However, life in the plantations was nasty, brutish and short. Governor Thomas Dale of Delaware around 1618 took offence to Richard Barnes uttering 'base and detracting words' against him. Barnes was ordered to be 'disarmed and have his arms broken and his tongue bored through with an awl and he shall pass through a guard of 40 men and shall be butted by every one of them and at the head of the troop be kicked down and footed out of the fort; and he shall be banished out of James City and the Island, and he shall not be capable of any privilege of freedom in the country.' This was in effect a death sentence, banishment. Seamstresses who sewed their ladies' skirts too high were whipped. Men who tried to escape were tortured to death. Piracy was a welcome release if the opportunity presented itself.

TOPGALLANT SAIL
The very top sail on a mast – changing this in a Force 9 gale was not a job to volunteer for.

TORTUGA
The most famous pirate island, just off north-west Hispaniola. It resembles a great 'sea-tortoise' or turtle, so was called by the Spanish Tortuga del Mar. Louis le Golif complained in his 'Memoirs of a Buccaneer' about having to fight two duels on Tortuga to keep suitors at bay. Its French governor finally imported hundreds of prostitutes to try and wean buccaneers away from matelotage, sodomy with their 'mates'. The Spanish in Santo Domingo regularly attacked the buccaneers in Western Hispaniola, and Tortuga was more easy to defend and escape from. It was later taken over by the French, and Petit Goave replaced it as a pirate haven from the late 17th century.

TORTURE
English law in pirate times allowed a child to be hung for stealing a crust of bread. It also allowed torture if one refused to plead at a trial. In 1725, the Scottish pirate Captain Gow was ordered to be pressed to death, (see Pressing) as he would not answer his accusers or make a plea. Upon hearing this sentence at Newgate, he quickly pleaded 'not guilty', but was still hung and displayed in chains at Greenwich.

One of the reasons that privateers and pirates of all nations were so cruel to Spanish captives was the nature of the Spanish Inquisition and its practices. Captives were routinely tortured to death. A revolting account from the Venetian Ambassador in Whitehall in 1604 records that 'the Spanish in the West Indies captured two English vessels, cut off the hands, feet, noses and ears of the crews and smeared them with honey and tied them to trees to be tortured by flies and other insects.'

TRADE WIND
A regular and steady wind in a certain direction, either perpetual or at a certain season of the year. The main trade winds are those regular winds due to the earth's motion and the action of the sun, between 30 degrees north and 30 degrees south of the equator. They were invaluable in the days of sail, those south of the equator blowing from the south-east, and those in the northern hemisphere coming from the north-east. The meeting of the Trade Winds just north of the Equator creates the 'Doldrums' where sailing ships can be becalmed for weeks waiting for a wind to carry them back into the Trades. They were known at the trade winds because their regularity assisted in trade. Thus 'feeling down in the doldrums' meant that sun-baked, listless crews became depressed at a lack of progress. The crews would often take to rowing boats and try to tow the ship towards windier conditions.

TRANSPORTATION

Because of the need for labour in the colonies, and the country's gaols were full to overflowing, a Royal Proclamation of December 23rd, 1617 allowed any felon except those convicted of murder, witchcraft, burglary or rape, to be transported to Virginia's tobacco plantations or to the West Indies sugar plantations. Women were particularly required as *'breeders'*. Thousands of children were also rounded up off London's streets and sent on the terrible passage. A 1627 letter notes that 1500 children had been sent to Virginia in the last year. A 17th century word for seizing was *'napping'*, and the napping of children (*kids*) to go as servants to America gave rise to the term *'kidnapping'*. Nearly all of the New World's colonists had a criminal background, or were there against their will. Two London merchants, John Jeffries and Robert Llewellin, had a contract to transport 200 *'passengers'* from Dublin to Virginia in the *Unity*. They could only find 14 suitable *'passengers'* in Irish prisons, so hired a press-gang to comb the city and meet the quota with innocent citizens of the right age and fitness. The *'Black Act'* of 1713 expanded the list of capital offences to over 50, including poaching fish, damaging trees, being caught in a game preserve or stealing a silver spoon. Kidnapping was not an offence. In 1717, an Act was passed allowing courts to sentence offenders directly to transportation, so a huge proportion of offenders were transported for periods of 7 to 14 years. Capital sentences could be transmuted to 14 years or life transportation. From 1720-1769, 70% of the Old Bailey's felons were transported, and 16 acts were passed establishing transportation as the sentence for crimes such as perjury. In the 1730's, 10,000 debtors were released to settle the new colony of Georgia. Conditions were almost as bad as the slave ships.

TRENCH MOUTH

Sailors ate off square wooden plates, trenchers, which could be easily stored. They were never washed, and usually became infested with worms, which could give one *'trench mouth'*. The trenchers were cleaned by wiping them with a piece of bread. If there was any type of dessert, the plate was turned over and the flat side used.

TRICING

Tying someone to the rigging to administer *'a taste of the rope's end'*, a flogging.

TROVE

Everyone has heard of *'treasure-trove'*. The author believes that the origin lies in the French *trouver* (to find), the same word as the Italian *trovare*.

TURN CAT IN THE PAN

This was used by Esquemeling to describe two black pirates who turned into *'villains'* by giving evidence for the Crown against their Captain, Bartholomew Sharp. The saying appears in Heywood's *'Proverbes'* of 1546, meaning to prove perfidious, or to change sides. It may be that cat comes from *'cate'*, or cake.

TURNIP-MAN

The Hanoverian George I declared upon his accession to the English throne that he would plant St James' Park with turnips and employ a man to hoe them. A popular ballad called *'The Turnip-Hoer'* was written, and his navy was known to Black Bart's crew as *'the Turnip-man's ships.'*

TURTLES

A common part of pirate diet, they could be kept alive on ships for fairly long periods by flipping them over on their backs, and keeping them covered from the heat and doused with water. They were the most common form of meat for ships in port, Governor Molesworth writing in 1684 of Port Royal, that it *'is what masters of ships chiefly feed their men in port, and I believe that nearly 2000 people, black and white, feed on it daily at Palisadoes Point, to say nothing of what is sent inland.'* The extent of the turtle hunting of the time is shown on today's maps, with Turtuguero in Costa Rica, Isla la Tortuga off Venzuela (Salt Tortuga), Dry Tortugas off the Florida Keys (cays), Ile de la Tortue off Haiti (Tortuga) and Green Turtle Cay in the Bahamas, etc.

Pirates turtling

URUCANA

The effects of the wind and Gulf Stream flowing north through the Caribbean.

VINEGAR-PISSER

Someone who *'pissed vinegar'* was disagreeable and surly.

WAD

Ball usually made of rope, pressed down the cannon barrel to keep the cannon ball and its charge in place in the rolling seas.

WAGGONER

Old sea atlas, named after Wagaenar, the early Dutch cartographer.

WALES

The reinforcing pieces of strong timber that go around a ship, a little above her water-line.

WALKING THE PLANK

There is absolutely no evidence of this ever having occurred with pirates, except in Plutarch's account of Cilician pirates around 100 AD making their Roman captives *'walk home'*.

WANKER
This increasingly common term of abuse is supposed to date from the 1940's, with an unknown origin, according to all the noted dictionaries the author has consulted. In Esquemeling's 'The Buccaneers of America', dated 1684-85 (1923 Routledge edition), we find the following description upon page 313 describing Captain Ringrose's shipwreck. Some Indians asked about six men in Ringrose's company who spoke a different language and kept apart from the British pirates. 'We told them they were 'Wankers', which is the name they commonly give to the Spaniards in their own language. Their next question was, if they should kill those Spaniards; but I answered them: "No, by no means; I would not consent to have it done." ' My supposition is, without any philological foundation, that the pirates used to call any Spanish man 'Juan-Carlos', and that the term for a group of Spaniards was 'Juan-Carloses', shortened to 'Wankers'. You heard it here first.

WAR OF JENKINS' EAR
Robert Jenkins (c.1700-1745) was a Welsh merchant captain. The Spanish guarda-costa boarded his brig, the Rebecca, in 1731 in the West Indies, and cut off his ear and sacked his cargo. He complained upon his return to England, and the British commander-in-chief in the West Indies confirmed this event. He then entered the East India Company as a captain, and was for sometime acting governor of St. Helena, a station on the Eastern trading route. In 1738, Jenkins told a House of Commons committee about his ear, producing it in front of them. There was a public outcry, leading to the 'War of Jenkins' Ear', which in turn developed into the War of Spanish Succession (1739-48).

WATCHES
Throughout recorded history, a 24-hour shipboard day has been divided into 'watches'. Generally, there was a larboard watch and a starboard watch. In English ships, the length of the watch was 4 hours, with the exception of the two dogwatches of 2 hours each.

WAVES
It is important to realise, as with storm forces, the types of seas that pirate ships faced. Small ships in high seas were the most unpleasant places on earth.

Wave code	Description	Height from trough to crest (feet)
0	Glassy Calm	0
1	Calm, ripples	0-1
2	Smooth, wavelets	1-2
3	Slight	2-4
4	Moderate	4-8
5	Rough	8-13
6	Very Rough	13-20
7	High	20-30
8	Very High	30-45
9	Phenomenal	Over 45, the centre of a hurricane

WELSH CRICKET
A louse, or a tailor. A 'Welsh fiddle' or 'Scotch fiddle' was an itch.

WELSH MILE
'Like a Welsh mile' meant long and narrow. As Max Boyce once famously remarked, Wales would be a massive country, 'bigger than England' if it was ironed out flat.

WET
Liquor, as in *'let's have a wet'*. As an adjective it meant that someone was under the influence of alcohol, or prone to drinking too much.

WHIPPING
This was the standard punishment of the times for vagrancy and begging, and could also be ordered by clergymen for *'offences against public decorum'*. The law stated that men, women or children should be stripped to the waist, tied to a whipping post or run through the streets at the back of a cart, and *'whipped until the body be bloody'.'* Females were publicly whipped until 1817, and men until 1850. The insane were routinely whipped, a *'therapy'* to bring them to their senses. Titus Oates was said to have received 2,000 lashes, being virtually flayed alive. A *'whip-arse'* was a school-master, and to *'lick on the whip'* or *'drink whip'* was to be thrashed severely.
'Ashley's Book of Knots' knot number 508 is a double overhand knot tied in a cat-o'-nine-tails and thence termed a 'blood knot': *'it may be double, treble, or even fourfold and is designed to add to the discomforts of whipping.* The 1801 'British Mariner's Vocabulary' tells us that a 'cat-o'-nine-tails' is *'nine cords about half a yard long fixed upon a piece of thick rope for a handle, having three knots on each at small intervals, nearest one end.'*

WHIP THE CAT
To become intoxicated, or *'whipcat'*. To *'whip'* was to drink extremely quickly. *'Whip-belly'* was weak alcohol. Also, *'whip the cat'* meant to play a practical joke.

WHIPSTAFF
Black Bart used a whipstaff to steer, and captured a ship with a new-fangled steering wheel, but its captain had taken the wheel ashore, much to his disappointment. Captain Henry Mainwaring, in his 'Seaman's Glossary' of 1623, wrote: *The Whippe is that Staff which the Steeresman doth hold in his hand, whereby he governed the helme, and doth Port it over from one side to another. It hath a Ring at one end, which is put over the end of the helme, and so comes through the Rowle, up into the Steeridge. In great Ships they are not used: for by reason of the Weight of the Rudder, and the Water which lies upon it in fowle weather they are not able to govern the helme with a Whippe, because conveniently there can stand but one Man at the Whippe.'* In the earliest days of sailing, the officer gave an order such as 'hard-a-starboard', meaning 'push the tiller or steering oar as far as you can to starboard', whereby the ship turned hard in the opposite direction, to port. From around 1450, however, a new form of steering was used. Ships had added castles to the main deck, so the steersman had to be lifted to a higher level. The deck had become so high above the rudder that the helmsman needed a remote way of turning the tiller, if he was to be on the deck and see the sails. The answer was the whipstaff, a stout piece of timber which passed through a hole in the deck to a pivot and from there to the end of the tiller. A mechanical advantage of about 4:1 was obtained at the cost of limited rudder movement. The helmsman stood with the whipstaff roughly vertical in front of, or beside, him. The whipstaff was pushed in the direction in which the ship was to turn. By the early 18th century, the ship's wheel was introduced on larger ships. As ship size had continued to increase, ships had become increasingly difficult to control. The steering wheel was connected to the tiller by block and tackle, which provided a considerable increase in mechanical advantage, a smoother rudder operation with less effort.

WHISKY GALORE
This book and film set in Scotland has its origins in fairly recent smuggling in the south-west

of Wales, of which the 16th century Sir John Perrot would have undoubtedly approved. *'On the night of the 30th January, 1894, a large merchant ship named the Loch Shiel, laden chiefly with cases of Scotch whisky for Australia, on making the Haven (Milford) for shelter, ran aground on the rocks at the back of Thorn Island, practically the northern boundary of West Angle Bay. On this occasion Mr Mirehouse, of Angle, and the crew of the lifeboat, did some brave work in rescuing the crew of the unfortunate ship, which ultimately became a total wreck. The cargo and wreckage floated about the harbour for weeks after, the Salvage of which did not all find its way to the Receiver of Wrecks.'* (Mason, 1905). Basil Hughes reported on the *Pembrokeshire Snippets* website that some local cottages walled over cupboards shortly after, and recounts whisky-related wedding festivities in the nearby village of Dale some time after the wreck.

WIND OUT OF HIS SAILS
A fast pirate sloop could bear down towards merchant, taking the *'wind out of his sails'* thus making him difficult to manoeuvre. This was usually preceded by a warning *shot across the bows*. The present term *'overbearing'* has the same nautical origin, meaning using a position of superiority.

WITH PLANKS A FLOAT
The term given to returning ships full of loot, so overloaded with bullion that the waves constantly swept over the deck planking. (This was later the main reason for the Plimsoll Line legislation - unscrupulous owners would deliberately overload ships to claim upon the insurance - men were easy to replace.)

WOODEN SHIPS
'were damp, dark, cheerless places, reeking with the stench of bilge water and rotten meat.' They always leak and are difficult to dry, so pirates often suffered from illnesses brought on by wet damp conditions and no dry attire. Additionally, a pirate ship sometimes needed twice the manning of a merchant ship, with men packed in like sardines. As well as carrying loot and more guns and munitions than the average boat, more people were needed to pose a threat in a fight. Pirates tried to keep the decks clean by washing them down with brandy, and to fumigate below decks by burning pitch and brimstone. The ships were full of disease, cockroaches, fleas and rats. However, rats were often used to supplement the diet of salt beef or pork crawling with maggots, foetid water, and mouldy, slimy bread.

WOOLDING
A particularly nasty piece of torture practised to try to get information from captives. One of Captain Morgan's men, present at the rape of Porto Bello, later wrote to the Secretary of State that *'it is a common thing among the privateers, besides burning with matches and such-like torments, to cut a man to pieces, first some flesh, then a hand, an arm, a leg, sometimes tying a cord about his head and with a stick twisting it till the eyes shoot out, which is called woolding.'* It was not invented by the buccaneers, but was a recognised part of the torture called *'cordeles'* by the Spanish, used in both secular courts and by the Inquisition to extract confessions.

YARD
Any spar horizontal to a mast – the yard-arm was the yard on either side of the mast, which was the easiest place to hang any miscreant from.

YELLOW JACK
Tropical fever or yellow fever, which turned the victims yellow with jaundice and made them

spew up black vomit. The *'Yellow Jack'* was therefore a flag flown by ships to indicate that there was disease aboard. *'Yellow Jack'* was also a particularly nasty term of abuse hurled at someone a pirate did not like.

ZEE-ROVERS
Dutch for pirates, copied in the English *'sea-rovers'*.

NOTE:
Peter Kemp's *'The Oxford Companion to Ships and the Sea'* is a fabulous compendium of shipping and sailing terms, almost a thousand pages of educative entertainment. As both my father and father-in-law went to sea as young lads, I have more than a passing interest in such matters. My uncle and father-in-law were torpedoed in World War II. The lady two doors down from where I was brought up, in Barri, lost four sons in the War at sea. Any mistakes in the above 'Pirate Terms' are mine, and I would be grateful if anyone can correct them for me, for possible future editions of this book. In the meantime, for definitions of the following, please refer to Kemp's glorious book. I always thought was *'futtock'* was a word made up by Barry Took for the camp pairing of Julian and Sandy on *'Round the Horne'* and *'Beyond Our Ken'* : *'mizzen futtock shrouds; jib-of-jibs, jibber the kibber,* **snotter***, sandbagger, naked, sheer legs, lady of the gunroom, scandalise, spanker, buttock lines, swallow the anchor, the wobbly eight, sandbagger, lee-fang, deadeye, loblolly boy, monkey jacket, baboon watch,* **baggywrinkle***, bagpipe the mizzen, joggle shackle, horse latitudes, fore topgallant standing halyard, bowline lizard, Kentish knock, Jack in the basket, galligaskins, jewel blocks, diamond shroud, cod-banger, bean-cod, lazy guy, bummaree,* **faggots***, hot chase, banyan days'*, and, of course the *'lower studding stay outer halyards'*.

CHAPTER II

THE EARLIEST WELSH PIRATES
THE THIRTEENTH CENTURY

WILLIAM MARSH, MARISCO fl. 1235 - 1242

Prince Madoc ab Owain Gwynedd was said to have sailed from Lundy Island to discover America around 1170, and it was used as a pirate sanctuary until the 1300's. William Marsh, son of a justiciar in Ireland, married the niece of the Archbishop of Dublin, and received a rich dowry. He was expected to have a long and successful career at court in London, but had an ungovernable temper. He murdered a king's messenger at Henry III's Westminster Palace in 1235. He was outlawed, and fled to Lundy, nominally a possession of his cousin, and until 1242 used it as his base to prey on Western shipping. Marsh also used Sully Island, near Penarth, as a base.

Marsh seized shipping from the Mull of Galloway down to Land's End, and became a friend of the King of Scotland for his effects upon English commerce and trade. At one time, Marsh was also arraigned for High Treason, as he had sent a servant to assassinate Henry III at his palace at Woodstock. This may have been at the instigation of the Scottish king. Marsh also traded with the monks of Margam Abbey*, where he sometimes stayed. His main income came from ransoming his captives, kept in a dismal damp dungeon on Lundy, rather than disposing of cargoes.

The coast of Devon was specially defended against Marsh's attacks, and some of his men and his wife were captured. Marsh thought that he was safe upon his Lundy stronghold. However, he was betrayed when one of his captured men, forced by the thumb-screw, told the royal forces that the weak point in his defences was held by a single guard, who did not like Marsh. Marsh was captured in May 1242 while eating his dinner, and taken in irons to the Tower of London. He and 16 colleagues were dragged by horses to the gibbet and hung, while other members of his crew were executed at Newgate. The new ship that he had been constructing at Lundy was taken to Ilfracombe to be finished and put into the Crown's service. (The *Marisco Tavern* is Lundy's pub - the island is now owned by the Landmark Trust, and a marvellous place for a holiday.)

*In 1289, the Prior of Goldcliffe Abbey in Gwent, was accused by a Bristol merchant of receiving several tuns of Bordeaux wine from his wrecked ship. The Vicars of Portishead and Ash in Somerset also shared in the booty.

FIFTEENTH CENTURY

COLYN DOLPHYN fl 1470

The Bristol Channel was a terrible place for piracy from the 13th-16th centuries, with Lundy island probably being the most popular haunt of ruffians. At the beginning of the 15th century the Breton pirate Colyn Dolphyn again used Lundy as his base and charged a toll on local shipping. Sir Edward Stradling of St Donat's Castle, Glamorgan, had two sons, William and Edward, who undertook pilgrimages to the Holy Land in the 14th century. Edward died there and his son, Harry, succeeded to the lands and castle of St Donat's. Harry's mother was the daughter of Howel ap Madoc ap Iestyn ap Gwrgan (Iestyn was the last native prince of Glamorgan), daughter of the Lord of Ruthyn, so the Stradlings now took the manorial arms of the Welsh princes. While travelling from the family's extensive Somerset estates back to Glamorgan, Sir Harry was captured on the Bristol Channel by Colyn Dolphyn, who asked for a massive ransom of 2,200 marks. Stradling was forced to sell his manors of Bassaleg, Rogerstone and Tregwilym in Monmouthshire, Sutton in Glamorgan, and two other manors in Oxfordshire, and never forgave the pirate.

Dolphyn operated from a base on Sully Island, as later did William Chick in the 1570's. Later, Stradling caught Dolphyn, local tradition saying that he was lured by the lights from the existing watchtower at St Donat's which was deliberately built to lure him. According to the notes of Taliesin Williams, '*he caused to be erected the watchtower, in the new park of St Donats, in which arms were placed; and men to watch, at night, for the sea-thief, Colyn Dolphyn, who too frequently cruised the Severn Sea, on ship-robbing intent. On one long winter's night, the watch-tower being in full light, Colyn Dolphyn drew towards it; mistaking it for Dunraven Place; and struck on the Nash Sands, until his ship went to pieces; but he and his men were taken, hanged and buried under the hillocks that are to be seen on a spot on the brink of the sea, near the castle. For this however, Sir Harry Stradling, it cannot well be devised why, was bitterly pursued at law by Henry VI.*"

Stradling's defence was that he gave the Breton to the villagers of Llanilltud Fawr to dispose of as they wished. He said that Dolphyn was buried up to his neck in nearby Tresilian Cove, while the crowd watched the tide come in. Harry Stradling had made a pilgrimage to Rome in 1475, and died at Cyprus on his way back from the Holy Land in 1476 or 1477. His heir Thomas died young, in 1480, and was succeeded by Edward, knighted at Tournai by Henry VIII. His son Sir Thomas became an MP, but was imprisoned in the Tower under Elizabeth for suspected Catholic leanings. He died in 1573 and was succeeded by his son Sir Edward (1529-1609). The direct line of Stradlings ended with him, and the Thomas Stradling who marooned Alexander Selkirk came from another branch of the family. St Donat's Castle was restored by William Randolph Hearst (Citizen Kane) and is now occupied by Atlantic College.

Taliesin Williams, son of Iolo Morganwg, wrote a poem, '*The Doom of Colyn Dolphyn*', about the event in 1837, based upon the local tradition that Dolphyn was 'given' to the villagers of Llanilltud Fawr (Llantwit Major) and hung by them. The three cantos, '*The Vase and the Huntsman*', '*The Shipwreck - The Trial*', and '*The Execution*' total 77 pages, so only an excerpt can be included, of the pirate's execution.

On the 'car', a wagon which is moved on, leaving the prisoner hanging, the pirate calls upon the Devil to save him. He breaks his chains, grabs the rope with one hand, and tries to untie himself from the noose. His hand is cut off, but his arm still reaches out…

> *"Come to my aid! Avert this fate!*
> *Our compact told a longer date.*
> *Thine am I Pledged by deed and vow!*
> *Supreme of Darkness! Nerve me now!"*
> *No more was heard: - but, while on high*
> *Fierce thunder rolled, and scowled the sky,*
> *He flung his hands apart! - the stroke*
> *Fetter and chain asunder broke.*
> *"God! And enough", exclaimed the Knight,*
> *"That was not done by mortal might!"*
> *The crowd receding at the sight,*
> *Exclaimed, - "The Foe prevails!*
> *Who, though evading mortal ken,*
> *Governs the doom of evil men; -*
> *The parting soul assails."*
> *And now, while moved the car along,*
> *Colyn sprang up with effort strong;*
> *Grasped with one hand the rope above,*
> *While - vain attempt! The other strove*
> *Its tie to loose; - but Dewry's brand*
> *Instant obeyed his Chief's command;*
> *And soon appeared the severed hand*
> *In useless grasp; - the crowd below*
> *Saw Colyn pendant to the bough.*
> *Then! Then! The fearful struggle came*
> *Of tortured soul in mortal frame!*
> *For oh! What agonies assailed*
> *His frame, ere victor Death prevailed!*
> *Each nerve convulsive sprang in throes!*
> *The bleeding arm still quivering rose!*
> *Distortive heaved his labouring breast!*
> *At last in Death's excruciate toil,*
> *Life found release from mortal coil:-*
> *And Colyn's soul-forsaken mould*
> *All haggard hung; grew stiff and cold…*

After 1545, Lundy was in control of a gang under the protection of Lord Seymour, High Admiral of England, who was after indicted for treason. After robbing the Dutch ship *Falcon* off Caldey in 1548, the pirates Cole and Stephens were captured in 1549, and a reward of £60 was shared between Rice ap Morgan, Philip Lower and Nicholas

Rest.. It had been pirate policy to befriend officials such as vice-admirals, sheriffs, customs officials and justices. Queen Elizabeth was forced to appoint four Piracy Commissioners in each maritime county in 1565, to not only deal with pirates but also the landsmen who aided their activities. Among the Welsh commissioners were the bishops of St David's and St Asaph, John Salesbury of Rug, Dr Ellis Prys (father of the privateer Tomas Prys), Sir Edward Mansell of Margam (father of Admiral Sir Robert Mansell q.v.) and Arnold Butler of Dunraven Castle, of a family notable for wrecking and smuggling. Three of the Herbert family of Glamorgan and Gwent were also appointed - men who virtually controlled piracy receiving in South Wales.

Footnote: For some years after 1610, Lundy was controlled by the pirate captain Thomas Salkeld, who styled himself 'King of Lundy'. Lundy Island features in ancient Welsh histories, and Michael Drayton wrote in his Polyolbion:

'England and Wales strive in this song,
To whether Lundy doth belong
When either's nymphs, to clear the doubt,
By music mean to try it out.
This while in Sabrin's Court, strong factions strangely grew
Since Cornwall, for her own, and as her proper due,
Claimed Lundy, which was said to Cambria belong,
Who oft had sought redress, for that her ancient wrong' ...
'Of all the inlaid isles her sovereign Severn keeps,
That bathe their amorous breasts within her secret deeps
To love her Barry much, and Scilly though she seem,
The Flat-Holm and the Steep as likewise to esteem,
This noblest British nymph yet likes her Lundy best' ...
'In this song Severn gives doom
What of her Lundy should become' ...
'Then take my final doom, pronounced lastly, this -
That Lundy like allied to Wales and England is.'

SIXTEENTH CENTURY

WILLIAM HUGHES fl. 1529

Piracy was prevalent in the Bristol Channel in the early 16th century: 'No Breton dared to come to Milford on account of robberies committed by a bark of Bristowe commanded by William Hughes and owned by Richard Fox and one Sunter of Bristowe.'

THOMAS CARTER fl. 1535

A Breton ship carrying salt and wine was taken off the Pembrokeshire coast by Carter in July 1535. The Deputy Vice-Admiral of Pembroke, Sir Thomas Jones of Abermarlais, discovered that the goods had been sold in the county. The Bishop of St David's, his Chancellor William Stradling and his Chaunter Thomas Lloyd were implicated, and ordered to attend the King's Council 'with a diligence', and ordered to satisfy the Breton owners and arrest the culprits. The Bretons were paid the value of their goods, and Carter was captured by Sir Richard Bulkeley of Beaumaris. Of the pirates imprisoned at Caernarfon Castle, five escaped, but Carter was taken to appear before Thomas Cromwell in London.

WALTER HERBERT fl. 1537

Captain Richard Hose's London ship, *Valentine*, put into Cogan (Penarth) in 1537, carrying wine, salt, tunny fish and alum. Hose was accused of failing to pay harbour dues, and put into prison. He was also carrying some Portuguese refugees, which did not help his case. Walter Herbert, Cardiff's Custom officer, illegally sailed the ship to Chepstow and sold the Valentine and its cargo. His defence was that he had been instructed by his Herbert kinsman, the Earl of Worcester. Thomas Cromwell released Walter in 1538, no charges being proven for this act of piracy. The Herbert family controlled south-east Wales at this time and for decades after. The Piracy Commissioners in 1565 included William Herbert of St Julian (Newport), William Herbert of Coldbrook, William Herbert of Swansea, Edward Mansel and Thomas Lewis of the Van (Caerphilly), all of whom were closely connected to the Herbert Earls of Pembroke, and all of whom were involved in incidents of piracy and receiving.

CAPTAIN GRIFFITH fl.1540

A Portuguese merchant, Peter Alves, engaged William Phelipp in 1540 to pilot the *Santa Maria Desare* from Tenby to Bastabill haven. Off the Welsh coast, Phelipp was attacked by a pirate ship named the *Furtuskewys*, with a crew of 35 men. The 30-ton pirate vessel was commanded by Captain Griffith and Robert Hyre. Alves was put ashore at Mumbles, and the *Santa Maria Desare* was sailed into Cork, where the pirates sold the ship and its cargo of flour, vinegar, salt and wines for 1524 crowns. Phelipp was a prisoner, and the Mayor of Cork was one of the main buyers. Alves complained to the king, and Richard Gowllys, the Mayor of Cork was ordered to return the ship to Alves. Gowllys refused, stating that he thought that the ship was Scottish, not Portuguese.

JOHN PHILLIPS (PHELYPPES) fl. 1540 - 'the first captain known to have committed piracy in the Americas'

In March 1540, Phillips left Portsmouth in the *Barbara*, heading for Brazil, with around 100 crewmen. In his crew were a dozen French sailors, who been involved in raids in the Americas. Phillips had the distinction of being the first British seaman to have practised piracy in the New World. Off Portugal's Cape St Vincent, Phillips took a 40-ton French barque carrying salt, and then a Spanish caravel with gold and amber from the Barbary Coast. He took the barque as the new *Barbara*, before putting into the Canary Islands for water and provisions for the Atlantic Crossing. The barque, or bark, had three masts, the first two being square-rigged and the after mast fore and aft rigged. It became the favoured pirate ship in the Caribbean, and they were sailed across to Africa and Madagascar, carrying up to 90 men.

In May, Phillips made landfall near Pernambuco (modern Recife, in Brazil), but found no ships to ransack, nor anything worth stealing from the natives. He headed northwest, for 'The Land of the Cannibals'. Eight men disappeared on shore, and he sailed on to Hispaniola. Off Santo Domingo, Phillips took a 300-ton Spanish vessel loaded with cow-hides and sugar. However, a Spanish galleon caused some damage to the *Barbara*. Phillips escaped to Western Hispaniola, and transferred their loot off the damaged *Barbara* to the Spanish ship. The Spanish crew were set ashore, and Phillips shared out gold between his men. After a stormy crossing back, reaching England in November, there were formal Spanish complaints, and several of the 32 surviving crewmen were arrested. However, it seems that no-one was tried. The insurers paid the *Barbara's* owners for her loss, although she had been lost committing piracy.

CAPTAIN OWEN fl.1540
In 1540, he was the captain of a pirate barque operating from Mount's Bay, and murdered a Breton crew off the Scillies. One of his crew recounted: '*Captain Owen called to Phillip the Welshman and to the other Welshman, speaking in Welsh, and at one or two of the clock in the afternoon the said Phillip called up the Bretons one after another to the number of seven men and brought every man to the waist of the ship and caused John the mariner of Weymouth to bind their hands on cross behind their backs. Then the same John by command of Phillip cast the seven Bretons overboard in the sea ... They were drowned with their jerkin on them, about 4 leagues from the land.*' Just two hours later, Captain Owen ordered the crew of another Breton hoy (a small coastal vessel) to be thrown into the sea.

WALTER VAUGHAN fl. 1542
Dunraven had the worst reputation for wrecking on the Glamorgan coast – its great Castle was unfortunately demolished in the 1960's, but it is an ancient site with an Iron Age fort overlooking the beautiful sandy beach of Southerndown. *Spencer's 'Annals of South Glamorgan'* tell us of Walter Vaughan, the 16th century Lord of Dunraven, who took to wrecking to supplement the income from his estates. From Bredwardine, he had inherited the estate from the last of the Butler family in 1541. To supplement his wasteful extravagances, he took to wrecking. His main accomplice was '*Matt of the Iron Hand*', a villain who had lost his hand in a previous fight at sea with Vaughan's men. Vaughan did not know that this hook-handed lieutenant secretly hated him and wished for revenge. One of the techniques used to lure ships onto the rocks was to fix lanterns to cattle. Ships in trouble would head towards the 'harbour' and get dragged onto a lee shore. On a dark and story night, after several years of luring ships to their fate with false lights, Matt eventually wrecked the boat he wanted more than any other. He reported his success to Walter Vaughan, who queried if there were any survivors. '*There was just the one, a Welshman from Dunraven*', Matt laughed back at him, as he thrust a severed hand into Vaughan's face. On the fingers was the ring of Vaughan's only son. Tradition states that Matt was then shot dead by the family harper, and Vaughan was so heart-broken that he sold the castle and left the area, never to return.

SIR JOHN WOGAN fl. 1542 - 1555

In the 1530's, Tenby had become a favourite haunt of Breton pirates. Around fifteen, including Captain John du Laerquerec, were taken when they came ashore to reprovision. Three boats were sent from to the pirate ship to rescue their captain: *'iii bootes came to the said tonne about midnight intending to have snatched the captain from them by force, but when they could not so have him, they shot their gonnes and blew up their trumpets and departed.'* Upon examination, the captain admitted *'he had taken from Englishmen, ropes of ships, mariners' apparel, v pieces of wine, fish, one crown of gold and xv half pens or pens of silver, iiiv daggers and a converture called in French "une port de ray"...'* His defence of his actions were that other St Malo pirates were much worse than him, such as *'John Hacque, who hath pilled and robbed many Englishmen'*. In 1542 Tenby features again, when Sir John Wogan, a former Sheriff of Pembroke, was suspected of complicity in gold stolen from a French ship. Later, in 1555 some pirates took a Breton merchant ship and took it to Tenby, to be arrested by Wogan. His next move was to sell the cargo and pocket the proceeds. John le Barthicke, the owner, petitioned the Privy Council, who ordered Wogan to return the money. In 1556, Welsh merchants petitioned about the pirate Mericke Morgan, and with piracy in the Bristol Channel and Irish Sea being worse than anywhere else in Britain, Elizabeth issued orders that all convicted pirates should be executed *'upon some cliffs near to the sea-side'*, their captains to be hanged in chains in view of the shipping lanes to discourage the others.

MICHAEL JAMES fl. 1546

Sailing the *Mary Figge* of Plymouth, he pillaged Flemish ships, and forced a Spanish ship sailing to Chester, to surrender in 1546. James put the crew under the hatches for two days and nights while he looted the cargo. He then put them in the bread-house before abandoning the ship, *'where they had no space to stand nor sit but did lie upon one another like hogs, fast bound with ropes and cords.'* James later claimed that he did this because the Spanish had tortured his father. He threatened to sink the ship with its crew tied up like this, but he later freed the Spaniards, and sold the cargo in Cardiff and Bristol. Several pirates named James are mentioned in piracy cases in 1546, along with James Hughes at Brighton and William ap Howell at Rye.

RICHARD VAUGHAN fl. 1546

Sailing out of Calais, he was reported as the ringleader of pirates in 1546 by the Mayor of Haverfordwest, having captured a Portuguese caravel, the *Sancta Maria de Leusa*, off the Pembroke coast, and disposing of the booty in Pembrokeshire and possibly also in Ilfracombe.

MORGAN MATTHEW fl. 1548

Probably from the famous Matthew family of Radyr, St Ffagan's and Llandaff, on Easter Day 1548 Morgan Matthew commanded the *Matthew of Cardiff (Mathewe de Kerdiff)* and the *Valentine* of Topsham, taking a Breton ship off the north coast of

Spain. The ship was sailing from Spain. The pirates *'fell in with spoiling and braking open of chests and within the space of half an hour they had rifled the said Breton; and the company departed with their spoil, being conveyed in bread-sacks.'* The nineteen pirates aboard the ship found that it was carrying the servants and baggage of the Portuguese Ambassador to France, Brasdellus Vetto. They looted six tables and silverware intended for the embassy - 880 ounces of silver flasks, flagons, porringers, platters, bowls and basins worth £220 at the time. Four cases of *'wild-fire'* for defending the ship were also stolen. The pirates kept their gains, although they were prosecuted, and were given a free pardon in 1551.

GRIFFITHS OF CEFNAMLWCH fl. 1563

Anglesey and Caernarfonshire and their associated islands were the most popular pirate haunts in North Wales, often supported by local gentry such as the Bulkeleys of Anglesey and the Griffiths family of Cefnamlwch on the Llyn Peninsula. In 1563 Captain Thomas Wolfall captured a prize with a cargo of wheat and rye, which he took to Enlli (Bardsey Isle). Griffiths boarded the prize to confiscate it, but Wolfall claimed that he was carrying a letter of marque issued by the Earl of Warwick. Griffiths appealed to Vice-Admiral Sir Richard Bulkeley, Sheriff William Griffiths and Griffith Davies, the keeper of the Armoury, for support, but they refused. Griffiths then plotted with John Thane to pretend to buy corn from Wolfall, and then attack the pirate ship with sixty men, in return for a payment to Thane of £30. Griffiths' plot was betrayed and corn and wheat were sold openly at Barmouth. John Wyn ap Hugh (q.v.) was one of his receivers. In September of that year, the pirate Captain Sergeant arrived at St Tudwal's Isle with two prizes laden with corn. One of the ships, complete with cargo, was bought openly by John Roberts of Caernarfon. John Griffiths of the Llyn took eight men and seized the *'pirate goods'* from Roberts in the name of the Queen and the Lord Admiral.

WELSH BUCCANEERS ON THE PELICAN 1570-1572 (1595?)

Although he lost his brother John, Francis Drake led a successful attack on Spanish ships, and took a mule train full of Peruvian silver worth 450,000 pesos, in the West Indies in 1571. He later renamed his ship The Golden Hind and circumnavigated the world with her from 1577 to 1581. The following is the last fragment of a long Welsh song by crew-member Lieutenant William Peilyn, dated at 1570 on the manuscript, but which must have been written later, during the early part of the voyage of Somers and Preston to the Indies in 1595. The poem is the story of a *pack of Welshmen ('bagad o Gymru')* and was found in the papers of a Rev. Bulkeley of Bryndu, as part of *'The White Book of Mechell'*. It was transcribed and modernised by Alfred Perceval Graves (an Irishman who considered himself a naturalised Welshman), who was the father of the poet Robert Graves. The ballad is dedicated to the Pelican, and *'The Ballad of the Welsh Buccaneers'* recounts *'what befell the Welsh sea rovers who adventured to the Indies at the behest of Elizabeth Tudor, to make reprisals, to annoy, and plunder the Spaniards.'* Robert Davie's account of the same voyage was published by Hakluyt in *'Principal Navigations'*, and corroborates the characters and events -

'of stirring episodes by flood and field,
of hairbreadth 'scapes in the imminent deadly breach.'

The crew which sailed from Plymouth in 1595 must have had many Welsh seamen, as
the concluding nine verses describe:
'Go tell them boldly, beauteous bird,
The Welsh are warriors splendid;
(Of Englishmen we lost a third,
Counting both killed and wounded.)

Captain Bilins, Hector-breast,
On land is our great guider,
In every perilous feat of arms
He was the foremost strider.

Captain Roberts seconds him,
Prince Jason was no prouder;
Like great Duke Theseus with his club
His foes he beats to powder.

Hugh Myddleton has done his share,
So hath each true lieutenant -
Salisbury* stout and Heilin rare -
Where'er we flew our pennant.

Robert Bilins, Sergeant Hughes,
Whipped the black foe like flummery!
Will Thomas, William Johnes and Hugh,
Behold the crew of Cymry!

Tell of our going to Newfoundland,
The cruel Gulf Stream over,
'Tis thence we'll come to Christendom
To meet fond friend and lover.

And if too far to the North we pass,
And thereby miss our sire-land
Then shall we sight Cape Clear aright
And rest awhile in Ireland.

Sure, when within your happy arms
You nursed us, mothers loving,
In faith how little did you dream
That we should thus be roving!
Our blessings on her, slender bird,
If Heaven befriend thy mission,

Greet all our kin kind Wales within
And tell them our condition.'

The poem begins with the author asking a pelican to take news from the West Indies
to Queen Elizabeth and *'famed Sir Roger Williams, that knight beyond compare'*, that the
Welshmen in the expedition were all well, *'although a third part of the English have died,
been killed, or have turned faint.'* *'Tell the Queen that we have not as yet come to a single
place - country, town or trim island, but that we have been victorious in every chase,
wherever her Grace's enemies were. First of all off the coast of Spain, the Enemy's own
country, we harried his ships as a hawk harries crows or chickens.'* After this, *'we sailed
along to Porto Santo, a strong and important island. We burnt the city and spoilt the land -
not till the crack of doom will it return to its former dignity.'* According to Davie's account
in Hakluyt, Somers had vanished chasing a Spanish ship when Preston decided to
attack Porto Santo. After getting over the first barricades, the pirates charged on to
find the Spaniards making another stand, *'from which they were repulsed by Captain
Roberts'*. Somers and Preston reunited at the Canaries, then reached Dominica on
May 8th, to rest and reprovision. Davie accounts: *the Indians came to us in canoes made
of a whole tree, in some whereof there were three men, in some four or six, in others twelve
or fourteen, and brought in them plantains, pinas and potatoes, and trucked with us for
hatchets, knives and small bead-stones.'* However, the Welsh bard saw matters very
differently:

'Cenavon cythreulig, geirwon hin ffyrnig
Ai crwyn yn baentiedig, Satan 'r un lun;
A weir yn eu ffroenau fal baeddod a dirieu
A'u safnau sy'n malu mwg ewyn.
Dyna'r creaduriaid gwaetha a geid
Y canibaliaid creulon;
Pobl ydynt fal eirth dig
Yn bwyta cig Cristnogion.'

(*'After we came to this country, there came to meet us a crowd of naked men with painted
skins, with bows in their hands, like devils: Hellish imps of fierce rude mien, their skins
painted like Satan's own. With wires in their nostrils like boars, they chanted their war-songs
with foam-flecked jaws. Although they were a great multitude, fearsome to gaze upon, we
tarried there to replenish our drinking water. They are the worst creatures to be met, cruel
cannibals; they are a race who, like ferocious bears, eat the flesh of Christians.'*)

According to Davie, the expedition next landed at Coche, and took some Spanish,
negroes and pearls, before the sea-dogs *'went a-fishing with a Seine-net, and took good
store of mullets and other fish; and amongst the rest drew ashore in the Seine a fish called by
the Spaniards Lagarto and by the Indians Caimon, which is indeed a crocodile, for it hath
four feet and a long tail and a wide mouth and long teeth and will devour men.'* Next, the
bard tells us that Caracas was taken:

'Yn Nghactacos eitha byd
Ynnill ffort ar lan y dwr
A dal y Gyfernwr hefydd'

'At Caraccos at the hither end of the word, where we won a fort at the water's edge, and caught the Governor too.' The governor had been sleeping in the woods, and was interrogated about the next objective, Santiago de Leon. He told them that the regular road had been deliberately blocked, as they had received news from spies in England that the expedition had been sent. However, there was 'the unknown way', used only by the Indians, but 'marvellous bad and very difficult to travel.' Captain Roberts cleared the way after leading another skirmish with Spanish soldiers, and Davie wrote: 'we marched until it was night over such high mountains as we never saw the like, and such a way as one man could scarce pass along … God knoweth, the mountains were so extreme high and so steep upright that many of our soldiers fainted by the way.' Davies related the assault upon Santiago, led by Captains Belings and Roberts, and the poem tells us that the expedition 'put to lie on his back every man within her.' The privateers demanded a ransom of 30,000 ducats to leave the city, but only 4,000 were offered, so they burnt the city to the ground. William Peilyn wrote 'we could not stay there long for want of succour', and the privateers headed back to their ships, burning a fort and Indian village en route.

However, towards the end of their exhausting march, they fell into a careful trap: 'After we had come (and a long journey it was!), we found our enemies, ten to one, all arrayed against us: some in our rear, some in front, some in a train on both our flanks; there was between us fierce fighting, yea, for four hours at a stretch. In their fury they kept shooting at us clouds of poisoned arrows, and we let the leaden bullets into their hides to pay back the score with interest. Thus for two long leagues we continued to gain ground by dint of arms, without stopping to pluck the arrows out of the flesh of our own wounded.' Peilyn finished his ballad here, saying that they intended to sail home via the Gulf and Newfoundland. Davie tells us that they sailed to Chicherichee where they took and burnt three Spanish ships, then took Coros by storm, then in the Bay of Laguna lost 80 men by 'the fluxe of the bellie'. At Jamaica, Captain Jones was sent in the Derling 'to discover some secret matter, in which discovery the gallant gentleman lost his life.' At Cuba they met up with Raleigh returning from Trinidad, and via Newfoundland dropped anchor in Milford Haven in September 1595.

The author cannot source the original Welsh poem, nor a full transcript, but Chapter VIII of 'The Welsh Elizabethans' by Frederick Harris (Pontypridd, 1924) adds much of the above information. Some of the places mentioned, such as 'Port y Saint yn Ynysoedd Dedwydd' (The Fortunate Isles) and 'Caractacos Tre Saint Iayan' are on the coast of Spain. Captain Jones, in 'The Derling' (see 'The Legend of Captain Jones') had been separated from the sister ship, but later joined the company and they set off for the West Indies on April 13th, reaching Dominica in May.

*JOHN SALISBURY fl. 1570-1591
This venturer from Gwyddlewern in Merioneth may be the buccaneer mentioned in Peilyn's poem. A 1591 'begging licence' was given to him by Lord Admiral Howard, stating in Welsh how the bearer had been a soldier and had diligently served Queen Elizabeth in France, Flanders, and 'on the seas of Morocco', on a ship called the 'Minion', sailing out of London. As the result of his bravery, Salisbury had lost the use

of one hand, and had suffered *'in his face, body and limbs eleven visible wounds'*. In seeking to heal his injuries, he had spent all his possessions, so the Queen's officials and all *'good devotional folk'* were adjured to help him by all means in their power. Drake took the Minion to the Indies in 1585 and 1586, and it was also involved at Cadiz, *'singeing the King of Spain's beard'* in 1587, before taking part in the fight against the Armada. The Moroccan reference is to when the Minion and nine other London ships fought for 6 hours off Gibraltar, against a fleet of Spanish galleys under Don Pedro de Acunha. *'Lieutenant Salibri'* who was mentioned in the poem above is otherwise possibly Captain John Salisbury who was among those ordered to take precautions against the feared Spanish invasion of 1597, who is known to have been killed while taking part in the rebellion of the Earl of Essex.

THE LEGEND OF CAPTAIN JONES
A book originally printed in 1631 was attributed to David Lloyd (1597-1663), but is sometimes attributed to Martin Lluelyn (1616-1682) and/or William Marshall (fl. 1617-1650). The 1671 frontispiece (E. Okes and Francis Haley, London printers) reads as follows:
The Legend of Captain Jones:
   Relating to his Adventure to sea, his First Landing, and Strange Combat with a Mighty Bear: His Furious Battel with his six and thirty Men, against the Army of Eleven Kings, with their Overthrow and deaths: His Relieving of Kemper (Quimper?) Castle: His Strange and Admirable Sea-Fight with Six Huge Gallies of Spain, and nine thousand Soldiers: His being taken Prisoner, and Hard Usage: Lastly, His being set at Liberty by the King's Command, and Return for England.

   Jones is apparently a historical figure, recounted in the above entry, and his exploits are the stuff of legend in this verse ballad, but the author has not been able to source a copy of the book for further research. There is a copy available from a USA rare books website at $1000.

MILES PHILLIPS fl. 1574-82
Another unknown sea dog, in the mould of David Gwynne, was the buccaneer Miles Phillips. (If the author was retired, or a full-time writer, or had more resources, Gwynn, Phillips and *'Captain Jones'* would all be researched in far more depth.) W.L. Clowes describes in *'The Royal Navy'* the 1568 attack by the Spanish fleet upon the Jesus, Minion and Judith in Vera Cruz bay. John Hawkins had been given Queen Elizabeth's permission to sail in 1567 for the African coast and the Caribbean, loaning him two of her warships. He gave command of the *'Judith'* to his young cousin Francis Drake. Off Africa, some French corsairs joined him, and they took some slaves off Portuguese caravels. The privateers became involved in tribal warfare in Sierra Leone, losing nine men, before sailing to the Spanish Main in 1568. He found it difficult to trade his slaves, and had several altercations with the Spanish authorities.

   John Hawkins had led the squadron around Hispaniola on its way to the Florida Channel, heading back to England. What followed ended all attempts by the English to ever trade peaceably with the Spanish in the Caribbean.

Hawkins rounded western Hispaniola, heading for the Florida Channel to sail north and recross the Atlantic for home before the hurricane season began. However, a tropical storm forced the fleet towards the western coast of Florida. The 'William and John' was separated from the fleet, and limped eventually back to Britain. The other ships were forced south towards the Gulf of Mexico, and the queen's 'Jesus of Lubeck', which Hawkins had sailed previously to the Caribbean, was damaged and leaking badly. He made for the nearest port, San Juan de Ulua, the place where mule trains took all the Mexican treasure for shipment to Spain. The Spanish allowed him to sail into the harbour, believing that it was the flota whose arrival was due any day. When they discovered, they were angry because of Hawkins' past reputation, despite his protestations of innocence. The very next day, 13 plate ships arrived. Hawkins was afraid to let them enter the harbour in case they destroyed his fleet, but knew he could not let them anchor outside in gale force winds. If the fleet was destroyed, there would be full-scale war between the nations. A compromise was reached, with hostages being exchanged, and Hawkins promised to leave. The harbour was full of merchant ships with cargoes of gold and silver to load aboard the flota.

Don Martin Enriques, the new Viceroy of New Spain, was on the flota, with orders from Phillip II to wipe out English prvateers. As a result he had exchanged 'worthless' sailors dressed up in gentlemen's finery as hostages, and that night began manoeuvring ships towards Hawkins, in violation of the truce. Hawkins' men noticed, and his second-in-command, the Spanish-speaking Robert Barret, was sent across to the Spanish flagship to complain. Barrett was thrown in the hold, and at sunrise the Spanish began firing from their fleet and from the shore batteries. For the whole day the battle went on, with two French corsairs aiding Hawkins. The Spanish flagship and another vessel were sunk. Spanish boarding parties were repeatedly repulsed, but the English ships were being reduced to match-wood by incessant fire. Hawkins' silver beer mug was shot out of his hand, one of the French ships was taken and the other dismasted, and the 'Jesus of Lubeck' had to be abandoned. Hawkins and the remaining crew rowed and swam to the 'Minion'. The battered 'Minion' and 'Judith' hung on until dusk and at night moved out of firing range. Drake disappeared with the 'Judith', and made it back to England, much to Hawkins' disgust. There were few provisions for the increased crew, and after a few fruitless days, Hawkins anchored off Tampico in the Gulf of Mexico, and put ashore 100 starving men, leaving them to their fate, so that the others could survive. Only 14 men reached Plymouth. 300 men and according to Drake 'two million crowns' worth of treasure had been lost.

The Spaniards soon captured the abandoned seamen, and the Inquisition tortured them extensively. Only two escaped, David Ingram and the Welshman Miles Phillips, whose account of his sufferings outraged Elizabethan England, and are recounted in Hakluyt's 'Voyages of the English Nation to America'. Phillips described how they ate parrots with cannibals, how the Spanish stripped them naked and put ropes around their necks, how they were whipped in the market-place and some tortured to death and others like himself sold as slaves. He was asked by the Spanish to interpret when Francis Drake came raiding the coast. (David Ingram had evaded the Spanish and trekked from Tampico in Mexico through hostile territory, all the way to St John's,

New Brunswick in Canada, to eventual safety.) Phillips eventually arrived at Poole in Dorset, after his escape, in 1582, after 14 years of imprisonment. The remarkable accounts by Hawkins and Phillips, from Hakluyt are appended. A Spanish website has been roughly translated by the author, which recounts the sufferings of Miles Phillips' colleagues: ' Of all the privateering expeditions, the most unfortunate was that of John Hawkins and the his nephew Francis Drake in 1568. In that year they sacked the fort of San Juan de Ulúa and the port of Veracruz, where the silver of Mexico was going to embark. Nevertheless, although causing the Spanish Navy a severe defeat, these " dogs of the sea", as they were known them then, not only lost almost all the booty, but also an important number of their men (approximately 200) were captured in Veracruz and Tampico. Some were sent to Spain and the others to Mexico City, where their presence was a great event. In the capital of New Spain, the healthy ones were jailed in the Orchard of the Marquess, while the wounded patients were given hospital care. Some time later, they were taken to work in groups to the manufacturers of the Texcoco, later as individuals or in pairs. They worked for distinguished Spaniards, such as estate and mine supervisors, carpenters, mules-train leaders, tailors, etc.

However, soon the question of the faith that they professed, became a problem. One by one the English were arrested and taken before the Inquisition, because the presence in New Spain of a so large a group of heretics seemed a serious danger to the faith of the indigenous Spanish Christians and their workers. Between 1572 and 1575 the Inquisition in Mexico questioned 38 Englishmen, and in all the names of about eighty compatriots were mentioned, who presumably were from Hawkins' fleet and still alive. Four of the sailors were burned on the bonfire, of these only two in the City of Mexico. (Robert Barrett was burned in Seville market plaza). Most of the condemned men were sentenced to retract their heresies in public, dressed as "San Benito", to walk barefoot with a candle in their hand, to undergo flagellation and to serve six to ten years in Spanish galleys. Some time later, by means of a plan designed by Hawkins to betray his queen, he managed to release his sailors jailed in Seville, and to obtain an indemnity of forty thousand for the lost ones in San Juan de Ulúa.

There were eight children between twelve and twenty years, that were exempted of being flagellated, but they were condemned to three or four years on watch in a monastery in the New Spain; at the end of these sentences most of them preferred to continue living in Mexico or Spain, and just two returned to England. Those that remained in Spanish territory, married with white or black or Indian women. They grew to love this land and forgot their homes in England.

Other incursions were carried out during the last quarter of the century, as much in the Gulf of Mexico as along the Pacific coastline. In general they were successful in terms of economic gain, but had few social repercussions, because they represented a sporadic and fleeting presence. Cavendish in 1579 and and Francis Drake in 1586, during their trips around the world, when journeying from the "South Sea" towards California, cast anchor in the bay of Huatulco, where they disembarked to supply themselves with food, and to sack the small town that existed there. In the case of one of these English expeditions, the Viceroy Enríquez despatched 200 soldiers to Acapulco, with orders for the naval authorities to persecute the privateers. **Miles Phillips**, one of the men Hawkins had left on the coast of the Pánuco in 1568, and who since that time had worked as a silk weaver in the country, *was sent to interpret. Nevertheless, although Drake had the intention to enter Acapulco and to burn the ships anchored there, he mis-navigated and continued sailing towards the coast of California. When some ships left to attack him, he was too far away.*

In the particular case of Thomas Cavendish, after the sacking of Huatulco he careened his ship in Mazatlán, ready to sail to Cabo San Lucas, in the middle of October, to wait for the arrival of the Manila galleon 'Santa Ana'. Cavendish captured it and obtained rich booty, the greatest thus far taken by the Elizabethan privateers. The loot was worth one hundred and twenty thousand gold pesos, damascus silks, food supplies, to a value of two million pounds.

In 1597 Villa de Campeche was occupied and sacked by pirates headed by William Parker, while Michael Geare loaded wood in the Gulf of Logwood. Christopher Newport made several trips that made to the Caribbean, and his greatest loot was from the raid carried out in 1599-1600. In a lucrative assault against Tabasco on the Gulf of Mexico he took control of 888 ounces of silver, currencies to the value of 200 pounds, 14 ounces of gold, leather and the bells of several churches....'

Britons like Drake, Hawkins and the Myddeltons could expect little mercy in Spanish hands. A 1604 report by the Venetian Ambassador in London reads: *'News arrived today that the Spanish in the West Indies have captured two English vessels. The Dons cut off the hands, feet, noses and ears of the crews and smeared them with honey and then tied them to trees to be tortured by flies and other beasts.'* In the previous 14 years there had been at least 160 privateering voyages from Britain to the Spanish Main, and the Spanish hated the English.

From *'Elizabethan Wales'* we read another version of what actually happened after San Juan de Ulua, mentioning other Welsh buccaneers:

'After his company had tried in vain to ward off the pangs of hunger by eating "hides, cats, rats, parrots, monkeys and dogs", Hawkins was obliged to maroon a hundred souls upon the coast of Mexico. Among these unfortunates were Richard Williams, Humphrey Roberts, and Thomas Ellis, and they were split up into two parties. Those of the party which included Williams, forced their way through the brambles and the long grass of the plains in search of a town. Sniped at and stripped naked by the Indians, stung by myriads of mosquitoes, they fell into the hands of the Spaniards, and were taken to the city of Mexico. There they had to face the terrors of the Holy Inquisition in all the pomp and grandeur of its bigoted might. They were cruelly racked and ceaselessly interrogated. At last the day dawned when they had to go up and receive sentence and punishment as interloping heretics. So, according to the vivid narrative of one of them, Miles Phillips to wit, Richard Williams and his companions were "arrayed in certain fools' coats, being called in their language San Benitos, which coats were made of yellow cotton with red crosses upon them both before and behind. So about 8 o'clock in the morning we set forth out of the prison, every man alone in his yellow coat, and a rope around his neck, and a great green wax candle in his hand unlighted, having a Spaniard appointed to go upon either side of every one of us; and so marching in this order and manner to the scaffold in the market-place." Upon the tiers in the market-place were seated the Viceroy and justices under the canopies of state, and behind them, row upon row, were seated the friars, white, grey and black, while the scarlet mantles of the inquisitors added a vivid dash of colour to the scene. After the heralds had proclaimed silence, the work of sentencing and executing began. Some were sentenced to death, and were burnt there and then; others were

sentenced to the galleys, and were whipped through the streets on horseback - "and all the way as they went there were some of the Inquisitors themselves and of the familiars of that rakehell order that cried to the executioners, 'Strike! Lay on these English heretics, Lutherans, God's enemies!' " Sickened by the sights he saw, Williams would seem to have recanted, for he was only sentenced to serve three years in a San Benito in a Carthusian monastery. His term served, he settled in the Spanish West Indies, prospered, and married a "rich widow of Biscay", who brought him a dowry of 4000 pesos.

In the meantime the other party of marooned Britishers, including Humphrey Roberts and Thomas Ellis, had passed also through great vicissitudes and suffering. The survivors, after a period of slavery in the wool-carding factories, found themselves at last at the Contractation House at Seville. There, on St Stephen's Day, 1570, Humphrey Roberts and six others tried to break prison, but they were caught and put in the stocks over Twelfth Tide. At last, like their comrades at New Mexico, they were arrayed in San Benitos and marched up before the Inquisitors at Triana. Humphrey Roberts and Thomas Ellis were both sentenced to the galleys, and the rigour of their doom may be read in the words of one of their fellow captives who escaped: "We were chained four and four together. Every man's allowance was 26 ounces of coarse black biscuit and water; our clothing for the whole year two shirts, two pairs of breeches of coarse canvas, a red coat of coarse cloth soon on and soon off, and a gown of hair with a friar's hod. Our lodging was on the bare boards and banks of the galleys; our heads and beards were shaven every month; hunger, thirst, cold and stripes we lacked none until our several terms expired." '

CAPTAIN HENRY ROBERTS fl. 1576 - 1595

In 1576, Roberts was in command of the *'Christopher of Dartmouth'*, when captured and taken to the Inquisition at Tenerife. *'Howbeit, Captain Roberts, by means of a friar was delivered out of prison (which cost him all the merchandise he brought with him in his ship) and so returned with dead freight to the sum of 200 pound.'* To compensate for this looting, letters of marque were issued to Andrew Barker of Bristol, whose ship it was, and in pursuance of these letters he and Roberts made their famous voyage to the Honduras in 1576. In 1581, Captain Roberts captured two Portuguese barques bound from Brazil, and in 1592 was again in the West Indies at Cavannas Harbour in Havana. His ship was the 140-ton *'Exchange'* of Bristol, and he sailed alongside a fleet owned by Master Watts and under Captain Lane. With other Welshmen, Roberts was on the Somers and Preston expedition to the Indies in 1595, when Porto Santo and Santiago de Leon were taken. Joined by the British privateers *Solomon* and *Jane Bonaventure*, many merchant ships were taken carrying *'sack, canary, muscadel, oil, hides, salsaparilla, indigo and balsamum.* Captain John Myddelton (q.v.) was also in Captain Roberts' company at Havana. According to Robert Davie, he was commanding the *Derling* when killed at Jamaica with Captain Jones on a secret mission in 1596 (see Welsh Buccaneers on the Pelican, above)

DAVID GWYNNE fl. 1588

There were many Welshmen who took part in the fleet that defeated the Spanish Armada, and W.H.K. Wright recorded in his tercentenary book 'Britain's Salamis' the following story. The Armada, upon leaving the mouth of the River Tagus, was hit by bad weather, and took three weeks to reach Cape Finisterre, where even fouler conditions scattered the fleet. One ship sank, and two others were in danger of foundering: 'On board of one of these there was a Welsh sailor, David Gwynne, who had been captured about ten years before and kept as a galley slave. The master of the galley asked Gwynne what was to be done. The Welsh sailor, who had already conceived an idea of escaping, told the captain that unless he wished his galley to go down he must take in sails and trust to oars alone, and, moreover, to give the rowers room to work, the soldiers must be sent below. This advice was accordingly acted upon, only a few soldiers being kept on guard over the rowers. The galley slaves had been allowed to make little toothpicks and other small articles to sell from any small bits of metal which came in their way, and in this way every man had managed to provide himself with a small weapon. At a signal from Gwynne the rowers dropped their oars and fell upon the sailors, Gwynne attacking and killing the captain.

They then attacked the soldiers and others who were closely packed in the hold and gained the mastery of the vessel. It was then seen that the other vessel was bearing down upon them, and Gwynne shouted to his comrades, who were relying upon him, "God has given us our liberty, and we must prove by our courage that we are worthy of the gift!" He steered his galley straight for the advancing vessel, boarded her, and, being joined by the galley slaves from the other ships, they quickly made short work of the Spaniards. Gwynne succeeded in navigating them to Bayonne, in France, where the 466 liberated slaves were warmly welcomed.

Harries' narrative continues thus: 'From another account we learn that several years before the Armada set out for the coast of England the Spaniards captured Gwynne, whom they consigned to the hulks of the great galley, the Vasana, where he slaved as a rower. There were four of these galleys, with low, open, waists and enormous turrets at stem and stern. The Diana, the largest of the quartet, foundered with all hands during the tempest. The Vasana, too, was in imminent peril, and the master was at his wits' end as to what should be done. In his extremity he consulted the Welshman, on whose experience and seamanship he knew he could rely. Gwynne at once saw the opportunity for which he had been waiting and was ready to improve it. He pointed out to the captain the impossibility of overtaking the Armada, the extreme probability of their going down as the Diana had done, and the necessity of taking in every rag or canvas and pulling in to the nearest port. The advice was accepted, and most of the soldiers were put under hatches, a few only sitting among the slaves. There had been a secret understanding among the unfortunate slaves for some time, and they were not, as supposed, entirely unarmed. They had been accustomed to making toothpicks and other trifling articles out of broken sword blades; every man amongst them thus provided himself with a stiletto.'

'At first', records J.L. Motley, in his 'History of the United Netherlands', 'Gwynne occupied himself with arrangements for weathering the gale. So soon, however, as the ship had been made comparatively easy, he looked around him, suddenly threw down his cap, and raised his hand to the rigging. It was a pre-concerted signal. The next instant he stabbed the captain to the heart, while each of the galley slaves killed the soldier next to him. Them, rushing below, they surprised and overpowered the rest of the troops and put them all to death. Coming again on deck, Gwynne descried the fourth galley of the squadron, called the

'Royal', commanded by Commodore Medrano, in person, bearing down upon them before the wind. It was obvious that the 'Vasano' was already an object of suspicion. "Comrades", said Gwynne, "God has given us liberty, and by our courage we must prove ourselves worthy of His boon." As he spoke there came a broadside from the galley 'Royal' which killed nine of his crew. David, nothing daunted, laid his ship close alongside the 'Royal' with such a shock that the timbers quivered again; then, at the head of his liberated slaves, now thoroughly armed, he dashed on board the galley, and after a furious conflict, in which he was assisted by the slaves of the 'Royal', succeeded in mastering the vessel, and putting all the Spanish soldiers to death.

This done, the combined rowers, welcoming Gwynne as their deliverer from an abject slavery which seemed their lot for life, willingly accepted his orders. The gale had meantime abated, and the two galleys, well conducted by the experienced and intrepid Welshman, made their way to the coast of France and landed at Bayonne, dividing amongst them the property on board the two galleys. Thence by land the fugitives, 466 in number, Frenchmen, Spaniards, English, Turks and Moors, made their way to Rochelle. Gwynne had an interview with Henry of Navarre, and received from that chivalrous prince a handsome present. Afterwards he found his way to England, and was well commended by the Queen. The rest of the liberated slaves dispersed in several directions.

This was the first adventure of the invincible Armada. Of the squadron of galleys, one was already sunk in the sea, and two of the others had been conquered by their own slaves. The fourth rode out the gale with difficulty, and joined the rest of the fleet, which ultimately re-assembled at Coruna; the ships having, in distress, put in at first at Vivera, Ribadeo, Gijon, and other northern ports of Spain. At the Groyne—as the English of that day were accustomed to call Coruna—they remained a month, repairing damages and recruiting; and on the 22nd of July 3 (N.S.) the Armada set sail: Six days later, the Spaniards took soundings, thirty leagues from the Scilly Islands, and on—Friday, the 29th of July, off the Lizard, they had the first glimpse of the land of promise presented them by Sixtus V., of which they had at last come to take possession.' .'

Harries goes on to tell us that in Watts-Dunton's 'Christmas at the Mermaid Tavern', at Walter Raleigh's right-hand side is a grizzled sea-dog, David Gwynne, 'a truthful son of truthful Wales', who told in verse his story of 'how he and the golden skeleton crippled the great Armada before it reached the Channel'.

The only other record that the author can find of David Gwynne is in the family history of the Hawkins family:

Before the Armada left the Tagus the Duke of Medina Sidonia, commander-in-chief issued his orders, in the first article of which there is a clear declaration "that before all things it was to be understood by all the officers and others, from the highest to the lowest, that the principal foundation and cause moving the King's Majesty to make and continue this journey or expedition had been and was to serve God, and to deliver a great many good people, oppressed and kept in subjection to sectaries and heretics, from eternal -sorrow, and to restore them to the unity of His Church." After such a declaration, what could be expected from these Spanish Missionaries, whose arguments were the ensigns of death and destruction ? The bigoted adventurers, thus spirited with a notion of doing God service, as well as of enriching themselves by the spoil of the English nation, had already conquered in their vain imagination.

And so, assured of a recompense whether they lived or died in so religious and advantageous a cause, they weighed and proceeded from the Tagus on the 15th May, and bent their course first for the Groyne. Before they had been long at sea they were scattered by a violent storm off Cape Finisterre. Two of the galleys were run into a port of France by the stratagem of **David Gwynn,** *an English (sic) slave, assisted by some of the Moorish slaves; and fourteen of their ships were drifted on to the Chops of the Channel, between Ushant and Scilly. Then, before they were met by the English fleet, a northerly wind conveyed them back to the Groyne (Corunna), where and in the neighbouring ports they and the rest of the fleet reassembled after the storm, in a disabled condition, to take in their soldiers and warlike provisions. This mishap proved disastrous to the Spaniards, but was nearly attended with fatal consequences to the English, by creating a report all over Europe, and a belief in the English Council, that the whole Spanish fleet had been destroyed. Walsingham, by order from the Ministry, in the Queen's name ordered four of the best ships to be sent back into port, supposing that the Spaniards could not repair their damages and proceed till the next year. But the Lord High Admiral not being so credulous, and still fearing the worst, would not agree and retained the vessels; alleging how dangerous it was to place themselves off guard in a matter of such importance, when they had no better authority than hearsay, adding that he would rather keep the ships out at his own charge than expose the nation to so great a hazard.*

However, this tale of derring-do appears to be government propaganda against the Spanish, much in the manner of today's 'spin-doctors' paid by the British tax-payer to make the government of the day look more successful than it actually is. Professor Laughton tells us that Gwynne was a slave on the *'Diana'* (not the *'Bayana'*), and that when the four galleys ran into difficulties in the bay, none of them foundered, except the *'Diana'* which ran aground trying to make Bayonne. The other three joined the fleet after sheltering at French ports. Gwynne and some other slaves escaped and reached La Rochelle, where Gwynne told English merchants that he urgently had to get home, as he had details of a plot by Lord Walsingham (the head of the secret service) to deliver Queen Elizabeth up to the Spanish. On his return to England, he was given the job of interpreter to examine Spanish prisoners from the Armada who had been shipwrecked off Ireland. However, one of the merchants returned to England and reported his slander to Walsingham, who acted promptly. Arrested by the Lord Deputy of Ireland, Gwynne was charged with the slander, and with embezzlement and robbery in Ireland. He was brought before the Privy Council, and disappears from history, but may have gone to the Low Countries to fight.

WELSH BUCCANEERS UNDER SIR FRANCIS DRAKE 1585 - 1595

In Drake's great voyage of 1585, sacking Santiago, San Domingo, Cartagena and St Augustine, his Sergeant Major was Anthony Powell, his Captain Matthew Morgan and Captain Robert Pugh was one of his two *'corporals of the field'.* Morgan led the vanguard at San Domingo and the rearguard at Cartagena, where Powell carried out the main attack, carrying the barricades in a terrific frontal charge: *'We soon found out the barricades of pipes and butts to be the meetest* (most suitable) *place for our assault, which, notwithstanding it was well furnished with pikes and shot, was, without staying, straightway attempted by us. Down went the butts of earth, and pell-mell came our swords and pikes together after our shot had first given their volley even at the enemy's nose.'* Powell died after leading the attack on St John's Fort in Florida, shot while chasing the fleeing Spaniards. In Drake's last voyage of 1595, Lieutenant Jones was killed by hostile Indians and Maurice Williams, *'one of her majesty's guard'*, was killed during the march on Panama.

JOHN CALLICE (CALLYS) - 'The most famous English (sic) pirate of the 16th century', 'The Most Dangerous Pyrate in the Realm'. fl. - 1571-1587

Gosse wrote in 1932 that John Callys was *'like many of his profession a man of birth and education. Among his relatives was the Earl of Pembroke, one of the leading peers of the realm. Callys first sailed as an officer of the Royal Navy under Sir John Berkeley, but afterwards turned pirate.'* From humble beginnings as a haberdasher's apprentice in Tintern, Callice looted ships in the Bristol Channel, the Scilly Islands, East Anglia and as far as Scotland. He moved to London when in his teens and became apprenticed to Alderman Bounds as a haberdasher, and then became a merchant, supplying the ships in the Pool of London. He may have been *'pressed'* when he joined the Navy in 1571, sailing first with Sir William Winter, and then under Sir John Berkeley. He was operating as a pirate in 1574, captaining *'The Cost Me Noughte'*. A kinsman of the great William Herbert, Callice built upon his connections with the Glamorgan gentry, and was an intimate friend of the Comptroller and Serjeant of the Admiralty at Cardiff - he even stayed at the serjeant's house when he came ashore. Callice also is known to have stayed with William Herbert and with Sir John Perrot's agent at Haverfordwest. Nevertheless, the Lords of the Admiralty referred to him as *'a notorious pyrate haunting the coasts of Wales'*, and was the unofficial leader of a bunch of pirate captains such as his crony *'Brother Battes'*.

In early 1574, he was master of *Elephant*, a royal ship, and took an Italian merchantman, the *Grace of God*, owned by Acerbo Velutelli, selling her cargo in Cardiff and Bristol. The heavily-armed *Oliphant (Elephant)* was owned by the courtier Sir Henry Knollys and appears to have been full of pirates. Fernando Fielding was captain and Simao Fernandes the Portuguese pilot. In December, a rich Portuguese ship was taken off the Azores, with sugar and exotic hardwoods. The Portuguese ambassador alleged that Fernandes had personally killed seven Portuguese seamen, but he was never charged. Later, in court in 1577, Callice stated that Fielding had sold him the ship for one hundred guineas, even though Knollys was the rightful owner. It seems that Callice was protecting Knollys' reputation in court. Callice then captained the *Elephant* until at least February 1576, but was captaining other ships from November of that year. Sir John Perrot (q.v.) was also a friend of Callice and his accomplice Hickes. Callice sold the *Elephant* to his pirate friend Captain Hickes around 1575. In 1576 Callice and Battes brought to Cardiff *Our Lady of the Conception*, a Spanish vessel laden with wool consigned to merchants in Bruges. The merchants complained to the Admiralty, who sent a man with orders to recover the wool from its receivers in Cardiff. However, we read of *'William Herbert of the High Street, and Robert ap Ifan disobeying process of the Court of Admiralty and misusing him that came with that process.'* Callice had headed north, and sold the remains of the wool in Denbigh, and the Lord Admiral reported to the Council that he '*was otherwise a notorious malefactor and had committed sundry great piracies*'. Certain dignitaries in Cardiff and Glamorgan, including the Sheriff, were ordered to London to explain their actions in not arresting Callice.

From 1574 to 1577 Callice had plundered anything that moved, especially in the Bristol Channel and off the South Coast of England, and several other captains joined his fleet, attracted by his success and the ineptitude and corruption of the authorities. From Holy Island to Yarmouth, the Scillies to Lundy he was known, and soon became master of the Bristol Channel. Cardiff was a particular centre for smuggling and piracy, probably because the powerful Herbert family controlled most of Glamorgan and south-east Wales. In south-east Wales, the Herbert Earls of Worcester, later to become the Earls of Pembroke, replicated Sir John Perrot's power-base in south-west Wales (see Walter Herbert and Morgan Matthew, above). Callice was free to move around Cardiff and dispose of his goods at will, because of his connections with the Herbert family.

Callice took major prizes from Denmark to the Azores, as well as off Cornwall and France. Simao Fernandes bought a small barque from William Herbert, Vice-Admiral of Wales, and joined with Callice's *Elephant* in April 1576. They jointly took a Portuguese caravel off the Canary Isles. The Privy Council assessed Callice as '*the most dangerous pyrate in the realm*', and pirates such as Heynes, Hickes, Bates, the Dutch Counte Higgenberte and the Portuguese Simon Fernandino acknowledged him as their leader. Gosse refers to Callice generally sailing alone, '*but sometimes joined forces with two foreign corsairs, Count Higgenberte and Symon Ferdinando Portingale**, or else with his old friend Captain Robert Hickes of Saltash, who was afterwards hanged.*' At this time Captain Gregory Penry of Tenby '*made no merchant's voyages by a long time, but hath kept the seas, taking and spoiling such things as he could meet withall*'. However, Fernandes was gaoled in May 1576 by South Wales admiralty officials. He claimed that he had made no profits from the Portuguese prize, so his backers turned against him. After a few months, William Herbert paid his bail, and the charges were dropped. Fernandes stayed in Cardiff, protected by Herbert, but the Portuguese sued to recover their goods. Callice also holed up in Poole and Lulworth Cove in the West Country, and brought into Cornwall the French *L'Esperance* in 1576 with its cargo of Gascony wine. He also took into Penarth Roads a homecoming Breton ship laden with Newfoundland cod which he had taken in the Straits of Belle Ile in Brittany.

Many Bristol Channel pirates were hanged in the late 1570's, including '*Brother Battes*'. The Bristol Channel pirates were nationally known, with captains Battes, Hicks, Fielding, Ward, Purser, William Chick and Tom Clarke being among the most prominent, operating from Cornwall to Cardiff, and from Pembroke to the east coast of Ireland. Prizes were brought into the shelter of Penarth Roads and goods transferred to Cardiff merchants. In North Wales, Bardsey (Enlli) and St Tudwal's Island were notable pirate haunts. The government was so annoyed with local officials in Wales that in 1576 they appointed a special Admiralty Commissioner, John Croft, to investigate why Callice was allowed to roam free. Croft arrested Robert Fresher in Cardiff, amongst Callice's '*aiders and retainers*' there. He then received intelligence that Callice had just left Cardiff for Newport and then to Penarth Roads, but Frost failed to receive support from the Mayor and Corporation of Bristol to arrest Callice. On his return to Cardiff he wrote in 1576 '*I required aide there for the apprehending of Callis' prize but I colde have none, nor any willingness offred me therein, althoughe in speche every sorte of people colde saie it were wll donne to take them; and there I founde certen knowledge that the Townesmen of Cardiffe and sondry gentlemen thereabouts did comonly buy and receave divers of the goods and spoiles brought there by Callis and his compplices, and gave them aide with victualles and other necessaries.*'

In December 1576 Croft discovered that Callice had returned to Cardiff with a stolen boat carrying '*sammon herrings and Manchester kersies*', with its crew '*kept as prisoner under the hatches*'. The Vice-Admiral of Monmouth, Sir William Morgan of Newport, sent a crew to pay Callice and took the prize to Newport. Morgan's crew refused to deal with Croft, who reported one man '*did not only utterly refuse to aid me but also obstinately did say that he did not care for the commission or me.*' Morgan's men carried on unloading the cargo, while the imprisoned crew called out from the holds for water and food. Croft implored the local JP's William Morgan of Llantarnam and Rowland Morgan of Machen to help in arresting the pirates, but they refused to act. The Privy Council later took no action against these magistrates, although Callice now took some French ships and a Danish ship. Under the pseudonym of Kanter, he boarded and took a ship in Helford Haven. After the Herberts, the Morgans were the most powerful family in these parts, and were linked by marriage to the Herberts. (In fact, the well-known pirate '*Brother Battes*' was a friend of William Morgan, and William Thickyns confessed the following dealings at Milord Haven: '*Battes had a ship of 160 tons and lay there with nothing in her but men and ordinance. He this deponent fell to practise with Captain Battes, first whether he should go with this deponent into Barbary upon certain good occasions, which this deponent did disclose to him, and he said yea with all his heart … and he said he would go with this examinant, but for all his former contracts with William Morgan Knight, who was so worshipful a gentleman that he could not find it in his heart to break his words to him.*' Morgan was one of the Vice-Admirals of Wales, governor of Dungarvan, Marshall in Ireland, and had recently bought 634 '*elephants' teeth*' off Battes.)

Fernandes was again arrested in February 1577, but released by Thomas Lewes, the Cardiff magistrate and a well-known conduit for pirate loot. A 1577 letter from a Haverfordwest JP to Sir John Perrot reads '*Cardiff is the general resort of pyrates and there they are sheltered and protected*'. Nicholas Herbert was Sheriff of Glamorgan at that time, and was a definite accomplice of pirates. Callice next took Peter Chamberlain's salt sloop, transferring to her 28 '*pieces of ordinance*', fitting her out as his ship, and disposing of the cargo and fittings along the ports of Pembrokeshire. Already the Privy Council had complained to Sir John Perrot (q.v.) about piracy in Pembrokeshire, on January 12th, 1577: '*Whereas their Lordships are given to understand that one John Callice, a notable pyrate frequenting that country and arriving lately at Milford, was lodged and housed at Haverfordwest, and being there was suffered to escape, their Lordships do not a little marvel at the negligence of such that are Justices in those parts that knowing the said Callice to be so notable an offender would suffer him to depart in that order.*' The local authorities had, however, *'for a show and colour of justice... apprehended some of the poorest and permitted the chiefest pyrates to depart'*, as they had put six of Callice's crew in gaol. The local authorities put the blame for Callice's 'escape' upon their counterparts in Cardiff.

Callice seemed to have spent some time at the Old Point House in Angle, Pembroke, now a fascinating pub sometimes cut off by the tide, and with a fire which has not gone out for hundreds of years. George Owen wrote of Caldey Island at this time that it was *'very fertile and yieldeth plenty of corn all their ploughs give with horses, for oxen the inhabitants dare not keep fearing the purveyors of the pirates.'* Robert Hicks of Cornwall sailed to join up with Callice in February 1577, and Callice took over command of his ship. They took three Scottish and a German ship off southern England. They headed north to link up with William Fenner, and off Elsinore captured the 300-ton Danish 8-gun ship Golden Lion. The prize was sailed to Weymouth for the cargo to be sold, and 15 Danish seamen were badly wounded.

However, Callice was finally captured on May 15th, 1577, by Edward Horsey, the Captain of the Isle of Wight. On his person was found the enormous sum of £22 and 7 shillings, which was later offered as a piece of incriminating evidence at his trial. He was conveyed to London *'under sure guard'* and lodged in the Tower of London, waiting trial by Dr Lewis of Abergavenny, Judge of the Admiralty. Callice was interrogated by Dr Lewis in the Winchelsea Prison, and insisted upon being called a gentleman, although he could not read or sign his name. His only possessions were those worth £10 a year at Tintern, which he had not seen since he was 11 years old. Callice had been charged with six major acts of piracy and many minor ones, and sentenced to hang. He was called *'a notorious malefactor who hath committed sundry great piracies'*. The pirate had no wish to hang in chains, and turned Queen's Evidence, his petition to the Queen reading *'I bewail my former wicked life, and beseech God and her Majesty to forgive me.... If she will only spare my life and use me in her service by sea and with those she can best trust, either to clear the coast of other wicked pyrates or otherwise, as I know their haunts, roads and maintainers so well, I can do more therein than if she sent ships abroad and spent £20,000. I send herewith particulars of the partakers of my pyracies and the maintainers of and victuallers of me and my companions.'* Callice gave a list of his supporters and 'receivers', including Thomas Lewis of the Van in Bedwas, and among his creditors was the deputy Vice-Admiral of South Wales. While the judges were deciding whether to execute him, the Regent of Scotland, Earl Morton, offered £500 for Callice's release, and the influence of several powerful men assisted his cause. Callice gave evidence against his receivers to help his cause. Callice had also written to Lord Walsingham to say that if he was spared, he would help rid the coast of pirates by giving particulars of their *'roads, haunts, creeks and maintainers'*. Among the *'maintainers'*, or receivers of smuggled and pirated goods was Lord O'Sullivan of Berehaven. Sir Francis Walsingham, the head of the secret service, ensured that Callice was released on a technicality. He needed Callice to exploit Fernandes' knowledge of the Caribbean and American coasts for an expedition he was planning with Humphrey Gilbert.

In 1577 the pirate leader William Chick was captured and turned informer when threatened with the thumbscrew and rack. Both Callice and Chick incriminated

Nicholas Herbert, Sheriff of Glamorgan (and John Callice's father-in-law!), William Herbert, the former mayor of Cardiff, Edward Kemeys of Cefn Mably Manor, and John Thomas Fleming of Flemingston. They did not suffer the same fate as the lesser pirates, of course. Callice knew all the corrupt officials in South Wales, and usually disposed of his goods through Cardiff. Robert Hickes took more ships in 1577, and hearing of Callice's capture, offered in a letter to surrender the *Golden Lion* (now renamed the *Neptune*), in return for the release of Callice. It reads: '... *wherefore I pray you send me word either by mouth or pen what you will wish me to do for you ... I will do it if the surrendering of the ship may by any means gain your liberty ... and I pray God send us both our hearts and a merry meeting.*' Hicks was captured in October 1577 and hung in chains in 1578 at Wapping Dock, after a trial by the Admiralty Court in London. Trial records show that he swindled Callice out of his share of the booty. Brother Battes was hung in this year, presumably following Callice's disclosures.

Callice had powerful friends. David Lewis, Judge of the High Court of the Admiralty, stated that influential men in Wales would not arrest a source of their profits - but '*will play bo-peep, seest me and seest me not.*' Vice-Admiral Sir William Morgan deliberately refused to help his local piracy commission. The Earl of Pembroke's Herbert family held the port of Cardiff, and the *arch-pirate* John Callice used to lodge with the High Sheriff of Glamorgan when he docked at Cardiff. The sheriff was Callice's father-in-law, and the controller and customs and the Admiralty port-sergeant were Herbert appointees. Callice had been safe there. The Clerk to the Council of Wales and the Marches, sent to Cardiff to buy Callice's plundered salt. The Mayor of Cardiff, Thomas Lewis, had also bought goods from Callice and his colleagues.

In July 1578 Callice was paroled, but quickly fled his parole officer to become the *Elephant's* pilot for his old comrade Sir Henry Knollys, on the North American expedition of Sir Humphrey Gilbert. The *Elephant* was Knollys' flagship of his three ships, and Fernando Fielding also was on the ship as a '*soldier-gentleman*'. Humphrey Gilbert assembled his fleet at Plymouth, while the *Elephant* carried on her privateering ways of the previous four years. Knollys and Callice defeated the pirate Robert Holbourne, capturing his ship and its French prize. They were stripped of booty, and Holbourne was released back in Plymouth. Knollys' other two ships were also practising piracy, so Humphrey Gilbert argued with Knollys. Knollys and Callice promptly took their small fleet to Ireland and the Isle of Wight, taking another French ship. Gilbert's great expedition broke up, and Knollys was investigated for his crimes in 1579, but no charges laid. His sister was married to the queen's favourite, the Earl of Essex. Walter Raleigh was due to captain the *Falcon* on the expedition, with Callice's associate Simao Fernandes as his lieutenant. Fernandes and Raleigh took a prize off the Cape Verde Islands, and Fernandes was Raleigh's pilot to the Americas in 1584, 1585 and 1587, serving also under Frobisher in 1588 against the Spanish Armada.

When one of Raleigh's captains took a French prize, it was turned over to John Callice, who returned it to its owners but kept the cargo. Raleigh took some of the booty, but most was smuggled ashore by Sir George Carey (the brother-in-law of Lord

Admiral Thomas Howard) in Hampshire, where he was Vice-Admiral, in charge of customs. When the French owners sued in the Admiralty Court, they lost because Callice and Carey had bribed the chief judge, Julius Caesar. Callice had powerful friends. Carey was a kinsman of Queen Elizabeth, who became Baron Hunsdon and embezzled huge amounts of money as treasurer for the Irish Wars.

The Admiralty Court awarded the owners of Callice's French prize £4000 in 1579, but Callice made no payment. (in modern times this would represent about £4 million). However, it appears that he did make a payment of around £505 to the owners of the Danish prize. The Danish ship had been taken in 1576 by William Fenner in a heavily-armed pinnace, in consort with John Callice. Callice took two ships off Hamburg in 1580, probably still funded by Knollys, and made his base South Wales. In 1582, William Fenner gained a commission to pursue pirates, and in August promptly hired his old colleague Callice as lieutenant, who then promptly took several merchant vessels. The 100-ton 'Gallion Fenner' of Chichester had a crew of 70 in 1582, probably three times as many as an equivalent merchantman, and twice as many as a naval vessel. After Fenner, Callice was in command, followed by the master (an expert seaman and 'lodesman'), then the owner, Edward Fenner. (Edward was a landlubber, so had little authority at sea). Next in the pecking order of command were the gunner, the master's mate, the boatswain and the purser, the gunner's mate, the boatswain's mate, the cook and his mate, the shipwright, six soldiers, three quartermasters and then 45 general hands, each of whom was assigned a specified number of shares in any loot taken.

In March 1583 Callice took two Scottish ships and sold their cargo at Plymouth. He kept one of the Scottish ships, the Falcon of Prestonpans and renamed it the Golden Chalice, but abandoned her to prevent his arrest. (Sir Humphrey Gilbert used it on his 1583 Newfoundland Expedition). On board the Falcon were two packs of religious books for James VI, which Callice sold for £40 to the Huguenot printer Vautrollier. In 1584, William Fenner was granted an extension to his licence, to take Spanish and Portuguese prizes, and Callice became his lieutenant on the Gallion Fenner, with 70 crew. Fenner's nephew Edward, the brother of Captain George Fenner, joined and in December they took a French warship. Callice was made captain of the prize. More ships were taken, mainly French, but also including a Portuguese sugar drover. In 1584, Peter Chamberlain, whose salt sloop had been taken by Callice eight years earlier, complained to the Admiralty that he had been robbed at sea 'by Count Helleburg and John Callice, pyrates.' William and Edward Fenner were arrested in 1585, after they had separated from Callice in stormy weather, but were never convicted. Edward and William both captained ships against the Armada, and William died during Drake's 1590 raid on Lisbon. Callice was later arrested in Ireland, but seems to have escaped again, capturing several French ships.

However, Callice was now finding that his base of operations, the Bristol Channel and Ireland were becoming more difficult to trade in, and he was still being chased for the 1579 £4000 judgement. Callice sometimes 1586 was pirating in the Orkneys, but lost his ship and all his belongings. He was reduced to serving as a seaman on the Minikin, a pirate ship owned by a Mr Bellingham. He practised piracy off the Barbary

Coast, and was killed in 1586 or 1587. According to Captain John Smith, the founder of Virginia (and of Pocahontas fame), *'this ancient pirate Collis, who most refreshed himself upon the coast of Wales… grew famous till Queen Elizabeth of Blessed Memory hanged him at Wapping'*, but it is far more likely that he died in a sea engagement after he joined the Barbary Corsairs. Gosse believes that he was hanged with two other active pirates off the coast of Wales, captains Pursser and Clinton.

The death of Henry VIII in 1547 had stimulated the rise of piracy. His widow's brother-in-law, Thomas Seymour was Lord High Admiral, and took half of what was looted, even seizing the Scilly Isles for himself. He attempted to marry Elizabeth Tudor, and under his rule the Admiralty Courts did not persecute pirates. From the 1550's to the 1570's, no pirate vessel had been taken while unloading cargo, in the secret and immune ports of Wales and the West Country. It seems that the pirates usually took around a fifth of the proceeds, while the receivers, with the support of the local lords, took 80%, which was 'dispersed' easily into the surrounding countryside. There were no warships on the Irish sea, and no regular patrols off the Welsh coast. The official guardship of the Vice-Admiral, the *'Flying Hart'*, was based at Newport until it was plundered by pirates in 1578. No pirate was taken at sea, and no prominent pirate ever arrested in Pembroke or Cornwall. Port officials turned a blind eye, or participated in piracy. Certain pirates who anchored in the Penarth Roads actually stayed with the local *'serjeant of the Admiralty'*. The building up of British sea power, culminating in the defeat of the Armada in 1588, meant that by the 1590's, piracy in the Bristol Channel was virtually suppressed. Pirates increasingly operated away from the British Isles, but outbreaks flared up until 1630. In that year Charles I tried to requisition a 30-ton barque with crew and provisions from the County of Glamorgan, but the local justices responded that not even Cardiff possessed a pinnace of that size. The only five ships that big had been captured by Moorish pirates, while taking Welsh butter to France and Ireland.

*Quote from Neville Williams *'Captains Outrageous'*, 1961
**In the Cardiff State Papers, Simon Ferdinando is mentioned twice in 1577, and noted as *'a portingall born.'*
Note: In the Cardiff State Papers for 1576 John Callice is noted as a *'pirate'*, as is 'John Callys' in 1577. Also in 1577 Ned Herbert, who sailed with Callice, is recorded as a pirate, along with William Chick (also recorded as Chicke), *'a great doer of mischief'*, *'late of Ipswich'*.
Footnote: there is a remarkable book, 'The Golden Challice', (C. L'Estrange Ewen 1939) recounting the story of John Callice in some depth, but the author could not source it by inter-library loan, nor spend the time at the British Library transcribing it.
Footnote: Captain Battes, Clarke and Hicks were all arrested in 1578. When Hicks took the *Jonas of Konigsberg*, its cargo of corn, wheat, rye, gunpowder, cable and timber was sold quite openly in Pembrokeshire ports. Morgan ap Howell, Mayor of Pembroke, was a receiver, and a Mr Thyckens stated that he was able to sell so openly because of the assistance of *'one Vaughan, a Vice-Admiral'*. Another pirate named Kyfte implicated Vaughan, Sir John Perrot's deadly enemy, saying that *'Vaughan was aboard all those pirates'*.

TOM CLARKE fl. 1577-78

Around the time when the pirate captains Hicks, Battes and Callice were using the Penarth Roads off Cardiff to lay up and dispose of loot, the most prominent local pirate was probably Tom Clarke, who owned a well-armed, fast sloop. With nine of his men, he is recorded as bursting into John Tracy's house in Penarth, armed with swords and calivers (guns), forcing Tracy and a companion to board his ship and stay overnight. The next day Clarke came ashore with Tracy and *'for feare'* he was given four quarters of mutton for provisions. On the next Sunday, a man carrying a sheep to a ship called the *Green Dragon* found that it had sailed, and *'in his return Captain Clarke's men fell upon him with their naked swordes and toke the wether from him by force.'* The *Green Dragon* was a local ship, and had sailed early because of the presence of Clarke's ship. The day before, its captain's cousin, Richard Herbert, had to pass near Clarke's men on his way to the *Green Dragon*, and *'the said Thomas Clarke saluted the said Richard with a glass of wine in his hand, and prayed him to come aboard, who so did, and there drunk with him and came forthwith to land without any bargaining or traffic at all'*. Edward Stradling, Thomas Matthew and John Borough, sailing from Barry to Cardiff, were rowing past Clarke's ship and the pirates *'called them aboard, but they refused to go, whereupon the men of war threatened to fetch them if they did not come; with that they went unto them and drunk with them till the tide was spent and so returned to Barry again.'* The pirates took as provisions six rabbits which were to be delivered to William Herbert of Cardiff. Clarke was eventually arrested in Penarth in 1578, and the Privy Council wrote to Sir Edward Stradling and Sir Edward Mansell commending their actions.

This followed a 'round-up' of Cardiff pirates in 1577. Hickes and Battes were hung, and Callice imprisoned, as London finally got to grips with the worst area for piracy in the whole of the kingdom. In March 1577, partly because of Callice's confessions, the Vice-President of Wales and the Marches was ordered by Elizabeth to appoint a strong commission to investigate *'certain disorders committed by pyrates'* in Glamorgan and Monmouthshire. This was a warning-shot across the bows of her half-brother, Sir John Perrot, in south-west Wales. The commissioners, Sir John Perrot, Fabian Phillips and Thomas Lewis, Mayor of Cardiff, were expressly desired by the Privy Council *'to take some pains therein'*. By April 3rd, Phillips and Lewis could report to the Council that they had examined up to sixty suspected pirates and their retainers in Cardiff. They doubted the integrity and commitment of Perrot and complained of his frequent absences. They also tried to hook Nicholas Herbert, Sheriff of Glamorgan. Upon being summoned to appear, he refused on the excuse that he had to be present at the Easter Assizes. Upon being informed, the Privy Council told him to attend the assizes and then travel directly to London to answer the charges brought against him.

The transgressors, led by Herbert, made a legal challenge *'for that in matters of spoils done on sea and what concerneth persons accessory by land there seemeth to be a difference in law.'* However, in June the Privy Council ordered the Judge of the Admiralty to consult with the Attorney General and Solicitor-General to ascertain the legal situation and call for new legislation if necessary. Lord Walsingham also wrote in June to the Attorney General *'to hasten his answer to the Council touching the fittest means to punish the aiders of pyrates about Cardiff.'* Many of the Cardiff transgressors were forced to travel to see the Privy Council, and in early 1578 the six ringleaders, including the Sheriff of Glamorgan, were heavily fined between £10 and £20 and bound over not to repeat their crimes.

SIR JOHN PERROT 1527 - 1592

Henry VIII had an illegitimate son by one of the royal ladies-in-waiting, Mary Berkeley. She married Thomas Perrot, of Haroldston near Haverfordwest, who was knighted as a 'reward' for the marriage. John was born at Haroldston, educated at St David's, and entered the household of the Marquis of Winchester. He was given massive estates in Pembrokeshire by his father. One of history's intriguing elements was the failure of Henry VIII to have a son by Catherine of Aragon, the former wife of his deceased brother Arthur. Mary Berkeley's success in giving Henry a male heir turned him against all of his wives in turn. Edward VI, Mary and Elizabeth I all acknowledged John Perrot as a half-brother, and a giant of a man, he strongly resembled his father. Henry VIII offered John a preferment, but died before he could award it, and John was a great friend of Edward VII, who made him a Knight of the Bath. In 1554, at a tournament for his half-sister Queen Mary Tudor and her husband Philip of Spain, he *'fought best of all'* of the Spanish and English grandees. Mary herself gave out the prizes, including *'a diamond ring of great value'*. However, he was denounced for his strong Protestantism and was imprisoned by Mary for a short time in the Fleet prison, before going overseas to serve under his friend the Earl of Pembroke. He returned when he knew that Mary was dying. Sir John was one of the four knights who carried Elizabeth I's canopy at her coronation, and was her great favourite.

As early as 1547, the 20 year-old Sir John Perrot was petitioned by John David to the effect that *'pyrates (it is commonly reported) are furnished, victualled, aided, received and succoured - all their goods openly sold in Cardiff.'* In 1552, Sir John as Vice-Admiral was sharply bidden by the Lordships of the Admiralty to send up to London one Phillip ap Rice, a pirate *'whom he and others in that countrie supporteth'*. There had been frequent reports of this Welsh pirate attacking shipping in the Bristol Channel, in consort with a Spaniard, John de Andreaca. To cover his back, Perrot promptly arrested William Rogers of Herefordshire and Captain Thomas Harys, who had plundered ten Flemish ships and sought a haven in Pembrokeshire. In 1554, the Admiralty was asking Perrot to chase the pirate Captain Jones, and in 1556 they asked the Sheriff of Pembroke to come to London to explain why he had not arrested the pirates Peter Heall and William ap Rees of Sandy Haven, William ap Rees of Haverfordwest and Philip ap Rees of Pyll. In 1555, the evocatively named *'Jones the Pirate'* took a Breton ship and brought it into Tenby to dispose of. Also in 1555, when pirates brought a captured ship into Tenby, Sir John Morgan, a former Sheriff of Pembrokeshire arrested the crew, but sold the cargo for his own profit. Presumably Perrot had his share. In 1556, Merrick Morgan was busy attacking ships off the Pembroke coast, while Sir John turned a blind eye. Perrot was reprimanded in 1564 when *'certain of Thomas Cobham's company stayed at Tenby'*, and the pirates stayed free because of the *'marvellous insufficiency'* of Perrot's deputy at Tenby, Sir John Parrot.

Cobham had seized the Spanish ship *Santa Catarina*, which became a full-blown international incident involving Phillip II of Spain. The situation was complicated for Sir John, as Thomas Cobham was the brother of Lord Cobham, Warden of the Ports. In 1565, Perrot was not re-appointed as Vice-Admiral or as a Special Piracy Commissioner.

Perrot had made vast wealth from as Vice-Admiral for the coast of South and West Wales, much from collusion with pirates, and built a great manor at Haroldston, and rebuilt Laugharne and Carew castles as manor houses. The harbour of Laugharne was noted as being safe for pirates to unload cargo at night. Haverfordwest, Tenby and Cardigan were also used by pirates, who stayed with Sir John's agents. Perrot was MP for Pembrokeshire, and mayor of Haverfordwest.

Queen Elizabeth next appointed him first Lord President of Munster in 1571, to suppress the Fitzmaurice Rebellion there, which he did within a year. From 1573, he was engaged in much litigation to increase his lands, having returned to Wales to lead '*a countryman's life*', as he informed his fellow-Welshman Lord Burghley. From 1574, as a member of the Council for Wales and the Marches, he was supposed to be actively involved in the suppression of piracy, and in 1575 made chief commissioner to suppress piracy in Pembrokeshire. He now made a pretence of appearing to act against pirates, proclaiming his intentions and imprisoning one of his own men for a short time in (comfortable) captivity at Pembroke. At the same time Robert Hickes, the accomplice of John Callice, was selling stolen corn openly from his ship the Jonas to the Mayor of Pembroke and respectable merchantmen. Perrot acted against Scottish interlopers, but actively encouraged piracy, while including in his reports to Whitehall incidents where he had 'accidentally' purchased illegal goods, as a defence against any informers. In 1576, he refused to take over a similar post for Glamorgan and Monmouthshire. A bitter feud had developed between Perrot and Richard Vaughan, chief commissioner for piracy in Carmarthenshire. Captain Hickes, already noted in the entry upon John Callice, had captured the *Jonas*, bound from Konigsberg to Lisbon with a cargo of corn, near Lands End. He brought his prize into Milford Haven, and began to sell the corn, and also cargo of salt which had previously been looted. Hickes dealt for 5 weeks with the whole spectrum of West Wales society, from a priest named Andrew buying enough corn for the winter, to George Devereux, uncle of the Earl of Essex, who bought 200 barrels of rye to illegally export to Spain. Perrot sent an unliveried retainer aboard to help Hickes keep account of his sales. The Mayor of Pembroke bought some corn and sent it in his ship the *Maudlen* to Galicia to offload. Another local vessel, the *George*, took corn to Portugal. Vice-Admiral Vaughan and Perrot both blamed the other. Perrot seems to have taken the biggest bribes, but also covered his tracks well, as he had made a record of Vaughan's trips to see Hickes. Vaughan had seen the chance to shine at last as a pirate-catcher. His first move was to go aboard Hickes' ship to haggle for a bribe, to avert suspicion. He then corresponded with Sir William Morgan of Abergavenny, the Vice-Admiral for South Wales, suggesting that Morgan send a warship, or come in his own *Flying Hart* to take the pirate ship. (A few months later the *Flying Hart* was plundered by pirates as it lay at Newport). Morgan declined to do anything. Vaughan recruited retainers at great expense from south-east Wales, as he knew most Pembroke men were loyal to Perrot, and twenty of his confederates were sent aboard Hickes' ship on the pretext of trafficking. Their watchword for the assault was to be *'he that is a friend unto John Callice, stand unto me!'*

However, Perrott had become increasingly uneasy about the constant traffic in the Haven between his supporters and Hickes. At the end of five weeks, he exploded into one of his famous rages while watching from an overlooking hill. He issued warrants to his servants to put an end to the trade, and tell Hickes to make his way out of the Haven. He may have received word that Morgan had been contacted by Vaughan, and was fearing the arrival of a naval vessel in his domain. Next to Hickes' ship was a pinnace loaded with 40 tons of wheat, which was Vaughan's bribe, and Sir John's men sailed it away. This alarmed Hickes' men, and all sixty of them quickly armed and prepared for action. Vaughan's men swiftly called off their plan, leaving Vaughan fuming. He had lost his bribe and his pirate and his glory. Hickes now began stripping the *Jonas*, *'not leaving a piece of rope the length of an arm'*, transferring everything to his own ship. Hickes intended to burn the ship, but the merchantman's Captain Rung protested, and bribed Vaughan to intercede. Rung sold the bare hulk to Perrot for just £10, enough for him and his crew to return to London. However, a French captive from the *Jonas*, Louis Bourdain of St Malo, was given to Sir John by Hickes as a *'present'* before he sailed off. Bourdain was sent to Little Newcastle (the birthplace of Black Bart Roberts) and ransomed. The Frenchman managed to escape as far as Swansea, but Sir William Herbert returned him to his cousin Sir John, and Bourdain was thrown into Carew Castle. He was fed only on a diet of dried fish and bread. 200 crowns was offered for him by his mother, and a Chester merchant creditor of Bourdain's offered £100. Perrot held out for a cargo of Gascony wine, and at great expense, Bourdain's brothers sent a cargo. However, before the ship reached Tenby, Bourdain had escaped again and was harboured by some of Vaughan's men at Pendine. Vaughan managed to take for himself 10 tuns of the Gascon wine, which was possibly his only victory in his dealing with Sir John. Poor Bourdain reached Cardiff, where he fell into the clutches of his Chester creditor.

The feud between the two local magnates grew, and in 1577 Vaughan tried to board a ship belonging to Davy Allen of Laugharne, lying off Laugharne, Perrot's private beach, with cargo for Perrot. He had ridden from Whitland on the advice of an informer that the boat was full of *'both murtherers and thieves'*, and rowed up to the ship, demanding to know its cargo. The crew yelled back *'that you shall not know, for none have to do here but Sir John Perrot.'* Vaughan noted ten men *'with culvers ready with fire in their cocks'* (i.e. ready to fire) and rowed away quickly. There were also two ships wrecked on Pendine Sands in a storm, and Sir John's men began collecting booty before Vaughan arrived with a fleet of 60 men in small boats from Tenby. After a squabble, Vaughan's men were forced to give up anything that they gathered off the wrecks. Vaughan himself had acquired two brass cannon and several bags of spice, which were *'confiscated'* by Perrot's followers, leaving Vaughan with *'nothing but shame and repulse.'* Next Vaughan tried to convert to Christian ways the wife of a Captain Johnson, who had put into Carmarthen with a prize, but she sold him some salt at an exorbitant price and then vanished with her husband. Perrot noted the details of the transaction in order to try and gain a legal hold over Vaughan. The noted Huguenot privateer Luke Ward, sailing under the flag of the Prince of Conde, put into Milford haven with a prize. Perrot being absent from the area, Vaughan invited him to a house he owned in Pembroke for a repast, but then surprised him by asking for his credentials. Ward had a properly accredited letter of marque, but was not inclined to let this devious man see it, roaring 'Thy betters have seen it"', and offered to fight a duel for his honour with Vaughan in a nearby field. However, Vaughan arrested Ward and some of his crew and imprisoned them. The satisfied Deputy-Admiral returned to Whitland, only to find that Sir John Perrot on his hearing the news, immediately released the privateers.

On yet another occasion in their ongoing dispute, Vaughan had come to Carew Castle to remonstrate with Perrot, who at the time was suffering from gallstones, and in no mood for a lecture from Vaughan. He reminded Vaughan that he had impaled the heads of 50 Irish rebels in Kilmallock market-place and had killed at least another 800 Irishmen, and was in a like mind. Vaughan came away insulted: 'His complaints were pooh-poohed: he protested that if any persons of lower rank did what Sir John did they would have been sent to prison. Perrot told him he did not know what he was talking about. Vaughan's dignity was touched: he had been the High Sheriff of two counties, etc. "Thou art a fool," quoth Sir John, and that endeth the interview.' In general, Perrot had the upper hand, which eventually drove Richard Vaughan into some kind of brainstorm. He lodged a bill of complaint against Perrot in Privy Council, and told crowds outside the Blue Boar in Holborn that 'Sir John better deserved hanging than any thief.' His bill was found to be so malicious that Vaughan was imprisoned and deprived of office in 1578. In that same year, Callice, Hickes and Bates were captured, and Perrot once again 'campaigned' against pirates as far as The Needles. However, he visited his friends at Falmouth during this voyage, the noted Killigrew pirate family.

In 1577, a privateer named Herbert, one of Perrot's servants, brought the prize Elephant into Pembrokeshire, followed by a Dutch ship laden with salt. It belonged to Peter Muncke, a merchant travelling with his ship. Herbert put ten of his men on the prize, but lost contact with it in a night storm. The prize sailed into Milford haven and anchored off Pembroke Ferry (near the present Burton Bridge). Muncke was taken to the mayor of Pembroke, and compelled him to offer his own stolen salt for sale, with his two pirate escorts passing themselves off as merchant associates. The mayor suspected from Muncke's demeanour that something was wrong, and contrived to talk to him in secret, when Muncke whispered that he was a prisoner and that half the ship and cargo would be the reward for his deliverance. The news was quickly transmitted to Sir John, while the mayor plied Muncke and the unsuspecting 'merchants' with lavish hospitality throughout the evening. At midnight the two drunken pirates and Muncke were put into a boat with some of Perrot's best men, and another few dozen armed men of Pembroke followed in another boat towards the prize. As they boarded, Muncke shouted for his men to rise up and lend a hand, and the pirates were soon overcome, with just three escaping in a small boat. Muncke must have thought that his wishes had come true, but after clapping the pirates in Haverfordwest gaol, in the old castle, Perrot took his half of the salt, and gave 5 tons of the remained to the mayor and his men *'for their pains and powder'*. Perrot also claimed all the ship's rigging and ordinance, and Richard Vaughan of Whitland seized the stripped ship's hull, broke it up and sold the timber. Muncke left, a saddened man. At the next Assizes, Perrot conveniently arranged the lack of a prosecutor, and Herbert's pirates were set free. Herbert seems to have been overthrown as captain after the loss of Muncke's ship, and approached his old master, Sir John, for employment. His answer was *'a torrent of oaths and threats'*, and the dejected Herbert cut his throat in a house in Haverfordwest.

In September 1579, Sir John commanded a squadron of five ships with orders to cruise off the west coast of Ireland and intercept any Spanish ships which might attempt to land. However, he only took one pirate ship, the *Derifold*. The first record of piracy in and around Newfoundland took place in 1582 when Sir John Perrot and Henry Oughtred launched a raid on Portuguese and Spanish fishermen around the Avalon Peninsula. To protect their vessels from these and other ships, Basque fish merchants began to apply for passports from the Lord Admiral of England.

Perrot was then appointed by Elizabeth Lord Deputy of Ireland from 1584 but was arrested on a false charge of treason in 1591 and sentenced to death. She had sent him to Ireland in command of a fleet to intercept a possible invasion of Ireland by the Spanish, but he had acted in a high-handed manner there, just as the Earl of Essex did when he followed him. Perrot's comments about his half-sister were reckless. She had appointed a Mr Errington to be clerk of the Exchequer in Ireland, and Sir John exclaimed *'this fiddling woman troubles me out of measure. God's dear Lady, he shall not have the office! I will give it to Sir Thomas Williams!'* Again, at the time of the Spanish Invasion of 1588, he was reported to have said *'Ah silly woman, now she will not curb me! Now she shall not rule me! Now, God's dear Lady, I shall be her white boy again!'* He added, when Sir John Garland brought him a letter from the Queen, *'This it is, to serve a base-born woman! Had I served any price in Christendom, I had not been thus dealt with!'* When told he must die, he exclaimed *'God's death! Will my sister sacrifice her brother to his frisking adversaries?'* Queen Elizabeth refused to sign the death warrant of her half-brother and planned to pardon him, but he died in 1592 in the Tower of London, aged 65.

His main accuser in his tribulations had been Sir Christopher Hatton, a powerful courtier, whose daughter Elizabeth had been seduced by Perrot. Despite his attainder, Perrot's vast estates were granted to his son, Sir Thomas Perrot. John's illegitimate son Sir James Perrot (1571-1630) was a literary man, who became an MP and Vice-admiral for Pembroke, suppressed piracy and wreckers, and was a founder member of the Virginia Company.

Footnote:

Caldey, the romantic island just off Tenby, features in the Queen Remembrancer Roll of 1562: *'Caldy, here the pirates are wont many times to victual themselves of sheep and other provisions some times without leave of the owners ... Milford is the great resort and succour of all pirates and enemies in storms whom the country cannot resist.'*

JOHN WYN AP HUGH OF BODVEL (d.1576)

Around the time that Sir John Perrot was actively encouraging piracy in the more prosperous south and south-west of Wales, North Wales was a poor region, which desperately needed income. Around Aberconwy, Nicholas Hookes (q.v.) controlled illicit trade. Hookes and local landowners used two islands off the Llyn Peninsula to control trade, Bardsey and St Tudwal. Captain George Morgan operated off the latter around 1565.

Descended from the noble house of Collwyn ap Tangno, John Wyn bore the royal standard of the Duke of Northumberland against Kett's Norfolk rebels at Mousehold Heath in 1549, and was rewarded with the grant of the holy island of Bardsey. John Wyn turned the Augustinian priory on Bardsey (Ynys Enlli - the Isle of 40,000 Saints) into a supplies store for pirates. His men on the island were *'at all times ready to deliver to all such pirates … victuals and necessaries, when and as often as they have need, receiving again of them for the same large recompense as wine, iron, salt, spices … which the pirates come by their desperate attempts, robbing and spoiling…'* John Wyn sold goods as far as 80 miles away, and his legal connections ensured that any proceedings against his captains were quietly dropped. He bought corn off the pirate Captain Wolfall, and excused his appearance upon Wolfall's ship in 1563 as *'Wolfall could speak no Welsh'* and needed an interpreter. When searchers went on board, they were prevented from carrying out their duties *'for John Wyn ap Hugh and William Glynne declared they had a commission for the like matters, being of more force and authority.'*

In 1567, Morgan ab Ieuan accused John Wyn of piracy from Bardsey. He claimed that John ap Wyn was causing problems for the people and instituted proceedings in Star Chamber. His Bill of Complaint begins: *'the people of Caernarfon have diverse and sundry times heretofore been troubled, molested, vexed, hindered and their great impoverishing and undoing for and by reason certain pyrates, arriving coming for and resorting to those quarters and confines.'* The sufferings were due to *'John Wyn ap Hughe, a man of evil disposition, defender and maintainer of all pyrates… he daily store … as well as all kind of beast necessary for victuals, as beefs, steers, wethers and other such like, as also with all kind of meal, bread and other necessaries.'* In 1569, John Wyn was again alleged to be using Bardsey Isle as the headquarters of a highly-organised nest of pirates. The pirate operated from the old Augustine priory in Bardsey Island, and from Beaumaris. His agent on Bardsey was William Morgan, whose duty was to be *'at all times ready to deliver to all such pyrates aforesaid, the said victuals and necessaries, when and as often as they have needs. receiving for the same large recompense – as wine, iron, salt, spices and all such things which the said pyrates by their desperate attempts robbing and spoiling, happen to come by.'* His father, Huw ap Richard ap Sion ap Madog of Bowrda, a bard and patron of bards, was buried on Bardsey.

PIRS (PERYS, PIERS, PYRS) GRIFFITH (GRUFFUDD) 1568-1628

The son of Sir Rhys Grifffith of Penrhyn Mawr near Bangor, on his father's death in 1580 he was made a ward of court. (A tradition is that he was a boy on one of the ships which accompanied Drake to the Straits of Magellan in 1577). In 1583, he was with Captain Koet and Tomas Prys when they took a prize off the coast of Africa. In 1588 he bought and provisioned a ship, and sailed from Beaumaris on April 20th, 1588. On his arrival at Plymouth on May 4th, he was honourably received by Sir Francis Drake. After fighting the Armada, Griffith joined Drake and Raleigh in expeditions against the Spanish in the West Indies. Pirs took the Spanish ship *Speranza* with its cargo of oil, olives and silk, landing at Aber Cegin in 1600. Pirs was arrested at Cork for piracy in 1603, and had to mortgage some of his estates to pay the heavy fines. It seems that he now liaised with Tomas Prys* (q.v.) of Plas Iolyn in privateering, and that further heavy financial penalties led to him losing some of his estates in 1614. By 1616 he was in the Fleet prison, and his lands had been taken by mortgagers such as the Myddletons. He had married Margaret, the daughter of Sir Thomas Mostyn, and was buried in Westminster Abbey.

*Tomas Prys was his best friend and kinsman, and wrote an ode entitled *'The Sending of the Porpoise to Prys Gruffydd to Turn Him from the Seas'*, recounting that the privateer *'on the deck of his ship, very doughty in his shining armour'* (Ar ei llong yn wrol iawn, Galw arno gloew ei harnais) had been away from home for years:

'Six years! Ah, how wearily they have dragged
Since his ship cleared the bar and bore away for the High Seas'.
(Chwe blynedd och ai blined
Ar llong er pan aeth ar lled
I foroedd uwch y forryd
Dros y bar ar draws y byd.'
Prys asked:
'May God grant him the chiefest treasure,
Grace to abandon the sea! ...
For, after all, sea-faring is only fit for wastrels,
Who own not a foot of land ashore!'

WILLIAM VAUGHAN, VALENTINE, BAUGH fl 1582

Using at least three names, he operated from Wales and Studland Bay, Dorset, and in 1582 took the 300-ton German ship *Salvator* of Danzig with Stephen Heynes* (a.k.a. Carless) as consort. Heynes tortured the crew so badly to discover where they had hidden their money that some of his own crew fell onto their knees to beg him to stop. The cargo of sugar and spices was sold openly at Studland in Dorset, and fresh cattle taken aboard. Like John Callice, Heynes had *'friends in high places'* among the rich aldermen and traders of London, and was friendly with Sir Christopher Hatton, the Vice-Admiral of Dorset. Heynes forced the German captain to borrow his ransom money from Francis Hawley. He also only released the Salvator to its owners upon the payment of a bribe. Heynes and Vaughan next took an English ship moored at Sandown, and its corrupt captain kept part of the cargo.

In 1583 Vaughan captured a ship loaded with Bibles, which he presented to priests and a deputy Vice-Admiral of Dorset, Francis Hawley. Hawley was noted for accepting stolen goods, and was later accused of asking pirate captains who moored off Studland Bay for protection money. He was offended when the pirate Clinton Atkinson (hanged 1583) did not give him an expensive looted tapestry which he had promised.

Hawley then asked another pirate to catch Atkinson for him, but Captain Thomas Walton refused. Walton, like Vaughan, sailed from Dorset and Wales, and in 1581 Vaughan had fired at him to keep him away from Studland Bay. Walton later sailed with another Welsh prate, Captain Ellis. William Vaughan was captured late in 1583, tortured to discover his accomplices, and hanged.

*Heynes in 1581 took the *'Esperance'* of Dieppe, which had been laden in Brazil with *'405 tons of Brazil wood, 12 puncheons of pepper, 6000 weight of cotton wool, 360 parrots* (q.v. in Terms), *54 munkeys, apes and other beasts.'* In June he was offering the monkeys for sale in Torbay.

THOMAS BEAVIN (BETHEWIN, BEVAN) d. 1583
Originally a shoemaker, he sailed from Welsh ports and Studland Bay. After a successful career between 1580 and 1583, he was captured by royal ships, and hanged in London.

SIR RICHARD BULKELY OF BEAUMARIS fl 1591
This Vice-Admiral of North Wales controlled Anglesey and much of Caernarfonshire. The other major landowner in Caernarfon was the Earl of Leicester, and one of his land agents, Owen Wood, of the Woods of Rhosmor, complained that Bulkeley had set up his brothers Charles and David as pirates. Wood was annoyed that Richard Bulkeley had 'tweaked' his nose in a Quarter Sessions. Wood brought his action to the Court of Star Chamber, claiming that Bulkeley had allowed Beaumaris to become a base for pirates such as Captain Purser, and had entertained the French pirate, Captain Henricke. Later, it was claimed that Sir Richard was present when Henricke was captured, but *'the said Sir Richard commanded his officers not to stay him... for he said he came to land at his request... whereupon the officer did let this pyrate go for they durst do no other.'* In 1591, Richard Bulkeley received a mild censure - he was a friend of Queen Elizabeth. Some years later, Bulkeley's brother-in-law, Griffith John Griffith, financed his son's piracy from Beaumaris, and his son was said to have buried treasure nearby. Griffiths' ship was impounded by the Admiralty, and old Richard Bulkeley craftily bought it for a minimal amount. Sir Richard Leveson was Bulkeley's successor as Vice-Admiral, and also allowed piracy to flourish.

CAPTAIN WILLIAM MIDLETON (MYDDELTON), GWILYM CANOLDREF c.1550 - c. 1600?
The son of Ffowc Midleton of Archwedlog, Llansannan, Denbighshire, he was a poet, soldier and sailor, who may have been educated at Oxford. His uncle was Richard Myddelton. He was educated by William Salesbury of Llansannor, the translator of the New testament in Welsh (see *100 Great Welshmen*). Midleton originally served under Henry Herbert, Earl of Pembroke, and composed and sang an elegy on the death of Catherine, Countess of Pembroke, in 1575. Catherine was Sir Philip Sidney's sister. In 1585-86, he was fighting with Leicester in the Netherlands, and was probably at Zutphen when Sir Philip Sidney perished. In 1589, William was in Portugal, fighting for Don Antonio's right to the throne. Lord Burghley seems to refer to him as a

privateer returning with a cargo of pepper in 1590. He now won renown as a brave sailor, and in 1591 *'has the honour of having saved the English fleet which was sent to the Azores to intercept the Spanish galleons.'* He had been sent by the Earl of Cumberland to ascertain the Spanish strength, and sailed incognito among its fleet for three days. They had ten times the number of ships of Lord Thomas Howard, who had laid an ambush off the Azores. Howard and Sir Richard Grenville were awaiting the arrival of the Spanish flota from South America. Howard managed to get most of the English fleet away in time, but Grenville waited for some men to leave shore for his boat. In the ensuing battle, Grenville's *Revenge* was destroyed. At some stage Midleton also buccaneered off the Barbary Coast, and described the casting away of the *'Toby'* in bad conditions: *'We committed ouselves to the Lord, and began with a doleful tune and heavy hearts to sing the 12th Psalm "Help, Lord for good and Godly men". Howbeit, before we had finished four verses, the waves of the sea had stopped the breaths of most of our men.'*

Sion Dafydd Rhys published a Welsh Grammar in 1592, acknowledging his debt to Midleton's learning. Midleton (as Gwilym Canoldref, his 'literal' bardic name) published in 1593 a book *'Bardhoniaeth, neu brydydhiaeth'* on the craft of the bards, and there are extant *awdlau, cywyddau* and *englynion* by him. Midleton wished to teach all his countrymen the poetic art, which had previously been confined to the professional bards. In 1603, his Welsh translation of the Psalms into *cynghanedd* verse was posthumously published. It appears that he had completed it on board ship while buccaneering in the West Indies in 1596. He was a Renaissance gentleman, a grammarian and poet who made a major contribution to Welsh literature in the 16th century. He claimed to be the first man, along with Thomas Price (Prys) and Captain Koet, to smoke tobacco in London. Tobacco leaves were twisted in the form of cigars. Tomas Prys refers to a dispute between Midleton and Sion Llwyd of Ial over a young lady. It may be that he was the Midleton who married Mary, the daughter of Stado Bruxell of Brussels, and died in Antwerp on March 27th, 1621, rather than around 1600.

DAVID MYDDELTON d. 1615

The Denbighshire Myddletons were descended from Rhirid Flaidd, Lord of Penllyn (d.1207), but adopted the English name after the marriage of Rhirid ap Dafydd to the daughter of Sir Alexander Myddelton of Shrophire in 1393. The Myddletons became a great family in North Wales, and Richard Myddelton, MP for Denbigh, had nine sons. Sir Thomas Myddelton (1550-1631) was the fourth son, who became an original shareholder in the East India Company, a partner in the chief buccaneering expeditions in the reign, a partner in his brother Hugh's New River Enterprise, and also in the Virginia Company. He was MP for Merioneth, bought Chirk Castle in 1595 with his buccaneering profits and from money-lending to shippers, was knighted in 1603 and became Lord Mayor of London in 1613. Hugh Myddleton of Ruthin used the profits from his gold-smithing, in the New River Project to bring fresh water to London. Their nephew was David Myddelton. His father and three uncles were heavily involved in the founding of the East India Company, and David sailed to the West Indies in May 1601. David was the youngest of four brothers, all of whom sailed in the initial voyages of the East India Company.

His captain, Sir Michael Geare (1566 - ?), had been a privateer since at least 1588, preying on Spanish shipping. In 1596, he shared command of the *Neptune* and its pinnace with the great pirate Christopher Newport. Newport then gave the pinnace *James* to Myddelton to command, as it was far better for shallow waters than his new ship *Archangel*. In the 1601 raid they took three prizes near Cuba, bringing two back to England but losing contact with the third at sea. The crew sold the third vessel in Morocco and dispersed. Geare then went off with Christopher Newport again, and David Myddelton joined the East India Company's Second Expedition (1604-1606). He was second captain of *Malice Scourge*, which he renamed the *Red Dragon*, after his homeland's flag. He commanded a ship on the Third Expedition (1607-1608), and sailed again to the East Indies in a single ship in 1609-1611. He was wrecked with three ships in April 1615 off Madagascar, all hands drowning.

(Myddelton Hall at Llanarthney near Llandeilo, was originally the property of David, brother of Sir Hugh Myddelton, before William Paxton bought and remodelled it.)

JOHN MYDDELTON 1563 - 1595?
He was another nephew of the wealthy Thomas and Hugh Myddelton. Although Hugh financed many buccaneering expeditions, it appears that John worked for other syndicates. Captaining the 50-ton *Moonshine*, he led raids on European vessels in 1586, 1590, and 1591, and was involved in the Azores Raid of 1586. In 1592 took a ship off Spain on his way to the West Indies. Here he linked up with Benjamin Wood, another of Raleigh's captains in the Azores Raid. Wood was commanding three of Lord Thomas Howard's ships, but one had been lost in a storm. Near Cartagena, John Myddelton tried to take a Spanish frigate which had run aground, but Myddelton was captured with 12 other privateers.

Released, probably ransomed, Myddelton was again active in the Caribbean in 1594, privateering for Sir John Watts. Watts made enormous profits from sponsoring privateers such as Christopher Newport, Thomas Lane and Michael Geare, prompting the Venetian Ambassador to call him 'the greatest pirate that has ever been in this kingdom.' Myddelton sailed in consort with the one-armed Christopher Newport around Trinidad and Guyana in 1594, and they took the town of Puerto Caballos in Honduras, without much booty to be shared. Myddelton then met up with other ships belonging to John Watts, captained by Richard Best in the 130-ton *Jewel* and William Lane. Off Havana, they took four prizes, including a caravel. However, the Spanish Governor sent two pinnaces which managed to capture Myddelton and seven others. He was taken to Spain in 1595 and never heard of again.

SEVENTEENTH CENTURY

THOMAS PRYS (PRICE) 1564? - 1634
His father was Elys Prys, 'The Red Doctor' of Plas Iolyn, the grandson of Rhys ap Meredydd (Rhys Fawr) who fought with Henry Tudor at Bosworth Field. Dr Elys Prys was one of the 'three adjudicators of Caerwys'. On his father's death in 1594, Thomas took the manor of Ysbyty Ifan and his father's clerical livings. In 1599, Thomas

became Sheriff of Denbighshire, then served with his mentor Robert Dudley, Earl of Leicester, in the Dutch Wars. (Sir Roger Williams, Sir Gelli Meyrick and Sir Thomas Morgan all were noted warriors in the Low Countries). In 1588, he was alongside Leicester in the army awaiting the Spanish Armada, and was present when Elizabeth I (see '100 Great Welsh Women') made her great speech at Tilbury. Prys fought in France, the Netherlands, Scotland, Spain and Ireland, and became an accomplished buccaneer. At the end of the 16th century he bought a ship, fitted it out for privateering and began raiding along the coast of Spain. One of his many 'cywyddau' reads in English 'For no mean period, I followed the seaways to Spain, across the world; I believed I had only to go to sea to come by all kinds of treasure.' He seemed happiest in later life as a pirate, living in his remote hide-out on Enlli (Bardsey Island), or in the merry company of poet friends at Llanrwst, near his estate of Yspyty Ifan. In the Llanrwst taverns, he describes the times when his fellow 'lions' used to roar under the effects of drink... 'When the beer begins to flow, then is pandemonium let loose in Llanrwst.' Of his friend David Salisbury of Llanrhaiadr, he said, 'no Christian man was more famed for his prowess in a fight', and of the ex-soldier Gawain Goodman 'if he once gets at all the wines of a town, he'll not come home without tripping: well I know how he can drink his share; if there's sack to be had, he'll not put up with gruel. A generous and a godly man is Gawain - when in his cups! Bu not so much as a pin will you get out of him till the pot has warmed his head.' Thomas Owen was 'that fierce, fiery-handed man of war', and his great friends Pyrs Gruffudd (q.v.) and William Midleton (q.v.) are also mentioned, the latter in relation to an impending duel because of a love affair.

A landowner, Thomas Prys was one of the first three men to smoke tobacco publicly in London, with his friend William Myddelton (q.v.) and Captain Coet. It was ransacked from a ship which the three captains took between the Canary Islands and Africa. Prys came to know London well, not only its great houses, but also its taverns and brothels, but tired of living there, and came to hate that city. In an extraordinary cywydd he explained to his son that London was Hell, and warned him against all officialdom. He had been in London as a soldier of Elizabeth, but left there to return to Wales. Thomas used his freedom as a nobleman to 'bring a breath of fresh sea air into the stalling cywydd'. His poem 'Cywydd y ddangos yr hildring a fu I wr pan oedd ar y mor' is a humorous account of his expedition, and one translated couplet reads 'Before I will, pill or part, Buy a ship, I'll be a shephart'. He also devoted some poems on his buccaneering to Pirs Griffith (q.v.), who was carrying out the same activities. He organised his activities from Bardsey Island (see John Wyn ap Hugh), but resided at Plas Iolyn. He had spent a great deal of time in London, dissipating his money in 'litigation and dissipation'. There is a vivid description of contemporary London in his collection of poetry 'Cywydd I ddangos mai Uffern yw Llundain.' Many of his poems are still extant, including many dedicated to 'Eiddig' (the jealous one). Two of his poems are entitled 'Ode to show that London is Hell' and 'Ode to show how a young man was cheated out of his money through drabbing and dicing when he first went to London.' Tomas describes a bawdy London of brothels and taverns, where 'life is short and precarious, the home of all the knavery and bawdery in the world...' and he is 'carousing with a drab at a tavern as boldly as you please.' The Welsh poem goes on about his 'going thence to the *shady quarter, bent upon gaming ('twas an easy job   to knock up against congenial companions in the city). Then to the dice-tables, warming to the game and calling a "sixer" on a poor cast... Detecting the wiles of "doctored" dice and swearing like a madman; perjuring oneself stoutly when found out; storming and blustering in no sweet terms, and brawling with naked weapons.'* In one of his poems he sends a porpoise to carry a message to his cousin Pyrs Gruffudd (q.v.) to give up piracy before it was too late. To some extent his rejuvenation of the *cywydd* verse form, with an injection of freshness and humour, enabled it to survive as the most frequently used and enjoyed of all the older Welsh verse forms in Welsh, in the present day.

WILLIAM HUGHES (HUGHS) fl. 1611
Richard Bishop of Yarmouth was a privateer from 1591, who sailed in consort with John Ward to Tunis in 1605. The Atlantic pirates elected Bishop the *'admiral'* of their confederation in 1608, with Captain Peter Easton as vice-admiral. In 1609, they commanded 9 ships and 1000 men based in Ireland. With impunity, the fleet plundered English and Dutch shipping in the Bristol Channel. In 1610, Captain Parker sold a three-quarter share of his confederation ship to Thomas Hussey, who now commanded the *Black Raven*, a captured 160-tom Flemish fly-boat with 23 guns. William Hughes was another of the pirate captains, as they were all summoned around Hussey's deathbed in 1611. Hussey gave the *Black Raven* and all his loot to Hughes. Bishop retired in 1611, and Easton became the pirates' admiral, leading a fleet of up to 17 ships. James I was reduced to offering the pirates a pardon, and allowed Dutch men-of-war to patrol British coastal waters in the hope that they would curb the pirates. However, Easton led his fleet in searching for their would-be destroyers, and took two of the Dutch fleet.

In August 1611, the confederacy broke up, and Hughes now sailed with Peter Easton and a Captain Harvey to West Africa, taking Dutch and English ships. Easton told a captured captain that he believed that Englishmen were no better than *'Turckes and Jews'*. The three captains then headed for Newfoundland, seeking more ships and bigger crews. They *'forced'* around 500 Britons and another six ships to join their flotilla, but several hundred men deserted in one Newfoundland raid, mainly because of Easton's unpredictable nature and cruelty. Easton returned to Sale (modern Rabat in Morocco) in 1612, and negotiated a pardon from the Duke of Savoy, Carlo Emanuele I. He retired under his protection to Villefranche, built a palace and married an heiress. Hughes' fate is unknown.

JOHN NORMAN fl. 1631
This pirate sailed into Pwllheli harbour in February 1631 and took a Scottish barque. Deputy Vice-Admiral Gruffydd Madryn, a cousin of John Griffiths, was unable to arrest him because of a lack of support. Norman repaired his ship at anchor, and the townspeople informed him that the Vice Admiral John Griffiths was on his way, so that he could escape. Captain Henry Mainwaring (q.v.) called Wales *'the nursery and store-house of pirates'* because of its natural hidden harbours and the ease with which they could escape to open seas.

SIR SACKVILLE TREVOR d. 1634

The brother of Sir John Trevor of Denbigh, he shared the patronage of Lord Howard of Effingham. Sackville commanded ships in the naval campaigns of 1596-1603, capturing four Spanish ships with valuable cargoes. Sackville was knighted at Chatham on July 3rd, 1604 by James I, for his valour. He married the widow of the Marshal of Ireland, who was killed at Blackwater in 1598. Sackville settled at Plas Newydd on Anglesey, and was elected the island's MP. In 1623, he was sent as a naval escort to Prince Charles in a journey to Spain, and he saved the future Charles I from drowning in Cadiz harbour. In 1627, the counties of Anglesey, Denbigh and Flint were ordered to supply Sackville with a 30-ton barque in preparation for a war with Spain. In June 1627, he won distinction in the failed expedition to relieve the Huguenots of La Rochelle. In September of that year, he led the flotilla which blockaded the mouth of the Elbe in support of Sir Charles Morgan's land force, aiding the King of Denmark. He died in 1634.

ADMIRAL SIR THOMAS BUTTON d. 1634

More of a naval man and an explorer, nevertheless he took part in some privateering adventures. He was the fourth son of Miles Button, Sheriff of Glamorgan (1565, 1571 and 1589) and of Margaret Lewis of The Van, Caerphilly. He was born near the site of the present Dyffryn House and its fabulous gardens, near St Lythans in the Vale of Glamorgan. He first went to sea in 1589, and then again in 1592 was at sea, seemingly sailing under Drake, Hawkins and Raleigh. With rapid promotion, in 1604 Button was given a pension for distinguished service in the West Indies and in Ireland by the Lord High Admiral. In 1609 he commanded a

Sir Thomas Button

ship, and in 1610 was a member of the company known as the 'Incorporated Discoverers' of the North-West Passage. It was formed under the patronage of Prince Henry to find a passage from the Atlantic to the Pacific around the north coast of America. After the death of Henry Hudson, Button was engaged by the merchants of London to follow up his discoveries, and commanded two ships, the *Resolution* and the *Discovery*.

Reaching Hudson's Straits in 1612, he became the first man to reach the west coast of America via that route, and had to over-winter as he was iced in. Losing a few men, the crew lived off ptarmigan which were plentiful in the area. He named the mainland New Wales, and also Button's Bay and Mansell's Islands. Nelson's River was named after the lost master of the *Resolution*. At 60 degrees latitude he found a current flowing in from the west which he believed to be the key to the North-West Passage, and called it Hubbart's Hope. However, his instructions forbade him to follow it, and he reluctantly returned home, to be knighted by James I. A year later his neighbour and cousin Captain Gibbon was sent out to explore the current, his mate being a man named Baffin, after whom Baffin's Bay was named.

He was then appointed Admiral of the Irish Seas, a position he held for most of the remainder of his life, except for the interlude of the Algerine Expedition of 1620-21, under the command of Sir Robert Mansell (the Welsh friend after whom he had named Mansell's Islands). Button was Rear-Admiral and complained to Mansell that he should have been Vice-Admiral instead of Sir Richard Hawkins. Mansell placated him by saying that he had not known at the time that Button was leaving his Irish post to join the venture. For most of the rest of his life, Button was chasing Barbary corsairs and Dunkirk and Biscay pirates off the west coast of Ireland in the *Antelope*, then in the *Phoenix*, and finally in the *Lion*. The *Lion* had 'twelve whelps', a squadron with many of his kinsmen as commanders, and scoured the seas from Kinsale to the Scilly Isles, from Dublin to Lundy and Bristol and St George's Channels. He had to mortgage his own estates around Cardiff to fit out these privateers, and he wrote in 1629 from Cardiff that he was 'kept back, not in so good a case as I was ten years ago, for then I owed nothing, but now for five years past receiving neither pension nor pay ... but in my house debarred from my wonted freedom by reason I have no means to pay what I owe (than which affliction of this latter not to be able to pay every man his own this world cannot lay a greater on me)... ' He feared that he and his family would have 'either to beg or starve' The Navy Board complained that he listened to no-one but Buckingham, but Mansell and the Earl of Denbigh always came to the defence of 'old Tom Button'. He took several prizes, which involved him in law-suits and also enabled him to defend himself and pay of some debts. He was in command of the *Convertive* and spotted four French ships chasing a small Welsh ship. He captured one, laden with salt and cognac, and intended to take it to Bristol. Prevailing winds meant that he landed it in Milford, and he spent many years in litigation as to the extent of his prize money. He was constantly asking for better guns for his 'whelps' in fighting the 'Turks' (the Barbary corsairs). In 1625, three 'Turkish' pirate ships took all the inhabitants off Lundy into slavery, and also kidnapped several people from Padstow and threatened to burn Ilfracombe.

His burial place is curiously unrecorded. Button married Mary, daughter of Sir Walter Rice of Dynevor. Their son Miles married Barbara, the heiress of Rhys Meurig of Cottrell Manor (the present golf course in the Vale), and their daughter Elizabeth married Colonel John Poyer, who executed by Cromwell at Covent Garden for defending Pembroke Castle with the Royalists. Sir Thomas Button himself was said to be a relative of Oliver Cromwell, whose real name was Williams.

DAVID JONES (see Davy Jones' Locker in TERMS) fl. 1636

In 1634, Charles I was bribed by some London merchants to give a secret privateering commission to capture ships below the Equator, from countries which did not have a peace treaty with England. One 'cover' commission was given to Richard Oldfield of the *Samaritan* and to William Cobb of the *Roebuck*, to 'range and discover' the African coast. Another 'secret' commission was a licence to plunder 'especially from the Cape to China and Japan, including the Red Sea, Persian Gulf and Coromandel Coast.' The last three areas broke the monopoly of the East India Company. When the seals were broken, off Cape Verde, Captain Oldfield asked to be put ashore as the expedition was plainly illegal.

David Jones was made sailing-master, and in effect was the real authority on board both ships. The two ships became separated, and the Samaritan foundered in the Comoros Islands off Madagascar. Captain Cobb began building a new sloop at Mohilla. The Roebuck, under Captain William Ayres, then took an Arabian junk in the Gulf of Aden. On September 5th, Ayres and Jones attacked the Indian ship Taufiqi in the Red Sea, although it had a sailing pass from the East India Company. Ayres seems to have led the crew in torturing the passengers and crew.

Jones was now in charge of a lightly manned, recently taken prize ship, filled with loot, accompanying Ayres in the 'Roebuck'. The outrage led to the East India Company commissioning two ships to seek out Ayres, Cobb and Jones. The East India Company ship 'Swan' under Captain John Proud took Ayres' ship, with Cobb now on board, in 1636 off the Comoros Islands. Jones knew he could not escape with his own heavily laden ship, so he scuttled it with all its incriminating evidence. The East India Company captain fined the privateers £10,000 in booty, and allowed them to keep the Roebuck. Two more Indian ships were taken in 1636, and the ship returned to England with £40,000 in loot in May 1637. Most of the booty was claimed by Charles I and the promoters, leaving about £10000 to be shared between the officers and 50 crew. Cobb and Ayres were arrested, but released, and briefly imprisoned in 1643. Jones disappeared from history.

NICHOLAS HOOKES (HAWKES) 'the great pyrate' d. 1637
In St Mary's Church, Conwy, there is a 17th century marble slab inscribed to Nicholas Hookes, and stating that he was the father of 27 children and himself a 41st child.
"Here lieth the body of Nicholas Hookes, of Conway, gentleman,
who was one-and-fortieth child of his father, William Hookes,
Esq., by Alice, his wife, and the father of 27 children. He died
20th of March, 1637."
Lewis Dwnn, in his 'Visitations of Wales' notes 'the great pyrate', the 15th son of a merchant in Conwy, who practised piracy and smuggling from bases at St Tudwal's Isle and Enlli (Bardsey Island). The author would welcome more information upon this intriguing and mysterious character. In 1653, the long poem 'Amanda' was published by the Royalist Nicholas Hookes, a recent graduate, who may have been a son of the pirate.

ADMIRAL SIR ROBERT MANSELL 1573 - 1653
Born at Margam in Glamorgan, he first went to sea with Lord Howard, and probably faced the Armada. He served with Sir Christopher Blunt's regiment when Howard and Essex sacked Cadiz in 1596, for which he was knighted. In 1596, Mansell was the captain of Essex's own ship in the 'Islands Voyage' of Essex and Raleigh. From 1599, he

was in charge of a small squadron operating off the Irish coast, reinforced in 1600 by Sir Richard Leveson. In that year, he fought a rapier duel with Sir John Heydon in Norfolk, and was reported killed, but after Essex's rebellion was engaged in arresting the Earl's accomplices. Given a squadron to guard the coast, he joined with Sir Amyas Preston (of the Preston and Somers 1595 Expedition fame), and they took six Portuguese 'Easterlings' laden with booty. In September 1602, Mansell intercepted six Spanish galleys, heading towards Flanders. He had waited for them off Dungeness, while his Dutch consorts patrolled Dunkirk and the Downs. The galleys fell into the trap. Two were rammed, two wrecked in a gale, and two taken by the Dutch. For this exploit, he was created Vice-Admiral of the Fleet, and Admiral of the Narrow Seas. Commanding Dutch and English ships, his fleet took more prizes, including a Portuguese carrack with a cargo of pepper in 1603. 'The proud Welshman' was given the honour of escorting the Spanish and French ambassadors from Calais to England on their 1603 peace mission, and prevented Admiral de Rosny from flying the French flag. In that year, he also escorted Sir Walter Raleigh from Winchester to his London trial. He was made Treasurer of the Navy in 1604 and Vice-Admiral of the Realm in 1618, and in 1620 led the Algerine Expedition in his flagship *Lion*. There were six men-of-war and thirteen armed merchant ships, but the engagement was inconclusive. The Barbary States centred on Algiers had a fleet of thirty ships and ten galleys.

A keen politician and speaker, he had been imprisoned briefly in the Marshalsea in 1613 for political disaffection. Mansell was MP for Kings Lynn in 1601 (the year after his nearby duel), for Carmarthen in 1603, Carmarthenshire in 1614, Glamorgan in 1623 and 1625, Lostwithiel in 1626, and again for Glamorgan 1627-28. He had a strong interest in glass manufacture, as shown when the application for a monopoly for the new process, of making glass from coal instead of wood, was granted in 1615. King James expressed his great wonderment '*that Robert Mansell, who had won so much honour on water should meddle with fire.*' He built several glass-works to protect his share of the monopoly, including one on the Tyne to make use of the abundant sea-coal in the region. His first marriage was to the daughter of the Lord Keeper, and his second to one of the Queen's Maids of Honour in 1617. He was one of the canopy bearers at the Queen's funeral in 1619.

CAPTAIN MAINWARING 1587- buried May 15th 1653 -
THE MOST FAMOUS SEA ROVER OF HIS DAY

From the Welsh borders in Shropshire, Sir Henry Mainwaring was the most famous of all the Jacobean pirates. The Mainwarings were an old Cheshire family, who had been in Shropshire and Cheshire since the early 12th century at least. The best account of his life is the two-volume account '*The Life and Works of Sir Henry Mainwaring*' edited by his descendant G.E. Mainwaring, and published by The Navy Records Society in 1920. The publication also includes Henry Mainwaring's '*Of the Beginnings, Practices and Suppression of Pirates*' and his '*The Seaman's Dictionary*'. Gosse (1932) says '*not only was he a most successful pirate himself, without equal in England*' but '*Mainwaring was one of those geniuses who lived at the wrong time. There can be little doubt that had he been born fifty years later, his fame would have equalled that of the great navigators Drake or Raleigh.*'

At the age of 15, Henry gained a degree from Brasenose College, Oxford, in 1602. After trying his hand at being a lawyer at the Inner Temple, then as a soldier in a volunteer regiment in the Low Countries, he went to sea as a privateer in 1611, aged just 24. He was given a commission by the Lord High Admiral to capture the troublesome pirate Captain Peter Easton (Eston). From 1610 the *'Pirate Admiral'* Easton was in command of a fleet of 40 ships, controlling Bristol Channel shipping from the mouth of the Avon. With ten ships Easton went to Newfoundland for fresh supplies, and at Harbour Grace took five ships, a hundred cannon, goods, and enlisted 500 English cod splitters to join his force. He was the first pirate to raid the Avalon coast of Newfoundland since Sir John Perrot.

Mainwaring could not capture Easton, who took advantage of the Duke of Savoy's offer of using the free port of Villefranche. Bonded warehouses were opened for the storage of his booty, and he retired to a palace there, in which he was reckoned to have £2,000,000 worth of gold stashed away. Mainwaring turned pirate as soon as he reached the Straits of Gibraltar. From a base at Marmora (Mehedia, near Rabat) and another at Broadhaven in Ireland he attacked Atlantic shipping. In 1612 the Lord High Admiral had given Mainwaring a letter of marque to savage Spanish ships in the Caribbean. In his 120-ton *Resistance*, Mainwaring sailed to Gibraltar and informed his crew that it was not really necessary to take the scurvy-ridden trip to the West Indies in order to hit the Spaniards. Mainwaring had bought the *Resistance* from the famed shipwright Phineas Pett, and wanted to get his money back quickly. He instead proposed to head for Marmora on the Atlantic Barbary Coast and use that as his base, to attack any *'Juan-Carlos'* (Spaniard) in sight.

Mamora was on the mouth of the Sibu River, not far from Sale. (Sale is modern Rabat in Morocco, and was the main pirate haven on the Atlantic coast. In the 1620's Barbary corsairs from Sale raided England for slaves, and held Lundy Island for two weeks). In return for protection, the British pirates at Mamora taught Moroccans gunnery and sailing, and shared their booty with them. Not until 1614 was it captured, by a huge Spanish expedition of 99 ships and 7000 troops. Mainwaring's privateers willingly agreed, to sail to this pirate paradise, and from the summer of 1613 to the summer of 1614, around 30 ships had been taken. The King of Spain sent the Duke of Medina to offer Mainwaring a high post in his own service plus money to join him, so as to stop the depredations on Spanish shipping. Mainwaring had refused to take any English prizes, but could not return to England, having over-ridden the authority of his letters of commission. The Spanish regarded him as the reincarnation of the fiendish *'El Draque'*, as *'hardly a ship passed his lair without either suffering damage or capture.'* At this time, the Duke of Florence and the Bey of Tunis respectively asked Mainwaring to privateer on their behalf, but he refused.

Like Easton, Mainwaring therefore had to go to Newfoundland to recruit amongst the disillusioned English cod-splitters and merchant seamen there. He led a fleet of eight ships, and pillaged the fishing fleets there for 4 months, in the company of Easton, his original target for capture. 1614 Records state that *'Captain Mainwaring with divers other captains arrived in Newfoundland the 4th June, having eight sails of war-like ships, one whereof they took at the bank, another upon the main of Newfoundland, from all*

*the harbours whereof they commanded carpenters, mariners, victuals, munitions and all
necessaries from the fishing fleet after this rate – of every six mariners they take one, and the
one-fifth part of all their victuals: from the Portugal ships they took all their wine and other
provisions, save their bread: from a French ship in Harbour Grace they took 10,000 fish;
some of the company of many ships did run away unto them. They took a French ship fishing
in Carbonear, and so after they had continued three months and a half taking their pleasure
of the fishing fleet, the 14th September 1614, they departed, having with them from the fishing
fleet about 400 mariners and fishermen: many volunteers, many compelled.'* Compulsion
was not usually used, except for *'sea-artists'* in the last resort. Usually, normal seamen
pretended that they had been 'forced' to join *'the sweet trade'*, and were given letters to
this effect by buccaneer and pirate captains. These letters were *'insurance policies'*
should they ever come to trial. Carbonear's first mention in history is due to
Mainwaring's raid - it is between Harbour Grace and Victoria on the Avalon Peninsula.

Mainwaring returned to Marmora, but found that the Spanish had taken his base
in his absence. He did not bother trying to storm its defences, as he knew that Easton
had retired to the safe port of Villefranche, under the protection of the Duke of Savoy,
Carlos Emmanuele I. There Mainwaring linked up with another exiled pirate captain
called Walsingham. Within six weeks, he had taken loot off the Spanish valued at
500,000 Spanish crowns, and brought its Mediterranean shipping to a virtual
standstill. The King of Spain despatched five warships, expressly to bring him back
dead or alive. Off Cadiz, Mainwaring's three ships decisively beat the Spanish flotilla,
however, which was forced to flee to Lisbon. The King now promised Mainwaring a
free pardon and 20,000 ducats a year to lead a fleet of Spanish ships, but he again
refused. The Bey of Tunis again offered a similar deal if Mainwaring would take the
Islamic faith and lead the barbary corsairs.

King James, with Catholic sympathies, was constantly being asked by the French
and Spanish ambassadors to stop Henry Mainwaring's depredations on their shipping,
so he sent an envoy to Mainwaring. The privateer was offered a free pardon to give up
piracy, with the (somewhat empty) threat that an English fleet would be sent to
capture him if he refused. Mainwaring returned to Dover in 1616 and he and his crews
were pardoned, and allowed to keep their booty.

Sir Henry now found a new role in capturing pirates, chasing the Barbary Corsairs
away from the British coast, and was knighted in 1618. In the same year he became a
Gentleman of the King's Bedchamber. In 1620 Mainwaring was appointed Lieutenant
of Dover Castle and Deputy Warden of the Cinque Ports and a year later was elected
an MP, ending his career as a Vice-Admiral. From 1618, he was not only a respected
courtier, but a friend of the King and Prince Charles. He also wrote a fascinating book
on piracy, *'Of the Beginnings, Practices and Suppresion of Pirates.'* As a naval
commissioner, he held command in several expeditions, and wrote more books,
including *'The Seaman's Dictionary'* in 1644, which for a century was the standard text
for naval terms (-see the definition for *whipstaffe* in Pirate Terms). Mainwaring, who
rose from a common pirate to knighthood and Admiral in the navy, summed up the
expediency of his times: *'The State may hereafter want such men who are commonly the
most serviceable in war.'*

MORRIS (MAURICE) WILLIAMS (fl. 1659-64)

He was noted in 'Terms' as having bought *La Abispa (The Wasp)*, a captured Spanish prize, by *'inch of candle'* in May 1659 at Cagway (Port Royal), Jamaica. It had been captured by the naval frigate *Diamond*, and renamed *Jamaica*. Williams then received a privateering commission from Governor Edward D'Oyley, who sold him five cannon and issued a proclamation allowing Williams to recruit sailors from the naval frigate *Marston Moor*.

Upon April 21st, 1664, Colonel Edward Morgan carried Charles II's instructions to Barbados to Sir Thomas Modyford. Modyford, a successful planter, and Governor of Barbados since 1660,was to be the new Governor of Jamaica, with Morgan as his deputy-governor. On June 1st Modyford landed in Jamaica, and followed the king's instructions by forbidding hostilities with Spain and ending the practice of issuing letters of marque. The privateers, including the redoubtable Captain Myngs, were reluctant to halt their trade, however.

In November 1664 the Welsh buccaneer Captain Morris Williams sent a note to Modyford. He offered to come in to Port Royal with a rich Spanish prize ship containing indigo, precious logwoods and silver, if security was given that it could be used to pay off his debts in Jamaica. Modyford refused to give him any promises, and Williams sailed in eight days later. The goods were seized, and the proceeds sent to the Spanish owner. This discouraged any other privateers from coming to Port Royal. However, it appears that Williams had previously carefully ransacked the prize before Modyford took it, as Modyford wrote in February 1665 *'The Spanish prizes have been inventoried and sold, but it is suspected that those of Morrice Williams and Bernard Nicholls have been miserably plundered, and the interested parties will find but a slender account in the Admiralty.'*

In April 1666, Williams took the 16-gun *Speaker* and with Edward Morgan sacked Saint Eustatius and Saba (see Edward Morgan). The English had received news that the Second Anglo-Dutch War had started. Morgan boarded Williams' *Speaker* as his flagship and set sail with five ships, another flotilla of 3 ships following on behind. Modyford wrote that there were about 650 men in the invasion force, *'chiefly reformed privateers, scarce a planter amongst them, being resolute fellows and well armed with fusils (muskets) and pistols.'* The Governor was pleased that the men went *'at the old rate of no purchase, no pay, and it will cost the King nothing considerable, some powder and mortar pieces.'*

COLONEL BLEDRI MORGAN fl. 1660

A kinsman of Henry Morgan, he was one of the most important buccaneers in Jamaica between 1660 and 1670. He commanded the rearguard of 300 men at the taking of Panama in 1670. In May 1671 he was appointed as Deputy-Governor of Providence Island by Sir James Modyford.

LIEUTENANT-COLONEL EDWARD MORGAN d. 1664

This buccaneer from a noble Welsh family was the uncle of Henry, so giving the lie to the claim that Henry was an indentured servant on his arrival in the Indies. He served as a mercenary in the 30 Years War in Germany, and married the daughter of the mayor of Lippstadt. In the English Civil War, he was a Royalist Colonel, and after the execution of Charles I, Morgan went into exile in Germany. On the Restoration of the Monarchy, he was named Lieutenant-Governor of Jamaica, deputy to Sir Thomas Modyford, arriving in the West Indies in the summer of 1664.

In 1665, when the Dutch declared war on England (The Second Dutch War), Governor Modyford commissioned Morgan to command a privateer's fleet against the French. Modyford gave commissions to the assembled pirates and buccaneers to attack the Dutch islands of St Eustacius (now St Kitt's, or St Christopher's Island), Saba, Tobago and Curacao. Edward Morgan had been given command of 10 ships and 500 men, most of them 'reformed prisoners', and including some condemned pirates who were reprieved and pardoned for the expedition. The crews mutinied before leaving Jamaica, but were pacified by the offer of an equal share of the spoils. Nine ships eventually met at Pinos Island, but there was disagreement on Morgan's plan of attack. Three ships deserted to attack Virginia, but the rest of the fleet sailed on to St Eustatius, arriving on 23rd July, 1665. Morgan, by now old and corpulent, collapsed during the fighting and died of a heart attack. His vice-commander Theodore Cary forced the Dutch colonists to choose between accepting English rule or leaving the island. A small military force was left on the nearby island of Nevis.

LIEUTENANT-COLONEL THOMAS MORGAN fl. 1665-1685
He sailed with Edward Morgan, and was left in charge of St Eustatia and Saba after they had been captured in 1665. In 1686 he commanded a company of buccaneers responding to a plea from Governor Wells of St Kitts, who was being attacked by the French. In a pathetic defence of the island, only Morgan's company emerged with credit, and Morgan was shot in both legs.
[Note: these early buccaneers tended to use a military title for operations on land, and revert to captain at sea].

CAPTAIN WILLIAM JAMES fl 1660-1663
A buccaneer operating off Jamaica and Tortuga, Governor D'Oyley of Jamaica gave him a 'let pass' for his frigate 'America' in May 1660. In 1663 James was in command of 70 men on the 6-gun frigate, on Commodore Myng's expedition to Campeachy, leaving Port Royal in January. However, Captain Mitchell in the Blessing, wrote that he failed to reach Campeachy: 'about 90 leagues this side of Campeche, he met three sail of the fleet, viz. Captain William James his ship, sunk in the sea by foul weather, who was the next best ship in the fleet to the Admiral (Myngl), and that many of their men in the fleet were dead.'

It appears that James was the buccaneer who discovered the true value of logwood (see Terms) for the privateers. 'Captain James carried off a Spanish prize full of logwood, being astonished upon reaching port at the high price his cargo fetched.' Until then, however, he had 'known so little of its real value that he had burned much of it for fuel on the voyage' to England. The Brethren of the Coast now started illicit logging operations along the Campeche coast, the Bay of Honduras and in Mexico's Laguna de Terminos.

CAPTAIN JAMES

This buccaneer captain was temporarily appointed 'President' of Tortuga Island by the Providence Company, while Governor Flood was in London defending himself against charges made by the island's planters.

CAPTAIN LEWIS fl. 1687 - 1726

It is not at present known if this Lewis actually existed, for it is difficult to find proof in any documents. It seems that Charles Johnson (Daniel Defoe) cunningly entangled his tale with that of Captain Bannister. Bannister had run away as a young man from Port Royal in June 1684, to take part in a privateering venture on a ship with 30 guns. He was caught and brought back on the frigate *Ruby*, and put on trial by Lieutenant-Governor Molesworth, but was surprisingly released by the jury on a technical offence. For the next 30 months Bannister was active in piracy, eluding Molesworth's frigates in the area. However, in January 1687 Captain Spragge sailed into Port Royal with Bannister and three other pirates hanging at the yardarm. Johnstone said that Lewis learned his trade from Bannister, and that he and another boy had been triced up to Captain Spragge's corvettes mizzen-peak, hanging *'like two living flags'* when he sailed in with Bannister's body. It was said that he was an accomplished linguist in the dialects of the Indians of the Mosquito Coast,

Bannister hanging from the yardarm

and that he was captured by the Spanish. He escaped from Havana in a canoe with some other prisoners, took a piragua, and with this captured a sloop used for the turtling trade. Somehow Lewis appears again in 1717 as one of the *'leading lights'* in the pirate community of Nassau. With 40 men on his sloop, he had next taken a *pink*, bound from Jamaica to Campeachy Bay, then Captain Tucker's 10-gun brig. Several ships were taken in the Leeward Passage, then when he careened in a South Carolina creek, some of his forced men ran away. In 1726, he operated off Virginia and South Carolina (- only New York and Boston were bigger towns than the port of Charleston, South Carolina, at this time-) selling the goods he had taken off Atlantic shipping. Defoe records that he had many French pirates with him, and the English crew were conspiring to maroon the French, so he put all the Englishmen in an open boat with only 10 pieces of beef for sustenance, and sailed off to Newfoundland with a crew of only French and blacks. He took several fishing boats, then careened, before anchoring In Trinity Harbour in Conception Bay. Several merchant ships were in harbour, including Captain Beal's 24-gun *Herman* galley, which he took. Beal told Lewis that if he sent his quartermaster ashore, he would be able to furnish him with provisions, but the quartermaster was imprisoned by Woodes Rogers, and cannon pointed at the harbour entrance to prevent Lewis or his prize *Herman* leaving port. At night, Lewis rowed from the *Herman* to his sloop, and managed to sail out, although damaged by cannon fire in the hull. Laying off the port, Lewis captured two fishing shallops, the captain on one of which was Captain Beal's brother. He told him that if his quartermaster was not released, all his prisoners would be executed, and the quartermaster was given a boat to row out to the pirates. The merchantmen in the harbour had sent a rider to St John's for the Welsh Captain Tudor Trevor in the HMS *Sheerness* man-of-war to capture Lewis's *Morning Star* but the pirate had sailed off just four hours before Trevor's arrival.

He took larger and larger French and English vessels, ending up with a French prize of 24 guns. Now in command of 50 men, he made it his flagship and named it the *Morning Star*. From Newfoundland, he sailed to the coast of Guinea, taking English,

Dutch and Portuguese ships. Sailing off African coast with 200 men, he was chasing Captain Smith's slaver from the Carolinas, when his main and foremasts were carried away, and he clambered into the main top, tore out a handful of his hair, and threw it into the gale, shouting 'Good Devil, take this till I come!' He eventually overhauled Smith's ship, and took it, but his superstitious sailors were unhappy with his 'consorting with the Devil'. They noted that after this event, he had caught up with his prize. There was now an another argument between the more numerous French pirates, and the English crew, and the French decided to leave under Captain Barre in a large sloop which had just been captured. They believed Lewis's *Morning Star* to be riddled with the teredos worm. They took ammunition and goods off Lewis's ship and moved away to anchor off the coast in a strong wind, beginning to store their goods. While they were thus unprepared, the angry Captain Lewis told his men 'They were a Parcel of Rogues, and he would make 'em refund; accordingly (Lewis) run along Side, his Guns being all loaded and new primed, and ordered him to cut away his (Barre's) Mast, or he would sink him. Le Barre was forced to obey. Then he ordered them all ashore; they begged to have Liberty of carrying their Arms,*

Captain Lewis giving a lock of hair to the Devil

Goods & co. with 'em, but he allowed 'em only their small Arms, and cartridge Boxes. Then he brought the Sloop along Side, put every Thing on board the Ship, and sunk the Sloop.

Le Barre and the rest begged to be taken on Board; however, tho' he denied 'em, he suffered le Barre and some few to come, with whom he and his Men drank plentifully. The Negroes on board (with) Lewis told him, that the French had a Plot against him. He answered, he could not withstand his Destiny; for the devil told him in the great Cabin, he should be murdered that Night. In the dead of Night came the rest of the French on board in Canoes, got into the Cabin and killed Lewis; they fell on the Crew, but, after and Hour and a Half's Dispute, the French were beat off, and the Quarter-master, John Cornelius, an Irish Man, succeeded Lewis.' Defoe goes on to describe Cornelius' exploits, who took Joseph Williams' slaver off the Guinea Coast before dying in Madagascar.

In 'The Pirates' Own Book' of 1837, there is a strange rhyme at the end of the chapter upon Lewis:
'He was the mildest-mannered man,
That ever scuttled ship or cut a throat;
With such true breeding of a gentleman,
You could never discern his real thought,
Pity he loved an adventurous life's variety,
He was so great a loss to good society.'

CAPTAIN JOHN JAMES (fl. 1699)

This Welshman commanded a pirate brigantine around Madagascar, and sometimes sailed with Ort Van Tyle, the New York merchant/privateer. Sailing in American waters in the galley Alexander, with Thomas Howard, later a noted pirate, as one of his crew, he had formerly plundered Atlantic shipping. It appears that he took up with Captain William Read on a 60-ton brig, transferring his galley's guns. A 200-ton ship was taken in the Persian Gulf, and in their eagerness to search for gold, the pirates threw a bale of trade goods overboard, in which had been hidden a great quantity of the metal. Read died, and James took over the 'small, crazy and worm-eaten brig', heading for Mayotte. Here they laid up, taking the mast out of the brig, and adding it to the one-masted 200-ton prize (a ship known as a grab). The new brig was given the name of James' former Alexander. Abandoning the old brig, provisions were taken on, and the pirates found a 12-oared boat, which had been washed ashore when the Ruby East -India Man had been lost at sea. They remained at Mayotte for six months, over the monsoon season, then sailed for Madagascar. James chased a French ship, and soon discovered it was also a pirate. 'They hailed each other, and received the same answer from each vessel, viz. "From the Seas"', so the ships joined forces. Captain Fourgette's ship, laden with liquor from Martinique, had been taken by George Booth at Ambonavoula. Fourgette had been intending to swap the alcohol for slaves with the pirates in Madagascar, but had been fooled by Booth. Booth and James now sailed together. 70 or 80 men of James' crew were taken on by the pirate Captain White's Speaker in Madagascar. Also the Alexander's guns were transferred to the Speaker at St Augustin Bay, so one can only assume that the ship was in poor condition. What happened to John James in unknown.

CAPTAIN EVAN JONES fl. 1699

This pirate flashes through history at Port Dauphin in the Indian Ocean, when he pulled into port and looted an Amercan slaver. He gave the ship to Abraham Samuel, the mulatto pirate and self-styled *'King of Port Dauphin, Tollannare, Farrawe, Fanquest and Fownzahira'*. Samuel sold it to four pirates from 1,100 pieces of eight (about $120,000).

THE EIGHTEENTH CENTURY

TOM COLLINS fl. 1695-1715

He appears to have been first a member of 'Long John' Avery's crew, probably arriving at Madagascar on the *Charming Mary* in 1695, and then ending his career by taking up slaving. Sailing for Captain Thomas White, Collins is also mentioned as one of Captain Booth's men by Defoe: *'As soon as the purser was ashore, he was taken Prisoner, by one Tom Collins, a Welchman born in Pembrokeshire, who lived on Shore, and had belonged to the Charming Mary of Barbadoes, which went out with a Commission, but was converted to a Pyrate; he told the Purser, he was his Prisoner, and must answer the Damage done to two Merchants, who were slaving. .. He was carried by Collins on board Booth's ship...'* Collins will have met the Welsh Captain Bowen (q.v.) at this juncture of his career. He was with Captain David Williams (q.v.) at Madagascar, captured by Ort Van Tyle when Thomas Howard tried to imprison the Dutchman. Both Welshmen, Collins with his arm broken, were forced to work as slaves for van Tyle. Collins controlled a great deal of the slave trade on the east coast in the years around 1715.

MR SAMUEL HOPKINS d. 1709

This buccaneer comes down to us in history as an apothecary who was first lieutenant to the remarkable Dr Thomas Dover (1660-1724). Dover qualified as a doctor at Caius College, Cambridge, and became a licentiate of the Royal College of Physicians in 1721. He had practised at Bristol, before sailing from that port. Dover was appointed 'second captain', Captain of the Marines (in deference to his position as part owner) to Captain Woodes Rogers on the 320-ton *'Duke'*. He was also appointed to the important position of President of the Council, which had to approve all decisions relating to the expedition, and his share of the booty would be far higher than the officers sailing with him. The pilot of the Duke was the noted former double-circumnavigator William Dampier. Dover also paid a great proportion of the costs of the 260-ton *'Duchess'*, under Captain Stephen Courtney, to be fitted out for the South Seas. (There was a separate Council of ship's officers for the *Duchess*, in case the ships became separated, but as long as they stayed together Captain Rogers, Captain Dover or Captain Courtney could call a single Council at any time).

The apothecary Samuel Hopkins had married Dover's sister Mary, and Dover appointed Hopkins as his first lieutenant, and also to assist in any medical duties when required. William Hopkins, perhaps another kinsman, was appointed by Dover as his Sergeant of Marines. The *Duke* and *Duchess* sailed for the South Seas on August 2nd,

1708. Neither Samuel Hopkins nor Dover had knowledge of sailing, but Dover had firmly insisted upon having a command as he had part-funded the venture.

After rounding the Horn, they moored off Juan Fernandez Island on the night of February 1st, 1709, and noticed a light on the deserted island. They rescued Alexander Selkirk, the prototype of Robinson Crusoe, and sailed north to take a Spanish ship, which was renamed the *Bachelor*. Dover was given command of the prize, and sacked Guayaquil in April 1709. Many of his men contracted the plague, after sleeping in a church where some victims had been recently buried. Dover bled each of around 100 ounces of blood. Dover's description of events is worth repeating: *'When I took by storm the two cities of Guaiaquil, under the (Equatorial) line, in the South Seas, it happened that not long before the Plague had raged amongst them. For our better security, therefore, and keeping our people together, we lay in their churches; and likewise brought thither the plunder of the city. We were very much annoyed with the smell of dead bodies. These bodies could hardly be said to have been buried, for the Spaniards abroad use no coffins, but throw several dead bodies one upon another, with only a draw board over them; so 'tis no wonder we received the infection.*

In a very few days after we got on board, one of the Surgeons came it to acquaint me, that several of my men were taken after a violent manner, with that languor of spirits. I immediately went among them, and to my great surprise, discerned what was the matter. In less than 48 hours, we had in our ships, 180 men in this condition. I ordered the surgeons to bleed them in both arms and to go round to them all with command to leave them bleeding till all were blooded, and then come and tie them up in their turns. Thus they lay bleeding and fainting, so long, that I could not conceive they could lose less than an hundred ounces each man.

If we had lost so great a number of our people, the poor remains would infallibly have perished. Now if we had recourse to Alexipharmicks such as Venice Treacle, Diacodium, Mithridate and such like good-for-nothing compositions, or the most celebrated Gascoyn's powder, or Bezoar, I make no questions at all, considering the heat of the climate, but we had lost every man. 'Tis surprising that Physicians can read so many authors, and overlook the most reasonable rules of Mankind, and imbibe principles which, were it not for fear of giving offence, I should say were contrary to common-sense.'

Only eleven men died, *'an astonishing feat of mediicine'* on board the two little crowded ships, with only about 20 able-bodied men, and Dover's reputation in the crews rose immeasurably. However, the most serious loss was Dover's kinsman Samuel Hopkins, who had been treating the victims for days. The plague combined with his fatigue to kill him. Hopkins had read prayers every day to the crew, and was recorded by Dover as *'a very good-tempered sober man, and very well loved by the whole ship's company'*. He was the first man to die, and Roger's account reads *'May 15. At 6 last night Mr Samuel Hopkins, Dr Dover's Kinsman and Assistant, died.'* *'May 19, about 10 in the Morning James Daniel our Joiner died'*. *'Thomas Hughes, a very good sailor'* died on May 21st, *'Thomas Morgan, a Welsh land-man, died the 31st of May'*, and the last man died of plague on the 4th of June. The only men not affected by the plague were the twenty men mentioned above, who did not go ashore.

Water was running short, and the bread was full of worms, when the weakened crew fortunately reached the Island of Gorgona to careen and take on fresh water. Two prizes were ransomed. Dover next took the famous *Acapulco*, with booty worth millions in today's money. He brought it back to Bristol in October 1711, after he and Hopkins had circumnavigated the world with Rogers. Woodes Rogers wrote 'A *Cruising Voyage Around the World*' and went on to be a notable Governor in the Bahamas.

Dover now moved to London, practising at the Jerusalem Coffee-house in Cecil Street, Strand. He wrote a popular book for physicians, recommending strongly the use of mercury in ailments, for which reason he became known as 'The Quicksilver Doctor'. He invented 'Dover's Powder' which included opium, which was still popular as a cure in the 1920's in the UK. The powder was made as following: '*Take Opium one ounce, Salt-Petre and Tartar vitriolated, each four Ounces, Ipecacuana one Ounce. Put the Salt-Petre and Tartar into a red-hot Mortar, stirring them till they have done flaming - Then powder them very fine; and after that, slice your Opium; grind these to a Powder, and then mix the other Powders with these. Dose from 40 to 60 or 70 grains in a glass of white wine Poset (made by adding port or sherry to milk and curdling it) going to bed, covering up warm and drinking a quart or three pints of the Posset. Drink while sweating.*' Gosse noted that he died aged 82, '*having invented Dover's powders, commanded a company of marines, rescued Alexander Selkirk, written a most extraordinary medical book, and for having been a successful pirate captain.*'

Prescriptions in Dover's time included concoctions of '*blood, fat, bile, viscera, bones, claws, teeth, hoofs, horns; pig's dung, cat's urine; the sexual organs, eggs, and excreta of various animals, the more unusual the better; bee-glue, cocks' combs, fur, feathers, isinglass, human sweat and placenta, the saliva of a fasting man, the hair of a menstruating woman; sponge, sea-shell, raw silk, spiders' webs, snake skin, scorpions, swallows' nests, hedgehog spines, wood-lice - there was hardly any limit to the inventiveness shown ... Gascoyne's was a favourite powder, composed of bezoar, amber, pearls, crabs' eyes, coral, and black top of crab claw; and there were scores of others, of which Dover's alone survives - and deserved to survive. In 1739, Joanna Stevens' remedy for the (gall) stone was bought "pro bono publico" by Act of Parliament for £5000 - the ingredients, including egg-shell, garden snails, swines' excreta, soap, and vegetable matter such as burdock and hips and haws.*' (- from *Dr Quicksilver* by L.A.G. Strong)

CAPTAIN HENRY JENNINGS (see Black Sam Bellamy and Paulsgrave Williams) fl. 1714

According to Gosse, '*this Welsh pirate had been a man of good position, education, and property before he took to piracy, which he did for the love of the life and not from necessity.*'

In 1714, the Spanish treasure fleet carrying the Royal taxes back to Spain ran into a hurricane, and was run aground on the shallow reefs of Florida. While the Spanish were attempting salvage operations, Jennings attacked and robbed the poorly defended salvage divers. He then established his base in Nassau in New Providence, where he could elude the Spanish navy. The harbour had two entrances, making it difficult for a single man-of-war to '*bottle up*' the port. There was ample fresh water, fish, turtle and wild game. The island was positioned ideally between the westbound shipping lanes carrying needed provisions from Europe, and the eastbound lanes

IN HOLBORN
Over againſt *Fetter-lane*, at the ſign of the Laſt, liveth a Phyſitian that through Gods bleſſing, cureth theſe following diſeaſes with honeſt Expedition and Concionable reſpect to the PATIENTS ability.

The FRENCH POX (to the cure of which there are many Pretenders, but few Performers, he cureth with Speed and Secreſie, and ſo much eaſe, that they may follow their occaſions, and not the neareſt Relation take notice of the cure.

The ISSUE at the YARD, commonly called the *Gonorrhea*, or *Running of the Reines*, (not alwaies got by Women, as ſome think) he Cureth ſafely, and ſoundly, from future danger.

Conſumptions.	Pain in the Back or Limbs.
All ſorts of Feavers.	Stoppage in the Urins.
Pain in the Head and Stomack,	Kings Evill. Falling ſickneſſe.
Such as cannot hold their Water	Worms. Ruptures.
Stone in the Bladder or Kidneys.	Rheumatick Defluctions.
Convulſions. Rickets.	Yellow Jaundice.
Ptiſick, or ſhortnſſe of breath.	Cankers, Ciatica.
Red hair may be changed,	Looſeneſſe,
Gouts ſeveral ſorts.	Sore Fys, Freckles.
Wind Cholick.	Piles and Emrods.
Sore leggs or old Ulcers.	Obſtructions of Women
Dropſies, as Tinpany, &c.	Immoderate Fluxes, with many
Barrenneſſe. Abortiveneſſe.	others, ſome not convenient,
Old Surfeits. Agues.	bers too tedious to be here inſerted.
Sinewes ſprain'd.	

He is to be ſpoken with from Two till Six in the afternoon.

taking gold and silver to Europe. Jennings was soon joined by other pirate captains, and a community of 2000 soon formed, living on ships, and in tents and huts. A Captain Stone, who was taken by Jennings, noted that he treated him civilly and stated that he would not harm Englishmen. Jennings' crew restricted their looting to 20 gallons of rum, for which they paid him handsomely.

Held in high esteem by his fellows in the Bahamas, becoming the unofficial Mayor of Nassau, and he presided at the meeting in 1717 when pirates gathered to discuss King George's offer of a pardon in 1717 (see Appendix A). Jennings was reported to have offered the new Governor of the Bahamas, Woodes Rogers 10% of all profits on the island, instead of the normal 8%, for looking the other way, but Rogers could not be tempted. After much discussion, Jennings declared that he would take up the king's offer of pardon, and around 150 other pirates then followed him in declaring the same intention. On the new Governor's arrival from England they received pardon certificates, although Johnson reflected that most of them returned to their evil ways, 'like a Dog to the Vomit.' Jennings' main ally in accepting the pardon and working with Governor Rogers, was Captain Benjamin Hornigold, who had taught Blackbeard piracy, and who later sailed with Paulsgrave Williams and Sam Bellamy. Hornigold turned into a notable 'pirate-chaser'.

WILLIAM LEWIS d.1718
There is also a Captain Lewis in Johnson's General History of the Pyrates. William Lewis was a former prize-fighter who operated from New Providence in the Bahamas. When Woodes Rogers offered the King's Pardon in July 1718, he accepted it. Like Howell Davies, he was sent by Rogers to trade for food in October, and like Davies, he mutinied. Three sloops were commanded by John Auger, Henry White and William Greenway, all pardoned pirates. Two days out from New Providence, yet another pardoned pirate, Phineas Bunce, led the mutiny at anchor off Green Cay, assisted by Lewis. Auger needed no convincing to join them, but Greenway was forced. They stripped Captain White and seven other crew members naked and marooned them on Green Gay. Several times over the next few weeks the pirates visited the islet, beating up the men, until they were rescued seven weeks later.

The three sloops were comprehensively beaten in a fight with the Spanish costa-garda at Long Island. Captain Phineas Bunce was wounded in battle and captured, but died before he could be hanged. Auger and around 15 men escaped ashore, but were recaptured by Benjamin Hornigold.

Another ring-leader of the mutiny, and yet another former pardoned pirate, was Dennis McCarthy. Wishing to be hanged in style at New Providence, in front of his former colleagues in piracy, he put on clean linen, tied his cap, neck, wrists and knees with long blue ribbons, and stepped onto the scaffold. He kicked off his shoes, having sworn not to die with his boots on. Also showing no remorse at the gallows, William Lewis asked for alcohol to toast his fellow prisoners and the crown in 1718. Defoe records 'William Lewis, aged about 34 Years, as he had been a hardy Pyrate and Prize-Fighter, affected an Unconcern at Death; but heartily desired Liquors to drink with his Sufferers on the Stage, and with the Standers by.' And of another Welshman hung with Lewis he records 'Thomas Morris, aged about 22, had been a very incorrigible Youth and Pyrate, and seemed to have very little Anxiety of Mind by his frequent Smiles when at the Bar, being dressed with red ribbons as Macarthy was in blue, he said, going over the Ramparts, "We have a new Governor, but a harsh one", and a little before he was turned off, said aloud, that he might have been a greater Plague to these Islands, and now wished he had been so.'

Captain Hornigold is particularly noteworthy in that he was the captain of Edward Teach (Blackbeard). He gave Blackbeard a captured sloop, and they sailed in consort from New Providence. In 1717 they took six ships off the coast of the North American colonies, then returned to the Caribbean, capturing a huge French ship laden with gold and jewels. Blackbeard took his share of the booty and adopted the prize as his ship, while the wealthy Hornigold returned to new Providence. There, he not only accepted the King's pardon, but became friendly with the new Governor of the Bahamas, Woodes Rogers, from July 1718. Among other pirates he captured Auger and William Lewis, before being sent by Rogers to Mexico, where his ship foundered on a hidden reef in 1719.

Note:

There was also a James Lewis, who was taken prisoner by the French, escaped to Spain and joined Captain 'Long Ben' Avery to capture the *Charles the Second*. Tried at the Old Bailey, he was hung in 1696.

JAMES WILLIAMS d. 1725

Williams was on the *George* galley sailing out of Amsterdam in 1724. From Santa Cruz on the Barbary Coast, they took on a cargo of beeswax to Genoa. However, with the Scots second mate John Gow (alias Smith or Goffe) Williams conspired among the crew to mutiny. After they left Genoa on November 3rd, 1724. Captain Ferneau of Guernsey, the chief mate and the surgeon were killed at night.

Gow was elected Captain and Williams chief mate, as the men decided to '*go on the account.*' The *George* was renamed the *Revenge*, armed with 18 guns, and an English sloop under Captain Thomas Wise was taken off the Spanish coast, filled with fish from the Newfoundland banks. Another prize, a Glasgow ship with a cargo of herrings and salmon was next taken. In Madeira, Gow presented the Governor with a box of Scotch herrings. A large French ship was next spotted, but Gow refused to chase and attack it. Williams accused Gow of cowardice, and fired his pistol into Gow's face in the ensuing argument, but it failed to go off. Two of Gow's pirates then shot Williams, severely wounding him in the arm and stomach. The next day, Captain Gow released some prisoners in an old sloop, manacling Williams and throwing him into the hold. The released captives were told to give Williams up as a pirate to the first English man-of-war they encountered. At Lisbon he was put on board HMS *Argyle* and taken to London.

Gow now sailed to the Orkneys to traffic in his stolen goods, but 11 men deserted. One bought a horse for three pieces-of-eight and rode to Kirkwall to surrender, and the other ten were taken prisoner near Edinburgh. After plundering the countryside, Gow ran the *Revenge* on rocks off the Isle of Eda, and his crew were captured. Gow and his crew were taken in chains to the Marchalsea prison, where they found Williams already incarcerated. Two attempts were made to hang Gow. On the same day, June 11th 1725, Williams was hanged at Newgate, and his body hung in chains at Blackwall Dock alongside that of his enemy Captain Gow.

CAPTAIN ROBERT JENKINS fl. 1731-38

The War of Jenkin's Ear (which merged into the War of the Austrian Succession, when France joined Spanish forces in 1744) was the result, amongst other things, of a minor confrontation between Spanish Guarda Costas and the Welsh Captain and crew of the Glasgow brig '*Rebecca*' in 1731. Captain Robert Jenkins claimed that, whilst in the Caribbean, his ship had been boarded by the Guarda Costa and his crew maltreated, and that the Spaniards had then cut off one of his ears. Additionally, he claimed he was tortured and threatened with death. Jenkins had relieved a Spanish salvage party of treasure that they were bringing up from a wrecked Spanish galleon. The guarda costa stopped British vessels, against the Treaty of Utrecht, because their trade laws prohibited British commerce with Spanish colonies. Although the incident occurred in 1731, it was only bought before Parliament in 1738, at a time when it was investigating Spanish depredations in the Caribbean. The situation in the Caribbean had been thought serious enough that four ships and two sloops had previously been despatched to the Caribbean to protect British commerce there. In 1738 Parliament was trying to ascertain the number of ships that had been taken by the Spanish.

Whether Jenkin's claims were true was by no means certain, but it was true that he had had part of his ear cut off, and his story was received with universal indignation. He told Parliament that the Spanish captain had given him back his ear, with the message that he would do exactly the same to the English King if he had the chance. Great Britain, aroused by the tales of mistreatment of her merchant seamen (notably the display by Robert Jenkins of his shrivelled ear to Parliament) and other hostile acts, declared war on Spain (19 Oct. 1739). Robert Walpole's declaration of war "*was received by all ranks and distinctions of men with a degree of enthusiasm and joy, which announced the general frenzy of the nation.*" There were no major actions fought during this war, although the declaration of war led to the despatch of Admiral Anson's squadron to attack the coast of South America, and Admiral Edward Vernon's fleet attacked Spanish territory in the Caribbean.

Basically, the war was one of commercial rivalry between England and Spain. By the Treaty of Utrecht (1713), which ended Queen Anne's War, Britain was allowed to participate in slave traffic with the Spanish colonies. A special Spanish fleet, however, interfered with this activity and the Spanish also objected to the English logwooders operating on the coast of Honduras. The other cause of the war was the continued dispute over the boundary of Spanish Florida in relation to Georgia. As soon as war was declared, Gov. James Edward Oglethorpe called on the citizens of Georgia and South Carolina to join in an invasion of Florida. The Spanish retaliated by attempting to invade those colonies by sea. The War of Jenkins' Ear (1739-1742) continued with an invasion of Florida led by Oglethope. He was protected on the west from the French by friendly Creek, Cherokee and Chickasaw Indians. He captured forts San Francisco de Pupo and Picolata on the San Juan River. From May to July he besieged St. Augustine, but broke off the attack when his rear guard was threatened by the Spanish. In the Battle of Bloody Marsh on St. Simons Island, one of the Sea Islands off the south-east coast of Georgia, the Spanish attacked Fort Frederica, which had been constructed by Oglethorpe in 1736 to protect the colony. The Spanish were repulsed in a bloody battle that was a decisive engagement of *The War of Jenkins' Ear*.

CHRISTOPHER BASSETT d. 1760

This Bonvilston man was related to the Bassetts of Old Beaupre castle, and around 1760 was given letters of marque to go privateering. In his brief career, he collected as much as £10,000 for one of his 'prizes'. He built a folly on The Gaer, at Bonvilston, with part of the proceeds.

LIEUTENANT PAUL LEWIS fl. 1763

While not strictly a pirate, rather a naval lieutenant turned highwayman, his story is of interest as his father was a Welsh clergyman, and the following description comes from 'The Complete Newgate Calendar' Volume IV, regarding his hanging at Tyburn upon May 4th, 1763:

'PAUL LEWIS was born at Hurstmonceaux in Sussex, and was the son of a worthy clergyman, who put him into a grammar school at a very early age. He had an ambition to become a fine gentleman. In his spirited attempts to attain that character he ran into debt with his tailor, to the amount of £150, which obliged him to run away and go to sea. There he had for some time behaved so well that he was made first a cadet, then a midshipman, and finally, a lieutenant in the Royal Navy.

He was at the taking of Senegal, the burning of the ships in Cancale Bay, the reduction of Cherbourg, the Battle of St Cas, the siege of Guadeloupe, and the engagement under Sir Edward Hawke, in all of which services he behaved with courage and activity. He had vices, however, not common to bravery, and very different from the irregular sallies of a high-spirited and strong passion. Paul was not only wicked but base, not only a robber but a scoundrel, of which he gave proofs while on board the fleet, particularly by collecting three guineas apiece from many of his brother officers, to lay in stores for a West India voyage, and then running away with the collection and commencing as a highwayman.

Having thus begun his iniquitous course of life, he went to a public-house in Southwark, stayed a great part of the day, and supped; and then, going to an inn, hired a horse, rode out between Newington Butts and Vauxhall, and stopped a gentleman and his son in a post-chaise and robbed them, returning to the public-house in Southwark. Being apprehended for this offence, he was brought to trial at Kingston, when, the people of the public-house swearing that he had not been absent from noon till midnight more than half-an-hour, he was acquitted.

After this he committed a variety of robberies. An accomplice and he having robbed a gentleman and lady in a post-chaise, near Paddington, the robbers rode some miles together and then agreed to part, to commit their depredations separately. Not long had they parted when Lewis stopped a gentleman, named Brown, and demanded his money. Mr Brown resisted the highwayman with such determined resolution that Lewis fired at him, but, happily, without effect.

At this juncture Mr Brown's horse took fright and threw him, but being little injured he soon recovered, and saw Lewis in the custody of Mr Pope, a constable, who had got him down and was kneeling on his breast - a circumstance that arose from the following accident. Mr Pope, riding on the same road, met a gentleman and lady who told him they had been robbed by two highwaymen, and desired him to be cautious, and he arrived at the critical spot a short time after the robbery was committed, and seized Lewis.

Pope desired Mr Brown to ride after the other highwayman who had been on the road, but at this instant Lewis rose, and, presenting a pistol, swore he would shoot Pope. The latter, however, was in no degree intimidated, but, knocking the pistol out of his hand, threw him down and secured him. The highwayman was conveyed to New Prison, where, having lain one night, he was taken before a magistrate, who committed him to Newgate. At an ensuing sessions at the Old Bailey he was brought to trial, and received sentence of death.

Such was the baseness and unfeeling profligacy of this wretch that when his almost heart-broken father visited him for the last time, in Newgate, and put 12 guineas into his hands, to defray is expenses, he slipped one of the pieces of gold into the cuff of his sleeve, by a dextrous sleight, and then opening his hand showed the venerable and reverend old man that there were but eleven, upon which he took from his pocket another and gave it to him, to make up the number he intended.

Arriving at Tyburn, he looked round him with a face of inexpressible anguish, and then addressed himself to the crowd in the following terms - "This dreadful sight will not, I believe, invite any of you to come here, by following my example; but rather to be warned by me. I am but 23 years of age, a clergyman's son, bred up among gentlemen - this wounds me the deeper; for to whom much is given, of them more is required."

THOMAS KNIGHT fl. 1783

A 1734 letter from local customs officers to the London authorities reads: 'At Aberthaw and Barry when any boat goes out to em from thence, the Owners of em have always a Spye on the officer; and when they find him on one side of the River of Aberthaw, they'll land what they have of the other; and by reason there's no Boat in the Service, not any boat on those acco'ts to be had for love or money, and the Officer obliged to go to a bridge *about two Miles round, they have time enough to secure the goods before he can get there. Nay, there is instances that they have run'd goods in the day time before the officers face in this Manner. At Barry tis the same case; if they find the officer on the Iseland they'll land the other side of the harbour. If the other Side of the harbour, they'll land on the Iseland, and the officers can't get over till the Tide is out, wich may be five or six hours; and there is so much Cover on the Iseland, and such conveniencys for hiding of goods the other side, that an Officer has but a poor Chance to meet with em after they are landed.'*

Until 1743, Customs Officers were unarmed, and always under-resourced to cope with desperate smugglers, who knew that capture was execution. As a result, many officials took the easy option and supplemented their meagre wages by accepting bribes. After 1743, however, we see continuous requests for decent boats to make reasonable patrols in coastal waters. On February 3, 1764, two Customs men were drowned when their boat returned from inspecting Flat and Steep Holm islands. There was also a case in 1773 when the local customs boat was in too poor a condition to police the activities on Flat Holm, and the King's officers refused to go out in rough seas.

In 1783, Thomas Knight moved from Lundy to make Barry Island his base for smuggling. He had a brig with 40 men and 24 cannon. The local Customs Officer, or *'searcher'* was Thomas Hopkins of Sully, who was absolutely powerless to control Knight's activities, but with reinforcements managed to push him back to Lundy around 1787. However, a Captain Arthur, even more of a rogue that Knight, then occupied Barry Island, and two expeditions were needed in 1788 to force him off the Island. The last use of the island as a smugglers' retreat seems to have been in 1791 when a crew operated the *'John of Combe'* from there.

O'NEILL

Until the 1850's, May 3rd saw the great event of *Llanilltud Festival*. It commemorated the date that the great pirate O'Neill attacked the town. The townspeople planned carefully to deal with his next attack, and hid in the gorse on both sides of the Col-huw valley as he approached the town. They then poured down the hills cutting off his retreat and in the melée several villagers, pirates and O'Neill himself were killed. His body was buried on the hillside there on the 3rd of May, and it became the town's holiday, *Annwyl Day* for centuries.

Each May 3rd *attackers* and *defenders* were selected from the neighbouring Boverton, Llanilltud and St Donats. Tents were placed in Colhuw valley and the 'pirates' would approach up the valley, to be beaten and captured by the defenders. The young men of Boverton and St Donats on horseback would lead the captured men and a great effigy of O'Neill, which was then burnt. The 'pirates', with blackened faces and eye-patches, would be led as prisoners through the town to the Court of Justice. There were sporting contests, dancing and singing, but the custom died out around 1850, the same time as the remarkable St Illtud's Feast Day celebrations – both should be revived.

CHAPTER III

CAPTAIN HENRY MORGAN (1635-1688) 'THE SWORD OF ENGLAND', 'THE GREATEST OF ALL THE BRETHREN OF THE COAST'

'Ho! Henry Morgan sails today
To harry the Spanish Main.
What a pretty bill for the Dons to pay,
Ere he comes back again.

Him cheat him friend of him last guinea
Him kill both friar and priest – O dear !
Him cut de t'roat of piccaninny,
Bloody, bloody buccaneer !'
-old West Indian ballad

Morgan as a young man

George Wycherley wrote 'Buccaneers of the Pacific' in 1924, praising the valiant exploits of buccaneers such as Drake, Dampier, Sharpe and Cooke. However, the Welsh Sir Henry Morgan, Governor of Jamaica, was called a 'murderous monster', a 'depraved, vicious, treacherous, almost unparalleled human brute, who was born of respectable people in Wales but deliberately chose the most evil life in his vicious age'. He was involved in 'shocking scenes of cruelty, torture, rape, murder, arson and every conceivable deviltry (sic) that he and his fellow-fiends could devise'. Thus Morgan was on a par with Pol Pot, Stalin and Hitler. Wycherley took all his facts from Esquemeling, a disaffected Dutchman who sailed under Morgan, and wrote of the events to please the enemies of Britain in Holland and Spain.

Henry was the eldest son of Robert Morgan of Llanrhymney. Llanrhymney (Llanrumney in the Anglicised version) was formerly in Monmouthshire, but is now on the outskirts of Cardiff, with the tidal river Rhymney forming an estuary. There is another Llanrhymney near Tredegar in Gwent. Both claim Henry as their son. The manor of Llanrhymney was in the ancient Hundred of Newport, and was the property of the Kemeys family before an heiress married a Morgan in the 16th century. Morgan's appearance in the West Indies is still shrouded in mystery. Even his birth is unclear. Morgans also lived at Pencarn near Newport and claimed him as an ancestor. They were descended from the 12th century Owen, son of the Lord of Caerleon. Thomas Morgan of Pencarn was known as 'the warrior' after commanding English forces overseas in the 1580's and 1590's. Thomas's nephew, Sir Matthew Morgan, was wounded at the Siege of Rouen in 1591. Sir Charles Morgan was a Privy Councillor for Charles I. And of course, the Morgan family held the great Tredegar House, just on the outskirts of Newport on the road to Cardiff. To make matters more obscure Morgan called one of his Jamaican plantations Llanrumney and the other Penkarne. He was remarkably touchy about his early history, suing the publishers of Esquemeling's book on buccaneers. This was the first recorded successful libel action in history. After the successful action in 1684, the English publishers had to add this rider to future editions: *'John Esquemeling hath mistaken the Origin of Sir Henry Morgan, for he was a Gentleman's Son of good Quality, in the County of Monmouth, and was never a Servant unto anybody in his life, unless unto his Majesty, the late King of England.'* One of Henry's uncles was Lieutenant-Colonel Edward Morgan, noted above, and another was Thomas Morgan, second-in-command to General Monck, and who became Governor of Jersey.

Most histories record that Morgan went as an indentured servant to Barbados, sailing on May 3rd, 1655, where he served his full seven years, before obtaining his freedom in 1662, and he then moved on to Tortuga before settling in Jamaica. The story prevalent in his lifetime was that he had been captured in Bristol and sold as a servant in Barbados. Esquemeling had a variant of this in that he had been sold by his parents as a boy to serve as a labourer in Barbados. He certainly was in Barbados before he appears in history in Jamaica. It seems that Esquemeling's popularity has obscured the facts. There was a *'Henry Morgan'* indentured in Bristol to sail to Barbados in 1655, but it was a rather common name in south-east Wales. (Cae-Paen field between Llandaff and Peterston was owned by a Henry Morgan in 1612). Morgan was far more likely a junior officer in an expedition sent to the West Indies by Oliver Cromwell under the incompetent General Venables. Yet another tale tells us that he was kidnapped as a boy in Bristol (this was a common occurrence), taken to Barbados and deserted his 'owner' when the Penn-Venables fleet reached there, recruiting for the attack on Hispaniola. Morgan had arrived in Barbados in 1655, aged around 20. The naval commander was the Welshman Vice-Admiral Penn, whose eldest son founded Pennsylvania and somewhat treacherously refused the Welsh settlers there an independent colony. The expedition of Penn and Venables (which left in 1654) was meant to capture Hispaniola from the Spanish, and nearly 7000 men landed at Santo Domingo on the south side of the island. Disease and incompetent leadership forced the army to withdraw.

The poorly-defended Jamaica was instead captured, in an otherwise poor campaign, and Morgan stayed there. Leslie, the earliest historian of Jamaica, noted soon after Morgan's death, that at this time Morgan *'saw the excess and debauchery of his Fellows, and that they became reduced to the lowest shifts by their lavish Expenses on their Arrival (in Jamaica), he, having Vast Designs in View, lived moderate and got together as much money as purchased a Vessel for himself; and having a fine Crew, put to Sea.'* Morgan spent the next few years taking part in successful attacks from the new British base in Jamaica, on Spanish towns in South America. Records show that Morgan was in at least two of the successful attacks led by Sir Christopher Myngs, being a ship's captain given commissions by Jamaica's new governor. There was an official 'cessation of hostilities' with Spain from 1658. However, the Spanish still captured British ships in the West Indies, and treated their crews as pirates. Thus it was an 'anything goes' situation off the Spanish Main and in the Caribbean, whereby the peace did not hold. The privateers of the time pleaded ignorance of any peace between the two countries.

SANTIAGO DEL HISPANIOLA 1659
Governor Elias Watts of Tortuga gave a commission to a party of four hundred seamen to sack Santiago in 1659, in exchange for a share of the plunder. They divided themselves up into four parties of a hundred men, with a captain appointed at the head of each. Henry Morgan was one of the men, who commandeered a French frigate from Nantes. The ship was so overcrowded, that the privateers took another two smaller boats on the way to Hispaniola, and landed at Puerta de Plata on Palm Sunday.

By Wednesday, hacking through forests, the force had reached their objective, St Jago (Santiago) in the island's centre. Just before dawn they attacked and the Governor offered a ransom of 60,000 pieces of eight to spare his life. For a day they looted the town, and on Thursday started back for the ships with the Governor, their captives, and all the loot they could carry. However, a force of a thousand Spaniards had been assembled and it cut off the buccaneer's retreat. Skirmishing was stopped by the threat to stab the Governor, and the buccaneers repeated their demand for his ransom. They boarded their ships unopposed, but freed all the captives without the ransoms, as all who took part made around three-hundred crowns each.

1660
With Cromwell's death and the restoration of the monarchy, the Royalist Edward Morgan was rewarded with the post of Lieutenant-Governor of Jamaica. Henry Morgan was becoming famous in his adventures in Jamaica, and began courting the eldest daughter of Edward, Mary Elizabeth. Edward was Henry's uncle, which again tells us that Henry came from a nobler background than his enemies described. Two of Henry's most trusted lieutenants and friends later married the sisters of Mary Elizabeth Morgan.

SANTIAGO DEL CUBA, CUBA 1662
There was peace between Britain and Spain from 1660, but the Council of Jamaica decided that it applied only to Europe. In 1662 Jamaica was under threat of attack by the Spanish of Cuba. Upon September 12th, the minutes of the Council proposed 'that men be enlisted for a design by sea with the "Centurion" and other vessels.' This 'design' was a buccaneering expedition to destroy St. Jago de Cuba (Santiago del Cuba), the nearest Spanish possession to Jamaica. It was seen as the focal point for the forthcoming Spanish invasion. Jamaica was surrounded by Cuba, Hispaniola, Mexico, Florida (also a Spanish possession) and the Spanish Main of South and Central America. Jamaica was the only British possession, with Barbados, in this vast area.

Morgan served as captain of his own small privateer under Captain (later Admiral) Myngs, who decided to assault the town and harbour with a fleet of eleven ships and thirteen hundred men. They sighted the castle of St. Jago on October 5th, but could not sail into the harbour because of the prevailing winds. The buccaneers landed in the dusk, with the men carrying fire-brands to see in front of them, to slash through the dense forests. By dawn they had covered just six miles, and were three miles from the fort. After breakfasting, they moved on to surprise the defenders, who had not expected that they could make such quick progress through the jungle. Only two hundred Spaniards, led by Governor Don Pedro de Moralis, defended the town entrance. They were supported by a five-hundred man reserve under Don Christopher de Sasi Arnoldo (-the unfortunate Governor who had lost Jamaica to the English in 1655). The buccaneers charged, and the Spanish fled.

The privateers (under a letter of marque from Lord Windsor, Jamaica's governor) took the famous citadel, El Morro. They demolished the town and fortress, and the fleet returned with vast booty to Jamaica. Some of the thirty-four guns were taken back to Jamaica, and the others thrown into the ocean. Six buccaneers were killed and twenty went missing. Some had been captured and sent to rot in Seville and Cadiz prisons in Spain, but were released in exchange for Spanish captives in November 1664.

CAMPEACHY (CAMPEACHE) 1663
Morgan then captained a ship under Myngs when he destroyed the town of Campeache on the Spanish Main (on the Mexican Coast). Twelve ships with around sixteen hundred soldiers were sent by the Council of Jamaica on January 9th and 10th to harry Cuba, Honduras and the Gulf of Campeache. After sailing a thousand miles, just ninety leagues from Campeache, a huge storm caused one ship to sink and another three to become separated from the fleet. However, on February 9th the remaining ships landed their men a mile or so from the city. The buccaneers used a hidden path shown to them by native Indians, and quickly took the city and all its forts except Santa Cruz. Myngs was wounded in three places by gunfire, as his force plundered and demolished what they could, including fourteen ships lying in the harbour. Thirty buccaneers were killed in a day of fighting. The Spanish counted their losses as 150,000 pieces of eight, and the damage done to the town and forts as costing another 500,000 to repair

Myngs left the Gulf of Campeache with the fleet on February 23rd, but did not return with the 'Centurion' to Port Royal until April 13th. The other ships came in a few days later. It appears that the fleet spent some days sharing out and disposing of booty rather than bring it back to Jamaica for the English royal family and assorted ship-owners to take their commission. Morgan now sailed out of Port Royal, flushed with success, with four other captains, and was not to return for almost two years.

1664
Henry's uncle, Colonel Sir Edward Morgan was appointed Deputy-Governor of Jamaica. Bledri Morgan, a distant cousin of Henry's, had come out also around 1662, and acted as one of Henry's lieutenants. Henry later married one of Colonel Morgan's daughters, Mary Elizabeth in 1666.

According to Edward Long's 'History of Jamaica', published in 1774, Henry cruised around Cartagena attacking shipping in 1664, and the minutes of the Executive

Council of Jamaica show a Captain Thomas Morgan raiding Central America, which must have been Henry. The small fleet had rounded the Yucatan Peninsula to the Gulf of Mexico. Landing at Frontera, they pirates marched 50 miles inland to sack Villahermosa. However, in their absence, their ships had been taken by the Spanish, so they had to capture two small Spanish boats and four coastal canoes to reach safety. They sailed and paddled against adverse currents for 500 miles to return around the Yucatan Peninsula and carry on raiding the coast of Central America. They took a rich town called Granada in what is now Nicaragua, in a surprise raid. The official report stated that more than a thousand Indians *'joined the privateers in plundering and would have killed the (Spanish) prisoners, especially the churchmen.'* Morgan returned a hero, with great riches to Port Royal. These events are recounted in more detail later in the text.

1665

Myngs was recalled with his royal men-of-war to England in 1665 because of the threat of war with Holland. Sir Thomas Modyford, the Governor of Jamaica was now forced to rely on privateers from Jamaica, Tortuga and Hispaniola for the defence of the island against Spain. Instead of operating under French letters of marque, these buccaneers now brought their spoils to dispose in Jamaica. King Charles II took a fifteenth of all proceeds, and the Duke of York as Lord High Admiral took a tenth, so the privateering was unofficially approved by the British Crown.

An official expedition this year sailed to the Dutch West Indies, as the English had declared war on the Dutch. Governor Modyford put the force of 650 men (mainly 'reformed prisoners' according to Modyford) and ten ships under Colonel Sir Edward Morgan. Lieutenant-Colonel Thomas Morgan, a distant relative from the great Tredegar House at Newport, was second-in-command. Modyford's plan was that the privateers destroyed the Dutch fleet trading at St Kitts, capture St Eustatius (St Kitts), Saba and Curacao, and on the homeward leg of the voyage rout the French settlements on Hispaniola and Tortuga. Just after the fleet sailed, Admiral De Ruyter with 14 ships attacked shipping at Barbados, and captured 16 merchant ships at Montserrat and Nevis.

Morgan's buccaneers proved troublesome, and had mutinied before their departure from Jamaica, refusing to sail until Morgan promised them an equal share of the plunder. After three months, the fleet attacked the tiny island of St Eustasius, east of the Virgin Islands, on April 23rd. Edward Morgan leaped out of a landing boat, ran up the beach towards the 450 defenders in the Dutch fort, and suffered a fatal heart attack. He was sixty years old and extremely corpulent. Thomas Morgan was shot in both legs, but the island was pillaged with very little plunder being found. Colonel Carey took command after the fort was taken and the governor surrendered. There were massive arguments over the sharing of the booty of 900 negro and Indian slaves, guns, livestock and cotton. Another party of 70 buccaneers crossed over to the island of Saba, only 4 leagues away, and secured its surrender also. The fleet returned in some disgrace to Port Royal, as the men were now again in a mutinous state, and could not be trusted to proceed to Curacao.

VILLA DE MOSA, HONDURAS, and GRANADA, NICARAGUA 1665

Somehow Henry Morgan was missing from the invasion fiasco of his uncle. He had been asked to organise Jamaica's militia and defences against the threat of Spanish invasion, and had then sailed in late 1663 on a 22-month voyage. Henry Morgan had

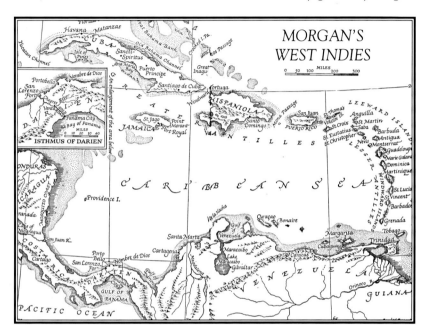

joined his fellow Welshman, Captain John Morris, and with Captain Jackman they sailed towards the peninsula of Campeache in Central America. Morgan wanted to fortify some islets as a preparation for sending for reinforcements and invading Mexico. However, Jackman and Morris were more short-termist in their thinking. They wanted plunder, and they wanted it immediately. Thus the little fleet sailed south and anchored in the mouth of the River Tabasco on the Gulf of Mexico, and a group of Indians offered to help them fight the hated Spaniards. Just 107 buccaneers landed, and the Indians guided them to Villa de Mosa (Vildemos), twelve leagues (almost 40 miles) inland. The town, mainly a trading station for cocoa, was undefended, and the invaders spent their time trying to find worthwhile valuables to plunder. The Spanish had left the town to set up an ambush for the privateers at the mouth of the river. Some 300 Spanish troops were eventually defeated by the better musketry of Morgan's men.

They then sacked the small fort and market at Rio Garta, near Belize, with just thirty men. The fleet then rounded the Yucatan Peninsula, and crossed the Bay of Honduras. Camping on Ruatan in the Bay Islands, they took on fresh water, and Morgan encouraged some men to stay there as settlers. An English patois is still spoken in Ruatan, where the main village is called Port Royal. Refreshed, Morgan,

Morris and Jackman now landed on the mainland to take Truxillo port. They harried the length of the Mosquito Coast, aided by local Indians. The privateers then sailed down to Nicaragua, anchoring at the entrance of the San Juan river. Indians told them that there were navigable lakes beyond, with the great city of Granada beyond them. One hundred buccaneers now rowed canoes to capture this fabled city of Granada. They were piloted by Indians, hiding in the islets on the river then on Lake Nicaragua by day, and rowing at night. The Indians were subject to a regime of controlled genocide by the Spanish, much like that practised by the French on the native Carib Indians in the West Indies. After five nights, Morgan was ready to attack this century-old settlement, with its seven churches and monasteries, and two colleges. The buccaneers reached the central plaza at dead of night, and overturned the 18 cannon they found there, and quickly took over the barracks and powder magazine. Three hundred inhabitants were herded as prisoners into the Cathedral. Another 3000 fled. For almost a day the buccaneers looted gold and silver plate, coins and jewels, more than they or their Indian helpers could carry. They sank all the Spanish boats, and were just about to set the Spanish free from the Cathedral before fleeing, when the Indians intervened. They wished to kill all the Spanish prisoners, especially the religious men among them. The pirate captains demurred. They told the Indians that the English did not intend ruling here, and that the Spanish vengeance would be terrible on their tribes, and the Indians reluctantly agreed to let them go.

This was a fabulous adventure, little recounted in history books, and rivalled Drake's exploits. It was the most audacious buccaneering adventure ever known in the West Indies. The crews were cheered back into Port Royal, but the captains were called before the Governor. Quizzed by Modyford, two of the captains produced obsolete letters of commission signed by Windsor back in 1662 before Modyford replaced him as Governor. On hearing of the booty, Modyford diplomatically wrote back to London that Central America was 'the properest place' to attack the Spanish. He gave his immediate approval to another expedition under Edward Mansvelt of Dutch Curacao, supported by Morgan. A soon as he knew of the St Eustatius fiasco, Modyford had persuaded the king to let him send for the reliable Mansvelt, and gave him the title of Admiral of the Brethren of the Coast, asking him to attack the Dutch, with the main target being the wealthy port of Curacao. Modyford had now been allowed to issue Letters of Marque, because of continued requests to England from the Council of Jamaica. Previously, Mansvelt had sailed under Portuguese privateering commissions. Mansvelt had already plundered Granada in Nicaragua, and Santo Spirito in Cuba and was the acknowledged *Commander of The Brethren of the Coast*.

1666 SANTA CATALINA, OLD PROVIDENCE (now Vieja Providencia, belonging to Colombia).

Morgan captained a ship under Admiral Mansvelt, and was made Vice-Admiral because of his attack on Granada. It appears that Morgan had assumed the leadership over Morris and Jackman in Nicaragua. Morgan was just thirty years old. In January 1666, Mansvelt waited in the cays off southern Cuba, for some of the harder types of buccaneer to join him. These men did not trust to land in Port Royal, such had been their crimes. Mansvelt then took the fleet of fifteen sail to Curacao, but lingered before pulling away. Perhaps he could not attack his own countrymen in the Dutch colony, and instead he took the small Spanish island of Santa Catalina, known as Old Providence, two-thirds of the way from Jamaica to the Isthmus of Panama. It appears that Mansvelt now left to try to repeat the exploits of Morgan, Jackman and Morris, once Santa Catalina had been occupied. Morgan went straight back to Jamaica, where Governor Modyford congratulated him, and Modyford's brother was appointed the new Governor of Santa Catalina in 1666.

1667

Mansvelt returned to Port Royal, but was welcomed with restraint by Modyford, who seemed to accept that Mansvelt was due to be replaced by Morgan in the esteem of the buccaneers. Mansvelt sailed on to Tortuga, where he suddenly disappeared. Authorities differ whether he was poisoned, or captured by the Spanish and tortured to death. The Spanish from Panama soon retook Santa Catalina, the vital line of communication between Jamaica and the mainland. Its English and French colonists were tortured, and the survivors were sent to work in mines on the Spanish Main. Morgan wrote to merchants and landholders in New England and Virginia, canvassing their support to retake the island. He wanted them to lobby Governor Modyford of Jamaica to give him a roving commission to attack the Spanish. However, Modyford was torn between his desire for a share of the plunder, and the fact that the previous Mansvelt expedition had been an official venture against a warring enemy, despite the fact that he attacked the wrong target and nationality. Unlike other privateers, living for the present, Morgan seems to have had a long-term vision of British control of the Caribbean – wherever he went, he wanted to settle. With the retaking of Santa Catalina by Don Juan Perez de Guzman, Governor of Panama, in 1667, Morgan seems to have decided that there were several keys to permanently wresting sovereignty from the Spanish. They were Old Providence (Santa Catalina), Panama City, Havana, Cartagena, Porto Bello, Maracaibo and Vera Cruz.

W. Adolphe Roberts described the importance of these targets. Old Providence was a small and fertile outpost near the Spanish Main, with plenty of water, which Morgan had already tried to settle. Havana in Cuba was the rendezvous for the galleons of the '*flota*' from all over the Spanish Main, before it returned on the annual voyage of the treasure-ships to Spain. Panama City is still the vital link between the Caribbean and the Pacific. Peruvian gold was taken up the Pacific coast to Panama, where it was unloaded and taken across the Isthmus of Panama by guarded mule-trains, to be shipped from Porto Bello to Seville via Havana. All of Mexico's loot came through Vera Cruz. Colombia and Venezuelan gold was shipped from Cartagena and Maracaibo.

1668

The thirty-three year old Morgan was now elected Admiral-in-Chief of the Confederacy of Buccaneers with the news of Mansvelt's disappearance and probable death. Gosse (1924) made the point that Morgan was '*a brilliant public speaker*', able to swing opinion of his pirate captains, a skill that served him well against political opponents in later life. Governor Modyford gave him an Admiral's commission in January, at the capital of Jamaica, St Jago, just twelve miles inland from Morgan's usual haunt of Port Royal. Immediately, Morgan sought out his Welsh colleague, John Morris. He found two French pirates with information upon Cuba. The pirates had sailed in a sloop from Tortuga, and cruised along forty miles of Cuban coastline. On this unsuccessful voyage, however, they had news of the size and disposition of the Spanish fleet, which was based at St Jago de Cuba (Santiago).The Frenchmen also told him that John Morris' barque had been sighted returning to Port Royal, after months at sea.

Morris returned with just a few captives and slaves, some rum and sugar, and a few bolts of cloth. The older buccaneer had not had a successful voyage. After unloading, Morgan approached Morris. His men only made about a hundred pieces of eight, each, with Morris receiving a few hundred, and Morgan taking a commission of another few hundred as Admiral of the Brethren. Morris told Admiral Morgan that he had left a fleet of privateers around the Cuban cays, five Tortuga-French and five English ships in total. Morris also told him of the increasing strength of the Spanish forces in the area around Cuba. That night in one of the bordellos, Morris is claimed to be the pirate who gave 500 pieces of eight, all his prize money, just to see a prostitute strip naked in front of his drunken men. The going rate at the time to spend a night with a white harlot was around 50 pieces of eight, and twenty for a negress.

If the author may digress here, there is a wonderful Rabelaisian description of this event in W. Adolphe Roberts' 1935 book 'Sir Henry Morgan': 'The barque which had just arrived was of about 100 tons, with a high poop and gunwales scooped to within a few feet of the water. She had sheered up against the beach, and planks were being laid to the serried piles which served as a dock. Being less ponderous than the boats noted by the observer Richard Blome, she was not forced to unload with 'planks a Float.' Her deck was crowded with men in cotton trousers and ragged shirts, their heads swathed in handkerchiefs that lacked the natty appearance of Morgan's red bandana.... These were the corsairs, among whom - in war attire - it was difficult to distinguish the officers from the crew.

Their prisoners, however, stood out vividly: a couple of livid-faced Spanish officers in rich silk costumes, lashed for pictorial effect with their backs to a mast; but, significantly, no Spaniards of lesser rank. Half a dozen male Negro slaves in chains. Twice that number of young Negresses, stark naked and strutting freely among their new masters. At the sight of the women, a howl of glee went up from the beach. There were shouts to send them ashore first, at which suggestion the followers of John Morris roared in hearty derision.

A diversity of trade goods were brought up from the hold, rushed across the planks and piled on the sand. The haul in this respect had not been important. There were bags of sugar, kegs of rum, bales of leaf tobacco and a few bolts of cloth, for which the usurious Port Royal merchants might be willing to pay 300 pieces of eight, the piece of eight being almost the exact equivalent of our dollar. It was clearly the booty of a single ship, and not a treasure galleon at that. The slaves and women, nevertheless, would fetch a pretty price.

Morgan took it all in, chuckling appreciatively. The black wenches filled his eye, and he was glad to see the two Spanish prisoners. Information that he wanted might be screwed out of them, though Modyford was so damned squeamish that physical torture was not to be thought of on Jamaican soil. He had long since made out his friend Morris in the throng, and as chief of the Confederacy he could have gone aboard to talk to him. But Morris was up to his gullet in work, and the High Admiral was contented to wait.

Before the cargo had been half unloaded, the swift tropical night came down like an eclipse. Lanterns were hung along the sides of the barque, and placed here and there on the round, flat tops of the piles... The job was finished at last, and Morris swaggered ashore, the nude Negresses walking behind him, their haunches swinging and their hard breasts puffed out. A squad of men on either side guarded them from the clutching hands of the crowd. At the end of the procession stumbled the male slaves in chains.

It now grew evident why the skipper had made such haste with the unloading, instead of waiting till the next morning. He wanted to cash in immediately the spoils. Competing merchants and brokers rushed up to him, and turned his head unused to figures with their jumbled estimates on this and that. In less than ten minutes, he had accepted a shamefully low figure for the trade goods. Bags of coins were thrust upon him before he could change his mind. He then disposed of the male Negroes at a relatively greater sacrifice, considering their value. But the women he stoutly refused to sell until the following day. Exasperated by an importunate customer, he explained with bellowing curses that he wanted to have some sport with the bitches around the taverns that night before he got rid of them.

Morgan edged through the crowd to his side, and jolted him in the ribs, laughing. "Egad, matelot!" he said, using the traditional buccaneer expression for a comrade. "There is no shortage of strumpets here. White ones to boot! A whole boatload of them have lately come out to us from London".

The other's eyes flashed with delight on seeing Morgan. A few incoherent growls postponed the eternal question of women. He was eager to tell the story of his raid, which, though it had only resulted in the capture of a coasting vessel, would enable him to pay each of his twenty men about 100 pieces of eight, with a few hundred for himself and, of course, a dividend for the Admiral. He had been lucky in finding a casket of money in the enemy commander's cabin. Almost as an afterthought, he added that he had left a fleet of ten buccaneer craft, half English and half French, cruising among the keys south of Cuba. Their captains had sent a message that they would follow Morgan in "any expedition which he chose to plan, so long as it gave promise of plenty of plunder."

The Admiral listened and nodded, keeping his own council as was his habit. Stalking with Morris up the street towards the taverns, he inquired simply about the Spaniards. Were their fighting ships active? Was there much danger of their coming to attack Port Royal?

Morris replied, blaspheming, that the ocean swarmed with the sails of the pestiferous Dons. But as for their venturing against so strong a place as Port Royal -

"Keep what opinions it may please you to have, yet spread the word that they are sure to be here anon," interrupted Morgan. "I am to see the Governor tonight, and I have a plan. Is there more to be learned from the Spanish officers you brought as captives?" "I flogged them and burned the soles of their feet with hot irons, yet they would not talk," answered Morris in disgust. "So I cut their tongues out." Morgan shrugged.

It would have suited him to go at once to visit Modyford, and to take John Morris along as a witness. Thus to spoil the orgy which John had been planning for weeks was not to be thought of, however. Morgan was not averse to the concession. He enjoyed orgies, despite the fact that he had been married for some years to his cousin Mary Elizabeth, daughter of the late Colonel Edward Morgan, a former Deputy-General of Jamaica.

The mob of buccaneers and their hangers-on growing more vocally riotous every minute, they arrived among the drinking-places and selected the same tavern where Morgan had had his rum in the afternoon. The first act was to divide the prize money - the purchase, as it was called in the current slang of the business - and this was done at a great mahogany table, Morris personally distributing the heaps of coins and receiving no complaints. There would be an additional share when the black wenches had been sold at auction on the morrow.

Shouts of joy resounded after the last man had been paid off. The pirates scattered to the bar and to smaller tables, where they yelled for liquor and immediately began throwing their money around without counting the change. More civilised meals than they ever had been having aboardship were ordered, too. The provender, even so, was limited to huge grilled beefsteaks and bread, with tropical fruit for dessert.

In an hour, the company was both gorged and intoxicated. Their appetites turned towards sex, and they bawled to the Negresses to dance. The latter had eaten heartily, but this did not prevent them from prancing around with energy and shamelessly slapping their buttocks, shaking their breasts, and exploding with jungle laughter. Whenever the fancy struck him, a man would get up, seize one of the cavorting females and drag her into the adjoining passage to be possessed. As the orgy heightened, the nearest open space upon the floor became good enough. Morgan shook with sardonic mirth. The mob of sightseers that jostled in the doorway and stood jammed outside every window looked on enviously....

Abruptly, the pirates tired of the Negresses. They called boisterously for white harlots, and presently a score of these came mincing in from bordellos in an adjoining street. They were dissipated-looking trollops, on whom the climate was telling; but they were dressed in what seemed fashionable and luxurious raiment to the men of the sea. Corseted snugly in high-waisted frocks that were slightly bouffant at the hips, and wearing small satin shoes, they paraded with a semblance of coquetry and conferred a favour when they sat upon knees encased in filthy, bloodstained cotton.

In the general outburst of enthusiasm, John Morris outdid his companions. He pounded upon the table and roared approvingly. He had evidently been nursing a secret nostalgia for white women. The men demanded more dancing, and the London strumpets complied giggling. But they had to have music played on a wheezy fiddle, and the only steps they knew were those of a sort of jig, and altogether it was not exciting. Inevitably, some lascivious fellow cried to them to take their clothes off, but this they would not do. They explained it was not a matter of virtue. They were not in the habit of displaying their charms for nothing, or in public places, merely that. They were not Negro slaves.

Morris declared that if they wanted money, they could have it. He scattered largesse on the floor, and his followers imitated him with fistfuls of reales and now and then a golden doubloon. The women gathered up the coins, but showed no disposition to oblige. "You!", the captain trumpeted, signalling out a chubby blonde. "A hundred pieces of eight to see you stripped here!" The girl cackled in absurd embarrassment, and shook her head. "Two hundred pieces of eight - five hundred!" Morris challenged. "Five hundred pieces of eight, for that!" she repeated, wondering. "Aye, God's wounds! I am a man of my word."

She hesitated, and then began to tear off her clothes. Soon she was mother naked, and gaining confidence she flaunted in a wide circle, her thick, pink body marked on the torso with welts made by the ribs of her corset. The buccaneers seethed and howled and foamed at the mouth, in unbridled jubilation at the spectacle. Morris, the most demonstrative of the lot, hammered on the table with both fists and fairly thundered his lustful satisfaction. He drew from his wallet the price agreed upon and paid it with a flourish.

Henry Morgan sat fingering his wisp of moustache and grinning faintly. That was a diverting show, he thought, but what crackpots men were! The greater part of Morris's dividend from the purchase spent just to see a London slut on the tavern floor without her clothes. Why, he could have had her for the rest of the night, stripped and bedamned to her behind a locked door, for a tenth of the sum....' (Thus the Welsh can claim to have invented the strip-show!)

Morgan reported the (false) news of the possible invasion fleet to Modyford. Morris next decided to join Morgan's commission from Modyford, to meet up with the ten ships off Cuba. Morgan took two of his own barques, and with Morris sailed off to the Cuban cays on March 30.

SANTA MARIA DE PUERTO PRINCIPE, PUERTO DEL PRINCIPE (now called CAMAGUEY) CUBA 1668

"Morgan's buccaneers attack Poerto Principe in 1668".

A treaty of peace had signed at Madrid on 23 May 1667, but the Spanish crown would not recognise British possession of Jamaica. Cromwell's force had only taken the island, more by accident than design, in 1655. In the West Indies Spain still claimed a monopoly of trade, maintained by armed forces. Modyford asked for a naval frigate to be sent to protect Jamaica, because of reports that a Spanish invasion army and fleet were being assembled in Cuba and Panama. When no response came, he had quickly commissioned Henry Morgan as Admiral in January 1668, to organise *'the brethren of the coast'* and *'to take prisoners of the Spanish nation, whereby you may gain information of that enemy to attack Jamaica.'*

The privateers off Cuba flocked to serve under a man of Morgan's reputation. By joining up with nine ships, he eventually had a fleet of twelve sail and over 700 men, 450 of whom were English. This seems to have been the time when the writer Esquemeling first sailed under Morgan. A Council of the Brotherhood was held at Twelve League Cays, a coral reef off the Cuban Province of Puerto Principe.

Morgan proposed a night attack on the great city of Havana, to cut links between Mexico and Spain. However, ex-prisoners who had escaped from Havana were of the opinion that it needed 1500 men to take the heavily defended port, and even then there was no guarantee of success. Unwillingly, Morgan had to accede to the democratic decision of the council. This was the 'code of the coast'.

The council was then swayed by a privateer who knew the town of Puerto Principe. Although 50 miles from the sea, it was rich, full of merchants dealing in hides, and not well defended. (It was called Puerto, or port, because the citizens of the port had moved inland years before because of constant buccaneer attacks). Morgan left his ships guarded and hidden amongst the cays off southern Cuba, and set off to trek fifty miles to attack Puerto Principe, said to be the second largest town on the island. Around six-hundred buccaneers marched through woodland to Puerto Principe, where the mayor (alcade) had raised a motley force of 800 soldiers, cavalry, citizens and slaves to defend the town. After a pitched battle of four hours outside the town, the alcade was killed, and the buccaneers moved in to fight their way through the town. Morgan herded all the survivors into the churches of La Merced and San Francisco.

For a week, the buccaneers tortured captives to find where plunder was hidden, and refused to feed the citizens locked in the churches. Pickings were small, to be shared between 600 hardened men. Four captives were released to get ransoms, but returned with nothing and asked for a fifteen day extension. Just then a negro messenger was captured by a forage party. Letters showed that the Governor of Santiago was on his way to rescue the Spanish prisoners. Morgan retreated to Santa Maria Bay, with his booty, and gave the Spanish just one day to find ransoms. With nothing coming in, he then made the pragmatic decision to ask for 500 cattle instead, to be brought to the bay, slaughtered, salted and carried aboard his ships. The desperate inhabitants in the churches agreed. Morgan took six eminent hostages, and the Spanish followed with a great herd of cattle the next day. The animals were slaughtered, butchered and salted quickly to prevent the meat from putrefying in the blazing heat.

In amongst the carnage, an incident occurred which threatened to turn the expedition into a mutiny. The greatest pleasure a boucanier could get was to suck the warm marrow out of the bones of freshly killed animals, and a Frenchman had put aside a pile of bones for himself. While his back was turned, an English privateer snatched the 'toute chaude' and started sucking it. A fight ensued, and the participants were ordered to settle it by duelling. While the Frenchman was talking to his seconds, the Englishman plunged a knife into his back, killing him, and a riot ensued. Morgan raced to the gory scene on the beach, and told the French that he would take the offender in manacles back to Port Royal, to be publicly hung there, as there was no time for a court-martial to be held.

The crews then quickly set sail to the Isla de las Vacas (Isle de Vaches, Cow Island), a small cay off south-west Hispaniola. This was his special rendezvous for dividing booty after expeditions, as some of his captains and crews could not return to Port Royal because there was a price on their heads. Treasure and goods came to only around 50,000 pieces of eight, making a small reward for each man after three months at sea and fighting the Spaniards. Around 200 Frenchmen returned to Tortuga, after asking Morgan to hand over the '*toute chaude*' robber, but he stayed with Morgan's forces.

RETURN TO PORT ROYAL

Morgan returned to another hero's welcome in Port Royal, with eight ships, three more than he left in. The buccaneers dispersed to spend their gains. At Town House, in Port Royal, Morgan now convinced Modyford that that he had frightened a large Spanish fleet from attacking Port Royal. After '*dispersing*' their fleet, only then he attacked Puerto Principe. It appears that the Spanish '*invasion*' was a red herring to get Morgan his letter of marque. Between 5% and 10% of the plunder went to Modyford, so he did not pursue the facts too closely. Governor Modyford was using his cut of pirate loot by quietly buying up enough Jamaican land to make him the largest plantation owner there. His payment from the Crown was infrequent or non-existent. However, Morgan's activities under the letter of marque seem to have been restricted to reprisals at sea, not on land, which caused problems in his later career.

To satisfy his standing as a man of his word, Morgan asked Modyford for an Admiralty Court to be convened, to fulfil his promise to the French whom he would need on future expeditions. The English '*toute chaude*' robber was duly '*swung off*' in public, and his corpse left on the gallows for months after. Morgan had kept his promise to his French comrades. It also appears that at this time Morgan's buccaneers were diverting Spanish resources from Florida, thereby not enabling it to be settled properly by the Spanish. Thus Spanish Florida never joined up with Spanish Texas, and the Spanish never pushed up into the American heartlands of the present USA. Morgan may have been instrumental in the eventual English take-over of the southern states of the USA.

PUERTO BELLO, PANAMA 1668

It now seems that Captain Jackman returned from pillaging Campeachy, bringing Morgan's fleet to nine vessels and 500 men in the Spring of 1998. Suitably prepared, in May 1998 the privateers sailed out of Port Royal, but neither Modyford nor the captains knew where Morgan was leading them. Morgan wanted no Spanish spies alerting his enemies of his potential targets.

Morgan's daring plan was to attack Puerto Bello, Portobello, the great Panamanian port, and the third largest and strongest city in the New World (after Havana and Cartagena). There were only two ways of sending goods from Panama to Porto Bello, and the overland route of 18 leagues could only be used in the summer. The other was by mule train to Venta Cruz, 7 leagues from Panama, then by water on the river Chagres to its mouth, 26 leagues away. If the river was high, this could be effected in 2 to 3 days, but in low water conditions, 6-12 days were needed. Winter rain and floods made the overland route impossible.

This was one of the ports where the annual '*flota*' assembled to carry the treasures of the Americas back to Spain, and thus had not one, but two reputedly invincible castles protecting the harbour entrance, with another castle in the city. Morgan knew there was no point in trying to sail into the port, where he believed the Jamaican invasion fleet was being prepared, so he decided to attack by surprise. In the last week of June he laid up his fleet, 120 miles west of Puerto Bello, and informed the crews of his target. While the privateers operated under the system of 'no prey, no pay', there was still a great deal of dissent about attacking the great port, and his French ships, with 250 men, sailed off, leaving him with just 450 buccaneers. He told his small band 'if our number is small, our hearts are great; and the fewer persons we are, the more union, and the better shares we shall have in the spoil !' (This speech struck such a chord among the Brethren of the Coast, that for generations after seamen used to sing a ballad with the words:'

'If few there be amongst us,
Our hearts are very great;
And each will have more plunder,
And each will have more plate.'

They paddled along the coast in twenty-three canoes, and landed at night at the mouth of the river Guanches, a few miles from Porto Bello. To the south-west of the town stood the magnificent castle of Santiago de la Gloria, and the smaller castle of San Jeronimo was also in the city. The harbour was fortified on either side, with the Fortress of San Fernando on the south, and on the north the 'impregnable' castle of San Felipe de Sotomayor. Both sides of the harbour were thus defended by cannons. Morgan knew that a frontal attack would have been fatal.

With an English guide who been a prisoner, they surprised and took a Spanish sentry, and learned that only 130 men were guarding the third castle, San Jeronimo in the city. The captured sentry called on the governor to surrender, shouting that the 'Luteranos' had an overwhelming force. The governor immediately fired a cannon, triggering an immediate buccaneer attack. Morgan reported 'We made our way into the town, and seeing that we could not refresh ourselves in quiet we were enforced to assault the castle, which we took by storm, and found well supplied with ammunition and provisions, only undermanned, being about 130 men, whereof 74 were killed, among whom the Castillano was one. In the dungeon were found eleven English in chains who had been there two years........ The Governor of the second castle refusing to permit our ships free entrance into the port, we were forced to attempt the taking of it, which ended in the delivering up of the castle and marching out with the colours flying, and the third castle immediately surrendered to five or six Englishmen.'

Esquemeling's account is very different to Morgan's. He recounts that Morgan gathered up monks, friars and nuns from his prisoners, and sent them first up the siege ladders to take the castle of La Gloria, where the alcade and many citizens were sheltering. Other reports say that the surviving Spaniards from the first fort were locked in the powder room and blown up. Morgan's followers had started looting after the success of San Jeronimo, but guns from La Gloria opened up on them, and the remaining citizens, so Morgan was able to restore order and attack La Gloria. A few men took San Fernando, while San Felipe appears to have kept its forces in for the fighting. La Gloria may have been taken using nuns and monks, but the buccaneers had heavy casualties. The Alcade (Castillano) refused to surrender although offered quarter, and it was impossible to take him prisoner, so he was shot. The troops from

San Felipe still did not leave the castle, perhaps because Morgan's nine ships were waiting outside the harbour.

Eventually the fleet moved in, and still the guns of San Felipe stayed silent. For fifteen days Morgan's men raped, pillaged and tortured, as noted by Esquemeling. However, in previous raids on Portobelo in 1668 and Providence Island in 1670, Morgan locked up and guarded female captives, so rape probably did not occur. Esquemeling hated Morgan and deliberately blackened his character. The surgeon Richard Browne, who was present at the attack, wrote in August 1671: *'What was in fight and heat of blood in pursuit of a flying enemy I presume pardonable. As to their women, I know or never heard of any thing offered beyond their wills. Something I know was cruelly executed by Captain Collier in killing a friar in the field after quarter given, but for the Admiral he was noble enough to the vanquished enemy.'*

Great treasure was taken, but the custom-house had little Peruvian bullion for the flota, so Morgan announced that he wanted 100,000 pieces of eight or the town would be destroyed with all its citizens. The temporary governor of Panama, Don Agustin de Bracamonte, came to retrieve the three *'impregnable'* castles, with 3000 soldiers. His vanguard was ambushed in a narrow canyon and he retreated. However, he refused to pay, so Morgan returned to the hapless inhabitants and told them of his plans to kill them unless they could find 100,000 pieces. Somehow the money was scraped together, Morgan spiked the guns of the forts and left the city.

Morgan wrote in his report to London that *'We further declare to the world that in all this service we lost 18 men killed and 32 wounded, and kept possession of the place 31 days; and for the better vindication of ourselves against the usual scandals of that enemy, we aver that having several ladies of great quality and other prisoners, they were proffered their liberty to go to the President's camp, but they refused, saying they were now prisoners to a person of quality, who was more tender of their honours than they doubted to find in the President's camp among his rude Panama soldiers, and so voluntarily continued with us till the surrender of the town and castles, when with many thanks and good wishes they repaired to their former homes.'* Covering his back, Governor Modyford added a codicil that Morgan should not have attacked the Spaniards on land, *'having commissions only against their ships.'*

Morgan took to Port Royal 500,000 pieces of eight, 300 slaves and a fortune in gold, silver and jewels. He was greeted like a king on his arrival. Modyford took a cut, Morgan 5%, the captains around 2000 pieces of eight and the men about 400 pieces of eight. 'Artists' such as surgeons, carpenters and navigators received around 1000 pieces of eight. The injured received, according to articles, 1000 pieces of eight for blindness, or for one eye 100 pieces. A lost arm or leg was worth 400-500 pieces of eight. If preferred, one slave equalled 100 pieces of eight in payment. There was wild rejoicing in London on hearing the account of Portobello. It was comparable in boldness to Admiral De Ruyter's attack on the British fleet on the Medway in the previous summer, when he burned several warships and towed the flagship *Royal Charles* back to Holland. With this humiliating defeat following just after the Fire of London and the Great Plague, Charles II needed some good news to placate his people. He listened politely to the protests of the Spanish Ambassador but refused to recall Jamaica's Governor, or return Morgan's booty.

MARACAIBO and GIBRALTAR, VENEZUELA 1669

Captain Morgan ignored Modyford's cautious strictures, and assembled another small fleet by the end of 1668 at Ile de Vache, his favourite rendezvous. By this time Morgan had effected the dress by which he is known. He wore a wig on formal occasions, much like his king Charles II, but his hair was cut short, and almost perpetually kept under a scarlet bandana. Like Charles, he called for his wig when he lay dying. He carried a plumed hat in his left hand, and wore a vest trimmed with silver, linen pantaloons, thread stockings, and shoes rather than boots. His silk and brocade coat was rarely worn as being too heavy and hot, but he always wore his cutlass, and usually carried a pistol in his belt.

Modyford now sent Morgan at the Isle de Vache the former royal navy frigate *Oxford*, under captain Edward Collier, with its 34 guns. The British Government had sent the *Oxford* to Jamaica specifically to be used as a privateer, to fill the royal coffers, and to keep Spain away from Jamaica. A French buccaneer sailed into the Isle de Vache, wishing to work with Morgan, but the treachery of Santa Maria Bay, and Morgan's insistence on total command, fouled up the negotiations. Morgan gave the French ship one last chance to join him, but they refused. However, running short of food on the Isle, the French had boarded a passing English merchant-man, taken some stores, and paid for them with fraudulent bills of exchange, drawn on Jamaica and Tortuga. Morgan invited the French captain and officers to come to his ship and dine to finally discuss whether they could come to an agreement. They were clapped in chains for thievery. Straight away, on January 2, 1669, Morgan called a council of war of his captains upon *Oxford*, his new flagship. He discussed the taking of Cartagena, the richest and strongest city of the Spanish Main. Sitting around a table on the quarterdeck, there was a great explosion, killing the French prisoners. A drunken gunner had shot a musket which ignited a powder barrel. The Oxford sank immediately, at Ile a Vache (Cow Island), off the southern coast of Hispaniola. 350 men died, including the all the captains sitting opposite Morgan at the conference table. In the bloody seas, other buccaneers cut the fingers off the floating corpses for their rings.

Richard Browne was the surgeon-general of Morgan's fleet, and recorded the explosion - '*I was eating my dinner with the rest when the mainmasts blew out and fell upon Captains Aylett and Bigford and others and knocked them on the head. I saved myself by getting astride the mizzenmast.*' (Although not kindly disposed towards Morgan, Brown noted his moderation towards prisoners, especially women, which seems to disprove Esquemeling's accusations). Morgan's miraculous reappearance prevented the fleet breaking up. Everyone thought him dead. He decided to blame the French prisoners for wrecking the ship, to get the English captains on his side. As there were no French survivors, this appeal to patriotism worked well. Their ship, the 24-gun *Le Cerf Volante*, was seized from the remaining crew, and Morgan found on it a commission from a Spanish governor, permitting the ship to '*cruise on the English pirates in what place soever they find them*'. Morgan, to try to atone for the loss of the warship *Oxford*, later sent *Le Cerf Volante* to Modyford as a crown '*confiscation*', and Modyford ratified this decision.

Admiral Morgan's new flagship only had 14 guns, but was the largest of his fleet of fifteen sail and 950 men. He gave up the idea of attacking Cartagena, and roamed the coasts of Cuba and Hispaniola, raiding on a *cut and run* basis. After a month or so, the fleet was dispersed. Some French privateers left to go on their *'own account'*, which left Morgan with only eight small ships and 500 men. Morgan could not return to Port Royal without booty, and luckily a French privateer who had attacked Maracaibo with the infamous L'Olonnois and Michel le Basque in 1666, joined them. He volunteered to guide the little fleet to Maracaibo in modern Venezuela.

They steered south to the island of Oruba, off Dutch Curacao, easily took it from the small garrison, and approached Maracaibo. After sailing up the triangular Gulf of Maracaibo. Morgan had to sail up a narrow strait, protected by the islands of Vigilias

One of Morgans's fleet

and Palomas, which had a garrisoned castle. The town was protected by this narrow inlet overlooked by Palomas fort, with which Morgan exchanged cannon fire all day. In a night assault by the privateers, the garrison ran away, leaving huge stocks of gunpowder, muskets and ammunition. Morgan spiked the 16 cannon in the fort, and tried to get his ships into the inlet, but the water was too shallow. They then set off in canoes to attack the fort that guarded the town, but this garrison had also fled. The town was abandoned, as mass hysteria had taken over with the approach of *'the conqueror of Puerto Bello'*. Just two years earlier, the gruesome L'Olonais had invaded the town. Just a few old and sick people remained. Anyone captured by forage parties was tortured by roasting, racks and thumbscrews to find more loot.

The town and area was ransacked for three weeks, but not enough treasure was found, so Morgan managed to get his ships over the sand bar in the inlet, and proceeded across Maracaibo Lake (an extension of the Gulf of Venezuela) for a hundred miles to attack Gibraltar. Here there was a spirited resistance from the fort's cannon, until the French guide led Morgan's men through woods to the landward side of the fort. The Spanish spiked their guns and fled to the hills. A slave volunteered to show Morgan where the treasure was hidden in a ship in one of the rivers that flowed into the lake, so 200 men were sent to take it. Morgan went with the other 250 privateers to capture the governor, who was on an island in another river.

Morgan at the Battle of Maracribo

TRAPPED

However, the governor had formed too good a defensive position, up a steep hill approachable only by a narrow track. Also, much of the treasure had been moved on, and some of the valuables taken were swept away with privateers and prisoners in a torrential flood. Morgan now spent four weeks trying to ransom some important prisoners and the two towns. He was forced to move on, taking some slaves and four of the most important hostages, as three Spanish men-of-war arrived outside Lake Maracaibo to blockade him. The great ships waited outside the sand bar at Vigilias and Palomas islands, so Morgan was trapped in the lagoon. Two of the frigates had 36 guns, and the other 24, and they had been sent out from Spain under Don Alonso del Campo with specific orders to exterminate Morgan and his men after the sacking of Puerto Bello. The Spanish repaired the Palomas fort guarding the harbour and put new troops in it, and waited for Morgan to try and break out from Lake Maracaibo into the Gulf of Venezuela. *Morgan the Welshman* was trapped.

It was this incident that proved to J. Leoline Phillips (Sir Henry Morgan, Buccaneer, 1912) that Morgan was '*a tactician and strategist of the highest order*'. He first sent his fastest boat to scout the situation. Its captain reported that Palomas fort was repaired, and there were three men-o-war with around 100 guns, with the flagship Magdalena's guns trained on the strait entrance. Morgan tried to bluff his way out, sending a Spanish prisoner, demanding a huge ransom not to burn Maracaibo and a free passage out into the open seas. The Spanish admiral, Don Alonso del Campo y Espinosa offered him an undisputed passage if he gave up his prisoners and slaves. Otherwise the Spaniard promised to fight him and follow him across the seas, or 'command boats to come from Caracas, wherein I will put troops, and coming to Maracaibo, will cause you utterly to perish, putting you every man to the sword.......... I have with me very good soldiers, who desire nothing more than to revenge on you and your people for the cruelties and base, infamous actions you have committed upon the Spanish nation in America'. (April 24, 1669).

The Welshman offered to compromise, as his men did not want to go home empty-handed, but the proposal was refused, so the buccaneers fell back to doing what they did best, fighting. The negotiations had given him time to plan, and to convince the other captains to follow his course of action. There was to be no surrender. All the men knew their fate if captured by the Spaniards - exquisite torture and death or the galleys. Morgan ordered the buccaneers to prepare a fireship (brulot) from one of the small Spanish ships captured at Gibraltar, and followed it out of the inlet on April 30th. Twelve volunteers manned the fireship, which was made to look like a warship. Slave drums were caulked black, and put into ports specially cut in the side of the ship. Dummy sailors were made and put in position. The English flag flew above this dummy privateer, which was loaded with pitch, tar, sulphur and gunpowder with short fuses. The deck planking had been loosened, so any explosion would hurl burning debris at the Spanish ships. Three ships of Morgan's fleet also had skeleton crews, one carrying Spanish males and slaves, one female captives and the most precious booty, and one just food, stores and merchandise. Another five ships were full of buccaneers, ready to fight to the death if the fireship was unsuccessful.

On the night of April 30, the buccaneers rode at anchor just inside the inlet, but at dawn on May 1st the small ships headed straight for the tall Spanish galleons. The dozen desperate privateers managed to grapple the fireship against Espinosa's flagship, the Magdalena. Rigging ropes were tarred to preserve them against salt water, and the decks were sealed with tar, so soon the Magdalena was ablaze, and exploded killing most of her 250-man crew. Espinosa escaped in a rowing boat to the shore. The other large Spanish man-of-war, the San Luis, was run ashore by her captain and set on fire, rather than fall into Morgan's hands. Morgan captured the remaining 240-gun frigate, La Marquesa, and made her his new flagship.

Esquemeling's almost contemporary description states: 'The fire ship sailing before the rest fell presently upon the great ship and grappled her; which the Spaniards – too late – perceiving to be a fire ship, they attempted to put her off, but in vain: for the flame seizing her timber and tackling soon consumed all the stern, the fore part sinking into the sea, where she perished. The second Spanish ship perceiving their admiral to burn, escaped towards the castle, where the Spaniards themselves sunk her, choosing to lose their ship rather than fall into the hands of those pirates. The third, having no opportunity to escape, was taken by the pirates.'

Unfortunately, the buccaneers were still trapped inside the inlet and could not get past the withering cannon fire from the fort, through the narrows to reach the Gulf of Venezuela. They attempted to retake the fort, but lost 60 dead. Morgan returned to threaten Maracaibo with burning, and took a ransom of 20,000 pieces of eight and 500 cattle, salted and loaded on the buccaneers' ships. There was further booty found in the wreck of the San Luis. He now threatened Espinosa that he would kill all his prisoners if he was not allowed to leave the Lake, but Espinosa refused. Morgan knew that dead hostages were no use whatsoever, so applied native cunning to the equation.

Morgan sent boats and canoes from his ships all day to the shoreline just out of cannon shot from the castle. Espinosa could see the boats full of heavily armed men leaving, but not landing. On the return he could see just a couple of rowers, as on each return trip the armed buccaneers hid in the bottom of the boats. The Spanish conferred and believed that there would be a massive attack on the castle in the night, as it appeared that the ships had been left almost empty, and that all the privateers were in the woods around the fort. Espinosa directed that most of the cannons and artillery be moved to face the landward side of the fort and prepare for battle. That night, Morgan ordered the anchor cables to be cut, and the flotilla drifted quietly out into the open seas on the ebb tide. The alarm was not raised until the little fleet was abreast of the fort, and then the buccaneers piled on every inch of sail, and were out of range before the Spanish had moved their cannon back to the ocean-facing side of the castle.

The estimate of the booty was 250,000 pieces of eight, including the value of all the prisoners and slaves. Those white prisoners unransomed were sold into bondage. The fleet returned to great rejoicing in Port Royal on 17 May, but Governor Modyford had to justify their actions inland, and so revoked the captains' letters of marque. They quietly bought plantations with their share of the booty, as the Crown took no action against them, and a state of peace was declared in Jamaica between Britain and Spain. Morgan spent some time on his first plantation, Danke's Lande, now known as Morgan's Valley, in Clarendon Parish, Jamaica. His ingenuity and determination earned Morgan the respect of all the 'Brethren of the Coast', and 'that is Harry Morgan's way' became a popular phrase for any feat of daring.

CAPTAIN PARDAL 1670

However, the Spanish Governor of Cartagena now gave a commission to a Portuguese privateer, Captain Manoel Rivera Pardal, who captured some small British ships and attacked the north coast of Jamaica. Governor Modyford now had real justification for giving Henry Morgan a new commission, without expecting any trouble from London. Pardal had even cruised along the south coast and outside Port Royal. On June 29th, 1670, Modyford's council passed a resolution making Henry Morgan 'Admiral and Commander in chief of all the ships of war belonging to this harbour' requiring him to draw up a fleet and defend the security of the island. At last the rider was added that he could 'land in the enemies Country as many of his men as he shall think needful; and with them march to such places as he shall be informed the said Magazines and Forces are.' Admiral Morgan could now not only issue commissions, but also attack inland with impunity, although he was still operating as a 'no purchase, no pay' privateer.

An extraordinary letter attached to the order asked Admiral Morgan to 'take Santiago de Cuba, to kill all male slaves, to send the women hither to be sold, to treat prisoners as ours have been treated, or rather, as our custom is, to exceed them in civility and humanity, endeavouring to make all people sensible of his (Morgan's) moderation and good nature, and his inaptitude and loathness to spill the blood of man.' This appears to have been engineered by Morgan, as not only the Modyford brothers but also his brother-in-law Lieutenant-Colonel Robert Bindloss, served on the Council. Morgan wanted to cover his own back, just like Modyford, as he became more diplomatically astute.

On July 2 1670 in Port Royal, the Town Crier had proclaimed the resumption of war with Spain. However, on July 8 in Madrid, peace was declared, although this was not known for months in the West Indies. Morgan was given his new commission on July 22, and he invited privateers to join him from his flagship *Satisfaction*, a 22-gun frigate that was formerly *Le Cerf Volante* captured by the *Oxford*. The former commander of the *Oxford*, Morgan's old friend Captain Edward Collier was made vice-admiral. Morgan made his headquarters as usual at Ile de Vache, while French, English and other privateers flocked to his flag. Apart from the old reliable John Morris, Morgan's cousin Bledri Morgan joined him at Bluefields Bay. Around ten ships then sailed on to Isle de Vache to join up with the more irregular buccaneers of Tortuga and elsewhere. Pardal's sister ship was now captured by Collier, commanding six ships, who had recently sacked two towns on the Spanish Main. Another three privateers captured and ransomed Granada in Nicaragua, and on their return to Port Royal were told by Modyford to join Morgan at Ile a Vache. With these nine ships and Morgan's *Satisfaction*, there were another 18 English privateers, the largest being the *Satisfaction* at 120 tons, and the smallest the *Prosperous* at 10 tons. Another seven French ships joined, to which Morgan gave letters of marque, the largest being the 100 ton *Catherine* with 14 guns and 110 men. This formidable buccaneer fleet, of 35 ships, had 1846 men and 239 guns.

On July 5th, Captain Pardal had landed at the western tip of Jamaica and had nailed the following challenge to a tree:

'I, *Captain Manoal Rivero Pardal, to the chief of the squadron of privateers in Jamaica. I am he who this year have done that which follows:- I went on shore in Caimanos, and burnt twenty houses, and fought with Captain Ary and took from him a catch laden with provisions and a canoe. And I am he who took Captain Baines, and did carry the prize to Cartagena, and now am arrived to this coast, and have burnt it. And I am come to seek General Morgan, with two ships of twenty guns, and having seen this, I crave he would come out upon the coast and seek me, that he might see the valour of the Spaniards. And because I had no time I did not come to the mouth of Port Royal to speak by word of mouth in the name of my King, whom God preserve. – Dated the fifth of July, 1670.'*

The Welsh Captain John Morris on the *Dolphin*, who had sailed with Morgan back in his early days, caught up with Pardal in his *San Pedro y la Fama*, sheltering from a storm in a bay off south-eastern Cuba. Admiral Morgan's fleet had been scattered by the storm on its way to the normal rendezvous. Pardal sent some men ashore to cut off Morris's retreat, and waited until dawn to attack. However, although outgunned 14 cannon to 10, and outmanned by 120 to 60, Morris attacked first at daybreak. The accuracy of the first broadside made the Spanish privateers abandon their guns, and Pardal's larger ship was grappled and he was fatally shot in the neck the firefight that followed. Surgeon Richard Browne was present, and wrote that '*so ended that same vapouring captain that so much amazed Jamaica, in burning the houses, robbing some people upon the shore and sent that insolent challenge to Admiral Morgan.*' Morris took the

Spanish frigate to supplement Morgan's fleet, and found Pardal's commission to attack English ships in his great cabin. The *Dolphin* itself was a former Spanish prize, only 50 tons, perhaps 50 feet long and with 10 guns, and the second largest ship in Morgan's fleet.

Modyford now wished Santiago de Cuba to be destroyed because Pardal had sailed from there to threaten Jamaican sovereignty. Morgan saw it as being a difficult harbour to break into, with little prospect of great booty, so roamed the Caribbean, attacking easy Cuban targets but not Santiago. He took foodstuffs on board in preference to plunder. A Spanish ship from Cartagena carrying maize was taken, and wild cattle were smoked in Hispaniola, until by mid-December he was ready for his real mission. He called in all his foraging ships, and announced to his captains on December 15th that they were going to take the treasure city of Panama. With Morgan's record of continuing success, they voted *aye* to the venture. The Calendar of State Papers records the personnel on the 29 English and 8 French ships sailing under Harry Morgan:

SHIP	CAPTAIN	TUNS	GUNS	CREW
Satisfaction frigate	Henry Morgan	120	22	140
Mary frigate	Thomas Harris	50	12	70
May-Flower	Joseph Bradley	70	14	100
Pearle	Lawrence Prince	50	12	70
Civillian	John Erasmus	80	12	75
Dolphin frigate	John Morris	60	10	60
Lily	Richard Norman	50	10	50
Port Royal	James Delliatt	50	12	55
Gift	Thomas Rogers	40	12	60
John of Vaughall	John Pyne	70	6	60
Thomas	Humphrey Thurston	50	8	45
Fortune (1)	Richard Ludbury	40	6	40
Constant Thomas	Coone Leloramell	60	6	40
Fortune (2)	Richard Dobson	25	6	35
Prosperous	Richard Wills	16	4	35
Abraham Oferenda	Richard Taylor	60	4	30
Virgin Queen	John Barnett	50	-	30
Recovery	John Shepherd	18	3	30
William sloop	Thomas Woodriffe	12	-	30
Betty sloop	William Curson	12	-	25
Fortune (3) ketch	Clement Symons	40	4	40
Endeavour (1)	John Harmanson	23	4	35
Bonadventure	Roger Taylor	20	-	23
Prosperous	Patrick Dunbar	10	-	16
Endeavour (2)	Charles Swan	16	23	0
Lambe sloop	Richard Powell	30	4	30
Fortune (4)	John Reekes	16	3	30

SHIP	CAPTAIN	TUNS	GUNS	CREW
Free Gift	Roger Kelly	15	4	40
St Catherine F	Tribetor	100	14	110
Galliardena F	Gascoone	80	10	80
St John F	Diego	80	10	80
St Peter F	Pearse Hanto	180	10	90
Le Diable Volante F	Desnangla	40	6	50
Le Serfe sloop F	Joseph	25	2	40
Le Lyon sloop F	Charles	30	3	40
Le St Marie F	John Linaux	30	4	30
	Totals	1585	239	1846

A fast ship had arrived at Isle de Vache, from Modyford, with the announcement of the Peace Treaty of Madrid. Morgan seems to have ignored it. One school of thought is that Modyford sent two packets of instructions. One was to go ahead with the expedition against the Spaniards, and not to open the other envelope giving details of the peace. Whatever the circumstances, a mere peace with Spain was not going to stand between Harry Morgan and the treasures of the Isthmus. Harry Morgan always had his 'way'.

OLD PROVIDENCE 1670
On December 21st, Morgan hove to off the west of Old Providence. According to Esquemeling, it had been converted into a formidable target, with a stone castle, Santa Teresa, and two forts, San Jeronimo and San José. There were forty-nine guns, but only 190 soldiers. One thousand buccaneers landed, but were met with heavy cannon fire from San Jeronimo. They spent the night shivering in the open, with no rations, before Morgan sent a flag of truce at dawn asking the governor to surrender. Morgan expected the standard refusal, and was going to return to his ships for more supplies before a fresh assault. Instead, the Governor proposed to surrender, subject to a subterfuge whereby he did not lose face to the Spanish authorities back home in Seville.

Morgan agreed to the stratagem, but stipulated that the first sign of treachery would lead to a *'no prisoners'* massacre. Morgan did not want to lose any of his precious force, all who would be needed for the Panamanian invasion. After a mock battle at the walls of San Jeronimo fort, the rest of the fleet disembarked some more of Morgan's men, to head for Santa Teresa castle. On his way from Santa Jeronimo from Santa Teresa, the governor was intercepted as planned, and *'captured'* as promised. He then led the buccaneers into Santa Teresa, and yielded his sword and surrendered both forts. All 190 soldiers were spared, and 270 civilians also unharmed. This civilised end to the engagement was a shame to the Spanish on the Main for years after. The prisoners were taken on to Chagres. There was no torture, and little looting, the main priority being to secure extra provisions and 30,000 pounds of gunpowder that was distributed across the fleet. The island's defences were thrown down and cannon spiked, except for the Castle of Santa Teresa, where Morgan left a small garrison. He still had hopes of settling the island, as before, because it was fertile, well-watered and near the mainland.

OLD PROVIDENCE 1670 and CHAGRES FORT 1671

Spanish prisoners had told Morgan that the Spanish were preparing for their expected invasion of Jamaica in Cartagena and Panama. A council of war of captains decided to attack Panama, taking the island of Old Providence on the way. The great fleet sailed on December 6, 1670, and over-ran the island just eight days later. It had been strongly fortified, but had too small a garrison to resist for long. Some Spanish deserters in the privateering fleet (the British and French navies held no monopoly on cruelty to their seamen) told Morgan that there was a fort on the River Chagres, on the approaches to Panama City. Without its capture, there could be no progress, so Morgan sent one of his most experienced captains, Captain Joseph Bradley of the *Mayflower*, to take it with three ships and 470 men. Bradley was made Vice-Admiral and told to take the fort as quickly as possible.

Captain Henry Morgan before Panama

Bradley knew the fort's capture was impossible from the sea, so he landed three miles away on December 27th, and hacked for miles through the jungle to reach a clearing opposite the main gate. Bradley stared at the earthen bank toped with wooden stakes, followed by a thirty foot deep dry moat, followed by another palisade, that was between his men and the fort. The only way across the palisades and gully was across a drawbridge, which was raised. The Spanish had a capable and confident Governor, Don Pedro de Lisardo, commanding 314 regular soldiers, 75 civilians and dozens of cannon. The buccaneers held a council of war, and decided to attack.

It is difficult to understand today, but privateers did not expect a long life – as Black Bart memorably commented fifty years later, '*a short life, and a merry one*' was what they expected. They were superb marksmen, and had a camaraderie, a '*brotherhood*' of equality where no man was supposed to let anyone else down. Driven on by Bradley, they stormed over the first palisade, into the ditch and up the second bank under withering cannon and small arms fire. In response they aimed accurately at the loop-holes in the fort's walls, and hurled grenades and fire bombs over the walls. Bradley had his legs shot off by cannon fire, and the privateers retreated to regroup before attacking again several times. At length they retired in the dusk, to tend their wounds and prepare for another assault at dawn.

The buccaneers were woken by explosions. They noticed flames coming from the fort. One of their fire arrows had started flames in a thatched roof, which had quickly spread across the fort, and most of Don Pedro's troops were engaged in putting out the spreading fires. Under cover of darkness, the privateers lit the two wooden palisades, which burnt quickly and caused gaps to appear in the walls, as the earth and rocks crumbled beneath the fires. The pirates again charged, with pikes and cutlasses, eventually taking the Citadel, where Don Pedro de Lisardo bravely refused to surrender and was shot dead. Bradley's 470 men had lost just 30 buccaneers but another 76 were wounded. 30 Spaniards, many wounded, were taken prisoner, and 360 killed (many had refused quarter, which usually meant a life of slavery for the soldiers who could not get a ransom). All the Spanish officers died in this bloody engagement. Now the way to Panama was open.

PANAMA 1671

HENRY MORGAN'S MARCH ON PANAMA - A.G. Prys-Jones

Morgan's curls are matted,
His lips are cracked and dry,
His tawny beard is tangled,
And his plumed hat hangs awry:
But his voice still booms like thunder
Through the foetid jungle glade
As he marches, bold as Lucifer,
Leading his gaunt brigade.

Twelve hundred famished buccaneers
Blistered, bitten and bled,
A stricken mob of men accursed
By the monstrous sun o'erhead:
Twelve hundred starveling scarecrows
Without a crumb to eat,
And not a drink for tortured throats
In that grim, festering heat.

Twelve hundred threadbare musketeers
Rotting in tropic mud
Where the reeking, fevered mangroves
Wreak havoc in their blood:
Twelve hundred febrile wretches,
A legion of the dead:
But Morgan in his blue brocade
Goes striding on ahead.

Twelve hundred tatterdemalions,
The sorriest, maddest crew
That ever the green savannahs saw

When the Spanish bugles blew:
Twelve hundred rattling skeletons
Who sprang to life, and then
Like a wild wave took Panama,
For they were Morgan's men.

Morgan's fleet sailed into Chagres on January 2, 1671. Morgan's *Satisfaction*, with three other ships, ran ashore because of the force of the winds, and were pounded to wreckage. The crews survived, and all the supplies were taken off them, however. Morgan's luck still held. However, Bradley was dying from his wounds, there were weevils in the grain, and maggots in the meat they had brought from New Providence. Morgan told his men to go out foraging for fresh supplies, before they started the next phase of the expedition. Some of the men wore the tattered redcoats of the Penn and Venables Expedition which took Jamaica in 1654, and will have known Morgan from that time.

With captured slaves, the fort was repaired, and 300 men were left there to guard the fleet. Major Richard Norman was made vice-admiral in place of Bradley, and put in charge of the defensive force. The ships were disposed in battle formation across the mouth of the River Chagres, with another 200 buccaneers on board. Morgan had heard that Don Alfonso del Campo y Espinosa, who had trapped him at Maracaibo, had a fleet in the area. The seven lowest draught ships, with 36 flat-bottomed river boats full of provisions, then set off up the river to Panama on January 8. Prisoners said that the river was navigable by such boats for five or six days, up to Venta de Cruz, just a day's march from Panama City. Unfortunately, unusually low waters, terrible heat, stinging mosquitoes and flies made the journey a nightmare. Fourteen miles into their journey, a Spanish force defending the river bank at Dos Bracas, fled at their approach. (This detachment of 250 men seems to have been sent by Governor Guzman to retake San Lorenzo. The sight of 1400 hardened buccaneers coming up the river obviously unnerved them). The privateers had to haul the boats through unforgiving jungle from one stretch of water to another, avoiding rapids, shallows and whirlpools. After four hard, miserable days, the boats and cannon were abandoned with a guard of 200 men under Captain Robert Delander, at a deserted Spanish defence post called Juan Gallego (near Gatun).

An advance party of 100 now used cutlasses to fight a path through the dense riverbank jungle, while 1100 men followed carrying provisions. The Spanish had burnt every defence post before them, taking all the provisions with them and destroying any crops. Morgan had ordered the buccaneers to make the expedition with almost empty packs of provisions, expecting easy foraging along the way, but within three days the men were starving. Two sacks of meal and some sacks of plantains were found in a cache, which Morgan confiscated at pistol point, and distributed among the sickest of the force. Fighting off mosquitoes, lurking alligators, snakes and malaria, the starving pirates resorted to chewing leather and leaves, until on January 14 they found a barn full of maize. The buccaneers crammed it into their mouths, knapsacks and pockets, and trudged on. An Indian ambush killed a dozen buccaneers, and Captain Thomas Rogers skirmished with a few Spaniards around this time.

Morgan's route to Panama

On 15 January, they reached the town of Venta de Cruz (Cruces), which was still burning. General Salado's troops had fired it and retreated. Apart from some stray dogs, there was nothing to eat. The only drink available was some Peruvian wine, which made some buccaneers so sick that they thought it had been poisoned. (Alcohol on an empty stomach has similar effects today!) Morgan knew it would be difficult to get back to the boats with no provisions, so he had no choice. He pressed ahead to Panama on the well-worn jungle path. They were now over half-way there, and the trek became much easier. Mule trains were used on this path by the Spanish to bring the riches from Panama to Venta de Cruz for river transport down to the 'flota' at Chagres. Guards had slow-burning fuses on their muskets, to fend off the ceaseless attacks from native Indians. On January 16, eight men were killed and ten wounded by arrows from either side of the path. Morgan ordered his men to spread out into the woods, where they were less of a target and could see the Indians.

After another two days of constant attacks by Indians and by Spanish scouts, the advance party reached open land. The next day, January 18, Morgan could see Panama and beyond it the glittering Pacific Ocean. Cattle grazing on the savannah of Matasnillos were slaughtered, for a great feast in preparation for the attack on their great prize, the richest city in The Americas. Spanish cavalry waited at a discreet distance from the invaders, shouting out 'perros' (dogs). Morgan set up sentries around low earthen banks and bivouacked for the night. There was still a day's march through the forest to reach the city, and he wanted his men fresh for the assault. Panama was not well-defended with fortifications. No-one expected it to be attacked. The citizens urged Guzman to meet the 'perros' outside the town to minimise damage.

However, Don Juan Perez de Guzman, Governor of Panama, made an oath in the Cathedral to die in the defence of the city, and priests and nuns prayed for victory against Morgan's savages. There were 2000 Spanish foot soldiers, some of whom were negroes and Indian natives, a few hundred cavalry and five field guns to defend the city. Ten days after leaving Chagres, on January 20, the 1200 swashbucklers faced the 2400-strong Spanish army. Morgan decided to attack on January 21, after resting his weary men, and drew up the buccaneers in three groups. There was a vanguard of 300 under Captain John Morris and Colonel Lawrence Prince, a main body of 300 under Morgan on the right and 300 under Collier on the left, and a rearguard of 300 under Colonel Bledri Morgan. Many of Morgan's followers were dressed in the red jerkins of Cromwell's New Model Army – they were veterans of the English Civil War. This lozenge formation was called by Morgan his 'tertia', with narrow gaps between the van, middle and rear sections.

The Spanish were drawn up in a stronger position, with cavalry on each wing, and the guns in front of them. On each flank they also had a herd of wild cattle with herdsmen, who were to be stampeded towards Morgan's little army. Morgan now checked the disposition of the Spanish and decided to try to outflank them with his advance guard. They crept through scrubby bushland, down a deep valley and circled a hill to get within musket shot of the Spanish wing. Guzman saw the danger and ordered the cavalry on that wing to charge the buccaneers, but a musket fusillade smashed the first charge apart. In the second, and final charge, the cavalry commander Don Francisco de Haro fell almost into the massed ranks of marksmen. The vanguard was still in its wedge formation, allowing for maximum firepower, and the cavalry had to charge into its front, because it was protected by a hill on one side and a swamp on the other. The outside ranks had knelt to shoot, just as in the English Civil War, then the next rank advanced to fire and so on. With no pikes, this rapid and accurate fire was the only way to have beaten the cavalry charges.

Guzman's infantry were ordered now to stand and fight, but some veterans under de Alcaudete had personally seen the results of the 'rape of Puerto Bello', and in their blind hatred charged without orders. They were joined by the rest, and pushed past the vanguard of John Morris aside to attack the right centre under Morgan. Captain Collier's men from the left centre joined the action and Guzman's army was dispersed. The attack by the cattle was easily repelled, as the rearguard buccaneers under Bledri Morgan aimed at the faces of the leaders, to turn the stampede back on the Spanish. De Alcaudete was wounded, and only Guzman appeared to remain on the field of battle, attended by a faithful negro servant and a priest, who entreated him to escape. Guzman reluctantly returned to Panama to marshal the defences, with thirty cannon covering the main streets, but the British and French soon over-ran the disheartened defenders. Casualties had been just five men killed and ten wounded against the Spaniards' four-hundred or so. A galleon full of bullion just managed to escape into the wide Pacific, carrying fleeing nobility and clergymen.

The retreating Spanish set fire to the main powder magazine in order to ruin the city, but Morgan's followers managed to keep the fires mainly under control for the next three weeks as they plundered the remaining buildings. Much treasure was dredged up from wells, dried out by the raging fires. (Esquemeling states that Morgan set fire to Panama, but a letter by Guzman exists stating that it was his order. The

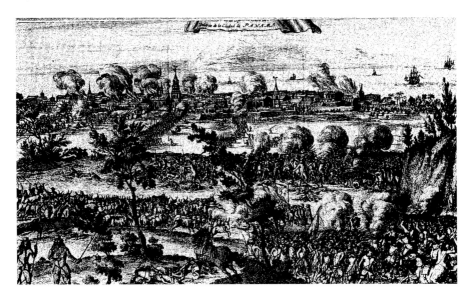

Morgan's sack of Panama

buccaneer William Frogge also stated that the Spaniards, not Morgan set fire to the city. Frogge also complained bitterly about the payout of £10 per man for this expedition, around £2000 in today's money*).

The pirates desperately searched for the famous Golden Altar of the city of San Jose, but assumed it had been taken by the escaping ship. It was covered with plates of solid beaten gold and worth an enormous sum. According to some sources, priests had covered it with white paint, which was scraped off several years later. As Morgan's men tortured priests to find its whereabouts, not much credence can be given to this story. The buccaneers also captured ships and towns in the surrounding Pearl Islands, taking booty and 3,000 prisoners to ransom. Morgan sent out the four fastest ships he could find in Panama harbour, to chase the escaping treasure galleon, but they only came back with another prize. At Taboga Island, this merchantman had valuable cargo and a chest with 20,000 pieces of eight. The buccaneers also captured slaves and Panamanian refugees on the island. For a month Morgan's men ravaged the area, torturing prisoners to find the whereabouts of treasure. A particular pleasure was hanging men by their testicles until they told the ruffians what they wanted to hear. Morgan seems to have fallen in love with one of the Spanish ladies travelling on the merchantman. He tried by all methods to seduce her, but, failing, released her. Two friars spent her ransom money upon freeing some religious colleagues, so Morgan hung them and sent her on her way on a mule. (This is Esquemeling's version of events).

So much plunder was taken that some factions of pirates were thinking of escaping with a share of the loot from Panama. Morgan heard of this, and ordered all the vessels dismasted and their sails and rigging burned. The buccaneers were becoming more difficult to control, fewer and fewer riches were coming from tortures, and the flow of ransoms was drying up. On February 14, 1671, the buccaneers loaded up their booty and set off for Chagres. Over 170 mules and horses were loaded down, as were all the captured slaves and Spanish families. At Venta Cruz (Cruces) they stopped to accept some ransoms in the form of meat, maize and rice as well as money. A rumour spread like wildfire among the buccaneers that Morgan was reserving some extra precious trophies, such as a solid gold shrine, for himself. To stamp the incipient mutiny out, Morgan had himself strip searched and his knapsack inspected, then ordered it to be done to all the rest of his men. Some old-timers and the French resented this bitterly, and disloyal mutterings about Morgan's leadership were still heard. After 12 days, the expedition arrived at San Lorenzo Castle at Chargres, on February 26th. Espinosa's fleet had not been sighted, and Norman's garrison in the fort welcomed him warmly, seeing the vast riches they would share in. Taking advantage of this, Morgan acted quickly and picked out several ringleaders of the potential mutiny and had them executed.

Morgan now sent the prisoners taken at Old Providence to Puerto Bello. They had been promised their freedom without ransom under the terms Morgan came to with their governor. A message was sent with the ship that San Lorenzo would be destroyed unless the Spanish authorities ransomed it. Don Alfonso de Alcaudete, recovered from his injuries on the plain of Matasnillos, refused to send anything. Morgan demolished the castle, spiking all the guns except the best which he took for his own ship. Morgan claimed that £30,000 was made in ransoms, but some of the other captains felt that he had made over £70,000 for the share-out at the end of the voyage. W. Llywelyn Williams estimated that the total value of all the plunder, including slaves, was 750,000 pieces of eight, the richest raid in history.

At Chagres, Admiral Morgan announced that the common pool could only pay out 200 pieces of eight, about £10 at the time, to each soldier and sailor who took part in the expedition, after deductions had been made for the King, the Lord High Admiral, officers, ship-owners, ships' surgeons and the like. All of the French and many English captains sailed off in disgust, to try to get more booty along the coast. Esquemeling was particularly scathing about Morgan's arithmetic …'*Morgan was deaf to all these and many other complaints of this kind, having designed in his mind to cheat them of as much as he could.*' Surgeon Browne also complained that Morgan did not give the men their fair share of the booty - he '*cheated the soldjer of a very vast summe.*'W. Llywelyn Williams however, thinks the share-out was about right, considering that the payments for injuries were higher than normal, captains took eight shares instead of five, Charles II took 10% and the Duke of York a fifteenth of the total. Henry Morgan's 1% share would have given him 7,500 pieces of eight. Esquemeling left Morgan at this time, to cruise the Honduras before joining the French buccaneers in Tortuga.

On March 12th, Morgan returned to Port Royal as a hero, with just 4 ships of his 35. Another 6 ships sailed into Port Royal shortly after, but Bledri Morgan sailed from Chagres to Old Providence, where he acted as governor for a time. However, Chagres had been captured by Morgan after unofficial news had come to Jamaica that there was peace with Spain. Morgan must have known by December 1, if only from Spanish captives, but he pleaded utter ignorance. Admiral Morgan submitted his report on

April 20th, and appeared before the council of Jamaica on May 31st to relate his voyage to Panama. It is noted that he received the formal congratulations of Modyford, and the approval of the council for carrying out his commission. Morgan had written in his report to Governor Modyford, *'thus was consumed the famous and ancient city of Panama, the greatest mart for silver and gold in the entire world.'* Modyford's brother wrote *'I think we are well revenged for their burning our houses on ye north and south side of this island.'* The Council met on June 10, 1671 and publicly thanked Morgan for carrying out his commission.

However, back in London, the Conde de Molina, the Spanish Ambassador to Whitehall, was incensed by Morgan's actions, and wanted him to face trial. Charles II was too weak financially to face another war, and tried to defuse the situation by ordering Sir Thomas Lynch to replace Governor Modyford, and send Modyford home as a prisoner. Morgan kept his head down, hoping that his account of events would be believed by the King. Lynch was indpendently wealthy, and indeed had loaned the king £50,000, probably in exchange for a knighthood. Unlike Modyford, he did not intend operating hand-in-glove with Morgan. The recent Asiento agreement meant that there were fortunes to be made in the slave trade taking negroes from Africa to the Spanish colonies. He had no need of privateers. Lynch arrived in Jamaica in June, showed his commission to the Council, and arrested Morgan's friend and patron, Governor Modyford.

Lynch had to take care in his dealings with Morgan, and seems to have been ambivalent about him. A letter to Lord Arlington written on July 2, 1671, says *'This voyage has mightily lessened and humbled them* (the privateers), *and they would take it for a great compliment to be severe with Morgan, whom they rail on horribly for starving, cheating and deserting them.'* But Governor Lynch, not Morgan's ally by any means, also wrote a letter to London which stated that *'to tell the truth of him, he's an honest, brave fellow, and had both Sir Thomas Modyford's and the Council's commission and instructions.'*

Governor Modyford was sent to London on August 22nd, in The *Jamaica Merchant*, kept in some comfort in the Tower of London for two years, then released to return to Jamaica as chief justice. Morgan, the hero of the Jamaicans, spent his time drinking and socialising in Port Royal and Santiago de la Vega. The scale and intensity of the raiding along the coast of South America in Morgan's years is incredible, when we think that inflation would increase these sums a thousand-fold:

Captains	Prize or Port	Value at the time
Christopher Myngs, with 12 ships and less than 500 men	1663 San Francisco de Campeche, Mexico	150,000 pesos (£37,500)
Edward Morgan with 6 ships and 300 men	1665 Oranjestad, St Eustatius	100,000 pesos (£25,000)
Francis L'Olonnais with 8 ships and 660 men	1667 Several ships, Maracaibo and Gibraltar, Venezuela	260,000 pesos (£65,000)
Henry Morgan with 10 ships and 500 men	1668 Puerto Principe, Cuba; Panama, Portobello	250,000 pesos (£62,500)

Henry Morgan with 8 ships and under 500 men	1669 Maracaibo and Gibraltar, Venezuela	120,000 pesos (£30,000)
Henry Morgan with up to 2000 men	1671 Panama City	120,000 pesos (£30,000)

The historian Edward Long in the 18th century estimated that Morgan's loot between 1669 and 1671 was as follows: Puerto del Principe 50,000 pieces of eight; Porto Bello 250,000 pieces; Maracaibo 250,000 pieces; and Panama 400,000 pieces - almost a million pieces of eight in three years. He went on '*Beside an immense quantity of silks, linen, gold and silver, lace, plate, jewels and other valuable commodities, which probably amounted to near as much more. By this means money grew to be in vast plenty, and returns easy to England, into which many hundred thousand of those pieces of eight were imported.*'

1672
However, Charles II eventually weakened to Ambassador Molina's insistence, and the veiled threat of a revenge Spanish attack on Jamaica, and in January 1672 Lynch received orders to send Morgan home to answer for his offences. Lynch put Morgan on an old royal frigate, the *Welcome*, which he *called 'an old vessel, and if taken in any distress of weather would be lost with all her men.'* He was obviously hoping that the problem would be solved at sea, and on April 4 she set of with the arrested Morgan on board. Morgan had prepared well, however, having sent to England a long memorandum on the necessity of encouraging privateers where there was no adequate naval protection for the colonies. He also canvassed all his friends for testimonials of recommendation to present to the King. The voyage took three stormy months, and Captain Keene reported to the cabinet's Lord Clifford that '*the two prisoners are still on board, but very much tired with their long confinement, especially Captain Morgan, who is very sickly.*' After a month at sea, food and water rapidly deteriorate, and there are severe outbreaks of scurvy and enteric illnesses. Morgan complained that after this voyage, and the cold and fogs of an English winter, he never regained his health.

On his arrival Morgan was immediately released pending trial. Charles owed him a great deal for the financial gains he had made, and for the fact that Morgan's victories had been the only success stories in his endeavours against Spain. Morgan was a popular hero in Britain, and between 1672 and 1675 was feted by Court and nobles, was seen smoking in fashionable coffee-houses, and also spent plenty of time in the dockside taverns and brothels where he probably felt more at home. John Evelyn noted in his Diary about Panama, that '*such an action has not been done since the famous Drake.*' Morgan and Modyford were feted everywhere, and Morgan told Evelyn at a dinner that with a thousand men he could capture the whole of the Spanish Indies for the King. The Third Dutch War had broken out, however, and every ship was needed to guard Britain.

Morgan met Christopher, Duke of Albemarle, the son of General Monck, and a relative of Modyford. Albemarle had helped with the release of Modyford from gaol, and promised he would also help Morgan. The Duke was close to Charles II because his father had engineered the return of the King to replace Richard Cromwell and the Reformation Government. Morgan was 37 and Albemarle 19, and they became life-long friends. The younger man seemed to recognise that Morgan had a great deal to teach him. Although the third richest man in England, after the King and the Duke of York, Albemarle was a kindred spirit to Morgan. He was married to Lady Ogle, but before Morgan arrived had been involved in a serious scandal. Whetstone Park was an low-class area of *bordels* (brothels) and *grog-shops* (taverns). Albemarle had gone to a brothel there on a Saturday night with some lesser lords, and the Duke of Somerset and the Duke of Monmouth (the same Monmouth who later led the bloody Monmouth Rebellion). A beadle (assistant constable) tried to enter the bordel to suppress the drunken noise and shenanigans, and was killed by a sword, allegedly by Albemarle. There was an outcry by the people of London, but Charles pardoned all the offenders, who continued to use Whetstone Park.

In 1672, Major-General Banister, Commander-in-Chief of the troops in Jamaica, wrote to Lord Arlington in Morgan's defence that Morgan '*is a well deserving person, and one of great courage and conduct, who may, with His Majesty's pleasure, perform good public service at home, or be very advantageous to this island if war should break out against the Spaniards.*' Arlington was one of King Charles' inner cabinet. All of Charles' closest advisors were now in the pro-Morgan faction at court.

1673 THE TRIAL

Morgan was tiring of London. It was soaking up his fortune, and there seemed to be no sight of a trial. He complained directly to the king that he wanted a hearing. There was no formal trial. Morgan and others gave evidence informally to the Lords of Trade and Plantations (which later became the Colonial Office), and the evidence was submitted to King Charles II. Modyford could prove that he had sent a messenger to the Isle des Vaches to tell Morgan that there was a truce with Spain. Morgan could prove that the messages were returned to Jamaica with their seals unbroken. The messenger had '*disappeared*', either by accident or design. No members of the expedition were called to account, to say where Morgan was when the messages were allegedly delivered. Morgan was then called before Charles to give a personal account, and answer a few questions. Deliberately or not, there was no real evidence against Morgan or Modyford.

In the dossier of evidence, there were some complaints, mainly about the sharing of booty, but his relative at the great Tredegar House in Monmouthshire, William Morgan, wrote strongly on his behalf about his '*relation and former near neighbour.*' '*He has had a very good character of him, and in the management of the late business of Panama he behaved with as much prudence, fidelity and resolution as could reasonably be expected, and at his return his services were approved by the then Governor and Council, and thanks ordered him, and all good men would be troubled if a person of his loyalty and consideration as to His Majesty's affairs in those parts should fall for want of friends to assist him.*' It was almost as if Morgan himself had written the letter.

Morgan's lobbying of past favours also had resulted in this evidence for the defence, from Major-General Banister, Commander of the Forces in Jamaica, and a member of the Council. Morgan had received '*a very high and honourable applause for his noble service therein, both from Sir Thomas Modyford and the Council that commissioned him.*' Albemarle, one of the most powerful political figures in England, had also lobbied tirelessly for his friend Morgan's acquittal. The only real danger to Morgan had come from the Spanish Ambassador. Even if Morgan had not known about the Treaty of Madrid, his commission did not give him the authority to fight on land and sack Panama City. Morgan's defence was that a phrase in his commission enabled him to '*do all manner of exploits*' in order to pay his men with captured goods and merchandise.

One of the English ministerial secretaries raised the point that by marching and giving battle in military formation, Morgan had '*arrogated the privileges of His Majesty's Army*' and thus made an official act of war. Morgan casually responded that he had to complete the work of Porto Bello, and prevent further attacks upon English shipping and upon Jamaica, indeed it had been '*a war to end war.*' The '*pestiferous nest*' of Panama had to be wiped out to stop Spanish aggression. He was also asked why he did not believe the Spanish when they told him that there was peace between the countries. Morgan replied that he had forgotten if anyone had told him that. He went on to say that he would have disbelieved it anyway, as all his experience showed him that the Spanish were liars. It was at this point that Charles was supposed to have said '*Oddsfish!*' and exploded with laughter, concluding the hearing.

As well as Albemarle, the Duke of Monmouth was a drinking companion of Morgan's. Monmouth was Charles' 'illegitimate' son by Lucy Walters, but was probably legitimate, and the heir to the throne (see '*100 Great Welsh Women*'). Morgan was wildly popular with the people of Britain, especially in London . He moved easily in Court circles. Charles had gained enormous riches from Morgan's expeditions. His brother James, Duke of York, as Admiral of the Fleet, had also made a fortune (although he was himself a Catholic). Charles quickly consulted with James and his inner advisors, the infamous CABAL of the lords Clifford, Arlington, Buckingham, Ashley and Lauderdale. The verdict was obviously '*not proven*'. Morgan's luck had held again, and the public reception was ecstatic. A few days later, King Charles summoned Henry to Court and knighted him. On November 20th, 1673, Charles II received Henry Morgan at Court in Whitehall, and gave him a snuff-box with the face of Charles set in diamonds. Morgan spent more and more time at court, looking for a suitable position back home in Jamaica.

1674

On January 24th, Charles appointed Charles Howard, Earl of Carlisle as Governor of Jamaica, to replace Lynch, the man who had arrested Morgan. On the same day, Henry Morgan was made Lieutenant-Governor of Jamaica. The letter confirming the appointment stated that Charles had a '*particular confidence in his loyalty, prudence and courage, and long experience of the Colony.*' These words were actually written by the philosopher John Locke, who was then Secretary to the Council of Trade and Plantations. In June, Sir Henry Morgan was also made Lieutenant-General of Jamaica's armed forces. Unfortunately Carlisle, a friend of Morgan's, wished to postpone his Governorship of the West Indies, and Lord John Vaughan was commissioned instead. Sir Henry's commission was then changed to make Vaughan his superior.

John Evelyn noted in his diary that Sir Thomas Modyford and Colonel Morgan were being entertained at Lord Berkeley's on September 21st, 1674. These two great friends were on their way 'home'. Sir Thomas Modyford had been appointed Chief-Justice of Jamaica. They obviously thought that they could easily 'sort out' Vaughan and once again control the island. The deposed Governor, Sir Thomas Lynch, was mortified that the two men he had arrested were coming back, Morgan laden with honours. In November 1674 he wrote to the Lords of Trade and Plantations about the increasing Spanish threat, no doubt hoping to rescind Charles' decisions 'One of the reasons of their coming is the noise of Admiral Morgan's favour at Court and return to the Indies, which much alarmed the Spaniards, and caused the King to be at vast charge in fortifying in the South Sea.'

1675

By a delicious irony, the ship that carried Morgan and Modyford to Jamaica in pomp was the *Jamaica Merchant*, which had taken Modyford to London as a prisoner back in 1671. On January 8, the frigate containing Vaughan and the ship containing Morgan and Modyford weighed anchor. Vaughan gave explicit instructions that they should keep close touch. Morgan and Vaughan seem to have hated each other from the start. Vaughan knew he had a larger-than-life character to keep in order. Morgan saw Vaughan as an inconvenience to his plans. The ships were separated on the first day out from England, for which Vaughan seems to have blamed Morgan. Morgan claimed that the anchor was stuck fast, and that Vaughan was out of range before they could set off. Although ostensibly on the same course, the ships never sighted each other again. The *Jamaica Merchant* made an incredibly fast crossing, not to Jamaica but to Morgan's old haunt of the Isle des Vaches. Morgan obviously wanted to meet someone at the favourite rendezvous, but also get to Jamaica before Lynch. However, on February 25th, his ship was wrecked at the Isle des Vaches. Whether the loss was contrived, or indeed the ship was wrecked at all, we do not know. Perhaps Morgan (and Modyford) were picking up some hidden loot stashed away in case things went awry in London.

Morgan later wrote to England that 'we had all perished, had I not known where I was'. Surprisingly, another vessel quickly picked Morgan, Modyford and the crew up, and he was in Port Royal on March 5th, still an astonishing nine days before the arrival of Vaughan's faster frigate, which had come the direct and quicker route. Morgan was a clever man, who would have been called a 'dashing rogue' in romantic potboilers. Welcomed in the taverns of Port Royal, Morgan rode almost immediately the twelve miles to the capital of St Jago, where with great relish he demanded a meeting of the Council which was held on March 7th. Sir Henry Morgan must have smiled when he gave his commission and formally deposed the bitter Governor Thomas Lynch. He asked the council if he could assume the Governorship and take command of the island, and took the chair for the rest of the meeting. On March 11th, at another

Council meeting in Port Royal, Morgan received the Great Seal of the Island, formally granting him the Governorship.

However, a vengeful Lord Vaughan finally arrived in Jamaica on March 14th, and the first of Morgan's terms of Governorship ended the next day. Vaughan hurriedly summoned a Council in Port Royal, took the Governor's oath, and Henry Morgan was sworn in as his Lieutenant. For the next three years the dour intellectual Vaughan (yet called by one of Samuel Pepys' friends 'one of the lewdest fellows of the age') argued constantly with the flamboyant hero Morgan. Morgan almost immediately accused Lynch of impropriety with a negro prize-ship, writing to England and calling him 'the greatest cheat of the age'. Vaughan allied with Lynch against Morgan, and said 'In the Downs I gave him orders, in writing, to keep me company, and in no case to be separated from me but by distress of weather; however he, God knows by what fate, coveting to be here before me, wilfully lost me.'

Rubbing salt into the festering wound of Morgan's popularity, the local parliament had granted him £600 'for his good services to the country during his Lieutenant-Governorship, but none to his successors'. The joyous Morgan then appeared on the Parliament floor to thank the representatives, which infuriated Vaughan enough to write home 'His particular ill conduct and wilful breach of his positive and written orders since the meeting at the Assembly, with other follies, have so tired me that I am perfectly weary of him, and I frankly tell you that I think it is for His Majesty's service he should be removed, and the charge (expense) of so useless an officer saved.'

Morgan now stayed away from the jibes of Vaughan and the capital of St Jago de la Vega as much as possible, sticking to his old friends in Port Royal. Vaughan saw him as being head of a 'de facto' second capital of the island. On September 20, 1675, Vaughan again wrote to Secretary of State Williamson telling tales: 'I am every day more convinced of his imprudence and unfitness to have anything to do with the Civil Government, and of what hazards the Island may run with so dangerous a succession. Sir Henry has made himself and his authority so cheap at the Port, drinking and gaming at the taverns, that I intend to remove thither speedily myself for the reputation of the Island and the security of the place.' Lord Vaughan was never made welcome at Port Royal, and never stayed for long, however. The Secretary of State showed little sympathy, and instead wrote to ask Morgan, not Vaughan, for a report on conditions upon the colony. Morgan answered that Vaughan would not let him contribute in Jamaica's government, so he could only send an incomplete account, but that he was as ready as any man to obey his King's commands.

1676

In early spring, Sir Henry halted the execution of a privateer called Deane, and Vaughan believed that he was also sending warnings to buccaneers rather than arresting them. By May he thought he had proof of Morgan's traitorous intentions, and wrote again to Secretary of State Williamson: 'What I most resent is, and which I consider as parts of my duty to lay before your Honour, that I find Sir Henry, contrary to his duty and trust, endeavours to set up privateering, and has obstructed all my designs for the reducing of those that do use that curse of life.'

Trying desperately to overthrow his second-in-command, the embittered Vaughan also wrote to the Lord Privy Seal, Lord Anglesea: *'I detected him (Morgan) of a most gross unfaithfulness in his trust, and a wilful breach and disobedience of my orders, only because they have obstructed his design of privateering....Since the trial of Deane he has been so impudent and unfaithful at the taverns and in his own house..... and has, with his brother (in-law) Byndloss, encouraged the King's subjects to take French commissions, fitted them out to sea, and been concerned with them in their ships and prizes. I know his imprudence and weakness lead him a long way, but believe his necessities do more, which would prove of sad consequence to the Island if there should be any devolution of Government .... His brother Byndloss agitates him in all he does, and I have therefore given him (Byndloss) no authority of any civil or military commission. He is a turbulent fellow, some years since he was surgeon of a ship, but never can be easy in any Government. It would be a good thing if the Governor had a private instruction to put him out of the Council.'*

Lieutenant-Colonel Robert Byndloss was Morgan's only open supporter on the eight-man Council of Jamaica, and this was Vaughan's last throw of the dice to get rid of this pair of scoundrels, who seemed to be openly flouting his authority. It was obvious at this time that Morgan was *'sailing close to the wind'* in his dealings with his former buccaneer associates. It was another thing for Vaughan to prove it, but he hurriedly called the Council together on July 24, 1676, citing the brother-in-law and asking them to answer charges.

MORGAN'S SECOND TRIAL

Whatever one feels about Admiral Sir Henry Morgan as a character, one cannot but admire his almost mischievous self-confidence. His humour tempered his natural arrogance, and this trial also shows his intelligence and native Welsh cunning. Morgan quietly sat through the list of charges, and was interrogated for a couple of hours by his peers on the council. Vaughan became quite vehement as he tried to rattle Sir Henry into making a mistake in his eloquent, and sometimes sophisticated answers. After all, Henry had been questioned by the King and the greatest in the land and found innocent of all charges. This jumped-up *land-lubber* was not going to get under his skin, instead he would slowly reel Vaughan in and watch him squirm. On the charge that Morgan had corresponded with *'monsieurs Puncay and Cussy'*, intending to collaborate with them to attack Spain, Vaughan had written proof. Also Morgan was known to have met on several occasions, in the drinking dens of Port Royal, with a French privateer named Prinier.

Things looked black for the old freebooter, but his answer was easy and assured. The Sieur de Pouancey (Puncay) had succeeded his uncle d'Ogeron as Governor of Tortuga and Western Hispaniola. The Comte de Cussy was de Pouancey's lieutenant, eventually to succeed him as Governor. They were the employees of Louis XIV, with whom Charles II had excellent relations. As a fellow senior official in the West Indies, what was wrong with diplomatic relations? If relations with the French were forbidden, where was the written order Were there any minutes or documents to prove this? Did anyone on the Council know of such an edict? (Morgan, when debarred from giving commissions to privateers, had sent them on to his friend d'Ogeron, and received a commission from him).

On the next charge of talking to the French pirate Prinier, Morgan explained that he was just carrying out political subterfuge. He wished to make sure through this men and his colleagues that the French were not issuing commissions to buccaneers. How else could he find out? By this time the majority of the Council were sensing a sea-change in the relative positions of authority of Lord Vaughan and Admiral Morgan. Morgan went on to offer his secretary's deposition that Morgan was totally innocent of dealing with privateers for his own ends. Morgan stated that Vaughan had never confided in him, and was out to ruin him '*for what reasons I know not.*' He finished his speech as follows: '*If I err in one tittle (small piece), then let me ever be condemned for the greatest villain in the world ..... I suckled the milk of loyalty, and if I would have sold one little part of it I might have been richer than my enemies will ever be.*'

Morgan sat down, satisfied and asked for some tobacco and rum while he watched the proceedings against Byndloss. While less loquacious, Byndloss gave the same, probably rehearsed, story. (Byndloss's descendants were left a fortune by Morgan in his will, on condition they took Morgan's surname in perpetuity, probably to make up for Morgan and his beloved Mary Elizabeth being unable to have children). The transcript of this executive enquiry was then sent to London, where Morgan's lobby was far closer to the locus of power than Vaughan's. The Council had seen that there was effectively no case to answer, and while the status quo reigned until Whitehall came to a decision, they knew that Vaughan had lost the running battle. Around this time also, the Lords of Trade and Plantations decided that the alleged pirate Deane was tried improperly, and ordered his release. Morgan had been vindicated over Vaughan, and when this verdict reached Jamaica in Autumn, most of the Council now openly sided with Morgan.

1677

In summer 1677, the official verdict to Morgan's trial came back to Jamaica. It was that The Lords of Trade and the Plantations had come to no resolution of the matter and would examine the case further. The Lords, along with Charles' Court, looked upon Morgan, now known as '*The Sword of England*', as the deputy for his friend the Earl of Carlisle. Vaughan was seen as a stop-gap Governor, holding the seat for Carlisle, and in the winter he was recalled as Carlisle decided to take up the office. Sir Harry had won the political and diplomatic battle at last.

1678 MORGAN'S SECOND TERM

On January 13, Carlisle received his commission, and in March Vaughan left Jamaica forever. On April 3, Morgan was sworn in as Acting Governor in Port Royal. One of the new Councillors was Sir Thomas Modyford, Morgan's old comrade. Chief Justice Modyford had used his '*cuts*' from privateering voyages that he had commissioned, to make himself probably the richest plantation owner in Jamaica. For three months Sir Henry ruled the island, until the Earl of Carlisle arrived on July 19th. Carlisle had previously received a confidential report underlining Morgan's popularity on the island, with the added benefit that Morgan always spoke well of Carlisle.

Morgan resumed his role of Lieutenant-Governor, and senior member of the Council. He built up his plantation interests, which were Penkarne in St George, Arthur's Land in St Mary, Danke's Land and Morgan's Valley. He became Judge-Admiral and first 'Custos Rotulorum' (the equivalent of a county's Lord Lieutenant) of Port Royal. Unfortunately Modyford, around seventy years old, died in 1679, about which time Morgan was drinking copious amounts even by his notable standards. From 1678-80, Morgan stood on the sidelines, not wishing to become embroiled in a bitter political battle between Carlisle and the Council. He was a friend of Carlisle's but a friend of Jamaica far more. Carlisle had been instructed by Charles II to change the pattern of law-making on the island, to standardise it with English law. The Assembly of the island could no longer make laws, but merely ratify Whitehall legislation, and could not reject any laws. The Council resented this, sending two Councillors to Whitehall to argue their case, and the Council was suspended. Morgan kept his counsel, neutral in the dispute and waiting to see which way the wind was blowing.

1680 THIRD GOVERNORSHIP

In May 1680, the Earl of Carlisle left Jamaica, and Morgan succeeded him. As Carlisle had dissolved the Assembly, Morgan was now in complete control of Jamaica. New elections could not be called until the two suspended Council members returned from London. Morgan packed the Council with his own supporters, and ruled for a year as a semi-dictator. For some reason, possibly previously agreed with Carlisle, he clamped down severely on all privateering. Morgan had huge debts, and saw his way to financial salvation by trading with Spain, rather than warring with it.

Port Royal was closed to 'illegal' vessels, and all privateers were offered to apply for pardons. Those who did not apply would be arrested, tried at the Admiralty Court, and hung. In July 1680, Morgan wrote to London asking for some small, quick frigates to stamp out the French buccaneers of Hispaniola, who were attracting Englishmen to become 'brethren of the coast'. True to his word, he captured Captain Jacob Everson and twenty-five of his crew at Bull Bay near Port Royal. His old cohort in crime, Everson, 'escaped', but some of the crew were executed. In another incident, Morgan heard of a strange ship in port. He invited the crew to dine with him, and over the free-flowing wine, out-vied them in buccaneering tales. They divulged the whereabouts of Spanish ships that were worth taking. Next morning, on leaving Morgan's hospitality, they were arrested by soldiers. After a short court hearing, seventeen pirates were 'swung off' at the end of the day. In the meantime, Colonel Samuel Long and William Beeston had argued successfully in Whitehall for a return to the Jamaican Constitution.

1681

In February 1681, Morgan could issue a writ to hold Assembly elections, and worked feverishly to get the new assembly to agree to seven years of 'contributions' to the London government of Charles II. However, in September he was astonished to discover that his old enemy Sir Thomas Lynch had again been given the

Governorship, with Morgan becoming once again Lieutenant-Governor. He had been intriguing against Morgan since his return to London, and probably gave Charles II yet another loan to secure the deal. No reason was given for his dismissal and Morgan was astounded and perturbed, fell once more into heavy drinking, and his health rapidly deteriorated. Like Vaughan, Lynch also complained of Morgan's dissolute behaviour, but the only witness who could be called against him was a female tavern-keeper who said she heard him say, as Morgan passed her door, 'God damn the Assembly.' Morgan now spent much of his time with his Tory cronies in the Loyal Club. Lynch complained: 'In his debauches which go on every night, he is much magnified and little criticised by the five or six little sycophants that share them ... In his drink Sir Henry reflects on the government, swears, damns and curses most extravagantly.'

Sir Hans Sloane, who accompanied Lord Albemarle to Jamaica, thought that Morgan had liver problems (caused by decades of neat rum), dropsy (oedema, or swellings) and chronic pulmonary 'phthisis' (tuberculosis, possibly caused by his journey under arrest to England years earlier). Henry organised a party of people around him as Tories, the loyalist party of Charles Stuart, while trying to parade Lynch as a royalty-hating Whig. However, Morgan's influence was waning with his health, and he kept as far away from the hated Lynch as possible.

1684

On October 10, Byndloss was removed from the Council for disorderly conduct. On October 12, with no supporters left in the Council, Morgan was also thrown off the Council on a variety of charges. Lynch had engineered a council full of his supporters. The Governor had organised the dismissal of the Welshman Cradock from the Council. Another Morgan supporter, Roger Elletson had been earlier moved off the Council, and he was now even forbidden to practise law. Captain Charles Morgan, Henry's cousin, brother-in-law and son of Sir Edward Morgan, was dismissed from his captaincy of Fort Royal. Lynch was in total command of Jamaica. In a last throw of the dice, Henry now sent Charles Morgan to England to protest about Lynch. Just at this moment, this only man to get the better of Sir Henry received terrible news. Lynch's wife and their two sons were drowned on the way to join him in Jamaica. Lynch died soon after the news, on August 24, 1684, and Hender Molesworth took over as Acting Governor.

1684 THE FIRST SUCCESSFUL LIBEL SUIT IN HISTORY

Johan Esquemeling, the Fleming who sailed under Morgan, wrote De Americaensche Zee Roovers in 1678. It was translated into Spanish and French and ran through many editions. Its immense success attracted two English booksellers, Thomas Malthus and William Crooke, who both published translations of the Spanish edition in 1684. Morgan read a copy of this History of the Bucaniers in Jamaica, and immediately instructed his London lawyer, John Greene, to force the publishers to retract the claims about his past. William Crooke complied immediately, promising to put a favourable insert on Morgan in the second edition. The legal action was dropped, especially as Crookes also issued a grovelling pamphlet which included:

'I have been credibly informed by certain gentlemen, who belong unto the acquaintance of Sir Henry, that several things are therein delivered, the which are both falsely reported by John Esquemeling, and wrongfully represented, and consequently are much redounding to the Disreputation and Dishonour of that Worthy Person, Sir Henry Morgan; For the Wounds of whose reputation by that Author, I have been, ever since my better information, both heartily sorrowful, and concerned in the sincerity of my mind; and in testimony thereof, have thought it convenient, by these times, humbly to solicit, and desire the pardon of that noble and generous Spirit, for as much as by me hath been contributed thereunto, by printing the English Translation.'

So far, so good, but Thomas Malthus was totally unwilling to settle. He seemed to have spread propaganda that Morgan was even more brutal than the book claimed, in order to create more interest and stimulate sales. Morgan and his lawyer seemed to hope the matter would just go away – Morgan could not afford litigation. It seems that Morgan did not mind much about the lies told about his behaviour - it was the slur on his pedigree that he cared about.

1685

However, in February 1685, the Catholic James II succeeded Charles II as King of England. As he was friendly with Spain, Morgan's alleged past as a murderer and torturer of the Spanish, without proper letters of marque, forced his lawyer to act quickly. The lawyer, John Greene, sought a special hearing by the new king, a *'coram rege'*. He set out to prove Esquemeling was a liar, and that Malthus had disseminated this *'certain false, malicious, scandalous and famous libel entitled 'The History of the Bucaniers'*. Morgan of course was *'of good fame and name, and against evil deeds, piracies and robberies'* and buccaneers were *'thieves'* of which he *'always had and still has hatred'*.

As James had personally profited from Morgan's buccaneering exploits, this line of attack could not really be disapproved by the King. Greene then went through the various libels in the book; that Morgan was a bond-servant, a pirate before he privateered under Mansvelt; the Puerto Principe accusations; and various tortures ascribed to Morgan. The lies were so great that the honest and loyal subject might even be tried and hung for piracy! The lawyer concluded his speech by asking for ten thousand pounds damages. Malthus was ordered to appear before the king, but refused to attend. Whether he believed that Morgan had a case, or he was *'warned off'* by some of Morgan's friends in London is unknown. King James refused to recommend an amount for damages, so the sheriffs of Middlesex summoned twelve men for jury service, who awarded Sir Henry £200, with costs, on May 27th. The action was reported in the London Gazette upon June 8th, and the principle that money could be awarded for literary libel had been made **legal precedent**.

Also in June, the Duke of Monmouth's rebellion was smashed at Sedgemoor. Christopher Monck, Duke of Albemarle (like Monmouth, a former drinking partner of Morgan's) fought for the king, and wanted the Governorship of Jamaica. Like Morgan, Albemarle desperately needed money – he had gambled, whored, drunk and frittered away most of his father's fortune. The Duke firmly believed that there was a Spanish treasure ship that could be salvaged, off north-east Hispaniola. The ship had foundered in 1659, and both Spanish and French expeditions had tried to find it. King Charles had loaned Albemarle a frigate and ninety-five men in 1682, but he had been unable to locate it. In 1685, a seaman had found some silver ingots, and one of gold, on the shores of Samana Bay, and James promised that Albemarle could try again.

1686
In March, an expedition sailed for the West Indies, mainly financed by Albemarle's depleted resources, and in May it was announced that he would be the new Governor of Jamaica. Morgan was overjoyed – this was a man he could work with. He had no friendship with Governor Molesworth, who was only really interested in working the Asiento treaty to his advantage. Molesworth was a factor of the Royal Africa Company, which now had a monopoly on the slave trade with Spain. He had no need for Morgan nor any other local leaders – he was too busy making money. Albemarle immediately called for Morgan and Byndloss to be reappointed to the Jamaica Council, but King James vetoed the proposal.

1687
Albemarle waited in England, waiting anxiously for the return of his two ships. In June 1687, they returned, carrying loot salvaged from the galleon to the value of a third of a million pounds. They could not carry any more bullion and had to return for more later. The newly rich Albemarle sent more ships out to salvage, and sailed to Jamaica for three days of roistering with Sir Henry. Morgan now assumed his rightful position as (unofficial) chief advisor to the Governor. Albemarle again proposed that Morgan join the Council of Jamaica, but King James prevaricated, saying that Morgan would have to return to England and plead his case. Morgan was ill, and feared that such a trip would kill him. Albemarle made yet another plea after lobbying Council support: *'One thing I have omitted to mention to your Lordships, as you will find by the minutes of the Council concerning Sir Henry Morgan, where the whole Council have desired me that I would favourable recommend him to your Majestie for re-admission into the Council which I earnestly do, and desire your Lordships will please to move it to his Majestie.'*

1688
In July, Albemarle and Morgan received news from Whitehall that Morgan was back on the Council. Morgan carried on drinking heavily, and frequented the lowest places in Port Royal. He was fifty-three years old, and Albemarle just thirty-five. Dr Hans Sloane gives us the account of Morgan's last days: *Sir Henry Morgan, aged about 45 (actually 53), lean, sallow coloured, his eyes a little yellowish and his belly jutting out or prominent, complained to me of want of appetite to victuals; he had a kicking or reaching to vomit every morning and generally a small looseness attending him, and withal was much given to drinking and sitting up late, which I supposed had been the cause of his present indisposition.'* After a temporary recovery, *'falling into the old course of life, and not taking any advice to the contrary, his belly swelled so as not to be contained in his coat, on which I warned him of his very great danger because he being so very weak and subject to looseness, there was no room for purging, medicines, which seems to be the greatest remedy for his*

Sir Henry Morgan

dropsy, threatening his life.' Frightened by this prognosis, Morgan called for the attentions of a negro medicine man, who *'plastered him all over with clay and water, and by it augmented his cough.'*

Henry had made his will in June, and died on August 25th at his Llanrumney estate in Jamaica. Governor Albemarle ordered a state funeral, with a salute of 22 guns, but died himself of jaundice and dropsy upon October 6th. *'The Sword of England'*, *'The Admiral of the Brethren of the Coast'*, *'Good Old Sir Harry'* was buried in Port Royal. In August 1688, Captain Lawrence Wright of HMS Assistance noted the occasion: *'Saturday 25. This day about 11 hours noon Sir Henry Morgan died, & the 26th was brought over from Passage-fort to the King's house at Port Royal, from thence to the Church, & after a sermon was carried to the Pallisadoes and there buried. All the forts fired an equal number of guns, we fired two & twenty and after we & the Drake had fired, all the merchant men fired.'* A few years later the historian Leslie noted *'he showed the world that he was qualified to govern as well as fight, and that in all stations of life, he was a great man.'*

The historian Edward Long wrote in 1774 that Sir Henry *'whose achievements are well known, was equal to any of the most renowned warriors of historical fame, in valour, conduct and success, but this gentleman has been unhappily confounded with the piratical herd.'* Twenty years later, another Jamaican planter, Bryan Edwards, criticised Esquemeling's treatment of Morgan, saying that *'By the kindness of a friend in this island I have had the opportunity of perusing some of Sir Henry Morgan's original private letters; and this I will say, that they manifest such a spirit of humanity, justice, liberality, and piety, as prove he has either been grossly traduced or that he was the greatest hypocrite living - a character ill-suited to the frank and fearless temper of the man.'* He also noted that the English translation of Esquemeling was not taken from the Dutch original, but from the Spanish translation, thereby further skewing opinion against Morgan. Sir Harry had an amazing and courageous life, but is virtually ignored in English history. One has to ask why. He joins a roster of Welsh heroes such as Owain Glyndwr and Owain Llawgoch who are virtually unknown Britons, probably because of the over-emphasis upon England at all levels of education.

Brigadier-General E.A. Cruickshank, in his 'The Life of Sir Henry Morgan' (1935, Macmillan Canada) fittingly ends his book thus: *'His talents as an organiser and administrator of a considerable fleet manned by volunteers, and his conduct as a leader of such a turbulent force in very daring undertakings were most remarkable. Skill in preparation and planning were combined with decision and dauntless courage in their execution. Francis*

Drake had not ventured to attack Puerto Bello. The formidable force sent out by Admiral Vernon seventy years later, having taken that place, declined to attempt crossing the isthmus for the capture of Panama. Morgan's outstanding ability as a commander is beyond dispute.'
    On June 7th, 1692, a huge earthquake and tidal wave destroyed most of Port Royal, killing most of the inhabitants and throwing the Port Royal cemetery into the sea.

'You was a flyer, Morgan,
You was the lad to crowd,
When you was in your flagship,
But now you're in your shroud'
-old Jamaican verse recounted to David Cordingley in 1966.

* The riddle of what happened to Morgan's 'treasure' has never been resolved. It was believed that he had concealed it somewhere between Panama and Jamaica, or perhaps a substantial portion went to King Charles. In the mid-1960's, the American marine archaeologist Robert Marx, working for the Jamaican government, found a treasure chest at Port Royal (see Port Royal in the *Pirate Terms* chapter). The wooden chest crumbled almost immediately, leaving only a brass lock, so no identification was made of its owner, except that the chest bore the crest of the Spanish king. It was filled with hundreds of silver coins, most minted at the silver centres of Potosi in Colombia, and Lima in Peru. They dated from Morgan's raid. Could there be more of Morgan's treasure to find at Port Royal? Or is there more loot on the Isle des Vaches?

FOOTNOTE - THE RECOVERY OF THE JAMAICA MERCHANT
A German team found the scattered timbers of what they think is the *Jamaica Merchant*, in just 16 feet of water off Haiti, and began diving there in 2001. The Haitian government granted a permit to dive, after many years of refusing any searches in the area. Klaus Keppler said *'We are now convinced that we can prove from the finds that the ship was commanded by Morgan. It is not just important because we believe it to be Morgan's vessel, but because as far as we know, it is the only pirate ship from the 17th century to be found.'* Monica Wetzke confirmed *'We have already found the ship's anchor, cannons and a few pieces of porcelain and coins. We know Morgan also used to steal a lot of his treasure from the inside of churches and that he had a stash in the caves on the island just by the sea. The porcelain which we found on the wreck was stuff which the crew would have used every day - plates and things of that sort. The coins are bronze, not gold or silver, and they are being examined by experts to tell us where they came from.'*

FOOTNOTE - CAPTAIN KIDD, HENRY MORGAN AND THE OAK ISLAND MONEY PIT
A document at the Public Records Office implies that William Kidd knew and *'resented'* Admiral Morgan - he may have been a member of the Brethren of the Coast who did not receive his fair share from Morgan's expeditions. A semi-literate Captain Dan Morgan of Bristol claimed direct descent from Henry Morgan, and wrote a letter to an antiques dealer called Hill Cutler in 1931. He claimed that Kidd's famed treasure

chest was the one used at the trial to prove Kidd was a pirate, because there was a skull and crossbones and a monogrammed K on the lid. He possessed this original chest, since one of his ancestors had been Kidd's gaoler at Newgate Prison, and had 'borrowed' the chest after the trial. A bible with a plaster skull fixed to it was in the bottom of the chest, but there was nothing in the false compartment under this. However, a man named Palmer now found a scrap of paper with a map, under the mirror on the inside box-lid. It showed the 'same' island as in earlier treasure maps, but with more detail, a red zig-zag joining crosses and dots laid over the map, and with the legend '*15SE and 50N, 36NE and 36NE ROCKS, 3 FEET BY THREE FEET BY FOUR*' There are dozens of books dealing with the search for Kidd's Treasure, and the above information is taken from George Edmunds '*Kidd - the Search for His Treasure*' 1996.

The Oak Island Money Pit, discovered in 1795, is by far the most baffling of all the 'buried treasure' sites around the world. (See '*The Oak Island Mystery*' by L&P Fanthorpe, 1995). Many attempts have been made to link Kidd to it, but Morgan's Raid on Panama in January 1671 led to huge confusion about the missing treasure. He had the time, resources, effective eadership and manpower to construct the Oak Island labyrinth. He may have been planning to retrieve the loot after the passage of the years, when suspicion had eased off. An editorial in *The Boston Journal of Commerce* in the early 1920's suggested that the booty was left by Morgan. Fanthorpe also mentions that the complex pit may be the work of Prince Madoc ab Owain Gwynedd, who is said to have landed at Fort Morgan in Mobile Bay in 1170 with Welsh settlers. (The Romano-Welsh goldmines at Dolaucothi were among the most advanced mines in the world, pioneering water engineering on a grand scale. Welsh gold, was what lured the Romans to Britain to supply the Imperial Mint at Lyons).

CHAPTER IV

DAVID WILLIAMS fl.1698 - 1709

The son of a Welsh farmer, he was more of a soldier than a pirate. He was recorded as being a morose character, who *'knew as little of the sea or of ships as he did of the Arts of natural Philosophy'*. A seaman on a merchant ship bound for India, probably the *Mary*, an East Indiaman out of Bristol, he was accidentally left on Madagascar. Williams found employment in fighting for native chiefs in an inter-tribal battle. He fought so well that he was befriended by the *'King'*, but a short time later this tribe was wiped out and Williams was taken prisoner. The King of this tribe, knowing of Williams' reputation, made him leader of his army, but Williams was again captured, by a King named Dempaino. He was made commander-in-chief of an army of 6000 men, and supplied with slaves, expensive clothing and all his needs.

Escaping, he sailed on the Rhode Island privateer *Pelican* in 1698, and then joined the *Mocha* under Robert Culliford, possibly around May 1698, when Culliford was at St Mary's Island off Madagascar. Culliford took £2000 in cash from a French ship there (to add to his previous tally of other European, Indonesian and Chinese captures), and took on about a hundred of the crew of his former captain, William Kidd. Culliford now sailed off in the *Mocha*, with Dirk Chivers' *Soldado* and the *Pelican*. Chivers and Culliford plundered the *Great Mohamed* in the Red Sea in September 1698. There was £130,000 in cash, each crewman receiving £700. Another prize was taken, and the ships sailed to St Mary's in February 1699.

In September 1699, the crew of the *Mocha* split up at Madagascar, sinking the *Mocha* when four British warships arrived. All of the 24 pirates, including Dirk Chivers, who took the offer of a pardon from the naval commander, seem to have been hanged in London, except for Culliford. Culliford was kept alive to testify against Samuel Burgess. At Madagascar, Williams had not trusted the pardon offer, and instead helped George Booth take a French ship. Booth's *Dolphin* was trapped at St Mary's Island in 1699, and burned, but its crew escaped to Madagascar. They then joined up with Williams' fellow-Welshman John Bowen (q.v.), and Williams sailed on the *Speaker* until it was wrecked in 1701. He returned to Madagascar, and joined Thomas Howard's *Prosperous* in 1702. However, he was accidentally left behind when Howard attacked a Dutch trader on the island.

According to Gosse, and details are entangled here, he was captured by the Dutch pirate Ort Van Tyle, who was sailing out on New York. Van Tyle was an associate of the Welsh pirate Captain James, and they both roamed the coasts off Madagascar and the Indian Ocean. He put his prisoners to work on his Madagascar plantation as slaves, and David Williams toiled there for 6 months before making his escape to a friendly tribe in the neighbourhood. He lived with Prince Rebaiharang's tribe for a year, then joined a Dutchman named Pro, who had a small settlement on the island. Williams was now arrested by a naval frigate, the HMS *Severn* in November 1703, but escaped with Pro, procuring a boat from the Comoro Islands in February 1704. The *Severn* and the *Scarborough* had been sent at the request of the East India Company of a '*search and destroy*' mission against the pirates infesting the waters around Madagascar.

Williams now joined Thomas White's pirates at Methalage, in Madagascar, and became Captain White's quartermaster in 1704. White had been captured with John Bowen back in 1698, and had been Thomas Howard's quartermaster. Williams was present when several more ships were taken in the Red Sea, as White sailed in consort with Captain Halsey, before dying of fever. White had married a local woman of Methelage, and died in her arms in 1708, reportedly of '*excessive drinking and other irregularities*'.

A Bostonian, Halsey had a commission to raid French and Spanish shipping in 1704, but turned from privateer to pirate in 1705, taking the 10-gun *Charles* to Madagascar. In 1706, he was deposed by pirate council for cowardice, when he refused to attack a large Dutch ship. However, when the Dutch ship attacked the *Charles*, he was quickly reinstated as captain.

Williams became John Halsey's quartermaster in 1707, making a fortune. Two coastal merchant ships were taken in February 1707 at the Nicobar Islands. At Mocha, in the Red Sea, in August 1707, the pirates attacked a fleet of five British ships, with a total of 62 guns. The fleet scattered, but Halsey took two of the vessels, with £50,000 worth of cash and cargo. In January 1708, the *Greyhound* arrived at Madagascar to trade alcohol and other provisions for the provisions taken from the British prizes. The *Neptune* also arrived in port to trade in liquor. However, a hurricane wrecked the pirate ships and their prizes. With the assistance of Samuel Burgess, first mate on the Scottish ship *Neptune*, and a former privateer, the pirates took over the *Neptune* and plundered the *Greyhound*. (Captain Culliford had testified against Burgess in his London trial, but he was mysteriously pardoned in 1702). Halsey became captain of the *Neptune*, and Burgess quartermaster, as his reward. On Halsey's death from fever in 1708, Burgess was voted out as quartermaster, and Williams became the captain of the *Neptune*, but another hurricane wrecked the ship before he could leave Madagascar. Undeterred, Williams and ten pirates fitted out a small sloop, and sailed for Mascarenas Island.

Missing the island, they sailed around Madagascar to Mathelage, where Williams laid the boat up for a year, dealing in slaves with Burgess and others. The local king, annoyed by Williams' irrational outbursts of temper, ordered him to leave, but prevailing winds meant that Williams could not reach his intended destination on the north of the island, but was forced into the port of Boyne, just a few miles from Mathelage, and still within the king's realm. Boyne was noted for its Arabian trade, and Williams anchored offshore, intending to see its Arab Governor. He took a canoe inshore and asked for directions to Kings Town, but an ambush had been laid. Defoe states that his 13-year pirate career came to an end in 1709: '*When they had left the*

Boyne, Williams and Meyeurs, a Frenchman, who also came ashore in the canoe, went to buy some Samsams, which are agate beads; and as they were looking over these goods, a number of the Governor's Men came about them, seized them both and immediately dispatched Meyeurs, Williams they bound, and tortured almost a whole day, by throwing hot Ashes on his Head and in his Face, and putting little Boys to beat him with Sticks; he offered the Governor $2000 for his life, but he answered he'd have both that and the money too; and accordingly when he was near expiring, they made an end of him with lances.' Williams' friend and benefactor, King Dempaino, revenged his death by sacking the Arab town and executing its chief with lances. Burgess had stayed in Madagascar and dealt in slaves with Williams and other captains, but was poisoned by a 'black chief' after an argument over prices.

CHAPTER V

CAPTAIN JOHN BOWEN d. 1704

Some sources call Bowen a Rhode Islander of Welsh descent, but he was born in Bermuda, possibly the son of one of the Royalist prisoners captured at the Battle of St Ffagans by the Parliamentarians in the Second Civil War. Moving to South Carolina, John Bowen became captain of a merchant vessel trading with the West Indies, but after some years was captured by French pirates. The French crossed the Atlantic to pillage the West African slave-coast, then went around the Cape to the island of Madagascar. Here they were ship-wrecked, and around eighteen months later Bowen and a few other survivors were picked up by the pirate Captain Read.

Read took a huge Arab ship in the Persian Gulf, but with little loot aboard, and around this time Bowen signed pirates' articles, despairing of ever returning to the Americas. He was now elected sailing-master, on account of his experience, and with Read, sailed in consort with the pirate captain George Booth off Western Madagascar. At the end of 1699, the two ships captured the *Speaker*, a strong 50-gun slave ship at Mathelage (now Majunga) off Madagascar's northwest coast. Booth now led the three ships and over 200 pirates to Zanzibar for supplies. In a quarrel with Arab soldiers, Booth and 20 pirates were killed there in late 1700. John Bowen was elected captain of the *Speaker* in his place. Bowen now took several ships off the Malabar coast in 1700, trading the goods in local towns.

Near the mouth of the Red Sea, Bowen took an Indian ship with £100,000 worth of booty in 1701 According to Jan Rogozinski, its value would be $50 million today. In November 1701, the *Speaker* took an English East Indiaman off Callequilon (Quilon), which was then sold on the Indian coast. According to Defoe, its Captain Conway had sailed from Bengal, and the loot was divided equally and sold to a Callequillon merchant, a merchant of Porca and a Dutch factor named Malpa. Returning to Madagascar, on January 7th, 1702 his ship was wrecked on St Thomas Reef off Mauritius, but most of the loot and crew were saved. Bowen gave Governor Roelof Deodati a huge bribe of 2,500 pieces of eight, for which he was warmly welcomed, and allowed to buy a replacement vessel. Bowen also gave the governor the wreck of the *Speaker*, with its stores and guns. The governor provided doctors, medicine and food to the shipwrecked pirates. Bowen bought and converted a Dutch sloop into a brigantine, and in the middle of March left the island, leaving the Governor a generous gift. (It appears that the remains of the *Speaker* have been found recently).

Defoe's account reads: '*Then (the Speaker) left the coast and sailed for the island of Madagascar, but in the way was lost on the island of Mauritius, on St Thomas's Reef, where* they were most courteously received and feasted, their sick carried into their fort and cured by their doctor, and a new sloop sold them. And (they were) supplied with all sorts of necessaries for their cutting her (the Sloop) and making her a brigantine, which they performed in the middle of March 1702 and took their leave of the Governor, giving him 2,500 pieces of eight ... and being invited to make Mauritius a place of refreshment, sailed for the island of Madagascar, where at a place on the east side, called Maritan (St Mary's) the captain with a gang settled themselves.' The wrecked Speaker had held 170 pirates and 30 Indian captives, but the sloop would not hold as many crew, so all the Indians and 12 seamen were left behind in Mauritius. Arriving at the French island of Reunion, several French pirates left the crowded ship. In return, a few settlers joined the pirates and sailed on to St Mary's.

In April 1702, Bowen returned to Madagascar, via Reunion and set up a camp at Maritan (St Mary's) on its eastern coast, where he built a fort. Governor Villiers recorded his arrival at Reunion on April 2nd. Bowen then took the Speedy Return, belonging to the Scottish Company of Africa, which had stopped to provision at Maritan, after taking on slaves at St Mary's. It was accompanied by the East India Company's Content, a brigantine also carrying slaves. Bowen and his men rowed up to the anchored ships at night, and took them with ease, overpowering the sleeping crew. Most of the 50 or so crew off the ships joined the pirates. Captain Drummond of the Speedy Return and Captain Stewart of the Content were released at St Mary's, and both seem to have died on the island. The loss of the Speedy Return was blamed upon Captain Thomas Green and the crew of the Scottish ship Worcester, which was trading along the Malabar coast at this time. On its return to Scotland, Green and 17 of his crew were convicted of massacring the Speedy Return's crew. Green and two others were hanged in 1705, before the error was realised and the rest of the crew pardoned. Israel Phipenny and Peter Freeland, two of Bowen's forced men, had escaped at Mauritius and had arrived in Portsmouth in March 1705. By the time the Mayor of Portsmouth had reported their affidavits to the secretary of State in London, and the Secretary had sent pardons by Express Coach to Scotland, poor Green had been dead for just a few hours.

Bowen now left Maritan with the Speedy Return and Content, having heard from Drummond's crew that Captain Honeycomb's galley Rook was lying at Mascarenas Bay, but it had left just before their arrival. Next, Bowen's consort brigantine ran aground off the west coast of Madagascar. It was refloated and caught up with the Speedy Return at Augustine Bay in Madagascar, but was so badly damaged that the pirates burnt it. In October 1702, the Speaker added the English ship Borneo to their list of vessels captured, and used several Indian and European merchants along the Malabar coast to trade their booty.

Next, Bowen sailed from New Methelage to Johanna and finally to Mayotte (Mayota), where he linked forces with Thomas Howard, captain of the Prosperous, around Christmas 1702. Bowen failed to capture the French ship Corbel after a chase, and headed for Mauritius, and then for the East Indies. The two ships took and looted a rich English East Indiaman, the Pembroke on March 10th 1703 at Mayotte. It was unfortunately stuck in its anchorage, and thus defenceless. Its captain had anchored her where the bay became dry when the tide ebbed. Bowen's men in two small boats approached her and asked to come aboard. *'Captain Weoley answered one of them might come only. Yet they both came rowing on and when they came under our quarter all their men at once started up with their arms guarded (ready to fire) swearing if any of us fired a shot they would do us no harm nor take anything from us. Captain Weoley ordered everyone to fire, which we did, and they at us … but we were not able to keep up with them, they firing six shot to our one … so we called for quarters which they gave, disarming every man and turning them into the head* (throwing them into the hold).' The *Pembroke* was looted, but the crew unusually voted not to burn her, although four pirates had been killed in the attack, along with the *Pembroke's* Chief Mate and another sailor.

Bowen kept the *Pembroke's* Captain Whalley (or Wooley) until October to serve as a pilot. (Whalley's letter to Mr Penning, head of the New East India Company of Calicut, sent in November 1703, gave Defoe his background information on John Bowen). The two pirate captains now separated, for Bowen to careen the *Speedy Return*, but rejoined a few months later in the Red Sea. Whalley wrote that the pirates went to Mathelage, returned to the Comoros and then sailed to the Highland of St Johns. In August 1703 Bowen and Howard took two Indian ships (returning to Surat from Mocha), worth £70,000 in the Red Sea, and some Moorish prizes. Howard's *Prosperous* took one and left it adrift off Daman without an anchor, and Bowen's *Speedy Return* took a larger ship and carried it to Rajapura in India. They shared the loot at Rajapura, and burned the *Prosperous* and *Speedy Return*, as they had become unsound. The captains converted Bowen's Indian prize, named it the *Defiance*, and set off in October 1703 with 56 guns and 164 pirates for the Malabar Coast. There were 50 Frenchmen, 43 Englishmen, and a mixture of Danes, Swedes and Dutchmen. 60 captured Indian crew were kept on board to perform menial tasks. According to Jan Rogozinski, the value of the two Indian ships was $100 million in today's money. Even after sharing this with Howard, it would mean that Bowen had taken the equivalent of $100 million in two years off Indian ships.

North of Cochin on the Malabar coast to dispose of their goods, the *Defiance 'anchored and fired several guns. But no boat coming off, the quartermaster (John North) went near the shore, and had conference by boat with the people, who next day brought off hogs and other refreshments … There came several Dutchmen aboard, and I saw no difference between their treatment of the pirates and any other ship.'* Here they came again upon the unfortunate *Pembroke*, and once again ransacked her. The pirates next put into North-West Harbour in Dutch-controlled, friendly Mauritius. Howard had remained with his men on the Indian coast, while Bowen sailed for the Mascarenes with 40 of his crew, intending to return home with their booty and escape piracy. According to Defoe, Howard and twenty of his crew were left on the Indian coast *'with what they had, and retired among the Natives, where Howard married a Woman of the country, and being a morose ill-natured Fellow, and using her ill, he was murdered by her Relations.'*

John Bowen sailed the *Defiance* to Mauritius and Reunion in February and April 1704. Six men left at Mauritius to retire. Bowen and several others were accepted as settlers at Reunion. Some of the French pirates who left Bowen's command at

Reunion were Guy Dumesnil, Joseph de Guigne*, George Christmas and Pierra Pradau. They were said to have been taken back to France by Baron de Pallieres' squadron in 1705. Unluckily, Bowen fell ill with an intestinal complaint, and died there after about six months in March 1705. 'The dry Belly ache' which carried Bowen off may have been the 'dry gripes', contracted by drinking rum held in lead containers. His goods were seized by the church and he was refused a Christian burial. He was known as Jean Bouin on the island. According to Gosse, Bowen had accumulated over a million dollars in coin, plus vast quantities of valuable merchandise. The East India Company seized the fortune that he left behind. About 200 of Bowen's men stayed on the Defiance and sailed on to St Mary's Island (just off the east coast of Madagascar), now under a former quartermaster, Nathaniel North.

* Joseph de Guigne, who disembarked at Reunion, had served Bowen on the Speaker, Speedy Return and the Defiance from 1697 - 1704. He was recorded as marrying on the island in November 1704, and later used his booty to buy land in three separate locations on Reunion.

NOTE ON THOMAS HOWARD, WHO SAILED WITH BOWEN
His nationality is unknown, but he may have been a Welshman who squandered his inheritance, and fled to Jamaica to escape his creditors. With some other seamen, he took a canoe, then took a small boat, then a sloop, gradually building up to taking a 24-gun ship, where he was elected quartermaster. In 1698 he was active off the North American coast, then crossed to the West African coast to plunder more ships.

However, the ship ran onto a reef off Madagascar in 1700. Most of the crew started ferrying heavier cargo off the ship to lighten it, and Howard took over the boat and sailed off with all the treasure. He was then abandoned ashore while hunting, until joining Captain George Booth. Booth had been a gunner on the Pelican, then the Dolphin from 1696, and had been trapped at St Mary's Island by the Royal Navy. The Dolphin was burned, but Booth had escaped to Madagascar with most of his men. The pirates seized a French ship which had put in to barter liquor and goods for slaves, and then met up with John Bowen.

In April 1700, Bowen and Booth took the Speaker, a 50-gun 450-ton slaver. Picking up provisions in Zanzibar, George Booth was attacked and killed by Arab troops, and John Bowen became captain. Bowen wrecked the Speaker in 1701, when Howard left him, returning to Madagascar and staying at St Augustine's Bay. Howard now seized the 36-gun Prosperous, was elected captain and rejoined Bowen in consort in 1702. The pair looted the Pembroke at Johanna Island (Anjouan) in the Comoros in March 1703. In August, the pirates again met up in the Red Sea, taking two Indian ships and over £70,000 in treasure. Dividing the loot at Rajapura, India, both Bowen's crew and Howard's men transferred to the largest Indian ship. Howard retired, and was killed by his in-laws, as noted above.

Footnote: Another notable sea-going Bowen was Captain Richard Bowen (1761-1797), who was killed in the action off Tenerife, when Nelson also lost his arm. He commanded the 32-gun frigate Terpsichore. Bowen took the first Spanish ship to be captured after Spain joined on the French side in 1796, the 34-gun Mahonesa, off

Malaga. He then took the 36-gun French frigate *Vestale* off Cadiz. After the battle of St Vincent, he took on the damaged 132-gun *Santissima Trinidad*, but was forced to break off the action when the rest of the Spanish fleet came to its assistance. '*Had he succeeded he might have become as big a hero as Nelson, who first won national fame in the same battle.*' Shortly after he was killed in the failed attempt to capture Santa Cruz.

'*Tom Bowling: A Tale of the Sea*' was a popular 1839 novel, supposedly based upon the life of Sir Richard Bowen. Ten year-old Tom is rescued from a drunken pedlar and given a home by the Rev. Mr. Monckton, whose daughter Susan teaches Tom the 3 *R's*. Aged 12, he goes to sea, where his courage, zeal and education attract the patronage of Nelson and Admiral Collingwood and leads to rapid advancement. He is posted captain aged just 20, marries Susan, and discovers that he is really the stolen son of a noble family. He serves through the Napoleonic Wars, and dies as Admiral Tom Bowling, Governor of Greenwich Hospital. The story is full of real actions and detailed accounts of life in the Royal Navy.

CHAPTER VI

PAULSGRAVE (PALGRAVE) WILLIAMS AND 'BLACK' SAM BELLAMY fl. 1715-1717

From Canterbury, where he had a wife and child, Samuel Bellamy left England in 1715 to look for sunken treasure off Florida. That summer, a dozen Spanish galleons had sunk in a hurricane. (Other sources proclaim him a Devon man, a sympathiser of James II.) The storm had hit the first Spanish treasure fleet to leave Havana for more than 8 years. More than 14,000,000 silver pesos were lying in shallow waters off the east Florida coast. The 24 year-old Bellamy met the 15-year-old Maria Hallett at Eastham Harbour, outer Cape Cod in 1716. He had promised to return from his voyage with diamonds and jewels to marry her. Bellamy courted her at the Great Island Tavern, on an island about 2 miles off Wellfleet. The remote tavern was well-known as an easy place for smugglers to trade their goods. Leaving Maria to seek his fortune, he came across the goldsmith Paulsgrave Williams, a man of good family and of Welsh stock.

It may be that he met Williams at the Great Island Tavern. It was built in 1712, and belonged to Israel Cole, who seems to have been married to Sam Bellamy's cousin. Somehow Cole had acquired £100,000 and large amounts of land before his death in 1724. The brilliant Benjamin Franklin was so disgusted with this news that he wrote an unflattering obituary in the New England Courant, on August 10th:
'Here lies old Cole; but how or why
He lived, or how he came to die,
His Son and Heir may best declare it,
Who's doubtly blessed with Father's spirit.
And who, when e'er he comes to breathe all
His useless Breath away, and leave all
To such another Son and Heir,
He may be thrown - but God knows where;
Perhaps in some black dark Hole
Where out of wood he extracts charcoal.'
No doubt the tavern witnessed many discussions amongst its smugglers and seafarers, regarding the Spanish sunken treasure - it attracted privateers like moths to a flame.

Williams was from Newport, Rhode Island, and his father had been the Welsh Attorney-General of that state. It may be that Williams was visiting relatives at Cape Cod. Married with two children, he financed the purchase of a sloop, and he and Bellamy took on 12 men to sail her. They sailed on to Florida then the Bahamas but were unsuccessful. The Spanish had hired Indian divers to bring up most of the

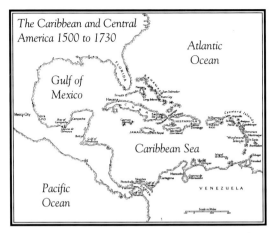

The Caribbean and Central
America 1500 to 1730

Atlantic
Ocean

Gulf of
Mexico

Caribbean Sea

Pacific
Ocean

treasure. All Bellamy's crew
retrieved were a few small items,
trawled by running grappling
hooks across the sea bed. Among
other captains searching with
Williams and Bellamy were the
Welsh Captain Evan James and
an out-of-work privateer,
Welshman Henry Jennings
(q.v.), both from Jamaica.
Captain Hornigold arrived from
the pirate's nest of Nassau in
Providence in the Mary. The
experienced Jennings was
particularly furious at his lack of success. He discovered that the salvaged coins were
being stored at a Spanish fort at Barra de Ays on Florida's coast, and marched his 300
men to its gates. Captain Jennings demanded the money, and the garrison commander
tried to bribe him to leave with 25,000 pieces of silver. Jennings instead drew his pistol
and threatened to shoot the hapless commander if the gates were not opened. The
garrison of Spaniards surrendered, on promise of quarter, and Jennings looted over
60,000 pieces of silver (other sources say 250,000 - it appears that the Spanish with
their Indian divers had managed to recover about 80% of the lost coins, so the higher
figure could well be accurate). Jennings had actually been commissioned by the
Governor of Jamaica to hunt pirates, but like everyone else along the coast, was
caught up in the 'treasure fever'.

Enthused by Jennings' success, by early 1716, Williams and Bellamy had decided to
'go on the account' in order to cut their losses. A crew member sewed a death's head
and crossed bones on a black flag, and Bellamy proclaimed 'This flag represents not
death, but resurrection. Never again will you be slaves of the wealthy. From this day, we are
new men - free men.' Almost all the crew assented, and over the next 15 months the
pirates were said to have taken over 50 ships. They traded in their slow salvage vessel
for two fast piraguas, sea-going canoes which could be manned with swivel guns. They
first operated off the coast of Belize, where the Mosquito Indian John Julian joined
them. Another recruit, Peter Cornelius Hoof, was a 33 year-old Swede who had spent
19 years on Dutch merchant ships along the Spanish Main. His knowledge of these
waters was invaluable.

In the Yucatan Channel, the piraguas took Captain Young's sloop, and forced him
to tow them to the west of Cuba, where the shipping lanes were busier. Crossing the
channel, Bellamy and Williams met with Henry Jennings, who had been 'fencing' his
Spanish treasure in Jamaica. Bellamy and Williams joined Jennings' flotilla of five
ships, to assist in his attack on the Spanish port of Baya Hondo, on the north coast of
Cuba. Jennings hated the Spanish with a vengeance, but would never attack English
ships. On April 3rd, 1716, the ships anchored off the bay, and send one of the canoes
to gather information about a large ship stationed there. The pirates' story was that

they needed to take on wood and water before carrying on their peaceful trading mission. The crew of the French interloper St Marie, under Captain L'Escoubett, told the strangers that they were dealing in expensive smuggled goods with the Spanish settlers. This heartened Jennings - capturing a smuggler did not constitute an act of piracy - but the Frenchman had 45 crew and no less than 16 cannon. However, Jennings saw no reason to risk bloodshed, and he was well aware of his horrible fate if he was captured and given to the Spanish, whose ships he had consistently attacked for the last few years. The pirates argued in council about the next move. His quartermasters George Dossitt and Francis Charnock, led the arguments against Jennings' 'cowardice'. However, it was all settled by one of the pirates shouting 'One and All' the pirate cry for sticking together. The others took up the cry, and Jennings was forced to attack.

Bellamy and Williams took a piragua each as the vanguard into the v-shaped harbour, as they were low and difficult to hit by French cannon fire. They were followed by sloops commanded by Jennings and John Ashworth. By 10pm in the black of night all four boats had moved to pistol distance from the St Marie. The pirates in the piraguas had stripped naked for battle, 'all in their skins or buff with naught on but their cartridge boxes and naked cutlasses and pistols'. They began to row furiously and a French sailor shouted, asking them what they were doing. The men in the piraguas swiftly swarmed onto the ship, and the French capitulated without firing a shot. One of the over-excited gunners on Jennings' crew accidentally fired a cannon, and a Frenchman was prevented from escaping to raise the alarm. The ship was ransacked, but its cargo was mainly fine French linen, a disappointing haul. However, the pirates found the ship's manifest, which stated that it was carrying 30,000 pieces of eight. Captain Escoubett claimed that he had hidden the silver ashore, and he and his crew were tortured until they admitted its hiding place on the ship. 28,500 pieces were found, of which Bellamy and Williams received a third. A canoe came into the harbour, and its captured crew told Jennings that another French interloper was trading at Porto Mariel, to the east. Captain Carnegie took his sloop and one of the piraguas, but by the time they reached the harbour, another pirate had taken the smuggler. It was the infamous Captain Benjamin Hornigold, the doyen of the pirate brethren. It was said that around a third of all pirate captains of these years had learned their trade off Hornigold.

Jennings took two sloops to search for Hornigold, leaving Bellamy and Williams with the treasure taken from the St Marie. On his return to Baya Hondo, having failed to find Hornigold, there was bleak news for Jennings. Bellamy and Williams had piled all his loot into the better of their piraguas and vanished. Captain Young had been unable to prevent them leaving, so Jennings sank Young's sloop, and also the piragua that Bellamy had left there. Bellamy and Williams now joined the pirate Captain Hornigold in June 1716. They found him off Cuba. Hornigold operated out of New Providence in the Bahamas, sailed with Blackbeard and had taught him piracy. Blackbeard had a sloop with 70 men and 6 cannon in Hornigold's flotilla. Hornigold disliked Jennings, and gave Bellamy the Marianne, a single-decked, speedy New England-built sloop, which could carry about 40 tons. The crew re-elected Bellamy as their captain. Hornigold, Blackbeard and three other captains anchored off Portobello in Cuba, to give support to a raid by Bellamy and Williams on the port. When they returned after a couple of days looting, they discovered that the flotilla had taken a ship with a cargo of logwood. There was a dispute over whether the ship should be looted or returned to its captain. It was a Dutch ship, but had an English captain, and Hornigold, like Jennings, had a policy of not attacking 'English' ships. The Pirate Council decided that the nationality of the ship was what mattered, and looted the cargo. Of the crew, a young man named John Brown (possibly a mulatto) willingly joined Bellamy.

A few days later, Bellamy intercepted two brigs carrying cacao en route to Vera Cruz in Mexico. They ransacked the brigs, and an Amsterdam-born man of mixed race, Hendrick Quintor, willingly joined Bellamy and Williams. In June 1716 Bellamy took Captain John Brett's ship. Hornigold would not allow the cargo to be taken off the English ship, but the crews took all its alcohol before releasing it. Then two pinks were captured off the Cuban coast, with four crewmen joining the pirates, before the flotilla, including Captain la Bouche (who sailed with Howell Davis), moved on to Samana Bay in Cuba to careen. There was again a dispute about Hornigold's policy of not taking English prizes, but Bellamy thought that all prizes were worth taking. Hornigold now sailed off in consort with Blackbeard, in August 1716, not wishing to pursue English ships. While Blackbeard, in *Queen Anne's Revenge*, was soon to die, Hornigold surrendered to a pardon in 1718 in the Bahamas, and turned into an efficient pirate-hunter for the new Governor.

Bellamy had effectively overthrown the most feared and efficient pirate of the time. John Fletcher was elected his quartermaster on the *Marianne*, William Main as sailing-master, and Jeremiah Burke as boatswain. (Two pirates named William Main sailed with Black Bart Roberts later, one being killed, and the other, a boatswain, badly burned and later hung). Olivier Levasseur, *La Bouche*, stayed with Bellamy, on his ship the *Postilion*, after serving Hornigold for the last few months. According to Shomette, the pirates now 'went on an orgy of plundering' in the Caribbean for several months. In some reports they took 50 ships in a year. The *Marianne* and its crew of 90 and six small cannon attacked a French man-of-war off Puerto Rico. By expert handling, they sailed their faster ship to the rear of the Frenchman, trying to board for an hour or so, without receiving a broadside from the 40-gun warship. However, after one pirate died and three were wounded, Bellamy broke off the courageous action.

In October 1716, a prison ship was captured off the Dominican Republic, and seven men joined the crew, including Simon Van Vorst of New York and a 'Dutch' tailor called Thomas Baker. In November, the *Bonetto* was taken between St Thomas and St Croix by the *Marianne* and *Postilion*. Captain Abijah Savage complained to the British governor of Antigua, who wrote to London asking for warships to 'disperse those vermin if possible.' A young passenger called John King begged to join the pirates, despite his mother's entreaties, whereby he threatened to murder her. He was welcomed with open arms by Bellamy. In December, after capturing more ships, the captains took the *Pearl* and the *Sultana* off Guadeloupe. The prisoners were put on the *Pearl* after it had been ransacked, and allowed to go free. Bellamy made the *Sultana* his flagship, and Paulsgrave Williams was made temporary captain of the *Marianne*, until they could go ashore and hold elections.

The next day, the *St Michael* was spotted 60 miles off the coast of Saba, and the *Sultana* caught her and took prime Irish beef and other cargo. Thomas Davis, the carpenter was forced to join (see later). The three ships now laid up at the uninhabited island of Blanquilla, off Venezuela, and Bellamy was formally re-elected as captain of the *Sultana*, and Williams elected him as commander of the *Marianne*. In February 1717, Howell Davis's later consort, La Bouche, accidentally went his separate way during a storm. He had gone off with 90 men to attack shipping off Curacao, but could not make a pre-arranged rendezvous. With about 120 men, the two remaining ships sailed for Spanish Town on the Virgin Islands, and sold some loot to John Hamann, a former pirate who sold smuggled and stolen goods to the Dutch on St Thomas. Some of the forced men escaped, and Bellamy threatened to burn Spanish Town if they were not 'returned'. The deserters were forced to re-embark, and Bellamy and Williams headed for the rich pickings of St Croix.

Governor Hamilton of Antigua had sent Captain Hume in HMS *Scarborough* to capture Bellamy. Hume found a pirate flotilla under Captain Kennedy at St Croix, and sank two ships, captured two, with one escaping. The survivors hid on the island and gave Bellamy the full story, joining his ships. Bellamy and his 180 pirates, ships filled with booty, headed west, stopping at the Dominican Republic, on their way to the Windward Passage. Spotting a three-masted galley in the distance, Bellamy followed it in the *Sultana*, hoping to be accepted as another merchant ship on the same route. However, as the *Sultana* gradually gained on it, the galley piled on sail, and heeled over hard to take maximum advantage of the wind. Being lightweight and low, with a narrow beam, the galley was a fast ship, and at one time Bellamy lost sight of it. However, he estimated its course and spotted it again the next day, slowly closing on it because of the extra weight of cargo that the merchant was carrying. Bellamy moved forward of the ship, and fired two cannon across its bows. It was a tense moment, for the galley had 50 crew and 16 cannon. However, its captain feared the 'no quarter' flag if he resisted, and hove to. Her captain was a former naval officer, with 13 years' experience in the transatlantic slave trade. He knew when not to fight.

Thus in February 1717 the pair captured Captain Laurence Prince's *Whydah* slaver, returning to London laden with gold, 'elephant tusks', coins, 'Jesuits' Bark' (cinchona, used for making quinine) sugar, molasses and indigo, valued at up to £30,000. There was also about £25,000 worth of booty from the sale of the slaves. Captain Prince had sold his 600 slaves for gold and silver in Jamaica, including gold dust and Akan tribal gold jewellery, and was also said to be carrying jewels including a perfect ruby the size of a hen's egg. The pirates had chased the fast *Whydah* for three days before catching up with it off Long Island in the Bahamas. Apart from firing two chase guns, there had been no resistance. It was a 100-foot galley, with 18 large cannons and about 12 swivel cannons. Swivel cannons were filled with shot for close range work to wipe out men on deck and in the rigging.

Upon examining the *Whydah's* cargo, Black Sam had shouted to his men, '*Lads, we've gotten enough! It's time to go home!*' Black Bellamy now wished to return to see

Maria Hallett in New England, with his promised gold and diamonds. Paulsgrave Williams likewise wished to return to his family on Block Island near Cape Cod. Bellamy by now cut a dashing figure, tying his long hair with a black silk bow, and wearing four pistols in the sash over his velvet coat. In the spring of 1717, it was time to head north for the summer, repair their ships and split the booty. The Whydah was anchored off Crooked Island to distribute the loot. It was now that Captain Prince was told by Black Sam that his ship was being commandeered. He knew the ship was new, from the ship's bell's inscription (later recovered at Cape Cod). He was informed that it had only carried out the 'triangular trade' once. It was hardly 'broken-in', and extremely fast when stripped of its cargo. The galley was only two years old, with two levels (not decks) upon each of which 300 slaves would have been chained in a supine position. The Captain of the Whydah was given Bellamy's old ship the Sultana to return home, with a 'present' of £20 from Black Sam. Thomas Davis asked to be allowed to sail with off with Captain Prince, but the pirates reneged on Bellamy's promise to let Davis go, took on six volunteers from the Whydah and forced another four men to join them. There was an election of officers for the new capture, and Bellamy was unanimously voted captain of the Whydah. Richard Nolan, one of Hornigold's men, replaced John Fletcher as quartermaster, John Lambert was elected sailing master and Jeremiah Burke boatswain. Williams was re-elected Captain of the Marianne. Converting the Whydah to be their 28-gun flagship (10 cannon were added from the Sultana), Bellamy and Williams sailed for Virginia in April, taking another four ships in the Caribbean. A pirate named Montgomery was named as captain of one of the refitted prizes. Near Haiti, off Petit Goave, they took the Jamaican frigate Tanner, which had been chartered by French merchants to take sugar and indigo to La Rochelle. There was also 5000 silver livres which were taken.

The crew had taken to calling themselves 'Robin Hood's Men', happy that the end was in sight of their pirating. Each of around 160 men had accumulated substantial plunder. There were another 20 'forced' men, possibly not entitled to loot. The quartermasters had informed the men that each had earned at least the value of a lifetime's work on shore. They flotilla sailed north for home and retirement. A bad storm hit Bellamy's ship and Williams' sloop and they headed for the shelter of the coast of the Carolinas, but were forced north and decided to head towards Rhode Island. The Whydah was leaking badly and running repairs were carried out, but the crews were heartened when Captain Beer's Boston sloop was taken off the Carolinas. Beer was ordered aboard the Whydah while his ship was looted, and pleaded to be given repossession of his ship. Bellamy consented, but was over-ruled by his crew. This democratic decision appalled Beer, who asked Bellamy 'Have you no control over your men? Or do they control you?' Bellamy's answer to Beer is recorded thus by Defoe: 'You are a devilish conscience rascal you! I am a free Prince, and I have as much authority to make war on the whole world as he who has a hundred sail ships at sea, and an army of 100,000 men in the field, and this my conscience tells me. But there is no arguing with such snivelling puppies who allow superiors to kick them about deck at pleasure, and pin their faith upon a pimp of a parson; a squab, who neither practises nor believes what he puts upon the chuckle-headed fools he preaches to. Damned my Blessed, I am sorry they won't let you have your *sloop again, for I scorn to do any one a mischief, when it is not for my advantage. Damn the sloop, we must sink her, and she might be of use to you. Tho' damn ye, you are a sneaking puppy, and so are all those who will submit to be governed by Laws which rich men have made for their own security.'* Williams now took the *Marianne* towards Block Island, and dropped off Captain Beer and his crew along the coast, and the other four ships headed on towards Cape Cod. The ships first waited for some time in the Chesapeake Bay in New England, as Bellamy had been informed that a man-of-war was cruising the coastline. Williams visited his mother and sisters, before heading north again to rendezvous with Bellamy. The plan was that they would meet at Green Island (now Richmond Island), off Maine's Cape Elizabeth. Defore relates at this time that a former 'stroller' (actor) put on a play for the crew's amusement, but some men woke from a drunken sleep and thought that the ship was being attacked and a fracas ensued, with at least one pirate dying.

In the meantime, disgraced by Maria Hallett's unexpected pregnancy, her parents had turned her out of their Wellfleet home to live in a hut on the beach near Eastham. Here she watched for Bellamy to return, only venturing out at night so that no-one could see her condition. Seven months after Bellamy had left her, Maria Hallett bore their baby boy. She delivered it herself in a barn belonging to John Knowles, and hid the child under straw to conceal him when she had to leave the barn. One day she returned to find John Knowles holding the dead infant in his arms. He had choked to death on a straw, and Maria was arrested by the Sheriff of Eastham for the crimes of pregnancy outside wedlock and neglect of her child. The gaoler left her door open, and she never faced trial. Locals avoided Maria's hut as they believed that she was a witch.

After the terrible storm which split up Bellamy's flotilla, Williams had headed for Block Island. He took a vessel loaded with wine off Cape Cod, after putting Beer and his crew ashore. The *Whydah* had almost sunk, but, on April 7th, Bellamy took the *Agnes* off Cape Charles, Virginia, taking rum, molasses, sugar and European goods. They let the ship and crew go - they wanted no extra '*baggage*' so close to their target life of plenty in retirement. The same day, Captain Bellamy took the Glasgow galley, *Mary Anne*, and Richard Nolan was given command of it - it was used as an store-ship, to lighten the *Whydah*. The third prize that day was the English pink *Endeavour*, out of Brighthelmstone, and the ship and crew were freed on April 12th.

It appears now that Williams met up with Bellamy off Maine, and they took a few more merchant ships. (Defoe records that then the flotilla fought a 36-gun French man-of-war in the mouth of the St Lawrence river, but there does not seem to have been the time for this.) On April 26th, 1717, Bellamy and Williams spotted another *Mary Anne*, out of Dublin, between Nantucket and George's Bank. They approached the unsuspecting *Mary Anne* carrying the King's ensign and pennant. Captain Andrew Crumpstey was ordered to strike his colours, and a boarding party under Thomas Baker took control. There were more than 7,000 gallons of Madeira wine on board, a fitting climax to a year when the crew had taken a prize on average every fortnight. Captain Crumpstey and four seamen were transferred to the *Whydah* with several bottles of Crumpstey's wine. The pirates on the *Mary Anne* were told to follow the *Whydah* towards Cape Cod, probably to fence some goods at the Great Island Tavern and to meet Maria Hallett. Paulsgrave Williams headed back to his wife and children in Newport, Rhode Island, in the *Marianne*.

The *Fisher*, a small sloop with deer hides and tobacco was taken by Bellamy around mid-afternoon on the 26th. It appeared out of dense fog off Chatham. Bellamy hailed its master Robert Ingols, and told him that he needed him to help navigate the treacherous coastal waters. There was an increasing swell, and in poor conditions, Bellamy ordered the *Fisher*, *Mary Anne* and *Whydah* to hang lanterns so that they did not lose sight of each other. The *Mary Anne* began to fall behind - most of its crew were drunk on Madeira wine. The *Whydah* had already sprung her mast in one spring storm, and the Newfoundland Banks are the setting for that wonderful book *'The Perfect Storm'* . A storm of those terrible dimensions now seems to have hit the flotilla. The *Mary Anne* was leaking, and lost the *Fisher* and *Whydah*. The *Fisher* also soon became lost in the fog and increasing storm. Both the *Fisher* and *Whydah* dropped their anchors to try and prevent being dragged onto the shore by 70 mph winds and 40 foot waves.

Driven north on April 26th 1717, the *Whydah* and the *Mary Anne* were wrecked in dense fog off Cape Cod. In 70 mph gales, and 40 foot waves, the ships had been forced towards the shore. Between 10 and 11 at night, the prize *Mary Anne* ran ashore at Orleans, Massachusetts, with 7 pirates and 3 of its original crew members who had been left on board the help sail her. The men stayed on board the pink, and the tide left it on the barren reef next morning. Arrested by a deputy sheriff, the 7 pirates were tried on October 18th before an Admiralty Court at Boston, and 6 were hanged a month later. Hanged at Boston were John Brown of Jamaica, Thomas Baker of Flushing, Holland, Peter Cornelius Hoof of Sweden, Simon van Vorst of New York, Hendrick Quintor (a black man born in Amsterdam), and Jean Shuan of Nantes, Brittany. Thomas South was reprieved as he had been 'forced' against his will.

That same night the *Whydah* had dropped its anchors, but was remorselessly dragged by the storm, currents and tides, so Bellamy ordered the cable to be cut. However, the ship had no chance of escaping off a lee shore as she was already in the breakers. Her mainmast broke a few hundred yards offshore, and the *Whydah* broke its back on a sandbar off Wellfleet, ten miles further up the coast from the *Mary Anne*. The *Fisher* was badly damaged but survived the storms. Bellamy drowned and only two of the 146 men aboard made the shore. Thomas Davis, the Welsh shipwright and carpenter, was acquitted as he had been 'forced'. The Indian pilot, John Julian (who seems to have been born on Cape Cod), of the Muscheta (Mosquito) tribe of Afro-Amerindians in modern Belize, was reprieved but seems to have been sold into slavery. Thomas Davis left a vivid account of the shipwreck which passed into Cape Cod folklore.

Williams on the *Marianne* had lost contact with Bellamy but came upon the site two days later, to salvage any bounty he could. A month later he took two more ships, and sailed into Cape Cod upon June 6th 1717 to launder his loot. He then vanished from history, a millionaire. Immediately after the *Whydah* was wrecked, the Governor of Massachusetts sent Captain Cyprian Southack (a mapmaker by training) to the site to try and mount a salvage operation. Poor weather made operations difficult, and the 'mooncussers', the wreck scavengers of Cape Cod, took anything of value which was washed ashore. (They were so called because they cursed the moonlight which lit up their nefarious deeds). Continuing foul weather buried the cannon under the shifting sands of the ocean, and Southack only managed to procure some rigging and cable before he gave up the attempt. Within two weeks, the ocean floor had buried the *Whydah* out of sight for almost three hundred years.

Southack instituted a door-to-door search of Eastham and a 30-mile radius, to try and find anything which had been looted, but failed dismally. Skilled contrabanders had plenty of hiding-places. However, Samuel Harding admitted that he had scoured the beach after dawn on April 26th, and hidden his findings on his Wellfleet farm. He refused to return it, but told Southack that during the stormy night of the 25th, there had been a furious pounding on his door. He found there an exhausted man, on the brink of death

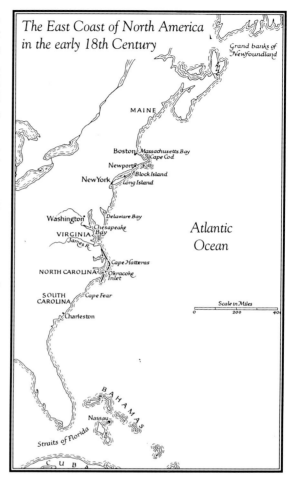

from cold and exhaustion. This was Thomas Davis, the carpenter on the *St Michael*, sailing from Cork to Jamaica. Just off Jamaica, Black Sam had taken the ship, looted it, and asked their crew to join him 'on the account'. Before leaving the *St Michael*, a buccaneer asked if there was a carpenter on board, and Davis reluctantly owned up to his trade. He was then '*forced*' as the pirates had great need of joiners to maintain and repair their ships. Davis appealed to Bellamy, but as he was unmarried, Bellamy denied him his freedom. However, Bellamy promised Davis that he would be allowed to sail away on the next prize he took. When Bellamy took the next prize, the magnificent *Whydah*, however, his angry crew reversed their captain's decision - carpenters were worth their weight in gold in keeping ships seaworthy and fast enough to catch, or escape from, other ships. One shouted after the voting at Davis '*Damn you, we would shoot you or whip you to death at the mast before we would let you go!*' Thus Thomas Davis worked on the *Whydah* until it was wrecked.

At first light, Harding took his wagon to the beach, and methodically stripped bodies of their valuables, and carted away anything else of value that was washed up. At least eight other *'Cape Codders'* were confronted by Southack for stripping bodies and hiding contraband, but all refused to give up any loot. All that Southack retreived was £263 worth of valuables from the beach, described in total at the Treasurer's Auction as *'Two anchors, two great guns and some junk'*.

The *Whydah's* cargo was said to be worth £20,000, and a Cape Cod treasure hunter named Barry Clifford began to excavate the site in 1984. It was the only sunken ship to be recognised as a genuine pirate wreck, before the finding of Henry Morgan's ship. (Marine archaeologists rate the finding of Morgan's *Jamaica Merchant* off Cows Island *'as dramatic as the discovery of the Titanic or the Bismarck'.)* Clifford had almost run out of funds when he found a coin dated 1684 at the site. The next year the ship's bell was found, and the discovery of the *Whydah* was confirmed. It was probably made by Evan Evans' Foundry at Chepstow, in Monmouthshire, and is marked *'THE + WHYDAH + GALLY + 1716'* . Gold ingots and hundreds of coins have been recovered, with the remnants of gold dust in casks. The gold coins were minted in Mexico and Peru, from melted-down pre-Columbian artefacts. Over 100,000 artefacts have been recovered, including a rare collection of gold jewellery from the Akan tribe of west Africa, which is on display at MacMillan Wharf in Provincetown. The force of the storm is indicated by the discovery of a silver teapot with a human shoulder bone wedged into it. Leather pouches and shoes have been recovered, last worn by pirates 300 years ago. 2000 coins have so far been found, the vast majority being *'pieces of eight'*, silver *'reales'* which date from the 1670's to 1715. Nine gold escudoes, *'doubloons'* have also been recovered, with some William III and Charles II English coins. Much of the jewellery had been cut up, and the gold bars and ingots bear the score marks of pirate knives, showing how the loot had been divided up between them. Recently Clifford has also found up to 18 ships including French warships and pirate vessels on a reef off Venezuela. This fleet was wrecked on May 3rd, 1678.

Postscript:
Barry Clifford, in his *'The Black Ship : the Quest to Recover an English Pirate Ship and its Lost Treasure'* (Headline, 1999), recounts what his Uncle Bill told him of the story of Black Sam and Maria Hallett: Bellamy had originally met Maria leaving Higgins Tavern in Eastham, when he followed the sound of singing to the local cemetery. *'Legend says that Maria walked up and down the beach looking for the body of Sam Bellamy. The bodies of more than an hundred pirates washed ashore in the days after the wreck and Maria examined every one. She never found her Sam and she never found peace. To this day, locals say that they can still hear her wailing for Sam Bellamy, from the cliffs of Eastham… There may be a surprise ending to this story. Some people claimed that after the wreck, a stranger turned up at Higgins' tavern near the cemetery where Bellamy first met Maria. He had long black hair and a deep scar across his face as if he had been struck by the blade of a cutlass. He was secretive about his purpose. When asked, he would simply say he was waiting for someone. He never took a job and never needed money. One spring day in 1720, the stranger went to the cemetery and sat underneath the apple tree, which was covered with a mist of blossoms. The stranger lay down and went to sleep. It was there, a few days later, that he, the man that some thought was Black Sam Bellamy, was found dead.'*

CHAPTER VII

CAPTAIN HOWELL DAVIS - 'THE CAVALIER PRINCE OF PIRATES' d. 1719

'Ah!' cried another voice, that of the youngest hand on board, and evidently full of admiration, 'he was the flower of the flock, was Flint!'
'Davis was a man, too, by all accounts,' said Silver. 'I never sailed along of him; first with England, then with Flint, that's my story; and now here on my own account, in a manner of speaking.' - 'Treasure Island', Robert Louis Stevenson, 1883.

"Howel Davis – the cavallier prince of pirates"

Milford Haven's Howell Davis was a Welsh pirate from Milford in Pembrokeshire, who preyed on shipping off the West African coast and in the Caribbean from July 1718 until June 1719. An expert in deception, Davis was killed in a skirmish with Portuguese troops on the West African Coast. Davis was virtually raised on a ship, coming to stature as chief mate of a slaver under Captain Skinner. In 1718, Davis was on Skinner's slaver snow *Cadogan* which was captured by Captain Edward England off the coast of Africa, en route from Nassau in the Bahamas to the island of Madagascar. Defoe wrote that England tried to get the good-natured, ever-smiling Davis to join his crew, but Davis *'resolutely answered that he would sooner be shot than sign the pirates' articles. Upon which England, pleased with his bravery, sent him and the rest of the men on board the snow (a small brig), appointing him captain in the room of Skinner (who had been shot) and commanding him to pursue his voyage. He also gave him a written paper sealed up, with orders to open it when he should come to a certain latitude..... This was an act of Grandeur like what princes practise to their admirals.... The paper contained a generous deed of gift of the ship and cargo to Davis and the crew, ordering him to go to Brazil, dispose of the lading to the best advantage and make a fair and equal dividend with the rest.'*

Skinner had been pelted with bottles by the pirates for being a brutal captain, before being put out of his misery by a musket-shot. Davis was a likeable, easy-going character, and easily had gained favour with England, and Davis wanted to sail on England's instructions to Brazil. However, most of the crew refused to follow this course of action, so Davis took the slaver on to Barbados, where he was charged with being a pirate and imprisoned for three months. Released for lack of proof, Davis found that his name had been blackened by the events, and could not get passage on any ship as a mate. He decided to head for the pirate stronghold of New Providence in the Bahamas, but Woodes Rogers had offered an 'Act of Grace' to the pirates at Nassau, and there was still no future for him. There were hundreds of former pirates now looking for 'honest' work there.

Governor Rogers took pity on him, and Davis sailed as an ordinary seaman on the *Buck*, a sloop full of New Providence's former pirates, with cargo for trading with Spanish and French possessions in the Indies. It sailed in consort with the *Mumvil Trader*. Rogers had few provisions, and the nearest island, Hispaniola, was in Spanish hands. He was surrounded by Spanish possessions which were not allowed to trade with him, and whose costagardas routinely tortured English seamen who fell into their hands. Rogers knew that if his expedition was stopped, it would have to fight the costagardas, so manned the ships *Buck* and *Samuel* with 'former' pirates, and filled the holds with barter goods. The Spanish colonists were willing to deal with pirates and merchants, as the Spanish monopoly of trade with them meant that they had to otherwise suffer high prices. The ships *Buck*, *Mumvil Trader* and *Samuel* left New Providence for Hispaniola in September 1718, anchored offshore and landed their cargo. Some sailors pretended to be filling casks with fresh water, so that any passing Spanish costagardas would possibly ignore them. Davis was still annoyed about his treatment - he knew that he would always be treated as a former pirate, with no chance of a mate's ticket.

Howell Davis, with former pirates Walter Kennedy, Dennis Topping, Thomas Anstis, Christopher Moody and William Magness, now saw their chance, and waited until Captain Brisk and the loyal members of his crew were asleep, then overpowered them. They transferred the remaining cargo from the *Mumvil Trader* onto the *Buck*, and sailed away to the north. The simmering and resentful Davis had started this mutiny at Martinique. There was no killing, merely a change of command, and most of the men who joined Davis were said to be Welsh and English. Davis was elected captain 'over a large bowl of punch.' According to Defoe: 'as soon as he was possessed of command, he drew up Articles, which were signed by himself and the rest, then he made a short speech, the sum of which was a declaration of war against the whole world.' He was voted captain with no opposition - the pirates thought the short, stocky Welshman 'pistol-proof'. He is later said to have 'played the (pirate) game because he was given the name'. The *Buck* was now careened with some difficulty at Coxon's Hole, a bay on the east of Cuba, as the pirates had no carpenter with them. With his crew of just thirty-five men, Davis then took a French ship. The *Buck* had followed the coast until Davis came across a 12-gun French ship at anchor in a sheltered creek. Davis fired a shot across the boat (not wishing to damage it), and some of its crew fled in a jolly-boat to the beach, there being no escape. While the vessel was being plundered, a larger, 24-gun French ship was spotted. Showing his native Welsh cunning, Davis then bluffed it into surrendering peacefully. He forced the prisoners on the first prize to pretend to be pirates and raised a dirty tarpaulin as a black flag. After a chase, the *Buck* caught up with the Frenchman, and after a couple of broadsides, the prize caught up with the action. Thinking it was outnumbered, the French ship struck its colours. Davis looted the two ships, transferring their equipment onto the *Buck*, then released them and their crews

Davis's sloops had only six light guns, and would find it difficult to capture a heavily-armed merchantman except by stealth, so the larger merchant ship was a fine acquisition, and they sailed into Privateer Bay, a hiding-place for pirates on the northern, uninhabited coast of Hispaniola. Impenetrable forests protected them from the Spanish settlers in the south of the island, and there were plenty of wild cattle for provisions. Now he decided to let the prisoners go. From the '*Buck*', Captain Brisk, his first and second mate, boatswain and two unfit seamen were put into Captain Porter's '*Samuel*'. A former pirate, Porter was also released, along with 17 of his crew who had families in New Providence. Porter sailed back to New Providence, and to the despair of Woodes Rogers, but other seamen were forced to stay with Davis, as he desperately needed crew members. One of those forced to stay was a young surgeon named Archibald Murray. Davis set sail for Cuba, where a Philadelphia ship was taken, then returned to Hispaniola. The busiest trade route in the West Indies was around Cape Franbarway, and more ships were captured. Upon one was a Welsh seaman called Richard Jones, who Davis wanted to join him, but who refused. A pirate gunner cut his leg, and the pirates repeatedly dropped him on a rope into the shark-infested seas, until Jones agreed to sign articles.

However, prizes were eluding the pirates, and Davis decided to cross the Atlantic and raid the African coast. He realised that his sloop needed to be properly careened. At a bay called Coxon's Hole in the east coast of Cuba, the '*forced men*' like Jones cleaned the *Buck*, and stripped her ready for pirate action. One side of the hull was scraped of barnacles, seaweed and other accretions, then coated with sulphur and brimstone to kill the teredos worms and their eggs, then covered with a protective tallow. Then the boat was hauled over to treat the other side, making the boat safer and faster at sea. Davis also had prepared plenty of '*boucan*', preserved strips of wild cattle meat, for the long voyage. A problem was that the '*Buck*' was fitted for 15 men, whereas he had a crew of over 60, so the ship reeked of sweat and sulphur. For this reason, his pirates preferred to laze ashore rather than in the comparative safety of the sloop. Davis now tacked through the Windward Passage, along the coast of Florida, until in the latitude of the Bahamas he took the trade wind to the Portuguese Cape Verde Islands. His trusted lieutenants, known as '*the House of Lords*' included the arrogant Walter Kennedy, the quartermaster John Taylor and the hot-tempered gunner Henry Dennis. These men were allowed privileges such as being on the quarterdeck, and had counselled Davis to set sail for Africa. Woodes Rogers had '*cleaned out*' Nassau, and Blackbeard had been killed - the Guinea Coast was a safer place to operate for the time being.

After the long crossing, Davis flew the English flag to enter the port of Sao Nicolau in early 1719, and pretended to be an English privateer with a letter of marque to fight the Spanish. He was welcomed, indeed '*caressed by the Governor and inhabitants.*' Davis had brought gold and goods in exchange for wine and apparel, and the Portuguese were only too happy to trade with the likeable *'merchant'*. Davis was invited to meet the Governor. The fort only had 12 guns, and Davis had left his stinking pirate sloop, stripped for action, well out to sea, when he first visited the governor. He wore a maroon velvet coat, silver-buckled shoes and a lace cravat, and his small bodyguard from the *House of Lords* dressed almost as ostentatiously. For five blissful weeks the pirates enjoyed themselves – *'no diversion was wanting which the Portuguese could show or money could purchase.'* However, Richard Jones, when fetching water, tried to limp away and hide in the coconut groves. Quartermaster Taylor spied him attempting to escape and chased after him through the undergrowth. He could not allow Jones to divulge that the *Buck* was a pirate ship. Eventually he caught up with the unfortunate Jones and tied his hands to take him back to the ship. A Portuguese officer reported this to the governor, but Taylor, with a smattering of Portuguese, explained that Jones was a pirate who had been captured and had escaped. Jones, who spoke no Portuguese, was taken back to the *Buck*, tied to the mast, and whipped by every person in the crew. Davis decided it was time to leave the island, provisioned the boat, and sailed to the Isle of May, where there were supposed to be rich pickings. Five pirates stayed and settled on the island, including a Monmouthshire man, Charles Franklyn who married a local girl. Franklyn was said to be *'so charmed with the luxuries of the place and the free conversation of the Women'*.

Off the Isle of May (Maio, in the Cape Verde Islands), Davis in February 1719, Davis sighted *'The Loyal Merchant'*, and sailing across its bows discharged chainshot at its crew, and stopping the ship. Davis ordered tits mate to come across to his ship, and questioned him on the sailing qualities of the merchantman, wishing to replace the small and slow *'Buck'*. Being slow to answer, the mate was badly beaten by the pirates, who hung him from the yardarm, and kept dropping him to the deck as he was about to pass out. *Lords* Dennis and Kennedy then *'woolded'* him (see Terms) and forced him to serve on the *Buck*. The *Buck* now took another seven Dutch and English prizes in the next few months, taking gold dust, ivory and slaves. One boat carried some welcome casks of rum, and one had a cargo of firearms. Eight heavy guns were taken off one merchantman, and used on a larger prize which they used to replace the *Buck*, which was now used as a consort ship. The new flagship was a two-masted brigantine with fore and aft rigging, which could take 26 cannon, and Davis named her the *Royal James*. Fore and aft rigging could be quickly altered to deal with different wind conditions.

Davis took the *Royal James* and the *Buck* to Gambia on February 23rd, and off Gallassee (later called Bathurst, and now Banjul) ran up merchant flags on the mastheads. He sailed past the Royal African Trading Company's fort of St James and ship the *'Royal Ann'*, up the Gambia River, to see Orfeur, the company agent. Taking the guise of Liverpool traders, Captain Davis, the ship's master and the surgeon *'dressed like gentlemen'* instead of the normal pirate dress. They took dinner with *'the Governor of Gambia Castle'* (this was possibly Orfeur), saying that they were *'bound for the river of Senegal to trade for gum and elephant's teeth (ivory).'* Davis had taken a *'hamper of European liquor'* to dinner, as a present for the Governor. The pirates took the opportunity to study the fort's defences, and the disposition and effectiveness of the *Royal Ann*. The fort was being rebuilt at Gallassee, and in the meantime Orfeur was conducting the Company's business from the *Royal Ann*. Orfeur suspected that the traders were not normal merchantmen, as they were too well-dressed. Some reports stated that the pirates suddenly drew pistols on the governor and relieved him of £2000 in cash after tying him to his chair, but the facts are different.

That night the pirates lowered boats and attacked Orfeur's men, but were met by a cross-fire from portholes. However, when Orfeur was wounded, he surrendered to the 60 pirates. Two pirates were injured, and they set the fort ablaze, looted the *Royal Ann*, and took another company ship lying alongside it. One of the men sheltering in the Fort of St James was to become Governor Plunkett who was captured by Black Bart, after his Sierra Leone fort at Brent (or Bence) island was bombarded. The pirates loaded up with ivory and bars of gold. (It appears that Davis totally destroyed the trading post, because George Lowther sailed as second mate in March 1721 of the Royal Africa Company ship '*Gambia Castle*', under Captain Charles Russell. She was '*carrying stores and a company of soldiers to the river Gambia, on the African coast, to garrison a fort some time before captured and destroyed by Captain Howel (sic) Davis, the pirate'*.) The badly-treated Welshman Richard Jones had actively taken part in the assault upon the fort and Royal Ann, and half of Orfeur's 14-man garrison joined Davis's men. They were malnourished, with a short life-span in the Tropics, and treated terribly by the Company.

For two nights Davis's crew caroused, but then another sloop nosed up the river towards the smoking fort. The ship flew no flag, and Davis prepared to send a shot across it. Captain Olivier *La Bouse* was commanding a 14-gun French pirate ship with sixty-four crew members, half French and half former slaves. He had formerly pirated with Captains Bellamy and Williams. He hoisted his Black Flag, fired a shot and almost attacked Captain Howel Davis, who was resting with his crew. Seeing the pirate flag raised, Davis swiftly hoisted his own, and hostilities were averted. Oliver le Vasseur, also known as *la Bouche* or *la Buse* (*the Buzzard*), apologised and the crews settled down to a week-long party. Both captains then agreed to sail down the coast together. On March 7th, they were guided by the master on the merchant vessel they had captured, through the treacherous channels of the River Gambia to the open ocean. The *Royal James* was followed by La Bouche's sloop, into the mists at the river's mouth. They came across Edward England's pirate ship, flying the black flag, but England declined to join their company and sailed on. Just a year later, La Bouche would join up with England on the account.

Davis allowed the merchantman to leave with its captain, but took his second mate, boatswain and five other crew. Two did not want to join and ran off into the forests, but Lord Taylor paid some Africans to find them. When they were hunted down they were brutally whipped by the pirates and thrown into the stinking hold. One who had suffered the same punishment, Richard Jones, was by now so highly thought of that he was elected boatswain by the pirates.

Arriving at Sierra Leone, they fired a broadside at a tall galley at anchor, which promptly hoisted its own Black Flag. The '*Mourroon*' was commanded by pirate Captain Thomas Cocklyn (from New Providence). Davis was annoyed that another pirate would spoil their chances of booty, but when Cocklyn heard that la Bouche was aboard, he invited Davis and la Bouche aboard his ship. Captain La Bouche was at New Providence Island in 1718, and had served on the same ship as Cocklyn. When Davis stepped aboard, a forced seaman rushed up to him and told him the story of William Hall. Cocklyn was known as a cruel captain, and Hall had been taken prisoner the previous day, on the 'Edward and Steed'. Hall was ordered by Cocklyn to release the foretop-sailsheet, and had climbed the shrouds too slowly for Cocklyn's liking. The boatswain shot him, not fatally, then climbed up after Hall, to cut at him with his cutlass, and his body dropped into the sea. The rest of the 'Edward and Steed' crew feared the same fate, and Davis swore at Cocklyn, calling him a fool. The law of the sea was that those who surrendered without struggling would not be harmed. La Bouche intervened as the two pirate captains circled each other, holding their cutlasses out. He put his arms around both and led them to Cocklyn's cabin for a drink. The three captains now formed up for a joint cruise 'on the account.' Their crews drank together for two days and on the third day they decided to head upriver to where six merchantmen had fled from Cocklyn. He already had captured two ships off Sierra Leone, the 'Edward and Steed', and Captain Elliott's 'The 'Two Friends', from Barbados.

Cocklyn was a vicious man, who had served with la Bouche under Christopher Moody. Moody had suspected Cocklyn of plotting against him, and had put him with other potential mutineers in a clapped-out galley, the 'Rising Sun', fully expecting it to sink. However, Cocklyn repaired it and renamed it the Mourroon. The rest of Moody's crew suspected that he had been withholding booty from them, deposed him and elected la Bouche as captain. Moody ended up in New Providence, where he joined Howell Davis's mutiny on the 'Buck'. Thus Moody was now in company with a man he had supported in mutiny (Davis), a man who had replaced him as captain (La Bouche), and a man whom he had thrown off his ship for plotting a mutiny (Cocklyn). Cocklyn suggested that he took the 'Two Friends' out for sea trials to see if it was suitable for replacing the 'Mourroon', while la Bouche and Davis stayed and blockaded the Royal African Company's Fort of Bence Island, in mid-river. (This location was later called Freetown, after British abolitionists settled freed slaves there in 1787). The two captains waited at sea, just out of the fort's gun range, to ensure that none of the merchantmen could slip away.

Suddenly, two cannon retorts were heard, and the pirates rushed to action stations. However, they soon began laughing - the shots had been fired by 'Crackers' John Leadstine, a private trader. He saluted each new pirate ship as he knew they would bring in cheap trade goods. His two brass cannon were surrounded by wooden cages in which he kept slaves for trade. La Bouche decided he did not wish to wait for Cocklyn, and despite Davis's protests, sailed toward Bence Island. Agent Plunkett organised cannon fire which tore through the mainsail and sprayed water over the sloop's decks, before la Bouche veered back to rejoin Davis. Davis's crew laughed at their efforts. Cocklyn now returned, with a boat that Davis had captured at Gambia, which he wanted to use as a store-ship. The pirate ships, all flying black flags, headed toward the fort, and the seamen abandoned the merchantmen for its relative safety.

The abandoned merchantmen were secured and taken. They were the 'Jacob and Jael' under Captain Thompson and the 'Society' trading from London; the brig 'Robert and Jane' under Captain Bennet, out of Antigua; the snow 'Parnel' under Captain Morris, and the 'Nightingale', both out of Bristol; and the 'Queen Elizabeth' under Captain Creighton. Goods, provisions, sails and guns were stripped from the boats, and barter terms agreed for the boats themselves with four of the captains. The two other boats were burned.

However, the pirates needed more booty, and believed that the fort held gold and Company money. At dawn the pirate ships began bombarding the fort, whose largest guns had rusted up. Davis sent Plunkett a cheeky message, asking if he had any spare gunpowder, ammunition or gold to lend him, and Plunkett retorted that he had no gold, but plenty of gunpowder and shot if Davis would care to come and collect it. However, Plunkett soon ran out of ammunition in the burning fort, and one wall had

The West Indies

been smashed in. He tried to take his men in canoes off the island but they were captured, and a furious Cocklyn put his pistol to Plunkett's head, cursing him. Plunkett responded with such a vile stream of invective at Cocklyn that the pirate was non-plussed and his men burst out laughing. Even the evil Cocklyn saw the funny side of this exchange, and spared Plunkett's life. The pirates stripped the fort of all its valuables, and forced some men to join them. Many did so willingly. There was an enormous party, and Plunkett was allowed to go back to his ruined fort. In the next few days, three more ships were taken as they sailed into the port, including the

'Sarah', which Cocklyn wanted to replace the Mourroon. The pirates spent their time selling off their loot to local traders, including 'Old Crackers'. Two men from the 'Mourroon' escaped into the local forests, and for a day the pirates searched for them, but Davis counselled that they would either return or die anyway. After three days, one was dead and the carpenter Henry Thrixton returned, starving and lacerated from the thorny jungle. Cocklyn wanted to torture and kill him, but Davis put him in safety on the Royal James to serve under him.

The three captains now agreed to leave Sierra Leone - pickings were slim as more and more ships knew that 'a new gang' of pirates was operating in the area. La Bouche and Davis allowed Cocklyn to refit the 'Sarah' with his guns and equipment from the Mourroon, and it was decided to split up the joint booty, which was kept in Cocklyn's store-ship. The other captains were afraid of Cocklyn making a 'soft farewell', leaving at night with all the accumulated loot. However, the pirates spotted a ship unexpectedly approaching, Captain Snelgrave's 'Bird', a London galley which had not heard of the pirate take-over of the port. The pirates hastily took their ships up-river, out of sight of Snelgrave, in order to entice him into port. By the time they had rigged ready for sailing out to sea, they might have lost their prey. In the calamitous rush to get up-river, they omitted putting out their camp-fires on the beach, and Snelgrave became suspicious. In the gathering dusk, he sent a pinnace to investigate, but the crew reported back that it was too dark to discover what had been happening. (Snelgrave's remarkable account of the capture, from his wonderful 'A New Account of some Parts of Guinea, and the Slave-Trade', published in 1734, is appended to this chapter. He recounts Davis as brave, 'my generous Friend', and humane, and records his death with some sadness).

Snelgrave took supper while pondering the findings of the search-party, and anchored off-shore. However, the officer of the watch rushed to him, reporting the sounds of rowing. Two boats containing 12 of Cocklyn's men, armed to the teeth, were close to the 16-cannon ship. Snelgrave ordered that 20 of his 45-man crew be woken and sent to the quarter-deck, and he hailed the two boats, asking who they were and what they wanted. The pirates shouted back that they were from Captain Elliott's 'Two Friends', out of Barbados. Snelgrave's crew had refused to arm themselves and go on deck, and the pirates shot at Snelgrave and began to board his ship. Snelgrave charged below to get help, but only a couple of loyal crewmen accompanied him, and they ran back up onto the deck, where one was shot. A grenade exploded, and his crew implored the unarmed Snelgrave to surrender, which he was forced to do.

Cocklyn's quartermaster was incensed by Snelgrave's decision to fight, for which the penalty was death, and he held a pistol against him. Snelgrave impulsively pushed the firearm away, but was shot in the arm. He turned to run, and was pistol-clubbed to the ground, and the situation looked bleak for him. The pirate boatswain said 'No quarter shall be given to any captain that offers to defend his ship', and lashed out with his cutlass, breaking its blade on the deck-rail. Luckily, Snelgrave's crew implored the boatswain to spare Snelgrave, one member crying 'For God's sake, don't kill our captain, for we were never with a better man.' Just then the pirate quartermaster returned from a quick inspection of the 'Bird's' splendid cargo, and announced that it was a fine prize. In the general exultation, Snelgrave was unusually spared, and the pirates fired their pistols into the night sky to celebrate. Snelgrave later wrote that Davis claimed that *'their reasons for going a pirating were to revenge themselves on base merchants and cruel commanders of ships'*.

However, Cocklyn had brought the *Mourroon* out to back up the assault by his men, and thought that the *Bird's* crew was firing. He ordered a broadside fired at the *Bird*, which unfortunately smashed its masts and sails, before he realised his mistake. Cocklyn next questioned Snelgrave upon the sailing qualities of the *Bird*, and requisitioned it, while boatloads of goods were ferried to the port's private traders, which included the Welshman Henry Glynn, an old friend of Snelgrave's. Snelgrave also told the pirates that Edward England, who had captured Davis and sailed with la Bouche, was still taking ships off the Gambia coast. Each of the boarding-party was given a fresh suit of clothes, and the look-out who first spotted the *Bird* was given a pair of pistols, while the three pirate quartermasters divided up the rest of the booty. Captain Snelgrave later wrote in his *'A New Account of Some parts of Guinea, and the Slave Trade'* that when Howell Davis captured his ship, his men drank the looted claret and brandy from bowls before throwing bucketfuls of the precious alcohol at each other, and ended up by swabbing the decks with the drink. (As Bart Roberts commented later, a pirate's life was to be a short and happy one.) Snelgrave also reported that *'Captain Howell Davis came in the river (Gambia) with a Black Flag showing, which said flag is intended to frighten honest merchantmen into surrender on penalty of being murdered if they do not'*

An 18 year-old who served under Davis tried to break open a chest when the quartermasters were assessing the spoils, but Cocklyn's quartermaster swung at him with a broadsword. The youth ran to the safety of Davis, who was sitting drinking in the *Bird's* captain's cabin with Cocklyn and la Bouche. The quartermaster swung again at the youngster, cutting him on the thumb, but also Davis on the hand. Davis was furious at this latest insult from Cocklyn or his crew. The youngster may have been at fault, but it was Davis's right to punish him. Back on the *Royal James*, he ordered that the guns were run out, and trained on the *Mourroon*. Cocklyn frantically sent his quartermaster on a boat from the *Bird* to apologise profusely to Davis.

It had been decided that la Bouche could replace his sloop with the *Bird*, and that Cocklyn could take the *Sarah* and leave the leaking *Mourroon*. Cocklyn renamed his new galley the *'Speakwell'*, and stripped the below-decks to allow 30 cannon to be installed. La Bouch renamed his new ship the *'Wyndham Galley'*, and fitted it with 24 guns. The apportioning of loot was finished, and quartermaster Taylor took the *Royal James'* share, but there was some ill-feeling, as Davis had more men that la Bouche or Cocklyn, who each received the same amount for their smaller crews. Each crew member had a single share of the ship's booty, officers took a share and a quarter, the quartermaster took a share and a half, and the captain two shares. A French ship was taken, and Cocklyn took such a dislike to its captain that he put a rope around his neck and repeatedly hung him from the yardarm and dropped him to the floor. The enraged la Bouche rescued his fellow-countryman, and Cocklyn pacified him by giving him the captain and ship. Meanwhile Davis, Dennis and Taylor discussed provisioning, weaponry and munitions as they prepared to leave the port.

Davis, Cocklyn and la Bouche first decided to visit the local harlots, and took three of Snelgrave's finest embroidered outfits to wear. Their crews were angry that they had taken the finery without asking, and stripped them off their backs. La Bouche's Welsh quartermaster, Williams, blamed Snelgrave for the presumption and wished to kill him, but Snelgrave wheedled his way out by flattery, addressing Williams as *Captain* Williams. Davis decided to calm tempers among the inebriated, bored crews by throwing a huge final party on board the *Royal James*. The revellers were so drunken during the feast that they did not notice a fire, which began with a dropped lamp near the rum stores. The sober Snelgrave organised a chain gang to work the pump and take buckets down the hold, and luckily doused the raging fires. There were 18 tons of gunpowder stored on the *Royal James*, and the pirates were so grateful for Snelgrave's efficiency and management that they wanted to take him with them as a pilot. Snelgrave argued piteously at this fate, and Davis spared him, giving him la Bouche's old sloop to sail home.

Howell Davis was now elected commodore by the pirates, with three pirate ships - the *Royal James*, the *Speakwell* and the Wyndham *Galley*, Cocklyn's store-ship the *Two Friends* and the captured 'Guinea Hen' in his fleet. The ships left Sierra Leone at the end of April, heading south and keeping near the shore. Cocklyn allowed its captain to sail off in the *Guinea Hen*, because it was slower than the rest of the fleet. Davis sailed around Cape Palmas, along the Ivory Coast, and on towards the Gold Coast. Thee were rich pickings there, with many ships carrying money and goods to four Royal African Company forts, to buy slaves for the Americas.

In the extreme heat, the pirates needed fresh water, but because of the lack of landing places and the heavy Atlantic rollers, relied upon native fishermen to supply them. Davis sent a longboat ashore with some men, guided by natives in their canoes, to whom he gave some old muskets. However, the natives eventually returned to the *Royal James*, with no white men among them. They said that the pirates had run off into the jungle. As one of the pirates had been with Davis since the *Buck* Mutiny, he knew this to be a lie, and that the men had been murdered for their weapons, but his crews were desperately short of water. Davis used his quartermaster, Taylor, as an interpreter to tell the native leader that they would need a second party to be led ashore. He then told Taylor in English to get heavily armed, take the best men, and force the natives to return to the *Royal James* with them. Casks were filled with fresh water by the natives at gunpoint, and they were forced back to the ship.

Taylor interrogated them as to the fate of the pirates, but could get no answer, so decided to use the blacks as target practice. In pairs they were hoisted in the air, with two teams competing for rum, to kill each swinging target first. Howell Davis watched thoughtfully, seeing how the men followed Taylor in his lust for blood, and knew that his time as captain was limited. Two days later another prize was taken, but with little booty, and his fate was sealed. One of Taylor's supporters proposed him as captain and Davis was deposed within minutes. However, he was then elected quartermaster in Taylor's place. Luckily for Davis, Taylor was another Cocklyn, a vindictive, vicious brute, and the crew soon tired of his bullying, capricious ways. Within a few days, they had voted again, and Davis was re-elected captain. In a fit of pique, Taylor joined Cocklyn's ship, with some of his supporters. The young Irishman, Walter Kennedy, was elected quartermaster on the *Royal James*.

La Bouche renamed his ship the *Duke of Ormond*, and Cocklyn's storeship, the *Two Friends*, sailed off one night in a *'soft farewell'*. At the end of May another ship was taken, but Davis now disagreed on the destination of the fleet with the other two captains. He wished to sail east to Principe, and as *'strong liquor stirring up a spirit of discord, they quarrelled'*. Howell Davis defused the situation, saying *'Hark ye, Cocklyn and la Bouche. I find by strengthening you, I have put a rod into your hands to whip myself. But I am still able to deal with you both. Since we met in love, let us part in love, for I find that three of a trade can never agree.'* Cocklyn, la Bouche and Taylor sailed off (- see the notes at the end of this chapter).

Davis now came upon the *Marquis del Campo*, formerly a British naval ship, out of Ostend with 30 guns, anchored off Cape Three Points. Pirates usually kept away from Dutch merchantmen because of their fighting reputation, but Davis probably felt he had something to prove after being deposed by his men recently. The first Dutch broadside killed nine pirates, and dozens more died in battle of their injuries. The fighting, in late May, lasted from noon until next morning. Both ships suffered severely. On capturing the Dutch ship, he made repairs and put 32 cannon and 27 swivel guns aboard and renamed it the *Royal Rover*. Unusually, none of the Dutch sailors were hurt when they surrendered. This was contrary to the pirate practice of 'no quarter' for those who dared to fight them. The wounded were taken ashore and tended by the surgeon Archibald Murray, while the *Royal Rover* was stripped to make a better fighting ship. Davis let the *Buck* go, and now had two very powerful ships to rove the seas. They passed the Royal African Company stronghold of Cape Coast Castle, heading towards Accra, towards another of its forts and ports, 15 miles away. Annambo (Anamabu) was not as important a slave-trading centre, and consequently was less well-defended.

On June 6th 1719, the *Royal Rover* and *King James* nosed into the slaving harbour of Annambo on the Gold Coast, flying the black flags, drums beating and trumpets blaring. The three English slave ships moored there, the *'Morris'*, the *'Royal Hynde'* and the *'Princess of London'* immediately struck their colours. The merchant captains were on shore, bartering for slaves, and the members of crew who did not escape in boats had no thoughts of bloody resistance. Davis took their cargoes of slaves, gold and ivory – like most pirates he always tried to avoid a fight and consequent damage to his ship, crew and the precious booty of the prize ships. Also there was always the chance of obtaining fresh crew members and *'sea-artists'*, or a better ship. Equally, merchant traders, although often well-armed, knew that if they surrendered immediately, quarter was nearly always given. They had no real desire to fight for the ship's owner or a hated captain. As a former merchant seaman and captain, Davis knew this, and had therefore deliberately drawn up his Ship's Articles to give quarter when it was asked for, that is when a *ship struck her colours* (lowered her flag). The Royal Africa Company's fort opened fire on the ships but its cannon were designed for short-range work against attacking natives. Pirate attacks were rare off this coast. The shot fell harmlessly out of range. Davis ordered his cannon to fire back, and the fort's guns fell silent, knowing the futility of the task. Davis leisurely finished looting the three slave vessels, and later gave one of them to the captain of the Dutch ship, releasing him and his crew.

One of the English ships captured was the *Princess of London*, a slaver whose third mate was a man of Pembrokeshire, like Davis. Something about the tall, dark John Roberts captured Davis' imagination, but he was proud of never having 'forced' a man to become a pirate. Davis had brought the *Royal Rover* up alongside the *Princess*, and its second mate, Stephenson, asked what he wanted. Captain Plumb and the first mate were hiding ashore. Davis told Stephenson to bring the carpenter Eastwell, the gunner John Jessup, John Owen, Thomas Rogers, James Bradshaw, William Gittus, and the third mate John Roberts on to the *Royal Rover*. Davis told them that some of them would be 'forced' to become pirates if there were not enough volunteers to replace the men he had lost in the fight against the *Marquis del Campo*. He sent the sailors back to the *Princess*, to allow them time to make a decision whether to join the pirate crew or not. ('*Black Bart*' Roberts soon became the most successful and feared pirate of them all). Eastwell decided to change sides, and the other men looked on as the three merchant captains, Plumb, Hall and Fenn, rowed back to their ships to negotiate with the pirates. They wanted to stop their ships being burnt, and to be left with enough crew to sail them back home.

Captain Blunt found that his *Princess of London* had been stripped bare. What Davis's new quartermaster Walter Kennedy could not find, Eastwell had eagerly directed him towards. Eastwell personally took Stephenson's hats and money from him, and threatened to shoot the mate if he did not tell him the whereabouts of 40 ounces of missing gold dust. Some slaves were also taken off the ships, to carry out menial labour on the pirate ships. Two Welshmen on the *Princess*, John Owen and Thomas Rogers, tried to take the ship towards the fort by hoisting sails, and were brought before Davis. He admired their bravery and made them join his crew. Davis now met the three merchant captains and asked for some of their crew members, as only Eastwell had volunteered his services, apart from the unfortunate Rogers and Owen. Fenn protested strongly, and in response Davis impressed all his crew except a cripple. He then gave Fenn's ship, the '*Morris*' to his thirty captured Dutch sailors from the *Marquis del Campo*, but kept a Scotsman, John Stewart from their crew.

Among the sailors forced to join from the *Morris* and the *Royal Hynde* was James Sail, who tried to escape, but was captured and taken on the *Royal James*. He again escaped, to the *Princess of London*, and upon this recapture was tied to the mainmast and whipped by crew members. Bradshaw, Jessup, Stephenson and Roberts were among those others taken from the *Princess* for Davis's crew. Sailing east, the next day the pirates plundered another Dutch ship bound for Holland. After just one broadside from the *Royal Rover*, it surrendered. It was a great prize, with the '*Governor of Accra on board, with all his effects*.' Apart from merchandise, there was over £15,000 in coin aboard. Davis now rid himself of the other two captured slavers, and let those that wanted leave his ships. However, Roberts and thirty-four other merchant seamen had to stay with Davis, who needed skilled seamen for his two great ships. Fenn and Plumb went with the *Royal Hynde* to Cape Coast Castle, and the Dutchmen sailed the *Morris* to Accra. Black Bart Roberts must have been bemused how easy the pirate life was, and he had heard of the bloodless trickery of Howell Davis in his past exploits. *'The Weekly Journal'* reported (April 9, 1720), *'The pyrates off the coast of Guinea in Africa have taken goods to the value of £204,000'*.

Davis seems to have been drawn towards Roberts, and consulted with him on sailing rigs and courses. Roberts, in his late 30's, had massive experience of the Americas and Africa and the *Slave Triangle*. Without accurate longitude in these times, experience and intuition could keep a ship on the Trade Routes and out of the *Doldrums*. Davis decided to head for the Portuguese island of Principe, a wealthy colony around 600 miles east-South-East of Annambo. More ships were taken on the Guinea Coast, but off Cameroon the *King James* was seen to be trailing about a mile behind. Davis immediately suspected Kennedy of plotting a *'soft farewell'*, but soon discovered that the ship was listing and the sailors working the pumps. Roberts suggested careening it in Cameroon Bay and repairing the rotting hull with fresh timber. However, the damage was so extensive that the *Royal James* had to be abandoned, and its rigging, cargo, provisions, guns, and men transferred to the *Royal Rover*.

The *Royal Rover* now sailed south to the Isle of Princes (Principe), where Davis hoisted navy flags and claimed to be captain of an English man-of-war sent to bring piracy to a halt in the area. Kennedy and Jones had wanted to attack by force rather than ruse, but were outvoted by the other pirates. A small sloop sailed up to the *Royal Rover* asking its business, and Davis responded that they were chasing the pirates which had been devastating the Guinea Coast. They were given permission to enter Principe's harbour. The Portuguese Governor officially welcomed Davis, and the pirates found a sandy cove to careen the ship. Davis was escorted on his pinnace to meet the governor by nine men in fresh white linen shirts and black trousers, and he dressed in a maroon velvet coat. Escorted by soldiers to see the Governor, he was granted the freedom of the island, while Davis in return promised that King George would reimburse any expenses.

In the evenings, the pirates spent their booty on women and drink in the little settlement on the main harbour. Because of their free-spending ways, the Governor must have soon known that they were pirates rather than the poverty-struck and impressed men of His Majesty's Navy. His suspicions must have been raised when the *Royal Rover* blocked a French ship's entry into the harbour, and Kennedy's boarding-party swarmed over it, looking for plunder. Davis explained to the Governor that the French ship had been trading with pirates, and that it had been seized in reparation by the English Crown. After another fortnight, during which the pirates became increasingly difficult to control, Davis and fourteen other men including his Lords, walked inland to a native village, upon hearing that some women might be available there. The women fled to the woods, and their chief complained to the Governor. To placate him, Davis invited the Governor to lunch on the Royal Rover, which was still anchored near the harbour entrance.

No-one knows whether Davis intended to repeat his feat at Gambia, when he attempted to trick the Governor, or just rest and carouse a while, as at the Cape Verde

Islands under its Portuguese Governor. It appears that the latter was the case – he would not have allowed his men to get out of hand if his motive had been to capture the Governor of Prince's Island by subterfuge. Tragedy now happened for Davis. Esquemeling recounts that a Portuguese negro swam ashore and told the Governor that he was to be invited on Davis' *Royal Rover* and held to ransom. It seems more likely however that the Governor was afraid of being reported to Portugal for consorting with, and profiting from pirates, on his poor little island. The Governor accepted the invitation, and invited Davis for a glass of wine at the fort before they were rowed to lunch on the ship.

Davis was called to the Government House on Sunday, the day before he was due to sail off. He took his ship's surgeon and several of the leading officers of the ship. (Esquemeling categorically states that he was going to capture the Governor, but this is unlikely, as this would mean risking the leadership of the *Royal Rover*). Davis took Kennedy, and nine other men. John Roberts was left in command of the *Royal Rover*, and Jones in charge of the pinnace, which would take the governor and his colleagues back to the *Royal Rover*. The building was empty, so Davis decided to return to his ship, but the party was ambushed by musketeers half-way down the hill. All but two of the party were killed, but it took five bullets and a cut throat to despatch Davis. He fired both pistols as he lay dying, so he died '*like a game-cock, giving a dying blow, that he might not fall unavenged.*'

Kennedy managed to escape to the waiting boats, and another pirate jumped off the cliffs and was luckily picked up by the pirates' longboat, just returning from a fishing expedition and alerted by the sound of musketry. The pirate escape and their revenge is described in the next chapter, upon Black Bart Roberts. The baton of captaincy now passed to his fellow Pembrokeshire man John Roberts, soon to become the most feared pirate in history, *Black Bart*. Howell Davis was known as '*the cavalier prince of pirates*', and according to Howard Pyle; '*The name of Capt. Howel Davis stands high among his fellows. He was the Ulysses of pirates, the beloved not only of Mercury, but of Minerva. He it was who hoodwinked the captain of a French ship of double the size and strength of his own, and fairly cheated him into the surrender of his craft without the firing of a single pistol or the striking of a single blow; he it was who sailed boldly into the port of Gambia, on the coast of Guinea, and under the guns of the castle, proclaiming himself as a merchant trading for slaves.*

The cheat was kept up until the fruit of mischief was ripe for the picking; then, when the governor and the guards of the castle were lulled into entire security, and when Davis's band was scattered about wherever each man could do the most good, it was out pistol, up cutlass, and death if a finger moved. They tied the soldiers back to back, and the governor to his own armchair, and then rifled wherever it pleased them. After that they sailed away, and though they had not made the fortune they had hoped to glean, it was a good snug round sum that they shared among them.

Their courage growing high with success, they determined to attempt the island of Del Principe - a prosperous Portuguese settlement on the coast. The plan for taking the place was cleverly laid, and would have succeeded, only that a Portuguese negro among the pirate crew turned traitor and carried the news ashore to the governor of the fort. Accordingly, the next day, when Captain Davis came ashore, he found there a good strong guard drawn up as though to honour his coming. But after he and those with him were fairly out of their boat, and well away from the water side, there was a sudden rattle of musketry, a cloud of smoke, and a dull groan or two. Only one man ran out from under that pungent cloud, jumped into the boat, and rowed away; and when it lifted, there lay Captain Davis and his companions all of a heap, like a pile of old clothes.

"The death of Captain Davis".

Capt. Bartholomew Roberts was the particular and especial pupil of Davis, and when that worthy met his death so suddenly and so unexpectedly in the unfortunate manner above narrated, he was chosen unanimously as the captain of the fleet, and he was a worthy pupil of a worthy master. Many were the poor fluttering merchant ducks that this sea hawk swooped upon and struck; and cleanly and cleverly were they plucked before his savage clutch loosened its hold upon them.'

The following is the full text of the report by Captain Snelgrave on his captivity under Howell Davis:

A New Account of some Parts of Guinea, and the Slave Trade
by Captain William Snelgrave, 1734

BOOK III
Containing an Account of the Author's being taken by Pirates, on the North part of the Coast of Guinea, in the Bird Galley of London, belonging to the late Humphrey Morrice Esq: who was sole owner of the said Ship. Interspersed with several Instances of the Author's many Deliverances, and narrow Escapes from Death, during the time he was detained Prisoner by the Pirates.

"In the beginning of November, in the year 1718, the late Humphrey Morrice Esq; Merchant of London, appointed me Commander of the Bird Galley, and gave me Orders to go to Holland, to take on board a cargo for the coast of Africa: having so done, we were unfortunately detained by contrary Winds, at Helvoet-Sluys, till the 10th day of December, when a violent storm arose, and in the night following forced our ship on shore, with several others. The ship, by the strength of the wind, and the height of the tide, was carried with a great force against the Dyke, or bank that secures the land from being overflowed by such high tides, which frightened the inhabitants thereabouts not a little. Moreover, the waves made her work so much on the ground where she was stranded, that when the tide had left her, we found she had set seven feet abaft (towards the stem of the ship) in the strand; but had the satisfaction to find, on examination, the ship had received no damage in her bottom. Having unloaded, and hired many Boers or peasants, to dig a trench of near 300 foot in length to the low water mark, we waited some time for a high tide; and then getting the ship off, carried her into Helvoet-Sluys pier.

Having refitted and loaded again, we proceeded on the voyage the latter end of January; but the wind changing by the time we were off the isle of Wight, and rising to a great storm westerly, we were forced into Spithead; where having lain some time, we sailed again with a fair wind, which carried us above 70 leagues to the westward of the Lizard. Here such a severe storm of wind coming up at southwest, obliged us to lie by, under a reefed mainsail; and it increased to such a violent degree, that we expected to be swallowed up every minute, by the great sea which ran mountains high; but it pleased God, that after 24 hours, it began to abate, and we received no other damage, than the loss of the ship's cut-water, which was washed away by the sea.

The wind (after this storm) remaining contrary a long time, with frequent hard gales, obliged us at last to go for Kingsale (Kinsale) in Ireland: Where having lain a few days, and repaired the ship's head, with other things that were out of order, we sailed from that place, with a northerly wind, the 10th day of March 1718-1719, and had a short and fine passage to the River Sierraleon; on the north coast of Guinea, in the latitude of 8 degrees 30 minutes, where we arrived the first day of April 1719: We met with nothing remarkable in our passage, except, that near the Canary Islands, we were chased by a ship whom we judged to be a Sallee-Rover; but our ship outsailing her, they soon gave over the chase.

There were, at the time of our unfortunate arrival in the above-mentioned river, three Pirate Ships, who had then taken ten English ships in that place. As it is necessary for illustrating this story, to give an account of how these three ships came to meet there, I must observe, that the first of them which arrived in the river, was called the Rising Sun, one Cocklyn commander, who had with him above 25 men. There having been one Captain Moody, a famous pirate, some months before, in a brigantine, which sailed very well, and took the Rising Sun, they were *morooned* by him, (as they call it) that is forced to board the ship, and deprived of their share of the plunder, taken formerly by the brigantine. These people being obliged to go away in her, with little provision and ammunition, chose Cocklyn for their commander, and made for the River Sierraleon; where arriving, they surprised in his sloop, one Segnor Joseph, a black Gentleman, who had formerly been in England, and was a person of good account in this country. This man's ransom procured the pirates a sufficient supply of provision and ammunition. Moreover, several Bristol and other ships arriving soon after, were likewise taken; and many of their people entering with the pirates, they had, when I fell into their hands, near 80 men in all.

The crew of the brigantine, who, with their Captain Moody, had thus forced their companions away in the Rising Sun, soon after repenting of that action, it bred great discontentment amongst them; so that they quarrelled with their captain and some others, whom they thought the chief promoters of it, and at last forced him, with twelve others, into an open boat, which they had taken a few days before, from the

Spaniards of the Canary Islands; and they were never heard of afterwards, doubtless they perished in the ocean. After this, they chose one La Bouse a Frenchman for their commander, who carried them to the River Sierraleon, where they arrived about a month after their parting from the Rising Sun.

At the first appearance, of this brigantine, Cocklyn and his crew were under a great surprise; but when they understood how Moody and some others had been served by them, they cheerfully joined their Brethren in Iniquity.

On the same day also arrived one Captain Davis, who had been pirating in a sloop, and had taken a large ship at the Cape Verde Islands. He coming into Sierraleon with her, it put the other two pirates in some fear, believing at first it was a Man of War: But upon discovering her black flag at the Main-top-mast-head, which Pirate Ships usually hoist to terrify Merchant-Men; they were easy in their minds, and a little time later, saluted one another with their cannon.

This Davis was a generous man, and kept his crew, which consisted of near 150 men, in good order; neither had he consorted or agreed to join with the others, when I was taken by Cocklyn; which proved a great Misfortune to me, as will appear afterwards. For I found Cocklyn and his crew, to be a set of the basest and most cruel villains that ever were. And indeed they told me, after I was taken, *'That they chose him for their Commander, on account of his Brutality and Ignorance; having resolved never to have again a Gentleman-like Commander, as, they said, Moody was.'*

Upon mentioning this, I think it necessary to observe in this place, that the Captain of a Pirate Ship, is chiefly chosen to fight the vessels they may meet with. Besides him, they choose another principal Officer, whom they call Quarter-Master, who has the general inspection of all affairs, and often controls the Captain's Orders: This person is also said to be the first man in boarding any ship they shall attack; or go in the boat on any desperate enterprise. Besides the captain and the Quartermaster, the pirates had all other officers as is usual on board Men of War.

I come now to give an account of how I was taken by them. The day that I made the land, when I was within three leagues of the river's mouth, it became calm in the afternoon. Seeing a smoke on shore, I sent for my first mate Mr Simon Jones, who had been formerly at Sierraleon, where I had not; *'Bidding him take the pinnace, and go where the smoke was, to enquire of the natives, how affairs stood up the river.'* But he replied *'it would be to little purpose, for no people lived there: As to the smoke we saw, he believed it might be made by some travellers who were roasting oysters on the shore, and would be gone before he could get a mile from the ship. Moreover, as night drew on, it would be difficult for him to find the ship again.'* Thinking this answer reasonable, I did not press him further, though I understood afterwards, there was a town where the smoke appeared. But I did not then in the least suspect that Mr Jones would have proved such a Villain as he did afterwards.

About five o'clock in the afternoon, a small breeze arising from the sea, and the tide of flood setting strong, we stood for the river's mouth. At sun-setting we perceived a ship at anchor, a great way up the river; which was the Pirate that took us soon after. The other two pirate ships, with their prizes, were hid from our sight by a Point of Land.

It becoming calm about seven o'clock, and growing dark, we anchored in the river's mouth; soon after which I went to supper, with the officers that usually eat with me. About eight o'clock the Officer of the Watch upon deck, sent me word, *'He heard the rowing of a boat.'* Whereupon we all went immediately upon deck; and the night being very dark, I ordered Lanthorns (lanterns) and Candles to be got ready, supposing that the boat might come from the shore with some white gentlemen, that lived there as free Merchants; or else from the ship we had seen up the river a little while before we came into anchor. I ordered also, by way of Precaution, the First Mate to go into the steerage, to put all things in order, and to send me forthwith twenty men of the quarter-deck with fire-arms and cutlaces (cutlasses), which I though he went about.

As it was dark, I could not yet see the boat, but heard the noise of the rowing very plain: Whereupon I ordered the second mate to hail the boat, to which the people in it answered, *'They belonged to the Two Friends, Captain Eliot of Barbadoes.'* At this one of the Officers, who stood by me, said, *'He knew the Captain very well, and that he commanded a vessel of that name.'* I replied, *'It might be so; but I would not trust any boat in such a place;'* and ordered him to hasten the First Mate (Jones), with the people and the arms upon deck, as I had just ordered. By this time our lanthorns and candles were brought up, and I ordered the boat to be hailed again; To which the people in it answered *'They were from America:'* And at the same time fired a volley of small shot at the ship, though they were then above a pistol shot from us; which showed the Boldness of these Villains: For there was in the boat only twelve of them, as I understood afterwards, who knew nothing of the strength of our ship; which was indeed considerable, we having 16 guns, and 45 men on board. But as they told me after we were taken, *'They judged we were a small vessel of little force. Moreover, they depended on the same good fortune as in the other ships they had taken; having met with no resistance: For the people were generally glad of an opportunity of entering with them:'* Which last (sentence) was but too true.

When they first began to fire, I called aloud to the First Mate, to fire at the Boat out of the Steerage Port-holes; which not being done, and the people I had ordered on deck with small arms not appearing, I was extremely surprised; and the more, when an Officer came and told me, *'The People would not take Arms.'* I went thereupon down into the Steerage, where I saw a great many of them looking at one another. Little thinking that my First Mate had prevented them from taking Arms, I asked them with some roughness *'Why had they not obeyed my Orders?'* Calling upon some brisk Fellows by name, that had gone a former Voyage with me, to defend the Ship; saying, *'It would be the greatest reproach in the World to us all, if we should be taken by a Boat.'* Some of them replied, *'They would have taken Arms, but the Chest they were kept in could not be found.'* The reason for this will be related hereafter.

By this time the Boat was along the Ship's Side, and there being no body to oppose them, the Pirates immediately boarded us; and coming on the Quarter-deck, fired their Pieces several times down into the Steerage, and shot a Sailor in the Reins (shoulders), of which Wound he died afterwards. They likewise threw several Granado-shells (grenades), which burst amongst us, so that 'tis a great wonder several of us were not killed by them, or by their Shot.

At last some of our People bethought themselves to call out for Quarter; which the Pirates granting, the Quarter-Master came down into the Steerage, enquiring, '*Where the Captain was?*' I told him, '*I had been so till now.*' Upon that he asked me, '*How I dared order my People to fire at their Boat out of the Steerage?, saying, that they had heard me repeat it several times.*' I answered, '*I thought it my Duty to defend the Ship, if my People would have fought.*' Upon that, he presented a Pistol to my Breast, which I had but just time to parry before it went off; so that the Bullet passed between my side and arm. The Rogue finding he had not shot me, he turned the Butt-end of the Pistol, and gave me such a Blow on the Head as stunned me; so that I fell upon my knees, but immediately recovering myself, I forthwith jumped out of the Steerage upon the Quarter-deck, where the Pirate Boatswain was.

He was a bloody Villain, having a few days before killed a poor Sailor, because he did not do something so soon as he had ordered him. This cruel Monster was asking some of my People, '*Where their Captain was.*' So at my coming upon Deck, one of them, pointing to me, said, '*There he is.*' Though the light was very dark, yet there being four lanthorns with candles, he had full sight of me: Whereupon lifting up his broad Sword, he swore, '*No Quarter should be given to any Captain that offered to defend his Ship,*' aiming at the same time a full stroke at my Head. To avoid it I stooped so low, that the Quarter-deck Rail received the blow, and was cut in at least an inch deep: Which happily saved my Head from being cleft asunder: And the Sword breaking at the same time, with the force of the blow on the rail, it prevented his cutting me to pieces.

By good Fortune his Pistols, that hung at his Girdle, were all discharged; otherwise he doubtless would have shot me. But he took one of them, and with the Butt-end endeavoured to beat out my Brains, which some of my People that were then on the Quarter-deck observing, cried out aloud, *For God's sake, don't kill our Captain, for we never were with a better Man!*' This turned the Rage of him and two other Pirates on my People, and saved my Life: But they cruelly used my poor Men, cutting and beating them unmercifully. One of them had his Chin almost cut off; and another received such a Wound on his Head, that he fell on the Deck as dead; but afterwards, by the care of our Surgeon he recovered.

All this happened in a few minutes, and the Quarter-master then coming up, ordered the Pirates to tie our People's hands, and told me, '*That when they boarded us, they let their Boat go adrift, and I must send an Officer, with some of my People in our Boat to look for theirs.*' Whereupon my First Mate, Mr Simon Jones, who stood by, offered to go: and the Quarter-master telling him, '*He must return quickly, otherwise he should judge that they had run away with the Boat, in order to go on Shore; and if they did so he would cut me to pieces.*' Mr Jones replied, '*He would not stay above a quarter of an hour, but return whether he found the Boat or not.*' Happily for me he soon found her, and returned (though it was very dark) in less time than he had promised.

Then the Quarter-master took me by the hand, and told me, '*My Life was safe provided none of my People complained against me.*' I replied, '*I was sure none of them could.*'

The Pirates next, loaded all their small Arms, and fired several Vollies for Joy that they had taken us: Which their Comrades on board their Ship hearing, it being then very near us, though we could not see it for the darkness of the night, they concluded we had made Resistance and Destroyed their People.

It will be proper to observe here, that soon after we had anchored in the mouth of the River Sierraleon, it became calm; and the Tide of Ebb beginning to come down, the Pirates cut their Cable, and let their ship drive down with the Tide towards us, from the place where we had seen her at anchor; having sometime before sent their Boat against the Tide of Flood, to discover us. The Ship being by that means come near us, and seeing our lights, without asking any questions, gave us a Broad-side with their great Guns; verily believing we had destroyed their Boat and People. This put the Pirates on board us into Confusion, which I observing, asked the Quarter-master, *'Why he did not call with the speaking Trumpet, and tell their Ship they had taken us?'* Upon that he asked me angrily *'Whether I was afraid of going to the Devil by a great Shot? For, as to his part, he hoped I would be sent to Hell one of these days by a Cannon Ball.'* I answered *'I hoped that would not be my Road.'* However, he followed my Advice, and informed their Ship, *'They had taken a brave Prize, with all manner of good Liquors and fresh Provisions on board.'*

Just after this, Cocklyn, the Pirate Captain, ordered them to dress a quantity of these Victuals; so they took many Geese, Turkeys, Fowls and Ducks, making our People cut their Heads off, and pull the great Feathers out of their Wings: but they would not stay until the other Feathers were picked off. All these they would put into our great Furnace, which would boil Victuals for 500 Negroes, together with several Westphalia Hams, and a large Sow with Pig, which they only (disem)bowelled, leaving the Hair on, This strange medley filled the Furnace, and the Cook was ordered to boil them out of Hand.

As soon as the Pirate-ship had done firing, I asked the Quarter-master's leave, for our Surgeon to dress my poop People who had been wounded; and I likewise went into the Steerage, to have my Arm dressed, it being very much bruised by the Blow given me by the Pirate-boatswain. Just after that, a person came to me from the Quarter-master, desiring to know, *'What a Clock it was by my watch?'* Which judging to be a civil way of demanding it, I sent it to him immediately: desiring the messenger to tell him, it was a very good going Gold Watch. When it was delivered to the Quarter-master, he held it up by the Chain, and presently laid it down upon the Deck, giving it a kick with his Foot, saying, *'It was a pretty Foot-ball'*: On which, one of the Pirates caught it up, saying, *'He would put it in the common Chest to be sold at the Mast.'*

I would not mention such trifling *Circumstances*, but that I judge they serve to show the Humours and Temper of these sort of People.

By this time I was loudly called upon to go on board the Pirate-ship. As soon as I came upon Deck, they hurried me over our Ship's side into the Boat; but when we arrived along the side of the Pirate-Vessel, I told them, *'I was disabled in my Arm, and so desired their help to get me into their Ship:'* Which was readily done. Then I was ordered to go on the Quarter-deck to meet their Commander, who saluted me in this manner. *'I am sorry you have met with bad usage after Quarter given, but 'tis Fortune of War sometimes. I expect you will answer truly to all such Questions as I shall ask you: otherwise you shall be cut to pieces; but if you tell the Truth, and your Men make no*

Complaints against you, you shall be kindly used; and this shall be the best Voyage you ever made in your Life, as you shall find by what shall be given you.' I thanked him for his good Intentions, telling him, *'I was content to stand on the footing he had proposed to me.'*

Having answered all his Questions, one of which was, *'How our Ship sailed, both large, and on a wind?'* I replying, *'Very well:'* He then threw up his Hat, saying *'She would make a fine Pirate man of War.'* When I heard that, I must own that I could not but be so concerned for having answered so truly in that particular: But then considering, that some of my People would no doubt have told them the same, and moreover, my Journal, when they looked into it, would have made it plainly appear, which might have proved my Destruction, I satisfied my Mind with these Reflections.

As, in this whole Affair, I greatly experienced the Providence of Almighty God, in his Goodness delivering me from the hands of these Villains, and from many Dangers; so the same good Providence gave me such a presence of Mind, that when I believed I was upon the Point of being killed, such Terrors did not arise, as I had formerly experienced, when in danger of Shipwreck (wreck). And though I fared very hard, and endured great Fatigues during the time I was there Prisoner; yet praised be God, I enjoyed my Health: Submitting with that Resignation to the Will of the Almighty, as a Man ought to do in such severe Misfortunes.

But to return to my Narrative, which the Remembrance of my past Dangers hath interrupted.

As soon as I had done answering the Captain's Questions, a tall Man, with four Pistols in his Girdle, and a broad Sword in his hand, came to me on the Quarter-deck, telling me, *'His name was James Griffin, and that we had been School-fellows.'* Tho' I remembered him very well; yet having formerly heard, it had proved fatal to some who had been taken by Pirates, to own any Knowledge of them; I replied, *'I could not remember any such Person by name.'* Upon that he remembered some boyish Pranks that had formerly passed between us. But I still denying any Knowledge of him, he told me, *'He supposed I took him to be one of the Pirate's Crew, because I saw him armed in that manner; but that he was a forced Man, and had lately been Chief Mate to Captain James Crichton of Bristol; who was then, with his Ship, in the Possession of the Pirates in the River, and had not been destroyed by them, at his earnest entreaty: That since being forced, they had obliged him to act as Master of the Pirate-ship; and the reason of his being so armed, was to prevent their imposing on him; for there was hardly any amongst the Crew of Pirates belonging to Captain Cocklyn, but what were cruel Villains; misusing much better Men than themselves, only for having the Misfortune to fall into their hands, as I had already experienced, and might find hereafter; but he would himself take care of me that night, in which would be my greatest Danger; because many of their People would soon get drunk with the good Liquors found in my Ship.'*

This generous Declaration was very acceptable to me, and I then readily owned my former acquaintance with him. Then he turned to Captain Cocklyn, and desired a Bowl of Punch be made. Which being done, the Captain desired Mr Griffin my Schoolfellow to show me the way to the great Cabin, and he followed himself.

There was not in the Cabin either Chair, or anything else to sit on; for they always kept a clear Ship ready for an Engagement: so a Carpet was spread on the Deck, upon which we sat down cross-legged. Captain Cocklyn drank my Health, desiring, *'I would not be cast down at my Misfortune, for one of the Boat's crew who had taken us had told him, My Ship's Company in general spoke well of me; and they had Goods enough left in the Ships they had taken to make a man of me.'* Then he drank several other Healths, amongst which was that of the *Pretender*, by the name of King *James the Third*, and thereby I found that they were doubly on the side of the Gallows, both as Traitors and Pirates.

It being by this time Midnight, my Schoolfellow desired the Captain, *'To have a Hammock hung up for me to sleep in,'* for it seems that every one lay rough, as they called it, that is, on the Deck; the Captain himself not being allowed a Bed. This being granted, I took leave of the Captain, and got into the Hammock, tho' I could not sleep in my melancholy Circumstances. Moreover, the execrable Oaths and Blasphemies I heard among the Ship's Company, shocked me to such a degree, that in Hell its self I thought there could not be worse; for though many Seafaring Men are given to swearing and taking God's Name in vain, yet I could not have imagined, human Nature could ever so far degenerate, as to talk in the manner those abandoned Wretches did.

After I was got into the Hammock, Mr Griffin, according to his Promise, walked by me, with his broad Sword in his Hand, to protect me from Insults. Some time after, it being about two a clock in the morning, the Pirate Boatswain (that attempted to kill me when taken) came on board very drunk, and being told I was in a Hammock, he came with his Cutlace (cutlass) near me. My generous Schoolfellow asked him what he wanted. He answered *'To slice my liver, for I was a vile Dog, for ordering my People to fire on their Boat; neither would I deliver my Watch when the Quartermaster first demanded it.'* Upon hearing that, I told Mr Griffin, *'The last was false, for I had immediately sent it by a Messenger, who only asked "what a clock it was?" supposing the Quartermaster expected it.'* Then Griffin bid the Boatswain keep his Distance, or else he would cleave his head asunder with his Broad Sword. Nevertheless, that bloody-minded Villain came on to kill me; but Mr Griffin struck at him with his Sword, from which he had a narrow escape, and then ran away. So I lay unmolested till day light. By that time the Fumes of the Liquor being gone off by Sleep amongst most of the Pirates, Mr Griffin complained to the Quartermaster and the Company, of the cruel Intentions towards me; representing, *'They ought to observe strictly that Maxim established amongst them, not to permit any ill usage to Prisoners after Quarter given.'* At the hearing of this, many of them voted for his being whipped, though he was a great favourite of several others. But though I wished him hanged in my Mind, yet I thought it prudent to plead for him, saying, *'I believed it was his being in Liquor that was the cause of his using me in that manner.'* So he received a general Order, not to give me the least Offence afterwards: Yet did that vile Wretch attempt once more to kill me, as shall be related in its due place.

I come now to relate, how Mr Simon Jones, my First Mate, and ten of my Men entered with the Pirates. The Morning after we were taken, he came to me, and said, *'His Circumstances were bad at home: Moreover, he had a Wife whom he could not love; and for these Reasons he had entered with the Pirates, and signed their Articles.'* I was greatly surprised at this Declaration, and told him, '*I was very sorry to hear it, for I believed he would repent when too late; and as he had taken this Resolution rashly, without communicating it to me, all I could say now would be to no Purpose; neither would it be proper for me, in the future, to have any Discourse with him in private.*' I saw this poor Man afterwards despised by his Brethren in Iniquity: and have since been informed, he died a few months after they left the River Sierraleon. However, I must do him the Justice to own, He never showed any Disrespect to me; and the ten People he persuaded to enter with him, remained very civil to me, and of their own accord, always manned the side for me, whenever I went on board any Ship they belonged to.

Several of these unhappy People soon after repented, and desired me to intercede for them, that they might be cleared again; for they durst (dared) not themselves mention it to the Quarter-master, it being death by their Articles: but it was too nice a matter for me to deal in; and therefore I refused them.

Some days after this, one of these poor Men, whose name was Thomas Wilders, discovered things to me, of which I only had a suspicion before. After cursing Mr Jones for persuading him to join with the Pirates, he said to me, '*That several times in the Night-Watch, before we came to Sierraleon, he had heard him say, "That he hopes we should meet with Pirates when we came to that River"*; which he then thought to have been spoken only in jest; but now he found it too true. As I seemed not to believe this, he called another of our People, who confirmed what he had told me. Then I asked them the Reason why the Chest of Arms was put out of the place where it usually stood at the Steerage; and where it was hid in the time we were taken. They answered, '*I might remember, that the Morning we made Land, I ordered the Steerage to be cleaned, to do which all the Chests there were carried between the Decks; and after the Steerage was cleaned, all the Chests were brought back into their places, except the Chest of Arms, which was left behind by the Mate's Order: That when I called to the People in the Steerage to fire on the Pirate-boat, supposing Mr Jones had delivered them Arms according to my Order, many of the Men would have broken the Chest open, but he prevented them, by declaring. "This was an opportunity he had wished for; and that if they fired a Musket, they would all be cut to pieces."* And they further assured me, that to induce them to enter with the Pirates, he had declared to them, '*That I had promised him to enter my self.*' Putting all this together, with what several of the Pirates told me afterwards, namely, *That he had been the chief occasion of their keeping my Ship*, it was a wonder that I escaped so well, having such a base Wretch for my principal Officer.

But to resume the thread of my Story.

As soon as the Fumes of the Liquor were gone out of the Pirates' heads, they all went on board the Prize, as they called my Ship, about eight a clock in the morning, it being the second day of April. Mr Jones, who had been my First Mate, went with them; and he having confirmed them in their intention of keeping the Ship for their own use, all hands went to work to clear the Ship, by throwing overboard Bales of Woollen Goods, Cases of India Goods; with many other things of great Value: So that before night they had destroyed between three and four thousand pounds worth of the Cargo. For they had little regard for these things, Money and Necessaries being what they chiefly wanted. The sight of this much grieved me, but I was obliged in prudence to be silent. For my Schoolfellow told me, I was still under the displeasure of many of them, on account of my ordering my People to fire on their Boat when they took me.

There were then residing at Sierraleon, several Englishmen who traded on their own accounts; and among the rest, one Captain Henry Glynn, who was since Governor for the Royal African Company at Gambia, and died there. This Gentleman was an honest generous Person, and of so much Integrity, that though he had suffered by the Pirates when they first landed, yet he would never accept any Goods from them, which they had often pressed him to receive for his own use. This Conduct, with an engaging deportment, so gained him the Good-will of the Pirates, that they were ready to oblige him in whatever he requested. Captain Glynn and myself having formerly been acquainted, as soon as he heard of my being taken, he engaged Captain Davis and Le Boose, the Commanders of the two other Pirate Ships, who were then on Shore at his House, to come on board with him to see me. I was very agreeably surprised with his coming that Afternoon, and both the Pirate captains that came with him saluted me civilly.

Captain Davis told me, 'He knew me', though I never could recollect where I had seen him; and I found, he did not care to tell, where he had seen me.

Soon after this, Captain Cocklyn with his Quarter-master and others, came from the Prize on board their old Ship, to compliment Captain Davis and the rest that came with him. After the Compliments were over, Captain Davis generously said, 'He was ashamed to hear how I had been used by them. That they should remember, their Reasons for going a pirating were to revenge themselves on base Merchants, and cruel Commanders of Ships. That as for the Owner of the Prize, he had not his fellow in London for Generosity and Goodness to poor Sailors, as he had formerly heard from others, and now from Captain Glynn: That as for my part, no-one of my People, even those that had entered with them, gave me the least ill Character: But by their respect since shown me, it was plain they loved me. That he indeed had heard the occasion of my ill usage, and of the ill-will some still bore me, was, because I had ordered my People to defend the Ship: Which he blamed them exceedingly for, saying, If he had the good fortune to have taken me, and I had defended my Ship against him, he should have doubly valued me for it: That as he was not in Partnership with them, he would say no more at present; but that he hoped they would now use me kindly, and give me some Necessaries, with what remained undestroyed of my pirate Adventure.' This was by no means relished by this pack of Miscreants; for in their hearts they hated Captain Davis, because he kept his Ship's Company in good order, they dreaded his Resentment. However Cocklyn, and the chief of his People putting a good face on the matter, invited him and Captain Glynn on board the Prize; and they two desiring I might accompany them, it was readily granted.

Soon after we were on board, we all went into the great Cabin, where we found nothing but Destruction. Two Scrutores (escritoires, or desks) I had there were broke into pieces; and all the fine Goods and Necessaries in them were all gone. Moreover two large Chests that had Books in them were empty; and I was afterwards informed, they had been all thrown overboard; for one of the Pirates, upon opening them, swore, 'There was Jaw-work enough (as he called it) to serve a Nation, and proposed they might be cast into the Sea; for he feared, there might be some Books amongst them, that might breed

Mischief enough; and prevent some of their Comrades from going on in their Voyage to Hell, whither they were all bound.' Upon which the Books were all flung out of the Cabin-windows into the River.

After the Company were all sat down in the Cabin, they were treated with all sorts of Liquors, and other things, that had once been mine: By this means the chief Pirates being put into a good humour, my friend Captain Glynn took the opportunity of begging the Quarter-master several Necessaries for me: Which being readily granted, they were tied up in Bundles, and Captain Glynn designed to take them on Shore with him to his House for me. But an unlucky accident happened, which made me lose them all again.

For some of Captain Davis's People were coming on Board at that time; one of them, a pert young fellow of eighteen, broke a Chest open to plunder it. The Quarter-master hearing of it, goes out of the Cabin, and asks the reason for his so doing; the young Man replied, 'As they were all Pirates, he thought he did what was right.' On that the Quarter-master strikes at him with his broad Sword, but the young man running away, escaped the Blow, and fled for protection into the great Cabin to his Master Captain Davis. The Quarter-master pursues him in a great Passion; and there not being room amongst so many of us, to make a stroke at him, he made a thrust with his Sword, and slit the Ball of one of the young Man's Thumbs, and at the same time Captain Davis upon the back of one of his Hands. Davis, upon that, was all on Fire, and vowed Revenge, saying, 'That though his Man had offended, he ought to have been first acquainted with it; for no other Person had a right to punish him in his Presence;' and immediately goes on board his own Ship. Where telling the Story to his Ship's Company, they all resolve to revenge this great injury done to one of their Comrades, and the Indignity shown their Captain. Upon that they slip one of their Cables, and began to heave on the other, in order to come and board Cocklyn's Ship, and destroy such a set of vile Fellows, and they called him and his Crew.

When Captain Davis went from the Prize, Cocklyn soon followed, and went on board his own Ship, to get all things in readiness to defend himself. Captain Glynn and myself only remained behind, and hoped quickly to have seen hot work between them; but Cocklyn having consulted his People, and judging they should be in no way able to cope with Captain Davis, hastily came on board the Prize again, and desired Captain Glynn to go on board Davis with him, in order to make up matters. My Friend would have refused this unpleasant Office, if he durst; but on his not readily complying, Cocklyn grew enraged. I, fearing the consequences, persuaded him to go: Which Cocklyn was so well pleased with, that he often spoke after of it to my advantage.

By the time they came on board Davis, his Ship was just on Cocklyn's Anchor; and though Captain Glynn was a well-spoken ingenious Man, he found it very difficult to compromise the Matter: which at last was done on these Terms; 'That Captain Davis and his Ship's Company, should have their share of Liquors and Necessities on board the Prize; and, That the Quarter-master, who had wounded the young Man belonging to Davis, should before all his Crew acknowledge his fault, and ask Pardon for the same.'

Night now approaching, Captain Glynn was obliged to go on Shore, without calling upon me for the Things he had begged, intending to come next day for them.

Being thus left on board the Prize, with only three or four of the Pirates, amongst whom the bloody-minded Boatswain (formerly mentioned) was one; and there being no Boat along the side at that time, I resolved to stay where I was all night, and not hail their Pirate-Ship to send their Boat for me.

The Pirate-Carpenter was then lying on my Bed in the State-Room; so I sat some time by myself in the Cabin, having a Candle by me on a Table. When he awoke, he civilly desired me to go and take some rest, saying, '*He feared I had not any since I was taken.*' I returned him thanks, saying, '*I would sit up till eight a clock:*' Whereupon he came and sat down by me on the Lockers, abaft in the Cabin.

The Boatswain came down soon afterwards, and being a little in Liquor, began to abuse me. On that the Carpenter told him, '*He was a base Villain,*' and turned him out of the Cabin. Soon after, a puff of Wind coming in at one of the Cabin Windows, put our Candle out; and the Carpenter and I rising up together, to blow the Candle in again, (but not being able to do it) we accidentally shifted places in the dark, he seating himself just over against the Cabin Door, where I sat before: and having no Tinder-Box, we were at a great loss how to light the Candle again.

While we were considering how to do it, the Boatswain came into the Steerage, and finding the Candle out, began to swear and rant, saying, '*I had put it out purposely, with design to go into the Powder-room undiscovered, and blow the Ship up.*' But the Carpenter told him, '*It was done by accident, and that I still sat by him on the Locker.*' So he came to the Cabin Door, and by the Star-light that came in at the Windows, perceived us sitting; but could not distinguish our Faces. Thinking I sat still in the Place where he had seen me before, he presented a Pistol, and drew the Trigger, swearing, '*At that instant, he would blow my Brains out.*' But by good fortune the Pistol did not go off, but only flashed in the Pan: by the Light of which the Carpenter observing that he should have been shot instead of me, it so provoked him, that he ran in the dark to the Boatswain: and having wrenched the Pistol out of his hand, he beat him, with that and his Fist, to such a Degree, that he almost killed him.

The noise that was made in this Fray (affray) being heard on board the Pirate-ship that lay close to us, a Boat was sent from her; and they being informed of the Truth of the matter, the Officer that was in her, thought fit to carry away this wicked Villain, who had three times attempted to murder me.

After this I slept soundly, having been much fatigued; but I was awaked early in the Morning by a great number of Captain Davis's Crew, who came on board to take part of the Liquors and Necessaries, according to Agreement. It was very surprising to see the Actions of these People. They and Cocklyn's Crew (for Le Boose's were not yet admitted) made such Waste and Destruction, that I am sure a numerous set of such Villains would in a short time, have ruined a great City. They hoisted upon Deck a great many half-Hogsheads of Claret, and French Brandy; knocked their Heads (bungs) out, and dipped cans and bowls into them to drink out of: And in their Wantonness threw full Buckets of each sort upon one another. As soon as they had emptied what was on the Deck, they hoisted up more: and in the evening washed the Decks with what remained in the Casks. As to bottled Liquor of many sorts, they made such havoc of it, that in a few days they had not one Bottle left: For they would not give themselves the trouble of drawing the Cork out, but nicked the Bottles, as they called it, that is, struck their necks off with a Cutlace (cutlass); by which means one in three was generally broke: Neither was there any Cask-liquor left in a short time, but a little French Brandy.

As to Eatables, such as Cheese, Butter, Sugar, and many other things, they were as soon gone. For the Pirates being all in a drunken Fit, which held as long as the Liquor lasted, no care was taken by any one to prevent this Destruction: Which they repented of when too late.

As for my things, which the Quarter-master had given my at Captain Glynn's Request, and which were accordingly bundled up; a company of drunken Pirates coming into the Cabin, and stumbling over some goods that lay on the Floor, they took them, with three of my Bundles, and threw them overboard; swearing, 'They had like to have broken their Necks by those things lying in their way.'

I had then but one Bundle left, in which was a black suit of Clothes, and other things which this Gang had spared. They being gone out of the Cabin, a Pirate, who was tolerably sober, came in soon after, and seeing my Bundle, said, 'He would see what was in it;' which in prudence I did not oppose. He then took out my black Cloth Clothes, a good Hat and Wig, and some other Things. Whereupon I told him, Captain Cocklyn's Quarter-master had given them to me, and I hoped he would not deprive me of them, for they were of no service to him in so hot a Country. But would be of great use to me, as I should soon return to England.' I had hardly done speaking, when he lifted up his broad Sword, and gave me a Blow on the Shoulder with the flat side of it; whispering at the same time these Words in my Ear, 'I will give you this Caution, never to dispute the Will of a Pirate: For, supposing I had cleft your skull asunder for your Impudence, what would you have got by it but Destruction? Indeed you may flatter yourself, I should have been put to death for killing a Prisoner in cold Blood; but assure yourself my Friends would have brought me off on such an Occasion.' I gave him thanks for his Admonition, and soon after he put on the Clothes, which in less than half an hour after, I saw him take off and throw overboard. For some of the Pirates seeing him dressed in that manner, had thrown several Buckets of Claret upon him. This Person's true name was Francis Kennedy. He was afterwards hanged at Execution-Dock, but he told me at the time he put my Clothes on, that his name was Sun; asking me, 'If I did not know his Father, who was the Commander of a Ship that used the Barbados Trade; and that if ever the old Dog fell in his way, he would kill him.' To which I answered, 'I knew no such Person.'

When night came on, I had nothing left of what had been bundled up, but a Hat and Wig. I must own, that whenever they plundered me, no Affront was offered to my Person; but several brought me Liquor, and Slices of Ham broiled, a Biscuit being my Plate; saying, 'They pitied my condition.' The Hat and Wig I had left, being hung on Pins in the Cabin, a person half-drunk came in about eight a clock a night, telling me, 'He was a great Merchant on Shore, and that his name was Hogbin.' But supposing him to be a Pirate, I said little to him. By this time these was a great Quietness in the Ship, most of the Pirates being dead drunk. After a little conversation, as Mr Hogbin was going out of the Cabin with my Hat and Wig on, he met Cocklyn's Quarter-master;

who knowing him not to be one of the Crew, asked him, *'How he came by the things he had on?'* To which the Fellow not returning a direct answer, the Quarter-master beat him very severely, for taking things he had no Right to: Then coming to me, he asked in a kind manner, *'How I had fared in the hurly burly of that Day?'* When I told him, *'I had lost all the Necessaries he had given my the Day before,'* he expressed much concern, and said, *'He would take care the next day to recover what he could for me.'* But he did not prove so good as his word.

The next day, which was the third since my being taken, Le Boose's Crew were permitted to come on board the Prize: Where they finished what was left of the Liquors and Necessaries; acting in the same destructive manner as their vile Brethren in Iniquity had done before.

Being quite weary of such Company, and understanding that the three Pirate Captains were on Shore at my Friend Captain Glynn's House, I asked leave of the Quartermaster to go to them; which he readily granted. On this I got into a Canoe, and as we rowed towards the Shore, we had like to be overset, through the drunkenness of the Pirates that was with us. If Providence had not prevented this Accident, we should undoubtedly have all been lost; for the Tide ran very strong, and several voracious Sharks were then near us.

When I came to Captain Glynn's, he and the Pirate Captains received me in a very civil manner; and upon telling them *'How I had lost all my Necessaries that had been given me;'* the Captains promised, That the next day they would do all they could, to recover some of them again for me. Then I begged a Shirt of my Friend Captain Glynn; for I had been three days without shifting (changing clothes), which is very uneasy in so hot a Country, where people sweat so much.

Being greatly refreshed with that clean Shirt, and having stayed all night with him, where I had more rest than I before had for a good while; next day I went on board, in company with the Pirate-Captains. Captain Davis desired Cocklyn to order all his People on the Quarter-deck, and made a Speech to them on my behalf; which they relished better that the one he had formerly made, It was resolved to give me the Ship they designed to leave, in order to go into the Prize, with the Remains of my Cargo which was undestroyed. And there being a large quantity of Goods likewise remaining in the several prizes, they concluded to give me them also: Which, with my own, were worth several thousand Pounds. One of the leading Pirates proposed to the rest, *'That they could take me along with them down the Coast of Guinea; where I might exchange the Goods for Gold: And if in order to make a quick Sale, I sold them at prime cost, I should get Money enough by them: That, no doubt, as they went down the Coast, they should take some French and Portuguese Vessels, and then they might give me as many of their best Slaves, as would fill the Ship: That then he would advise me to go for the Island of St Thomas in the West Indies, a Freeport belonging to the Danes, and sell them there, with the Vessel: And after rewarding my People in a handsome manner, I might return with a large sum of Money to London, and bid the Merchants defiance.'*

This proposal was unanimously approved of by them: But it struck me with a sudden damp (sweat), apprehending it would be fatal to me. So I began to insinuate, *'It would not be proper for me to accept of such a quantity of other Peoples' Goods, as they had so generously voted for me:'* And going on to give my reasons, I was immediately interrupted by several of the Pirates, who began to be very angry, that I did not readily accept of what had been proposed, so much to my advantage, as they thought; for many of them were so ignorant, as to think their Gift would have been legal.

On this, Captain Davis said, *'I know this Man, and can easily guess his thoughts concerning this matter; for he thinks, if he should act in the manner you have proposed, he shall ever lose his Reputation. Now I am for allowing every body to go to the Devil their own way; so desire you will give him the Remains of his Cargo, with what is left of his private Adventure, and let him do with it what he thinks fitting.'*

This was readily granted, and they advised me to take Le Boose's Brigantine, which he had then just quitted, (having fitted one of the Prizes for a Pirate-ship for him and his Crew) and carry her along the side of my Ship, in order to save the Goods then left undestroyed in her; allowing me some of my own people to do it. By this means we saved a considerable part of the Cargo, but of my private Adventure not above thirty Pounds Sterling: for that chiefly consisting in Necessaries and Liquors, with fine Goods, was soon destroyed by them: One instance out of many I shall give. The Pirates took several pieces of fine Holland, and opening them, spread them on the Deck; and being almost drunk, lay down on them: Then others came and threw Buckets of Claret upon them, which rousing them up, and the Hollands being thereby stained, they flung the Pieces overboard.

Captain Davis likewise obtained for me, that I might lie on board the 'Two Friends' Captain Elliott of Barbados; whom they had taken and forced to be their Store Ship; and that I might go on shore when I pleased, to my Friend Captain Glynn's house, on condition I should return whenever they sent for me.

And now, the Tide being turned, they were as kind to me, as they had been at first severe. So we got the Brigantine the side of the Prize, and as Bale-goods and cases came to hand, we got them into her; only now and then we lost some, by the ill-nature of two or three leading Pirates: For if we could not receive the Goods so fast as they expected, with the few People I had of my own then with me, they would let them drop overboard.

The same they did by a quantity of Irish Beef, the first day after I was taken; for they despised it, having found so much English, in the several Prizes they had met with in the River. This sight moved me to entreat Captain Cocklyn to give me the Irish Beef they were going to throw overboard; for the use of my poor People that had not entered with them. But I being then under the high Displeasure of him and his crew, he brutishly replied, *'There is Horse-beans enough in the Prize to serve you and your People six months.'* To which I answered, *'It was coarse diet.'* But answering thus put him into a Passion, and I held my Tongue, and the Beef was cast into the Sea.

In this place I think it is proper to acquaint the Reader, What danger all the Prisoners were in by a false Report brought on board the Prize Ships that afternoon. For it was confidently averred by some Negroes, *'That one of their Crew was murdered, by two Captains, whose names were Bennet and Thompson, who had been obliged to fly into the woods from the rage of the Pirates.'* And they added, *'That these two Gentlemen, coming to the House of one Mr Jones (who lived a great way up the River) to seek for*

Provisions, they there met with the person whom they had killed.' Upon this report the Pirates resolved to revenge themselves on us who were their prisoners. *'Which obliged me to argue with them, and observe how great a cruelty it would be, to punish us who were wholly innocent, for the faults of others.'* Moreover I said, *'The report might be false, it coming from the Shore-Negroes; and I hoped at least they would defer their resentment against us, till they had a more certain account of the matter.'* This calmed their Rage a little, when, to our great Joy, the Person who was reported to be killed, came on board soon after; and told his Comrades, that he had met with Captain Bennet and Thompson at Mr Jones' House, who threatened him; from which the report arose that they had killed him; but that they had not otherwise misused him: So on this their passion was calmed.

As I have mentioned these two Captains Bennet and Thompson, I shall give an account of their Misfortunes, which I had afterwards from their own Mouths. Captain John Bennet, being bound from Antegoa (Antigua) to the Coast of Guinea, was taken at Cape de Verd Islands by Davis. Who, after plundering him, restored him his Ship; and he went into the River Sierra Leon, where Captain Thompson was arrived before him. Upon Cocklyn the Pirate's coming into the River, they carried their Ships a good way up, to a place called Brent's-Island, being the Settlement of the Royal Africa Company; where one Mr Plunket was Governor. Having got their Ships very near the Shore, they made a Battery thereon, and having landed Ammunition, resolved with their People to defend themselves to the utmost; thinking at that time they would remain faithful. Le Boose being arrived in his Brigantine, and hearing that several Ships were up the River, he resolved to have one of them for his use; so he went up to attack them, and they bravely defended themselves against him: But, soon after, Cocklyn coming with his Ship to the assistance of Le Boose, their People began to falter; and these gallant Captains were, for saving their Lives, obliged, with Mr Plunket, and several of their Officers, to fly into the Woods: Where, for many Weeks, they remained, having nothing to subsist on but Rice, with now and then some Oysters, which they got by night from the River side: neither durst they appear near the place where the Pirates were (as long as they remained there) for they had vowed to cut them to pieces, if ever they fell into their hands. Moreover, their Ships were burned, and Le Boose took for his own use, one Captain Lamb's Ship, which at that time lay farther up River. I thought proper to relate this, in order to set the story in a better light, though it happened some weeks before I was taken.

But now, to return to my Subject, I was relating, how we were employed in saving what Goods we could. This took us up four days; and I slept every night on board the 'Tender' commanded by Captain Elliot, who was very kind to me, and had a great ascendant over the leading Pirates: so that he seldom had the Company of the common sort, having orders to drive them away, whenever they came on board him. And I have often been amazed, to hear and see what he has done to some of them when they have been impudent; beating some of them, and saying, *'He was sure he would see them hanged in due time at Execution-dock.'* However, by this means we were generally easy on board him, which was no little satisfaction to me in my Circumstances.

About this time the Quarter-master, who took me, fell sick of a Fever; which increasing, he sent to speak with me: And having desired all present, except myself, to withdraw, he told me, *'That at the time I was taken, he designed to have killed me, when he presented the Pistol to my breast; begging I would forgive him his cruel Intention:'* Which I readily doing, he further said, *'That he was a most wicked Wretch, having been guilty of all manner of abominable Crimes; and that now believing he should die, his Conscience sadly tormented him, fearing he would be punished, as he deserved, in Hell-fire, which so often in their vile discourse he had made light of.'* Upon hearing that, *'I exhorted him to sincere Repentance; telling him, the Christian Religion assured us of God's Mercies, if we are truly penitent; and I instanced the goodness of God to myself, in that he was graciously pleased to preserve me, the night I was taken, from being murdered by him and others; which great Mercies I believed were shown me, because I put my Hope and Trust in Almighty God; and exhorted him to do the same.'* But he replied, *'O, Sir, my heart is hardened; however I will endeavour to follow your good counsel.'* As he was going on, expressing his sorrow for his former course of Life, some of the Pirates broke in upon us, to ask him, *'How he did?'* So he called his Boy, and, as a mark of his Good-will towards me, ordered him to take the Key of his Chest, and let me take out what Necessaries I would. Accordingly I took that opportunity of providing myself with Shirts, Stockings, and several other things. As I was taking them out, a Pirate coming from the Deck, and knowing nothing of the Quarter-master's order, called out aloud; *'See how that Dog is thieving there: He does it as cleverly as any Rogue of us all.'* But being told, *'It was with the Quarter-master's leave,'* he came and helped me bundle the things up, and I sent them on board the Tender. These were the first Necessaries which I could call my own, since my Misfortune.

The Quarter-master that evening falling into a Delirium, died before morning in terrible Agonies; cursing his Maker in so shocking a manner, that it made a great Impression on several new entered Men: and they afterwards came privately to me, begging, 'that I would advise them how to get off from so vile a Course of Life, which led them into Destruction of both Body and Soul. Some of them proposed to fly into the Woods, and remain there till their Ships were gone, if I would promise to protect them afterwards; but this being too nice (i.e. tricky) a matter for me to meddle with at that Juncture, I declined it; Exhorting them in general, Not to be Guilty of Murder, or any other Cruelty to those they should take. For if ever they should, by a general consent, resolve to embrace the King's Pardon, it would be a great Advantage to them, to have the unfortunate people they had taken to give them a good Character in that respect.'

Having mentioned the King's Pardon, I shall here relate what I before omitted, with relation to his late majesty's Proclamation, for a *Pardon to Pirates, that should surrender themselves at any of the British Plantations, by the first of July 1719.* This Proclamation I had on board, with a Declaration of War against Spain. The Quarter-master finding them amongst my Papers, and not being able to read, he brought them to me, the next day after I was taken, and 'bid me read them aloud to all present;' which I did: But there being Rewards offered in the proclamation, to those that should take or destroy Pirates; so much for a Captain; and in proportion so much for the other Officers and common Pirates; this put them into such a Rage, that I began to apprehend myself in some Danger. But Captain Cocklyn ordering silence to be made, bid me read the other Paper, which was *The Declaration of War against Spain*. When I had read it, some of them said, 'They wished they had known it before they left the West Indies.' From thence I took occasion to observe to them, 'That if they thought fit to embrace his Majesty's most gracious Pardon, there was not only time enough for them to return to the West Indies, (there still being three Months to come of the time limited in the Proclamation) but now that War was declared against Spain, they would have an opportunity of enriching themselves in a legal way, by going a privateering, which many of them had privately done.' This seemed to be relished by many: but several old Buccaneers, who had been guilty of Murder and other barbarous Crimes, being no ways inclined to it, they used the King's Proclamation with great contempt, and tore it in pieces. I thought myself well off, that no Resentment or ill-usage was shown me on this occasion.

Amongst the several Pirates, that came to consult me, 'How they should get off.' There was one Ambrose Curtis, who was in a bad state of Health, and generally walked the Deck in a Silk Night-gown. This person finding me shy in answering his Questions, he told me, 'Though I had forgotten him, yet he had not me; for he was eleven years ago at Sea with my Father, who had used him severely for being an unlucky Boy: That I might remember, my Father died in Virginia, and I commanded the Ship afterwards, and brought her home to England; having been very kind to him, except in one thing, which was, That he having confessed to me, he was a Servant, and run away from his Master, I refused to pay him his Wages, till he brought a person who gave me Security that I should not pay them twice; and then he had his Wages to a farthing: Adding, 'he had told this to several leading Pirates, who had persuaded him to revenge himself on me; but as I had been kind to him, and in his Conscience he believed I was in the right, to demand Security when I paid him his Wages, so he bore no ill-will to me on that account; and when my necessaries came to be sold at the Mast, he would buy some of them for me;' in which he proved as good as his word.

But as to his Questions about getting off, I replied as I had done to others; 'Assuring him, if ever it came into my power to serve him, I would not spare for Money or Pains to do it.' But this poor fellow died, before the Pirates left Sierraleon.

I hope the Reader will pardon me for mentioning several things, which are not so coherent as I should wish; as also several little incidents. The reason why I mention them is, because I think they display the true humours and ways of these Miscreants.

Amongst my Adventure of Goods, I had in a Box three second-hand embroidered Coats. One day the three Captains, coming on board the Prize together, enquired for them, saying, 'They understood by my Book such Clothes were in my Ship.' I told them, 'They were in a Box under the bed place in the State-room. So they ordered them to be taken out, and immediately put them on. But the longest Coat falling to Cocklyn's share, who was a very short Man, it almost reached as low as his ankles. This very much displeased him, and he would fain have changed with Le Boose, or Davis: But they refused, telling him, 'As they were going on Shore amongst the Negroe-Ladies, who did not know the white Men's fashions, it was no matter. Moreover, as his Coat was Scarlet embroidered with Silver, they believed he would have the preference of them, (whose Coats were not so showy) in the opinion of their Mistresses. This making him easy, they all went on Shore together.

It is a Rule amongst the Pirates, not to allow Women on board their Ships, when in Harbour. And if they should take a Prize at sea, that has any Women on board, no one dares, on pain of death, to force them against their inclinations. This being a good political Rule to prevent disturbances amongst them, it is strictly observed. So now being in a Harbour, they went on Shore to the Negroe-women, who were very fond of their Company, for the sake of the great presents they gave them. Nay, some white Men that lived there, did not scruple to lend their black Wives to the Pirates, purely on account of the great Rewards they gave.

The Pirate Captains having taken these Clothes without leave from the Quarter-master, it gave great Offence to all the Crew; who alleged, 'If they suffered such things, the Captains would in future assume a Power, to take whatever they liked for themselves.' So, upon their returning on board next Morning, the Coats were taken from them, and put into the common Chest, to be sold at the Mast. And it having been reported, 'That I had a hand on advising the Captains to put on these Coats,' it gained me ill-will in particular of one Williams, who was Quarter-master of Le Boose's Ship. He seeing me in the Tender's Boat, going on board a French Ship lately taken, where he then was, he swore, 'That if I came there, he would cut me to pieces, for the advice I had given to the Captains.' But Captain Elliott, who was then in the Boat, whispered me, saying, 'Don't be afraid of him, for it is his usual way of talking. But be sure you call him Captain, as soon as you get on board.' It seems this Villain had been Commander of a Pirate Sloop; who, with a Brigantine, two years before, took Captain Laurence Prince in the Whidaw Galley near Jamaica; and now being Quarter-master, which he did not like, he loved to have the Title of Captain given him. So when I came into the French Ship, I addressed myself to him, saying, 'Captain Williams, pray hear me upon the point you are so offended at.' Upon that he gave me a slight Blow on the Shoulder, with the flat of his Cutlace, swearing at the same time, 'he had not the heart to hurt me;' When I told him how the affair had really happened, which he had been so angry about, he gave me a Keg of Wine, and was my Friend ever after.

The French Ship just now mentioned, fell into their hands about a fortnight after I was taken by them, in this manner. It was not bound for Sierraleon, but having not had an Observation for several days, because the Sun was near their Zenith, they made land unexpectedly; and not knowing whereabouts they were, but seeing several Ships in the River at an Anchor, they came boldly towards them.

I was then on board Captain Cocklyn's old Ship; for they had not quite fitted mine for their use, not having at that time any Guns mounted; so I saw the great fear and confusion that was amongst them. My Mate, who had entered with them, said, 'He believed, by the Ship's coming in so boldly, it was the Launceston Man of War of forty Guns, whom we had left in Holland. For he had heard me say, she was to follow us to the Coast of Guinea.'

Happy it would have been for us and many more, if it had been so. For had that, or even a smaller Ship of twenty Guns, with the King's Commission, come in at that time, or any other, whilst I was in their hands, I am persuaded they would have easily destroyed them. For the new-entered-men had little Courage; and the far greater part of both old and new Pirates, were so much in drink, that there could have been no Order of Conduct amongst them in an Engagement. So that it would have been very easy to have subdued them, and prevented that terrible Destruction, which happened to above one hundred Sail of Ships, that fell afterwards into their Hands, in their going down the Coast of Guinea: Together with those Damages that happened a good while after in the East Indies, by some of this Gang; and the great Ravage made by Roberts (who rose out of Davis's Ashes) till he was happily destroyed by Sir Chaloner Ogle in the Swallow Man of War. But the reason why no timely care was taken to prevent so great a Destruction, is not proper for me to mention in this place.

As I had no business to be on board the Pirate Ship in time of Action, I asked Captain Cocklyn's leave to go on board their Tender, which he readily granted. Just as I was going, several of my people who had entered with him, said, 'They would go along with me, for they had never seen a Gun fired in anger.' Cocklyn hearing that, told them, 'That now they should learn to smell Gunpowder, and caned them heartily.

So I went on board Captain Elliot, where I soon saw the French Ship taken. For coming so unexpectedly into the Pirates' hands, they made no Resistance: And because their Captain did not strike (his colours) on their first firing, they put a Rope around his Neck, and hoisted him up and down several times to the Main-yard-arm, till he was almost dead. Captain Le Boose coming at that instant, luckily saved his Life: And highly resenting this their cruel usage to his Countryman, he protested, 'he would remain no longer in Partnership with such barbarous Villains.' So, to pacify him, they left the Frenchmen with the Ship in his care; and after the Cargoe was destroyed, they cut the Ship's Masts by the board, and run her on Shore, for she was very old, and not fit for their purpose.

After the affair of the French Ship was over, I was employed for several days, in landing out of the Brigantine the Goods that had been given me, out of my own Ship's Cargoe, and carrying them to my Friend Captain Glynn's House; in which both he and I worked very hard. For my own People that did not enter with the Pirates, were mostly obliged to work on board the Prize, in fitting her for them; and the Natives who served Captain Glynne at his House, were grown so insolent by the large quantity of Goods given them by the Pirates, that they would do nothing but what they pleased. However, at last, with much trouble we got them housed.'

By this time, which was about the 20th of April, the Ship the had taken from me was completely fitted, and the next day was appointed to name her, to which Ceremony I was invited. When I came on board, the Pirate Captains told me, 'It was not out of Disrespect they had sent for me, but to partake of the good Cheer provided on this occasion:' So they desired I would be cheerful, and go with them into the great Cabin. When I came there, Bumpers of Punch were put into our Hands, and on Captain Cocklyn's saying aloud, 'God bless the Windham Galley, we drank our Liquor, broke the Glasses, and the Guns fired.

The Ship being Galley-built, with only two flush Decks, the Cover of the Scuttle of the Powder-room was in the great Cabin, and happened at that time to be open. One of the after-most Guns blowing at the Touch-hole, set fire to some Cartouchboxes, that had Cartridges in them for small Arms, the Shot and Fire of which flew about us, and made a great smother. When it was over, Captain Davis observed, there had been great Danger to us from the Scuttle's being open; there being under, in a Room, above twenty thousand weight of Gunpowder. Cocklyn replied, 'He wished it had taken fire, for it would have been a noble blast, to have gone to hell with.'

Then all going upon Deck, three Prizes that remained undestroyed, were ordered to be burned; upon hearing that, I privately represented to Captain Davis, 'How hard it would be upon us who were Prisoners, to remain in that Country, without necessaries, and without Food to subsist on: Besides, there was no manner of Prospect of our getting away quickly; That to the many Obligations I owed him, I hoped he would add one more, and by his Interest, at least save one of the Vessels, for us to return to London in: That as he had several times hinted to me, how much he disliked that course of Life, hoping he should have an opportunity of leaving it in a short time; so I wished he would put it in my power, to report to his Advantage, the good deed I then requested of him; for, in my Opinion, next to Murder and Cruelty, too often practised by Pirates, nothing could make them more odious to the World, than their destroying, out of mere Wantonness, so many Ships and Cargoes, as had been done by Cocklyn and Le Boose's Crews; in which I knew he had no hand: And if he would be pleased to secure my entire Liberty, at the same time that he pleaded for one of the Vessels for us, it would be a double Obligation on me to Gratitude, in case it ever fell into my power to serve him.'

This he readily promised, and by his Management the Ships were saved from being burned, and they made a Bonfire only of the old Rising Sun, being the Ship they had quitted for mine: And now obtaining, through Captain Davis's means, my entire Liberty, I went on Shore to my friend Captain Glynn's House again.

Two days after this Captain Elliot sent his Boat for me, desiring I would forthwith come on board his Ship, because he wanted much to speak with me. I had too many obligations to this Gentleman to refuse going, (tho' I had a sort of aversion). Upon coming on board, he privately represented to me, 'That I knew he had been obliged against his will by the Pirates, to receive into his Ship a great quantity of other People's Goods; for which he might hereafter be called to an account; therefore he desired I would give him a Certificate, testifying the Truth of it.' Knowing this to be true, I readily complied; for he was a very honest Man, as appeared soon after. For the Pirates compelling him to go to go out of the River with them, as their Tender, he took the first opportunity of getting away from them, which he did in a Tornado, or sudden Gust of Wind, that arose in the Night; and having the good fortune to succeed in his attempt, he made a good Voyage for his Owners, with Slaves to Barbadoes; where he fell sick and died.

While I was in his Ship, the three Pirate captains called along the side. Not expecting to see me there, they seemed very glad of it, and invited me to go and sup with them on board Captain Davis. This I declined, being desirous of going on Shore to Captain Glynn's. But Captain Davis insisting on it, I thought it prudent to comply; that I might not lose that gentleman's Good-will, who had been so kind to me.

After we had been some time on board his Ship, Supper was brought about eight a

clock in the Evening; and the Musick was ordered to play, amongst which was a
Trumpeter, that had been forced to enter out of one of the Prizes. About the middle
of Supper, we heard upon Deck an outcry of 'Fire!', and instantly a Person came to us,
and said, 'The Main-hatch-way was all in a Flame'; so we all went upon Deck.

At that time, besides the Pirate Ship's Crew, who were mostly drunk, there was on
board at least fifty Prisoners; and several Boats along the side, into which many People
jumped, and put off. I being then on the Quarter-deck, with the Captains, observed
this to them; but they all in confusion said, 'We know not what to do in the matter:'
Upon that I told them, 'If the sober People were allowed to go away with the Boats, no
one would endeavour to save the Ship; and we that were left should be lost, (for the
other Ships were a Mile from us, and the Tide of Flood then ran so strong, that their
Boats could not row against it to save us:) So I proposed to them, 'to fire the Quarter-
deck Guns at the Boats which had just put off, to oblige them to come on board again;'
which being instantly done, it so frightened the People in them, that they forthwith
came back; and all that were able, and not drunk, lent their helping hand to put out
the Fire; which by this time was come to a great head in the Ship's hold.

After this I went down into the Steerage, where I saw one Goulding, who was
Gunner's mate, and a brisk active Fellow, put his head up the After-hatch-way, calling
for Blankets and Water; 'which if not brought immediately, (he said) the Bulk-head of
the Powder-room would be fired, and the Ship soon blown up.' Observing the
Stupidity of the People about me, who stood looking on one another, I caught up
several Blankets and Rugs which lay scattered about, and flung them to him, and so
did others by my example. Then I ran out of the Steerage upon Deck, where meeting
with some People who were sober, I got them to go over the side, and draw up Buckets
of Water; And others handing them to Goulding, who had by this time placed the
Blankets and Rugs against the Bulk-head of the Powder-room, he flung this Water on
them, and thereby prevented the Flames from catching the Powder, and consequently
from blowing up the Ship, which must otherwise have happened: For there was on
board as least thirty thousand pounds of Gunpowder, which had been taken out of
several Prizes, it being a Commodity much in request amongst the Negroes.

There was still great Confusion amongst us, occasioned by the darkness of the
Night, and the many drunken People, who were not sensible of the great danger we
were in: Moreover, the People in the Hold gave us as yet no Hopes of their getting the
Mastery of the Fire. So I went again on the Quarter-deck, and considered with myself,
if the fire could not be conquered, as I could not swim, I should have no chance of
being saved: and even those that could, would, I knew, be exposed to be torn to pieces
by voracious Sharks, which abound in that River: So I took one of the (wooden)
Quarter-deck Gratings, and lowered it by a Rope over the Ship's side, designing to get
on that, if I should be forced to quit the Ship. For tho' the Boats had been once
obliged to come back, yet it being a dark Night, some People, unperceived, had
slipped again away with them, and were quite gone away.

Whilst I stood musing with myself on the Quarter-deck, I heard a loud shout upon
the Main-deck, with a Huzza, 'For a brave blast to go to Hell with', which was repeated
several times. This not only much surprised me, but also many of the new entered

Pirates; who were struck with a Panic Fright, believing that the Ship was just blowing up, so that several of them came running on the Quarter-deck, and accidentally threw me down, it being very dark. As soon as I got upon my Legs again, I heard these poor Wretches say, in a lamentable Voice, one to another; 'Oh, that we should be so foolish as to enter this vile course of Life! The Ship will be immediately blown up, and we shall suffer for our Villainies in hell Fire.' So that when the old hardened Rogues on the Main-deck, wished for a blast to go to hell with, the other poor wretches were at the same time under the greatest Consternation at the thoughts of it.

The Apprehension of the Ship's being just ready to blow up, was so universal, that above fifty People got on the Bolt-sprit, and the Sprit-sail-yard, thinking they should have there a better chance for their Lives: But they much deceived themselves, so had so great a quantity of Powder as was at that time on board, been fired, it would have blown them up to Atoms.

There was one Taylor, master of this Pirate Ship, as brisk and courageous a Man as ever I saw; (who afterwards commanded the Cassandra, and English East India Ship, and carried her to New Spain, where he and his Crew separated). This Person, with fifteen more, spared no pains to extinguish the Fire in the Hold; and tho' they were scalded in a sad manner by the Flames, yet they never shrunk till it was conquered; which was not till near ten a clock at night, when they came upon Deck, declaring the Danger was over: So the Surgeons were called to dress their Burns. This was joyful News to us all on Deck, for we little expected to escape.

I shall now relate how this Fire happened, from which our Deliverance was almost miraculous. About half an hour after eight a clock in the evening, a Negroe Man went into the Hold, to pump some Rum out of a Cask; and imprudently holding his Candle too near the Bung-hole, a Spark fell into the hogshead, and set the Rum on fire. This immediately fired another cask of the same Liquor, whose Bung had been, through carelessness, left open: And both the Heads of the hogsheads immediately flying out, with a report equal to that of a small cannon, the fire ran about the Hold. There were twenty casks of Rum, with as many Barrels of Pitch and Tar, very near the place where the Rum lay that was fired; yet it pleased God none of these took fire, otherwise it would have been impossible for us to escape.

After this was over, I was obliged to stay on board till Morning, all the Boats being run away with. In that time Goulding, the Gunner's Mate, told the Pirate's Crew several things to my Advantage: 'How I had handed the Blankets to him, and ordered Water to be thrown on them; which saved the Bulk-head, where the Powder lay, from being fired, and consequently the Ship from being blown up.' So now I was more than ever in their favour: For several of them desired me to come on board the Windham Galley, the day things were sold there at the mast, and then they would be kind to me. Likewise Captain Davis pressed me to come, asking me, 'Whether the gold watch that was taken from me was a good one?' To which I answering 'It was very good, at that time.' He then said, 'He would buy it for his own use at any rate.'

While he and I were talking thus, one of the Mates came half drunk, on the Quarter-deck, saying to him, 'I propose on behalf of the Ship's Company, that this Man shall be obliged to go down the Coast of Guinea with us; for I am told we cannot have a better Pilot.' This was a great surprise to me; but my generous Friend Davis soon put me out of pain. For he told him, 'They wanted no Pilot:' and the fellow still insisting on my going, Captain Davis caned him off the Quarter-deck, and I heard no more of it: For soon after I went on Shore to my Friend Captain Glynn's House.

Two days after this, a small Vessel came into the River, and was taken by them. It was called the Dispatch Captain Wilson, belonging to the Royal Africa Company. Mr Simon Jones, formerly my First Mate, who had entered with the Pirates (as I have before related) told them, on this occasion, 'That he had once commanded a Ship, which was hired and freighted by the Royal Africa Company; and that he had been very unjustly used by them; so he desired the Dispatch might be burned, that he might be revenged of them.' This being immediately consented to, and forthwith ordered to be executed, one John Stubbs, a witty brisk Fellow, stood up, and desired to be heard first; saying, 'Pray, Gentlemen, hold a little, and I will prove to you, if this Ship is burnt, you will thereby greatly serve the Company's Interest.' This drawing everyone's attention, they bid him go on: Then he said, 'The Vessel has been out these two years on her Voyage, being old and crazy, and almost eaten to pieces by the Worms; besides, her Stores are worth little; and as to her Cargoe, it consists only of a little Redwood and Melegette-pepper; so if she should be burned, the Company will lose little; but the poor People that now belong to her, and have been so long on the Voyage, will lose all their Wages, which, I am sure, is three times the value of the vessel, and of her trifling Cargoe; so that the Company will be greatly obliged to you for destroying her.' The rest of the Crew being convinced by these Reasons, the Vessel was spared, and delivered again to Captain Wilson and his People, who afterwards came safe to England in it.

The 29th of April, such of the Pirates as were my Friends, sent me word on Shore, 'That the Sale of Necessaries was to begin that day in the afternoon, in the Windham-galley, Captain Cocklyn.' So I went on board in a large Cannoe, belonging to two Men who lived ashore, who went at the same time with me. At the Sale, several of the Pirates bought many Necessaries that had been mine, and gave them to me. Likewise, Mr James Griffin, my Schoolfellow, was so civil as to beg from those who were not so kind to me, as he hoped they would have been. The two white Men that went with me in the Cannoe, minded their own business so well, that they got several great Bundles of Clothes and Goods, which they put into the Cannoe with mine.

By this time several Pirates being half drunk with Brandy, looked over the side, and seeing so many Bundles in the Cannoe, which they supposed to be all mine, they swore, 'I was insatiable, and that it would be a good deed to throw them overboard.' This my kind Schoolfellow hearing, he came and told me of it; advising me, to go immediately on Shore, which I accordingly did; and it proved very happy for me. For soon after my Watch was put up for sale, and many bidding for it, some of them out of Spite to Captain Davis, it was run up to one hundred pounds, which he paid down. One of the Pirates being greatly vexed at it, said, 'He believed the Cases of the Watch were not good Gold'; and calling for a Touch-stone, he tried them on it. The Touch looking of a copperish Colour, (as indeed all the Gold-cases of Watches do on the touch, by reason of the quantity of Alloy put in to harden them) this pretence served the turn of this Villain; who thereupon exclaimed against me, saying, 'I was a greater Rogue than any of them, who openly professed Piracy; since I was so sly, as to bring a base Metal Watch, and endeavour to put it off for a gold one.'

This Speech procured me the Anger of many, who knew no better; they believing every word of what he said to be true. And tho' Captain Davis laughed at it, yet several swore, 'If I had not been gone on Shore, they would have whipped me.' And as their Drunkenness increased, they talked of sending for me to be punished for so great a Villainy, as they called it. But my Schoolfellow apprehending they would really offer me some Violence, was so kind as to send me word of what had passed, by a white Man living on Shore, who was then on board; advising me to go into the Woods, for they should sail quickly out of the River.

The next morning early, which was the last day of April, as I was just going to follow his advice, I was agreeably surprised by the arrival of one Mr James Bleau, my Surgeon, whom they designed to take by force with them. This honest Man had been very cast down at it, and had often desired me to intercede for his liberty. Accordingly I had done it, representing, 'That he grieved himself so much, that if he did not die quickly, yet he would be of no use to them.' But this had no effect. However, at last, a fortunate Accident cleared him, when he least expected it; for that very evening, after I was come on Shore, the Surgeon of the French Ship entered with them; whereupon they gave Mr Bleau his Liberty the next morning.

Mr Bleau brought us the agreeable News, that the three Pirate Ships, with their Tender, were under sail, going out of the River. This gave us all on Shore the highest Satisfaction; for I had been in their hands a Month, and many others much longer. Mr Bleau, whom I have here mentioned, lives now at Woodford-Row on Epping Forest, where he follows his Business.

I shall now inform the Reader, what became of my kind Schoolfellow Griffin, and my generous Friend Davis. The first took an opportunity of getting out of the hands of the Pirates, by taking away in a Boat from the Stern of the Ship he was in, when off the Road of Annamaboe, on the Coast of Guinea. He was driven on Shore there, unperceived in the night time; and from thence went to Cape Coast Castle, belonging to the Royal Africa Company; from which place he went Passenger to Barbadoes, in an English Ship, where he was taken with a violent Fever and died.

As to Davis, having discovered, a few days after they left the River Sierraeon, a Conspiracy to deprive him of his Command, which was carried on by one Taylor, that was the Master of the Ship under him, he timely prevented it: But he and some others left their Ship, and went on board the Windham Galley, Captain Cocklyn, by whom he found Taylor had been set on to displace him. This causing him to leave their partnership, he took a few days after one Captain Plumb in the Princess of London, whose second mate Roberts, so famous afterwards for his Villainies, entered with him; and Davis's Crew, after plundering the Ship, restored her to Captain Plumb again. After this captain Davis went to the Island Princess, belonging to the Portuguese, which lay in the Bay of Guinea. Here the Pirates gave out, 'They were a King's Ship'; but the People soon discovered what they were by their lavishness, in purchasing fresh Provisions with Goods; but the Governor winked at it, on account of the great Gains he, and others of the Chief of his People made by them. But at last putting him in mind, 'That if this Affair should come to the King of Portugal's ear, it might prove his ruin'; he plotted how to destroy Davis and his Crew, in order to colour over what he had so basely permitted, in allowing them a free trade, after discovering they were Pirates.

Captain Davis being one day on Shore with the Governor, he told him, ' They designed to sail from the Island in three Days, and that he would come, and take his leave of him the day before.' Accordingly he went on a Sunday morning, taking with him his first Surgeon, the Trumpeter, and some others, besides the Boat's Crew. At their coming into the Governor's House, they saw no body to receive them; so they went on, till they came to a long Gallery fronting the Street. Here the Governor's Major-Domo presently came to them, saying, 'His Master was at his Country-House, but he had sent a Messenger to him, when they saw Captain Davis coming on Shore, and no doubt he would soon be in Town. But the Surgeon observing, that many People had got together in the Street, with Arms in their hands, he said to his Captain, 'I am sure we shall see no Governor today', and advised him immediately to go away. So Davis and the Surgeon went out of the House; whereupon the Major-Domo called to the people in the Street, to fire at them. The Surgeon and two more were killed on the spot, and the Trumpeter was wounded in the Arm, who seeing two Capuchin Friars (from whom I had this Account at the Island Princess) fled to them. One of them took him in his Arms to save him, but a Portuguese came, and shot him dead without any regard to the Friar's Protection. Captain Davis, tho' he had four Shots in divers Parts of his Body, yet continued running towards the Boat: But being closely pursued, a fifth Shot made him fall, and the Portuguese being amazed at his great Strength and Courage, cut his Throat, that they might be sure of him.

The Boat's Crew hearing the firing, put off in good time at some distance from the Shore; and seeing the Portuguese advancing to fire at them, they rowed on board their Ship; where relating what had happened, as they supposed, to their Captain, and to the rest on Shore, it set the Pirates all in a flame; and they directly chose Roberts as their Commander, vowing a severe revenge on the Portuguese.

The Water was so shallow, that they could not get their Ship near the Town; so they prepared a Raft, on which they mounted several Pieces of Cannon, with which they fired at the place: but the Inhabitants having quitted it, and all the Houses being of Timber, they did little damage to the Town. Neither durst they land to burn the Place, for fear of the great number of People, whom they perceived in the Bushes with small Arms: So, they returned to their Ship, and the next day sailed out of the Harbour.

Thus fell Captain Davis, who (allowing for the Course of Life he had been unhappily engaged in) was a most generous humane Person. And thus Roberts arose, who proved the reverse of him, and did afterwards a great deal of mischief in the West Indies, and on the Coast of Guinea; till he and his Crew were happily suppressed by Sir Chaloner Ogle, in the Swallow Man of War, and in the Engagement, Roberts, and several of his People were killed. But as there is 'An Account of the Pirates' published, in which the principal Actions of Roberts are related, I shall say nothing more of him here; but go on to relate what is not mentioned in the aforesaid Book.

As soon as it was commonly known, that the Pirates were sailed from Sierraleon, Captain Bennet and Thompson, with several others that had been obliged to keep in the Woods, as I have formerly related, came to Captain Glynn's Hose. There we all consulted about preparing the Bristol Snow, which the Pirates had spared at my entreaty, so as to make it fit for us to return to London in. There was with us one Captain David Creichton, in the Elizabeth of London, laden with dyeing wood; whom the Pirates had taken not long before me. Him they plundered, and would have destroyed, but by the Interest of Mr James Griffin, who had been chief Mate with the Captain's Brother, the Ship was spared. In this Ship Captain Creichton took as many People as he possibly could, in order to spare our Provisions, and sailed a few days after the Pirates left the River Sierraleon, for London: We that were left behind, sent notice by him to our Owners of the great Misfortunes that had befallen us.

Then applying ourselves to fit the Bristol Snow, whom a worthy Person, one Captain John Morris, commanded, we found we should be in very great want of Provisions, considering how many poor People desired to go home with us. Upon that Captain Glynn sent a small Sloop belonging to him, to fetch Provisions from the River Sherberow, where the destroying Pirates had not been. From thence she returned in a few days, with a good quantity; and one Captain Nisbet having found under his Ship's Ballast in the Hold, several Casks of Beef; which had not come to the knowledge of the Pirates (otherwise it would no doubt have been destroyed, as most part of his Cargoe was) he was so kind as to spare me as much of this Beef as he possibly could; and I drew a Bill on my Owner for the value of it.

Lastly, knowing that large quantities of Goods had been given by the Pirates, to all the white Men residing on Shore upon their own Accounts, we all went in a body to demand them. Messieurs Mead and Pearce, who were in Partnership, very readily and honourably delivered up all they were possessed of: But others did not follow their Example, for they only showed us what Goods they thought proper, of which I allowed them one third part for salvage.

So I shipped what I had recovered from them, with the other Goods the Pirates had given me formerly out of Captain Morris's Vessel; and then we embarked in her, being above sixty Passengers, besides six Masters of Ships, whose Vessels had been destroyed, or fitted for the use of the Pirates. We left the River Sierraleon the 10th of May and, after a tedious Passage, occasioned by the Ship's bad sailing, we came safe to Bristol, the first of August 1719.

On my landing at the Key (quay), Mr Casamajor, Merchant of that City, delivered me a Letter from my Owner, the late Humphrey Morrice Esq; who had received mine by Captain Creichton, with the account of my Misfortune, a few days before we arrived at Bristol. Mr Morrice, in his Letter, was pleased to comfort me under so severe a Trial, as I had undergone, assuring me, 'He would immediately give me the Command of another Ship; (which accordingly he most generously did soon after) and that he had ordered Mr Casamajor, his Correspondent, to supply me with Money, to distribute amongst my poor Sailors, who had returned with me to Bristol; in order to enable them to go to their several Habitations' which was in several Parts of England.

.... This ends the narrative of Snelgrave, the final third book in its entirety, in which the account of Howel Davis's death is probably the truest account we have. Humphrey Morrice was a founder-member of the New Royal Africa Company, on September 27th, 1672, so had a long history of slave-dealing. Other founders were Charles II's brother, James, Duke of York (later James II), Prince Rupert, the Earls of Shaftesbury, Craven and Arlington, and the Welshmen Henry Griffith, Thomas Lewis, Simon Lewis, Richard Middleton, John Middleton, Robert Morris, John Morgan, Lord Powis, William Roberts, Gabriel Roberts, Henry Richards and Godfrey Richards.

NOTES ON THE OTHER PIRATES WHO APPEAR IN THE ACCOUNT OF HOWELL DAVIS
(notes on Thomas Anstis appear under the Bartholomew Roberts chapter)

EDWARD ENGLAND
Jasper Seagar (Edward England) was mate on a sloop from Jamaica to Providence which was taken by Captain Christopher Winter in 1717. His sailing skills and friendliness were such that he was given his own sloop, sailing out of New Providence. However, after Woodes Rogers' amnesty there, he sailed off to the coast of Africa, where he took Howell Davis in the snow *Cadogan*. After his crew tortured Captain Skinner, as recounted above, he gave the *Cadogan* to Davis. England next took the *Pearl*, and exchanged it for his sloop, renaming her the *Royal James*. Several ships were taken off the African coast, then off the Azores and Cape Verde Islands. Returning to Africa in 1719, England took ten ships between the River Gambia and the Cape Coast. Four were burned, four released after being plundered, and the *Mercury* and *Elizabeth and Katherine* were fitted out as pirate ships. Renamed the *Queen Anne's Revenge* and the *Flying King*, they were given to Captain Lane and Captain Robert Sample, who took them to the Caribbean. England now took the galley *Peterborough*, which he kept, and the *Victory*, which he released. At Cape Coast castle, he tried to take the *Wida* and the *John*, but they sailed under the protection of the fort's guns. On Whydah roadstead, he discovered that Olivier la Bouche had been taking any plunder available. He then careened his ships, renaming the *Peterborough* as the *Victory*. It was captained by John Taylor, one of Howell Davis's former pirates. In an isolated bay in Ghana, Johnson says '*they lived there wantonly for several Weeks, making free with Negroe Women, and committing such outrageous Acts, that they came to open Rupture with the natives.*' After of month's roistering, the two ships sailed around the Cape of Good Hope, and arrived at Madagascar in January 1720. Off the Malabar coast several Indian vessels were captured, and a Dutch vessel taken and used as a 34-gun pirate ship renamed the *Fancy*. The *Royal James* was given to the Dutch captain.

At Johanna Island (Juanna), the *Victory* and *Fancy* came across Captain James Macrae's *Cassandra* and the *Greenwich* from England and a Dutch East Indiaman from Ostend. The *Cassandra* fought back strongly while the other ships fled. The *Cassandra* and *Fancy* were both grounded, and pounded each other with broadsides for several hours. Macrae suffered 37 casualties, and more than 90 pirates were killed before

Macrae escaped to the shore, leaving £37,000 worth of booty. Macrae hid for 10 days, and then took a chance. He went aboard the *Victory* and asked for mercy. In the Great Cabin, England pleaded for Macrae's life, but Taylor was adamant that he had to die. However, England plied Taylor with more and more rum, until Taylor agreed. The *Fancy* was so badly damaged that she was given to the English captain, which further annoyed Taylor. (Macrae with his 47 surviving crew had a terrible 7-week journey in the semi-derelict ship before they reached the safety of Bombay). England was seen as weak, and in early 1721 he was marooned on Mauritius with three other crewmen. John Taylor sailed off as the new pirate captain. One of the men marooned with him was the model for Long John Silver, being '*a man with a terrible pair of whiskers and a wooden leg, being stuck around with pistols.*' Fashioning a small boat out of driftwood, the marooned men managed to sail to St Augustine Bay, Mauritius. England lived for a short time off the charity of others, before dying in late 1720 or early 1721.

JOHN TAYLOR
A fierce member of Howell Davis's '*House of Lords*', he was in Edward England's crew which took a 30-gun vessel off Africa in 1719. He was given command of the *Victory*, and after some success off India with England, he marooned him for the clemency that he showed to Captain Macrae of the *Cassandra*. Taylor now took some Indian, Arab and European prizes. Taylor paid the Dutch governor of Cochin a huge bribe in order to stay there, and he and his men spent the entire month of December 1720 carousing in relative safety. He then went to careen the fleet at Mauritius and St Mary's Island, and Olivier la Bouche took over as captain of the *Victory*. Taylor in the *Cassandra* and La Bouche moved on to Reunion, where they captured a Portuguese carrack which had put in for repairs. *Nostra Senhora de Cabo* was carrying the retiring viceroy of Goa with all his accumulated treasure, diamonds valued at £500,000, and £375,000 in value of rare oriental products. This was a huge windfall, and the two pirate ships and the Portuguese prize sailed back to Madagascar, where 240 pirates shared about a million pounds in accumulated plunder. Johnson wrote that each man received up to 42 diamonds. The *Nostra Senhora de Cabo* was renamed the *Victory*, and the old *Victory* was burned.

Being informed that a Royal Navy squadron was being sent to Madagascar, Taylor and La Bouche spent some time in East Africa, deciding to split up in December 1722. Some pirates returned to Madagascar and burned the *Victory* (the former *Nostra Senhora de Cabo*), to destroy evidence, before vanishing into the townships with their loot. Taylor took the *Cassandra* and 140 pirates to Panama in May 1723, and exchanged the *Cassandra* with the governor in exchange for pardons. Each pirate still had around £1200 in gold and silver, plus his diamonds. It seems that Taylor became a captain in the Panamanian costa-garda. Interestingly, Captain Christopher Winter, originally responsible for Edward England's pirate career, was also a captain of the Hispaniola (Cuba) costa-garda in 1723, and was accused of robbing English ships and taking Jamaican slaves off the plantations.

OLIVIER LE VASSEUR, LA BOUZE, LA BUSE (THE BUZZARD) LA BOUCHE (The Mouth)

Possibly from Calais, La Bouche was a small man with a limp, who sailed from the pirates' nest of New Providence in 1716, cruising with another pirate ships commanded by Benjamin Hornigold and later by Samuel Bellamy (q.v.) With Bellamy and Paul Williams, he captured English and French ships off the Virgin Islands, but their ships were separated by a great storm early in 1717. In July 1717 Captain John Frost was chased by La Bouse for 12 hours, who caught up with him at 9 in the evening, in a ship of 20 guns and with a crew of 170 men. To force Frost to surrender, La Bouse fired a broadside of *'double round and cartridges, and a volley of small shot'*, so each of 10 guns was loaded with two cannon balls and a bag of partridge shot. The bombardment, combined with the firing of muskets and landing of grenades, forced Frost to surrender his wrecked ship.

La Bouse left his New Providence base when Woodes Rogers became governor of the Bahamas in July 1718, although he accepted the King's Pardon. *The Buzzard* then made for the easier targets of the coast of West Africa. Edward England found thin pickings at this time along the coast, because La Bouche had scared away much of the merchant shipping. In Spring 1719, La Bouche joined up with Howell Davis and Thomas Cocklyn, as recounted in the entry on Howell Davis. He had borne down on Davis, only to see Davis also raise the black flag. They met Thomas Cocklyn a few weeks later. The three pirates took the galley *Bird* at Sierra Leone, which was given to La Bouche to replace his brig, but the three captains argued and parted. Cocklyn, Taylor and la Bouche joined up with Edward England's pirates, and took some merchantmen off the Cape Coast, then sailed a hundred miles west to the Portuguese fort at Ouidah. There they took the English *'Heroine'*, two Portuguese and a French ship. Later in 1719, they all sailed to Madagascar. In 1720 La Bouche commanded the 250 ton *'Indian Queen'* with twenty-eight guns and ninety crew. He was still sailing with Taylor in 1722, on the other side of Africa, around Madagascar.

Making from the Guinea Coast for the Red Sea, he was wrecked on Mayotte in the Comoros Islands in 1720. Early in 1721, La Bouche met up again with Taylor when he landed at St Mary's Island to careen, and Taylor gave him command of the *Victory*. Off Reunion, the took vast treasure off a Portuguese carrack (see the entry on Taylor), and divided up the booty back at St Mary's. His capture of *Virgen del Cabo (La Vierge du Cap)* with Taylor is noted above, and during his ten-year pirate career it is said that he took spoils estimated at £300 million in today's money. In the Bishop of Goa's treasure ship, they found *'rivers of diamonds, a large quantity of gold bars, cascades of gold coins and cases and chests of sacred church vessels.'* It included the diamond-encrusted, golden *'Fiery Cross of Goa'*, an opulent crucifix which, it is said, took three men to lift.

Some of the crew stayed at St Mary's, but La Bouche and Taylor sailed on, in 1722 plundering the Dutch garrison at Fort Lagoa. Le Vasseur was supposed to have hidden his share of the treasure on an island in the Indian Ocean. On sailing from Guinea Coast to the East Indies, Captain La Bouche lost his ship near Madagascar on the Island of Mayotta. La Bouche and about forty of his men started building a new ship and the rest of the crew left in canoes and joined pirates led by Captain England at

Johanna. Olivier la Bouche retired on the islet of Bel Ombre near Mahe in the Seychelles. He seems to have been offered an amnesty by the French government. However, he realised that he would have to give up his booty, and the Buzzard turned them down. He carried on sporadic piracy, until captured by the French man-of-war *Meduse* off Fort Dauphin. He was trapped, tried and sentenced to death after resuming piracy. On the scaffold on the French island of Reunion, he flung a coded message into the crowd, crying *'Find my treasure he who can!'* La Bouche was hanged at Reunion Island or Mahe on July 17th, 1730.

The Buzzard's code seems to have surfaced in the Seychelles, the French islands 1,100 miles north of Reunion, soon after WWI. In 1948 Reginald Cruise-Wilkins, a former British army officer, bought the cryptogram, believing that it showed La Bouche's treasure to be buried at Bel Ombre Bay on Mahe, the main island in the Seychelles. He spent the rest of his years searching for the booty, finding what he thought was an 18th century pirates' graveyard and dozens of artefacts contemporary with la Bouche. He presumed that a group of up to 250 men stayed there between 1725 and 1729, a time when the Buzzard apparently vanished from history. The Seychelles were uninhabited until the middle of the 18th century. On his death-bed in 1977, Cruise-Wilkins claimed that he was only 6 yards or so from finding the loot. In 1988, his son John resumed the search, upon hearing that a metal object the size of a table had been traced by a remote survey of Bel Ombre. At the bay, there is a series of carvings of birds, snakes, female genitalia and a human nose. Reginald Cruise-Wilkins thought that these were related to the cryptogram, but others believe that it is indecipherable or a fraud.

'Seychelle Nation' Report
Hunter prepares to enter tunnel he believes holds treasure worth £100 million
Treasure hunter John Cruise-Wilkins Thursday blasted an eight-foot tall rock of similar length at Bel Ombre, which he said stood at the entrance to a tunnel where pirates hid treasure worth £100 million around the year 1721.

He told Nation that once the rubble from the now-broken, formerly turtle-shaped rock was cleared, he would gain access to the treasure, which he hoped included the *golden Sacred Fiery Cross of Goa*, stolen by buccaneer Olivier Le Vasseur, better known as *La Buse*, and another pirate, from a Portuguese ship in April 1721.

He said that following Greek mythology and signs at the site, and going by "known" practices of pirates, he was convinced that the rock had been deliberately placed on that spot to block the entrance to the tunnel by the pirates, who were executed in 1730 in Reunion for their theft.

Mr Cruise-Wilkins said it appeared that the search his late father started in 1949 would soon be over, adding that a German firm was funding his exploration which had ran into hundreds of thousands of rupees.

The Treasure Islands of The Indian Ocean - website information
These islands, located some one-thousand miles east of the African mainland, were so named after a Minister of Finance during the reign of Louis XV, Vicomte Moreau de

Seychelles. There is some evidence that these islands may have been known about or
visited in the Middle Ages by Arab traders from the Arabian peninsula and Persian
Gulf, sailing to and from ports in East Africa before the Monsoons. The period of
Portuguese exploration in the Indian Ocean records the sighting of the Amirantes
group by Vasco da Gama on his second voyage to India in 1502 or 1503. Previously,
in 1501 or 1502, the island of Farquhar, formerly called John de Novo, may have been
discovered by the Portuguese explorer of that name. 1501 is also the date on the first
map showing what are believed to be the main group of islands. On the morning of
January 19, 1609, twenty-eight days out of Zanzibar, boatswain Jones of the brig
Ascension under the command of General Alexander Sharpleigh passed the word
"land ... one point off the starboard bow." This British expedition financed by private
merchants was known as `The Fourth Voyage of The East India Company'. Two
company traders, John Jourdain and William Revett were on board ship. Their orders
were to sail around Africa's Cape of Good Hope with the object of establishing trade
relations with Aden and Surat. The ship was attacked by natives near the Portuguese
island of Pemba. The aim of the natives was to capture the ship and turn it over to the
Portuguese. On escaping from Pemba, the brig ran straight into the northeast
monsoon. The prevailing winds made it virtually impossible to steer the Ascension to
the next port-of-call, Aden and Surat. It was during this off-course stretch that land
was sighted. Looking for fresh water, they sailed among a "cluster of islands" at the
time mistaken for the Amirantes, but clearly identifiable by log and journal entries as
Mahe and adjacent islands. First landings were made on North Island and Silhouette.
On North Island, the men found many giant land tortoises, the larger ones weighing
between five and six hundred pounds. The men took eight tortoises for the purpose as
recorded by boatswain, Mr. Jones, in the ships log: "The tortells were good meate, as good
as fresh beefe, but after two or three meales our men would not eate them, because they did
looke soe uglie before they were boyled." William Revett recorded in his journal: "we
founde land turtles of such bignes which men would think incredible; of which our company
had small lust to eat of, being such huge deformed creatures and footed with five claws lyke
a beare." On the morning of the third day, January 22, the ship dropped anchor in a
bay sheltered from the monsoon winds on the leeward side of the largest island. The
next day, the ship's skiff was lowered and the crew, in charge of boatswain Jones and
accompanied by John Jourdain and William Revett, went ashore. The description of
their landing place as recorded in their journal entries fits the bay of present day Port
Victoria. The bay teemed with fish and sea turtles, and they spotted some crocodiles.
An account of this shore excursion was recorded in the 'Journal of John Jourdain',
published by the Hakluyt Society. He wrote: "within a pistol shot of the shore where we
rode as in a pond from the 22nd to the 30th ditto; in which time wee watred and wooded at
our pleasure with much ease; where wee found many coker nutts, both ripe and greene, of
all sorts, and much fishe and fowle and tortells and many soates with other fishe. As alsoe
aboute the rivers there are many allagartes (crocodiles); our men fishinge for scates tooke one
of them and drewe him aland alive with a rope fastened within his gills. Within two miles
where we roade, there is a good tymber as ever I sawe of length and bignes, and a very firme
timber. You shall have many trees of 60 and 70 feete without spriggs except at the topp, very

bigge and straight as an arrowe. It is a very good refreshing place for wood, water, cooker nutts, fish and fowle, without any feare or danger except the allagartes for you cannot discerne that ever any people had bene there before us." The Ascension left the islands on February 1, arriving in Aden April 7. The ship's log and Jourdain and Revett's journals are the first record of Europeans landing in the Seychelles. With the departure of the Ascension, the islands remained dormant among the warm waters of the Indian Ocean. Located outside the usual spice trading routes to India and the Far East, they remained unexplored and barren of human habitation for more than a hundred years. Although visited by pirates in the 18th century, the islands continued in their isolation from the rest of the world.

Towards the end of the 17th century the British Navy cracked down on the many pirates, who had been active in the West Indies and the Spanish Main, driving them into new territory for the practice of their nefarious trade. Tales of the wealth of the Orient seems to have taken them into the Indian Ocean where an abundant scattering of uninhabited islands provided ideal refuge and hiding places from the law. Between 1700 and 1720 no less than eleven of their ships that used to sail in the Caribbean were identified in Indian Ocean waters. It was highly unlikely that the archipelago, with its ample supply of fresh water, magnificent trees for masts and spars, and safe anchorages would escape their notice. It was in 1721 that the notorious pirate **Olivier Le Vasseur**, also known as La Buse (The Mouth) visited the islands in his ship *Le Victorieux*. He was accompanied by the equally infamous English pirate Taylor in his ship *Defence*. Other pirates, such as Kidd and Conduit, may also have been visitors. More than likely, the islands were only used as a temporary refuge from the law or as a hiding place for plundered loot. The pirates' main centre of operation continued to be Madagascar. It was there that the middlemen from New York were ready to buy the loot at bargain prices. The era of the Indian Ocean Buccaneer came to an end shortly after La Buse was captured by the French Navy and hanged from the yard-arm of a ship in Reunion harbour on July 7, 1730. There is nothing as fascinating as a historical mystery. There is a beach on the south coast of Mahe that is named Anse Fourbans (Pirate's Cove). The north-east coast of Praslin is known as Cote d'Or (Gold Coast). These places were so named by the colonists who arrived 30 to 40 years after the pirates ceased their operations in the Indian Ocean. Cote d'Or is primarily associated with La Buse and Anse Fourbans with pirates in general. Pirates, treasure, and islands are ingredients in the minds of many people that conjure up fantasies of high adventure in exotic places.

It is rumoured amongst the Seychellois that the fortunes of at least two island families can be attributed to the accidental unearthing of wine jars filled with coins. One was purportedly found on Therese Island and the other near the site of St. Elizabeth Convent in Victoria. There is also a rumour that during the construction of the Seychelles International Airport, a treasure chest full of gold and jewels was unearthed by the contractor. What happened to it? No one knows. But these cases are insignificant compared to, what some believe, is a treasure worth millions of pounds that La Buse is said to have buried at Bel Ombre on Mahe. There was one man who had searched for this treasure for more than a quarter century, with no reward except for the excitement of the search. The adventure of seeking with hope and expectation is a reward in itself. The only authentic find so far that has been documented has been 107 silver coins, a few forks and spoons, two shoe buckles and a boatswain's whistle. Those items were found on Astove Island in 1911. Since then, even the government's share has been mysteriously pirated away with only the written record remaining as proof of the find.

CHAPTER VIII

JOHN ROBERT - BARTHOLOMEW ROBERTS - BARTI DDU – BLACK BART
'THE GREAT PYRATE', 'THE BLACK CAPTAIN', 'THE LAST AND MOST LETHAL PIRATE'

WHAT I HEARD IN THE APPLE BARREL

Black Bart –
"The last and most
lethal pirate".

'No, not I,' said Silver. 'Flint was cap'n;
I was quarter-master, along of my timber
leg. The same broadside I lost my leg, old
Pew lost his daylights. It was a master
surgeon, him that ampytated me – out of
college and all – Latin by the bucket, and
what not; but he was hanged like a dog,
and sun-dried like the rest, at Corso
Castle. That was Roberts' men, that
was, and comed of changing names of
their ships – Royal Fortune and so on.
Now, what a ship is christened, let her
stay, I says.'
-    'Treasure Island' by Robert
Louis Stevenson, 1883.
(Roberts moved his ship's name at
least 5 times. He took over Davis's
Rover, then the *Rover* was lost as
Kennedy sailed it away from the
African coast. Off the Newfoundland
coast Roberts then took a Bristol galley, mounting 16 guns and naming her the
Fortune. Then he swapped her for a French ship of 26 guns, which he also named the
Fortune. In 1720, the Fortune was replaced with a captured French ship of 42 guns,
named the *Royal Fortune*, and then off the African coast he took the *Onslow* and
refitted her as the *Royal Fortune*.)
      Only three real pirates were mentioned in *Treasure Island* – Captain England and
the two Welsh captains, Bart Roberts and Howell Davis. Gosse, in his 1932 'The
History of Piracy' notes that Black Bart Roberts *'seems to attain most nearly to the
popular pirate of fiction'*. He paints a pen-picture of the Welshman thus: *'He was*

remarkable, even among his remarkable companions, for several things. First of all, he only drank tea, thus being the only recorded teetotaller known to the fraternity (of pirates). Also he was a strict disciplinarian and on board his ships all lights had to be out by 8pm. Any of the crew who wished to continue drinking after that hour had to do so upon the open deck. But try as he would this ardent apostle of abstemiousness was unable to put down drinking entirely.

If Roberts had lived today, he would probably have been the leading light on the council of a local vigilance society. He would allow no women aboard his ships; in fact he made a law by which any man who brought a woman on board disguised as a man was to suffer death. Nor did he permit games of cards or dice to be played for money, as he strongly disapproved of gambling. Being a strict Sabbatarian, he allowed the musicians to have a rest on the seventh day. This was as well, for the post of musician on a pirate ship was no sinecure, since every pirate had the right to demand a tune at any hour of the day or night. He used to place a guard to protect all his women prisoners and it is sadly suspicious that there was always the greatest competition amongst the worst characters in the ship to be appointed sentry over a good-looking woman prisoner. No fighting was permitted amongst his crew on board ship. All guards had to be settled on shore, the duellists standing back-to-back armed with pistol and cutlass, pirate fashion.

Bartholomew dressed for action, surprisingly, was the very beau of pirates. A tall, dark man, he used to wear a rich damask waistcoat and breeches, a red feather in his cap, a gold chain round his neck with a large diamond cross dangling from it, a sword in his hand and two pairs of pistols hanging at the end of a silk sling flung over his shoulders.' This is the picture of the **most successful pirate of all time.**

In 1924, in his 'The Pirate's Who's Who', Gosse had written 'If a pirate is to be reckoned by the amount of damage he does and the number of ships he takes there can be no doubt that Captain Roberts should be placed at the very head of his profession, for he is said to have taken over 400 vessels. The only man who can rival him is Sir Henry Morgan, but Morgan, although in some ways an unmitigated blackguard, was a man of much greater outlook than Roberts ever was, and, moreover, was a buccaneer rather than a pirate.'

And Patrick Pringle, in 'Jolly Roger', puts the Welshman's 'career' as a pirate into true perspective: 'Most of the Guinea pirates were exceptionally daring, and one of them was possibly the most daring pirate who ever lived. His name was Bartholomew Roberts, and he bestraddles the Age of Piracy like a colossus. A Welsh poet has honoured "Black Barty", but he has never become a household name like Kidd or Blackbeard. I cannot imagine why. Not only was he immeasurably bolder, braver, and more successful - not only is his story far more exciting and dramatic - but in his lifetime he achieved a far greater fame. For nearly three years he was feared more than any other man at sea. Moreover, Johnson, on whose history most popular pirate books are based, did Roberts full justice, giving him five times as much space as Blackbeard or any other pirate ... the story of Roberts (is) one of the best documented in pirate history. This is very fortunate, for Roberts was of considerable historical as well as personal importance. **He was not only the greatest of the pirates, but he was virtually the last.** ...Captain Ogle was knighted for destroying Roberts. I think this is the only case of such an honour being granted for taking pirates, and it is a measure of the importance that was attached to the event. Bartholomew Roberts was indeed the terror of the seas, and the news of his death was acclaimed by Governors in places as far apart as New York, Port Royal, and even Bombay.... It was said that the end of "the great pirate" would be the end of the great days of piracy. It was, too.'

John Robert was born in the peaceful hamlet of Little Newcastle (Casnewydd Bach, which Daniel Defoe described as 'Newybagh'), a few miles south of Fishguard (Abergwaun), Pembrokeshire, in 1682. His father was probably George Robert, noted in the Pembrokeshire Hearth Tax list of 1670. A metal memorial on an old stone on the village green reads:

CAS NEWYDD BACH	LITTLE NEWCASTLE
Yn y pentref yma y ganed	In this village was born
BARTI DDU	BLACK BARTY
y mor-leidr enwog	the famous pirate
1682-1722	1682-1722

(Mor-leidr literally means 'sea-robber')

John Robert went to sea aged 13, in 1695, but vanished from history, until we find him working as mate on a Barbados sloop in 1718. He probably served in the Royal Navy during the years 1702 to 1713, when the War of Spanish Succession brought hostilities between Britain and Spain. From 1713, he then served on slave-ships, signing on in Barbados, one of thousands of seamen left jobless when the wars ended.

1718

Our first real record is that John Robert is mate of a sloop in Barbados. These were times of pirate mayhem in the Caribbean, with the notorious Edward Teach, Blackbeard, in the fore. The pirate John Plantain maintained that he sailed from Rhode Island on the privateer sloop *Terrible*, with the Welshman John Williams as captain, and Bart Roberts as mate. On the way to West Africa, and off its coast, several prizes were taken. A Dutch slave ship, the *Fancy*, was taken and given to Edward England, who was an experienced ship's mate. England now wanted the squadron to sail to the Indian Ocean, but Roberts strongly disagreed. There was a meeting, and some pirates voted to stay with Roberts in Africa, while others went with England on the Fancy and Victory. Only Plantain gives this account, but it may well be that Roberts was known as a former pirate when he was captured by Howell Davis.

1719
THE SLAVE TRADE

It is in Spring 1719, that John Robert, later known as John Roberts, explodes into maritime history. Under Captain Abraham Plumb, he had sailed to the Guinea Coast of West Africa, as third mate on the galley *Princess of London*. His ship left England in November, 1718, sailing in consort with Captain Snelgrave's *Bird* (captured by Howell Davis), and traded along the Guinea coast. His wage was less than £3 a month, and he had no chance of promotion to his own ship's captaincy in the Merchant Navy. A superb navigator and handler of men, he was condemned to roam the seas working for fools, risking his life on every voyage, in terrible conditions on slave ships. One of the reasons for his going on the account was '*to get rid of the disagreeable Superiority of some masters he was acquainted with — and the Love of Novelty and Change.*' Since the peace with Spain in 1713, many English ships were licensed by the Royal African Company of London to carry slaves from Africa to the Spanish colonies in the New World. (The Asiento Clause in the Treaty of Utrecht gave Britain this '*right*'). The Royal Africa Company, with its President King George 1, was granted the monopoly on trade in both goods and '*black ivory*' by the Crown in 1718.

The *Princess* had discharged its trade goods (see *Middle Passage* in 'Pirate Terms') in Annambo on the Gold Coast in the Gulf of Guinea. Annambo was one of a number of forts along this coast which also acted as trading stations. It was also the main slaving depot of the Royal Africa Company. The Company received a 10% tax off the owners of the *Princess* for the right to sell goods and buy slaves, gold and ivory. In early June Captain Plumb and John Robert were supervising the taking on of slaves to replace the trade goods they had disposed of. The slaves were destined for the islands of the West Indies and possibly for the Spanish settlements in the New World. There were two other slave ships at harbour with it, when two pirate ships approached bearing black flags.

THE TAKING OF ROBERTS

The three merchant ships immediately lowered their colours. The pirate ships were full of armed men, and they could expect quarter for not resisting. Merchant seamen had no affection for their owners anyway – most had been impressed into service, or driven into it by poverty, and a life at sea was generally short and unpleasant. The pirates were led by Captain Howell Davis, a Welsh Jacobite from Milford Haven, a few miles from John Robert's home (see Howell Davis). His ship was the *King James* (because of his Jacobite leanings), with 26 guns. His consort was a recently captured Dutch ship, now called the *Royal Rover*, with 32 cannon and 27 swivel guns. Davis looted the three slave ships, then gave one to the captain of the Dutch ship he had overcome. Michael Mare of Ghent joined from the Dutch ship. He then sailed out to sea with Roberts' *Princess* and the other slave ship.

The next day, Davis gave chase to, and captured an extremely rich Dutch ship, which surrendered after one broadside. Davis gave quarter to the enemy, as he had stipulated in his Ship's Articles. Roberts must have watched bemused at the ease with which this pirate seemed to take prizes. Davis sold off the three captured ships, and asked all those who wanted to join his crew to say so. Roberts demurred for a while, but Davis was keen to have a fellow-Pembrokeshire man and expert sailing-master with him. Roberts was almost exactly the opposite of the happy-go-lucky extrovert Davis, although he came from only a few miles away from Davis's home town of Milford. Davis was a typical short, stocky Welshman, but Roberts was taller than all his colleagues, lean and brooding, black hair and clean-shaven, with a '*black*' or sombre aspect, according to Defoe. Eventually Roberts and 34 other crewmen from the slavers joined. The *Princess's* second mate Stephenson joined with Roberts. Davis boasted that he forced no man to join him. Roberts' reluctance could have been because he wanted to be seen to be *'forced'* to join the pirates – then there was some hope of mitigation of sentence if captured. John Jessup of Wisbech also voluntarily joined from the *Princess* (another John Jessup later joined the crew).

THE DEATH OF DAVIS

Travelling down the Guinea Coast, past the Bight of Biafra and the Bight of Benin, Davis took more ships, but off Cameroon the *Royal James* was leaking badly, still damaged by battling with the first Dutch ship a few weeks earlier. The *King James* was abandoned, and the crew transferred to the *Rover*, which Davis renamed the *Royal Rover*. They had to careen the ship in Prince's Island, in the Gulf of Guinea, off Spanish Guinea. With just one ship, it had to be fast and seaworthy. Besides, there were women and drinking dens in this Portuguese enclave. Howell Davis claimed that he was captain of an English man-of-war, chasing pirates out of the local seas. His ship was saluted by the fort's twelve cannons overlooking the harbour, and Davis was greeted personally by the Governor of Prince's Island.

No one really knows whether Davis intended just to careen his ship, spend his loot, or attack the island, as in his previous raids. Careening was a laborious, and necessary process, carried out every three months or so. (See *Careen*). On a sandy beach, the topmasts were taken down (and perhaps replaced) and all the guns removed. By blocks and tackles, the ship was attached to trees (or another ship) and pulled over onto her side. The hull was then cleared of debris, repairs made, and coated with tallow and pitch. The process was repeated on the other side. This hard work was often accompanied by evenings of whoring, gambling and drinking.

The Governor probably suspected Howell Davis was a pirate, but there were huge profits to be made from trade with such a ship. Pirates had few outlets for their stolen merchandise, accepted low prices, and usually spent the proceeds very quickly. The Royal Rover was to leave harbour after a few weeks, on a Monday morning. Davis had promised to pay the Governor a farewell visit on the Sunday morning, and went with his chief surgeon and a handful of other crew. There was no-one at the Government House, and on his return the party was ambushed. Three were immediately killed, including the surgeon. Davis was shot four times but still fought back. After the fifth bullet wound he fell to the ground, but still managed to shoot and kill two Portuguese soldiers. The Portuguese swarmed over his dying body and cut his throat to ensure he was dead.

Just two pirates managed to escape the ambush. The fearless quartermaster, Walter Kennedy, managed to flee to the waiting boat, which was rowed quickly to the *Royal Rover*. Without a captain, there had to be an election of someone agreed by the whole crew. However, Davis' ship was very different from other pirate vessels. The hardest and most experienced pirates, such as Thomas Anstis (who later captained his own pirate ship), and Valentine Ashplant (the former captain of a brig), had formed themselves into what they called *The House of Lords*. *Lord* Christopher Moody had already captained a pirate crew. They had assumed powers not available to the rest of the crew, or *Commoners*. They could go ashore at will, walk the quarter-deck and

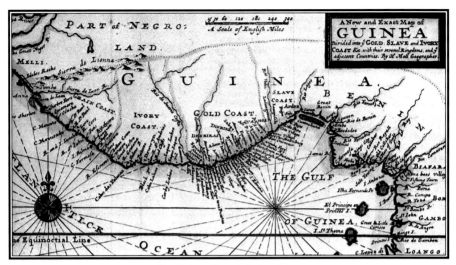

The Guinea Coast in Roberts' time

parley with the captains of prize ships. They referred to each other as '*my fellow noble*' and greeted others as '*my noble lord*'. It was this *House of Lords* which first debated who among them should be the new captain. In all other ships, the crew were not by-passed in this manner in such important discussions.

ROBERTS MADE PIRATE CAPTAIN

The *Lords* were furious and wanted revenge – Davis had been an intelligent leader and had led some profitable voyages, with very little bloodshed. Kennedy was discussed as a captain, but he was a hard taskmaster, and the merits of *Lords* Henry Dennis and Thomas Anstis were also debated. *Lords* Ashplant, Moody, Topping, Phillips and Sutton also could have claims to be the next captain, but the over-riding quality apart from bravery in a captain had to be navigational skills. Daniel Defoe gives us the text of the speech that Lord Dennis made to the assembled Lords in their Council: '*It is not of any great significance who is dignified with the title of commander, for really, and in truth, all good governments have, like ours, the supreme power lodged with the community, who might doubtless revoke and depute authority as suited interest or humour. We are the original holders of this claim and should a captain be so saucy as to exceed prescription at any time, why, down with him! It will be a caution after he is dead to his successors of what fatal consequences any sort of assuming may be. However, it is my advice, that, while we are sober, we pitch upon a man of courage, and skilled in navigation; one who by his counsel and bravery seems best able to defend this commonwealth, and ward us from the dangers and tempests of an unsuitable element, the sea, and the fatal consequences of anarchy; and such a one I take Roberts to be. A fellow, I think, in all respects worth your esteem and favour.*' Only Lord Simpson, known as '*Little David*', did not applaud – he wanted the captaincy himself. This West countryman grumbled: '*I do not care whom we choose captain so he is not a Papist, for against them I have conceived an irreconcilable hatred, for my father was a sufferer in Monmouth's Rebellion.*'

Roberts had only been aboard for six weeks, but must have tremendously impressed the *House of Lords*. They knew that Davis had desperately wanted Roberts to join them, and an outside candidate from the *House of Commons* kept the *House of Lords* as it was. Anyway, any captain could be deposed by popular vote at any time, so they had little to lose if Roberts did not prove '*pistol-proof.*' Lord Dennis referred to this fact at the start of his speech. The *House of Commons* unanimously agreed, and Roberts accepted with this short speech:

'*Since I have dipped my hands in muddy water and must be a pirate, it is better to be a commander than a common man.*' He was also sure to tell his new crew that '*he neither feared nor valued any of them*'. They soon found out that he did not suffer fools gladly - his rages at ineptitude, inefficiency drunkenness or poor seamanship became legendary. However, he was forced to tread easily with the *Lords* in the first few months of his captaincy. He became more autocratic with them as time went on and success bred their complacency.

Captain Roberts later justified his going '*on the account*': '*In an honest service said he, there is thin commons (poor food and drink), low wages and hard labour; but in a pirate life there is plenty and satiety, pleasure and ease, liberty and power, and who would not balance creditor on this side when all the hazard that is run for it, at worst, is only a fore-look or two at choking (dying). No, a merry life and a short one shall be my motto.... Damnation to him who ever lived to wear a halter.* ' (This seems to be the origin of the phrase, '*a short life and a merry one*').

THE ATTACK ON PRINCE'S ISLAND

The new ship's surgeon and other officers were next appointed to replace those lost at Prince's Island. After this it was down to the serious business of avenging the death of Howell Davis. Some pirates had wished to leave the island, but the fort's guns covered the harbour exit, although they did not cover the harbour itself. The Governor expected the pirates to flee, and their guns would be primed, and trained upon the harbour exit. Roberts counselled prudence, stating that they could bombard the fort from where they were, with no fear of retaliation. The *Royal Rover* swung around and its cannonade started pounding the fort. One of the *Lords*, Walter Kennedy, had been voted as one of Roberts' lieutenants, and he now led a band of thirty men up the hill to attack the fort. The settlement on Prince's Island was only a couple of streets with wooden shacks, and the fort guarded both this and the harbour. The *Royal Rover* fired broadsides at the fort, while the pirates attacked under this cover, but the Portuguese fled before they reached the walls. The fort was fired, and its 12 cannon thrown into the sea. Kennedy's band returned, as agreed to the ship.

The Pirate Council then decided that it wanted to take the town as well. Roberts, being the captain only in times of aggression (or being chased) agreed, but only on condition that the town could be taken at minimum risk. To get to the settlement on land would mean passing through dense forest, perfect for an ambush. The Royal Rover could not sail into the shallow inner harbour without stripping itself of goods and armaments, leaving the pirates defenceless if things went wrong. He therefore took a French sloop which had been captured by Kennedy, stripped it of everything removable and mounted three cannon and two swivels on it. He put seven other guns on rafts which the French ship towed towards the town. Once in the harbour, the town was bombarded at length, until it had been virtually levelled and the remains were burning. For good measure, two Portuguese ships in the harbour were also ransacked and set alight. Roberts restored the French ship to her captain and sailed southwards, away from '*The Isle of Princes*' and its burning settlement. Davis had been revenged. It was the second week of July, 1719. Roberts took the *Royal Rover* into an inlet near Cape Lopez for refitting, where a forced man named Rogers attempted to escape and was clapped in irons and then soundly whipped.

MORE PRIZES

Almost immediately after leaving the inlet, on July 27th, off the Bight of Biafra Roberts came upon a Dutch merchantman, the '*Experiment*', sailing from London under Captain Cornet. This was a slaver, or '*blackbirder*', of the Royal Africa Company like the *Princess* that Roberts had been serving on, just eight weeks earlier. Seamen hated working on these ships, and sickness was rife in the Bight of Benin and the Gulf of Guinea. Black Bart fired a couple of shots across the '*Experiment's*' bows, then hauled up the black flag. The *Experiment* struck its colours. Kennedy now shouted at the sailing-master, Thomas Grant, to

Black Bart Roberts

row across to board the *Royal Rover*. When on board, Kennedy began furiously shouting at Grant, asking him where the valuables were. Grant answered quite reasonably that they were still aboard the *Experiment*. He hit and threatened to kill Grant, whose life was saved from the quartermaster by other pirates. The hot-headed Kennedy supervised the ransacking of the merchant, and found little - Captain Cornet had handed over 50 ounces of gold and some coin. Roberts now wanted to keep the *Experiment* as a storeship, but Kennedy, after burning the '*Experiment's*' yawl in a fit of pique, then set fire to the ship as well. Most of its crew joined Roberts, and the others including Cornet and Grant imprisoned on the *Rover*.

The next day, a small Portuguese merchantman was plundered, and just two days later Roberts took the *'Temperance'* under Captain Sharman. It still had a cargo of British pots and pans that Sharman had been trying to barter for slaves. Roberts gave him the Portuguese ship, and kept the *Temperance*. There was now a pirate council about the next destination. Roberts knew that Edward England, and probably la Bouche and Cocklyn were still operating off Africa, so decided to head for Brazil where there would be less competition. Some men wanted to head for Madagascar, and the pirates headed down to the island of St Thomas (Sao Tome), but found no new prizes. They now carried on south-west to the island of Annabona for fresh water and provisions. The Council met again, to decide whether to go to the East Indies (Java, Sumatra, etc.), or west across the Atlantic to Brazil. Roberts won the vote. The long voyage to the coast of Portuguese Brazil on the Southern Trades was taken in August 1719. In just three weeks Roberts, by use of the cross-staff, long-staff, quadrant, hourglass and logline, landed exactly where he wanted in Brazil. In these days when there was no way of calculating longitude, it was a superb example of seamanship, and Roberts further earned the crew's respect. At a small, uninhabited island off its coast, Fernando de Noronha (Ferninadino), they quickly boot-topped (partially careened) the *Royal Rover*. For weeks they cruised the shore, unaware that the Portuguese trade with Brazil was very minor, and that other pirates had been active along this coast, scaring off any potential shipping. In this climate, Roberts began to lose his aura as a *'lucky'* captain amongst his bored crew.

THE PORTUGUESE TREASURE FLEET

Roberts had kept the ship away from sight of land, but simply cruised the Brazilian coast for several weeks. He did not want to alert the Portuguese that he was in the area. With no luck, the pirates then agreed to head for the far busier waters of the Caribbean, the international cross-roads of Atlantic traffic. In September, they came upon the Lisbon Fleet of 32 ships laden with gold, silver, hides, tobacco and sugar. These armed merchantmen were lying-to at Bahia de Todos dos Santos (the Bay of All Saints) in Brazil. The fleet was waiting for its escort to Lisbon, two Portuguese men-of-war with seventy guns apiece, to finish their preparations for the Atlantic Crossing. Two forts trained their guns over the fleet, which had over 500 cannon and over 1000 men. The *Lords* decided to turn tail before they were spotted by the Portuguese. Roberts, conscious of the murmurings of discontent, stated that they would attack. He seemed to know that his days as captain would have been numbered, without a quick success. There followed an attack which for sheer audacity rivalled that of Francis Drake on Cadiz or of Henry Morgan on Portobello.

Black Bart quietly outlined his plan to the disbelieving pirates. Roberts sent a party in a boat to capture some Portuguese pilots to assist him, and then ordered his men to stay quiet and below decks. It was a moonless, dark night, which would assist their endeavours. Because of Roberts' incredible track-record, although short, the crew must have agreed to this outrageous attack. Once attack was under way, all decisions were the captain's until his death in action. *Lord* Henry Dennis, who had also been Howell Davis's gunner, inspected and prepared each cannon for action. Dennis stayed as Roberts' gunnery expert throughout his career. The pirates prepared their weapons and grappling-hooks and ropes. However, Captain Roberts knew he could not take on all forty-two ships. He had to find the most wealthy ship, take it quickly and flee before the other merchantmen, or the men-of-war, trapped him. Kennedy guided the *Royal Rover* slowly to the nearest heavily-laden vessel. Once alongside, all the pirates came up on deck with their cutlasses and muskets, and threatened to give no quarter, unless the captain told them which was the richest ship. Anstis had led the party and took the captain back to Roberts. The frightened captain took the easy option and pointed to the biggest ship, the *Sagrada Familia* (*Holy Family*). As yet no-one suspected that a pirate ship was in the harbour. Roberts coolly and calmly took the Portuguese captain and crew upon his ship, bound them and sailed on, towards the *Sagrada Familia*, its Vice-Admiral and its forty cannon.

THE TAKING OF THE *SAGRADA FAMILIA*
In hailing distance of the treasure galleon, Roberts ordered the Portuguese Captain to ask the Vice-Admiral to come aboard the ship for urgent news. The response was that he would, but obviously the captured captain had given a warning, as the Portuguese crew made ready for action. Roberts immediately ordered a full broadside, sailed quickly within grappling distance and boarded the prize. The boarding party was again led by the Irishman, Lieutenant Kennedy, who lost just two men in a brief but bloody battle. A tow-line was attached to the 36-gun *Sagrada*, and Kennedy then towed the slow and unwieldy treasure galleon out of the bay. All over the fleet, guns were firing, and one of the men-of-war began closing with the slow, unwieldy *Rover* and *Sagrada*. Roberts fired at it from the *Royal Rover*, and the man-of-war amazingly stopped its pursuit. Eastwell shouted from the crow's-nest that it was waiting for the other man-of-war to catch up, which was stationed on the other side of the fleet. With dawn breaking, Roberts escaped out to the open sea. The *Weekly Journal* reported in 1720 on the action '*The Lisbon Fleet from the Bay of All Saints, Brazil, has arrived. But one vessel of 36 guns was taken by a pyrate ship (formerly an English hog-boat) and two others plundered.*' The third boat's identity is unknown. The rest of the Spanish fleet had arrived in Lisbon on the 21st January 1720, carrying 759,000 octaves of gold dust, 164,000 moidores of gold (plus unspecified amounts of gold, including some for the king), 164 slaves, 205 raw hides, 11,000 rolls of tobacco, 950 chests of sugar, 92 barrels of honey, 22,000 hides, unspecified amounts of hardwoods, 128 baskets of cake-sugar and 7,800 chests of sugar.

The pirates made off with the galleon plus 40,000 *moidores* (*moeda d'oura, money of gold*), jewellery, sugar, skins, tobacco, silver plate and the diamond-studded gold cross designed for the King of Portugal. Roberts now started wearing two brace of pistols in a red silk sling over his shoulder, and a cutlass. Until his death he went into battle also wearing a scarlet damask waistcoat and breeches, a crimson plumed hat and the massive chain with the King of Portugal's jewelled cross on it. This red silk outfit, with the huge diamond cross, gave him his epithet by French merchants and pirates of *Le Joli Rouge* (the pretty red), probably the origin of *The Jolly Roger*. About this time he started to be known as Bartholomew Roberts, or *Black Bart*. (Bartholomew Sharp was

The West Indies

another famous pirate of the day, so perhaps Roberts was aping him. The other explanation is that he was trying to escape the identity of John Robert, in case he ever returned to Wales).

DEVIL'S ISLAND AND THE SIXTH PRIZE

Roberts now sailed north and north-west, past the Amazon estuary to the Iles du Salut off Surinam. The pirates anchored at Ile du Diable, Devil's Island and Cayenne Island off Guyana, and had a debauched time for two weeks. Now the former is renowned as the former French prison colony and the *Dreyfus Affair*, but then it was a Spanish possession. The Spanish Governor of Guiana apparently welcomed this sudden influx of wealth into his territories. Surgeon Murray tended to the injured from the *Sagrada* battle, while the Portuguese prisoners rotted in the hold. The pirates had now acquired huge wealth to add to their previous acquisitions under Davis, and Roberts had his fiddler and trumpeter play through the days to celebrate.

In October 1719, Roberts moved to the mouth of the river Surinam, and easily took a small Rhode Island sloop under Captain Cane. Cane told them that there was a far larger Rhode Island brig, with a much better cargo sailing towards Surinam. Back on the island, Roberts sent the *Royal Rover* to a nearby islet to be careened, while he checked the stores with his boatswain. He next wished to sail north to the West Indies, and provisions were needed. However, 30 crew members, under Eastwell, Rogers and Hews, deserted in a longboat which was soon recaptured. Ashplant wished to maroon them - the standard punishment - but Roberts desperately needed to keep his crew, and Kennedy relished whipping the deserters, paying particular attention to the ringleaders, whom he left half-dead. They were locked up in the hold, to reflect upon their misdemeanours. A mast-head was now sighted on the horizon, and thinking it to be the ship that Cane had promised, Roberts took forty of his best men in the sloop and raced after it. The *Royal Rover* was still laden with cargo and much of the treasures of the *Sagrada Familia*, so was neither fast nor worth the risk of losing. There were no provisions on the sloop, which he had renamed the *Fortune*, as they had been transferred to the *Royal Rover*. Black Bart lost sight of the quarry, and was becalmed for eight days, ending up ninety miles offshore. The *Royal Rover* had returned to Devil's Island, and the carousing pirates were blissfully unaware that a naval man-of-war, the *Seaford*, was now patrolling the West Indies. Two more naval sloops, the *Rose*, and the *Shark*, were also on their way from England.

DESERTION
Roberts was in a dilemma - he was becalmed, with no provisions in his haste to chase the merchantman. There were no creeks or inlets for mooring for his stricken ship. The *Fortune's* only boat was rowed back to order the *Royal Rover* to come and assist.

The crew were near death's door from lack of water, and despite rationing of food and water Roberts had to rip up some planking to make a raft to go ashore and bring in water. Roberts had sent Moody and five others for assistance, but they returned a few days later with bad news. Lieutenant Walter Kennedy had vanished, taking the *Royal Rover* and the *Sagrada Familia* with him. Back on the coast of Guiana, Black Bart decided that Ship's Articles must be drawn up,

Bart Roberts

and signed by all the crew. Many of the crew had been with Howell Davis. They had had a good run under these two Welsh captains, and it was only because of Portuguese and Irish treachery that events had ever misfired. The hardened cadre of Howell Davis's 'Lords' (Valentine Ashplant, Henry Dennis, William Magness, Christopher Moody, Richard Hardy, Thomas Sutton and Thomas Anstis) were still with Roberts. They unanimously decided to ban all Irishmen from ever sailing with them, and Bart became an implacable enemy of everyone and everything Irish.

However, it seems with hindsight that Kennedy had not deserted. Moody had reached Devil's Island to find that Kennedy had vanished, leaving no message. However, the 24 year-old Kennedy had seen his captain and the *House of Lords* vanish over the horizon, and had expected them back within 24 hours at the most. He had two ships stacked with treasure trove from half-a-dozen captures, and dozens of Portuguese prisoners. The 30 men who had tried to desert and whom he had badly beaten were also chained in the hold, and many forced men who were looking for any opportunity to escape. The pirates wanted to leave the island, and after 11 days Kennedy sailed for the West Indies. Although he was young and no navigator, it seems that the crew elected him captain because of his strength of character. Because of the crew shortage, Kennedy transferred all the loot to the *Royal Rover*, and gave the *Sagrada Familia* to Captain Cain. Kennedy believed that the *Fortune* must have been captured or sunk. Cain took the *Sagrada Familia* and the Portuguese prisoners to British Antigua and gave it to Governor Hamilton of the Leeward Islands. After Kennedy's 'desertion', the despondent Black Captain drew up his famous '*articles*' to be kept by the crew, and signed by all new members. Each pirate signed the articles, as Black Bart commented '*for the greatest security it is in everyone's interest to observe these articles if he is minded to keep up so abominable a combination (profession)*'

THE ARTICLES OF CAPTAIN ROBERTS
According to Charles Johnston (Daniel Defoe), writing just four years later, in 1724, '*The following, is the Substance of the Articles, as taken from the Pyrates' own Informations.*

I
Every Man has a Vote in Affairs of Moment; has equal Title to the fresh Provisions, or strong Liquors, at any Time seized, and may use them at Pleasure, unless a Scarcity make it necessary, for the Good of all, to vote a Retrenchment.

II
Every Man to be called fairly in Turn, by List, on board of Prizes, because, (over and above their proper Share) they were on these occasions allowed a shift of Cloathes (change of clothes): But if the defrauded the Company to the Value of a Dollar, in Plate, Jewels or Money, MAROONING was their punishment. This was a barbarous Custom of putting the Offender on Shore, on some desolate or uninhabited Cape or Island, with a Gun, a few Shot, a Bottle of Water, and a Bottle of Powder, to subsist with, or starve. *If the Robbery was only betwixt one another, they contented themselves with slitting the Ears and Nose of Him that was Guilty, and set him on Shore, not in an uninhabited Place, but somewhere, where he was sure to encounter Hardships.*'

III
No Person to Game at Cards or Dice for Money

IV
The Lights and Candles to be put out at eight a-Clock at Night: If any of the Crew, after that Hour, still remained inclined for Drinking, they were to do it on the open Deck; which *Roberts* believed would give a Check to their Debauches, for he was a sober Man himself, but found at length, that all his Endeavours to put an End to this Debauch, proved ineffectual.

V
To keep their Piece (firearm), Pistols, and Cutlass clean, and fit for Service: In this they were extravagantly nice, endeavouring to outdo one another, in the Beauty and Richness of their Arms, giving sometimes at an Auction (at the Mast) 30 or 40 pounds a pair, for Pistols. These were slung in Time of Service, with different coloured Ribbands, over their Shoulders,

in a Way peculiar to these Fellows, in which they took great Delight.

VI

VI No Boy or Woman to be allowed amongst them. If any Man were found seducing any of the latter Sex, and carried her to Sea, disguised, he was to suffer Death; so that when any fell into their Hands, as it chanced in the *Onslow,* they put a Sentinel immediately over her to prevent ill Consequences from so dangerous an Instrument of Division and Quarrel; but here lyes the Roguery; they contend who shall be Sentinel, which happens generally to be one of the greatest Bullies, who, to secure the Lady's Virtue, will let none lie with her but himself.

VII

To Desert the Ship, or their Quarters in Battle, was punished with Death or Marooning

VIII

No striking one another on board, but every Man's Quarrels to be ended on Shore, at Sword and Pistol, thus: The Quarter-Master of the Ship, when the Parties will not come to any Reconciliation, accompanies them to Shore with what Assistance he thinks proper, and turns the Disputants Back to back, at so many Paces Distant: At the Word of Command they turn and fire immediately, (or else the Piece is knocked out of their Hands:) If both miss, they come to their Cutlashes (cutlasses), and then he is declared Victor who draws the first Blood.

IX

No man to talk of breaking up their Way of Living, till each had shares a 1000 pounds. If in order to this, any Man should lose a Limb, or become a Cripple in their Service, he was to have 800 Dollars, out of the publick Stock, and for lesser Hurts, proportionately.

X

The Captain and Quarter-Master to receive two Shares of a Prize; the Master, Boatswain, and Gunner, one Share and a half, and other Officers one and a Quarter.

XI

The Musicians to have Rest on the Sabbath Day, but the other six Days and Nights, none without special Favour.

These, we are assured, were some of Roberts' Articles, but as they had taken Care to throw over-board the Original they had signed and sworn to, there is a great deal of Room to suspect, the Remainder contained something too horrid to be disclosed to any, except such as were willing to be Sharers in the Iniquity of them; let them be what they will, they were together the Test of all new Comers, who were initiated by an oath taken on a Bible, reserved for that Purpose only, and were subscribed to in the Presence of the worshipful Mr Roberts.'

Roberts was the only known teetotaller amongst pirate captains – his 'House of Lords' were known from their Howell Davis days as hardened drinkers (related in Captain Snelgrave's account that they took his ship off Guinea, drank the claret and brandy, threw alcohol at each other and ended up swabbing the deck with what was left) – so control was difficult for him. He also observed the Sabbath, again marking him out as a very different kind of leader.

1720 - TO THE WEST INDIES AND FOUR MORE PRIZES

Roberts seems to have been a changed man after what he saw as Kennedy's desertion. He did not seek counsel as much as previously from the Lords. He withdrew even more from his men. 'Lord' Christopher Moody, who had previously captained pirate ships, was voted sailing master until a more experienced man could be taken. 'Lord' Thomas Anstis was voted quartermaster to replace Kennedy. Jones and Dennis were re-elected boatswain and gunner. Roberts' little sloop was repaired where he had broken up the decking to make a raft. Black Bart had christened the his little sloop Fortune, and the Council decided to sail, as agreed previously, to the West Indies. There was a better chance of gaining provisions, and thousands of hiding places around the cays. Roberts also knew the area from his days as mate on the Barbados sloop.

The pirates desperately needed success after the loss of their huge treasure. Sailing past Trinidad, they spied the sloop Philippa anchored of Laquary Roads. Roberts held his distance during the night. Captain Daniel Greaves was below decks suffering from gout, but his mate John Wransford noticed a canoe approaching from the Fortune, just after dawn on January 10th, 1720. Greaves shouted at Wransford and the crew to fire their pistols at the canoe, and stop its occupants getting near the Philippa. Anstis swore at the sailors that if there was any more firing they would all be killed, and the guns fell silent. On board, Anstis announced to Captain Greaves that he was 'impounding' his boat, and the sloop was sailed to join the Fortune at Sandy Point. Roberts saw no benefit in exchanging ships - although he desperately needed a better ship like the mighty Royal Rover - and contented himself with transferring the cargo.

They took two guns, a 60-gallon cask of rum, 300 pounds of sugar, firearms, food and some slaves for menial tasks. Three of Greaves' men also wished to join, including a large man known as 'Little David' Sympson, who was to become one of the leading Lords. Luckily at this time for Roberts, the Royal Navy was preoccupied with the war with Spain, from the West Indies to the American Colonies. Near Deseada Island, close to Guadeloupe, another two merchant vessels were taken and stripped of provisions. Because of merchant distress on Jamaica and Barbados, the Leeward Isles Governor Hamilton asked Captain Rose in the Seaford to turn from anti-Spanish duties, and search for Roberts, but he could not find him. There were five Royal Navy ships stationed on and around Jamaica, with 148 guns between them, and another nine stationed at Barbados, the Leeward isles, Virginia and New York. However, because of logistical problems, there were only ever around 6 naval ships at sea, covering the open sea from Newfoundland to the Tropics, with the thousands of islets and creeks and inlets where pirates could be hidden.

Off Barbados, an inwards-bound Bristol trader was taken, although it had ten guns. Apart from clothes, gunpowder, oatmeal and beef, Black Bart gained five seamen who decided to join 'on the account'. The prize and its remaining crew was ordered not to sail for three days, and when it eventually reached Barbados, the Governor was informed that Black Bart was active nearby in the Caribbean. More ships were taken by Roberts by February 12th, 1720, including the Benjamin from Liverpool, and on the 18th the Sloop Joseph, commanded by Bonaventure Jelfes. However, these were little prizes to the conqueror of the Portuguese treasure-ship, and other pirates such as 'Jolly

Jack' Rackham were also scouring the nearby seas. The day after taking the *Joseph*, Roberts spied a small sloop, the *Sea King*, and chased it. Roberts hoisted the black flag, expecting the boat to make a run for it, but it turned towards him and hoisted its own black flag. Its pirate captain was Montigny la Palisse. Roberts' *Fortune* needed to be replaced desperately by a bigger, faster boat, and he took la Palisse as a partner to cover his weakness until he could acquire a better ship.

THE BARBADIAN EPISODE
Because of the losses to trade, Captain Witney was now ordered to take the naval ships *Rose* and *Shark* to the Leeward Isles and help Captain Rose search for Roberts, and Whitney sailed to Antigua after an 8-day delay because of sickness in his crews. Captains Roberts, La Palisse and Rackham took a few more prizes off Barbados, and the traders of Barbados decided something had to be done, as Governor Lowther had no wish to help them. (It was rumoured that he had dealt with pirates in the past, and had been recalled to London in 1714 on corruption charges, and in 1720 to be accused of taking bribes. In October 1720, he was found guilty in London on several accounts. Lowther was charged with imprisoning naval captains to prevent their chasing pirates, and found guilty of allowing trade with a Spanish ship despite the Navigation Act, and of misappropriating £28,000 of Barbadian funds.)

The merchants petitioned Lowther on February 19th, 1720 that they had to take steps to avoid certain ruin and defend themselves; as *'a certain pyrate sloop carrying 12 guns and manned with 70 men hath lately taken several vessels to windward of this island and still lyeth there to intercept their trade.'* Barbados and Jamaica were the only real British colonies in the West Indies. Lowther decided that he had to allow the petition, such was the resentment of men losing their livelihood. Governor Lowther had no men-of-war close to call to his aid, so he allowed the traders to fit out a Bristol galley, the *Summersett*, captained by the Bristolian Owen Rogers with 16 guns and 130 men (other sources give 20 guns and 80 men); and a sloop the *Philippa* commanded by Daniel Greaves, with 6 guns and 60 men (another source gives 10 guns and 60 men). The Governor gave a Letter of Marque (commission) to Captain Rogers of Bristol for the expedition against Roberts. Rogers on the galley was made Commodore, and Captain Greaves took command of the sloop. The two privateers made all speed to find Black Bart and the *Fortune*.

Rogers and Greaves left the harbour on February 22nd, and 2 days later caught up with a small French pink off Barbados. Its mizzen mast and part of its main mast had been cut down by Roberts, and its captain told Rogers that Roberts now had a smaller consort sloop, formerly from Virginia. Rogers now prepared the *Summerset* for action, bringing portable bulwarks up to the quarterdeck to minimise cannon damage, stringing netting up to impede boarding parties, and setting hammocks around the masts to disguise marksmen from the pirates. However, Greaves had fallen sullenly silent since realising that there were now two pirate ships, and refused to prepare for action. On February 26th, the two sloops were sighted, charting a course towards their two 'merchantmen'.

Rogers and Greaves now sailed on slowly alongside each other, pretending to be normal merchantmen, then suddenly piled on full sail, as if to flee the pirates. Greaves steered his ship into the protection of Rogers' port side, as Roberts approached its starboard, and Rogers fired at the *Fortune*. Now Rogers sailed past the *Fortune*, exposing the *Summersett's* starboard to a broadside, knowing that the *Fortune* would then itself be exposed to a broadside from Greaves' *Philippa*. The *Fortune's* broadside, from point-blank range, tore into the *Summersett*, killing men. Musket fire was exchanged. Black Bart's band played. Another cannon ball hit the *Summersett*, from la Palisse's *Sea King*, which promptly fled the action. However, Greaves did not fire at Roberts, and Black Bart took advantage of his luck to circle around to approach the stern of the *Summersett*. This was the easiest way to take a ship, throwing bombs of sulphur and tar onto the merchantman's deck, which would suffocate and blind its crew and its marksmen in the rigging. Swivel guns would spew glass and nails across its decks. Few guns could be brought to bear on the *Fortune*. The *Fortune* was towing a small boat full of pirates armed to the teeth, which would swarm up the sides of the *Summersett* to aid the direct attack from the boarding party. The *Philippa*, under the cowardly Greaves, moved further away from the impending action, and Roberts changed course slightly to deliver another broadside to the merchantman. However, as Roberts approached the stern, he veered away. It may have been that Black Bart thought that the *Summersett* had been damaged and could be taken by easier methods than a boarding party, or that he had spotted the hammocks, nets, barricades and numbers of men that were on this 'innocent' trading ship. Obviously she was no mere merchantman - was she a naval ship in disguise? Would the *Philippa* rejoin the fray when he had boarded and the *Fortune* was defenceless? Was it a trap? After la Palisse had fled, he had to make sure of his course of action.

The two gun decks of the *Summersett* fired into the *Fortune*. Its drummer was hit and fell off the roundhouse. Musket and pistol fire was exchanged, with pirates in the unprotected towed boat also being hit. Rogers now realised that Greaves in the other ship would not join him in the action, and altered course to yet again hit Roberts with a broadside. The lightly armed *Fortune* was hit below the waterline and now in great trouble. Some of its depleted crew were sent down to effect running repairs, and at least two of them were drowned as they lost their footing, as Roberts desperately tacked the *Fortune* to try and get away from the withering fire. The *Summersett* positioned itself for one last broadside to finish off the limping *Fortune*, and amazingly, the *Philippa* returned to the action, stationing itself between the *Summersett* and the *Fortune*, so that Rogers could not fire without hitting Greaves's sloop. Rogers believed that either Greaves would fire a last broadside into the *Fortune*, or board the severely damaged ship.

However, Greaves did nothing. Roberts took advantage, hauling up full sail. The *Fortune* came up alongside, fired a shot across the *Phillipa's* bows and hoisted Roberts' *Black Flag*. It seems that the raising of the flag was a decoy to pretend that the pirates intended to stay and fight to the death. However, Black Bart had no choice against crews that were on commission to kill him, and *cut and run*. Greaves' *Philippa* did not give chase. The *Summersett* galley gradually closed on the *Fortune*, and kept up fire from its bow chaser, killing more of Bart's crew. The pirates had to throw precious guns and heavy cargo overboard to eventually outstrip the privateers. Rogers fumed at losing his prize. By dusk Roberts had lost Rogers, but had to effect urgent repairs to his bloody ship and to tend to his wounded and dying. Almost half the crew had died or were wounded, and since Archibald Murray had left, there was no surgeon to amputate or prevent gangrene. Men were anaesthetised with rum, until they died. From henceforth Bristolians and Barbadians were added to Black Bart's pet hate of Irishmen, formerly incurred by what he thought was Kennedy's treachery. All were singled out for special treatment if captured.

The 'Weekly Journal', June 25th, 1720, noted the action as follows: *From Portsmouth in New Hampshire they tell us that a brig arrived there from Barbados in 22 days and reported that a Bristol galley and a sloop were fitted out to take a pirate ship of 12 guns that lay to windward of the island; they came up and engaged her but the pirate having a great number of men on board gave them such a warm reception that they were obliged to go back to Barbados without her. In this engagement many men were lost on both sides.'*

THE MARTINIQUE GOVERNOR
The *Fortune* sailed for 200 miles, not daring to land on St Lucia or Martinique, losing 20 men on the way. The *Fortune* landed at Dominica to make repairs, and more men died. Over half of Roberts' 70 men had perished because of the sea fight. He dared not stay long, because if their presence was reported, the French governor of nearby Martinique would send a force to destroy them. For two days they bartered with natives, took on water and provisions and cut timber to repair the *Fortune*, desperately trying to conceal their presence. Then their lookouts sighted a group of 13 naked, unarmed men. Robert Butson explained that they had been landed by the sloop *Revenge*, out of Antigua, and that this costagarda had marooned them there without clothes, food, or equipment, 3 weeks earlier. A *'garde de la coste'*, the French sloop *Revenge*, had put down thirteen Englishmen from two New England trading ships there. They included Joe Mansfield (a deserter from the *Rose*), James Phillips and Robert Butson, all later hanged at Cape Corso. Anstis had badly wanted them to join the depleted pirate force, but Roberts had told the unfortunate men that he would not *force* any of them to become pirates. The sailors eagerly signed Roberts' Articles - they desperately needed to escape the island. Within an hour, the *Fortune* made heavy way towards the relative safety of the Grenadine Islands.

However, the French Governor of Martinique had discovered that the pirates were on Dominica. Just 12 hours after the *Fortune* limped away, two armed sloops from Martinique landed and discovered from the natives that Roberts had just eluded them. Roberts and his men sailed in the unseaworthy *Fortune* to Carriacou, just 20 miles north of Grenada in the Windward Isles. He knew that the ship would be hidden on all sides by high land, while he quickly careened it and the carpenters made repairs. Roberts knew that time was of the essence - his sloop had too few guns (after jettisoning some to escape the *Summersett*), to fight properly at sea in these hostile waters. Some men were still wounded, and were fortified by a diet of land-tortoise.

Roberts now called his *Lords* to Pirate Council. He had decided that attacking ships at sea was pointless. It was a lottery as to what they would be carrying, and the fact

Black Bart's personal flags

that the merchantmen *Summersett* and *Philippa* were in fact heavily armed privateers, meant that appearances could now be deceptive. A far better plan of action would be to attack ships at anchor, and to loot the riches of the ports which supplied them. The *Lords* agreed, and the new strategy was to be followed. During this week, spirits rose, despite the lack of taverns and women, but lookouts noted that the two sloops from Martinique were combing the surrounding islands, and that they had to move quickly before they were penned in. The *Fortune* left in early March, just a half-day before the French chasers sailed into the bay. This event added Martinicans to Bart's hate-list. Around this time he had his famous flag made. Designed by himself, his personal jack-flag always now flew in action – it portrayed Black Bart holding a sand-glass and a flaming sword in each hand, with each foot resting on a skull marked *ABH* and *AMH* – 'A Barbadian's head' and 'A Martinican's Head'. His intention was to hang the governors of both islands. His personal ensign, or Jolly Roger, showed Roberts holding an hour-glass with a skeleton. The skeleton also holds a flaming lance, or arrow, and there is a heart dripping three drops of blood under the hour-glass.

THE NEWFOUNDLAND BANKS
Roberts took the *Fortune* north, through the West Indies, past the American colonies, and up towards an area which had not suffered from much piracy in these times. Newfoundland was the centre of the fishing industry, with many small vessels, and no men-of-war patrolling. It would be easy pickings after the problems of the African coast and the West Indies. Also, his old *Fortune* would be at huge risk during the worst of the hurricane season, towards August and September if he stayed in the West Indies. Indeed, he just escaped an early hurricane. On June 15th of that year, the man-of-War *Milford* was lost off Cuba escorting a Jamaican fleet to England, with another 14 ships it was escorting. In summer, the northern traffic across the Atlantic increased. The King's ships stayed at their stations, and the majority were in the West Indies.** In June 1720, naval ships were clustered at the West Indies. Jamaica had the fourth rate man of war *Mary* (320 men, 60 guns); the fifth rate *Adventure* (190,40); *Mermaid* (135,30); and the sloop *Happy* (80,14). Barbados had the 5th rate *Milford* (155,30). The Leeward Islands had the 6th rate *Rose* (115,20) and the sloop *Shark* (80,14). Off Guinea, the 5th rate *Royal Anne* Galley (190,40) and the *Lynn* (190,40) were stationed. The American mainland was protected by the following sixth raters: *Rye* off Virginia (115,20); *Flamborough* off Carolina (115 20); *Phoenix* off New York (100, 20) and *Squirrel* off New England (100, 20). The 5th rate *Kinsale* (135,30) was being used to take despatches to and from North America.

With the French and Spanish sloops and 'coastguards' (revenue cutters) also posing a threat, the West Indies had been a dangerous place for Black Bart. Off the English colony of North America, he could acquire a better ship, at the very least. It seems that he sold his slaves and some goods in New England on the way up to Newfoundland, where he captured and looted around a dozen vessels including a pink, by mid-June 1720. There were too many captives now, so he sent all those unwilling to join him on a captured brigantine to Newfoundland. They obviously raised the alarm. In June he raided the small harbour of Ferryland, and burned the largest ship, the Admiral's, as a warning to the townspeople not to become involved. Another ship was looted. There was no resistance to this unexpected threat from any ship or the port.

Roberts plundered some more shipping, as he headed south, and sent a message to the major port of Trepassey that he was about to visit them. Now that the coastal towns knew that a pirate ship was in the area, it was pointless trying to nose into any harbours by stealth, as when he took the Sagrada Familia. He also knew that crews and their masters would tend to stay ashore, rather than risk their lives. On June 21st, Roberts unfurled his black flag of skull and cutlass, set his musicians playing, fired a broadside and roared into Trepassey harbour, Newfoundland. There were 1200 men from 22 sloops in the harbour, but few were aboard their ships. With just 70 men and ten guns, Roberts had made directly for the Bideford Merchant, under Admiral Babidge, one of the richest men in Newfoundland. Babidge scrambled onto a dinghy to escape, and Thomas Anstis led the boarding party aboard the biggest ship in the port. The Fortune fired a broadside into the wooden houses along the harbour-side, but there was no reaction.

Roberts sent a message that all the captains were to come to the Fortune, and berated them that they had not defended their ships, nor welcomed him as a distinguished guest. It seems that the recent deaths in battle had affected Black Bart's state of mind. As an example, he tied Babidge to the mast and had him flogged. He told them that at the sound of his morning gun, they must come to the Fortune every morning, to help him oversee the looting of their ships, otherwise the boats would be burned. Roberts disabled every boat to stop any escapes, except for a two-masted, square-rigged Bristol 16-gun brig under Captain Coplestone. It was the ideal replacement for the Fortune. Batches of up to 50 pirates were allowed ashore at night to enjoy the local taverns and prostitutes, but Roberts stayed aboard, supervising the conversion of the brig to his liking. By late-June, Black Bart was ready to leave. He told the captains that he intended to sail to St Mary's, where he could commandeer a good ship belonging to a Mr Hall. As he prepared to depart, he reneged on his promise, and burned all the boats in the harbour.

The Weekly Journal reported the event as follows: 'A pyrate in a small sloop of 12 guns and 160 men entered Trepassy on Tuesday the 21st inst., and made himself master of the said harbour and of all the ships there, being 22 sails and 250 shallops. He made the masters all prisoners and beat some of them heartily for their cowardice for not making any resistance. The Admiral, one Babidge, in the Bideford Merchant, suffered most because he and all his hands left their ship with jack, ensign and pendant flying, his guns all loaden, in order to defend themselves but the pyrate was close alongside him, struck his colours, hoisted their own, and fired all his guns. They cut his masts and several others close by the deck. He cut all the other ships' cables in junks and their shrouds. He seized one Copleston's ship for himself, and set all the ship's carpenters to work to fit her for this purpose. They threatened to burn all the rest and to hang one of the masters at least for their incivility in not waiting upon him to make him welcome at his entrance. He destroyed about 30 sail, French and English, on the Banks.'

Black Bart now repeated the act in St Mary's harbour, and a letter from the small port of Placentia near Trepassy stated: 'There are many ships drove in here by the pirates who infest our coast and in one of our next ports they have burnt and destroyed 26 ships and a great number of fishing craft. Those pirates have now destroyed near 150 boats and 26 ships at Trepassy and St Mary's which, if a communication had been cut overland (roads through the thick forests), it had not been a two-days march to have rescued these harbours where the pirates have been repairing their ships for 14 days past, not could any vessel sail from hence to reprieve them if we had any ships of force.' Even the Governor of New England was moved to report of 'The Black Captain', 'one cannot withhold admiration for his bravery and cunning.'

Roberts returned to Trepassey immediately. He also recruited some cod-splitters, who were only too happy to leave their terrible jobs. Many men joined Roberts' crew from his Newfoundland ravages. West Country fishing vessels brought over every year many poor labourers who were paid low wages, and who by contract had to pay for their voyage back to England. By day they fished, split and dried fish and warded off the bitter winter evenings by drinking 'black strap' (a vicious combination of rum, molasses and chowder beer). The cost of the 'black strap' meant that many could not afford their way back home, and were compelled to agree articles of servitude that kept them on the island over the winter. Their new masters now charged them exorbitant prices for food and clothing, so that they were 'bound' to them for the next season's hard labour, and so on and so on. It is no wonder that these poor men readily joined the pirates or sometimes seized a small boat or shallop and traded 'on their own account'.

A pirate was flogged by Anstis for trying to conceal a bolt of cloth for himself. Now Black Bart feared no-one. He came across a French flotilla of six sail near the Newfoundland Banks and captured them all. He chose the best of the French ships, a square-rigged brigantine and transferred all the guns from his new flagship to the new ship, which he called the Good Fortune. With 28 guns, it was a powerful ship, and he set his Fortune galley adrift. The next day he came across the Fortune again, and put his French prisoners on it. He said he would only 'force' English sailors to go on the account with him. Although it did not handle as well as the Fortune, the Good Fortune was a powerful ship, in which they could enter action stations with far more confidence. More boats were taken, including another four French vessels, during which time Montigny la Palisse unexpectedly rejoined him, apologising for his actions off Barbados.

After the hard work in the Gulf of Guinea and the West Indies, taking ten ships, Bart had now taken another sixty merchant ships and one-hundred and fifty fishing vessels, in just a few weeks. Among the vessels recorded taken in June and July were the *Expectation* of Topsham, and a brigantine from Teignmouth. Joseph Nossiter joined from the *Expectation*. Among those captured and sunk in July were the brigantine *Thomas* of Bristol, the pink *Richard* of Bideford, the *Willing Mind* of Poole, the *Blessing* of Lymington, and the *Happy Return*. James Harris joined from the *Richard*. The boatswain Thomas Wills, who loved reading, also joined Roberts from the *Richard*. John Parker and Hugh Harris joined from the *Willing Mind* and Robert Crow from the *Happy Return*. John Walden of the *Blessing* joined, who would feature strongly in Black Bart's later career. A Dutch ship was taken after resistance off Cape Broyle, and its crew pleaded successfully to Roberts not to burn their ship.

MORE NEWFOUNDLAND PRIZES
On July 13th Captain Thomas Cary (Curry) on the sloop *Samuel* was bound for Boston from England. Seeing two ships approaching, he did not expect pirates this far north, and surrendered immediately upon the hoisting of the black flags, the musicians playing and the firing of warning shots. Roberts and la Palisse took over £10,000 worth of goods and threatened the passengers to make them tell where their valuables were hidden. Charles Johnson wrote in 1724: *'The Samuel was a rich ship, and had several Passengers on board who were used very roughly, in order to make them discover their Money, threatening them every Moment with Death, if they did not resign every Thing up to them. They tore up the Hatches and entered the Hold like a Parcel of Furies, and with Axes and Cutlashes, cut and broke open all the Bales, Cases and Boxes, they could lay their Hands on; and when any Goods came on Deck, that they did not like to carry aboard, instead of tossing them into the Hold again, threw them over-board into the Sea; all this was done with incessant Cursing and Swearing, more like Fiends than Men. They carried with them Sails, Guns, Powder, Cordage, and £8,000, or £9,000 worth of the choicest Goods; and told Captain Cary that they should accept no Act of Grace; that the King and Parliament might be damned with their Acts of Grace for them; neither would they go to Hope Point (London) to be hanged a-sun-drying as Kidd's and Bradish's crews were, but if we are captured we will set fire to the powder with a pistol, and all go merrily to Hell together.'* 'The Boston News Letter' also commented that the pirates behaved *'like a parcel of furies, breaking open every bale and packing-case aboard the Samuel in search for plunder.'* The pirates took their time, fearing no-one, to ensure that they properly stripped the ship. Captain Cary noted that they took 48 hours to despoil the *Samuel*.

His men took two heavy cannon, sails, powder, rope, and forty barrels of gunpowder, before a bejewelled, crimson-frocked Roberts stepped aboard the *Samuel*, asking for men to join him. Since taking up a pirating career, the Black Captain had totally transformed from a dour ship's mate to a dandy. Several joined Roberts, including Hugh Menzies, pleading to Captain Cary would he would state that they had been *'forced'*. Anstis found the *Samuel's* mate, Harry Glasby, hiding in the hold, and he was thrown into the sea, and then made to join Roberts' crew for his deception. This was extremely rare for Roberts, who had boasted that, like Howell Davis, he never took a man against his will. He must have been in dire need of another experienced sailing-master to take the weight off his shoulders. Roberts would only

Newfoundland Fish-splitters

allow experienced seamen to join his ships. One of the House of Lords commented to Captain Cary at this time that *'if we are captured, we will set fire to the powder with a pistol, and all go merrily to Hell together.'*

Bart was discussing whether to burn the ship on July 15th, when a new sail was spotted on the horizon, and the *Samuel* was left with Captain Cary, while the *Sea King* and *Good Fortune* gave chase to take a merchant snow from Bristol under Captain Bowles. On July 16th, the *Little York*, out of Virginia was taken, on the same day as the Bristol sloop *Sidbury*. From the *Sidbury*, two men named William Williams, Roger Scott and a William Fernow gladly joined Roberts' crew. The day after, the Bristol snow *Phoenix* was taken, making six merchantmen in five days. Richard Harries and David Littlejohn joined from the *Phoenix*. Roberts now had a crew of *'sea-artists'*, skilled seamen who left miserable lives to join a successful ship. All were *'forced'*, but this was a voluntary farce as some sort of defence in the event of their capture. On July 18th, Roberts took Captain James Phillips' *Little York*, out of Bristol, off Virginia when William Taylor, Thomas Owen and James Greenham joined. On the same day Captain Thomas's *Love* of Lancaster was also captured off Virginia, when John Jaynson joined. Thus Roberts had taken 8 ships in 7 days. Also in July he took a ship of 26 guns and its consort sloop, with 200 men on both ships, back on the Newfoundland Banks

In October, *Appleby's Original Weekly Journal* reported that *'two light men-of-war are ordered for Newfoundland in quest of Roberts and other pirates who continue to commit great depredations on our merchant ships that way.'* It was too late for the *Rose* and the *Shark*, which sailed from the West Indies up to Newfoundland to eradicate *'the pyrates that infest there.'* *'That Great Pyrate'* had disappeared.

BACK TO THE CARIBBEAN
Black Bart was now famed from Britain to America, from the West Indies to the coast of Africa. He had sensed that it was time to move. It was thought that he had gone to Africa or Madagascar, or had been lost at sea. The Governor of New England had noted that *'one cannot with-hold admiration for his bravery and courage'*, while the Governor of Virginia fulminated against him. The Royal Africa Company and the Admiralty changed their policies towards piracy, under pressure from London merchants. *The American colonies started to wonder if they were better off as an*

independent country instead of paying taxes for a non-existent defence. The Royal Navy made the case that it needed more investment from the Government to help trade and retain the colonies. Forces were gathering that would spell the end of the '*Golden Age of Piracy*'.

In fact, Roberts had unfinished business with the governors of Martinique and Barbados. Booty had dried up as transatlantic shipping almost halted, as did shipping along the North American coast. With the winter approaching, his men wanted to return to the sunny climes of the Caribbean, now that the hurricane season had ended there, where there were hundreds of hidden bays to drink and while away their hours. Harry Glasby (Gillespie) was appointed sailing-master, and had invaluable knowledge of these coastal waters. He also altered the rigging of the *Good Fortune* to make it almost as fast and manoeuvrable as la Palisse's sloop. The dour Northerner Glasby, bemoaning his lot, was curt with Roberts and Anstis, but friendly with the coarse Londoner Lord Valentine Ashplant. One day a pirate hit Glasby to the deck, being tired of his stubborn, unfriendly attitude. Ashplant leaped on the offender and half-strangled him before being pulled off. After that day, no-one harmed Harry Glasby.

Roberts now had Anstis to run the ship and Glasby to sail it. He dressed up in his lace and crimson finery and freshly powdered wigs every day, rested in his Great Cabin, or walked the quarter-deck, incessantly drinking tea. He had taken over 100 ships, the most successful pirate in history, and he promised his drink-sodden crew a thousand captures. It is difficult to know what forces drove Roberts - he was still a teetotaller, an outsider who did not consort with tavern harlots, a thoughtful, brooding tall man who had the crew's respect as being '*pistol-proof*'. Roberts was in no hurry to reach the West Indies. In August, Captain Wallace Fensilon's sloop was taken off South Carolina, with supplies of fresh water and 8 hogsheads of rum. James Clements joined Roberts' crew, along with Fensilon's mate and carpenter. Before Fensilon reached Virigina, Captain Jack Rackham also boarded him and stripped the ship of its few remaining provisions.

Roberts made for the island of Deseada (Desirade, off Guadeloupe in the Lesser Antilles) to get fresh provisions, and to barter his booty ashore with smugglers. A hurricane hit them before they reached its shelter. The top-sails were furled hastily. In the storm La Palisse's *Sea King* vanished. A cannon broke loose on the *Good Fortune* and smashed into the gunwhales. Sailing the gale out, Roberts reached the tiny island to find it deserted. There were traces of camp fires and of boats being drawn up in the sand, but no smugglers. Roberts decided to make for Carriacou again to careen the *Good Fortune*. Incredibly, on the journey, la Palisse linked up with him again. On September 4th, the pirates sailed into the lagoon to find a merchant captain, Robert Dunn of the sloop *Relief*, catching turtles there. Friendly negotiations were held with the merchant captain, while the three crews feasted on turtle stew. Dunn later reported that the pirates had kept him prisoner for 3 weeks, supplying fresh turtles to them, and that their ships had 28 and 6 guns. Valentine Ashplant concocted his favourite variation of rumfustian for a party. He mixed eggs, beer, sherry and gin, added brown sugar, cinnamon and nutmeg and heated the brew until it was ready to drink.

Over the days, Dunn's sloop was loaded with goods that the pirates wished to sell, which he would take to sell at Basseterre on St Christopher (St Kitts). The *Good Fortune* was careened and repaired, and Roberts agreed to meet Dunn off St Kitts on September 26th. The deal was that the pirates should take half of the revenue, otherwise they would burn the settlements on St Kitts. Black Bart renamed the *Good Fortune* as the *Royal Fortune*, and renamed the *Sea King* the new *Good Fortune*. While the pirates lazed and drank on the beach, three forced men tried to escape on the 17th, but were quickly caught on the 18th, on the small island. On September 19th the pirates took a French sloop carrying brandy and wine. On here was held the trial of the three deserters. After being flogged, two were pardoned by the Pirate Council, but the third was condemned to marooning as an example. Towards the end of September he was stripped naked and put ashore on a half-mile islet, with just a few trees for cover. Anstis threw him a flask of water, a musket, one lead ball and a small amount of powder so that he could shoot himself. It appears that this man was the luckless Richard Luntly, a carpenter captured by Howell Davis on the Guinea Coast. Now in Roberts' crew, he had been heard conspiring with other forced men to take the ship and sail her to the West Indies and freedom. Reported to Roberts and the quartermaster, '*immediately all hands were called up to know what they should do with us, some of them was for shooting us, others not, and so they consented to put us on a desert island.*' Rescued by an English ship, the unlucky Luntley was tried for consorting with the '*great Pyrate Roberts*' at an Admiralty Court in Scotland. He complained '*we were forced men, compelled by force of arms to do things that our conscience thought to be unlawful*', but he was condemned and hung at Leith on January 11th, 1721.

It appears that the luckless Captain Cane was again captured around this time, and rum and sugar taken from him. The *Royal Fortune* sailed on to reach the waters off St Kitts at dusk on September 25th. Roberts waited all day in Basseterre Roads upon the 26th, but suspected Dunn of betraying him when he saw the cannon in the forts covering Basseterre harbour being moved. Fort Smith, overlooking one side of Basseterre, had better fortifications and firepower than another fort at Bluff Point, on the other side of the harbour, so Black Bart decided to attack on the Bluff Point side. Militiamen were despatched to all four forts on the island by its governor, Lieutenant-General Christopher William Mathew, who was suspicious of the strange ship lying outside the harbour. While Mathew was preparing the defences, Roberts hoisted his new pennant with the Barbadian and Martinique skulls, and early in the morning sailed swiftly into the harbour. All the ships anchored in the Road immediately struck their flags att he sound of Roberts' musicians and the sight of his ships. A ship's boat rowed towards them, and asked what they wanted. The two *sea-artists* upon it, the Mary and Martha's mate Bridstock Weaver, and its boatswain George Smith, were swiftly made to sign Roberts' Articles, as five ships were quickly looted. In the harbour, one ship under Captain Fowles was grappled as she briefly fought back.

Captain Wilcox of the *Mary and Martha* argued with the boarding party, and for his impertinence, his ship was burnt. Captain Cox's *Greyhound* was also burnt, because Owen Rogers had a hatred for ships from the port where he had been press-ganged.

The *Greyhound's* Welsh mate, James Skyrme, became an important member of Black Bart's crew, and willingly signed articles for *Barti Ddu*. Another of the five ships, Monsieur Pomier's French sloop, was towed out to sea, as Roberts considered using it for his own purposes. Roberts wanted to take Captain Hingstone's new ship, as it had a steering-wheel instead of the traditional whipstaff, but Hingstone had taken the wheel ashore with him. Captain Henry Fowles of the fifth vessel discovered that Roberts needed fresh meat, and offered to send a letter asking for sheep and goats to be brought to the harbour-side. The letter was dated September 27th, 1720. Fowles informed Roberts that Dunn had not been treacherous. He had been caught unloading his smuggled goods two days before, and was threatened with hanging. He told the governor that if he was hung, the island would be attacked. Thus Mathew began his preparations at about the same time as the pirates hove into view. Roberts was now in control of the town, and wanted to provision his ship for a quick getaway, before he allowed his men ashore to get roaring drunk. As evening approached, he moved the *Royal Fortune*, the *Good Fortune* and the Pomier's and Hingstone's ships out to sea, out of the range of the forts' gunnery.

Carcasses were shipped to the pirates, but Hingstone refused to send his precious steering wheel, so his ship was set alight. Some of Hingstone's seamen were sent with messages from Roberts. One was to the Governor of nearby Nevis, stating that Roberts intended to visit him next and burn the settlement, because he had hanged some men from the *Royal Rover* some months before. The other letter was for Governor Mathew of the Leeward Islands. Captain Hingston gave this letter from Roberts to Lieutenant-Governor Mathew, which reads:

Royal Fortune
September 27th, 1720
'This comes expressly from me to let you know that had you come off as you ought to a done and drank a glass of wine with me and my company I should not harmed the least vessel in your harbour. Farther it is not your guns you fired that affrighted me or hindered our coming on shore but the wind not proving to our expectation that hindered it. The Royal Rover you have already burnt and used barbarously some of our men, but we now have a ship as good as her, and for revenge you may assure yourselves here and hereafter not to expect anything from our hands but what belongs to a pirate. As farther, Gentlemen, that poor fellow you have in prison at Sandy Point is entirely ignorant and what he hath was gave him and so prey make conscience for once let me beg you and use that man as an honest man and not as a C. (Criminal) If we hear any otherwise you may expect not to have any quarters to any of your island.*
Yours,
(signed) *Bartholomew Roberts'*

It seems that the 'criminal' referred to was one of his old crew from the *Rover*, left behind by Kennedy.

Mathew had worked through the night bringing 13 new cannon in from the other forts and repositioning them to defend the bay much better. The next morning the *Royal Fortune* re-entered Basseterre to take back Captain Fowles and two of his men, but were hit by seven cannon balls from the fort. His 13 guns, including the 24-pounder, fired two rounds before Roberts escaped, his sails ripped. He gave Wilcox Pomier's sloop, left Fowles' boat at anchor and headed towards Nevis for his next assignment, knowing that Basseterre was now a lost cause. However, prevailing winds forced him to change his mind. The crew needed money, after Captain Dunn's unfortunate capture, and Roberts decided to fix up the *Royal Fortune* and reprovision at St Bartholomew's, the 8-mile square French possession of St Barthelemy. Its governor has precious few resources, and little fresh water, and the rocky scrub yielded little food. He therefore was known to be susceptible to giving leniency to pirates, in return for trade. The grateful inhabitants of the island took all the treasure from Newfoundland to St Christopher's, into a warehouse, and the pirates gave them generous terms. The governor was presented with a gold chain worth more than a year's salary by Roberts. The pirates accepted not just coin, but payment in kind at the two small taverns and with the women of the island. For three weeks the pirates roistered happily ashore, but Bart kept a heavily-armed night-watch on each of his ships, to prevent desertion by the forced men, or a *soft farewell* by some disaffected pirates.

Roberts next took his ships to Tortola in the Virgin Islands, and took a 22-gun brig there. He converted it to the new *Royal Fortune*, and gave the furious captain his rotting hulk in exchange. On October 25th the new *Royal Fortune* was at St Lucia, near Martinique, and looted an English brig lying there. He also took Monsieur Courtel's sloop to act as a storeship, and prevent the *Royal Fortune* and *Good Fortune* being weighed down when chasing merchantmen. In total, fourteen English and French ships were taken between October 23 and 26, 1720. A hundred miles north of St Lucia, Roberts' small fleet came across a Dutch ship. The Dutch interloper had 30 guns and 90 men lay in harbour of St Lucia. Suddenly there was cacophony of noise and banging as the 32-gun *Royal Fortune* and 18-gun *Sea King* sailed into the harbour under the black flag.

However, the Dutchman, faced with 350 pirates, still did not strike its colours, and prevented grappling by using booms and fenders. There followed a 4-hour gun battle – with many lost on both sides, but the beleaguered Dutch ship had no room to manoeuvre. Roberts knew that the larger 'interloper' would definitely resist vigorously even against 350 pirates, and carried on a broadside battle, while Courtel's storeship/sloop and the *Good Fortune* tried to attack its poorly defended stern. (Dutch 'interlopers' were forbidden to trade with the British, under the Navigation Acts, but were known to carry large amounts of gold and coin). After a horrendous, bloody encounter, the Dutchman was boarded, and her crew all killed. La Palisse went on to loot 15 vessels in the nearby harbour, and Roberts' bloodthirsty crews went on an orgy of vengeance for their recent losses, slaughtering every Dutchman they found aboard the ships.

The great Dutch ship was taken by Black Bart to be his new flagship, again called the *Royal Fortune*. A deserter from the Royal Navy's *Rose*, John Mansfield, volunteered to join Roberts, but proved to be a terrible drunk. Roberts' fleet now comprised the 48-gun *Royal Fortune*, the large Tortola brig, the St Lucia sloop and la Palisse's *Good*

Fortune. He was at the zenith of his powers. The *Royal Fortune* held 180 hardened pirates and *sea-artists*. It had seven 2-pound and 3-pound guns in its bows; four 4-pound minions on each side; six falconers on each side, each firing 6 pounds of shot, twelve half-ton demi-culverins, each firing 8-pound cannon balls, and four massive 12-pound cannon - 44 guns in total, with a vast assortment of types of shot with different uses from disembowelling men to bringing down rigging. The French Leeward Isles Governor reported that in 4 days at the end of October 1720, Black Bart had '*seized, burned or sunk 15 French and English vessels and one Dutch interloper of 42 guns at Dominica'*.

The *Mary and Martha* of St Christophers was now taken again, under a different captain, Wilson in December 1720, when George Smith of Wales joined the pirate crew. Martinique's governor had heard of Roberts' new pennant featuring his head, and wrote anxiously several times to the Governor of Nevis, asking that Captain Whitney's *Rose* be sent to protect them. The London Journal reported in January 1721, '*we are in expectations of hearing of a bloody action with the pyrates in the West Indies, three of His Majesty's ships well-manned being gone from Barbadoes in quest of them upon information of the place of their rendezvous*. Roberts was again becoming nervous - he sensed that forces were moving against him. In Dominica he had let it be known that his next target was St Eustatia, but stayed near, but out of sight of Dominica, wondering where to go. Back north was unattractive - the weather was bad. Africa beckoned once again, from where he could explore the Red Sea and the Indian Oceans. Preparing for Council, the ships sheltered in a hidden Dominica Bay. After a couple of days, Harry Glasby and two other men tried to escape but were hunted down as they climbed the hills to reach the townships on the other side of the island.

The jury was all for hanging, shooting or marooning them for desertion until Lord Valentine Ashplant stood up and stated '*By God, Glasby shall not die, damn me if he shall'*. He sat down and smoked his pipe, ignoring his fellow '*Lords'* on the jury. The other pirates had unanimously agreed, and shouted that they must die, whereupon Ashplant again removed his pipe to stand up, and argued '*God damn ye gentlemen, I am as good as the best of you, damn my soul if I ever turned my back to any man in my life, or ever will, by God; Glasby is an honest fellow notwithstanding this misfortune, and I love him, Devil damn me, if I don't. I hope he'll live and repent of what he has done; but damn me, if he must die, I'll die alongside with him.'* He then pulled out his brace of pistols and pointed them at the judges, who agreed that Glasby should be acquitted. The other two unfortunates were tied to the mast and shot dead, however, not having as effective a defence counsel to support them. Glasby was never to be allowed ashore again. Ashplant seems to have been listened to, as he was the chief brewer or distiller on ship - he had a genius for making something alcoholic and potable out of anything that was available, and thus a man of some importance.

In mid-November, Roberts sailed north towards the Bermudas, to pick up the currents and winds for Sierra Leone and Africa. Again, he was one step ahead of his pursuers. The brig was leaking, and with the sloop was left to drift away. *Appleby's Original Weekly Journal* commented in March 1721 '*A pirate of 40 guns and 2 smaller ships caused havoc on the coast of Carthagena and St Martha (in the West Indies). They have taken several rich French ships from Petit-Guaves and 2 Dutch and about 5 English ships and sloops. But we hear since that the pirates have left for Cuba and design to go from there to Martinique. They take any nation's ships. What exploits our men-of-war have done against them we hear but little.'*

Near the Bermudas, the pirates bore down upon Captain Thomas Bennett's *Thomas Emanuel*, which immediately surrendered. After looting, it was towed as a storeship, but its captain reported that its lightened weight put it in danger of sinking, in heavy and worsening seas. A boat was sent to rescue Bennett and his men, and the towrope was cut. Heading towards Africa, Roberts was going to land and reprovision on the Cape Verde Islands, when he saw two merchantmen off the coast and headed to intercept them. However, they were escorted by two Portuguese men-of-war, one with 40 guns and the other 80. La Palisse veered off again, repeating his previous cowardly departure, while Roberts attacked, remembering the glory of Bahia. The Portuguese naval ships piled on full sail and fled. Roberts chased the merchantmen but found that he was being pushed by the winds away from the islands and their precious water supply. Desperately he and Jones calculated that they could just reach the most southerly island, Brava. However, constantly adverse great winds meant that they missed it. Gillespie (Glasby) now tried to bring the *Royal Fortune* around again, and failed, leaving them heading back towards the Americas. The contrary winds meant that they could no longer find a safe nearby landfall, so there was no choice but to return to the Caribbean and wait for more favourable winds to take them again to Africa. Roberts calculated their quickest landfall to be Surinam, 700 leagues (2100 miles) away, using the favourable north-easterly Trade Winds. They had one hogshead (63 gallons) of water, rationed to one cupful a day for the 124 men. After a few days the ration was a mouthful a day. Men drank their own urine over and over until it was almost black. They wetted their lips with sea-water so that they could open their mouths to speak. Those that ate too much died horrible deaths. The wiser and older pirates, the *Lords*, rationed themselves to one mouthful of bread a day, and just rested in whatever shade they could find. Those who drank sea-water died in agony. Sails were rigged to catch and trap sea-mists at night as precious water. Fever and dysentery racked the ships. Water rations dropped to a swallow a day. Anstis guarded the near empty water barrel, while the men died agonising deaths.

At last la Palisse and Roberts reached the mouth of the River Maroni in Surinam, a remarkable navigational feat for men who were close to death. They had no water at all for the last two days of sailing. They headed north. In December 1720, they landed on Tobago to reprovision. With the latest acquisition, Roberts felt strong enough to try and capture his hated enemy, the governor of Martinique, who had tried to capture him in Carriacou. Despite the pull of 'hiraeth', he could never return to Pembrokeshire - he was now too famous. (Hiraeth is a Welsh word, difficult to describe, which is the longing for home felt by Welshmen outside their country. Many expatriates return to Wales, thus there are not the huge colonies of Irish and Scots in former English colonies. There are 40,000,000 people in the USA who declare Irish ancestry, against 2,000,000 Welsh. The Welsh are the salmon of the world). A pardon may be extended to other, lesser, pirates, but not to Roberts. The English, French,

Spanish and Dutch - the day's great international powers - all wanted his blood. The Americas offered no outlet. As he drank his tea, he knew that his position was only as secure as the next successful capture. After filling up with loot, the pirates then wanted to spend it in an orgy of onshore drunkenness and whoring. Then it was off to sea again, avoiding men-of-war and increasing anti-pirate activity, looking for increasingly heavily-armed merchantmen, and the cycle repeated itself. He was forever trapped as a pirate. Roberts seemed to celebrate his safe arrival back in the New World by going on a terrific rampage. His original plan to try to make for Africa was forgotten. He wanted to go out in a blaze of glory.

1721
In early January, Bart sailed quickly (and presciently) to avoid Barbados and headed for Pigeon Island, just a mile off St Lucia, and on the 13th he found a sloop and a brig anchored in a small bay. Captain Benjamin Norton's Rhode Island brig, the *Sea King*, was stripped of its guns, and used to replace la Palisse's clapped-out sloop. Captain Richard Simes' Barbados sloop, the *Fisher*, was chased, ran aground and unfortunately caught fire. Captain Norton offered, like Captain Dunn, to trade some of their plunder at Rhode Island. The old *Good Fortune* was burnt, and the *Royal Fortune* and new *Good Fortune* for the next two weeks took some more trading ships off St Lucia, forcing some more men to join them to replace those they had lost on the dreadful Atlantic crossing. He took a much-needed surgeon off one boat, possibly from Captain John Rogers' sloop the *Saint Anthony*. He allowed Captain Simes and some prisoners to sail off on one captured sloop, along with Captain Bennett, who was lucky to have survived the crossing from Cape Verde to Surinam.

While there, two sloops, one under Captain Porter, and the *Adventure* under Captain Tuckerman came onto the island. According to Defoe, they greeted the great Pirate Roberts with the following message: '*We have heard of your fame and achievements, and we have put in to learn your art and wisdom in the business of pirating, since we are of the same honourable design as yourself. We hope, that with the communication of your knowledge, we shall also receive your charity as we are in want of necessities for such adventures.*' Not averse to such flattery, Barti gave them powder, guns and provisions, and swapped eighteen of his captured negroes for four white pirates, including the Welshman John Coleman who wanted to join his crew. Off Dominica, a Dutch interloper was taken after a brief fight. *El Puerto del Principe* from Flushing was now towed behind Roberts' ship while it was decided what to do with her.

The fleet of two great brigantines (the *Royal Fortune* and *El Puerto del Principe*), another brig (the *Good Fortune*) and two small pirate sloops, now sailed towards Guadeloupe, and approached Basseterre with no colours flying. The *Royal Fortune* hoisted French colours, sailed into the harbour and fired across a French flyboat which was anchored out of reach of the fort's guns. As its crew fled in boats, a tow-line was attached, and the prize was taken out to the open seas. Roberts now took his crews for '*rest and recreation*' in Hispaniola, and '*boot-topped*' the *Royal Fortune* and the *Good Fortune*, one after the other. He seems to have suspected that the seas were too quiet for comfort. While Captain Whitney, in the *Rose* was not particularly interested in battling with pirates, more in lucrative dealing with them, Captain Durrel in the *Seahorse* was a far different 'kettle of fish'. At Boston the Council had suggested that he went down to protect the West Indian colonies, and he had just missed Roberts off Barbados in early-January. Roberts had seemed to have sensed there was a problem at this time, and had piled on sail to keep away from the Barbadian shipping lanes. Durrell could not reach Roberts off Martinique because of prevailing winds, and while he waited at Barbados, he sent for 90 more men and more munitions from Massachusetts. While waiting, Durrell had press-ganged 86 Barbadians by early February. At this time, the Admiralty had sent the *Swallow* and *Weymouth* to Africa to protect the slave-trade from piracy.

While Durrell was frustrated in his attempts to reach Martinique, Black Bart moved his fleet to careen properly on Mona, just off Puerto Rico, but sea conditions meant that he landed a hundred miles away, at Bennet's Cay, in Bahia de Samana, Eastern Hispaniola. Porter and Tuckerman left for Jamaica, where they were thought of as honest merchantmen. For a week the pirates lazed, sang, gambled and drank Valentine's Ashplant's potent 'rumbullion', while the brigs were careened properly, finishing off the earlier 'boot-topping'. Dan Harding joined from the *El Puerto del Principe*. The pirates revelled the nights away. Although Roberts did not drink, and hated his crew drinking at sea, he did not mind them carousing in secret places such as Bennet's Cay. While the mayhem was going on, Harry Glasby and nine other forced men tried to escape, but became lost in the dense forests. They returned after three days, professing that they had got lost chasing pigs. Luckily they were believed, and lived to tell the tale. Roberts now trusted Captain Norton a little more, and asked him to examine the cargo of the *El Puerto del Principe* with him, with the intention of fencing it in Rhode Island. Porter and Tuckerman rejoined Roberts. Their 'front' as merchantmen in Port Royal, Jamaica, was crumbling. Local people had discovered that Porter and his brother had been in New Providence to accept Woodes Rogers' Pardon to all pirates, and Tuckerman had been previously imprisoned for assisting in the escape of the pirate Stede Bonnet. (Bonnet was an unusual man, a gentleman estate-owner who had turned to piracy as an optional career to escape his nagging wife). Tuckerman was later taken to London on piracy charges, but his fate is unknown.

Norton was given the *El Puerto del Principe* and a skeleton crew of his own trusted men who would not talk to the authorities, to sail to Rhode Island, full of 'normal' trading goods like food, cocoa, ironmongery, cloth and flour which were not needed by the pirates. All 'incriminating' goods such as gold and jewellery were left with Roberts. An agreement was made that they would return with cash for Roberts in 6 weeks, meeting off South Carolina, where Roberts would refill the brig's hold with more captured goods. It seems that Roberts now had a trusted, and far less risky, channel of distribution for his gains. Captain Norton now sailed his great ship to Tarpaulin Cove, New England, but his protestations that Black Bart had 'given' him the ship were unfortunately not believed.

In February Roberts took the sloop *Mayflower*, and Joseph Moore joined his crew, and soon after Black Bart took a ship off Guadeloupe, with 600 hogsheads of sugar, and set fire to her. On February 18th, Roberts moved in on the harbour of St Lucia yet again, seeing another large Dutch interloper, with 75 men and 22 guns, lying in the roads. The settlement's inhabitants witnessed a fierce battle which lasted for hours, with the Dutchman putting out fenders and booms to prevent the *Royal Fortune* boarding. Gunner Dennis fired a close broadside, and the *Good Fortune* attacked its stern with swivel guns, ensuring that the decks were clear of crewmen to defend against the inevitable boarding party. Resistance was futile, and Anstis, wearing a bright yellow bandana, was seen to be attaching tow-ropes to the ship. The few survivors were killed, and the capture was repaired by Roberts' carpenters. Anstis, Richard Jones and the seasoned members of the *House of Lords* now took over the ship, while the *Royal Fortune* and *Good Fortune* were sent southwards for a later rendezvous. Roberts had a debt to repay in Martinique.

Roberts cheekily took the 22-gun Dutch interloper as a decoy, under Dutch colours, alongside the harbours of Martinique. He slowly sailed past Vauclin, Sainte Marie, Morrain and St Pierre, Schoelcher and the Fort de France. This was a sign for the islanders that there were cheap Guinea slaves available from this unlicensed trader, a chance to make some quick profits. Bart then went to St Luce, an isolated bay in the south of Martinique, where the Martinican vessels always came to make their illicit trades. Sloops were fitted out to go and fetch the slaves, and one by one they approached Roberts' ship over a few days. 14 boats, laden with gold and coin for barter were captured in this way, and were also filled with tradable goods. Roberts threw each captain and crew into the hold. These islanders were now badly abused by Roberts' crew, some being suspended from the yard-arms for target practice. His feelings towards Martinique had festered, and Roberts did not attempt to stop the cruelty. Every sailor was whipped or killed. Thirteen of the sloops were burned, and the remaining captives put on the fourteenth sloop, and told to tell the governor that Roberts 'hoped we should always meet with such a Dutch trade as this was'.

Around this time Christian Tranquebar was on a Danish ship attacked by Roberts in two vessels, and reported that Roberts' ship was manned by 180 white men and 48 French Creole blacks, and that his consort brig was crewed by 100 white men and 40 French blacks. On the *Royal Fortune*, Roberts had mounted 42 cannon, from 4-pounders to 12-pounders, plus another 7 guns. The Governor of Martinique now implored Governor Hamilton of Antigua for aid. Hamilton thus wrote to the Lords Commissioners for Trade and Plantations that 'The Great Pyrate Roberts' was wreaking havoc around the islands, and that the French Governor-General in the Caribbean wished to act jointly to dispel the pirates. The HMS *Rose* was in the area under Captain Witney, after moving down from guarding the New England coast, but showed little interest in facing up to the *Royal Fortune* and *Good Fortune*. Witney wrote to Hamilton saying that that Roberts was off Deseada and that he was waiting for the snow *Shark* to join him before attacking the *Great Pirate* Roberts. Hamilton responded requiring Witney to protect the islands, but Captain Witney sailed away from any possible point of contact with Roberts. Witney's men were probably in a state of near-mutiny, like most naval ships of this time, and he was almost certainly engaged in illicit trades to pay them. Naval crews, because of shortage of funds, were often paid in credit notes, which were worth less than half their value when eventually exchanged for cash. The majority of the men were pressed into service, half-starved, beaten, living in filthy cramped conditions, over-worked, disease-ridden, and not allowed to ever leave the ship for fear of desertion. Some of the more 'enlightened' captains ferried a boatload of prostitutes to the ship when it arrived at port, to alleviate the boredom. Most naval and merchant captains hated and brutalised their crews. When a ship was taken, its crew were always asked about their treatment by its officers. A tyrannical captain was usually killed by the pirates in their empathy for their former lives.

Black Bart and his crews now spent a month on St Barthelemy, during which time he took Captain Andrew Kingston's galley Lloyd, with 12 guns and 18 men off Antigua on March 26th. Poor Kingston was then taken again on March 27th by a rare Spanish pirate ship, and marooned when they found his boat had already been ransacked. Fortunately he and his men were seen by a passing trader and taken to St Christopher's, where the reluctant Captain Whitney was persuaded to take the Rose out to look for Roberts. Captain Kingston recounted his travails in a letter sent on April 24th from St Christopher's (St Kitts) to his London employers: 'I am sorry to give you this account of my great misfortune with this voyage. On 26th of March I made the island of Desirade about 11 o'clock of noon and soon after saw two sail standing the same course as I did. I made the best of my way from them, but about 8 at night they came alongside me. I was then about 4 leagues (12 miles) off Antigua. They fired at me, being pyrates, one a ship of 36 guns and 250 men and 50 negroes; the other a brig of 18 guns, 46 men and 20 negroes; these I could not withstand. They had been but 2 days upon that station before they saw me, and are both under the command of Captain John Roberts. They carried me into Bermuda (actually, it was Barbuda, just north of Antigua), there kept me 5 days, and what of the cargo was not fit for their purpose, they threw overboard. They took away most of my rigging and sails, all my anchors, blocks, provisions, powder, small arms etc., and 12 of my men, and then carried me to the northward that I might not come into these islands to give an account of them; and the 1st of this instant (April 1st) they left me in latitude 30 degrees North in a very sad condition. I hope the ships bound from London to Jamaica after me may escape the said Roberts: for he designed to keep the station and destroy all ships that come to these islands which may fall into his hands. They left me without any manner of clothing; and Roberts brought my brother (the chief mate) to the gears and whipped him within an inch of his life by reason he had concealed 2 gold rings in his pocket. This is the dismal account I am to give of this voyage. A. Kingston'

The pirates now left St Bathelemy to rendezvous with Norton off the Carolinas, chasing a ship into New Providence harbour on the way. However, a British man-of-war was stationed there, and three pirate longboats creeping up on the merchantmen were spotted, and the chased trader moved closer to the naval ship. The pirates returned to the Royal Fortune. At this point, a forced man, Joseph Slinger, jumped from the Royal Fortune as she started to move off, and swam for hours until he drifted ashore with the tide to safety. Roberts now stationed himself off Charleston, South Carolina, but Captain Norton did not appear with the expected returns from his trading. La Palisse, in frustration with waiting, returned to the West Indies in a captured sloop. Roberts was not sorry to see him go. Twice in battle he had vanished from the scene *'at a rate of knots'*. *Lord* Thomas Anstis was given the *Good Fortune* after la Palisse's defection, but he complained that it was difficult to sail, because it was carrying Norton's second cargo, ready for another round of trading..

Norton was not to come, and Roberts was fuming with waiting for someone he had trusted. Norton had left the laden *El Puerto del Principe* at Naushon in the Elizabeth Isles, then gone on to Rhode Island to let his trader friends know, so they could bring their empty sloops out to Naushon to do (illegal) business. The excitement was so great at the prospect of being able to *'fence'* the proceeds of the *Great Pyrate* for the foreseeable future, that too many people in the tiny colony became involved, and Governor Cranstone of Rhode Island soon found out the truth of the matter. The Royal Navy's Lieutenant Hamilton was sent to Tarpaulin Bay, to find Norton's friends loading up their sloops with cocoa, sugar and bolts of cloth. Norton would not allow Hamilton on his ship, and Hamilton returned to the Governor for fresh instructions. The traders sailed off to their separate landing places. Then the sheriff of Bristol County, Massachusetts appeared and impounded the *El Puerto del Principe* and another trader's sloop, and took them to Rhode Island. Benjamin Norton had managed to escape on the arrival of the sheriff.

The pirates became restless. La Palisse had left. Anstis did not like the *Good Fortune*. He had been a popular quartermaster on the *Royal Fortune*, but had been replaced by the pugnacious and disliked bully, David Sympson. The *Lords* had been increasingly annoyed by Roberts' growing autocratic manner - he listened to Council less and less, in line with his growing success as a pirate captain. The crews were bored. The food and drink were bad. They wanted to go ashore, or return to the warm climes of the West Indies. The money they had been reliant upon from Norton seemed to have disappeared. Tempers frayed with the waiting. Roberts responded to the growing tension by offering to fight a duel with anyone, with sword or pistol, *'for he neither valued or feared any of them.'*

At this time Roberts finally lost his temper badly, with a crewman who insulted him. The man had been helping load fresh water onto the *Royal Fortune*, but drunkenly mishandled a cask, which had fallen back into the longboat and hurt one of the landing-party. Roberts swore at the culprit, and he swore back and spat at Roberts. Incensed, Black Bart shot the drunk on the spot. The Welshman Thomas Jones, one of Howell Davis's original crew, was also bringing in water when it happened, and he cursed Roberts for killing his friend. As Roberts had fired his pistols, he ran Jones through with his sword, but Jones furiously lashed out with his knife, and as Bart ducked away, he fell over a gun-barrel. Thomas Jones fell on him and repeatedly thrashed Roberts over the gun barrel, before he could be dragged off. The crew was divided upon which action to take, but most sided with the honour of the captaincy, and the quartermaster Sympson decided that the punishment for Thomas Jones was to be two lashes from each member of the crew when his sword-wound healed.

Roberts' position was becoming precarious, and he needed success. On April 9th the *Jeremiah and Ann* was taken, and Robert Johnson and William Shurin joined

Roberts. In his defence at his trial, Johnson was later to call witnesses to claim that he was so drunk that he had to be hoisted out of his own ship 'in tackles' to join the pirates. In April 1721 Roberts took a French man-of-war of 32 guns and 9 swivel guns with 140 crew off the Leeward Islands. It seems that it had not been keeping an adequate watch, because it was taken very quickly by the *Royal Fortune* and *Good Fortune*. Roberts was extremely pleased with the prize, for it was carrying the Governor of Martinique. True to his word, Roberts had him promptly hanged from the year-arm of the French ship. Walter Kennedy at his trial in 1721 stated that *'Roberts could have no peace of mind if only for murdering the French governor.'* Roberts kept the ship, and called it the *Sea King*, marooning its crew. He could now look for the head of the Governor of Barbados, and make his personal pennant a statement of fact, with both governors' skulls displayed on it. A few days later a Virginia merchantman was taken, and the *Royal Fortune*, *Good Fortune* and *Sea King* set course for Africa, as had been decided in the West Indies. Prevailing winds and currents made the passage from New England and Newfoundland to Africa or Europe easy.

By Spring 1721 there was little left to plunder in the Americas. The *Royal Fortune*, *Sea King* and *Good Fortune* were *'filled to the gunnels'* with gold and booty, and Roberts knew that there was trouble brewing for him along the coastlines of the Americas if he tried to trade his loot. The Governor of the Leeward Islands was lobbying for more men-of-war to be sent to protect shipping against Roberts. Governor Spotswood of Virginia had erected 54-gun batteries along his coast specifically to prevent Roberts attacking. He had discussed matters with the *House of Lords*, who had wanted to return south, but had his way and at the beginning of April set sail for Africa. He was not driven away - most merchant shipping would not approach the area, and prizes were becoming harder to take. His crew was getting restless. Roberts knew that his crews needed a fresh challenge, and knew that the Royal Navy was becoming more active in the West Indies and along the American colonies coastline, so he decided to make for Brava island in the Cape Verde Islands, and maraud the Guinea coast.

THE DESERTION OF ANSTIS
However, the aggrieved Thomas Jones went with some other pirates to the *Good Fortune*, captained by Thomas Anstis, one of Howell Davis' old *House of Lords*. Anstis was disaffected because Roberts was becoming prouder and less approachable, probably becoming mentally unstable with the problems of holding together a bunch of psychopathic alcoholics over three years. The brig *Good Fortune* was just being treated like a supply ship, and a tender for loot. On April 18th the disaffected Anstis, Jones and a hundred crewmen and forty French negroes stole away into the night, away from Roberts forever, with most of his bulkier loot.

The 180 men (and 48 Creole negroes) on the *Royal Fortune* were not overly worried, as their ship was fully provisioned and by far the better fighting ship. Roberts on April 17 in the mid-Atlantic had taken the Dutch *Prince Eugene* under Captain Bastian Meake, and then a small snow was also captured. In the mid-Atlantic in May the Dutch snow *Christopher*, captained by Nicholas Hendrich was seized. Off Cape Verde the galley *Norman* was then taken in May 1721, when Benjamin Jeffries and

John Little joined Black Bart. One account is that poor Jeffries did not wish to go on the account, saying *'None who could get their bread in an honest way would be in such an account'*, and for his impudence was whipped six times by each member of the crew. However, it was Roberts' proud claim that he never 'forced' anyone to join him. Gosse's account is as follows: *'Roberts allowed those of the crew who did not wish to join the pirates to return to the Norman, but Jefferys had made such friends on the pirate ship that he was too drunk to go, and also was abusive in his cups, telling his hosts that there was not one man amongst them. For this he received six lashes from every member of the crew, "which disordered him for some weeks." But Jefferys eventually proved himself a brisk and willing lad, and eventually was made bosun's mate.'* The Dutch *Royal Fortune* was left at Cape Verde because of leaks, and its guns and booty taken on the French *Sea King*, which became the new *Royal Fortune*.

Deciding to trade their booty for Guinea gold, Roberts moved on towards the Sierra Leone coast of Africa. He did not yet know that the men-of -war *Swallow* and *Weymouth* had escorted a fleet of East Africa Company ships to Africa and that both were off Sierra Leone. However, as they cruised east 700 miles from Cape Three Points to the island of Principe, Black Bart had moved to Sierra Leone, 800 miles north-west of Cape Three Points. His luck had held out. In June, 1721, two French ships guarded the gum trade at Senegal. One had 10 guns and 65 men, and the *St Agnes* had 16 guns and 75 men. They chased Roberts, thinking he was a Dutch interloper, an unlicensed trader. As soon as Roberts raised his Black Flag, and ran out his 40 cannon, they surrendered. The *Comte de Toulouse* was renamed the *Ranger*, and the smaller ship *St Agnes* named the *Little Ranger* and used as a storeship. There was now a pirate council for officers of the new prizes. *Lord* David Sympson was dismissed as quartermaster because the pirates thought him too much of a bully. On the *Royal Fortune*, under Black Bart were 'Lord' William Magnes as quartermaster, the Welshman James Philips was boatswain, 'Lord' Henry Dennis (as always) was gunner, and the forced Harry Glasby (Gillespie) was nominated and elected as sailing-master. Thomas Sutton became captain of the *Ranger* for a short time before he was deposed by a vote, with William Main as boatswain. The Welshman James Skyrme was then elected captain of the *Little Ranger*. Black Bart, as overall commander of the flotilla, reminded his crews that they had no surgeon, and one was desperately needed.

Roberts had sailed into the mouth of the Senegal River on June 12th - the *Swallow* had left just six weeks previously, and the government agent Plunkett could do nothing from his rebuilt Brent (Bence) island fort. Black Bart's crew was welcomed with a celebratory fusillade from the brass cannon of *Old Crackers*, the private trader in anticipation of doing some lucrative business. On that June day in1721, Roberts took a merchant ship in Frenchman's Bay. He anchored in an inlet with a long narrow inlet near the Cape, which is now known as Pirates' Bay and then careened the fleet of the *Royal Fortune* and the three new prizes. The Sierra Leone river has a large mouth with small hidden bays on either side, excellent for cleaning and watering vessels. Many outward-bound ships also used the mouth of the river for taking on water, so there were plenty of ships to be taken in the area. Local traders bartered with the pirates, the local tribes were friendly and some of Howell Davis' old crew from

1719 knew the best places for local women. 'Old Crackers' (John Leadstone), a former pirate, had been a friend of Davis, and not only traded but ran the best brothel in the area. There were thirty traders on the mainland, and in Rio Pungo Benjamin Gunn lived a hermit-like existence (he was later to become famous as the character Benn Gunn in Treasure Island). These ruffians exchanged slaves, dye-woods and *elephants' teeth* (ivory) for alcohol, guns and the like. Over the next two months, Roberts did lucrative business with around 30 local traders.

The Royal Africa Company had a very weakly defended fort on Brent Island, so it seems the coast was made for Black Bart's company. Roberts was now told that the Royal Africa Company had asked for men-of-war to come to the area, after the depredations of Captains Davis, England, Cocklyn and La Bouche. The two third-raters, the *Swallow* under Captain Challoner Ogle and the *Weymouth* under Captain Mungo Herdman had left the area in April and were not expected back until Christmas, so Roberts felt doubly safe – friendly natives, plenty of places for his men to expend their energy and money, and no Royal Navy vessels for at least six months. (Incidentally, Alexander Selkirk was serving in the *Weymouth* - see Stradling in the section on *Pirate Terms*).

There was a rumour that Bart buried his personal treasure from the Caribbean on the Isles of Idols off Sierra Leone, known as Los Islands at this time. In July, Roberts sent a boat to the fort on Brent Island asking for gold dust, powder and ball-shot. Governor Plunkett informed the pirates that he had no gold, but plenty of powder and ball if Roberts would come for it. Plunkett had been captured by Howell Davis and some of the *House of Lords* two years previously. Roberts took three ships and bombarded the fort for a few hours. When the fort ran out of ammunition to return the cannonade, Plunkett rowed to hide on the nearby small island of Tombo, but was soon captured and brought before Roberts at the fort. With his natural hatred for the Irish after the Kennedy desertion, Black Bart berated the old man harshly for having foolishly resisted. Plunkett, an old Africa hand, exploded with such a tirade of oaths and curses that the House of Lords roared with appreciative laughter. Most of the watching pirates were doubled up in laughter, seeing their feared captain being outsworn by the fearless Governor. Even Roberts eventually saw the funny side of things, and after exhausting his vocabulary allowed Plunkett to have his fort back, after the warehouses had been ransacked. (Plunkett had previously been under attack by Howell Davis in Gambia in 1719, and this same story is related with regard to Thomas Cocklyn and Plunkett). Plunkett had nowhere to go. All boats were guarded, and some slave ships burnt.

Two men joined Roberts' company from the fort. William Watts was one, employed by Captain Glynn, a trader who was a former pirate and knew Cocklyn, La Bouche and especially Howell Davis. Roberts spent several days in the company of his fellow-Welshman Glynn, recounting their anecdotes of Howell Davis. The other man taken aboard is notable in that he was too much of a drunken thug for even Robert's crew of reprobates. William Davies had beaten up the second mate on the galley *Ann* at Sierra Leone, in a drunken rage, and deserted to join the negroes in the shanty town. They gave him a wife, who he immediately sold in order to buy punch. After spending

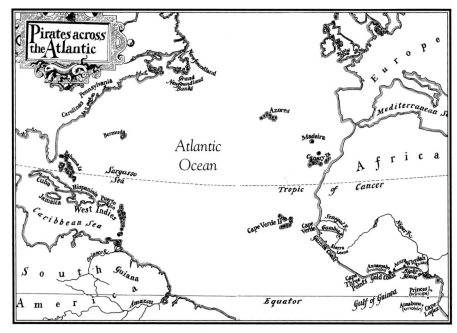

The Pirate Seas

his money he sought protection from Governor Plunkett, but his wife's relatives soon came for compensation. Plunkett surrendered Davies to them, stating that they could cut his head off as far as he was concerned. Plunkett was obviously a wise judge of character. The negroes then sold him to Senor Joseph, a negro trader and landowner, who indentured him for two years. Soon after joining Roberts' ship, the *House of Lords* and *House of Commons* decided unanimously to get rid of Davies. However, it appears that he managed to hang on in service, as he was later tried and hung at Cape Corso Castle. William Williams tried to escape with two other forced men into the jungle, but was recaptured and whipped. The other two men probably died in the jungle, killed by natives or wild animals.

During June and July, the pirates drank, caroused, gambled and fornicated while their musicians played. The musicians looked forward to Sunday, the day that Roberts had decreed was free of music. Otherwise, they were at the inebriated pirates' beck and call at any hour of the night or day. Any ship that came into port was taken, so that the news of their whereabouts could not reach the *Swallow* or *Weymouth*. Sensing that the Royal Navy might visit, Roberts now took the Royal *Fortune* and the *Ranger* away from Sierra Leone at the end of July, with Lord Sutton commanding of the *Ranger*. Plunkett despatched messages to the captain of the *Providence*, noting the traders who had dealt with Roberts: Glynn, 'Old Crackers' , Lamb, England, the Presgrove brothers, Bonnerman, Warren, and another Welshman, Pierce. Roberts was not to know that the *Weymouth's* crew was anchored off Principe, with its crew suffering terribly, many dying from yellow fever from mid-July to the beginning of September.

At the end of July, the Dutch galley *Semm* was taken at Axim, with little booty except some cloth, but several men were forced, including Charles Bunce and Robert Armstrong. Armstrong had deserted from the HMS *Swallow* eight weeks earlier at Cape Three Points. Upon August 6th, Captain John Tarleton's *Liverpool* galley was taken off Sestos, with Robert Hays joining up. Sometime in August, the *Martha*, Captain Lady's snow from Liverpool, was captured off Cape la Hou, and Joshua Lee joined Roberts' men.

Off Point Sestos in Liberia upon August 8th, the pirates took the Royal Africa Company frigate-slaver *Onslow*, bound for Whydah and Cape Coast Castle. A 410-ton ship, it carried 12 guns, with cargo valued at £9000, destined for Cape Coast Castle. Captain Michael Gee had stopped at Sestos on the pretext of taking on fresh food and water, but in reality pursuing his private trading interests. Anchored alongside was Captain Canning's *Robinson* from Liverpool. With many of the crew ashore, possibly trading for slaves, William Magness, Roberts' quartermaster, easily took the moored ships. Lord Sympson 'showed off' to the fifty or so merchant seamen and passengers, shouting that he was as bold a pirate as Roberts, and bullying the passengers with his cutlass. Mrs Elizabeth Trengrove was travelling to Cape Coast Castle to join her husband, and William Mead made advances to her, forcing off her hooped petticoat. Another pirate, John Mitchell, smashed mead over the head with his flint-lock, and told her that she would be safe from pirate advances in the gun-room. The brutal 'Little David' Simpson followed her, leering and telling his fellow 'Lords' that he would stand sentinel and safeguard her honour. As was the practice of the time, the pirate who chose to carry out such 'guard-duties' expected something in return, and she was raped three times by him over the next few days. This awful event would come back to haunt Mrs Trengrove.

Roberts next came on board. Black Bart asked if anyone of the would join him, and stated that no-one would be forced. He mentioned to a by-stander *'I must oblige these fellows with a show of force.'* After a mock show of being *'forced'*, many crewmen did join, such as Phillip Bill, William Petty, Abraham Harper, Peter Lesley, William Wood, Edward Watts, John Horn, James Crombie and John Stevenson, and he impressed two Royal Africa Company agents named Thomas Castell and Edward Crispe. (Castell survived to give evidence against the pirates in the Cape Corso trial). Abraham Harper, a cooper, now had the job of removing all the casks and cooper's tools from prizes. Some soldiers captured were going to serve in the castle garrison, on a wage of £13 a year in local currency only (so savings were useless), and could only look forward to a miserable native diet of plantain and 'canky'. They wanted to join the pirates, but Roberts' crew was reluctant to take on 'landlubbers'. Eventually they were allowed to join, but only with a 'quarter-share' of any plunder, compared to the usual one share for a pirate. The Reverend Roger Price, a Welshman, was also asked to join, and take a share of the booty. All in return that Roberts asked was that he said prayers and made punch. He refused, and the pirates returned his confiscated property. He also claimed goods belonging to other passengers, which were returned to them later. However, Roberts kept three prayer-books of Price's, and his corkscrew. Bart informed the minister that his men led a dissolute life but he tried to keep them in order on a Sunday, allowing no rowdiness, evil-doing or games.

The *Onslow* was a well-built 410-ton frigate, and became the fourth 'Royal Fortune' as the old one was leaking. It was mounted with 40 guns, the gunwales highered for extra protection, and its deck-houses pulled down. Johnson describes Roberts' carpenters *'making such alterations as might fit her for a Sea Rover, pulling down her bulkheads, and making her flush, so she became, in all respects, as complete a ship for their purpose as any they could have found; they continued to her the name of Royal Fortune and mounted her with 40 guns.'* The bulkheads, or internal walls between decks were taken away, as there was no need to store cargo. A clear space was needed for working the guns, as in a man-of-war. Making her flush meant that the forecastle was removed and the quarterdeck lowered or removed, giving a flat weather-deck, suitable for fighting and boarding.

Captain Gee was given the old *Royal Fortune* when the work was completed. The new *Royal Fortune* hoisted French colours, as there was no knowing where the Royal Naval vessels were cruising, and moved on up the Bight of Benin to Jacquin for a short stay. (The frigates were still at Principe, Prince's Island, at this time, careening. The

"Roberts' crew carousing at old Calabar River".

crews were suffering from venereal diseases and malaria, and at least 50 had died from each ship. Captain Ogle was forced to press crewmen off local shipping and purchase slaves in order to get a full complement of crew.) The pirates forced the *Onslow's* surgeon, Hamilton to join them on the *Royal Fortune*, and took another surgeon, George Willson from Captain Tarlton's ship off Assinie near Cape Coast Castle, and put him on the *Ranger*. Willson and two others escaped from Sutton a few days later, by a subterfuge of pretending to get new drugs off one of the prize vessels. Their small sailboat made for the coast before Sutton could do anything.

The fleet moved on to Old Calabar in the Bight of Biafra (Nigeria) to careen. Roberts had gleaned from captured despatches that the two men-of-war were still at Principe. On Oct 1st Roberts boarded the *Joceline* under Captain Arthur Loane and made him pilot their ships up the tricky river with its 13 feet draught. Once up the Calabar River, they were out of sight of the Navy. Roberts generously paid Loane for his services. He could be useful again, so there was no point in plundering his ship. Robert Haws joined up with Roberts. Bart found two ships lying inland. From the galley slaver *Mercy* he impressed the musicians, and yet another surgeon, William Child. (Musicians were carried on slavers to while away the time of the slaves, and entertain the crew). Israel Hynde of Bristol joined him as did Cuthbert Gross, John Griffin (a much-needed carpenter) and Thomas Giles. He also captured Captain Rolls' slave galley, the *Cornwall*, and impressed some more men, including a hunch-backed musician, James White, the Welshman David Rice and the

Bristolian surgeon Peter Scudamore. This surgeon quarrelled with Lord Moody, who did not want him. However, Roberts had found a real friend in Scudamore, who was the only surgeon to voluntarily sign articles on record. Scudamore was arrogant, but intelligent, and Roberts came to enjoy his cultured company, while the surgeon took to the life of a pirate like a duck to water.

From captured despatches on these two prizes, Roberts now discovered that the men-of-war were over 200 miles away at Principe, so he decided to move on again to trade with another port. With goods to trade, Roberts moored his three ships and three prizes on October 1st off the native township of Calabar, and forty men went ashore under cover of his forty guns. 2000 hostile natives lined up to face them – they did not deal with white men in this part of modern-day eastern Nigeria, and were rightly suspicious of the pirates' motives. After a few fusillades of musket-shot and showers of spears, both sides had lost a few men, but Robert's men stayed their ground. The local tribe retreated, and the pirates kept on firing at them, then set fire to the town. There was now a stand-off – the pirates were not welcome on land, and the natives would not come near them. Several pirates were killed, and the natives retreated back into the jungle, with their much-needed goods and provisions. The attack was still being recounted 200 years later by locals in their tribal legends. From now on Bart sent a pinnace full of pirates on a regular basis to the mouth of the Calabar, looking for the opportunity to board merchantmen lying at anchor in the estuary, perhaps taking on water. It was now that Scudamore showed himself to be a 'true' pirate, cursing Captain Rolls and hoping that he would drown as he was a 'great rogue'. The surgeon took his medicines, scales and knives off the Cornwell, before that ship, the Mercy and the Joceline were returned to their captains. The unfortunate Elizabeth Trengrove left the clutches of Sympson to carry on her journey.

Roberts went off to careen 400 miles south at Cape Lopez, where John Jessup deserted and vanished. The squadron then moved on to a safer careening site at Annabon, a small island 200 miles from the Cape. Jessup had been a shipmate of Roberts when he had first been taken by Howell Davis, and was a proficient gunner, but was frequently so drunk that he had missed out on his share of plunder. When the Summersett had been taken in 120, he had distinguished himself, but now was regarded by Roberts and his fellow-pirates as a hopeless sot. The aggrieved Jessup was picked up on the Gabon Coast by a Dutch trader, whose captain did not believe the story that he had been marooned. Unluckily for Roberts, Jessup was taken to the Swallow at Cape Coast Castle. Here, clapped in irons, he turned informer and told Captain Ogle all about the movements of Black Bart, and his intention to ravage the Gold Coast next. By now 280 men had died on the Weymouth, and the vast majority of its 240-man crew had to be press-ganged, for it to now accompany the Swallow towards the Gold Coast. On October 20th, both men-of-war left Principe, piling on full sail, to chase Roberts.

On Dec 14th, 1721 the Dutch galley Gertrouycht, under Captain Benjamin Kreeft was taken at Gabon, in a crazy drunken attack. The pirates strung sausages, which had been made by Kreeft's wife, around their necks. The men went ashore to hunt for fresh meat, hunting for buffalo, then reprovisioned and traded at Annabona Island

(Palagula). Roberts now moved off to Cape La Hou (French Ivory Coast), with the more competent Welshman Skyrme now replacing *Lord* Sutton as captain of the *Ranger*, after Sutton resigned.

1722

On January 2nd, the *Elizabeth,* under Captain Joseph (or John) Sharp, was pursued and taken by the three pirate ships, off Jacquesville on the Ivory Coast. On board was the missing surgeon, Richard Willson. He managed to convince Sutton and Roberts that his boat had been blown onto the beach at Cape Mesurado. The pirates fortunately believed him, as he had been forced to live in miserable conditions there for five months, and they always needed surgeons. His old ship under Captain Tarlton had found him after a few weeks, feverish and starving, but refused to take him aboard. A French ship then picked him up, but abandoned Willson at Sestos, as they were afraid of his fever spreading to the rest of the crew. A negro trader took the starving, penniless Willson on as a bond-servant, working as a slave clearing land, until Captain Joseph Sharp ransomed Willson's indenture for £3 and 5 shillings. Willson was nursed back to health by the surgeon Adam Comrie on the *Elizabeth.* Willson and Scudamore now persuaded Roberts that Comrie should be forced to join the crew as another surgeon, as they were sure that Hamilton would desert as soon as he had a chance.

Willson now noticed on the *Royal Fortune* the forced mate Thomas Tarlton of Liverpool, the brother of the captain who had abandoned him at Mesurado. Captain Tarlton's slaver *Tarlton* had been taken four days before the *King Solomon.* Tarlton was therefore badly beaten up by Roberts and other pirates. This was unusual - but happened because he was a brutal mate according to his crew, some of whom had joined Roberts – usually Bart just threatened captains with *'I'll blow your brains out!'*

Roberts captures 11 merchantmen off Africa

Lords Moody and Harper wanted to shoot Tarlton, who was hidden under a sail by some fellow-Liverpudlians. With their constant success, Roberts was finding it increasingly difficult to restrain his crews - he seems to have become resigned to his fate from this time. Roberts had no escape - so many people knew him, that he could not retire anywhere in anonymity and safety. As a teetotaller and Christian, he must have despaired at the way his life was going - there was no escape *in the bottle* for Black Bart. With continued success, his crews were spinning out of control - they thought they were invincible, and at the same time he could not control their perpetual drinking, which made them far less efficient as seamen. Roberts was trapped in a web of his own making.

As the *Elizabeth* was being ransacked, the *Hannibal* of London, under Captain Charles Ousley was taken. The pirates virtually trashed it, because of the lack of plunder on the small ship, causing £2000 worth of damage. Lord Richard Hardy was so annoyed at the *'day's takings'* that he broke his cutlass on the Captain's head, who died soon after. Without Roberts' influence on the spot, the Lords were fast getting out of control. Roberts let Captain Sharp take the emptied *Elizabeth* away - Sharp was a good captain to his men, and had been kind to Willson. The *Hannibal* was to be used as a hulk to store loot as the pirate fleet was careened. Comrie signed articles and was voted to become the *Royal Fortune's* surgeon, and Willson served Skyrme as surgeon on the Ranger. The pirates did not vote for Hamilton as they knew he could not be trusted, and did not care for Scudamore's arrogance - he had even struck Lord Moody when they had previously quarrelled. However, Roberts liked him and they needed Scudamore, as a surgeon who was not likely to try and escape. The *Ranger's* crew voted as a man for Scudamore to be transferred off their ship to join Roberts on the *Royal Fortune*.

Upon January 4th, the Dutch *Vlissingen*, (Flushingham), with Captain Gerrit de Haen was taken at Grand Bassam. Sixteen pirates boarded, and obliged the captain and mate to join them for a drunken feast, when they pretended to sing in Spanish and French out of a Dutch prayer-book. On the next day, the sloop *Diligence*, under Captain Stephen Thomas, was taken at Cape Appolonia. A second sailor named John Jessup joined Roberts, off the prize. Upon January 6th, the 200 tons *King Solomon* of London, a 12-gun slaver with a Welsh Captain, Joseph Traherne, was taken off Cape Appolonia. William Magness, quartermaster, again led a long-boat to take it, as the *Royal Fortune* could not tack near enough to it. Captain Traherne shouted *'Defiance'* and fired a musket at the approaching pirates, but his men were half-hearted in supporting him. The pirates called out that any resistance would meet with *no quarter*, the King Solomon's Welsh bosun, William Phillips, led the crew in asking for quarter against the captain's wishes. It was not worth sailors risking their lives for the Royal Africa Company, as the pirates knew full well – only the captain was a financial loser if the ship was seized. In 1723, partly because of Phillips' actions, an Act of Parliament was passed punishing seamen who would not defend their ship against pirates. John Lane, John King and Samuel Fletcher joined up from the *King Solomon*. Roberts was pleased with the booty, and asked Traherne *'How dared you fire? Didn't you see the two ships commanded by the famous Captain Roberts?'*

The pirate John Walden addressed the recalcitrant Captain Traherne 'Captain, what signifies this trouble of yo-hoping and straining in hot weather ? There are plenty more anchors in London and, besides, your ship is to be burned' – he then cut the anchor cable. Walden was a hot-headed and argumentative man, known as 'Miss Nanny' by the crew, as noted above. (One noted writer on pirates believes that 'Miss Nanny' was an 18th- century term for a homosexual, but this author cannot find any such reference. The writer uses this to make the connection that Walden was Robert's lover, but again there is nothing to prove this allegation. Surely this 'fact' would have been noted in the interrogations and trial transcripts of above 200 men if it was the case. To this author, it seems that Roberts was asexual, if anything). Phillips helped Scudamore, Walden and Magness ransack the boat and showed little love for his former captain, encouraging the pirates to hit him. What cargo they could not take, they threw overboard. More men had joined Roberts' crew, including more soldiers. Peter de Vine, who had sailed under Stede Bonnet on the pirate sloop Revenge, joined willingly. The drunkard Joe Mansfield found a beautiful crystal glass, which Lord Moody promptly seized. When Mansfield protested, Moody threatened to blow his brains out. Scudamore took the medical equipment and supplies, and argued with another pirate over a backgammon table. Magness was forced to intervene, and Scudamore took the table, before returning for Captain Traherne's quilt and bolster. Surgeon Willson was so preoccupied with looting that he omitted to dress a pirate's wound, and Roberts threatened to cut his ears off. The Welsh bosun Phillips was forced for his seamanship skills, and the ransacked King Solomon allowed to go free. Philips later testified that he signed Roberts' Articles because a pistol had been laid pointing at him on the table, as if to say that if he did not sign, he would be shot.

The pirates now heard that HMS Swallow had at last left Principe. Roberts realised that he had to sail on away from the vicinity of Cape Coast Castle, and headed for Whydah, the busy port where the Portuguese paid for slaves in gold. The Royal Africa Company's Williams Fort was 3 miles inland, and could not guard the port with its guns. The Swallow and Weymouth were very near at this time, but luckily for Roberts, had veered away to anchor off Cape Corso on January 7th. Ogle was disappointed that his provisions from England had not arrived. Some of these supplies had been looted off the King Solomon by Black Bart only the day before, unknown to him. Captain Ogle now heard that Roberts had just taken a French ship off Axim, and that three pirate vessels, presumably those of Roberts, had taken a galley off Axim Castle and another Royal Africa Company ship. The captains surmised that Roberts would leave the Gold Coast and head for Whydah (Ouidah) on the Bight of Benin, and set off from Cape Coast on January 10th to capture him there. Whydah was the richest port in West Africa. The King of Dahomey lived six miles inland with his hundred wives, and exacted a toll to the value of 20 slaves from each of the blackbirders who picked up slaves there. The corpulent king sent contingents of spearmen into the interior to raid villages and bring young men and women to the slave-ship captains. His avarice was such that he sold the slaves naked, without their 'arse-clouts' (loin-cloths). Slaves were kept at Wydah in a stinking storehouse known as 'The Trunk'. A Guinea slaver wrote 'the negroes were put into a booth, or prison, built for that purpose, near the beach, *all of them together; and when the Europeans are to receive them, they are brought out into a large plain, where the surgeons examine every part of everyone of them, to the smallest member, men and women all being stark naked.'* Wounded, sick and those with venereal diseases were rejected, and the rest branded and replaced in cages. In the Niger Delta, slaves were herded into a huge cage known as a *barracoon.* However, the Royal Africa Company hoarded its slaves in huge stone castles along the shore, usually in rock dungeons.

On Jan 11th, 1722 Black Bart sailed into Whydah roadstead, flying his personal colours, and immediately took 12 slave ships. Hearing the drums and music, 5 Portuguese, 4 French and 3 English *blackbirders* struck their colours immediately when they saw Roberts' black flags. The French ships each had around 30 guns and 100 men. The ships included the *Carlton* of London, under Captain Allright, the *Porcupine* under Captain Fletcher and the *Hardey* under Captain Dittwitt. All the captains fled ashore in their tenders when they saw Robert's flotilla enter the harbour. The ships had been stripped to take maximum cargoes of slaves across the Atlantic, and had little to loot. However, Roberts knew that their captains had gold to pay for negroes. Only the *Carlton* had taken on its slaves, and its captain could only raise 40 ounces of gold dust to retrieve his ship. The Royal Africa Company's agent loaned him 100 ounces to release the ship. All except the *Porcupine* agreed to be ransomed for 140 ounces of gold each. The pirates even gave the captains of galleys such as the *Sandwich* receipts for the gold-dust, stating on one: *'This is to certify whom it may or doth concern, that we GENTLEMEN OF FORTUNE have received 8 lbs. of Gold-Dust for the ransom of the Hardey, Captain Dittwitt commander so that we discharge the said ship.*

Witness our hands this 13th January 1722
Batt. Roberts
Harry Glasby'

This may have been at the honest Glasby's request, but the Portuguese captains were given the identical dubious receipts but jokingly signed by Lords Sutton and Simpson as 'Aaron Whifflington' and 'Sim. Tugmutton'

The *Porcupine,* however, was an interloper, an illegal trader. Her slaves were already chained up, and her captain ashore settling his bills. Captain Fletcher refused to negotiate with the pirates. Roberts gave the order to unchain the slaves and transport them to his ships, then burn the *Porcupine.* In the boarding party was Miss Nanny, John Walden, who was furious at having to do this slow and tedious job of unshackling the leg and wrist irons, while the other freebooters were happily drinking themselves into oblivion after an easy day's work. To Roberts' horror, he set fire to the slaver before the unfettering was finished, and all eighty natives died. Some screaming negroes, chained in pairs, *'jumped over-board from the Flames, were seized by Sharks, a voracious Fish, in plenty in the Road, and in their Sight, torn Limb from Limb alive. A Cruelty unparalleled.'* Roberts' control was now extremely tenuous – success had bred contempt for any discipline among the harder members of his crews. He could not punish them, for the offence had not occurred in battle. Outside battle conditions, the quartermaster was in real control of the ship.

Also, some of Roberts' crew took the *Comte de Thoulouze*, although it had been ransomed, and mounted extra guns on her from the other French ships. (This seems to be another *Comte de Thoulouze*, as the ship captured in June was a naval warship). 18 French sailors were also put on her, to return to Whydah if it was not a fast ship. It was a former privateer from St Malo, so the pirates obviously liked *the cut of its jib*, and intended to test its suitability at sea. Thomas Diggle was among the men forced to join Roberts. On one of the English ships, Roberts' men found a letter from Director-General James Phipps of Cape Coast Castle. (He was on a salary of £2000 per year, plus bribes or *'dashees'* from illegal traders, *interlopers*). It was meant for The Royal Africa Company agent on Whydah, Mr. Baldwin, informing him that Roberts had been spotted off Cape Three Points, and that the man-of-war *Swallow* was chasing him towards Whydah. Black Bart addressed his crew, telling them that there was no point in risking anything by staying and fighting the *Turnip-man's* ship (see Terms). The crew easily agreed with this sense, and the three ships sailed off towards Annanbona Island to hole up.

The *Swallow* missed Roberts by just two days when it sailed into Whydah on the 15th. Surgeon Hamilton was left at Whydah, as the pirates had no need of a surgeon who hated being with them. Roberts sailed out in the *Royal Fortune*, Skyrme in the *Ranger*, Captain Bunce in the *Little Ranger*, and followed by the captured *Comte de Thoulouze*. On the day they left, Roberts took the sloop *Wida* of London, under Captain Stokes, off Jacquin. Stokes had tried to avoid Whydah because he had known the pirates were there and was unfortunate they caught up with him on his escape route to Grand Popo. The *Wida* was burnt and its crew taken aboard – they wanted no-one to inform the *Swallow* of their whereabouts. Roberts had by now lost many men to disease contracted at Calabar and elsewhere. A great proportion of his men had never encountered a serious battle. Many of the *Lords* were perpetual drunkards, perpetually quarrelling with their teetotal captain. Roberts had no way out.

Throughout November and December, the third-raters chased up and down the African coast, following up merchant reports regarding Roberts' whereabouts. The *Weymouth* then left to pick up some goods held illegally by the Dutch at Des Minas, while the *Swallow* returned to Cape Coast Castle. There, Chaloner Ogle read two despatches that three suspicious ships had been seen at Whydah. Ogle had been delayed in reaching Whydah because he had helped two local ships at Accra, and did some personal business with a trader called Little Betty Morris. General Phipps was furious at this because on the night of January 14th the *Swallow* had nosed into Little Popo to be told that Roberts was at Whydah by a French boat. On the 15th Ogle found the burned hulk of the *Porcupine* and the other ships at anchor that Roberts had ransomed. Ogle and Hill were now given information that the pirates had gone to Jacquin, 7 leagues away, so moved there, before returning to Whydah to take on more men. Captains Ogle and Hill were now scouring inlets as they realised that the *Comte de Thoulouze* would need careening and refitting, and that the pirates needed water.

Ogle had been tardy in approaching Roberts thus far, but had been told of the fortune in gold aboard the *Royal Fortune*. Knowing that Roberts' ships were laden with booty changed the equation for Chaloner Ogle, aboard his 50-gun man-of-war. He

Captain Chaloner Ogle

directed the *Swallow* a thousand miles to Gabon, where he had captured Roberts' man, Jessup, but found no signs of Roberts. Ogle then interrogated the pirate prisoner, John Jessup, who was held in chains in the *Swallow's* hold. Jessup explained that he had not escaped from the Gabon estuary area, but from Cape Lopez, a hundred miles south. Roberts' days were numbered. However, it had been a reasonably successful two or so years. A modern estimate of the fortunes earned by Roberts and his crews is over £100,000,000. The *Sagrada Familia* alone was worth over £5,000,000. He virtually stopped international trade wherever he went.

THE TAKING OF THE GREAT RANGER

The *Comte de Thoulouze* had proved a fine sailer, but needed further fitting out and careening, as the naval commanders had rightly ascertained. It was to join Roberts' fleet, renamed the *Great Ranger*, under Captain Skyrme who had been commander of the *Ranger*. The *Ranger* was now called the *Little Ranger*. While the refitting was being done, there were duels ashore. Discipline was now a major problem – Roberts could not keep his crew sober any longer, and quarrels kept flaring up in the three overcrowded ships.

On February 5th, at daylight, after tracking around Prince's Island, Roberts' ships were sighted at Cape Lopez. The informer Jessup had told Ogle that he had escaped at Cape Lopez, and that it was a favourite resting place for Roberts. The *Great Ranger* (the former *Comte de Thoulouze*) was on its side, ready to be careened, as was the *Royal Fortune*. From the cliffs, Roberts spotted Ogle's ship in the distance and judged that it was a Portuguese trader. The *Swallow* moved away to avoid a shallows known as Frenchman's Bank, so Roberts assumed it was a merchantman attempting to flee from them. Ogle had wanted to attack the pirates as they rested in a drunken stupor, and raged at his helmsman until the situation was explained to him. Ogle had been forced out to sea again, to make a long tack to run into the bay again. Roberts rapidly ordered the *Great Ranger* to be righted, and a party of 20 men from the *Royal Fortune* boarded it. The *Royal Fortune* needed more work on her keel, and the *Little Ranger* was a store-ship, not really equipped for chasing and fighting. Ogle could not believe his luck - he could pick off the ships one by one.

Skyrme was sent off to chase the '*merchant*', hopefully to procure some sugar for making punch. Ogle cleverly kept up the deception, allowing the *Ranger* to slowly gain on him until the two ships were out of sight of Roberts and Roberts could not hear any cannon. (Three miles is the maximum distance of sight to the horizon, for anyone standing on a beach). Ogle closed off all his gun-ports, pretending to be a merchantman and put on all sail, but allowed Skyrme to slowly close on him. When Skyrme was in musket-shot, Ogle ordered the lower guns to be run out, and its 32-

pounders raked the *Great Ranger* with cannon shot into its rigging and below the water line. Skyrme realised his mistake, and fired a broadside back. In the exchanges, Captain Skyrme had a leg shot off. The pirates, waved on by Skyrme and his cutlass, were encouraged to board the naval vessel. Their topmast fell down, so they had no option – they could not outsail it. However, the new crew members and forced men were unwilling to suffer any more casualties – the *Great Ranger* was almost dead in the water and being straddled with chain shot and musket shot. Surgeon Comrie worked desperately on the wounded and dying, while Lord Valentine Ashplant and boatswain Hynde urged on the less committed pirates. A forced man, Lilliburne, ran down to the powder-stores with a musket, determined that no pirate would blow the ship up to prevent their capture. Hynde's arm was blown off. After four hours of fighting, from 11 – 3, Skyrme was forced to ask for quarter as his men deserted their posts to escape the deadly hail of missiles. When promised quarter, Skyrme ordered the black flags to be thrown into the water. Ashplant weighted them and did so. The opinion among Roberts' men was that he would soon come and rescue them. Skyrme had lost ten men, and another 20 like himself were very seriously wounded. However, as the navy was preparing to board, there was a great explosion, tearing a hole in the *Great Ranger's* side.

As the boarding-party came across to the *Great Ranger*, an explosion ripped out the great-cabin. The Welshman John Morris, with other hardened pirates Roger Ball and William Main, had decided to blow up the ship. They overpowered Lilliburn, and Morris fired his pistol into the remaining powder, but there was too little left to hole the hull. Four pirates including William Main and Roger Ball were badly burned, and Morris and another died horribly. Ball had been blown through the side of the boat, and rescued from the sea. The boarding party found 23 negro slaves and 16 French prisoners on board. Around 30 pirates were dead or terribly wounded, leaving around 30 new and pressed crew members. Most of the battle-hardened 'Lords' of Howell Davis were still on the *Royal Fortune*, with '*The Great Pirate*' Roberts. The Swallow's surgeon John Atkins, treating the blackened William Main, noted the silver whistle on a ribbon around his neck, and said '*I presume you are the boatswain of this ship*'. Main answered '*Then you presume wrong, for I am the boatswain of the Royal Fortune, Captain Roberts, commander.*' He averred that there were 120 'clever fellows' on the *Royal Fortune*, and he wished he was with them. Ball refused to be treated, and that night became delirious, shouting that Roberts would come and save them all. Ogle's response was the typical naval one of the day - he ordered the terribly burned man to be flogged in the morning. During his flaying, Ball still shouted back, and was whipped again. He fell into a coma and died the next day.

Ogle thought about burning the disabled *Great Ranger*, but realised that he did not want the prisoners and wounded on the *Swallow*. He therefore spent the night repairing it, and sent it to Princes Island with the French prisoners and four of his own men. By evening on February 6th, he was ready to go for Roberts, with his crew in fine fettle – they had not lost a man. On February 9th, Captain Thomas Hill was sailing the Neptune off Cape Lopez, a 200-ton pink with 10 guns. Roberts, in the newly careened *Royal Fortune*, easily took her, with £4000 in goods and stores, and put the crew and passengers of the burned *Wida* (Jan 13th) on her. There was plenty of alcohol on the *Neptune*, and a drunken Captain Bunce of the *Little Ranger*, said that he would salute Skyrme on his return with a 13-gun salute. Roberts was waiting for Skyrme to return before he could take to the seas again.

THE END

On February 10th Black Bart was sitting down calmly in his great-cabin breakfasting with Captain Hill and no doubt wondering where Skyrme was. He was anchored in the lee of Parrot Island, off Cape Lopez on the Guinea Coast. Possibly, Skyrme was spending his time ransacking the prize at sea rather than towing it back with him. Eating salmagundy, there was tea for Roberts and beer for Hill. The crew was drunk on the liquor taken from Hill's ship, when a ship was seen to be approaching. Roberts probably thought it was Skyrme returning. As Ogle saw the third ship, the *Neptune*, he guessed that Robert's crew would be dead drunk, celebrating, and was again correct. Most were asleep with hangovers, except a few pressed men, Harry Glasby the reluctant sailing-master and Roberts the teetotaller.

Ogle approached carefully, so as to give the appearance of a merchantman, and flew a French flag. However, a deserter from the *Swallow*, Armstrong, rushed into the great cabin and told Roberts that it was his old naval man-of-war. The pirates from the *Little Ranger* were ordered to join the *Royal Fortune* immediately. Roberts was almost trapped, and his men were is a desperate condition. Lords Magness and Dennis rushed around, kicking senseless pirates awake and hurrying them on board the *Royal Fortune*.

Lord Simpson was instructed to find out from Armstrong the *Swallow's* firepower and its weaknesses in sailing, and the Royal Fortune hurriedly hove to, Roberts exclaiming 'it is a bite' (deception). Roberts had very little time as the *Swallow* was almost upon her. It was on its second long and cautious tack through the shallows, and Black Bart managed to cast anchor by 10.30. He left the *Little Ranger* filled with treasure. He had decided to set all sail and pass next to the man-o-war, to assess her firepower. Armstrong had told him that the Swallow was a good ship going into the wind, but slow when sailing with the wind. Robert's men were not yet ready to return cannon fire, and Roberts could then assess whether to make a run for it into the open seas. He had to risk a full broadside, which unnerved Johnson. Roberts told Magness and Dennis that he would not try to board the Swallow, as his men were not fit for action. If the newly careened *Royal Fortune* passed the Swallow, the odds were that she could be outsailed. If the *Royal Fortune* was disabled, he could swing her onto the nearby cliffs and most of his men could escape into the forests. As the sails were set he went and dressed himself in his usual attire for battle. He finished dressing in his matching crimson coat and breeches, both with the same gold damask pattern, white ruffled lace shirt, and a long red feather in his hat. His expensive pistols were carried in a red silk shoulder strap, and he wore a great diamond-crusted gold cross.

On deck alongside Black Bart, the former 3rd mate on the *Princess*, was Stephenson, who had been the *Princess's* 2nd mate, and Roberts ordered his helmsman Johnson towards the oncoming man-of-war. The wind was from the shore, and the stratagem could work. At 11 in the morning the first broadside of the *Swallow* was fired from a pointblank range of 20 yards. Dennis had managed to reply with 20 cannon. The *Royal Fortune* passed, as the Swallow drifted towards the shore. However, the top of the *Royal Fortune's* mizzen topmast was felled and interfered with the mainsail. The panicking Johnson swung to starboard, disobeying Black Bart's instructions to keep a straight course. The *Royal Fortune* lost way, as it was directly behind the *Swallow's* stern. The *Swallow* tacked around to catch up with the almost becalmed *Royal Fortune*, taking its wind off the land. Black Bart cursed the helmsman and watched and waited as the *Swallow* inexorably made ground on him. He knew that his sails could not fill out until the *Swallow* came alongside him, and its 32-pounders smashed into his ship, and its other cannon, muskets and swivels destroyed his rigging and men on deck. He now knew that there would be several point-blank broadsides before the *Royal Fortune* could shake off the Swallow. Dennis prepared his gunners, while Magness roared around the deck urging his men on. The scarlet-clad Roberts watched, not moving amongst the hysteria. He was the easiest target on deck - it was almost as if he was waiting for his death.

The first broadside did tremendous damage, but even worse was the constant bombardment of swivel guns sweeping chainshot and grapeshot across the decks. Marksmen in the Swallow's rigging picked off Roberts' crew. The scarlet captain fell over a cannon, killed instantly by grapeshot in his throat. Stephenson, who had taken over as helmsman from the cowardly Johnson, shouted at Bart to '*stand up and fight like a man*', then burst into tears when he found Black Bart was dead. '*Miss Nanny*' Walden's leg had been blown off. Black Bart's body was weighed down and thrown overboard, following his previous instructions. Only two more pirates were killed after Roberts' death - he was their only leader. One appears to have been his second mate from the Princess, Stephenson, as he was not tried at Cape Corso. As he had been made steersman instead of the useless Johnson, the fate of the *Royal Fortune* was probably sealed with his death. Harry Glasby took over as helmsman and urged the pirates to surrender, but confused and leaderless, they decided to sail off. The Swallow caught them, probably because of Glasby's deliberate bad steersmanship or poor winds. Roberts' body was hoisted overboard by Magness and Stephenson after his express wish, but no-one came forth to take his place. The *Lords* descended into a drinking frenzy as the *Swallow* raked their ship with fire for two hours. The main mast came down. A few leaderless pirates fought courageously, but were hampered by the drunks, cowards and forced men. At two o'clock Lord Magness asked for quarter, or else they would blow up the ship. Ogle agreed. Yet another Welshman on the crew, the boatswain James Philips, now tried to blow the ship up with a lighted taper, shouting '*Let us all go to Hell together!*', but was restrained by Glasby and Captain Stephen Thomas (captured with the Diligence on January 5th - he was later acquitted on piracy on the grounds that '*it was unlikely that a master of a vessel at £6 a month should be a volunteer amongst such villains*'). Magness threw the Ship's Articles into the sea, but Roberts' black flags were pinned to the deck by a broken mast. As the boarding party arrived, a deserter from HMS *Rose*, Joe Mansfield, temporarily woke up from his drunken coma and shouted for the pirates to help him board and capture the *Swallow*. On board the Royal Fortune, Ogle found '*an English ensign jack and Dutch pennant and ye black flag hoisted at the mizzen peak.'* Roberts had used captured Dutch flags when posing as a Dutch interloper and capturing 14 French traders at Martinique.

Charles Johnson, in his 1724 'A General History of Pyrates' noted: *'The Account of Roberts runs into greater length than that of any other Pyrate... because he ravaged the seas longer than the rest... having made more Noise in the World than some others.'* Roberts seemed to have kept his command longer than any other pirate captain, pillaging the Caribbean for eighteen months and the Guinea Coast for a further eight. From a £3 per month third mate on a slaver, he wreaked more havoc and made more money than any pirate before or since. His death ended *'the Golden Age of Piracy'.*

Howard Pyle, in his 1891 *'The Buccaneers and Marooners of America'*, wrote: *"He made a gallant figure,"* says the old narrator, *"being dressed in a rich crimson waistcoat and breeches and red feather in his hat, a gold chain around his neck, with a diamond cross hanging to it, a sword in his hand, and two pair of pistols hanging at the end of a silk sling flung over his shoulders according to the fashion of the pyrates."* Thus he appeared in the last engagement which he fought—that with the Swallow—a royal sloop of war. A gallant fight they made of it, those bulldog pirates, for, finding themselves caught in a trap betwixt the man-of-war and the shore, they determined to bear down upon the king's vessel, fire a slapping broadside into her, and then try to get away, trusting to luck in the doing, and hoping that their enemy might be crippled by their fire. Captain Roberts himself was the first to fall at the return fire of the Swallow; a grapeshot struck him in the neck, and he fell forward across the gun near to which he was standing at the time. A certain fellow named Stevenson, who was at the helm, saw him fall, and thought he was wounded. At the lifting of the arm the body rolled over upon the deck, and the man saw that the captain was dead. "Whereupon," says the old history, "he" [Stevenson] "gushed into tears, and wished that the next shot might be his portion." After their captain's death the pirate crew had no stomach for more fighting; the "Black Roger" was struck, and one and all surrendered to justice and the gallows. Such is a brief and bald account of the most famous of these pirates. But they are only a few of a long list of notables, such as Captain Martel, Capt. Charles Vane (who led the gallant Colonel Rhett, of South Carolina, such a wild-goose chase in and out among the sluggish creeks and inlets along the coast), Capt. John Rackam, and Captain Anstis, Captain Worley, and Evans, and Philips, and others—a score or more of wild fellows whose very names made ship captains tremble in their shoes in those good old times.. And such is that black chapter of history of the past—an evil chapter, lurid with cruelty and suffering, stained with blood and smoke. Yet it is a written chapter, and it must be read.''

AFTERMATH

Of the 152 men on board, 52 were negro slaves. Only 3 men were killed on the *Royal Fortune*, and none on the *Swallow*. Ogle stole a great deal of gold-dust from Bart's great-cabin. £2000 of gold dust was recovered from the *Royal Fortune*, and Ogle went to Cape Lopez on February 12 to raid the *Little Ranger's* gold dust, jewellery and cash. However, the *Little Ranger* was empty. All the pirates' chests had been broken open. Captain Hill had departed in the Royal Africa Company ship *Neptune*, and in August gave back 50 ounces of gold-dust, but the vast majority of Roberts' fortune disappeared. This seems to have been the origin of the persistent story that Roberts buried his treasure on the Ile de Los Idols, north-east of Sierra Leone. Some of Roberts' men appear to have escaped into the woods in the mayhem, having been left onshore, and operated in West Africa in the 1720's intermixing with the Kru tribe. 45 of Roberts' captured crew had been 'black saylors, commonly known by the name of gremetoes', mariners from the Sierra Leone and Liberia region. The Kru were well-known for their skill in handling long canoes at sea, and for their independent leadership of slave revolts if captured. Intriguingly, it was noted in the early 19th century that 'a Kru makes a bad slave, because they know that if they are enslaved, they will commit suicide immediately.'

The *Swallow* stayed to boot-top and take on water at Cape Lopez, and sailed with the *Little Ranger* on February 18 for Princes' Island to rendezvous with the *Great Ranger*, which they met on February 22. Ogle set course for Cape Coast Castle, but a tornado at St Thomas Isle meant that he lost his prize ships. Most prisoners were on the *Swallow*, and it became difficult to keep control of the ship. The *Swallow's* crew had been divided between four ships. The pirates were manacled and guarded night and day. Hungry, they shouted that they would not have enough weight on them to hang. Young Sutton, the master-gunner, complained bitterly about being chained next to a pirate who was praying to go to Heaven. Sutton responded '*Did you ever hear of any pirate going thither ? Give me Hell, it's a merrier place. I'll give Roberts a salute of thirteen guns at its entrance.*' Sutton then made a formal complaint to have the pirate removed from his side or his Prayer Book confiscated.

In this dark atmosphere, Lords Ashplant, Magness and Mayer plotted to take over the Swallow and kill its officers. A mulatto boy was used to carry messages, but two prisoners chained next to Lord Ashplant heard of the plot. The surgeon George Willson, who joined from the *Stanwich*, betrayed the pirates in an attempt for clemency. Guards were doubled on the prisoners, and it was discovered that several had already broken their shackles. Roberts had been a shrewd judge of men after the Walter Kennedy lesson, and had called Wilson a double-rogue and threatened to cut off his ears in the past. Off Cape Corso, a French ship from Nantes struck its colours upon sighting the *Swallow*, thinking that Roberts was still in charge – he struck terror from beyond the grave. The prisoners were placed in the slave dungeons at Cape Coast Castle.

A report in *The Weekly Journal* on February 24th, 1722, reads: '*Tis computed that within five years past the pyrates have taken 140 English vessels on the Coast of Newfoundland and Africa. The report of the taking of the Weymouth man of war by Roberts the pyrate proves groundless.*' HMS *Weymouth* sailed into the Castle on March 26th, and the three prize ships rode out the storm and eventually made it to Cape Coast Castle upon April 3, two weeks after the *Swallow's* arrival. The *Royal Fortune* also survived the tornado and then took fresh food and water at St Thomas Isle before following on to the Castle. However, the pirate surgeons Scudamore and William Child had a free run of the ship to look after the wounded on board. Scudamore entreated the slaves on board to mutiny, using his smattering of their language, and the other prisoners willingly agreed to fight rather than be hanged. There was only a skeleton crew on board, but the day before the mutiny William Childs revealed the plan to an officer, and Scudamore was chained up.

Meanwhile, upon March 1st the Neptune moored at Cabinda (Angola) to take on 400 slaves, which were sold in August in Barbados. Captain Hill surrendered 50 ounces of gold here to the Governor, to avoid being prosecuted as a pirate, but still made a handsome profit from the affair. Both Ogle and Hill blamed each other for the disappearance of gold-dust. Ogle wrote that 300 pounds of gold-dust had been found. What was in the *Royal Fortune* and what was in the *Little Ranger* will never be known, but both Hill and Ogle profited enormously.

THE TRIAL AT CAPE CORSO CASTLE, THE BIGHT OF BENIN - THE GREATEST PIRATE TRIAL OF ALL TIME

This started on March 28th, 1722 with a Vice-Admiralty Court consisting of Captain Mungo Herdman, Lieutenant John Barnsley and Second-Lieutenant Charles Fanshawe, all from H.M.S. *Weymouth*, plus the Company agents Francis Boye, Henry Dodson and Samuel Hartease, Captain William Menzies of the Company ship *Chandos*, and The Honourable James Phipps, Director-General of the Company. Interestingly, the Registrar of the Court was the Swallow's surgeon, John Atkins, who recounted the capture of the pirates to Daniel Defoe. Because of legal technicalities, the only charges proceeded with, concerned the attack on H.M.S. *Swallow*.

The court was then filled with sixty-nine prisoners taken from the *Great Ranger*, commanded by Captain James Skyrme, who was barely alive. Most pirates admitted that they had signed the Pirate Articles and taken plunder, but all stated that they had been 'forced' into the life by Captain Roberts. The Frenchmen, and sailors recently taken from the *Whydah* and *Porcupine* all denied taking Pirate Articles.

The prisoners were taken out, while the Court decided what actually constituted an act of piracy. It was decided that newly-entered men might be precluded if they had not shared any booty, nor voluntarily taken or robbed a ship. Then the prisoners from the *Royal Fortune* came into court, of whom eight-seven were charged with piracy. Thomas Castell, a Company agent forcibly impressed from the *Onslow* in 1721, gave evidence that all the pirates who boarded the *King Solomon* did so voluntarily.

Ninety-one pirates were found guilty and seventy four acquitted. Captain Skyrme and most members of the 'House of Lords' were found 'Guilty in the Highest Degree', and the President of the Court, Captain Herdman pronounced:

'Ye and each of you are adjudged and sentenced to be carried back to the place from whence you came, from thence to the place of execution without the gates of this castle, and there within the flood marks to be hanged by the neck till you are **dead, dead, dead**. And the Lord have mercy on your souls'...........'After this ye and each of you shall be taken down, and your bodies hung in chains.' ('Records of the High Court of the Admiralty').

Herdman sentenced fifty-two of Bart Roberts' crew to death, twenty men to an effective death sentence in the Cape Coast mines, and sent another seventeen to imprisonment in London's Marshalsea Prison. Of these seventeen, thirteen died in the *Weymouth* in passage to London, The four survivors were eventually pardoned while in Newgate Prison. Two 'guilty' sentences were 'respited'. Of the fifty-two pirates hung at Cape Coast, nearly half were Welsh or West Countrymen, and most of the others indentured servants or poor white colonists. Fifteen pirates had died of their wounds on the passage to Cape Corso Castle, and four in its dungeons. Ten had been killed in the *Ranger*, and three in the *Royal Fortune*. Thus ninety-seven of Roberts' crew had died. The seventy negroes on board the pirate ships were returned to slavery.

THE END OF THE HOUSE OF LORDS

Surgeon Atkins's account of the hangings is repeated in Defoe's *'History of the Pyrates'*.

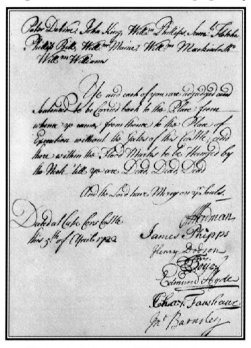

Warrant for the hanging of 19 of Roberts' crew

The first six to hang were the hardened 'Lords' Sutton, Simpson, Ashplant, Moody, Magness and Hardy. Atkins offered his services as a priest, but even Sutton, who had been suffering dysentery for days, ignored him. They called out for drinking water, and complained that *'We are poor rogues, and so get hanged while others, no less guilty in another way, escaped.'* Loosened from their shackles, they walked carelessly to the gallows. 'Little David' Simpson spotted poor Elizabeth Trengrove in the huge crowd, who he had ravished when the Onslow was taken in August 1721. He shouted *'I have lain with that bitch three times, and now she has come to see me hanged.'* The executioners did not know how to hang men, and tied their hands in front of the 'Lords'. Lord Hardy stated calmly *'I have seen many a man hanged, but this way of having our hands tied behind us I am a stranger to, and I never saw it before in my life.'*

Later hangings saw many of the men admit their sins, especially surgeon Scudamore, the only ship's doctor to have willingly joined any pirate ship. He asked for two days reprieve to read the scriptures, and was allowed to sing the 31st Psalm on the gallows before being swung off. A young man known as *'Captain'* Bunce also confessed to his sins, and blamed the liveliness and vivacity of his nature. He ended his speech from the gallows with the following words: *'I am now extremely afflicted because of the injuries I have done to all men, and I beg theirs and God's forgiveness. I exhort you here present to remember the Creator in the days of your youth and guard betimes so that your minds take not a wrong bias. I stand here as a beacon upon a rock to warn erring mariners of danger.'* (The gallows stood on a rock.)

Eighteen of the bodies were dipped in tar, encased in a frame of iron bands, and hung from gibbets in chains from nearby Lighthouse Hill, Connor's Hill and Catholic

Mission Hill, so that they could be seen by ships as a warning to pirates. Others were simply left hanging for the birds to eat. In Robert Louis Stevenson's *'Treasure Island'* is the following passage:

'You've seen 'em, maybe, hanged in chains, birds about 'em, seamen pointing 'em out as they go down with the tide .... And you can hear the chains a-jangle as you go about and reach for the other buoy.'

CAPTAIN CHALLONER OGLE

This architect of Roberts' defeat now took the HMS *Weymouth* and HMS *Swallow*, with their three prizes, back to Cape Lopez to clean the boats and take on water before heading across the Atlantic to Port Royal, Jamaica. However, lying at anchor there, they suffered a massive hurricane on August 28th, 1722. Only four men-of-war and two merchant-men survived, and about fifty other boats sank, including the *Royal Fortune* and *Little Ranger*. The town was itself devastated and around 300 people died there. This was almost exactly 30 years after the huge earthquake which tipped Henry Morgan's grave into the sea.

The naval ships were refitted and returned to England in April 1723, and Challoner Ogle was knighted by George I for killing Roberts, the only occasion any naval captain was knighted for such a deed. At the Admiralty Court, Ogle now petitioned for the *Great Ranger* to be the ship and effects of pirates, so he could partition its spoils. The prize and spoils were assessed at a value of just £5,364, of which the Court took £280 in expenses, Ogle was granted £3,144, and £1940 was to be distributed among the officers and crew of the Swallow as *'head-money'*. The worth of the gold-dust and valuables was not assessed, but Ogle computed it at just a few pounds per man, which he refused to pay until ordered to do so a year later, with the *'head-money'*.

On April 3rd, 1725, more than 3 years after the capture, the *'London Journal'* reported that the *Swallow's* officers and men had been paid the declared rate due to them under royal proclamation for taking of pirates. It noted *'it is remarkable that none of the Officers and crew of the said ship knew they were entitled to the said bounty, till the publishing of a book entitled "A General History of Pyrates", where the said Proclamation is taken notice of."* Thus Captain Johnson (Daniel Defoe) was responsible for them received their money off the arrogant Ogle. His men were furious with Ogle, who they rightly suspected of creaming off much of the booty, and unanimously petitioned Lord Berkeley, First Lord Commissioner of the Admiralty to intercede with King George. Ogle steadfastly refused to reapportion the shares, even when the Admiralty Secretary forwarded to him another letter stating that the King would be pleased to see a second distribution. Ogle finally responded by refusing on the grounds that he needed more money now that he had been made a knight of the realm by the King. The Admiralty tried once again in 1726 to force some money out of him, but Challoner Ogle repeated the same excuse. He wrote that he hoped that the Lords of the Admiralty would appreciate that the money which he had retained would be needed to help him keep up the dignity befitting his state. This rogue was made Commander-in Chief and sent to Jamaica in 1732, and promoted to Rear-Admiral of the Blue fleet (see Terms) in

1739. In 1742 he was in charge of the West Indies Fleet, then made Admiral of the White, retiring as a full Admiral and Commander-in-Chief of the Royal Navy. He died in 1750, one of the original London 'fat cats'.

FOOTNOTE ON WALTER KENNEDY

On December 15th, 1719, the Royal Rover took the 'Sea Nymph'. Off Barbados, it was spotted by Kennedy, and after a 7-hour chase Captain Bloodworth's New York snow was captured. It was kept alongside the Royal Rover for 8 days, until it was given back to Bloodworth, along with 16 forced men who wanted to return. Howell Davis's forced surgeon, Archibald Murray, was amongst those to receive their freedom. They reached Barbados on Christmas Day, 1719, and Murray testified against Kennedy's pirates at Edinburgh 11 months later. A mulatto who had served with Roberts was hanged in Virginia in March 1720, and was possibly one of Kennedy's deserters. This was a rare event, as usually black pirates were put into slavery at this time. Kennedy set course for Ireland for remaining the crew to disperse, but his poor navigation wrecked them in Scotland. Most of the crew were captured and executed, but Kennedy found his way to Dublin. Later, in London, he set up a brothel in Deptford, and also had a sideline in burglary. One of his dissatisfied harlots informed that he was a robber, and in prison he was recognised as a pirate and hanged.

FOOTNOTE ON THOMAS ANSTIS

Howell Davis, Thomas Anstis, Christopher Moody, Dennis Topping, Walter Kennedy and William Magness were all together on the Buck, and conspired to take that ship into piracy. Upon Davis' death, they all served under Black Bart, until Topping's death in battle, Kennedy's defection in October 1719, and Anstis' desertion on April 18th or 21st, 1721. Anstis had become tired of Roberts' increasingly autocratic manner, and had left Black Bart as their ships approached Africa. Anstis believed that there were better prospects in the West Indies. In the 18-gun brig Good Fortune he then captured several ships around Hispaniola, Martinique and Jamaica, increasing the size of the crew. During this time he 'abused and wounded' a Captain Doyle of Montserrat, who had tried to prevent a female passenger from being raped. She was killed and thrown overboard. In Johnson's lurid writing, which may or may not be true, 'twenty one of them forced the poor Creature successively, afterwards broke her Back and flung her into the Sea.'

After careening, the brutal Anstis made for Bermuda and captured the Morning Star, which was refitted with 21 guns and 100 men. John Fenn, a former member of Black Bart's crew, was given the captaincy of the captured ship, as Anstis was used to the handling of the Good Fortune. However, both crews wished to give up piracy as there had been little treasure taken, and Anstis and Fenn drew up a petition for pardon, claiming that they had been forced by Black Bart. They waited for a response to an island off the south-west of Cuba, and according to Johnson, for nine months 'they passed their time in Dancing and other Diversions' including mock trials. When no answer had been received by August 1722, the Good Fortune and Morning Star went to sea, and found off a merchantman that there was no interest from the authorities in giving them a pardon. Anstis and Fenn thus returned to piracy.

Fenn wrecked his ship on the Grand Caymans, and the *Good Fortune* anchored while Anstis tried to recover the crew. Unfortunately for Anstis, two men-of-war, the *Hector* and *Adventure*, came across them. Anstis cut his cable and fled, but the Royal Navy was on the point of taking him when the wind dropped. The heavy warships were becalmed, while the *Good Fortune's* crew desperately rowed her to safety. Sailing to the Bay of Honduras to careen, Anstis took three more ships and burned them all to leave no trace of his whereabouts. With too many prisoners aboard, the merchant Captain Durfey attempted to take the *Good Fortune*, but was beaten off.

In early December, a large frigate was taken. Encumbered by prisoners and loot, Anstis decided to keep her, and mounted her with 24 guns, giving its captaincy to Fenn again. Fenn had been disabled fighting for Black Bart, with only a single hand, and a poor record in captaincy, having lost the *Morning Star*. More prizes were taken in the Bahamas, before the ships went to Tobago to careen and refit in April 1723. The man-of-war *Winchelsea* came across them, and burned all the ships except for Anstis' *Good Fortune* which escaped in the nick of time. John Fenn fled into the woods, but was captured a day later and hanged at Antigua. Soon after, several recent recruits and forced men mutinied, killing Anstis and his officers, and put the ship into Curacao.

PARTIAL LIST OF SHIPS TAKEN BY THE BLACK CAPTAIN

The following table gives us about 220 ships and 250+ fishing boats that were taken by Roberts - nearer 500 prizes than the 400 accorded in most textbooks.

Date	Ship	From	Captain	Where taken
Spring 1717	Dutch, taken by Davis			
Spring 1719	Davis killed at Principe			
Spring 1719	Roberts in command - attacked Principe - took French ship and two Dutch sloops			
Early July	Careened			Near Cape Lopez
2nd week in	Experiment			
July 1719	(renamed Fortune)	London	Cornet	Off Guinea Coast
1 day later	Merchantman	Portugal		
2 days later	Temperance	Bristol?	Sharman	
August 1719	Careened			Ferninandino off Brazil coast
Sept 1719	Attacked 42-ship Lisbon treasure fleet - took Sagrada Familia and two other Portuguese ships	Lisbon		Bahia de Todos, Brazil
Oct 1719	Sloop	Rhode Island	Cane	Surinam
Oct 1719	Careened Royal Rover			Islet near Devil's Island
Oct 1719	Royal Rover and Sagrada Familia disappear under Kennedy			
January 10, 1720	Philippa sloop		Daniel Greaves	Laquary Roads, Trinidad
Feb 1720	2 sloops			Off Guadeloupe

Date	Ship / action	Home port	Captain	Location
Feb 1720	10-gun trader	Bristol		Off Barbados
Before Feb 12 1720	Benjamin	Liverpool		
Feb 18 1720	Joseph sloop		Bonaventure Jelfes	
Feb 19 1720	Chased pirate Sea King		Joined La Palisse	
Feb 1720	Pink	French		Off Barbados
Feb 26 1720	Roberts attacked by Summersett and Philippa			
Feb 1720	Repaired at Martinique, then careened at Cariacou	Picked up marooned pirates from Revenge		
May to mid-June 1720	about a dozen vessels' including a pink and a brig			Off coast of North America
May 1720	Expectation	Topsham		Newfoundland Banks
June 1720	Ferryland harbour, Newfoundland, looted one ship and burned Admiral's ship			
June 1720	Phoenix snow	Bristol	J. Richards	Newfoundland Banks
June 1720	Brigantine	Teignmouth, Devon	Peet	Newfoundland Banks
June 21 1720	Trepassey harbour - 22 sloops and 250 fishing boats, inc. Bideford Merchant	Replaced Fortune with Capt. Copplestone's brig	Admiral Babidge	Newfoundland
June 1720	St Mary's Harbour - took at least another 4 sloops and several fishing boats			Newfoundland
June 25 1720	Sidbury sloop	Bristol	William Thomas	Newfoundlandd Banks
June-July 1720	French fleet of 6 ships taken	French flagship renamed Good Fortune		North America coast
July 1720	4 more French ships			North America coast
July 1720	Brigantine Thomas	Bristol		Banks
July 1720	Richard pink	Bideford	Jonathan Whitfield	Banks
July 1720	Willing Mind	Poole		Banks
July 1720	Blessing	Lymington		Banks
July 1720	Happy Return sloop		William Taylor	Banks
July 1720	A ship of 26 guns and its consort sloop			Banks
July 14 1720	Samuel sloop		Cary	Off New England coast
July 15	Snow	Bristol	Bowles	Off New England coast
July 18	York, or Little York	Bristol	James Phillips	Off Virginia
July 18	Love brig	Lancaster	Thomas	Off Virginia
August 1720	Success sloop		Fensilon	Off South Carolina
August 1720	Storm, careened at Cariacou			

Date	Ship / Event		Captain / Owner	Location
Sept 4 1720	Relief sloop		Robert Dunn	Cariacou, Grenadines
Sept 19 1720	French sloop			
Sept 1720	sloop	Rhode Island (captured again)	Cane	
Sept 1720	Thomas brigantine			
Sept 26-27 1720	Mary and Martha, plus 6 ships at Basseterre inc. Capt. Cox's Greyhound sloop, Capt. Hingstone's ship, M. Pomier's French ship, Capt. Cox's Greyhound and Capt. Henry Fowles' ship	Liverpool	Wilcox	St Kitts
Sept-Oct 1720	Sheltered at St Bathelemy			
Oct 1720	22-gun brig captured	Renamed Royal Fortune		Tortola, Virgin Islands
Oct 25	English brig			St Lucia, near Martinique
Oct 25	sloop	As storeship	M. Courtel	St Lucia
Oct 23-26	14 English and French ships			Off Martinique
Oct 1720	Dutch interloper with 30 guns, plus 15 ships looted in harbour	Interloper became new Royal Fortune		St Lucia harbour
Dec 1720	Mary and Martha (again)	St Kitts	Wilson	
Dec 1720	Thomas Emanuel		Thomas Bennett	Bermudas
Dec	Aborted transatlantic crossing near Cape Verde Islands, returned to Surinam after a 4000 mile round journey			
Jan 13 1721	Sea King sloop (Capt. Richard Simes Barbados sloop, the Fisher, caught fire)	Rhode Island	Benjamin Norton	Off St Lucia
Jan-Feb	Several sloops to replace the crew lost in the Atlantic crossing			
Jan 1721	Saint Anthony sloop		John Rogers	
Jan 1721	flyboat			Basseterre harbour
Jan-Feb 1721	Boot-topping in Hispaniola, then careening in Bennet's Cay			
Feb 1721	Mayflower sloop			Off Martinique
Feb 1721	sloop			Off Guadeloupe
Feb 18 1721	Dutch interloper			St Lucia harbour
Feb 1721	14 Martinican traders	Martinique - 13 were burned		St Luce Bay, Martinique
March	Rested on St Barthelemy			
March 26	Lloyd galley		Hingston	Off Antigua
April 1721	Roberts fights with Thomas Jones			
Apr 9 1721	Jeremiah and Anne			West Indies
Apr 1721	French man-of-war with 41 guns and 140 crew	Roberts is said to have hung the Governor of Martinique		Off Leeward Isles
April 1721	merchantman	Virginia		
April 17	Prince Eugene	Dutch	Bastian Meake	mid-Atlantic

April	small snow			mid-Atlantic
April	Set course for Africa, Anstis deserts April 18			
May 1721	Dutch snow Christopher		Thomas Heindrich	mid-Atlantic
May 1721	Norman galley			Off Cape Verde
June 1721	St Agnes warship and Comte de Thoulouze warship	French, guarding the Senegal gum trade		Off Senegal River, Sierra Leone
June 1721	Merchant ship	French		Frenchman's Bay, Senegal
June 12	A French ship, three other ships looted and several burned			Brent Island
End July	Semm Galley	Dutch		Off Axim
August 1721	Robinson	Liverpool	Canning	Off Grain Coast
August 6	Stanwich galley	Liverpool	Tarlton	Off Sestos
August 8	Onslow	London	Gee	Off Sestos
August	Martha snow	Liverpool	Lady	Off Cape la Hou
August 1721	Ship?	Dutch?		
September	Careened in Old Calabar			Bight of Biafra
Oct 1 1721	Joceline		Loane	Calabar River
Oct 2 1721	Mercy galley			Calabar River
Oct 5	Hannibal	London	Charles Ousley	Calabar River
Oct 1721	Cornwall galley		Rolls	Calabar River
Oct 1721	Running battle with Calabar natives			
Dec 14 1721	Geetruyt, or Geertrouycht galley	Dutch	Benjamin Kreeft	Gabon
Jan 2 1722	Elizabeth		Joseph Sharp	Jacque Jacques
Jan 2 1722	Tarlton	Liverpool	Thomas Tarlton	Assinie
Jan 3	Hannibal		Ousley	
Jan 4	Vlissingen (Flushingham)	Dutch	Gerrit de Haen	Grand Basaam
Jan 5	Diligence sloop		Stephen Thomas	Cape Appolonia
Jan 6	King Solomon	London	Joseph Traherne	Cape Appolonia
Jan 11	Porcupin Carlton (Charlton)	London	Fletcher	Whydah
	Hardey On Jan 11, apart from the 3 English slave ships, 5 Portuguese and 4 French were also taken		Allright Dittwitt	
Jan 11	Comte de Thoulouze	French privateer	There may have been two ships of this name - see June 1721	Whydah
Jan 13 or 15	Whydah (Wida) sloop	London	Stokes	Off Jacquin
Feb 5-6	The Ranger is taken by Ogle at sea			
Feb 9	Neptune		Thomas Hill	Cape Lopez
Feb 10	The final battle - Roberts dies			

PRISONERS TAKEN FROM THE RANGER and GOOD FORTUNE - THEIR FATE

R = taken from the Ranger. RF = taken from the Royal Fortune	Place of Birth	Taken from	With Bart from	Age at Trial	Verdict
Michael Mare (Maer) R	Ghent	In the Rover when Dutch from 1717	1718	41	Guilty - hung at Cape Corso Castle April 11th 1722
Martin (or Marcus) Johnson RF	Smyrna (Greece)	Rover when Dutch like Michael Mare	1718	21	Guilty - hung at Cape Corso Castle April 11th 1722
'Lord' Richard Hardy R	Wales	With Howel Davis	1718	26	Guilty - hung in chains at Cape Corso Castle April 3rd 1722
'Lord' Henry Dennis R	Bideford	With Howel Davis	1718	–	Guilty - but reprieved and sentenced to 7 years working in a plantation for the Royal Africa Company.
'Lord' Valentine Ashplant R	Minories, London	With Howel Davis	1719	32	Guilty - hung in chains at Cape Corso April 3rd, 1722
Robert Birdson R	Cornwall	With Howel Davis	1718	30	Guilty - died in prison?
'Lord' William Magness (Magnus) R	Minehead	With Howel Davis	1718	35	Guilty - hung in chains at Cape Corso April 3rd, 1722
'Lord' Christopher Moody RF	–	With Howel Davis	1718	28	Guilty - hung in chains at Cape Corso April 3rd, 1722
'Lord' David Sympson RF	North Berwick	Capt. Greaves Philippa of Trinidad	Jan 10th 1720	36	Guilty - hung in chains at Cape Corso April 3rd, 1722
'Lord' ThomasSutton RF	Berwick	With Howel Davis	1718	23	Guilty - hung in chains at Cape Corso April 3rd, 1722
John Jessup (1)	Wisbech	Taken with Roberts by Howel Davis	Feb 1719		Surrendered at Princes Island - Guilty - petitioned successfully for Royal Africa Company Indenture
Hag. Jacobson RF	Bristol	Dutch ship at Surinam	1719	30	Guilty - hung in chains at Cape Corso April 11th 1722
Joseph Moor(e) RF	Mere, Wiltshire	May Flower sloop	Feb 1720	19	Guilty - hung at Cape Corso Castle April 11th 1722
Josecph Nositer (Nossiter) RF	Sidbury, Devon	Expedition of Topsham	May 1720	26	Guilty - hung at Cape Corso April 16th, 1722
Joe Mansfield	Orkneys	Deserter from Rose, picked up at Dominica with Philips and Butson	June		Guilty but reprieved as he gave information on Scudamore's plot, although other sources state he was hung on April 16th at Cape Corso
James Philips (Phillips) RF	Antigua	Revenge pirate sloop Dominica	June 1720	35	Guilty - hung in chains at Cape Corse April 20th , 1722
Robert Butson	Ottery St. Mary, Devon	Revenge pirate sloop	June 1720	30	Guilty - hung at Cape Corso April 16th, 1722
William Williams (1) RF	Plymouth	Sidbury of Bristol Capt. William Thomas, at Newfoundland	June 25th 1720	40	Guilty - hung April 9th, 1722 although he had previously tried to escape from Roberts at Sierra Leone
William Williams (2) RF	Holland	Sidbury sloop	June 1720	30	Guilty - hung April 16th, 1722
William Fernon RF	Somerset	Sidbury	June 1720	22	Guilty - hung in chains at Cape Corso Castle April 11th, 1722
Roger Scot(t) RF	Bristol	Sidbury	June 1720		Guilty - reprieved to serve the Royal Africa Company for 7 yrs.

William Main R	–	Capt. Peet's Brigantine	June 1720	28	Guilty - hung at Cape Corso April 9th, 1722
Richard Harris (Harries) R	Devon or Cornwall	Capt. Richards' Phoenix snow of Bristol	June 1720	45 the oldest	Guilty - hung at Cape Corso April 16th 1722
D. Littlejohn R	Bristol	Capt. Richards' Phoenix snow of Bristol	June 1720		Guilty - reprieved to serve the Royal Africa Company
Thomas How R	Barnstaple Devon	Joined from Trepassey fishing boat Newfoundland	June 1720		Guilty - reprieved to serve the Royal Africa Company for 7 years
John Phillips (Philips) RF	Alloa	Fishing boat Newfoundland	July 1720		Guilty - hung in chains at Cape Corso Castle Aprill 11th, 1722
James Harries RF	Jersey	Capt. Jonathan Whitfield's Richard pink	July 1720	28	Sent for trial at Marshalsea
Harry Glasby		Capt. Cary's Samuel sloop off New England	July 1720		Acquitted
Hugh Menzies RF		Capt. Cary's Samuel	July 14th 1720		Acquitted
Thomas Owen RF	Bristol	Capt. Phillips' Little York of Bristol	July 18th 1720		Guilty - reprieved and sold to the Royal Africa Company
William Taylor RF	Bristol	Little York of Bristol	July 18th 1720		Guilty - reprieved to serve the Royal Africa Company
James Greenham R	Marshfield Gloucester	Little York of Bristol	July 18th 1720		Guilty - successful petition to Royal Africa Company indenture
John Jaynson R	Lancaster	Love of Lancaster	July 18th 1720	22	Guilty - hung at Cape Corso Castle April 11th, 1722
James Clements RF	Brisol	Capt. Fensilon's Success sloop	July 1720	20	Guilty - hung at Cape Corso Castle April 11th, 1722
Herman Hunkins R		Success sloop	July 1720		Sent for trial at Marshalsea
John Parker RF	Dorset	Willing Mind of Poole	July 1720	22	Guilty - hung at Cape Corso Castle April 11th, 1722
Hugh Harris R	Corfe Castle, Devon	Willing Mind sloop	July 1720		Guilty - reprieved to serve the Royal Africa Company
William Mackintosh R	Canterbury	On Newfoundland Banks	July 1720	21	Guilty - hung at Cape Coast Castle April 9th, 1722
Thomas Willis R		Richard of Bideford	July 1720		Acquitted
George Smith RF	Wales	Mary and Martha	July 1720	25	Guilty - hung at Cape Corso April 20th, 1722
John Walden (1) R	Whitby	Mary and Martha	July 1720	24	Sent for trial at Marshalsea
John Walden (2) RF	Somerset	Blessing of Lymington	July 1720	24	Guilty - hung in chains at Cape Coast Castle April 23rd, 1722
Robert Crow RF	Isle of Man	Capt. Williams Taylor's Happy Return sloop	July 1720	24	Guilty - hung at Cape Corso Castle April 13th 1722
Christopher Lang R		Thomas brigantine	Sept. 1720		Sent for trial at Marshalsea
James Skyrme R	Somerset	Greyhound sloop of Bristol	Oct. 1720	44	Guilty - hung in chains at Cape Corso Castle April 13th 1722
John Mitchel R	Shadwell, London	Norman galley	Oct. 1710		Guilty - reprieved and sold to the Royal Africa Company
T. Withstandenot R		Norman galley	Oct. 1720		Acquitted
Peter la Fever R		Jeremiah and Anne	April 9th 1721	20 ind efoe	Acquitted

William Shurin R	Wapping, London	Jeremiah and Anne	April 1721	20 ind efoe	Guilty - reprieved to serve the Royal Africa Company
Robert Wilbourne RF		Capt. Whitby's Jeremiah and Anne	April 1721		Acquitted
Robert Johnson RF	Whydah	Jeremiah and Anne	April 1721	32	Guilty - hung at Cape Corso April 20th, 1722
William Darling RF		Jeremiah and Anne	April 1721		Acquitted
William Mead RF		Jeremiah and Anne	April 1721		Sent for trial at Marshalsea
Thomas Diggles RF		Capt. Thomas Heindrich's Christopher Dutch snow - mid Atlantic	April 1721		Acquitted
Ben Jeffreys (Jeffries) RF	Bristol or Devon	Norman galley of Cape Verde	May 1721	21	Guilty - hung at Cape Corso April 20th 1722
John Francia RF		Sloop at St Nicholas	April 1721		Acquitted
Dan Harding RF	Congresbury Somerset	Dutch interloper, El Puerto del Principe, St. Lucia	April 1721	26	Guilty - hung at Cape Corso Castle April 11th 1722
John Coleman RF	Wales	Adventure sloop	April 1721	24	Guilty - hung in chains at Cape Corso April 20th 1722
Charles Bunce RF	Exeter	Dutch galley Semm	April 1721	26	Guilty - hung at Cape Corso April 16th, 1722
R. Armstrong RF	London	Dutch galley, deserter from HMS Swallow	April 1721	34	Guilty - hung as a deserter from the foreyard on HMS Weymouth
John du Frock RF		Capt. Hingston's Lloyd galley off Antigua	May 1721		Sent for trial at Marshalsea
William Champnies RF		Lloyd galley	May 1721		Acquitted
George Danson RF		Lloyd galley	May 1721		Acquitted
Isaac Russel RF		Lloyd galley	May 1721		Sent for trial at Marshalsea
William Watts R	Irish	With Capt. Josse at Sierra Leone	July 1721	23	Guilty - hung in chains at Cape Corso April 20th 1722
William Davis (Davies) R	Welsh	With Capt. Glynne at Sierra Leone - deserter from the Ann Galley	July 1721	23	Guilty - hung in chains at Cape Corso April 20th, 1722
Abraham Harper RF	Bristol	Capt. Gee's Onslow at Sestos	Aug. 1721	23	Guilty - hung at Cape Corso Castle April 11th, 1722
Peter Lesley (Lashley) RF	Aberdeen	Onslow at Sestos	Aug. 1721	21	Guilty - hung at Cape Corso April 16th, 1722
Thomas Watkins RF		Onslow at Sestos	Aug. 1721		Acquitted
Philip Bill RF	St. Thomas Isle	Onslow at Sestos	Aug. 1721	27	Guilty - hung at Cape Corso Castle April 9th, 1722
Joseph Stephenson (Stevenson) RF	Whitby	Onslow at Sestos	Aug. 1721	40	Guilty - hung at Cape Corso Castle, April 16th, 1722
James Cromby RF	Wapping London	Onslow at Sestos	Aug. 1721		Guilty - petitioned to indenture at Royal Africa Company
Thomas Garret RF		Onslow at Sestos	Aug. 1721		Acquitted
George Ogle RF		Onslow at Sestos	Aug. 1721		Sent for trial to Marshalsea
Thomas Stretton R		Onslow at Sestos	Aug. 1721		Acquitted
William Petty R	Deptford	Onslow at Sestos	Aug. 1721	30	Guilty
Michael Lemmon R		Onslow at Sestos	Aug. 1721		Acquitted
William Wood R	York	Onslow at Sestos	Aug. 1721	27	Guilty - hung at Cape Corso April 20th, 1722
Edward Watts R	Dunmore	Onslow at Sestos	Aug. 1721	22	Guilty - hung in chains at Cape Corso April 20th, 1722

John Horn R	St. James London	Onslow at Sestos (a soldier)	Aug. 1721		Guilty - reprieved to serve the Royal Africa Company
Robert Hays RF	Liverpool	Capt. John Tarleton's Liverpool galley	Aug. 1721	20	Guilty - hung at Cape Corso April 20th, 1722
James Barrow R	Liverpool	Capt. Lady's Martha snow of Liverpool off Cape la Hou	Aug. 1721		Sent to Marshalsea for trial
Joshuah Lee R	Liverpool	Martha snow	Aug. 1721		Guilty - reprieved to serve the Royal Africa Company
Roger Gorsuch RF		Martha snow	Aug. 1721		Acquitted
John Watson RF		Martha snow	Aug. 1721		Acquitted
Robert Hartley (1) R		Capt. Canning's Robinson of Liverpool off Grain Coast	Aug. 1721		Acquitted
James Crane R		Robinson of Liverpool	Aug. 1721		Sent for trial to Marshalsea
George Smithson R	Wales	Capt. Tarleton's Stanwich galley of Liverpool off Sestos	Aug. 1721	24	Acquitted
Roger Pye R		Stanwich galley	Aug. 1721		Acquitted
Robert Fletcher R		Stanwich galley	Aug. 1721		Sent for trial to Marshalsea
Robert Hartley (2) R	Liverpool	Stanwich galley (a gunner)	Aug. 1721		Guilty - reprieved on petition to serve a Royal Africa Company Indenture
Andrew Rance R		?	Aug. 1721		Sent for trial to Marshalsea
Cuthbert Goss R	Plymouth	Dutch ship	Aug. 1721	21	Guilty - hung within the flood-marks at Cape Corso Castle April 20th, 1722
Thomas Giles R	Minehead	Mercy galley of Bristol at Calabar	Oct. 1721	26	Guilty - reprieved to serve the Royal Africa Company
Israel Hynde R	Aberdeen or Bristol	Mercy galley	Oct. 1721	30	Guilty - hung in chains at Cape Coast Castle April 13th, 1722
William Child RF		Mercy galley surgeon	Oct. 1721		Acquitted
John Griffin RF	Blackwall London	Mercy galley carpenter	Oct. 1721		Guilty - reprieved into 7 years slavery for the Royal Africa Co.
Peter Scudamore RF	Welsh but 'of Bristol'	Capt. Rolls' slave galley Cornwall at Calabar	Oct. 1721	35	Guilty - hung in chains at Cape Corso Castle April 13th, 1722
Christopher Granger		Cornwall galley at Calabar	Oct. 1721		Acquitted
Nicholas Brattle RF		Cornwall galley at Calabar	Oct. 1721		Acquitted - a musician
James White RF		Cornwall galley	Oct. 1721		Acquitted - a musician
Thomas Davis RF		Cornwall galley at Calabar	Oct. 1721		Acquitted
Thomas Sever RF		Cornwall galley at Calabar	Oct. 1721		Acquitted
Robert Bevins RF		Cornwall galley at Calabar	Oct. 1721		Guilty
T. Oughterly RF		Cornwall galley at Calabar	Oct. 1721		Guilty
David Rice RF	Welsh but 'of Bristol'	Cornwall galley	Oct. 1721		Guilty - sentenced to 7 years in the Royal Africa Company Plantations

Name	Origin	Ship	Date	Age	Verdict
Robert Haws RF	Yarmouth	Capt. Loane's Joceline on the Calabar River	Oct. 1st 1721	31	Guilty - hung at Cape Coast Castle April 11th, 1722
William Church R		Gertruycht of Holland	Dec. 14th 1721		Acquitted - a musician
Phillip Haak R		Flushingham of Holland	Jan. 1722		Acquitted - a musician
William Smith R		Capt. Joseph Sharp's Elizabeth	Jan. 2nd 1722		Acquitted
Adam Comry R		Elizabeth	Jan. 2nd 1722		Acquitted - the surgeon testified against George Wilson and Scudamore
William May RF		Elizabeth	Jan. 1722		Acquitted
Edward Thornden RF		Elizabeth	Jan. 1722		Acquitted
Peter de Vine R	Stepney	Capt. Trahern's King Solomon off Cape Appollonia	Jan. 6th 1722	42	Guilty - hung at Cape Corso Castle April 9th, 1722
John Johnson R	Near Lancaster	King Solomon	Jan. 1722	22	Acquitted but Gosse says hung
John Stodgill R		King Solomon	Jan. 1722		Acquitted
John Lane (Line) RF	Lambert St. London	King Solomon (a soldier)	Jan. 1722		Guilty - indentured for 7 years to Royal Africa Company
Sam Fletcher RF	East Smithfield	King Solomon	Jan. 1722		Guilty - indentured to Royal Africa Company on petition
William Phillips RF	Lower Shadwell London	King Solomon	Jan. 1722	29	Guilty - hung at Cape Corso Castle - April 9th, 1722
Jacob Johnson RF		King Solomon	Jan. 1722		Acquitted
John King RF	Shadwell London	King Solomon	Jan. 1722	20	Guilty - reprieved to serve the Royal Africa Company
Benjamin Par RF		Capt. Kanning's Robinson	Jan. 1722		Acquitted
Josiah Robinson R		Capt. Thomas Tarlton's Tarlton at Cape la Hou, Assinie	Jan. 2nd		Acquitted
John Arnaught R		Tarlton	Jan. 1722		Acquitted
John Davis R		Tarlton	Jan. 1722		Acquitted
Henry Graves R		Tarlton	Jan. 1722		Sent for trial to Marshalsea
Thomas Howard R		Tarlton	Jan. 1722		Acquitted
John Rimer R		Tarlton	Jan. 1722		Sent for trial to Marshalsea
Thomas Clephen R		Tarlton	Jan. 1722		Acquitted
George Wilson RF		Tarlton	Jan. 1722		Guilty - execution witheld on the King's pleasure, as he informed
Edward Tarlton RR		Tarlton	Jan. 1722		Acquitted
John Jessup (2) RF	Plymouth	Capt. Stephen Thomas' Diligence sloop	Jan. 5th 1722	20	Guilty - hung at Cape Corso April 20th, 1722
Hugh Riddle RF		Diligence sloop	Jan. 1722		Acquitted
Stephen Thomas RF		Diligence sloop	Jan. 1722		Acquitted
Henry Dawson R		Whydah sloop at Jacquin	Jan. 1722		Acquitted
William Glass R		Whydah sloop	Jan. 1722		Acquitted
James Cosins R		?	Jan. 1722		Sent for trial to Marshalsea

William Guineys R		Capt. Fletcher's	Jan. 11th		Acquitted
		Porcupine	1722		
Richard Wood RF		Porcupine	1722		Acquitted
Richard Scot RF		Porcupine	1722		Acquitted
William Davison RF	Wales	Porcupine	1722	23	Acquitted
Sam Morwell RF		Porcupine	1722		Acquitted
Edward Evans RF		Porcupine	1722		Acquitted
Thomas Roberts RF		Capt. Allwright's	Jan. 11th		Acquitted
		Charlton (or Carlton)	1722		
John Richards RF		Charlton	1722		Acquitted
John Cane RF		Charlton	1722		Acquitted

'Lords' Hardy, Moody, Magness, Ashplant, and Sutton had served with Howell Davis. It is significant that these were the first six men hung, all on April 3rd, and all six were then displayed in chains. They showed contempt for the hangings, and complained that the inexperienced hangmen tied their hands in front of them, instead of behind, as was the custom. In the mass hanging of 14 pirates upon April 11th, Jacobson, Philps and Fernon were transferred into chains. The next batch of prisoners to be hung in chains were the one-legged Skyrme, 'Nanny' Walden and Israel Hynde, both of whom had lost arms in the final fight, and the rogue surgeon Scudamore. These four were the only executions on the 13th of April. In another mass hanging of 14 men on the 20th, another 5 men were hung in chains - Edward and William Watts, William Davies, James Phillips and John Coleman. Thus a total of 18 pirates in chains was the grim sight for ships entering the harbour, for several months after. Stevenson may refer to the sight in *Treasure Island* - 'You've seen 'em, maybe, hanged in chains, birds about 'em, seamen pointing 'em out as they go down with the tide … And you can hear the chains a-jangle as you go about and reach for the other buoy.'

Thomas Jones had returned to England and was incarcerated in the Marshalsea, where he died. Of the 17 men committed to the Marshalsea Prison in Southwark, 13 died on the homeward trip on HMS Weymouth. Of the two respited, George Willson died soon after on the Cape Coast, and the other received the King's Pardon.

18 impressed men from the French ship at Whydah in February 1722 were taken off the *Ranger* and acquitted. The acquitted musicians had 'served as Musick on board the Royal Fortune, being taken out of several merchant ships, having had an uneasy life of it, having sometimes their Fiddles, and often their Heads broke, only for excusing themselves, as saying they were tired, when any Fellow took it in his Head to demand a Tune' (trial transcript)

Roger Ball died of burns caused by John Morris exploding gunpowder in the Royal Fortune. Another William Main in the crew was blown up on the Royal Fortune. 10 men were killed in the Ranger and 3 in the Royal Fortune.

Fate	No. of men	Notes
Executed	52	In 1722 at Cape Corso Castle: 6 on April 3rd; 6 on April 9th; 14 on April 11th; 4 on April 13th, 8 on April 16th, 14 on April 20th
Guilty, and sentenced to Death, reprieved on petition to 7 years' **Servitude** for Royal Africa Company	20	All seem to have died before their 7 years were completed
To **Marshalsea** Prison	17	13 died on the voyage
Respited	2	1 died, 1 pardoned
Acquitted	74	
Negroes	70	52 on Royal Fortune, 28 on Ranger - some were slaves and some were seamen
Died en route to Cape Corso	15	
Died in Cape Coast Castle	4	
Killed on Ranger	10	
Killed on Royal Fortune	3	
TOTAL Crew Members	267	

Footnotes:

1. Among Roberts' pirates captured by Challoner Ogle was John Place in 1722. Not far off Cape Coast Castle, in October 1748, he led a mutiny on the HMS *Chesterfield*, wishing to settle a colony. He was hanged. (see *Mariners' Mirror*, 47, 1961). When the captain and most of the officers were ashore, the first lieutenant took the ship to sea, to turn pirate. However, the *Chesterfield* was recovered by the boatswain, who sailed it to the West Indies. The first lieutenant and lieutenant of marines were shot, and the carpenter, his mate and three others hanged.

2. The nature of equality aboard pirate ships, with blacks being treated as equal, was known in the early 18th century. In 1715 the ruling Council of the Colony of Virginia worried about the 'connections' between the *"Ravage of Pyrates"* and *"an Insurrection of the Negroes."* They were right to be concerned. By 1716 the slaves of Antigua had grown *"very impudent and insulting"* and reportedly many of them *"went off to join those pirates who did not seem too concerned about colour differences."* These connections were trans-Atlantic; stretching from the heart of Empire in London, to the slave colonies in the Americas and the 'Slave Coast' of Africa. In the early 1720s a gang of pirates settled in West Africa, joining and intermixing with the Kru—a West African people from what is now Sierra Leone and Liberia, renowned both for their seamanship in their long canoes and when enslaved for their leadership of slave revolts. The pirates were probably members of Bartholomew Roberts' crew who had fled into the woods when attacked by the Navy in 1722. This alliance is not so unusual when you consider that of the 157 men who did not escape and were either captured or killed on board Roberts' ship, 45 of them were black — probably neither slaves nor pirates but *"Black saylors, commonly known by the name of gremetoes"* — independent African mariners primarily from the Sierra Leone region, who would have joined the pirates *"for a small demand of wages."* We can see the way these connections were spread and the how the pirates' legacy was disseminated even after their defeat in the fate of some of those captured on Roberts' pirate ship. *"Negroes"* from Black Bart's crew grew mutinous over the poor conditions and *"thin Commons"* they received

from the Navy. *"Many of them"* had *"lived a long time"* in the *"pyratical Way"*, which obviously for them had meant better food and more freedom.

3. The remnants of Roberts' pirates who intermarried with the Kru Tribe, may have some connection with *Palm Wine* music, which is believed to have its origins in the *Kru* tribe of Liberia, and combines elements from Caribbean Calypso with local melodies and rhythms. *The music was so called because the music could be largely heard in clubs where palm-wine was usually served without limitation. The music could be heard in bars along marina areas enjoyed by sailors and crewmen. Palm Wine guitarists had a tremendous impact on most African guitarists of today and their influence can be heard in both Highlife and Soukous guitar players. Presently Pine Wine music is on the decline, the last well known artist being S.E. Rogie who died in 1994. However Palm Wine music originated, it is an expression of the day-to-day life of ordinary people, the music of their hearts. It tells of people's joys and sorrows, pleasures and displeasure, success and disappointments. The word Palm Wine is used to describe a milky white liquid tapped from the Palm tree. It has 2 percent alcohol, it is cheap and it makes a mellow natural high. When people gather around the fire to share life experiences, some are shy and bashful, but after drinking a few glasses of Palm Wine, it brings them out.*

America's formula-driven music industry has been unkind to most African musicians. It beckons with the promise of enormous riches, then rebuffs with a calculated closed-mindedness. *Palm Wine guitar music is like folk music or blues. In Palm Wine music people sing heart-to-heart songs, what they feel. They drink a little to feel happy, and what they drink is Palm Wine. The wine is a sweet milky sap from a variety of palm tree plentiful in West Africa.* The music is a blend of rural tradition and urban acculturation. Fortified by the arrival of cheap acoustic guitars, and the musical exchange fostered by sailors plying the waters along the Gulf of Guinea and Sierra Leone who staffed the apparatus of colonialism up and down the coast, it took root in the twenties and thirties. The sailors, many of whom were from the Kru tribe of Sierra Leone and Liberia, brought sea shanties and records from other lands. Krios, the comparatively well-educated descendants of an amalgam of Africans of varying ethnicity, freed from slavery and repatriated to the colony of Freetown (now Sierra Leone's capital), carried music from post to post throughout British West Africa. Freetown in the fifties and sixties was a particularly good place for musicians. There were always parties to play for in the bustling capital, and a variety of bars competed for customers with the lure of live music. Recording, too was becoming a means of generating both income and a measure of fame. European record companies had representatives roaming West Africa in search of talent; the British company Decca even had a mobile studio, which periodically visited Freetown.

4. 'The Black Captain' should be made into a Spielberg movie. 'Black Bart' was a film starring Dan Duryea and Yvonne de Carlo. Unfortunately, it was a Western about a stagecoach robber who termed himself Black Bart, Charles Bowles, from Norfolk, England. He served the Union Army at Vicksburg and was wounded before the Siege of Atlanta. For eight years he plagued Wells Fargo with a string of at least 28 robberies. Boles operated on foot with an unloaded shotgun and never robbed stagecoach passengers or drivers. Between robberies he lived in San Francisco, and disappeared from the Palace Hotel, Visalia, California in 1888 and was never heard of again. The 1996 book 'Black Bart, Boulevardier Bandit: The Saga of California's Most Mysterious Stagecoach Robber and the Men who Sought to Capture Him', by George Hoeper, recounts the story.

CHAPTER IX

JOHN PHILLIPS (PHILIPS) d. 18th April 1724

John Phillips was probably forced from the *Inven*, the first prize captured by Thomas Anstis in the *Good Fortune*, a day after he and Thomas Jones deserted Bart Roberts (-see the footnote on Anstis in the entry on Howell Davis. Another source says that this John Phillips had originally been captured along with Bart Roberts by Howel Davis). Anstis had not wished to sail for Africa, and Jones had been involved in a brawl with Roberts. Phillips was needed by the pirates as a carpenter. Soon the pirates took the *Two Sisters*, under Captain Richards, and headed for Martinique. However, narrowly escaping from two French men-of-war off Montserrat, the next we hear of the *Good Fortune* is in the *Weekly Journal* of January 13th, 1722:

'*Our merchants have received the following advice from St Christophers dated October 15th, 1721, that they were in daily expectation of the arrival of the new governor, with some men-of-war along with him which they very much wanted. That the Hector man-of-war, Captain Brand, having buried most of her crew could then do but little service. That several pirate ships infested the coast where one carrying thirty guns and 400 men some days before had engaged two French men-of-war. She carried a black flag at her top-mast-head. The action took place off Montserrat but she got away from them and bore away from Antigua. That five men newly come in there that did belong to the Inven, Captain Ross, from Cork in Ireland, having on board 600 barrels of beer besides other provisions which ship was taken off Martinico by a pirate sloop well mounted with 140 men. That Colonel Doyley of Montserrat with his family was on board the said vessel and was very much cut and wounded by the pirates. That 21 of these brutes had forced a woman passenger one after another and afterwards broke her back and threw her into the sea.*' Doyley had been attacked for trying to defend the woman - the story shows how remarkable the discipline of Captain Bart Roberts was, regarding the safety of women.

Anstis and Jones next captured Captain Marston's ship carrying alcohol and provisions, and five men joined the crew, before taking Captain Smith's *Hamilton* in late June 1722. At Mohair Key, the crew laid up for a few weeks, to drink their way through the liquor and careen the Good Fortune. They returned the looted and stripped *Hamiton* to its captain, and headed for the Gulf of Campeachy, taking two Spanish ships on the way, with meagre returns. One was driven ashore at Campeachy and one was burned. Strangely, the next ship they encountered was Captain Smith's *Hamilton* again. It had been captured by a Spanish privateers, and was being taken into Cuba when the Spaniard ran aground. Jones asked Smith if he had been looking for his empty bottles, before he was put into an open boat with his remaining crew, and the *Hamilton* was burnt. On October 21st, the rich *Don Pedro* was looted off

Hispaniola, the first decent prize since Anstis and Jones had deserted Roberts. £3000 in goods was taken, and its surgeon forced, after a short battle when two of its crew were killed. A few days later, the *Morning Star* was captured, 32 guns were transferred to her, and the one-handed John Finn was elected captain. The *Morning Star* and *Good Fortune* took Captain Lubbock's *Portland* in December, then two more small prizes before taking Captain Ellwood's *Nightingale*, at anchor of Tortuga. This was April 1722, and while the pirates careened, Montigny la Palisse and those former members of Roberts' crew must have mused upon the poor 'luck' of Anstis as a leader. Roberts concentrated on specific areas to hunt, whereas Anstis seemed to have no strategy but to rely on ships passing at sea. Some wanted to steal the *Good Fortune*, and Anstis was replaced in an election as its captain by Bridstock Weaver. The unhappy pirates allowed Ellwood to sail off in the *Nightingale* upon condition he took the following petition for pardon to Governor Lawes of Jamaica and return with an answer:

To His Most Gracious majesty, by the Grace of God, of Great Britain, France, and Ireland, Defender of the Faith

The Humble PETITION of the Company, now belonging to the Ship Morning Star and Brigantine Good Fortune, lying under the ignominious Name and Denomination of Pyrates, Humbly sheweth:

That we your Majesty's most loyal Subjects have, at sundry Times, been taken by Bartholomew Roberts, the then Captain of the aforesaid Vessels and Company, together with another Ship, in which we left him, and have been forced by him and his wicked Accomplices, to enter into, and serve, in the said Company; as Pyrates, much contrary to our Wills and Inclinations: and we, your loyal Subjects utterly abhorring and detesting that impious Way of Living, did, with a unanimous Consent, and contrary to the Knowledge of the said Roberts or his Accomplices, on, or about, the 18th Day of April, 1721, leave, and ran away with, the aforesaid Ship Morning Star and Brigantine Good Fortune with no other Intent and Meaning than the Hopes of obtaining toy Majesty's most gracious Pardon.

And that we, your Majesty's most loyal subjects, may with more Safety return to our native Country and serve the Nation, unto which we belong, in our respective Capacities, without Fear of being prosecuted by the Injured, whose Estates have suffered by the said Roberts and his Accomplices, during our forcible Detainment, by the said Company. We most humbly implore your Majesty's most royal Assent, to this our humble Petition. And your Petitioners shall ever pray etc.

The forced carpenter, John Phillips, and Thomas Jones, sailed with Ellwood with the petition, as they were both confident of a reprieve. Jones had fought against Roberts and escaped from him, and Phillips had been forced as an 'artist'. Governor Lawes sent the petition to London, having received it on July 6th. By the time the various authorities in London had decided to pardon the pirates, the August deadline given by the pirates had passed, and they returned to piracy. Phillips managed to return to England on the *Nightingale*. Learning that some of his co-pirates under Anstis had been taken to gaol in Bristol, he panicked and quickly decided to try to sail to Newfoundland, leaving Topsham harbour. Having failed to gain a pardon, Phillips had remained 'under cover' in Bristol, as he felt that his story of being 'forced' would not be believed. (Thomas Jones, the old comrade of Howell Davis, who had personally fought Bart Roberts, and had deserted with Anstis, was one of those arrested - he was sent to the Marshalsea Prison in London, and later executed). Upon landing at Peter Harbour Phillips deserted his ship, and became a splitter in a cod-fishery. The work was terribly hard, in freezing conditions, but was safer and easier than being a merchant seaman in those days. Roberts had easily recruited such men in his raids on neighbouring Trepassy, and Phillips soon grew tired of an honest life. He had tasted the fruits of the easy life of piracy, and it beckoned him stongly.

On August 29th, 1723, with William White he stole a small schooner belonging to a William Minors (or Minott), off Saint Pierre Island. White was one of Minors' crewmen. Sixteen disaffected men had plotted the capture, but only four turned up, so they sailed away with three others, Phillips being chosen as captain. White had no position, but John Nutt was sailing-master, James Sparks the gunner, and Thomas Fern the carpenter. Articles were drawn up, and in the absence of a Bible, they swore them over a hatchet. Defoe enumerates Phillips' articles on board the *Revenge*:

1. *Every Man shall obey civil Command; the Captain shall have one full Share and a half in all Prizes; the Master, Carpenter, Boatswain and Gunner shall have one Share and a quarter*
2. *If any Man shall offer to run away, or keep any Secret from the Company, he shall be marooned, with one Bottle of Powder, one Bottle of Water, one small Arm and Shot.*
3. *If any Man steal any Thing in the Company, or game to the Value of a Piece of Eight, he shall be marooned or shot.*
4. *If at any Time we should meet another Marooner (that is, Pyrate) that Man shall sign his Articles without the Consent of our Company, shall suffer such Punishment and the Captain and Company shall think fit.*
5. *That man that shall strike another whilst these Articles are in force, shall receive Moses' Law (that is, 40 Stripes lacking one) on the bare Back.*
6. *That man that shall snap his Arms, or smoke Tobacco in the Hold, without a Cap to his Pipe, or carry a Candle lighted without a Lanthorn, shall suffer the same Punishment as the former Article.*
7. *That Man that shall not keep his Arms clean, fit for an Engagement, or neglect his Business, shall be cut off from his Share, and suffer such other Punishment as the Captain and the Company think fit.*
8. *If any Man shall lose a Joint in Time of an Engagement, he shall have 400 Pieces of Eight, if a Limb, 800.*
9. *If at any Time we meet with a prudent Woman, that Man offers to meddle with her, without her Consent, shall suffer present Death.*

By taking several small fishing boats, Phillips added to his crew. A former pirate named Burrill became boatswain. One of his prisoners from a merchantman was the ex-pirate John Rose Archer, who had served under the infamous Blackbeard, Edward Teach, in 1718. Archer was quickly made quartermaster. Phillips called his ship the *Revenge*, and in October 1723 captured another Welshman, William Phillips. In that month, the brig *Mary*, another brig, a Portuguese brig and the sloop *Content* were taken, with reasonable takings off each prize. From the *Content*, its first mate John

Master, William Phillips, William Taylor and James Wood were 'forced'. The crew holed up and careened in a small bay on Barbados for several weeks, but ran desperately short of provisions, so returned to sea.

Phillips spotted a large 12-gun Martinican ship with 35 crew, and was forced to attack it for much-needed supplies. It tried to outsail the *Revenge*, which took almost a day to overhaul her, and after bitter fighting it was taken. Four of the survivors, one a surgeon, were impressed as pirates, and the ship reprovisioned. Two more ships were taken, then the *Revenge* was careened again, in Tobago. Anstis had careened there with Phillips, and Phillips wanted more men for his crew. Some pirates had hidden there in the recent past, members of the crews of Anstis and Finn when they were attacked. However, he only found one marooned negro, Pedro, who said that the other men had been taken off by a man-of-war. The *Revenge* now beat a hasty retreat when a man-of-war was spotted by Burrill, taking on water nearby, and the four French prisoners were left behind.

Several more ships were taken, with more violence than was necessary. They included a sloop from New York, a Virginia ship under Captain Haffam, three Jamaican sloops, a snow and a Portuguese ship bound for Brazil. In February 1724, John Phillips put William Phillips and four others on board Captain Laws' captured snow, with Thomas Fern as captain, ordering them to sail in consort with the *Revenge*. One night, the consort attempted to elude the *Revenge*, but was chased for several hours and taken in a savage battle. James Wood was killed. William Phillips had to have his left leg amputated. There was no ship's surgeon, so John Rose Archer, with some experience of these matters, sawed Phillips' leg off. He then used a red-hot axe to cauterise the stump. However, he burned too much of Phillips' body away from the wound area, leaving terrible injuries. William Taylor had also been injured in the leg. Heading north from Tobago, a Portuguese ship and three sloops were taken, and Fern again tried to escape in one of the sloops. He was shot by Captain Phillips, in accordance with the ship's articles, and another seaman a few days later for the same offence. Over 30 French, English, American and Portuguese ships were taken in nine months in the West Indies and along the Atlantic Coast.

On February 7th, 1724, Captain Huffan's ship was taken off North Carolina. The navigator Harry Gyles was forced, as was Charles Ivemay, but John Masters was allowed to leave, as he had a wife and children who would starve without his income. On March 25th, another two ships were taken, one under another John Phillips, and one under Captain Robert Mortimer. On March 27th, Mortimer struck Phillips with a hand-spike in the shoulder, while trying to lead a mutiny. But his men stood by and Phillips slashed him with his sword three times, then Nutt and Archer hacked at his prostrate body before Burrill kicked it and ordered Mortimer's crew to throw his body overboard. John Salter's sloop off the Isle of Sabloes was next taken on April 4th, and kept as a prize. Captain Caldwell's schooner was also captured and Phillips was about to scuttle it when he discovered that it was owned by the Mr Minors who had 'supplied' him with the *Revenge*, so he let it go. A ship under Captain Dependance Ellery was taken, but it had tried to out-run the pirates, so they forced the unfortunate master to dance until he dropped with exhaustion. Ten vessels were shortly taken, with the following masters, Joshua Elwell, Samuel Elwell, Mr Combs, Mr Lansley, James Babston, Edward Freeman, Mr Start, Obadiah Beal, Erick Erickson and Benjamin Wheeler. In early April 1724, Phillips took two ships travelling from Virginia to New York. From the *Dolphin*, Edward Cheeseman and John Filmore, (the great-grandfather of President Millard Fillmore) were forced to become pirates. Phillips replaced his ship with the *Dolphin*, which was a better sailer, a sloop out of Cape Ann.

Phillips sailed back up to Newfoundland, intending to take on more crew from the disaffected cod-splitting fraternity, and off Nova Scotia took Andrew Harradine's brand-new sloop on April 17th. Harradine quickly discovered that over half the crew were forced men, and were anxious to be rid of Phillips. A day later, Harradine, Fillmore, Cheesman and some other forced men attacked the pirates with axes and hammers. The desperate Phillips tripped over, and was killed by Captain Harridan's hatchet. Phillips' head was cut off, pickled and tied to the mast-head. Archer and the few pirates were overpowered. The gunner James Sparks and John Nutt were thrown overboard by Edward Cheeseman in the mutiny. The remainder of John Phillips' crew were chained up, and Harridan took the ship to land in Boston on May 3rd. Cheeseman and Fillmore were tried in Boston on May 12th and acquitted, while Archer and White were found guilty. Phillips and Burrill's heads, pickled in Newfoundland, were exhibits at the trial. Some of Phillips' personal treasures were awarded by the court to Fillmore, including silver knee-buckles, shoe buckles, a tobacco box, a silver-hilted sword and two gold rings.

Archer, William Phillips and William White were hung on Bird Island in Boston Harbour on June 2nd. They were ministered to in their last days by a fierce Boston theologian, of whom John Jameson remarked in 1923 that '*Cotton Mather ministered to them in their last days, adding, one would think a new horror to death*'. The amputee William Phillips was somehow reprieved after conviction, as was William Taylor. The negro Pedro was acquitted, as was another impressed negro known as Pierro, and three impressed Frenchmen, John Baptis, Peter Tafferey and Isaac Lassen.

CHAPTER X

JOHN EVANS d. 1723

John Evans was a mate on ships sailing from Jamaica, and became master of a sloop sailing out of Nevis. As jobs dried up with piracy prevalent in the West Indies, he took to robbery with four other disenchanted seamen, in order to support themselves. The only alternative was being pressed into harsh naval service or being indentured as a bond labourer on the plantations. They took a canoe out of Port Royal harbour in September 1722, and began stealing from houses near the shores of Jamaica. After a few weeks, they came across a small Bermudan sloop lying at Dun's Hole, which they took. Evans stepped aboard and announced to the crew that he was captain of their vessel, 'which was a piece of news they knew not before'. The pirates sailed it to a small hamlet, and Evans celebrated by spending three *pistoles* on alcohol for his crew. The landlord invited Captain Evans to call again, pleased with his generosity. This Evans did, in the middle of that same night, ransacking the tavern for liquor and goods to put to sea. The next day, Evans sailed for Hispaniola, in the sloop, which he now named the *Scowerer*.

They took a Spanish sloop on the very next day, the crew being able to share a sum of £150 per man. Evans then made for the Windward Isles. Off Puerto Rica they captured Captain Diamond's *Dove*, on its way from new England to Jamaica. The *Dove's* mate, with navigational knowledge, was forced to join the pirates, along with three other men. They gave the Dove back to Captain Diamond, and put into one of the Windward Islands for water and provisions.

On January 11th, 1723, Captain Mills' 200-ton *Lucretia and Catherine* was taken, off the island of Deseada. Evans then took his men to the islet of Avis, wishing to careen the *Scowerer*. However, before they could start, they spotted a merchant sloop and gave chase, but without success, being slowed in the pursuit by the *Lucretia and Catherine*. Evans now decided to carry out a desperately needed careening at the nearby island of Ruby, but before this managed to capture a Dutch sloop. They let the *Lucretia and Catherine* go, and kept the sloop as it was a better ship. The *Scowerer* and the sloop now headed for the north of Jamaica, where they captured a sugar drover, then moved on to the Grand Caymans, intending to careen both ships.

Before landfall, Captain Evans and the *Scowerer's* boatswain exchanged insults, and the boatswain challenged Evans to a duel. They waited for the sloop to catch up with them before making landfall, but the boatswain refused to go ashore and fight Evans. The angry Evans hit him around the head and shoulders with his cane, as his honour was at stake, but the boatswain drew a pistol and shot the captain in the head. The bosun then jumped overboard and tried to swim to the shore to escape the incensed crew. The *Scowerer's* longboat caught up with the bosun, and took him back aboard the ship. The majority of the pirates wished to torture him, but two of the crew were so angry that they shot him before he could be tied down. The crew could not decide upon a captain to replace the unfortunate Evans, and split £9000 in booty amongst the 30 of them, drifting back into anonymity on the various islands in British possession.

CHAPTER XI

WILLIAM WILLIAMS - LLEWELLIN PENROSE 1725
or 1727 - 1790 or 1791

There is no doubt that this man was a privateer, who was marooned in South America, before finding his way to America, where he married and lost two sons at the Battle of Bunker's Hill against the English army. He was also a respected painter, and was influential in the career of the great American painter, Benjamin West. His semi-autobiographical novel, 'The Journal of Llewellin Penrose - Seaman', lays claim to be the *first American novel*. He died in almshouses in Bristol. Williams' career is a fascinating story of an unknown privateer, a great artist, important in American Colonial painting, and an original novelist who influenced Edgar Allan Poe. The author is beginning a book upon Williams, which will be complemented by the original text of his novel, and will hopefully be published in 2004. Thus, the following information has all been taken from the public domain, preparatory to an in-depth study of the Welsh pioneer.

   The Dictionary of Welsh National Biography down to 1940, published by the Honourable Society of Cymmrodorion in 1959, gives the following entry on **WILLIAMS** (*alias* **PENROSE**), **LLEWELLIN**

(1725-?), SAILOR AND PAINTER. Williams was his family name, but he took the name 'Penrose' from a shipbuilder or sea-captain of his acquaintance.* Born in May 1725, near Caerphilly, Glamorgan, he was the elder son of two children of a sailor, who later lost his life in a storm off the Dutch coast. Williams attended a grammar school in Bristol, where he first developed his love of painting. On the remarriage of his mother, the family lived for some time in Worcestershire and Monmouthshire before returning to an unspecified town in South Wales. Unhappy because of his step-father's insistence that he should enter the legal profession, Williams ran away from home in September 1744, and made for Bristol, passing through Pyle,** Glamorgan, on his way. Thereafter for many years he led an adventurous life at sea and in America, where he spent some years amongst the Indians.

   During this period of his life, he met the artist Benjamin West, who later attributed the development of his artistic ability in some measure to his contact with Williams in Philadelphia. Returning in indigent circumstances to London and then to Bristol, he was befriended by Thomas Eagles, who placed him in the Merchants' Alms House in Bristol. On Williams' death, Eagles inherited all his books and also the manuscript of a 'Journal' containing adventures based partly upon Williams' experiences amongst the Indians. This was published in 1815, under the title 'The Journal of Llewellin Penrose, a seaman.' The date of his death is unknown.'

*Editor's Note: This is patently wrong. There were so many Jones, Williams, Evans and Davies surnames in Wales, that they were known by their vocation, e.g. David Davies 'Top-Sawyer', or Jones 'the milk', or from their location, as in Llewellin Penrhos, anglicised to Penrose.

*This is quite obviously to this author Pill in Newport, named after the *pwll* (pool or harbour) of St Gwynlliwg of the 6th century, and now corrupted to Pillgwenlly. Newport's St Woolo's Cathedral likewise is the Anglicisation of St Gwynlliwg's)

Williams Family Of Craven County website information from Jerome Williams
My 3x great Grandfather was William Joseph Williams 1759-1823. He lived his last years in New Bern and is buried in Cedar Grove Cemetery. William Joseph Williams came to New Bern from Charleston, S.C. around 1804. He'd been a regular visitor to New Bern for about 25 years before that. He was born in New York City the Son of William Williams 1727-1791(Artist, Musician, Author of the first American novel, "Penrose", friend of Benjamin Franklin, tutor of Benjamin West, etc.) and Mary Mare (Sister of John Mare, Jr. 1738-1804, Artist, Merchant, moved to Edenton, member of first North Carolina Cabinet with Governor Caswell, co-founder of UNC, organised NC Masons, etc.)...

It is generally conceded that Edgar Allan Poe, the American genius, who died in poverty in 1849, aged 40, was the pioneer of detective story writing, with his bizarre masterpiece, "Tales of Mystery and Adventure". An outstanding tale was Edgar Allan Poe's *"The Gold Bug"* – a weird account of the recovery of Pirate Captain Kidd's treasure through the deciphering of a mystically devised parchment. When the story was published in 1841, it won a prize of $100 and saved Poe's household from near starvation. He undoubtedly got his idea for the plot of *"The Gold Bug"* from another extraordinary narrative written some years before at the Merchant Venturers' Almshouses, King Street, Bristol, by an old sailor named Llewellyn Penrose, who had been given refuge there by the Merchant Venturers.

In Bristol, it is quite reasonable to claim, was penned the work to which modern mystery fiction really owes its inception. Penrose was a strange character, declaring that his story was true and based on his own actual experiences, but how far that was so must ever remain a mystery. It was towards the close of the 18th century that a reputable citizen of Bristol, Thomas Eagles, met in the streets of the city one day an elderly down-at-heel old man who, from his speech, had obviously known better days. *"I am alone in the world,"* he told Mr Eagles. *"I have lost my wife and children. My two sons were killed at the battle of Bunker's Hill in the American Civil War. I have nothing to live for. I want a place to die in. Can you get me a pass for St Peter's Hospital, the old Poorhouse on Castle Park. Will you do that much for me?"*

In the course of further conversation Eagles found that the aged mariner had travelled in remote parts, was a man of taste and ability and something of an artist. He finally managed to get him lodgings at the Almshouses in King Street and there Penrose lived in comparative comfort for some years. He was often invited to Thomas Eagles's house for dinner and talked of art and literature and regaled the family with mystifying stories of his travels and adventures.

When he died he left all his possessions, a few books and two old manuscripts to his benefactor. One of the manuscripts was entitled *"The Journal of Llewellyn Penrose,* a Seaman." Mr Eagles read it aloud to his sons. It proved so engrossing that one of the boys missed the coach which was to have taken him to school in order that he might remain at home the next evening to hear the end of Penrose's marvellous adventures. Eagles copied out the manuscripts and took it to London. John Murray, the famous publisher, offered him £200 for it. Two well-known artists drew illustrations for it and it was brought out in book form. Lord Byron, the poet, said of it: "*Penrose kept me up half the night and made me dream the other half. It has all the air of truth – most entertaining and interesting.*"

Now in this "*Journal*" Penrose relates that he ran away from his native place near Caerphilly in 1744 and made his way to Bristol. From the port he sailed on a privateering voyage in the ship *Recovery* against the Spaniards. They lost part of the crew in a fight with a Spanish vessel and stood away for Santa Catarina in Brazil. They then chased another Spanish vessel but she eluded them. Sighting land at sunset the next day, they took it for the Main; hove to and started to fish for their supper. Penrose and two others jumped into one of the ship's boats to follow a tortoise. It was dark when they returned, "*I was very drunk,*" writes Penrose, "*and lay in the boat and fell asleep.*" He woke to find himself alone and the ship gone! In astonishment and dread, he rowed for the shore near at hand, landed and began to walk about. It was a wild country of palmetto trees and shrubs. He saw two Indians, a man and a woman; hid from them and wandered further, to find that he was on a small island. He sighted other land about five miles distant. He pushed off, made for this shore and landed. He came to a bluff overgrown with trees; discovered a lagoon abounding with fish. Strange birds of luxuriant plumage rose above him like a veritable cloud. He was in a land such as he had never seen before. And its people were as strange and mysterious as the land itself. So began his adventures there.

One day, accompanied by a Dutchman who had arrived from the Main, he came upon a roughly set up pyramid of stones. Beneath them was a skeleton and a sealed glass bottle.

The skull of the skeleton was fractured, and they inferred from this that it had belonged to "some poor unfortunate Spaniard, negro or mulatto," who had been sacrificed by superstitious pirates in order that his spirit might be a kind of *guardian to preserve their treasure until their return.*

In the bottle were three papers. One was inscribed with names in a circle like the points of a compass. There was a drawing of a human head, hands and feet and cross-bones.

There were also numerals and an arrow indicating a spot where treasure was buried. They deciphered this cryptic diagram as PAINTER."

Williams was his family name, but he took the name 'Penrose' from a shipbuilder or sea-captain of his acquaintance. Born in May 1725, near Caerphilly, Glamorgan, he was the elder son of two children of a sailor, who later lost his life in a storm off the Dutch coast. Williams attended a grammar school in Bristol, where he first developed his love of painting. On the remarriage of his mother, the family lived for some time in Worcestershire and Monmouthshire before returning to an unspecified town. Unhappy because of his step-father's insistence that he should enter the legal profession, Williams ran away from home near Caerffili in September 1744, and made for Bristol, passing through Pyle, Glamorgan, on his way. Thereafter for many years he led an adventurous life at sea and in America, where he spent some years amongst the Indians. During this period of his life, he met the artist Benjamin West, who later attributed the development of his artistic ability in some measure to his contact with Williams in Philadelphia. Returning in indigent circumstances to London and then to Bristol, he was befriended by Thomas Eagles, who placed him in the Merchants' Alms House in Bristol. On Williams' death, Eagles inherited all his books and also the manuscript of a 'Journal' containing adventures based partly upon Williams' experiences amongst the Indians. This was published in 1815, under the title 'The Journal of Llewellin Penrose, a seaman.' The date of his death is unknown.'

Williams achieved some fame as an American painter, with the following Columbia Encyclopaedia entry: **Williams, William, American painter:**

c.1710–c.1790, American painter, b. England. He probably led a seafaring life before settling (c.1747) in Philadelphia, where he was Benjamin West's first instructor in painting. He designed the building and in 1759 painted scenery for the first Philadelphia theatre. After painting in New York City in 1775, Williams probably returned (c.1780) to England. He died in a Bristol almshouse, leaving a partly autobiographical manuscript, The Journal of Llewellin Penrose; this was published in 1815. His richly coloured paintings have a lively naïveté and romantic charm; among those known to be his are portraits of Deborah Hall (Brooklyn Museum., N.Y.) and Benjamin Lay (Historical Society of Pennsylvania).

In the same artists' encyclopaedia, part of the entry upon Benjamin West mentions Penrose/Williams: West, Benjamin 1738-1820 The farmhouse in which he was born is still standing near Swarthmore, in what is now called Delaware County, Pennsylvania. According to the life by John Galt, which was written from information supplied by West himself, his early life was marked by many remarkable and prophetic circumstances. At seven years old he drew his baby niece in her cradle in red and black chalk. He received his first instructions in art from a Cherokee, and obtained from him his first colours, which were the red and yellow used by the Indians. To these his mother added a stick of indigo, and so completed the chord of what were then called the three primary colours. He shaved a cat to make his brushes, and his early artistic efforts so astonished a merchant named Pennington that he gave him a box of colours. He also gave West some brushes and a piece of canvas on which the boy painted a composition from three engravings by Guercino, also given to him by his admirer. This picture was still in existence, and was exhibited by the side of his large picture of 'Christ Rejected' sixty-seven years after it was painted. **At nine years old he burst into tears at the sight of a landscape by an artist of Philadelphia named Williams, and declared his intention of being a painter.** His father and mother were Quakers, but they and the Society of Friends at Springfield were so convinced of the greatness of the lad's gifts that after solemn deliberations they allowed him to adopt art as a profession. When eighteen years old his mother died, and he set up as a portrait-painter at Philadelphia, and afterwards at Lancaster and New York. Then, with the assistance of £50 from a merchant named Kelly, he went to Italy....'

APPENDICES

APPENDIX A

The 1717 Act of Grace, whereby most of the major British pirates (including Paul Williams) in the Caribbean surrendered, is reprinted here:

By the King
A PROCLAMATION for Suppressing of PYRATES

"Whereas we have received information, that several Persons, Subjects of Great Britain have, since the 24th Day of June, committed divers Pyracies and Robberies upon the High-Seas, in the West-Indies, or adjoyning to our Plantations, which hath and may Occasion great Damage to the Merchants of Great Britain, and others trading into those parts; and tho' we have appointed such a Force as we judge sufficient for suppressing the said Pyrates, yet the more effectually to put an end to the same, we have thought fit, by and with the Advice of our Privy Council, to Issue this our Royal Proclamation; the said Pyrates, shall on, or before, the 5th of September, in the Year of Our Lord 1718, surrender him or themselves, to one of our Principal secretaries of State in Great Britain or Ireland, or to any Governor or Deputy Governor of any of our Plantations beyond the Seas; every such Pyrate and Pyrates so surrendering him, or themselves, as aforesaid, shall have our gracious Pardon, of, and for such, his or their Pyracy, or Piracies, by him or them committed, before the fifth of January next ensuing. And we do hereby strictly charge and command all our Admirals, Captains, and other Officers at sea, and all our Governors and Commanders of any Forts, castles, or other Places in our Plantations, and all other our Officers Civil and Military, to seize and take such of the Pyrates, who shall refuse or neglect to surrender themselves accordingly. And we do hereby further declare, that in Case any Person or Persons, on, or after, the 6th day of September, 1718, shall discover or seize, or cause or procure to be discovered or seized, any one or more of the said Pyrates, so refusing or neglecting to surrender themselves as aforesaid, so as they may be brought to Justice, and convicted of the said offence, such Person or Persons, so making such discovery or seizure, or causing or procuring such Discovery or Seizure to be made, shall have and receive as a Reward for the same, viz. for every Commander of any private Ship or Vessel, the Sum of 100l. for every Lieutenant, Master, Boat-swain, Carpenter, and Gunner, the sum of 40l. for every inferior Officer, the sum of 30l. and for every private Man, the sum of 20l. And if any Person or Persons, belonging to, and being Part of the Crew, of any Pyrate Ship and Vessel, shall, on or after the said sixth Day of September, 1718, seize and deliver, or cause to be seized and delivered, any Commander or Commanders, of such Pyrate Ship or Vessel, so that he or they be brought to Justice, and convicted of the said Offence, such Person or Persons, as a Reward for the same, shall receive for every such Commander, the Sum of 200l. which said Sums, the Lord Treasurer, or the Commissioners of Our Treasury for the time being, are hereby required, and desired to pay accordingly.

Given at our Court, at Hampton-Court, the fifth Day of September, 1717, in the fourth Year of our Reign.
GEORGE R.
God save the KING."

APPENDIX B
THE WHITE WOMEN OF LUNDY (from a Welsh website)

Looming dim and mysteriously through shrouding mists of morning, the storm-cliffs and wave-riven rocks of Lundy looked like grim and voiceless wardens of unrecorded romances and forgotten tragedies. Scarred with grisly seam and haggard cleft, the dark and barren granite ridges, hurled in wild disorder on the sparse shingle, caught the first red gleam of the summer daybreak. Above, on the bare and wind-blown heights now capped with cloud-reefs, all was cold and grey and unfriendly. Below, among the lesser cliffs, fantastic coves and shadowy grottoes, myriads of sea-birds whirled wildly, as though glad to welcome the return of sunrise. All the jagged ledges and jutting rocks were swarmed with them, and the morning air was filled with their wild and discordant screams. In the words of an old chronicler, it is *"so immured with rocks, and impaled with beetle-browed cliffs, that there is no entrance but for friends."*

Drayton in his Polyolbion sings -
"England and Wales strive in this song,
To whether Lundy doth belong
When either's nymphs, to clear the doubt,
By music mean to try it out.
This while in Sabrin's court, strong factions strangely grew
Since Cornwall, for her own, and as her proper due,
Claimed Lundy, which was said to Cambria to belong,
Who oft had sought redress, for that her ancient wrong."
He then goes on -
"Of all the inlaid isles her sovereign Severn keeps,
That bathe their amorous breasts within her secret deeps
To love her Barry much, and Scilly though she seem,
The Flat-Holm, and the Steep as likewise to esteem),
This noblest British nymph yet likes her Lundy best."
The decision appears in the next canto -
"In this song Severn gives doom
What of her Lundy should become."
In conclusion, the poet sings -
"Then take my final doom, pronounced lastly - this,
That Lundy like ally'd to Wales and England is."

Around the peninsula of Lametor and Rat Island, the silver green waves of the Atlantic rolled surging against the cliffs, and at their base the surf foamed and frothed ceaselessly. The ruins of Marisco Castle looked gloomy and grand as the clouds lifted, and the first faint sunbeams worked curious traceries thereon. It was a day to be remembered by the few islanders that remained on Lundy. Before the troubled times of the Great Rebellion, and when it was almost deserted by its hereditary owners, Lundy was known as one of the very worst of pirates' nests. It afterwards became the refuge for people during the civil wars. Echard, the old English historian, states that after Lord Say and Sele *"had lived to see his fine ambition defeated by the supremacy of Cromwell, he sought a voluntary retreat, or rather imprisonment, in the isle of Lundy."* Later on, the island regained its old reputation as the headquarters of pirates and desperadoes, and a safe resort for criminals and adventurers of all nationalities.

In 1663, reports were sent to the Admiralty that *"pirates and desperadoes"* had *"established themselves there,"* and that *"one Captain Pronoville, a Frenchman, having grown desperate, had fixed himself at Lundy, and was doing great damage to merchants."* For three years Pronoville had been playing havoc in the Golden Bay, as Barnstaple Bay was called, because of the numberless prizes gained there by pirates. On this June day in 1666, when the Atlantic rollers caught the first flush of sunrise, and over the vast green water wastes the earliest golden glory of the summer sunshine rippled in quivering radiance, two white-sailed skiffs, with sea-birds wheeling in their wake, rounded Rat Island and entered the roads. Pronoville, the pirate, standing on the heights like a bird of prey, sent down his minions to demand the cause of the intrusion of the strangers. Buccaneer as he was, he felt fearful of spies - of other pirates coming to share the island, and above all he was much afraid of his powerful rivals the Dutch. "*It looks like the Dutch,*" said he, scanning the skiffs. Then he descended from the lordly heights above the sea, and went down to the roads. "*Who may ye be?*"' thundered Pronoville to the three men just landed. "*We be peaceable Welshmen, come over to see some of our relatives that do live in the island,*" said the spokesman of the party. Pronoville had doubts, whereupon the Welshmen produced satisfactory proofs in support of their statement, so they were allowed to pass in peace to the Gannet's Coombe to their relatives, who gained their living as feather "*pluckers.*" The three men were the sons of the veritable master of the Mumbles (a suburb of Swansea) man-o'-war, which, he said, was armed with "three leatherin' guns and a handspik'." They came to see and befriend their only sister Mary Marriner, formerly Llewellyn, who had recently been widowed and left in ill circumstances. When the Welshmen reached Mary's home in Gannet Coombe, a thoroughly Celtic greeting took place. It was "*Oh dear, dear, an' here you be, come to see your poor sister;*" and "*Didn't I know it was you?*" and then in Welsh, "*Look, look, my little children.*" Then amid tears and sobs and smiles, the Welsh element subsided, and order once more resumed its sway. It was pleasant for Mary Marriner in Gannet Coombe, because her brothers had brought "*plenty of money*" and spent it freely. In their rude manner all this "*spendin'*" was intended to assuage the soul agonies of the widow, and still the sorrows of the orphans. After a few days had passed, Pronoville was disposed to seek the society of these Welshmen, and, before the week was out, he spent the greater part of his time with them. One day, while Pronoville and the Welshmen were regaling themselves with undiluted spirit in Gannet Coombe, the wary old sea-pirate suggested that the visitors should "*have a try*" at his own profitable profession. "*You'd make money ding-dong,*" said Pronoville, slapping one of the men on the shoulder. "*Don't know so much about that,*" said Jacob Llewellyn. "*It would take a long time to learn, an' by the time I did know the way how, I'd be ready for my grave.*" Pronoville laughingly scorned the idea. "*You're a young man yet,*" said he with a friendly poke. "*Not so young,*" said Jacob. "*I'm on the wrong side of sixty now*". "*Then you had better have a try at my game,*" Pronoville said to the other Welshman. "*Well,*" said Reuben Llewellyn, "*it's uncommon kind of you to give us a chance, and, if my brother Pharaoh would join, I don't mind trying, an' see what'll come of it.*" "*What do you say, Pharaoh?*" asked Pronoville. "*I've a mind to try, but I'd like to take a few days to think over it,*" said Pharaoh.

"By all means," said Pronoville.
It was agreed that three days hence decision should be made. That night, in the Gannet Coombe, Jacob was by no means agreeable. He disliked the idea of Welshmen leaguing with wicked "*sea-thieves and robbers,*" and went so far as to say that there never had been any Welsh pirates, or wild rovers and robbers. Whereupon he was reminded of the Welsh buccaneers, who had scoured the seas, and scourged the merciless taskmasters of the far West. "*Let's turn buccaneers,*" said Reuben; "*it's a fine game, Pharaoh*". "*Ay, ay!*" responded Pharaoh.
Mary Marriner, listening to this conversation, observed that although Jacob appeared to be opposed to the proposition, there was a curious twinkling in his eyes, and secret satisfaction with the course his brothers intended to pursue. And she moreover observed that, although Jacob fretted and fumed when any of the "*pluckers*" were present, he rubbed his hands and chuckled to himself when the brothers sat alone. The three days passed, and Pronoville came for the answer. "*Agreed,*" exclaimed Reuben and Pharaoh Llewellyn. "*What about yourself?*" asked Pronoville, addressing Jacob. "*I'll have nothing to do with it; no, not I,*" said Jacob. "*When they do begin their work I'll go back to Swansea.*" "*Work will begin next week,*" said Pronoville, " *Time means money.*"

He rubbed his hands and chuckled gleefully. Like the spider luring the fly, the old sea-rover loved to catch the unwary, and laid his plots accordingly. He saw that the Welshmen had money to spend, and, if anybody could get it out of them, he would. He wanted partners with money badly just now. "*Trade had been dull,*" he told himself - not revealing the fact to his new partners - and he wanted more craft and crew. The Dutch were gradually becoming powerful rivals, and he feared they would take his "*Golden Bay*" prizes from him; and again, he wanted younger men to fill his place in a trustworthy manner when, work-weary, he might wish for rest and temporary leisure. Not that he - the intrepid sea-robber - ever intended retiring from business, not he!
"*The sea's my bonnie bride,*
And whatever may betide,
I will never leave her side.
Never! Never! Ho! ho! ho!"
sang Pronoville.
New life and fire filled the Frenchman's heart, and he went about ordering his men with the air and importance of a monarch who has augmented his army. "*It's a grand thing to be bold, fearless, intrepid, daring, and - honourable, isn't it, Pharaoh?*" asked the pirate, sturdily beating his breast. "*That it is,*" responded Rueben. "*Ay, indeed,*" added Pharaoh. But they did not see where the "*honourable*" came in. "*We begin with the tide on Monday,*" said Pronoville. "*My plans are laid, and all will be ready for action by Sunday evening.*" That night in the Gannet Coombe, Mary Marriner was sad and poor spirited. Her own brothers, sons of her own mother, were going to "*bemean*" themselves by "*taking to*" a nefarious trade. It was more than she cared to contemplate, and, before her brothers retired for the night, she gave them "*a piece of her mind.*" Mary Marriner spoke warmly, as one who bitterly disliked even the very thought of it, and she concluded her attack by declaring her intention of packing up her belongings," and quitting Lundy when Jacob returned. "*When are you going?*" she asked Jacob.
"*In a week or two,*" he replied.
"*Are you going to stay here so long as that!*" exclaimed Mary, almost screaming. "*Will you look on at such dreadful wickedness?*" Mary was in a perfect rage. Seeing this, Jacob whispered a few words in Welsh, which had the effect of instantly and completely subduing her. With the tide on Monday, Pronoville, accompanied by his new partners Reuben and Pharaoh, commenced "*business,*" and apparently with great success. As trade increased, Pronoville grew lazy, and in course of time he drank heavier and oftener, sometimes he would remain for days carousing in his headquarters with boon companions, while Reuben and Pharaoh worked. Jacob returned to Swansea, but Mary, after all, remained to look after her brothers. Meanwhile, rumours floated among the islanders that somebody had seen a ghost flitting about the ruins of Marisco Castle, and strange rappings and noises were heard in different parts of the island. As time passed the spirit rappings increased, and the ghost had taken a partner.
Pronoville did not believe a word of it. There always were strange noises in Lundy, he said. It was "*the noisiest hole in the world,*" and, "*as for ghosts,*" he did not believe in such "*old womanish inventions,*" they were not worth thinking about. Pronoville continued to drink heavier, and the more he drank the worse his nerves grew. "*I'm getting shaky,*" he said to Reuben one September day, when, from the great sapphire rollers, the Atlantic sent the foam flying over the Templar Rock, and the storm-wind sent the salt-spray fleeting like mist over wide wastes of heather and countless hillocks of drift. Confusion reigned supreme in Lundy.
The wind roared wildly in the Devil's Chimney; the tide seethed and whirled around the Cheeses; the long and heavy swells broke in furious cataracts on the Shutter Rock, and rolled huge boulders to and fro in the darkness of the caverns under the Devil's Limekiln. Against the inky black sky innumerable white and grey winged sea-birds appeared in bold relief, as they soared aloft, and with wild notes and shrieks rejoiced in the storm, while the din of wave-warfare reverberated

among the grim precipices that towered in to the rain-drifts and clouds above. In the lonely recesses of that wild and wave-washed island, fresh additions were already being made to the numerous relics of wrecks stored there, while the rain on land, and the storm at sea, boded further calamity.

Captain Pronoville and his French crews were holding revelry at the headquarters, while the tide rolled "*mountains high*" into Rattles Bay, and the relentless rain lashed the ruined towers of Marisco Castle. Although Pronoville found Reuben and Pharaoh and their money useful, he did not trust them so implicitly as his own dearly-loved Frenchmen, and, on the other hand, his Welsh allies shrank from the "*foreign*" orgies of the notorious pirate. Reuben and Pharaoh returned to Gannet Coombe, there to wait until the storm passed. Mary Marriner catered for them in the generous and hospitable manner known to country folk in general, but to Welsh housewives in particular. The storm lingered, and on the third day it increased almost to a hurricane. One day during this period of storm, Pronoville experienced what he termed a "*strange feeling*," but, in truth, it was a fright. Early in the afternoon, during a pause of the rain, the wily old sea rover crept up to his grey and weather-beaten outlook, Marisco Castle. There he remained until the gathering twilight warned him it was high time to return to Rattles Bay.

While looking out to the wild wave-distance, he heard the sound of a wailing voice calling slowly in a long-drawn, husky tone - "*Pro-no-ville.*" Again it wailed, almost groaned, "*Pro-no-ville!*" "*It is my fancy,*" said Pronoville, "*and perhaps the wind helps it.*"

He knew all his men, in fact all the inhabitants on the island called him captain. Not a person would venture to address him only by his surname. But he disliked the wailing voice, and, putting his fingers in his ears, he swore loudly and strongly about the weather in general and the wind in particular. Then he started to ascend the stairs. As he reached the top, which formed a sort of landing, he saw emerging from one of the rooms a gliding figure going ghostlike into an adjoining apartment. Pronoville started back in terror. He had seen the ghost! But he was not going to be "*humbugged*" he said, so, taking courage, he followed the figure, to find the room which he entered quite empty! Then he descended the stairs, and before reaching the ancient portal, that voice, that blood-curdling wailing voice, called, "*Pro-no-ville!*" again, and yet again. Like one soul-driven, Pronoville rushed away. His fingers were in his ears, and, as if to drown all recollection, he swore vehemently. For some reason best known to himself, he turned to look back, and there, horror of horrors! standing in the ruined window of the room which Pronoville thought to be empty, was the ghost! There it stood waving its long shadowy arms in the windy twilight, like a wraith of the mist, or a hag of the night.

Pronoville fled in terror, and his men down in Rattles Bay stared aghast to see their "*intrepid*" captain rushing amongst them as "*if he had seen the ghost,*" they said. Pale to the lips, scared and trembling from head to foot, the pirate entered the quarters, and none dared question him as to the cause of his commotion. The storm continued with almost unabated fury, and Pronoville did not go to his outlook for nearly a week. When next he visited the citadel, he saw the ghost, and heard the wailing voice as before. Worse still, the ghost glided after him, and he ran wherever he could, as if for dear life, down to Rattles Bay. Three weeks passed, during which the wraith continued to persecute the sea-rover, and, in due course, as the rumour had it, the ghost appeared with a partner. Those - and they were few - who dared gaze at the ghosts, likened one of them to a tall, thin, and extremely shadowy person accompanied by a short, spare, and smaller figure. Both were women, and both wore their long hair floating far down beyond their waists.

In due course the ghosts came to be called the "*White Women,*" and they held their own, as though they had taken possession of the solitary and sea-girt Castle of Marisco. Through the dreary and moonlight nights of grey and shivering October - through the dense fogs and rain-drifts of November - through the darkness and desolation of December, strange noises, mingled with unearthly wailings, were heard, and the ghosts maintained their sway. In time the islanders came to be afraid to venture out once the brief daylight began to wane, while the *"bold, fearless, intrepid, daring - and honourable"* Pronoville and his French crew fairly *"shook in their shoes"* with terror whenever they had to go to Marisco Castle, which was both store and ammunition room, as well as their *"look out."* Only the sea birds - the gulls, the shoveler ducks, the snow-buntings, and the *"white-fronted geese"* - were fearless. The peregrine falcon soared high and haughtily above the ghostly tracks, and the snow-white gannets remained loftily immovable and indifferent, as though leagued against wraiths and the spirit-world in general, and the *" White Women"* in particular. Still the ghosts continued their mysterious walks abroad.

Even when the whirling snow flung its pure shroud over the lonely island, and the leaden sky looked down upon the steel-blue sea, those wraiths haunted the place. Men grew fearful, women shuddered, and children crept into the corners when the first footfall of mysterious night - so like death - appeared. Great grey waves thundered in Rattles Bay, and men shivered in the morning. Dense white mists crept through the desolate and lonely coombes, and the women sighed and looked scared in the twilight. White foam-flakes were driven by the wind far inland, and the children cried in the starless and moonless nights. Lundy was like No-Man's Land, where ghosts in passing greet one another on their way with the melancholy cry, *"Whither-ay-whither?"*

When the winds of March had passed, and April with her tears and smiles wandered along the earth, a surprise came to the island. *"I told you so,"* exclaimed Reuben. *"It's never her,"* said Pharaoh. *"What are you talking about?"* asked Pronoville. *"Enough, I should think,"* said Pharaoh. *"Don't you see in the offing the Mumbles man-o'-war?"* Pronoville swore. *"My father means friendly,"* said Reuben. Pronoville, persecuted by the ghosts, was in *"no mind"* to be agreeable or to see strangers. In came the Mumbles man-o'-war, with its *"three leatherin' guns and a handspik',"* and the master thereof landed. He was warmly welcomed by his sons, who were overjoyed to see him. Pronoville's men *"took to him"* at once. Even Pronoville got to like him in a day or so. Davy Prosser, one of the men of the Mumbles man-o -war, was told of the ghost.

"I do know more about it than our cap'n," said he, in a confidential tone to Pronoville over their grog. *"Yes, indeed. Thirty years ago Admiral Nutt, the great buccaneer, was Lord of Lundy. `Twas he did infest the Narrow Seas; and I was in one of the Government `whelps' that was chasing him. Old Nutt caught us, an' we, the crew of the Little Sally, was kept on Lundy for months"*. *"What then?"* asked Pronoville. *"We did see what the island people did call the `White Women of Lundy.' `Tis a bad sign when they do come, so we did hear then. When the `White Women' do prowl about, it do mean coming dangers loss, ruin, sickness, and sometimes - death."* The pirate shivered. His luck seemed to have departed with the coming of the *"White Women."*

All his courage had long since forsaken him. He had grown strangely restless, moody, fearful, and tremulous, and worse so because of the deep draughts of ardent spirits quaffed to keep off their disembodied contemporaries. The Mumbles man-o'-war came as a boon and a blessing to Pronoville. He would be equal with those detested *"White Women."* They should not any longer be forewarners of danger, loss, ruin, sickness, and - he shuddered to think of it - perhaps death! Life became insupportable, and the old pirate's nerves were hopelessly shattered. In May he quitted Lundy for ever.

He sailed with his partners, Reuben, Pharaoh, their father, Davy Prosser, and Mary Marriner, in the Mumbles man-o'-war, bound for Swansea. Before reaching Wales, Pronoville, seized by a strange *"brain fever"* died, raving in his death agony, *"The White Women - the White Women - see, they're following us! "* They buried him in the sapphire waves of Swansea Bay, and his body went to be the prey of those terrors of the sea to which he had committed so many unfortunate mortals. Then, and not before, it was known in Lundy and elsewhere that the *"White Women"* were Reuben and Pharaoh Llewelyn, who for a heavy bribe, willingly offered by merchants and other sufferers by piracy, invented a ruse whereby to rid the island of the renowned and intrepid but wily Captain Pronoville.

His crew remained in Lundy, but their sway was of short duration, for on the 3rd of June 1667, the collector of Barnstaple wrote to the Board, *"that some small Flushing privateers, which lie skulking under the island of Lundy, have taken six small barks coming from Ireland laden with bullocks, sheep, wool, and tallow;"* and a few days later, a report was sent to the Admiralty by John Man, *"that French privateers, lying at Lundy Island . . . took a trow, kept the master, and sent the men ashore at Barnstaple to procure money for the redemption of the vessel and lading, taking out of her a hundred sheep and other provisions for themselves."* A later report states that *"three privateers at Lundy put terror into all the vessels; much shooting had been heard for three or four days."* On the 21st of June very few of Pronoville's men remained, for the officer in charge of the district wrote to the Admiralty: *"Lundy Island is very slenderly guarded, four or five men from a vessel riding on a cross wind crept over the gates, and went to the people's houses before they saw anybody. If the Dutch should take the island it would block up the Severn, and a dozen good men would secure it from the world."* The Mumbles man-o'-war's men lived to a good old age, and they never grew weary in telling the story of the *"White Women of Lundy."*

APPENDIX C
This is taken from an American website:

The Legend of Thomas Lacy and the Pirate
The story of Thomas Lacy capturing a pirate, reputedly Blackbeard, has come down through the generations. The furthest back it goes is to the Rev. William Sterling Lacy, a man of outstanding character and the source of much correct information on the family. This story has been suspect because of the claims that it was the pirate, Blackbeard, who was captured and slain. This could not possibly be because Edmond Drummond, a.k.a. Edward Teach a.k.a. "Blackbeard" was born 1680-1690 and was killed 22 November 1718 in a fight with Lieut. Robert Maynard and company.

The incredibly true story has now surfaced, much of it consistent with the important facts in William Sterling Lacy's version. It was found by Gene Lacy doing an on-line search in the Virginia Colonial Records Project on the Homepage of the Library of Virginia. The Library spent the years between 1955 and 1985 visiting more than one hundred libraries and archives in Great Britain, Ireland, and France to survey the collections. They subsequently obtained microfilm on 14,704 Survey Reports, and acquired 963 reels of microfilmed documents. It was among these documents that the story of Thomas Lacy and the pirate surfaced. First we present the story as told by William Sterling Lacy. This is taken from Hubert Wesley Lacey's book, "The Thomas Lacy III Family of Hanover and Buckingham Counties, Virginia". COPY OF OLD PAPER WRITTEN BY WILLIAM STERLING LACY, SON OF REV. DRURY LACY. ORIGINAL IS IN THE POSSESSION OF ALFRED P. JONES, M..D. OF ROANOKE VA.

Passing through the upper end of Luta Prairie about the year 1828 or '29, I stopped at the house of old Mr. Wm. Rice; he said he was 85 or 86 years of age, and brother of Rev. David Rice, one of the first Presbyterian Ministers of Kentucky. His mind was unimpaired, his memory remarkable and he was esteemed a consistent Christian man. He told me that when a small boy, he saw my ancestor who emigrated from Wales, and was then residing in Hanover Co., Va., remarking that he was one of the oldest and tallest men he ever saw; his name was Thomas Lacy. He told me his history was very peculiar, that when a young man he embarked on board a vessel from Wales with other emigrants, with a view of settling in Virginia; that during the voyage he was captured by a notorious pirate who went under the familiar name of Black Beard, but whose name was Taike; that every passenger on board was made to walk the plank with the exception of Thomas Lacy, who the pirate swore was too fine a looking fellow to be drowned and that he would impress him into his service and make a noble pirate of him.

A short time after the pirate put into Ocracoke Sound, and cast anchor on a desolate coast, where he was in the habit of trading with some lawless accomplices. A man of suspicious character, I think by the name of Minnis, applied to the Governor of Virginia, then residing on Jamestown Island, to aid him in fitting out a large Merchant Vessel and collecting a large number of desperate adventurers with a view of capturing the pirate. He was induced to do this, from the fact that a very large reward had been offered by the British Government and several of her colonies for the capture of the pirate. It seems that Minnis was acquainted with the habits of Black Beard and knew at what time he would be on the coast. The vessel was fitted and crew collected. Immediately on entering Ocracoke Inlet the vessel was so fitted to appear almost a wreck. Taking advantage of a favourable wind and tide she sailed slowly under ragged sails and crippled masts to where the piratical vessel lay, only four or five men on deck making signals of distress as they approached the pirate. All the men, completely armed, hid under the hatches of the vessel. The pirate seemed amused at her slow approach, supposing they had her entirely in their power. The piratical vessel was anchored over a half mile from shore. At this time nearly half the crew were on shore trading as above mentioned. As soon as she reached the pirate she was grappled and drawn up alongside of her. Instantly all the hatches were thrown up and armed men in large numbers rushed on the deck of the pirate. At this instant Thomas Lacy drew his cutlass and shouting with trumpet-voice, "I am a true man. I am a prisoner", began to cut down the pirates on the right and left.

This circumstance increased their panic and threw them into some confusion so that they were quickly overcome by superior numbers. Not one would surrender and every one was slain. Black Beard recognised Minnis and cursed him as a traitor and was soon after killed.

They then proceeded with their prize to Jamestown where the good Conduct of Thomas Lacy being reported to the Governor, he gave him a share of the prize money, and a tract of land on the frontier in which is now Hanover Co., saying he would make a fine Indian fighter. In a few years after Thomas Rice sailed from Wales and settled in the same neighbourhood of Thomas Lacy. Thomas Lacy married his daughter to whom he had been engaged before leaving Wales.

This Thomas Rice was the ancestor of this William Rice who gave me the above narrative. Signed: William S. Lacy

FROM THE COLONIAL RECORDS PROJECT-LIBRARY OF VIRGINIA
Survey Report No. 4385

13 May 1700 This document contains 21 depositions sworn before the Court of Oyer & Terminer for the trial of pirates in Virginia before Peter Beverly, Clerk of Arraigns. Some of the depositions are sworn by individual mariners, others by groups of mariners from different ships captured by Lewis Guittar. All ships were outward bound from Virginia, except the Pennsylvania Merchant, which was inbound from England. On 17 April (1699) the BALTIMORE was captured; on 18 April the GEORGE of Pennsylvania bound for Jamaica. The master of the FRIENDSHIP of Belfast-Hans Haniel-was killed when the pirates fired on his ship. On 28 April 4 ships were captured within the Cape of Virginia including the PENNSYLVANIA MERCHANT, and the INDIAN KING of Virginia and the NICHOLSON. The PENNSYLVANIA MERCHANT WAS BURNT. The crews taken prisoner were confined in the hold of the pirate ship which was call LA PAIX (PEACE); some other being made to throw cargoes of tobacco and other goods to Lyn-Haven by the pirates. On 28 April Captain John Alread, Commander of H.M.S. ESSEX having heard of the pirates' exploits came ashore and informed H. E. Francis Nicholson H.M. Governor General of Virginia and Captain Passenger of H.M.S. SHOREHAM that there was a Pirate in Lyn-Haven Bay. Whereupon captain Passenger and His Excellency, together with Captain Alread and Peter Hayman Esquire, went aboard H.M.S. SHOREHAM and in coming out of the James River engaged the Pirate ship. Captain Guittar fought under a blood red flag. Peter Hayman Esquire was slain. After an engagement which lasted 6 to 8 hours John Lympany, a passenger from the PENNSYLVANIA MERCHANT, was ordered by Lewis Guittar to swim aboard the SHOREHAM to inform H. E. the Governor that there were English prisoners aboard his ship and that they and the ship would be blown up unless H. E. was prepared to grant Quarter to Guittar and his men if they surrendered. The Governor gave his promise. About 124 pirates were taken prisoner and some 25 to 30

pirates were slain. Between 40 and 50 English prisoners were liberated. Survey Report No. 4378 Part I contains two documents 17 and 18 relating to charges of Piracy against Lewis Guittar and others and 18 also relates to a charge of Piracy against David Evand and Turlagh Sulivan and others.
8 November 1700. The warrant for the execution of Lewis Guittar and members of his crew for Piracy upon the High Seas.
21-21 October 1700. Not of Judgment at Sessions, sentencing Lewis Guittar and a number of his crew to death.
Survey Report No. 5918
An Admiralty memorial, dated 12 September 1701, recommending an allowance of 23 shillings a month for 5 months to Thomas Lacy and William Woolgar for the capture of the French pirate Lewis Guittar, within the Cape of Virginia.
Survey Report No. 6672
Lords of the Admiralty to the Navy Board. 17 September 1701. By direction of the Lords Justices, their Lordships ordered the Navy Board to pay Thomas Lacey and William Woolgar each five months pay as A.B. of the Royal Navy as a gratuity for their voluntary service on board H.M.S. SHOREHAM, Capt. Passenger, in her action with a pirate ship off the Capes of Virginia.
Conclusion: Thomas Lacy was listed as a sailor from one of the ships that was captured on the 28th of April 1699. Of the three ships captured, only the Nicholson was reported as leaving crew behind in its attempt to escape from the pirate. The above report makes it clear that Thomas Lacy served on the Shoreham during the battle. Thus, we conclude that he was a seaman aboard the Nicholson, was left in port in the hasty departure, volunteered to serve on the Shoreham and received his reward for this service. Research has not made it clear whether or not Thomas Lacy was captured by Guittar or whether he served on the Shoreham during the capture.

APPENDIX D

Probably the most intriguing court-case in the world is the one involving the heirs of the Welsh privateer Robert Edwards, and the ownership of a large chunk of Manhattan real estate. He was given 77 acres of what is now the heart of Manhattan, by Queen Anne for his services in disrupting Spanish shipping. His will gave the area to the Cruger brothers, on a 99-year lease, with the understanding that it would revert back to his heirs after that. Somehow the land has ended up in the hands of Trinity Church, one of New York's biggest landowners. The land is valued at $680 billion. It includes 'ground-zero' (the site of the World Trade Centre), Broadway and Wall Street). Robert Edwards was born in Pontypridd, the son of William Edwards of Llanymynech.

THE EDWARDS FORTUNE
From the book
"The Edwards Family of Northampton"

For over seventy-five years many thousands of Edwards' in America, England, Wales and elsewhere laid claim to a big section of Manhattan Island that makes up an area three quarters of a mile long and four blocks wide in mid-town New York City. It was worth many millions. This story occupies a place in the history of the Edwards family, because it **IS** a part of our history. It was no wisp of smoke, a leaf fluttering in the breeze or the telling of an old folk tale. It was something real and **ALMOST** tangible. There were visions of the receipt of substantial sums of money that would pay off mortgages, build fine homes or educate the children. This thought and hope and dream persisted until the middle 1950's. There would be little point in going any further with the story except for several facts that make it worthwhile. One of these is the magnitude of the fortune involved and the number of people who participated in the effort to recover it.

Basically, the story is: Robert Edwards acquired two large tracts of land on Manhattan Island, one of 66 acres, another of 77 acres. He leased them in June of 1778 to John and George Cruger. Immediately thereafter he embarked for England and the ship and passengers were lost in a terrible storm at sea. The lease expired in 1877 and title to the land and buildings on it, then extremely valuable, reverted to his heirs that he named in the lease. It was only necessary to identify the heirs, take possession of the properties and divide the wealth among those then living.

This lease is reproduced below:

Manhattan Island, June 1, 1778

Know all men by these present: That I Robert Edwards, on this day lease to John and George Cruger 77 acres 3 rods and 32 perches, beginning at a stake set in the ground at high water mark, near Bestavern, Fittlegil, and running east along Prince Street 1000 feet; thence northwesterly in a zigzag course along part of old Jan's land to Christopher Street to high water mark 547 feet; thence south along the Hudson River along the lines of high water mark 2,276 to the point and place of beginning. Said land being leased for 99 years at 1,000pounds and a pepper-corn yearly rental. Said land to be held by Johnand George Cruger and their heirs so long as contract is fulfilled; otherwise it must revert to me or my living heirs, and at the expiration of the 99 year lease said land together with all improvements shall revert to my lawful heirs, which will be descendants of my brothers and sister which are as follows: William Edwards, Jacob Edwards, Leonard Edwards, Joshua Edwards, John Edwards, Thomas Edwards and Martha Edwards. (This was Thomas, Sr. our ancestor)

Witness my hand and seal this June 1, 1778 Witness: "Robert R. E. Edwards" Anthony Barclay "John Cruger" Nicholas Bayard "George Cruger"

The area involved includes some of the most expensive real estate on earth, including some of New York's most valuable buildings. A court action in 1934 described it in present day terms as: *Beginning at a point between West St. and Washington St. in New York City, Borough of Manhattan, running in a line parallel with Christopher St. which is three blocks to the north in a northeasterly direction to a point west of Broadway, thence south to a point north of Clarkson St. and Varick St; thence southeast in a staggered line crossing Clarkson, Hudson and Greenwich Sts. to a point north of King and Washington Sts., then northwest along Washington Street to the point of beginning.*

An article in the Raleigh News & Observer on Feb. 21, 1924 said that the area included the City Hall, Federal Building, Metropolitan Life Insurance Building, the Singer Building, the New York Stock Exchange and Wall Street, and adds *"which is without doubt one of the most valuable estates in the United States of America without an owner and which the heirs are now fighting to regain"*. The value of the area described is no myth. The 1924 article stated *"now said to be valued at $400,000,000."* Its present value is impossible to estimate but would be in the billions. It was enough to make the Edwards family feel that any portion of it would put them at ease for life.

If you will check the attached records, you will find that the Thomas Edwards named on the lease is a direct descendant of our ancestral family in Wales, and a direct ancestor, of our Tennessee—Arkansas, Edwards family. The story, as developed by Fannie Mae Edwards Claud, the member of our family who carried the burden of the fight for over thirty years, is in part, as follows:

Robert Edwards was one of the three brothers, Robert, Jacob and John, who came to America from Wales. Jacob settled in Tidewater, Virginia but later returned to England and died there. Robert and John came to Northampton County. John bought 267 acres there. Robert was not married and lived with John and his wife Elizabeth. Elizabeth died after the birth of their son and John returned to England and died, leaving the farm in Northampton to his son Samuel. Robert traded in real estate for some time, then went to New York and invested his money in land there. He leased it for 99 years and embarked for England. The ship and all passengers were lost in a storm.

This should have been a simple matter to reclaim this land, but there were problems. The lease was not found recorded in New York. There are stories that records were altered to eliminate it. A newspaper article in Nashville, Tennessee dated August 11, 1950 says that records found in an old trunk by Mrs. Nancy O. Smith indicate that a sheepskin original now lies in the Trinity Church vault. Trinity Church became deeply involved in the story. There is little reference to the existence of the original lease in court records and Fannie Mae did not record where she got the copy that she had or who gave it to her. There were plenty of shenanigans pulled on the heirs by unscrupulous persons during the recovery effort and this lease could have been prepared especially for them. It must be admitted that this lease could have been a hoax. The description of the land could have been obtained from an old court case for they began the recovery effort even before the termination of the lease.

When the lease expired in 1877 the country was electrified by an inquiry from someone from New York about the heirs of Robert Edwards. Peyton Neale Clarke said in 1897 that it was a newspaper advertisement calling on the heirs to communicate with certain parties in New York City. Dorothy Ann Edwards wrote in 1885 that the governor of New York advertised for the heirs. From the information available it seems that various groups made an investigation and were informed that it would cost many thousands of dollars to make the necessary search both in America and in England and Wales and that possession would be disputed. No one came up with the money and the matter rested for several years,a s far as any action being taken.

All over the country Edwards claimants appeared. Trinity once said there were five thousand. Associations were formed to lend organisation and raise money in places like Detroit, Missouri and as far west as Denver. There was a Colorado Edwards Heirs Association who consolidated with others in 1930 to form the "International Consolidation of Edwards Heirs". The board of directors were from Canada, Mississippi, Oregon, Missouri, Ohio, Oklahoma, Tennessee, Indiana, Michigan, Louisiana, South Carolina, Alabama and Texas. The headquarters of the association later moved to Nashville, Tennessee. The Edwards Family Claimant's Association was formed in Wales. Bruce Edwards has a clipping from the Wales Daily Mail dated Sept. 14, 1953 stating *"there are 500 members of the Association, mostly working people from South Wales, all one big family, really, stemming from Old Thomas Edwards of Merthyr. The claimants maintain that through his family old Thomas' son Robert left behind in the U. S., land, on which Manhattan and Broadway now stand. He also left behind rich industrial tracts in South Wales. The American fortune, they say, is worth about 280,000,000 pounds and is growing each week. In this country there is a fortune held in Chancery, about 50,000,000 pounds".* The total of the fortune on both sides of the Atlantic was enormous. The Edwards of Northampton County, North Carolina hired a lawyer to investigate their claim. He went to New York, sold them out and returned home to convince them that they had no right to it and prevented them from entering any claim. The name of the lawyer, a Judge, is given repeatedly in Bruce Edwards' files, but is not used because he has descendants too.

Bruce also has a deathbed confession of the Judge which took place in1911. The confession was to Tom Odom who made the affidavit show below and dated Dec. 5, 1924, witnessed by Rev. C. E. Edwards and notarised by J. G. Eanes, Notary Public. The story is told below.

When the Judge was dying he showed such agony the doctor saw that he had something on his mind that was worrying him and he asked him if he had anything he wanted to say before he passed on. "Yes", he replied, *"call in some witnesses quick. I have a confession to make. Get Tom Odom if you can, his wife is an heir".* The following is what he said:

"In 1877 when the Robert R. E. Edwards 99-year lease expired in New York I told the heirs if they would give me two hundred and fifty dollars that I would go to New York and straighten out the estate for them and that they pay me more when the estate was settled, and they readily trusted me. The heirs had confidence in me, they trusted me and I betrayed them. I meant to do the right thing, I don't know what made me do such a foolish thing as I did, but the New York people hated to give up the improvements they had put on this land and they persuaded me. They talked mighty nice and sweet until I had signed their papers and accepted the large sum of money they paid me and then they made it plain that if I ever betrayed them it meant death for me. They told me there was nowhere that I could hide where they could not find me and that they would get me even if I went into the ground. I was in Hell the minute after I signed those papers and accepted that cursed money and I have been in Hell ever since. I have never been

able to enjoy one cent of that money. I was afraid to use it; I couldn't sleep, something was always after me. On my way home from New York I was in distress, not knowing how to face the heirs, but knowing them like I did and knowing how honourable and fine they were, I made up this tale before I reached home. I told them I found out the estate was not theirs and I insinuated that they were trying to get something that did not belong to them. I hurt them, I hurt them plenty and God has made me suffer for it. These heirs are the descendants of Samuel Edwards who died in 1790; He was the son of John Edwards who came from England with his brother Robert Edwards and settled in Northampton County. Tell all the heirs I am sorry for what I did and tell them the property is rightfully theirs and they can get it. I did not sign any papers to keep them from getting the property. I couldn't sign any papers to keep them from getting their own property".

Apparently the Cruger brothers never paid any rent on the land to anyone. It can be assumed that no one ever asked for it. Robert Edwards was dead and it is possible that none of his heirs ever knew of the lease. The Crugers are supposed to have sub-leased all or part of the land to the Trinity Corporation around 1800, and it built the church and established a graveyard on the land, according to the suits filed. Some suits against Trinity claimed that title to the land descended to the heirs of Thomas Hael and his son-in-law Robert Edwards. Trinity countered with the claim that the land was granted to them by Queen Anne of England in 1705 and presented grants to prove it, but with such vague descriptions that they were open to question.

Fannie Mae Edwards Claud took up the fight for the North Carolina Edwards again by asking Tom Odom to tell the story of the Judge again exactly as he remembered it. She then typed it and had him sign it and had C. E. Edwards witness his signature. She attested to both signatures before a notary. She then took an affidavit on Feb. 10,1925 from S. J. Calvert, Register of Deeds for Northampton County about two lawyers coming that day to examine County records about Robert Edwards. He quotes the lawyers as saying "*Every damn thing here is against us and if those heirs ever get in court we will lose everything*". On the next day she took a notarised statement from Charles Eaton Edwards, giving the family history as he had heard it from his father and written it down at the time. She obtained copies of deeds, the will of Samuel Edwards probated in 1790 and others, and built a firm claim to a part of the fortune.

Now comes double-cross number two. She had attended a meeting in Portsmouth, Virginia of Edwards heirs in 1924 and was impressed with the sincerity of a certain lawyer. She furnished him copies of her claim. She initiated correspondence with various claimants who recommended another lawyer, and she entrusted the latter with the claim for her family. She did not keep copies of her letters in the early years, but did later; those of this attorney to her are in Bruce's files. Later she wrote:

"*He wrote me to meet him at the Monticello Hotel at Norfolk a certain date and to come alone. Not knowing what it was all about and being tied down on the job I did not go, but found out later they got a pay-off. This is not fair and just. If I had gone I would have been paid but the other heirs would have been left out. This is not right in the sight of God or man…it seems that Trinity would be glad to payoff the heirs for the land after they had it free over a hundred years…*" She named the two lawyers in another statement and said "*…….they and others were paid off at the Monticello Hotel, Norfolk, Va. in 1925.The heirs got nothing*".

In 1930 the International Consolidation of Edwards Heirs filed suit in New York. The suit failed, as others had before, for the simple reason that the State of New York had a Statute of Limitations that provided that if no claim was made within fifteen years after the expiration of a lease by the lessor or his heirs, the occupants or possessors of the property received full title by adverse possession. The property was theirs no longer. The Judge had done his work well.

In 1947 Fannie Mae resumed the fight. She wrote to the mayor of New York City who replied that he could not give her any information. She appealed directly to the Trinity Corporation, stating the family claim and asking for justice. Their attorney, Mr. Shepard, wrote her that the

Supreme courts of both New York State and the United States had up-held their title and they would not recognise any claim against it. She wrote him again in 1948. He replied, *"...I may say that I am constantly receiving letters from all parts of the world from people claiming an interest in the property owned by Trinity Church..."* but insisted that there was no possibility of recognising her claim.

A suit was filed against Trinity by British subjects residing in England, Canada and New Zealand. This case was dismissed. Fannie Mae then employed John F. X. Brown, an attorney in New York, in October of 1948 and paid him a fee. He reported at length in January of 1949, citing court cases, saying that the case was hopeless. She wrote the Department of Justice in Washington in June of 1949. She also wrote the Chief Post Office Inspector, President Harry S. Truman, the American Arbitration Association in New York, to the Honourable W. M.Tuck, Governor of Virginia, to the Lord Mayor of Cardiff, Wales; all to no avail. In 1953 another suit was filed by the Hael Heirs and the New York Sunday News gave the entire story a spread in the Dec. 13, 1953 issue. The case was dismissed. In 1954 Fannie Mae made another appeal to Mr. Shepard, attorney for the Trinity Corporation. His answer was courteous but firm on April 23,1954: *"The courts have definitely held that any possible claims are barred by the Statute of Limitations. It would, therefore, be useless to discuss the matter any further."*

History records many more attempts to reclaim this Edwards property, but I think this should be enough to show that any further pursuit of this would be useless. So the quest for the Edwards fortune ends? Was it just a fantasy? It was no fantasy. It was as real as the paper this is written on. The records are there to prove it. Our loss is Trinity's gain and it makes a good story even if it does end in heartbreak.

APPENDIX E

(from **The Complete Newgate Calendar, Vol. II**)
DICK HUGHES
A Robber whose thoughtful Wife bought the Rope to hang him.
Executed at Tyburn in June, 1709.

THIS great villain, Richard Hughes, was the son of a very good yeoman living at Bettws, in Denbighshire, in North Wales, where he was born, and followed husbandry, but would now and then be pilfering in his very minority, as he found opportunity. When he first came up to London, on his way money being short, necessity compelled him to steal a pair of tongs at Pershore in Worcestershire, for which he was sent to Worcester Jail; and at the assizes held there, the matter of fact being plainly proved against him, the judge directed the jury to bring him in guilty only of petty larceny; and accordingly, giving in their verdict guilty to the value of ten pence, he came off with crying carrots and turnips, a term which rogues use for whipping at the cart's tail.

After this introduction to further villainy, Dick Hughes, coming up to London, soon became acquainted with the most celebrated villains in this famous metropolis, especially with one Thomas Lawson, *alias* Browning, a tripe man, who was hanged at Tyburn on Tuesday, the 27th of May, 1712, for felony and burglary, in robbing the house of one Mr Hunt, at Hackney. In a very short time he became noted for his several robberies; but at last, breaking open a victualling-house at Lambeth, and taking from thence only the value of three shillings, because he could find no more, he was tried and condemned for that fact at the assizes held at Kingston-upon-Thames; but was then reprieved, and afterwards pleaded his pardon at the same place. Now being again at liberty, instead of becoming a new man he became rather worse than before, breaking open and robbing several houses, at Tottenham Cross, Harrow-on-the-Hill, a gentlewoman's house at Hackney, a gentleman's at Hammersmith, a minister's near Kingston- upon-Thames, a tobacconist's house in Red Cross Street, and a house on Hounslow Heath. Burglaries being the masterpiece of Dick Hughes's villainy, he went chiefly on them; till at last, breaking open and robbing the house of one Mr George Clark, at Twickenham, he was apprehended for this fact, and committed to Newgate.

Whilst he lay under condemnation, his wife, to whom he had been married in the Fleet Prison, constantly visited him at chapel. She was a very honest woman, and had such an extraordinary kindness for her husband under his great afflictions that when he went to be hanged at Tyburn, on Friday, the 24th of June, 1709, she met him at St Giles's Pound, where, the cart stopping, she stepped up to him, and whispering in his ear, said: *"My dear, who must find the rope that's to hang you - me or the sheriff?"* Her husband replied: *"The sheriff, honey; for who's obliged to find him tools to do his work?"* *"Ah! "* replied his wife, *"I wish I had known so much before; it would have saved me twopence, for I have been and bought one already."* *"Well, well,* said Dick again, *"perhaps it mayn't be lost, for it may serve a second husband."* *"Yes,"* quoth his wife, *"if I have any luck in good husbands, so it may."*

Then, the cart driving on to Hyde Park Corner, this notorious villain ended his days there, in the thirtieth year of his age; and was after anatomised at Surgeons' Hall, in London.

APPENDIX F
(from the Newgate calendar)
WILLIAM DAVIS, THE GOLDEN FARMER
Who was Farmer and Highwayman for Forty-two Years
without his Neighbours suspecting. Executed
20th of December, 1689

THE Golden Farmer was so called from his occupation and from paying people, if it was any considerable sum, always in gold; but his real name was William Davis, born at Wrexham, in Denbighshire, in North Wales, from whence he removed, in his younger years, to Salisbury, in Gloucester-shire, where he married the daughter of a wealthy innkeeper, by whom he had eighteen children, and followed the farmer's business to the day of his death, to shroud his robbing on the highway, which irregular practice he had followed for forty- two years without any suspicion among his neighbours.

He generally robbed alone, and one day, meeting three or four stage-coaches going to Salisbury, he stopped one of them which was full of gentlewomen, one of whom was a Quaker. All of them satisfied the Golden Farmer's desire excepting this precisian, with whom he had a long argument to no purpose, for upon her solemn vow and affirmation she told him she had no money, nor anything valuable about her; whereupon, fearing he should lose the booty of the other coaches, he told her he would go and see what they had to afford him, and he would wait on her again. So having robbed the other three coaches he returned, according to his word, and the Quaker persisting still in her old tone of having nothing for him it put the Golden Farmer into a rage, and taking hold of her shoulder' shaking her as a mastiff does a bull, he cried: *"You canting bitch! if you dally with me at this rate, you'll certainly provoke my spirit to be damnably rude with you. You see these good women here were so tender-hearted as to be charitable to me, and you, you whining whore, are so covetous as to lose your life for the sake of mammon. Come, come, you hollow-hearted bitch, unpin your purse-string quickly, or else I shall send you out of the land of the living."* Now the poor Quaker, being frightened out of her wits at the bullying expressions of the wicked one, gave him a purse of guineas, a gold watch and a diamond ring, and they parted then as good friends as if they had never fallen out at all.

Another time this desperado, meeting with the Duchess of Albemarle in her coach, riding over Salisbury Plain, was put to his trumps before he could assault her Grace, by reason he had a long engagement with a postilion, a coachman and two footmen before he could proceed in his robbery; but having wounded them all, by the discharging of several pistols, he then approached to his prey, whom he found more refractory than his female Quaker had been, which made him very saucy, and more eager for fear of any passengers coming by in the meanwhile; but still her Grace would not part with anything. Whereupon by main violence he pulled three diamond rings off her fingers, and snatched a rich gold watch from her side, crying to her at the same time, because he saw her face painted: "*You bitch incarnate, you had rather read over your face in the glass every moment, and blot out pale to put in red, than give an honest man, as I am, a small matter to support him on his lawful occasions on the road,*" and then rode away as fast as he could, without searching her Grace for any money, because he perceived another person of quality's coach making towards them, with a good retinue of servants belonging to it.

Not long after this exploit, the Golden Farmer meeting with Sir Thomas Day, a Justice of Peace living at Bristol, on the road betwixt Gloucester and Worcester, they fell into discourse together, and riding along he told Sir Thomas, whom he knew, though the other did not know him, how he was like to have been robbed but a little before by a couple of highwaymen; but as good luck would have it, his horse having better heels than theirs, he got clear of them, or else, if they had robbed him of his money, which was about forty pounds, they would certainly have undone him for ever. "*Truly,*" quoth Sir Thomas Day, "*that would have been very hard; but nevertheless, as you would have been robbed between sun and sun, the county, upon your suing it, would have been obliged to have made your loss good again.*"

But not long after this chatting together, coming to a convenient place, the Golden Farmer, shooting Sir Thomas's man's horse under him, and obliging him to retire some distance from it, that he might not make use of the pistols that were in his holsters, presented a pistol to Sir Thomas's breast, and demanded his money of him. Quoth Sir Thomas: "*I thought, sir, that you had been an honest man.*" The Golden Farmer replied: "*You see your Worship's mistaken, and had you had any guts in your brains you might have perceived by my face that my countenance was the very picture of mere necessity; therefore deliver presently, for I am in haste.*" Then, Sir Thomas Day giving the Golden Farmer what money he had, which was about sixty pounds in gold and silver, he humbly thanked his Worship, and told him, that what he had parted with was not lost, because he was robbed betwixt sun and sun, therefore the county, as he told him, must pay it again. One Mr Hart, a young gentleman of Enfield, who had a good estate, but was not overburdened with wit, and therefore could sooner change a piece of gold than a piece of sense, riding one day over Finchley Common, where the Golden Farmer had been hunting about four or five hours for a prey, he rides up to him and, giving the gentleman a slap with the flat of his drawn hanger over his shoulders, quoth he: "*A plague on you! How slow you are, to make a man wait on you all this morning. Come, deliver what you have, and be poxed to you, and go to hell for orders!*" The gentleman, who was wont to find a more agreeable entertain merit betwixt his mistress and his snuff-box, being surprised at the rustical sort of greeting, began to make several sorts of excuses, and say he had no money about him; but his antagonist, not believing him, made bold to search his pockets himself, and finding in them above a hundred guineas, besides a gold watch, he gave him two or three slaps over the shoulder again with his hanger; and at the same time bade him not give his mind to lying any more, when an honest gentleman desired a small boon of him.

Another time this notorious robber had paid his landlord above forty pounds for rent, who going home with it, the goodly tenant, disguising himself, met the grave old gentleman, and bidding him stand, quoth he: "*Come, Mr Gravity from head to foot, but from neither head nor foot to the heart, deliver what you have in a trice.*" The old man, fetching a deep sigh, to the hazard of losing several buttons of his waistcoat, said that he had not above two shillings about him; therefore he thought he was more of a gentleman than to take a small matter from a poor man. Quoth the Golden Farmer: "*I have not the faith to believe you; for you seem by your mien and habit to be a man of better circumstance than you pretend; therefore open your budget or else I shall fall foul about your house*".

"*Dear sir,*" replied his landlord, "*you cannot be so barbarous to an old man. What ! Have you no religion, pity or compassion in you? Have you no conscience? Have you no respect for your own body and soul, which must be certainly in a miserable condition, if you follow unlawful courses?*" "*Damn you !*" said the tenant to him, "*don't talk of age and barbarity to me; for I show neither pity nor compassion to any. Damn you, don't talk of conscience to me! I have no more of that dull commodity than you have; nor do I allow my soul and body to be governed by religion, but interest; therefore, deliver what you have, before this pistol makes you repent your obstinacy.*" So, delivering his money to the Golden Farmer, he received it without giving the landlord any receipt for it, as his landlord had him.

Not long after committing this robbery, overtaking an old grazier at Putney Heath, in a very ordinary attire, but yet very rich, he takes half-a-score guineas out of his pocket, and giving them to the old man he said there were three or four persons behind them who looked very suspicious, therefore he desired the favour of him to put that gold into his pocket; for in case they were highwaymen, his indifferent apparel would make them believe he had no such charge about him. The old grazier, looking upon his intentions to be honest, quoth: "*I have fifty guineas tied up in the fore-lappet of my shirt, and I'll put it to that for security.*" So riding along, both of them check by jowl, for above half-a- mile, and the coast being clear, the Golden Farmer said to the old man: "*I believe there's nobody will take the pains of robbing you or me to-day; therefore, I think I had as good take the trouble of robbing you myself; so instead of delivering your purse, pray give me the lappet of your shirt.*" The old grazier was horridly startled at these words, and began to beseech him not to be so cruel in robbing a poor old man. "*Prithee,*" quoth the Golden Farmer, "*don't tell me of cruelty; for who can be more cruel than men of your age, whose pride it is to teach their servants their duties with as much cruelty as some people teach their dogs to fetch and carry?*" So being obliged to cut off the lappet of the old man's shirt himself, for he would not, he rode away to seek out another booty. Another time this bold robber, lying at an inn in Uxbridge, happened into company with one Squire Broughton, a barrister of the Middle Temple, which he understanding, pretended to him that he was going up to London to advise with a lawyer about some business; wherefore, he should be much obliged to him if he could recommend him to a good one. Counsellor Broughton, thinking he might be a good client, bespoke him for himself. Then, the Golden Farmer telling his business was about several of his neighbours' cattle breaking into his grounds and doing a great deal of mischief, the barrister told him that was very actionable, as being *damage feasant*. "*Damage feasant,*" said the Golden Farmer; "*what's that, pray, sir?*" He told him that it was an action brought against persons when their cattle broke through hedges, or other fences, into other people's grounds, and did them damage. Next morning, as they both were riding toward London, says the Golden Farmer to the barrister: "*If I may be so bold as to ask you, sir, what is that you call 'trover' and 'conversion'?*" He told him it signified in our common law an action which a man has against another that, having found any of his goods, refuses to deliver them upon demand, and perhaps converts them to his own use also. The Golden Farmer being now at a place convenient for his purpose — "*Very well, sir,*" says he, "*and so, if I should find any money about you, and convert it to my use, why then that is only actionable, I find.*" "*That's a robbery,*" said the barrister, "*which requires no less satisfaction than a man's life.*" "*A robbery!*" replied the Golden Farmer. "*Why then, I must e'en commit one for once and not use it; therefore deliver your money, or else behold this pistol shall prevent you from ever reading Coke upon Littleton any more.*" The barrister, strangely surprised at his client's rough behaviour, asked him if he thought there was neither heaven nor hell, that he could be guilty of such wicked actions. Quoth the Golden Farmer: "*Why, you son of a whore, thy impudence is very great, to talk of heaven or hell to me, when you think there's no way to heaven but through Westminster Hall. Come, come, down with your rhino this minute; for I have other guess customers to mind, than to wait on you all day.*" The barrister was very loath to part with his money, still insisting on the injustice of the action, saying it was against law and conscience to rob any man. However the Golden Farmer, heeding not his pleading, swore he was not to be guided by law and conscience any more than any of his profession, whose law is always furnished with a commission to arraign their consciences; but upon judgement given they usually had the knack of setting it at large. So putting a pistol to the barrister's breast, he quickly delivered his money, amounting to about thirty guineas, and eleven broad-pieces of gold, besides some silver, and a gold watch.

Thus the Golden Farmer, having run a long course in wickedness, was at last discovered in Salisbury Court; but as he was running along, a butcher, endeavouring to stop him, was shot dead by him with a pistol; being apprehended nevertheless, he was committed to Newgate, and shortly after executed, at the end of Salisbury Court, in Fleet Street, on Friday the 20th of December, 1689; and after-wards was hanged in chains, in the sixty-fourth year of his age, on Bagshot Heath.

Footnote: According to the WDNB, Davis was born in 1627 at Wrexham, moving at an early age to Sodbury, Gloucestershire, where he married the daughter of a wealthy innkeeper. They had 18 children, and Davis became a successful farmer. He hid his further profession, as a highwayman from his wife, almost to the end of his days. He began by picking out farmers on their way to pay rent, and those who had made money selling their beasts and produce at markets. According to one account he was at one time a corn-chandler in London's Thames Street, selling by day and robbing farmers at night. He was tried at the Old Bailey in December 1690 and hung in that year, according to the WDNB, not 1689 as in the Newgate Calendar. His exploits led to the publication of leaflets, posters, chapbooks and even a play. Not a pirate, buccaneer or privateer, but Wales' only well-known highwayman, whom the author has included in this book on a whim.

APPENDIX G

THOMAS STRADLING, ALEXANDER SELKIRK AND ROBINSON CRUSOE

Buccaneers under Captain Watling were scared off the uninhabited Juan Fernandez Island in January 1681, and in their haste left a Mosquito Indian called William behind. He had been in the woods, hunting for wild goats. On March 22nd, 1684, buccaneers under Captain Cook of the *Batchelor's Delight* and Captain Swan of the *Cygnet* came into sight of Juan Fernandez. Some of Cook's men had sailed under Watling, and wanted to send a boat ashore to look for William. Dampier related in his journals that he went ashore on this boat with another Mosquito Indian named Robin. *'Robin, his countryman, was the first who leaped ashore from the boats, and, running to his brother Mosquito-man, threw himself flat on his face at his feet, who, helping him up and embracing him, fell flat with his face on the ground at Robin's feet, and was by him taken up also. We stood with pleasure to behold the surprise, tenderness, and solemnity of this interview, which was exceedingly affectionate on both sides; and, when their ceremonies were over, we also, that stood gazing at them, drew near, each of us embracing him we had found here, who was overjoyed to see so many of his old friends come hither, as he thought, purposely to fetch him. He was named Will, as the other was Robin; which names were given them by the English, for they have no names among themselves, and they take it as a favour to be named by us, and will complain if we do not appoint them some name when they are with us.'*

William had seen the buccaneers anchor and had killed three goats which he dressed with vegetables, preparing a treat for them when they landed. The Spanish had known that William was on the island for three years and had tried to trap him and find where he was holed up. *'He had built himself a hut, half-a-mile from the sea-shore, which he lined with goats' skins, and slept on his couch or barbecu (wooden hurdle) of sticks, raised about two feet from the ground and spread with goats' skins.'* The goats were left there by the Spanish to multiply and supply fresh meat (much like the wild hogs and cattle in other islands), and there was fresh water flowing at two places on the island.

He had been left on the island with just a musket, knife, a little powder and some shot. Dampier tells us that *'when his ammunition was expended, he contrived by notching his knife to saw the barrel of his gun into small pieces, wherewith he made harpoons, lances, hooks and a long knife, heating the pieces of iron first in the fire, and then hammering them out as he pleased with stones.'* Fishing lines were made from the skins of seals laboriously cut into thongs and knotted. He had no clothes left, and wore a goatskin around his waist.

The crews reprovisioned with goats, wild vegetables, fish, sea-lions and seals, before they weighed anchor on April 8th. It seems that William fits the lifestyle of Daniel Defoe's 'Robinson Crusoe' perfectly. Dampier's Journals were published in 1697 and 1699 and Defoe's book in 1719. However, most people believe that the Robinson Crusoe story was inspired by Alexander Selkirk, a Scot marooned by a Welsh buccaneer on the same island.

Dampier features again in this version. In late summer 1704, he was captain of the privateer *St George*, with Thomas Stradling was captaining the consort ship *Cinque Ports*. In September, the Cinque Ports needed caulking was put into Juan Fernandez for repairs, where the ship's master Selkirk and the captain Stradling had a blazing row. Dampier said that the repairs were not good enough and that the ship would leak badly. He shouted that if Stradling insisted on setting sail in her, he could *'go to the bottom alone'*. In high dudgeon, Stradling left Selkirk ashore with his sea chest. Selkirk thopught that other men would join him, forcing Stradling to change his mind, but as the ship's boat pulled away from the beach, he shouted to Stradling that he had changed his mind. Stradling shouted back that he had not changed his, and Selkirk was marooned.

At first he expected the ship to return, read copiously from his Bible, prayed for rescue and almost starved, before he realised that this was to be no short sojourn. A resourceful man, he must have known that William had survived here for three years a decade ago, and he set to the job in hand. Two grass-covered huts were built and lined with goat-skins, one for living in and one for cooking. He replaced his worn-out clothes with goatskin garments fashioned using a nail as a needle and unravelled stockings for his thread. He wore out his knife, but made fresh blades from iron barrel-hoops left on the island. When his ammunition ran out, he ran down goats on foot to kill them.

On January 31st, 1709, Dampier was sailing under Woodes Rogers after rounding Cape Horn, trying to put into Mas a Tierra, one of the Juan Fernandez Islands. The privateer ships *Duke* and *Duchess* could not get closer than twelve mile away, because of winds, so it was decided to send a pinnace ashore. The crew were sick, and seven had succumbed to scurvy. Fresh water, vegetables and meat were urgently needed. The pinnace took hours to get within three miles of the island, and at nightfall a huge bonfire was seen on the coast. The pinnace returned to the *Duchess*, thinking that the French or Spanish were on the island.

Next morning Captain Rogers could see no enemy ships at either bay on the island, and managed to get closer to the islands before the ship's yawl was sent out with seven armed men. It did not return, so Rogers risked sending the pinnace to the island, with chosen musketeers on board. It did not return for hours, and Rogers hoisted signal flags. When the pinnace eventually came back, it was loaded with fresh crayfish and a barefoot, bearded semi-intelligible man dressed in goat-skins. He was asked how long he had been there and answered four years and four months – he had kept the time by marking wood. He was asked his name and replied with difficulty, Alexander Selkirk, master of the *Cinque Ports*. Dampier then came forward to fill in the details. When Selkirk saw Dampier, he asked to be put ashore again, but was talked out of it.

Rogers used this period to help his crew recuperate. Apart from the seven who died, there were another suffering from scurvy, of which two could not be saved. Ashore they found turnips and parsley planted by previous parties of buccaneers, and there was abundant wild cabbage, flocks of goats and all the crabs. Lobsters and crayfish they could eat. Rogers' men pronounced that seal tasted as good as English lamb, and picked their teeth clean with sea-lion's whiskers, forgetting the horrors of the rounding of Cape Horn. After six weeks, on February 14th, Rogers continued upon his remarkable circumnavigation of the world.

Meanwhile, after leaving Selkirk, Stradling soon discovered that his ship was foundering, as Selkirk had predicted, so he was forced to run it aground in the Mapella Islands. The Spanish threw the survivors into dungeons in Lima for six terrible years.

It is believed that Daniel Defoe was Captain Charles Johnson, who wrote the definitive history of pirates. It was also believed that Defoe's 'Robinson Crusoe' was based on Alexander Selkirk, the Scot from Largo in Fife. Defoe had read William Dampier's 'Voyage Round the World', and also Woodes Rogers' account, with the same title. Both give the story of Selkirk. Defoe's latest biographer, Richard West, makes absolutely no mention of Johnson, and believes that Robinson Crusoe was not based upon Selkirk.

A DISCOURSE WRITTEN BY ONE MILES PHILLIPS, ONE OF THE COMPANY PUT ASHORE IN THE WEST INDIES BY MASTER JOHN HAWKINS IN THE YEAR 1568, CONTAINING MANY SPECIAL THINGS OF THAT COUNTRY AND OF THE SPANISH GOVERNMENT, BUT SPECIALLY OF THEIR CRUELTIES USED TO OUR ENGLISHMEN, AND AMONGST THE REST, TO HIMSELF FOR THE SPACE OF FIFTEEN OR SIXTEEN YEARS TOGETHER, UNTIL BY GOOD AND HAPPY MEANS HE WAS DELIVERED FROM THEIR BLOODY HANDS, AND RETURNED TO HIS OWN COUNTRY. ANNO 1582.

THE FIRST CHAPTER.

WHEREIN IS SHOWN THE DAY AND TIME OF OUR DEPARTURE FROM THE COAST OF ENGLAND, WITH THE NUMBER AND NAMES OF THE SHIPS, THEIR CAPTAINS AND MASTERS, AND OF OUR TRAFFIC AND DEALING UPON THE COAST OF AFRICA.

Upon Monday, being the 2nd of October, 1567, the weather being reasonable fair, our General, Master John Hawkins, having commanded all his captains and masters to be in a readiness to make sail with him, he himself being embarked in the Jesus, whereof was appointed for master Robert Barret, hoisted sail and departed from Plymouth upon his intended voyage for the parts of Africa and America, being accompanied with five other sail of ships, as namely the Minion, wherein went for captain Master John Hampton, and John Garret, master. The William and John, wherein was Captain Thomas Bolton, and James Raunce, master. The Judith, in whom was Captain Master Francis Drake, now Knight, and the Angel, whose master, as also the captain and master of the Swallow, I now remember not. And so sailing in company together upon our voyage until the 10th of the same month, an extreme storm then took us near unto Cape Finisterre, which lasted for the space of four days, and so separated our ships that we had lost one another, and our General, finding the Jesus to be but in ill case, was in mind to give over the voyage and to return home. Howbeit, the eleventh of the same month, the seas waxing calm and the wind coming fair, he altered his purpose, and held on the former intended voyage; and so coming to the island of Gomera, being one of the islands of the Canaries, where, according to an order before appointed, we met with all our ships which were before dispersed. We then took in fresh water and departed from thence the 4th of November, and holding on our course, upon the 18th day of the same month we came to an anchor upon the coast of Africa, at Cape Verde, in twelve fathoms of water, and here our General landed certain of our men, to the number of 160 or thereabouts, seeking to take some negroes. And they, going up into the country for the space of six miles, were encountered with a great number of the negroes, who with their envenomed arrows did hurt a great number of our men, so that they were enforced to retire to the ships, in which conflict they recovered but a few negroes; and of these our men which were hurt with their envenomed arrows, there died to the number of seven or eight in very strange manner, with their mouths shut, so that we were forced to put sticks and other things into their mouths to keep them open; and so afterwards passing the time upon the coast of Guinea, until the 12th of January, we obtained by that time the number of one hundred and fifty negroes. And being ready to depart from the sea coast, there was a negro sent as an ambassador to our General, from a king of the negroes, which was oppressed with other kings, his bordering kings, desiring our General to grant him succour and aid against those his enemies, which our General granted unto, and went himself in person on land with the number of 200 of our men, or thereabouts, and the said king which had requested our aid, did join his force with ours, so that thereby our General assaulted and set fire upon a town of the said king his enemies, in which there was at the least the number of eight or ten thousand negroes, and they, perceiving that they were not able to make any resistance, sought by flight to save themselves, in which their flight there were taken prisoners to the number of eight or nine hundred, which our General ought to have had for his share; howbeit the negro king, which requested our aid, falsifying his word and promise, secretly in the night conveyed himself away with as many prisoners as he had in his custody; but our General, notwithstanding finding himself to have now very near the number of 500 negroes, thought it best without longer abode to depart with them and such merchandise as he had from the coast of Africa towards the West Indies, and therefore commanded with all diligence to take in fresh water and fuel, and so with speed to prepare to depart. Howbeit, before we departed from thence, in a storm that we had, we lost one of our ships, namely, the William and John, of which ship and her people we heard no tidings during the time of our voyage.

THE SECOND CHAPTER.

WHEREIN IS SHOWED THE DAY AND TIME OF OUR DEPARTURE FROM THE COAST OF AFRICA, WITH THE DAY AND TIME OF OUR ARRIVAL IN THE WEST INDIES, ALSO OF OUR TRADE AND TRAFFIC THERE, AND ALSO OF THE GREAT CRUELTY THAT THE SPANIARDS USED TOWARDS US, BY THE VICEROY HIS DIRECTION AND APPOINTMENT, FALSIFYING HIS FAITH AND PROMISE GIVEN, AND SEEKING TO HAVE ENTRAPPED US.

All things being made in a readiness at our General his appointment, upon the 3rd day of February, 1568, we departed from the coast of Africa, having the weather somewhat tempestuous; which made our passage the more hard, and sailing so for the space of twenty-five days, upon the 27th March, 1568, we came in sight of an island called Dominique, upon the coast of America, in the West Indies, situated in fourteen degrees of latitude, and two hundred and twenty-two of longitude. From thence our General coasted from place to place, ever making traffic with the Spaniards and Indians, as he might, which was somewhat hardly obtained, for that the king had straitly charged all his governors in those parts not to trade with any. Yet notwithstanding, during the months of April and May, our General had reasonable trade and traffic, and courteous entertainment in sundry places, as at Marguerite, Corassoa, and elsewhere, until we came to Cape de la Vela, and Rio de la Hacha (a place from whence all the pearls do come). The governor there would not by any means permit us to have any trade or traffic, nor yet suffer us to take in fresh water; by means whereof our General, for the avoiding of famine and thirst, about the beginning of June was enforced to land 200 of our men, and so by main force and strength to obtain that which by no fair means he could procure; and so recovering the town with the loss of two of our men, there was a secret and peaceable trade admitted, and the Spaniards came in by night, and bought of our negroes to the number of 200 and upwards, and of our other merchandise also. From thence we departed for Cartagena, where the governor was so strait that we could not obtain any traffic there, and so for that our trade was near finished, our General thought it best to depart from thence the rather for the avoiding of certain dangerous storms called the huricanoes, which accustomed to begin there about that time of the year, and so the 24th of July, 1568, we departed from thence, directing our course north, leaving the islands of Cuba upon our right hand, to the eastward of us, and so sailing towards Florida, upon the 12th of August an extreme tempest arose, which dured for the space of eight days, in which our ships were most dangerously tossed, and beaten hither and thither, so that we were in continual fear to be drowned, by reason of the shallowness of the coast, and in the end we were constrained to flee for succour to the port of St. John de Ullua, or Vera Cruz, situated in nineteen degrees of latitude, and in two hundred and seventy-nine degrees of longitude, which is the port that serveth for the city of Mexico. In our seeking to recover this port our General met by the way three small ships that carried passengers, which he took with him, and so the 16th of September, 1568, we entered the said port of St. John de Ullua. The Spaniards there, supposing us to have been the King of Spain's fleet, the chief officers of the country thereabouts came presently aboard our General, where perceiving themselves to have made an unwise adventure, they were in great fear to have been taken and stayed; howbeit our General did use them all very courteously. In the said port there were twelve ships, which by report had in them in treasure, to the value of two hundred thousand pounds, all which being in our General his power, and at his devotion, he did freely set at liberty, as also the passengers which he had before stayed, not taking from any of them all the value of one groat, only we stayed two men of credit and account, the one named Don Lorenzo de Alva, and the other Don Pedrode Revera, and presently our General sent to the Viceroy to Mexico, which was threescore leagues off, certifying him of our arrival there by force of weather, desiring that forasmuch as our Queen, his Sovereign, was the King of Spain his loving sister and friend, that therefore he would, considering our necessities and wants, furnish us with victuals for our navy, and quietly to suffer us to repair and amend our ships. And furthermore that at the arrival of the Spanish fleet, which was there daily expected and looked for, to the end that there might no quarrel arise between them and our General and his company for the breach of amity, he humbly requested of his excellency that there might in this behalf some special order be taken. This message was sent away the 16th of September, 1568, it being the very day of our arrival there.

The next morning, being the 17th of the same month, we descried thirteen sail of great ships; and after that our General understood that it was the King of Spain's fleet then looked for, he presently sent to advertise the General hereof of our being in the said port, and giving him further to understand, that before he should enter there into that harbour, it was requisite that there should pass between the two Generals some orders and conditions, to be observed on either part, for the better contriving of peace between them and theirs, according to our General's request made unto the Viceroy. And at this instant our General was in a great perplexity of mind, considering with himself that if he should keep out that fleet from entering into the port, a thing which he was very well able to do with the help of God, then should that fleet be in danger of present shipwreck and loss of all their substance, which amounted unto the value of one million and eight hundred thousand crowns. Again, he saw that if he suffered them to enter, he was assured they would practise all manner of means to betray him and his, and on the other side the haven was so little, that the other fleet entering, the ships were to ride one hard aboard of another; also he saw that if their fleet should perish by his keeping them out, as of necessity they must if he should have done so, then stood he in great fear of the Queen our Sovereign's displeasure; in so weighty a cause, therefore, did he choose the least evil, which was to suffer them to enter under assurance, and so to stand upon his guard, and to defend himself and his from their treasons, which we were all assured they would practise, and so the messenger being returned from Don Martine de Henriquez, the new Viceroy, who came in the same fleet, and had sufficient authority to command in all cases both by sea and land in this province of Mexico or New Spain, did certify our General, that for the better maintenance of amity between the King of Spain and our Sovereign, all our requests should be both favourably granted and faithfully performed; signifying further that he heard and understood of the honest and friendly dealing of our General towards the King of Spain's subjects in all places where he had been, as also in the said port; so that to be brief our requests were articled and set down in writing, viz.—

1. The first was that we might have victuals for our money and license to sell as much wares as might suffice to furnish our wants.

2. The second, that we might be suffered peaceably to repair our ships.

3. The third, that the island might be in our possession during the time of our abode there, in which island our General, for the better safety of him and his, had already planted and placed certain ordnance, which were eleven pieces of brass; therefore he required that the same might so continue, and that no Spaniard should come to land in the said island having or wearing any kind of weapon about him.

4. The fourth and the last, that for the better and more sure performance and maintenance of peace, and of all the conditions, there might twelve gentlemen of credit be delivered of either part as hostages.

These conditions were concluded and agreed upon in writing by the Viceroy and signed with his hand, and sealed with his seal, and ten hostages upon either part were received. And farther, it was concluded that the two Generals should meet and give faith each to other for the performance of the promises. All which being done, the same was proclaimed by the sound of a trumpet, and commandment was given that none of either part should violate or break the peace upon pain of death. Thus, at the end of three days all was concluded, and the fleet entered the port, the ships saluting each other as the manner of the seas doth require. The morrow after being Friday, we laboured on all sides in placing the English ships by themselves and the Spanish ships by themselves; the captains and inferior persons of either part offering and showing great courtesy one to another, and promising great amity upon all sides. Howbeit, as the sequel showed, the Spaniards meant nothing less upon their parts. For the Viceroy and the governor thereabout had secretly on land assembled to the number of one thousand chosen men, and well appointed, meaning the next Thursday, being the 24th of September, at dinner time to assault us, and set upon us on all sides. But before I go any further, I think it not amiss briefly to describe the manner of the island as it then was, and the force and strength that it is now of. For the Spaniards, since the time of our General's being there, for the better fortifying of the same place, have upon the same island built a fair castle and bulwark very well fortified; this port was then, at our being there, a little island of stones, not past three foot above water in the highest place, and not past a bow's shot over any way at the most, and it standeth from the mainland two bow-shots or more, and there is not in all this coast any other place for ships safely to arrive at; also the north winds in this coast are of great violence and force, and unless the ships be safely moored in, with their anchors fastened in this island, there is no remedy, but present destruction and shipwreck. All this our General, wisely foreseeing, did provide that he would have the said island in his custody, or else the Spaniards might at their pleasure have but cut our cables, and so with the first north wind that blew we had had our passport, for our ships had gone ashore. But to return to the matter. The time approaching that their treason must be put in practice, the same Thursday morning, some appearance thereof began to show itself, as shifting of weapons from ship to ship, and planting and bending their ordnance against our men that warded upon the land with great repair of people; which apparent shows of breach of the Viceroy's faith caused our General to send one to the Viceroy to inquire of him what was meant thereby, who presently sent and gave order that the ordnance aforesaid and other things of suspicion should be removed, returning answer to our General in the faith of a Viceroy that he would be our defence and safety from all villainous treachery. This was upon Thursday, in the morning. Our General not being therewith satisfied, seeing they had secretly conveyed a great number of men aboard a great hulk or ship of theirs of nine hundred tons, which ship rode hard by the Minion, he sent again to the Viceroy Robert Barret, the master of the Jesus—a man that could speak the Spanish tongue very well, and required that thosee men might be unshipped again which were in that great hulk. The Viceroy then perceiving that their treason was thoroughly espied, stayed our master and sounded the trumpet, and gave order that his people should upon all sides charge upon our men which warded on shore and elsewhere, which struck such a maze and sudden fear among us, that many gave place and sought to recover our ships for the safety of themselves. The Spaniards, which secretly were hid in ambush on land, were quickly conveyed over to the island in their long boats, and so coming to the island they slew all our men that they could meet with without any mercy. The Minion—which had somewhat before prepared herself to avoid the danger—hailed away, and abode the first brunt of the three hundred men that were in the great hulk; then they sought to fall aboard the Jesus, where was a cruel fight, and many of our men slain; but yet our men defended themselves, and kept them out: so the Jesus also got loose, and, joining with the Minion, the fight waxed hot upon all sides; but they having won and got our ordnance on shore, did greatly annoy us. In this fight there were two great ships of the Spaniards sunk and one burnt, so that with their ships they were not able to harm us; but from the shore they beat us cruelly with our own ordnance in such sort that the Jesus was very sore spoiled, and suddenly the Spaniards, having fired two great ships of their own, came directly against us; which bred among our men a marvellous fear. Howbeit, the Minion, which had made her sails ready, shifted for herself without consent of the General, captain, or master, so that very hardly our General could be received into the Minion; the most of our men that were in the Jesus shifted for themselves, and followed the Minion in the boat, and those which that small boat was not able to receive were most cruelly slain by the Spaniards. Of our ships none escaped save the Minion and the Judith, and all such of our men as were not in them were enforced to abide the tyrannous cruelty of the Spaniards. For it is a certain truth, that whereas they had taken certain of our men at shore, they took and hung them up by the arms upon high posts until the blood burst out of their fingers' ends; of which men so used there is one Copstowe and certain others yet alive, who, through the merciful Providence of the Almighty, were long since arrived here at home in England, carrying still about with them (and shall to their graves) the marks and tokens of those their inhuman and more than barbarous cruel dealing.

THE THIRD CHAPTER.

WHEREIN IS SHOWED HOW THAT, AFTER WE WERE ESCAPED FROM THE SPANIARDS, WE WERE LIKE TO PERISH WITH FAMINE AT THE SEA, AND HOW OUR GENERAL, FOR THE AVOIDING THEREOF, WAS CONSTRAINED TO PUT HALF OF HIS MEN ON LAND, AND WHAT MISERIES WE AFTER THAT SUSTAINED AMONGST THE SAVAGE PEOPLE, AND HOW WE FELL AGAIN INTO THE HANDS OF THE SPANIARDS.

After that the Viceroy, Don Martin Henriques, had thus contrary to his faith and promise most cruelly dealt with our General, Master Hawkins, at St. John de Ullua, where most of his men were by the Spaniards slain and drowned, and all his ships sunk and burnt, saving the Minion and the Judith, which was a small barque of fifty tons, wherein was then captain Master Francis Drake aforesaid; the same night the said barque was lost us, we being in great necessity and enforced to move with the Minion two bow-shots from the Spanish fleet, where we anchored all that night; and the next morning we weighed anchor and recovered an island a mile from the Spaniards, where a storm took us with a north wind, in which we were greatly distressed, having but two cables and two anchors left; for in the conflict before we had lost three cables and two anchors. The morrow after, the storm being ceased and the weather fair, we weighed and set sail, being many men in number and but small store of victuals to suffice us for any long time; by means whereof we were in despair and fear that we should perish through famine, so that some were in mind to yield themselves to the mercy of the Spaniards, other some to the savages or infidels, and wandering thus certain days in these unknown seas, hunger constrained us to eat hides, cats and dogs, mice, rats, parrots, and monkeys, to be short, our hunger was so great that we thought it savoury and sweet whatsoever we could get to eat.

And on the 8th of October we came to land again, in the bottom of the Bay of Mexico, where we hoped to have found some inhabitants, that we might have had some relief of victuals and a place where to repair our ship, which was so greatly bruised that we were scarce able, with our weary arms, to keep out the water. Being thus oppressed, by famine on the one side and danger of drowning on the other, not knowing where to find relief, we began to be in wonderful despair. And we were of many minds, amongst whom there were a great many that did desire our General to set them on land, making their choice rather to submit themselves to the mercy of the savages or infidels than longer to hazard themselves at sea, where they very well saw that if they should all remain together, if they perished not by drowning, yet hunger would enforce them, in the end, to eat one another. To which request our General did very willingly agree, considering with himself that it was necessary for him to lessen his number, both for the safety of himself and the rest. And, thereupon, being resolved to set half his people on shore that he had then left alive, it was a world to see how suddenly men's minds were altered, for they which a little before desired to be set on land were now of another mind, and requested rather to stay, by means whereof our General was enforced, for the more contenting of all men's minds, and to take away all occasions of offence, to take this order: first he made choice of such persons of service and account as were needful to stay, and that being done, of those which were willing to go, he appointed such as he thought might be best spared, and presently appointed that by the boat they should be set on shore, our General promising us that the next year he would either come himself or else send to fetch us home. Here, again, it would have caused any stony heart to have relented to hear the pitiful moan that many did make, and how loth they were to depart. The weather was then somewhat stormy and tempestuous, and therefore we were in great danger, yet, notwithstanding there was no remedy, but we that were appointed to go away must of necessity do so. Howbeit, those that went in the first boat were safely set ashore, but of them which went in the second boat, of which number I myself was one, the seas wrought so high that we could not attain to the shore, and therefore we were constrained— through the cruel dealing of John Hampton, captain of the Minion, and John Sanders, boatswain of the Jesus, and Thomas Pollard, his mate—to leap out of the boat into the main sea, having more than a mile to shore, and, so to shift for ourselves, and either to sink or swim. And of those that so were, as it were, thrown out and compelled to leap into the sea, there were two drowned, which were of Captain Bland's men.

In the evening of the same day—it being Monday, the 8th of October, 1568—when we were all come to shore, we found fresh water, whereof some of our men drank so much that they had almost cast themselves away, for we could scarce get life in them for the space of two oror three hours after. Other some were so cruelly swollen—what with the drinking in of the salt water, and what with the eating of the fruit which we found on land, having a stone in it much like an almond, which fruit is called capule—that they were all in very ill case, so that we were, in a manner, all of us, both feeble, weak, and faint.

The next morning—it being Tuesday, the 9th of October—we thought it best to travel along by the sea coast, to seek out some place of habitation—whether they were Christians or savages we were indifferent—so that we might have wherewithal to sustain our hungry bodies, and so departing from a hill where we had rested all night, not having any dry thread about us, for those that were not wet being thrown into the sea were thoroughly wet with rain, for all the night it rained cruelly. As we went from the hill, and were come into the plain, we were greatly troubled to pass for the grass and woods, that grew there higher than any man. On the left hand we had the sea, and upon the right hand great woods, so that of necessity we must needs pass on our way westward through those marshes, and going thus, suddenly we were assaulted by the Indians, a warlike kind of people, which are in a manner as cannibals, although they do not feed upon man's flesh as cannibals do.

These people are called Chichemici, and they used to wear their hair long, even down to their knees; they do also colour their faces green, yellow, red, and blue, which maketh them to seem very ugly and terrible to behold. These people do keep wars against the Spaniards, of whom they have been oftentimes very cruelly handled: for with the Spaniards there is no mercy. They, perceiving us at our first coming on land, supposed us to have been their enemies the bordering Spaniards; and having, by their forerunners, descried what number we were, and how feeble and weak, without armour or weapon, they suddenly, according to their accustomed manner when they encounter with any people in warlike sort, raised a terrible and huge cry, and so came running fiercely upon us, shooting off their arrows as thick as hail, unto whose mercy we were constrained to yield, not having amongst us any kind of armour, nor yet weapon, saving one caliver and two old rusty swords, whereby to make any resistance or to save ourselves; which, when they perceived that we sought not any other than favour and mercy at their hands, and that we were not their enemies the Spaniards, they had compassion on us, and came and caused us all to sit down. And when they had a while surveyed, and taken a perfect view of us, they came to all such as had any coloured clothes amongst us, and those they did strip stark naked, and took their clothes away with them; but they that were apparelled in black they did not meddle withal, and so went their ways and left us, without doing us any further hurt, only in the first brunt they killed eight of our men. And at our departure they, perceiving in what weak case we were, pointed us with their hands which way we should go to come to a town of the Spaniards, which, as we afterwards perceived, was not past ten leagues from thence, using these words: "Tampeco, tampeco, Christiano, tampeco, Christiano," which is as much (we think) as to say in English, "Go that way, and you shall find the Christians." The weapons that they use are no other but bows and arrows, and their aim is so good that they very seldom miss to hit anything that they shoot at. Shortly after they had left us stripped, as aforesaid, we thought it best to divide ourselves into two companies, and so, being separated, half of us went under the leading one of Anthony Goddard, who is yet alive, and dwelleth at this instant in the town of Plymouth, whom before we chose to be captain over us all. And those that went under his leading, of which number I, Miles Phillips, was one, travelled westward—that way which the Indians with their hands hadd before pointed us to go. The other half went under the leading of one John Hooper, whom they did choose for their captain, and with the company that went with him David Ingram was one, and they took their way and travelled northward. And shortly after, within the space of two days, they were again encountered by the savage people, and their Captain Hooper and two more of his company were slain. Then again they divided themselves; and some held on their way still northward, and other some, knowing that we were gone westward, sought to meet with us again, as, in truth, there was about the number of five-and-twenty or six-and-twenty of them that met with us in the space of four days again. And then we began to reckon amongst ourselves how many we were that were set on shore, and we found the number to be an hundred and fourteen, whereof two were drowned in the sea and eight were slain at the first encounter, so that there remained an hundred and four, of which five-and-twenty went westward with us, and two-and-fifty to the north with Hooper and

Ingram; and, as Ingram since has often told me, there were not past three of their company slain, and there were but five-and-twenty of them that came again to us, so that of the company that went northward there is yet lacking, and not certainly heard of, the number of three-and-twenty men. And verily I do think that there are of them yet alive and married in the said country, at Sibola, as hereafter I do purpose (God willing) to discourse of more particularly, with the reasons and causes that make me so to think of them that were lacking, which were with David Ingram, Twide, Browne, and sundry others, whose names we could not remember. And being thus met again together we travelled on still westward, sometimes through such thick woods that we were enforced with cudgels to break away the brambles and bushes from tearing our naked bodies; other sometimes we should travel through the plains in such high grass that we could scarce see one another. And as we passed in some places we should have of our men slain, and fall down suddenly, being stricken by the Indians, which stood behind trees and bushes, in secret places, and so killed our men as they went by; for we went scatteringly in seeking of fruits to relieve ourselves. We were also oftentimes greatly annoyed with a kind of fly, which, in the Indian tongue, is called tequani; and the Spaniards call them musketas. There are also in the said country a number of other kind of flies, but none so noisome as these tequanies be. You shall hardly see them, they be so small: for they are scarce so big as a gnat. They will suck one's blood marvellously, and if you kill them while they are sucking they are so venomous that the place will swell extremely, even as one that is stung with a wasp or bee. But if you let them suck their fill, and to go away of themselves, then they do you no other hurt, but leave behind them a red spot somewhat bigger than a flea biting. At the first we were terribly troubled with these kind of flies, not knowing their qualities; and resistance we could make none against them, being naked. As for cold, we feared not any: the country there is always so warm.

And as we travelled thus for the space of ten or twelve days, our captain did oftentimes cause certain to go up into the tops of high trees, to see if they could descry any town or place of inhabitants, but they could not perceive any, and using often the same order to climb up into high trees, at the length they descried a great river, that fell from the north-west into the main sea; and presently after we heard an harquebuse shot off, which did greatly encourage us, for thereby we knew that we were near to some Christians, and did therefore hope shortly to find some succour and comfort; and within the space of one hour after, as we travelled, we heard a cock crow, which was also no small joy unto us; and so we came to the north side of the river of Panuco, where the Spaniards have certain salines, at which place it was that the harquebuse was shot off which before we heard; to which place we went not directly, but, missing thereof, we left it about a bow-shot upon our left hand. Of this river we drank very greedily, for we had not met with any water in six days before; and, as we were here by the river's side, resting ourselves, and longing to come to the place where the cock did crow and where the harquebuse was shot off, we perceived many Spaniards upon the other side of the river riding up and down on horseback, and they, perceiving us, did suppose that we had been of the Indians, their bordering enemies, the Chichemici. The river was not more than half a bow-shot across, and presently one of the Spaniards took an Indian boat, called a canoa, and so came over, being rowed by two Indians; and, having taken the view of us, did presently row over back again to the Spaniards, who without any delay made out about the number of twenty horsemen, and embarking themselves in the canoas, they led their horses by the reins, swimming over after them; and being come over to that side of the river where we were, they saddled their horses, and being mounted upon them, with their lances charged, they came very fiercely running at us. Our captain, Anthony Goddard, seeing them come in that order, did persuade us to submit and yield ourselves unto them, for being naked, as we at this time were, and without weapon, we could not make any resistance—whose bidding we obeyed; and upon the yielding of ourselves, they perceived us to be Christians, and did call for more canoas, and carried us over by four and four in a boat; and being come on the other side, they understanding by our captain how long we had been without meat, imparted between two and two a loaf of bread made of that country wheat, which the Spaniards calledd maize, of the bigness of one of our halfpenny loaves, which bread is named in the Indian tongue clashacally. This bread was very sweet and pleasant to us, for we had not eaten any for a long time before; and what is it that hunger doth not make to have a savoury and delicate taste? Having thus imparted the bread amongst us, those which were men they sent afore to the town, having also many Indians, inhabitants of that place, to guard them. They which were young, as boys, and some such also as were feeble, they took up upon their horses behind them, and so carried us to the town where they dwelt, which was distant very near a mile from the place where we came over.

This town is well situated, and well replenished with all kinds of fruits, as pomegranates, oranges, lemons, apricots, and peaches, and sundry others, and is inhabited by a great number of tame Indians, or Mexicans, and had in it also at that time about the number of two hundred Spaniards, men, women, and children, besides negroes. Of their salines, which lie upon the west side of the river, more than a mile distant from thence, they make a great profit, for it is an excellent good merchandise there. The Indians do buy much thereof, and carry it up into the country, and there sell it to their own country people, in doubling the price. Also, much of the salt made in this place is transported from thence by sea to sundry other places, as to Cuba, St. John de Ullua, and the other ports of Tamiago, and Tamachos, which are two barred havens west and by south above threescore leagues from St. John de Ullua. When we were all come to the town, the governor there showed himself very severe unto us, and threatened to hang us all; and then he demanded what money we had, which in truth was very little, for the Indians which we first met withal had in a manner taken all from us, and of that which they left the Spaniards which brought us over took away a good part also; howbeit, from Anthony Goddard the governor here had a chain of gold, which was given unto him at Cartagena by the governor there, and from others he had some small store of money; so that we accounted that amongst us all he had the number of five hundred pesoes, besides the chain of gold.

And having thus satisfied himself, when he had taken all that we had, he caused us to be put into a little house, much like a hog sty, where we were almost smothered; and before we were thus shut up into that little cote, they gave us some of the country wheat called maize sodden, which they feed their hogs withal. But many of our men which had been hurt by the Indians at our first coming on land, whose wounds were very sore and grievous, desired to have the help of their surgeons to cure their wounds. The governor, and most of them all, answered, that we should have none other surgeon but the hangman, which should sufficiently heal us of all our griefs; and they, thus reviling us, and calling us English dogs and Lutheran heretics, we remained the space of three days in this miserable state, not knowing what should become of us, waiting every hour to be bereaved of our lives.

THE FOURTH CHAPTER.

WHEREIN IS SHOWED HOW WE WERE USED IN PANUCO, AND IN WHAT FEAR OF DEATH WE WERE THERE, AND HOW WE WERE CARRIED TO MEXICO TO THE VICEROY, AND OF OUR IMPRISONMENT THERE AND AT TESCUCO, WITH THE COURTESIES AND CRUELTIES WE RECEIVED DURING THAT TIME, AND HOW IN THE END WE WERE BY PROCLAMATION GIVEN TO SERVE AS SLAVES TO SUNDRY GENTLEMEN SPANIARDS.

Upon the fourth day after our coming thither, and there remaining in a perplexity, looking every hour when we should suffer death, there came a great number of Indians and Spaniards armed to fetch us out of the house, and amongst them we espied one that brought a great many new halters, at the sight whereof we were greatly amazed, and made no other account but that we should presently have suffered death; and so, crying and calling to God for mercy and for forgiveness of our sins, we prepared ourselves to die; yet in the end, as the sequel showed, their meaning was not so; for when we were come out of the house, with those halters they bound our arms behind us, and so coupling us two and two together, they commanded us to march on through the town, and so along the country from place to place toward the city of Mexico, which is distant from Panuco west and by south the space of threescore leagues, having only but two Spaniards to conduct us, they being accompanied with a great number of Indians, warding on either side with bows and arrows, lest we should escape from them. And travelling in this order, upon the second day, at night, we came unto a town which the Indians call Nohele, and the Spaniards call it Santa Maria, in which town there is a house of White Friars, which did very courteously use us, and gave us hot meat, as mutton and broth, and garments also to cover ourselves withal, made of white baize. We fed very greedily of the meat and of the Indian fruit, called nochole, which fruit is long and small, much like in fashion to a little cucumber. Our greedy feeding caused us to fall sick of hot burning agues; and here at this place one Thomas Baker, one of our men, died of a hurt, for he had been before shot with an arrow into the throat at the first encounter.

The next morrow, about ten of the clock, we departed from thence, bound two and two together, and guarded as before, and so travelled on our way toward Mexico, till we came to a town within forty leagues of Mexico named Mesticlan, where is a house of Black Friars, and in this town there are about the number of three hundred Spaniards, both men, women, and children. The friars sent us meat from the house ready dressed, and the friars and men and women used us very courteously, and gave us some shirts and other such things as we lacked. Here our men were very sick of their agues, and with eating of another fruit, called in the Indian tongue, Guiaccos, which fruit did bind us sore. The next morning we departed from thence with our two Spaniards and Indian guard as aforesaid. Of these two Spaniards the one was an aged man, who all the way did very courteously entreat us, and would carefully go before to provide for us both meat and things necessary to the uttermost of his power. The other was a young man, who all the way travelled with us, and never departed from us, who was a very cruel caitiff, and he carried a javelin in his hand, and sometimes when as our men with very feebleness and faintness were not able to go so fast as he required them, he would take his javelin in both his hands and strike them with the same between the neck and the shoulders so violently that he would strike them down, then would he cry and say: "Marches, marches, Engleses perros, Luterianos, enemicos de Dios;" which is as much to say in English, "March, march on you English dogs, Lutherans, enemies to God." And the next day we came to a town called Pachuca, and there are two places of that name, as this town of Pachuca, and the mines of Pachuca, which are mines of silver, and are about six leagues distant from this town of Pachuca towards the north-west.

Here at this town the good old man our governor suffered us to stay two days and two nights, having compassion of our sick and weak men, full sore against the mind of the young man his companion. From thence we took our journey, and travelled four or five days by little villages and Stantias, which are farms or dairy houses of the Spaniards, and ever as we had need the good old man would still provide us sufficient of meats, fruits, and water to sustain us. At the end of which five days we came to a town within five leagues of Mexico, which is called Quoghliclan, where we also stayed one whole day and two nights, where was a fair house of Grey Friars, howbeit, we saw none of them. Here we were told by the Spaniards in the town that we had not more than fifteen English miles from thence to Mexico, whereof we were all very joyful and glad, hoping that when we came thither we should either be relieved and set free out of bonds, or else be quickly despatched out of our lives; for seeing ourselves thus carried bound from place to place, although some used us courteously, yet could we never joy nor be merry till we might perceive ourselves set free from that bondage, either by death or otherwise.

The next morning we departed from thence on our journey towards Mexico, and so travelled till we came within two leagues of it, where there was built by the Spaniards a very fair church, called Our Lady Church, in which there is an image of Our Lady of silver and gilt, being as high and as large as a tall woman, in which church, and before this image, there are as many lamps of silver as there be days in the year, which upon high days are all lighted. Whensoever any Spaniards pass by this church, although they be on horseback, they will alight and come into the church, and kneel before this image, and pray to Our Lady to defend them from all evil; so that whether he be horseman or footman he will not pass by, but first go into the church and pray as aforesaid, which if they do not, they think and believe that they shall never prosper, which image they call in the Spanish tongue Nostra Signora de Guadaloupe. At this place there are certain cold baths, which arise, springing up as though the water did seethe, the water whereof is somewhat brackish in taste, but very good for any that have any sore or wound to wash themselves therewith, for as they say, it healeth many; and every year once upon Our Lady Day, the people used to repair thither to offer and to pray in that church before the image, and they say that Our Lady of Guadaloupe doth work a number of miracles. About this church there is not any town of Spaniards that is inhabited, but certain Indians do dwell there in houses of their own country building.

Here we were met by a great number of Spaniards on horseback, which came from Mexico to see us, both gentlemen and men of occupations, and they came as people to see a wonder; we were still called upon to march on, and so about four of the clock in the afternoon of the said day, we entered into the city of Mexico by the way or street called La Calia Sancta Catherina; and we stayed not in any place till we came to the house or palace of the Viceroy, Don Martin Henriques, which standeth in the middest of the city, hard by the market place called La Placa dell Marquese. We had not stayed any long time at this place, but there was brought us by the Spaniards from the market place great store of meat, sufficient to have satisfied five times so many as we were; some also gave us hats, and some gave us money; in which place we stayed for the space of two hours, and from thence we were conveyed by water into large canoas to a hospital, where certain of our men were lodged, which were taken before the fight at St. John de Ullua. We should have gone to Our Lady's Hospital, but that there were also so many of our men taken before at that fight that there was no room for us. After our coming thither, many of the company that came with me from Panuco died within the space of fourteen days; soon after which time we were taken forth from that place and put all together into Our Lady's Hospital, in which place we were courteously used, and visited oftentimes by virtuous gentlemen and gentlewomen of the city, who brought us divers things to comfort us withal, as succats and marmalades and such other things, and would also many times give us many things, and that very liberally. In which hospital we remained for the space of six months, until we were all whole and sound of body, and then we were appointed by the Viceroy to be carried unto the town of Tescuco, which is distant from Mexico south-west eight leagues; in which town there are certain houses of correction and punishment for ill people called obraches, like to Bridewell here in London; in which place divers Indians are sold for slaves, some for ten years and some for twelve. It was no small grief unto us when we understood that we should be carried thither, and to be used as slaves; we had rather be put to death, howbeit there was no remedy, but we were carried to the prison of Tescuco, where we were not put to any labour, but were very straightly kept and almost famished, yet by the good providence of our merciful God, we happened there to meet with one Robert Sweeting, who was the son of an Englishman born of a Spanish woman; this man could speak very good English, and by his means we were holpen very much with victuals from the Indians, as mutton, hens, and bread. And if we had not been so relieved we had surely perished; and yet all the provision that we had gotten that way was but slender. And continuing thus straightly kept in prison there for the space of two months, at the length we agreed amongst ourselves to break forth of prison, come of it what would, for we were minded rather to suffer death than longer to live in that miserable state. And so having escaped out of prison, we knew not what way to fly for the safety of ourselves; the night was dark, and it rained terribly, and not having any guide, we went we knew not whither, and in the morning at the appearing of the day, we perceived ourselves to be come hard to the city of Mexico, which is four and twenty English miles from Tescuco. The day being come, we were espied by the Spaniards, and pursued, and taken, and brought before the Viceroy and head justices, who threatened to hang us for breaking of the king's prison. Yet in the end they sent us into a garden belonging to the Viceroy, and coming thither, we found there our English gentlemen which were delivered as hostages when as our General was betrayed at St. John de Ullua, as is aforesaid, and with them we also found Robert Barret, the master of the Jesus, in which place we remained, labouring and doing such things as we were commanded for the space of four months, having but two sheep a day allowed to suffice us all, being very near a hundred men; and for bread, we had every man two loaves a day of the quantity of one halfpenny loaf. At the end of which four months, they having removed our gentlemen hostages and the master of the Jesus to a prison in the Viceroy his own house, did cause it to be proclaimed, that what gentleman Spaniard soever was willing, or would have any Englishman to serve him, and be bound to keep him forthcoming to appear before the justices within one month after notice given, that they should repair to the said garden, and there take their choice; which proclamation was no sooner made but the gentlemen came and repaired to the garden amain, so that happy was he that could soonest get one of us.

THE FIFTH CHAPTER.

WHEREIN IS SHOWED IN WHAT GOOD SORT AND HOW WEALTHILY WE LIVED WITH OUR MASTERS UNTIL THE COMING OF THE INQUISITION, WHEN AS AGAIN, OUR SORROWS BEGAN AFRESH; OF OUR IMPRISONMENT IN THE HOLY HOUSE, AND OF THE SEVERE JUDGEMENT AND SENTENCES GIVEN AGAINST US, AND WITH WHAT RIGOUR AND CRUELTY THE SAME WERE EXECUTED.

The gentlemen that thus took us for their servants or slaves, did new apparel us throughout, with whom we abode doing such service as they appointed us unto, which was for the most part to attend upon them at the table, and to be as their chamberlains, and to wait upon them when they went abroad, which they greatly accounted of, for in that country no Spaniard will serve one another, but they are all of them attended and served by Indians weekly, and by negroes which be their slaves during their life. In this sort we remained and served in the said city of Mexico and thereabouts for the space of a year and somewhat longer. Afterwards many of us were by our masters appointed to go to sundry of their mines where they had to do, and to be as overseers of the negroes and Indians that laboured there. In which mines many of us did profit and gain greatly; for first we were allowed three hundred pezoes a man for a year, which is three score pounds sterling, and besides that the Indians and negroes which wrought under our charge, upon our well using and entreating of them, would at times as upon Saturdays when they had left work labour for us, and blow as much silver as should be worth unto us three marks or thereabouts, every mark being worth six pesoes and a half of their money, which nineteen pesoes and a half, is worth four livres, ten shillings of our money.

Sundry weeks we did gain so much by this means besides our wages, that many of us became very rich, and were worth three thousand or four thousand pezoes, for we lived and gained thus in those mines some three or four years. As concerning those gentlemen which were delivered as hostages, and that were kept in prison in the Viceroy his house, after that we were gone from out the garden to serve sundry gentlemen as aforesaid, they remained prisoners in the said house, for the space of four months after their coming thither, at the end whereof the fleet, being ready to depart from St. John de Ullua to go for Spain, the said gentlemen were sent away into Spain with the fleet, where I have heard it credibly reported, many of them died with the cruel handling of the Spaniards in the Inquisition house, as those which have been delivered home after they had suffered the persecution of that house can more perfectly declare. Robert Barret also, master of the Jesus, was sent away with the fleet into Spain the next year following, whereafter he suffered persecution in the Inquisition, and at the last was condemned to be burnt, and with him three or four more of our men, of whom one was named Gregory and another John Browne, whom I knew, for they were of our general his musicians, but the names of the rest that suffered with them I know not.

Now after that six years there fully expired since our first coming into the Indies in which time we had been imprisoned and served in the said countries, as is before truly declared in the year of our Lord one thousand five hundred and seventy four, the Inquisition began to be established in the Indies very much against the minds of many of the Spaniards themselves, for never until this time since their first conquering and planting in the Indies, were they subject to that bloody and cruel Inquisition. The chief Inquisitor was named Don Pedro Moya de Contreres, and John de Bouilla his companion, and John Sanchis the Fischall, and Pedro de la Rios, the Secretary, they being come and settled, and placed in a very fair house, near unto the White Friars, considering with themselves that they must make an entrance and beginning of that their most detestable Inquisition here in Mexico to the terror of the whole country, thought it best to call us that were Englishmen first in question, and so much the rather for that they had perfect knowledge and intelligence, that many of us were become very rich as hath been already declared, and therefore we were a very great booty and prey to the Inquisitors, so that now again began our sorrows afresh, for we were sent for, and sought out in all places of the country, and proclamation made upon pain of losing of goods, and excommunication that no man should hide or keep secret any Englishman or any part of their goods. By means whereof we were all soon apprehended in all places, and all our goods seized and taken for the Inquisitors' use, and so from all parts of the country we were conveyed and sent as prisoners to the city of Mexico, and there committed to prison in sundry dark dungeons where we could not see but by candlelight, and were never more than two together in one place so that we saw not one another, neither could one of us tell what was become of another. Thus we remained close imprisoned for the space of a year and a half, and others for some less time, for they came to prison ever as they were apprehended. During which time of our imprisonment at the first beginning we were often called before the Inquisitors alone, and there severely examined of our faith, and commanded to say the pater noster, the Ave Maria, and the creed in Latin, which God knoweth a great number of us could not say otherwise than in the English tongue. And having the said Robert Sweeting who was our friend at Tescuco always present with them for an interpreter he made report for us in our own country speech we could say them perfectly, although not word for word as they were in Latin. Then did they proceed to demand of us upon our oaths what we did believe of the sacrament, and whether there did remain any bread or wine after the words of consecration, yea or no, and whether we did not believe that the Host of bread which the priest did hold up over his head, and the wine that was in the chalice, was the very true and perfect body and blood of our Saviour Christ, yea or no, to which if we answered not yea, then was there no way but death. Then would they demand of us what we did remember of ourselves, what opinions we had held or had been taught to hold, contrary to the same whiles we were in England; to which we for the safety of our lives were constrained to say that we never did believe, nor had been taught otherwise than as before we had said. Then would they charge us that we did not tell them the truth, that we knew to the contrary, and therefore we should call ourselves to remembrance and make them a better answer at the next time or else we should be racked and made to confess the truth whether we would or no. And so coming again before them the next time, we were still demanded of our belief whiles we were in England, and how we had been taught, and also what we thought or did know of such of our company as they did name unto us, so that we could never be free from such demands, and at other times they would promise us that if we would tell them the truth, then should we have favour and be set at liberty, although we very well knew their fair speeches were but means to entrap us to the hazard and loss of our lives; howbeit God so mercifully wrought for us by a secret means that we had that we kept us still to our first answer, and would still say that we had told the truth unto them, and knew no more by ourselves nor any other of our fellows than as we had declared, and that for our sins and offences in England against God and our Lady, or any of His blessed saints, we were heartily sorry for the same, and did cry God mercy, and besought the Inquisitors, for God's sake, considering that we came into those countries by force of weather, and against our wills, and that never in all our lives we had either spoken or done anything contrary to their laws, that therefore they would have mercy on us, yet all this would not serve, for still from time to time we were called upon to confess, and about the space of three months, before they proceeded to their severe Judgement, we were all racked, and some enforced to utter that against themselves which afterwards cost them their lives.

And thus having gotten from our own mouths matter sufficient for them to proceed in judgement against us, they caused a large scaffold to be made in the midst of the market-place in Mexico, right over against the head church, and fourteen or fifteen days before the day of their judgement, with the sound of a trumpet, and the noise of their attabalies, which are a kind of drums, they did assemble the people in all parts of the city, before whom it was then solemnly proclaimed that whosoever would upon such a day, repair to the marketplace, they should hear the sentence of the Holy Inquisition against the English heretic Lutherans, and also see the same put in execution. Which being done, and the time approaching of this cruel judgement, the night before they came to the prison where we were, with certain officers of that holy hellish house, bringing with them certain fools' coats which they had prepared for us, being called in their language St. Benitos, which coats were made of yellow cotton and red crosses upon them, both before and behind; they were so busied in putting on their coats about us and in bringing us out into a large yard, and placing and pointing us in what order we should go to the scaffold or place of judgement upon the morrow, that they did not once suffer us to sleep all that night long.

The next morning being come, there was given to every one of us for our breakfast, a cup of wine, and a slice of bread fried in honey, and so about eight of the clock in the morning, we set forth of the prison, every man alone in his yellow coat and a rope about his neck, and a great green wax candle in his hand unlighted, having a Spaniard appointed to go upon either side of every one of us; and so marching in this order and manner towards the scaffold in the market-place, which was a bow-shot distant or thereabouts, we found a great assembly of people all the way, and such throng, that certain of the Inquisitors' officers on horseback were constrained to make way, and so coming to the scaffold we went up by a pair of stairs, and found seats ready made and prepared for us to sit down on, every man in order as he should be called to receive his judgement. We being thus set down as we were appointed, presently the Inquisitors came up another pair of stairs, and the Viceroy and all the chief justices with them. When they were set down and placed under the cloth of estate agreeing to their degrees and calling, then came up also a great number of friars, white, black, and grey, about the number of 300 persons, they being set in the places for them appointed. Then was there a solemn Oyes made, and silence commanded, and then presently began their severe and cruel judgement.

The first man that was called was one Roger, the chief armourer of the Jesus, and he had judgement to have 300 stripes on horseback, and after condemned to the galleys as a slave for ten years.

After him was called John Gray, John Browne, John Rider, John Moone, James Collier, and one Thomas Browne. These were adjudged to have 200 stripes on horseback, and after to be committed to the galleys for the space of eight years.

Then was called John Keies, and was adjudged to have 100 stripes on horseback, and condemned to serve in the galleys for the space of six years.

Then were severally called the number of fifty-three, one after another, and every man had his several judgement, some to have 200 stripes on horseback and some 100, and some condemned for slaves to the galleys, some for six years, some for eight, and some for ten.

And then was I, Miles Phillips, called, and was adjudged to serve in a monastery for five years, without any stripes, and to wear a fool's coat or San Benito, during all that time.

Then were called John Storie, Richard Williams, David Alexander, Robert Cooke, and Horsewell, and Thomas Hull. These six were condemned to serve in monasteries without stripes, some for three years, and some for four, and to wear the San Benito during all the said time. Which being done, and it now drawing towards night, George Rivelie, Peter Momfrie, and Cornelius the Irishman were called, and had their judgement to be burnt to ashes, and so were presently sent away to the place of execution in the market-place, but a little from the scaffold, where they were quickly burnt and consumed. And as for us that had received our judgement, being sixty-eight in number, we were carried back that night to prison again, and the next day in the morning, being Good Friday, the year of our Lord, 1575, we were all brought into a court of the Inquisitors' Palace, where we found a horse in readiness for every one of our men which were condemned to have stripes, and to be committed to the galleys, which were in number sixty, and so they, being enforced to mount up on horseback, naked, from the middle upward, were carried to be showed as a spectacle for all the people to behold throughout the chief and principal streets of the city, and had the number of stripes to every one of them appointed, most cruelly laid upon their naked bodies with long whips, by sundry men appointed to be the executioners thereof, and before our men there went a couple of criers, which cried as they went, "Behold these English dogs, Lutherans, enemies to God," and all the way as they went, there were some of the Inquisitors themselves, and of the familiars of that rake- hell order, that cried to the executioners, "Strike, lay on those English heretics, Lutherans, God's enemies;" and so this horrible spectacle being showed round about the city, and they returned to the Inquisitors' House, with their backs all gore blood and swollen with great bumps. They were then taken from their horses and carried again to prison, where they remained until they were sent into Spain to the galleys, there to receive the rest of their martyrdom; and I, and the six other with me, which had judgment and were condemned among the rest to serve an apprenticeship in the monasteries, were taken presently and sent to certain religious houses appointed for the purpose.

THE SIXTH CHAPTER.

WHEREIN IS SHOWED HOW WE WERE USED IN THE RELIGIOUS HOUSES, AND THATWHEN THE TIME WAS EXPIRED THAT WE WERE ADJUDGED TO SERVE IN THEM, THERE CAME NEWS TO MEXICO OF MASTER FRANCIS DRAKE'S BEING IN THE SOUTH SEA, AND WHAT PREPARATION WAS MADE TO TAKE HIM; AND HOW I, SEEKING TO ESCAPE, WAS AGAIN TAKEN AND PUT IN PRISON IN VERA CRUZ, AND HOW AGAIN I MADE MINE ESCAPE FROM THENCE.

I, Miles Phillips, and William Lowe were appointed to the Black Friars, where I was appointed to be an overseer of Indian workmen, who wrought there in building a new church, amongst which Indians I learned their language or Mexican tongue very perfectly, and had great familiarity with many of them, whom I found to be a courteous and loving kind of people, ingenious, and of great understanding, and they hate and abhor the Spaniards with all their hearts. They have used such horrible cruelties against them, and do still keep them in such subjection and servitude, that they and the negroes also do daily lie in wait to practice their deliverance out of that thraldom and bondage that the Spaniards do keep them in.

William Lowe, he was appointed to serve the cook in the kitchen; Richard Williams and David Alexander were appointed to the Grey Friars; John Storey and Robert Cooke to the White Friars; Paul Horsewell the Secretary took to be his servant; Thomas Hull was sent to a monastery of priests, where afterward he died. Thus we served out the years that we were condemned for, with the use of our fools' coats, and we must needs confess that the friars did use us very courteously, for every one of us had his chamber, with bedding and diet, and all things clean and neat; yea, many of the Spaniards and friars themselves do utterly abhor and mislike of that cruel Inquisition, and would as they durst bewail our miseries, and comfort us the best they could, although they stood in such fear of that devilish Inquisition that they durst not let the left hand know what the right doeth.

Now after that the time was expired for which we were condemned to serve in those religious houses, we were then brought again before the Chief Inquisitor, and had all our fools' coats pulled off and hanged up in the head church, called Ecclesia Majora, and every man's name and judgement written thereupon with this addition—HERETIC LUTHERAN RECONCILED. And there are also all their coats hanged up which were condemned to the galleys, with their names and judgements, and underneath his coat, HERETIC LUTHERAN RECONCILED. And also the coats and names of the three that were burned, whereupon were written, ANN OBSTINATE HERETIC LUTHERAN BURNT. Then were we suffered to go up and down the country, and to place ourselves as we could, and yet not so free but that we very well knew that there was a good espial always attending us and all our actions, so that we durst not once to speak or look awry. David Alexander and Robert Cooke they returned to serve the Inquisitor, who shortly after married them both to two of his negro women; Richard Williams married a rich widow of Biskay with four thousand pezoes; Paul Horsewell is married to a Mestiza, as they name those whose fathers were Spaniards and their mothers Indians, and this woman which Paul Horsewell hath married is said to be the daughter of one that came in with Hernando Cortes, the Conqueror, who had with her in marriage four thousand pesoes and a fair house; John Storie he is married to a negro woman; William Lowe had leave and licence to go into Spain, where he is now married. For mine own part I could never thoroughly settle myself to marry in that country, although many fair offers were made unto me of such as were of great ability and wealth; but I could have no liking to live in that place where I must everywhere see and know such horrible idolatry committed, and durst not once for my life speak against it; and therefore I had always a longing and desire to this my native country; and to return and serve again in the mines, where I might have gathered great riches and wealth, I very well saw that at one time or another I should fall again into the danger of that devilish Inquisition, and so be stripped of all, with loss of life also, and therefore I made my choice rather to learn to weave Groganes and Taffataes, and so compounding with a silk weaver, I bound myself for three years to serve him, and gave him one hundred and fifty pesoes to teach me the science, otherwise he would not have taught me under seven years' prenticeship, and by this means I lived the more quiet and free from suspicion.

Howbeit I should many times be charged by familiars of that devilish house, that I had a meaning to run away into England, and be an heretic Lutheran again; to whom I would answer that they had no need to suspect any such thing in me, for that they knew all very well that it was impossible for me to escape by any manner of means; yet notwithstanding I was called before the Inquisitors and demanded why I did not marry. I answered that I had bound myself at an occupation. "Well," said the Inquisitor, "I know thou meanest to run away, and therefore I charge thee here upon pain of burning as an heretic relapsed, that thou depart not out of this city, nor come near to the port of St. John de Ullua, nor to any other port;" to the which I answered that I would willingly obey. "Yea," said he, "see thou do so, and thy fellows also; they shall have the like charge."

So I remained at my science the full time and learned the art, at the end whereof there came news to Mexico that there were certain Englishmen landed with a great power at the port of Acapulco, upon the South Sea, and that they were coming to Mexico to take the spoil thereof, which wrought a marvellous great fear among them, and many of those that were rich began to shift for themselves, their wives and children; upon which hurly-burly the Viceroy caused a general muster to be made of all the Spaniards in Mexico, and there were found to the number of seven thousand and odd householders of Spaniards in the city and suburbs, and of single men unmarried the number of three thousand, and of Mestizies—which are counted to be the sons of Spaniards born of Indian women—twenty thousand persons; and then was Paul Horsewell and I, Miles Phillips, sent for before the Viceroy and were examined if we did know an Englishman named Francis Drake, which was brother to Captain Hawkins; to which we answered that Captain Hawkins had not any brother but one, which was a man of the age of threescore years or thereabouts, and was now governor of Plymouth in England. And then he demanded of us if we knew one Francis Drake, and we answered no.

While these things were in doing, there came news that all the Englishmen were gone; yet was there eight hundred men made out under the leading of several captains, whereof two hundred were sent to the port of St. John de Ullua, upon the North Sea, under the conduct of Don Luis Suares; two hundred were sent to Guatemala, in the South Sea, who had for their captain John Cortes; two hundred more were sent to Guatelco, a port of the South Sea, over whom went for captain Don Pedro de Roblis; and two hundred more were sent to Acapulco, the port where it was said that Captain Drake had been, and they had for captain Doctor Roblis Alcalde de Corte, with whom I, Miles Phillips, went as interpreter, having licence given by the Inquisitors. When we were come to Acapulco we found that Captain Drake was departed from thence, more than a month before we came thither. But yet our captain, Alcalde de Corte, there presently embarked himself in a small ship of threescore ton, or thereabout, having also in company with him two other small barques, and not past two hundred men in all, with whom I went as interpreter in his own ship, which, God knoweth, was but weak and ill-appointed; so that for certain, if we had met with Captain Drake, he might easily have taken us all.

We, being embarked, kept our course, and ran southward towards Panama, keeping still as nigh the shore as we could; and leaving the land upon our left hand, and having coasted thus for the space of eighteen or twenty days, and were more to the south than Guatemala, we met at last with other ships which came from Panama, of whom we were certainly informed that he was clean gone off the coast more than a month before; and so we returned back to Acapulco again, and there landed, our captain being thereunto forced, because his men were very sore sea-sick. All the while that I was at sea with them I was a glad man, for I hoped that if we met with Master Drake we should all be taken, so that then I should have been freed out of that danger and misery wherein I lived, and should return to mine own country of England again. But missing thereof, when I saw there was no remedy but that we must needs come on land again, little doth any man know the sorrow and grief that inwardly I felt, although outwardly I was constrained to make fair weather of it.

And so, being landed, the next morrow after we began our journey towards Mexico, and passed these towns of name in our way, as first the town of Tuatepec, fifty leagues from Mexico; from thence to Washaca, forty leagues from Mexico; from thence to Tepiaca, twenty-four leagues from Mexico; and from thence to Lopueblo de Los Angelos, where is a high hill which casteth out fire three times a day, which hill is eighteen leagues directly west from Mexico; from thence we went to Stapelata, eight leagues from Mexico, and there our captain and most of his men took boat and came to Mexico again, having been forth about the space of seven weeks, or thereabouts.

Our captain made report to the Viceroy what he had done, and how far he had travelled, and that for certain he was informed that Captain Drake was not to be heard of. To which the Viceroy replied and said, surely we shall have him shortly come into our hands, driven on land through necessity in some one place or other, for he, being now in these seas of Sur, it is not possible for him to get out of them again; so that if he perish not at sea, yet hunger will force him to land. And then again I was commanded by the Viceroy that I should not depart from the city of Mexico, but always be at my master's house in a readiness at an hour's warning, whensoever I should be called for. Notwithstanding that, within one month after, certain Spaniards going to Mecameca, eighteen leagues from Mexico, to send away certain hides and cuchionelio that they had there at their stantias, or dairy houses, and my master having leave of the secretary for me to go with them, I took my journey with them, being very well horsed and appointed; and coming thither, and passing the time there at Mecameca certain days, till we had certain intelligence that the fleet was ready to depart, I, not being more than three days' journey from the port of St. John de Ullua, thought it to be the meetest time for me to make an escape, and I was the bolder presuming upon my Spanish tongue, which I spake as naturally as any of them all, thinking with myself that when I came to St. John de Ullua I would get to be entertained as a soldier, and so go home into Spain in the same fleet; and, therefore, secretly one evening late, the moon shining fair, I conveyed myself away, and riding so for the space of two nights and two days, sometimes in, and sometimes out, resting very little all that time, upon the second day at night I came to the town of Vera Cruz, distant from the port of St. John de Ullua, where the ships rode, but only eight leagues; and here purposing to rest myself a day or two, I was no sooner alighted but within the space of one half hour after I was by ill hap arrested, and brought before justices there, being taken and suspected to be a gentleman's son of Mexico that was run away from his father. So I, being arrested and brought before the justices, there was a great hurly-burly about the matter, every man charging me that I was the son of such a man, dwelling in Mexico, which I flatly denied, affirming that I knew not the man; yet would they not believe me, but urged still upon me that I was he that they sought for, and so I was conveyed away to prison. And as I was thus going to prison, to the further increase of my grief, it chanced that at that very instant there was a poor man in the press that was come to town to sell hens, who told the justices that they did me wrong, and that in truth he knew very well that I was an Englishman, and no Spaniard. Then they demanded of him how he knew that, and threatened him that he said so for that he was my companion, and sought to convey me away from my father, so that he also was threatened to be laid in prison with me. He, for the discharge of himself, stood stiffly in it that I was an Englishman, and one of Captain Hawkins's men, and that he had known me wear the San Benito in the Black Friars at Mexico for three or four whole years together; which when they heard they forsook him, and began to examine me anew, whether that speech of his were true, yea or no; which when they perceived that I could not deny, and perceiving that I was run from Mexico, and came thither of purpose to convey myself away with the fleet, I was presently committed to prison with a sorrowful heart, often wishing myself that that man which knew me had at that time been further off. Howbeit, he in sincerity had compassion of my distressed state, thinking by his speech, and knowing of me, to have set me free from that present danger which he saw me in. Howbeit, contrary to his expectation, I was thereby brought into my extreme danger, and to the hazard of my life, yet there was no remedy but patience, perforce; and I was no sooner brought into prison but I had a great pair of bolts clapped on my legs, and thus I remained in that prison for the space of three weeks, where were also many other prisoners, which were thither committed for sundry crimes and condemned to the galleys. During which time of imprisonment there I found amongst those my prison fellows some that had known me before in Mexico, and truly they had compassion of me, and would spare of their victuals and anything else that they had to do me good, amongst whom there was one of them that told me that he understood by a secret friend of his which often came to the prison to him that I should be shortly sent back again to Mexico by wagon, so soon as the fleet was gone from St. John de Ullua for Spain.

This poor man, my prison fellow, of himself, and without any request made by me, caused his said friend, which came often unto him to the grate of the prison, to bring him wine and victuals, to buy for him two knives which had files in their backs, which files were so well made that they would serve and suffice any prisoner to file off his irons, and of those knives or files he brought one to me, and told me that he had caused it to be made for me, and let me have it at the very price it cost him, which was two pesoes, the value of eight shillings of our money, which knife when I had it I was a joyful man, and conveyed the same into the foot of my boot upon the inside of my left leg, and so within three or four days after that I had thus received my knife I was suddenly called for, and brought before the head justice, which caused those my irons with the round bolt to be stricken off, and sent to a smith in the town, where was a new pair of bolts made ready for me of another fashion, which had a broad iron bar coming between the shackles, and caused my hands to be made fast with a pair of manacles, and so was I presently laid into a wagon all alone, which was there ready to depart, with sundry other waggons to the number of sixty, towards Mexico, and they were all laden with sundry merchandise which came in the fleet out of Spain.

The wagon that I was in was foremost of all the company, and as we travelled, I being alone in the wagon, began to try if I could pluck my hands out of the manacles, and as God would, although it were somewhat painful for me, yet my hands were so slender that I could pull them out and put them in again, and ever as we went when the wagons made most noise and the men busiest, I would be working to file off my bolts, and travelling thus for the space of eight leagues from Vera Cruz we came to an high hill, at the entering up of which (as God would), one of the wheels of the wagon wherein I was brake, so that by that means the other wagons went afore, and the wagon man that had charge of me set an Indian carpenter at work to mend the wheel; and here at this place they baited at an ostrie that a negro woman keeps, and at this place for that the going up of the hill is very steep for the space of two leagues and better, they do always accustom to take the mules of three or four wagons and to place them all together for the drawing up of one wagon, and so to come down again and fetch up others in that order. All which came very well to pass, for as it drew towards night, when most of the waggoners were gone to draw up their wagons in this sort, I being alone, had quickly filed off my bolts, and so espying my time in the dark of the evening before they returned down the hill again, I conveyed myself into the woods there adjoining, carrying my bolts and manacles with me, and a few biscuits and two small cheeses. And being come into the woods I threw my irons into a thick bush, and then covered them with moss and other things, and then shifted for myself as I might all that night. And thus, by the good providence of Almighty God, I was freed from mine irons, all saving the collar that was about my neck, and so got my liberty the second time.

THE SEVENTH CHAPTER.

WHEREIN IS SHOWED HOW I ESCAPED TO GUATEMALA UPON THE SOUTH SEA, AND FROM THENCE TO THE PORT OF CAVALLOS, WHERE I GOT PASSAGE TO GO INTO SPAIN, AND OF OUR ARRIVAL AT THE HAVANA AND OUR COMING TO SPAIN, WHERE I WAS AGAIN LIKE TO HAVE BEEN COMMITTED PRISONER, AND HOW THROUGH THE GREAT MERCY OF GOD I ESCAPED AND CAME HOME IN SAFETY INTO ENGLAND IN FEBRUARY, 1582.

The next morning (daylight being come) I perceived by the sun rising what way to take to escape their hands, for when I fled I took the way into the woods upon the left hand, and having left that way that went to Mexico upon my right hand, I thought to keep my course as the woods and mountains lay still direct south as near as I could; by means whereof I was sure to convey myself far enough from that way which went to Mexico. And as I was thus going in the woods I saw many great fires made to the north not past a league from the mountain where I was, and travelling thus in my boots, with mine iron collar about my neck, and my bread and cheese, the very same forenoon I met with a company of Indians which were hunting of deer for their sustenance, to whom I spake in the Mexican tongue, and told them how that I had of a long time been kept in prison by the cruel Spaniards, and did desire them to help me file off mine iron collar, which they willingly did, rejoicing greatly with me that I was thus escaped out of the Spaniards' hands. Then I desired that I might have one of them to guide out of those desert mountains towards the south, which they also most willingly did, and so they brought me to an Indian town eight leagues distance from thence named Shalapa, where I stayed three days; for that I was somewhat sickly. At which town (with the gold that I had quilted in my doublet) I bought me an horse of one of the Indians, which cost me six pesoes, and so travelling south within the space of two leagues I happened to overtake a Grey Friar, one that I had been familiar withal in Mexico, whom then I knew to be a zealous, good man, and one that did much lament the cruelty used against us by the Inquisitors, and truly he used me very courteously; and I, having confidence in him, did indeed tell him that I was minded to adventure to see if I could get out of the said country if I could find shipping, and did therefore pray him of his aid, direction, and advice herein, which he faithfully did, not only in directing me which was any safest way to travel, but he also of himself kept me company for the space of three days, and ever as we came to the Indians' houses (who used and entertained us well), he gathered among them in money to the value of twenty pesoes, which at my departure from him he freely gave unto me.

So came I to the city of Guatemala upon the South Sea, which is distant from Mexico about 250 leagues, where I stayed six days, for that my horse was weak, and from thence I travelled still south and by east seven days' journey, passing by certain Indian towns until I came to an Indian town distant from Mexico direct south 309 leagues. And here at this town inquiring to go to the port of Cavallos in the north-east sea, it was answered that in travelling thither I should not come to any town in ten or twelve days' journey; so here I hired two Indians to be my guides, and I bought hens and bread to serve us so long time, and took with us things to kindle fire every night because of wild beasts, and to dress our meat; and every night when we rested my Indian guides would make two great fires, between the which we placed ourselves and my horse. And in the night time we should hear the lions roar, with tigers, ounces, and other beasts, and some of them we should see in the night which had eyes shining like fire. And travelling thus for the space of twelve days, we came at last to the port of Cavallos upon the east sea, distant from Guatemala south and by east 200 leagues, and from Mexico 450 or thereabouts. This is a good harbour for ships, and is without either castle or bulwark. I having despatched away my guides, went down to the haven, where I saw certain ships laden chiefly with canary wine, where I spake with one of the masters, who asked me what countryman I was, and I told him that I was born in Granada, and he said that then I was his countryman. I required him that I might pass home with him in his ship, paying for my passage; and he said yea, so that I had a safe conduct or letter testimonial to show that he might incur no danger; for, said he, "it may be that you have killed some man, or be indebted, and you would therefore run away." To that I answered that there was not any such cause.

Well, in the end we grew to a price that for 60 pesoes he would carry me into Spain. A glad man was I at this good hap, and I quickly sold my horse, and made my provision of hens and bread to serve me in my passage; and thus within two days after we set sail, and never stayed until we came to the Havana, which is distant from port de Cavallos by sea 500 leagues, where we found the whole fleet of Spain, which was bound home from the Indies. And here I was hired for a soldier, to serve in the admiral ship of the same fleet, wherein the general himself went.

There landed while I was here four ships out of Spain, being all full of soldiers and ordnance, of which number there were 200 men landed here, and four great brass pieces of ordnance, although the castle were before sufficiently provided; 200 men more were sent to Campechy, and certain ordnance; 200 to Florida with ordnance; and 100 lastly to St. John de Ullua. As for ordnance, there they have sufficient, and of the very same which was ours which we had in the Jesus, and those others which we had planted in the place, where the Viceroy betrayed Master Hawkins, our general, as hath been declared. The sending of those soldiers to every of those posts, and the strengthening of them, was done by commandment from the King of Spain, who wrote also by them to the general of his fleet, giving him in charge so to do, as also directing him what course he should keep in his coming home into Spain, charging him at any hand not to come nigh to the isles of Azores, but to keep his course more to the northward, advertising him withal what number and power of French ships of war and other Don Anthony had at that time at the Tercera and isles aforesaid, which the general of the fleet well considering, and what great store of riches he had to bring home with him into Spain, did in all very dutifully observe and obey; for in truth he had in his said fleet 37 sail of ships, and in every of them there was as good as 30 pipes of silver, one with another, besides great store of gold, cochineal, sugars, hides, and Cana Fistula, with other apothecary drugs. This our general, who was called Don Pedro de Guzman, did providently take order for, for their most strength and defence, if needs should be, to the uttermost of his power, and commanded upon pain of death that neither passenger or soldier should come aboard without his sword and harquebuse, with shot and powder, to the end that they might be the better able to encounter the fleet of Don Anthony if they should hap to meet with them, or any of them. And ever as the weather was fair, this said general would himself go aboard from one ship to another to see that every man had his full provision according to the commandment given.

Yet to speak truly what I think, two good tall ships of war would have made a foul spoil amongst them, for in all this fleet there were not any that were strong and warlike appointed, saving only the admiral and vice-admiral. And again, over and besides the weakness and ill- furnishing of the rest, they were all so deeply laden, that they had not been able (even if they had been charged) to have held out any long fight. Well, thus we set sail, and had a very ill passage home, the weather was so contrary. We kept our course in manner northeast, and brought ourselves to the height of 42 degrees of latitude, to be sure not to meet with Don Anthony his fleet, and were upon our voyage from the 4th of June until the 10th of September, and never saw land till we fell with the Arenas Gordas hard by St. Lucar.

And there was an order taken that none should go on shore until he had a licence; as for me, I was known by one in the ship, who told the master that I was an Englishman, which (as God would) was my good hap to hear; for if I had not heard it, it had cost me my life. Notwithstanding, I would not take any knowledge of it, and seemed to be merry and pleasant that we were all come so well in safety. Presently after, licence came that we should go on shore, and I pressed to be gone with the first; howbeit, the master came unto me and said, "Sirrah, you must go with me to Seville by water." I knew his meaning well enough, and that he meant there to offer me up as a sacrifice to the Holy House. For the ignorant zeal of a number of these superstitious Spaniards is such that they think that they have done God good service when they have brought a Lutheran heretic to the fire to be burnt; for so they do account of us. Well, I perceiving all this, took upon me not to suspect anything, but was still jocund and merry, howbeit I knew it stood me upon to shift for myself. And so waiting my time when the master was in his cabin asleep, I conveyed myself secretly down by the shrouds into the ship boat, and made no stay, but cut the rope wherewithal she was moored, and so by the cable hailed on shore, where I leapt on land, and let the boat go whither it would. Thus by the help of God I escaped that day, and then never stayed at St. Lucar, but went all night by the way which I had seen others take towards Seville. So that the next morning I came to Seville, and sought me out a workmaster, that I might fall to my science, which was weaving of taffaetas, and being entertained I set myself close to my work, and durst not for my life once to stir abroad, for fear of being known, and being thus at my work, within four days after I heard one of my fellows say that he heard there was great inquiry made for an Englishman that came home in the fleet. "What, an heretic Lutheran (quoth I), was it? I would to God I might know him. Surely I would present him to the Holy House." And thus I kept still within doors at my work, and feigned myself not well at ease, and that I would labour as I might to get me new clothes. And continuing thus for the space of three months, I called for my wages, and bought me all things new, different from the apparel that I did wear at sea, and yet durst not be over bold to walk abroad; and after understanding that there were certain English ships at St. Lucar, bound for England, I took a boat and went aboard one of them, and desired the master that I might have passage with him to go into England, and told him secretly that I was one of those which Captain Hawkins did set on shore in the Indies. He very courteously prayed me to have him excused, for he durst not meddle with me, and prayed me therefore to return from whence I came. Which then I perceived with a sorrowful heart, God knoweth, I took my leave of him, not without watery cheeks. And then I went to St. Mary Port, which is three leagues from St. Lucar, where I put myself to be a soldier in the King of Spain's galleys, which were bound for Majorca and coming thither in the end of the Christmas holidays I found there two English ships, the one of London, and the other of the west country, which were ready freighted, and stayed but for a fair wind. To the master of the one which was of the west country went I, and told him that I had been two years in Spain to learn the language, and that I was now desirous to go home and see my friends, for that I lacked maintenance, and so having agreed with him for my passage I took my shipping. And thus, through the providence of Almighty God, after sixteen years' absence, having sustained many and sundry great troubles and miseries, as by this discourse appeareth, I came home to this my native country in England in the year 1582, in the month of February in the ship called the Landret, and arrived at Poole.

MILES PHILLIPS

Books

The following are representative of the books consulted for this publication.

Clinton Black 'Pirates of the West Indies' Cambridge 1989
F.B.C. Bradlee 'Piracy in the West Indies and its Suppression' Essex Institute 1923
Aubrey Burl 'That Great Pyrate' Alun Books 1997
James Burney 'History of the Buccaneers of America' 1816 Aberdeen University Press reprint   1949
Calendar of State Papers, Colonial Series, Eyre and Spottiswoode
Chappell 'History of the Port of Cardiff'
Barry Clifford and Paul Perry 'The Black Ship' Headline 1999
David Cordingley 'Under the Black Flag', Random House 1995
David Cordingley 'Pirates: From the Americas to the Far East' Salamander 1996
Captain A.G. Corse 'Pirates of the Eastern Seas' Frederick Muller
E.A. Cruickshank 'The Life of Sir Henry Morgan' Macmillan of Canada, Toronto 1935
George Francis Dow and John Henry Edmonds 'The Pirates of the New England Coast 1630-1730'
Marine Research Society, Salem Massachusetts 1923
Charles Ellms 'The Pirates' Own Book' Portland 1844
J. Esquemeling 'The History of the Buccaneers' first published in English 1684
Robert Falconer 'Falconer's Marine Dictionary' 1780
Peter Gerhard 'Pirates of the pacific' University of Nebraska 1995
Philip Gosse 'The History of Piracy' Cassell 1932
Philip Gosse 'The Pirate's Who's Who' Burt Franklin 1924
C.H. Haring 'Buccaneers in the West Indies in the 17th Century' Methuen 1910
Captain Charles Johnson (Daniel Defoe) 'A General History of the Pyrates' 1724
Peter Kemp 'The Oxford Companion to Ships and The Sea' Oxford University Press 1979
Peter Kemp and Christopher Lloyd 'Brethren of the Coast' The Windmill Press 1960
James Lydon 'Pirates, privateers and Profits' Boston 1971
G.E. Mainwaring 'Life and Works of Sir Henry Mainwaring' Navy Records Society 1920
David Marley 'Pirates and Privateers of the Americas' ABC-CLIO 1994
Jennifer Marx 'Pirates and Privateers of the Caribbean' Krieger 1992
David Mitchell 'Pirates: An Illustrated History' Dial Press 1976
P. Pringle 'Jolly Roger' Museum Press' 1953
Marcus Rediker 'Between the Devil and the Deep Blue Sea' Cambridge 1987
Stanley Richards 'Black Bart', Christopher Davies, 1966
Jan Rogozinski 'A Brief History of the Caribbean' 1992
W. Adolphe Roberts 'Sir Henry Morgan' Hamish Hamilton 1933
Frank Sherry 'Raiders and Rebels' Henry Morrow 1986
Dava Sobel 'Longitude – the True Story of a Lone Genius Who Solved the Greatest Scientific Mystery
of His Time', 4th Estate paperback edition 1998
Captain William Snelgrave 'A New Voyage to Guinea, and the Slave-Trade' 1744
Spencer 'Annals of South Glamorgan'
L.A.G. Strong 'Dr Quicksilver 1660-1742 - the Life and Times of Dr Thomas Dover' Andrew Melrose
1955
W. Llewelyn Williams Sir Henry Morgan, the Buccaneer, Transactions of the Honourable Society of
Cymmrodorion, Session 1903-1904, published 1905.
Neville Williams 'Captains Outrageous' Weidenfield and Nicholson 1962
Alexander Winston 'No Purchase, No Pay' Eyre and Spottiswoode 1970
George Woodbury 'The Great Days of Piracy' Elek Books 1954
George Wycherley 'Buccaneers of the Pacific' The Bobbs-Merrill Company 1924

REVIEWS OF OTHER PUBLICATIONS FROM WALES BOOKS (GLYNDWR PUBLISHING)

100 GREAT WELSHMEN - T.D. Breverton ISBN 1-903529-034 £18.99, 376 pages illustrated (April 2001)
Welsh Books Council 'Book of the Month'
Review from The Western Mail, May 11th 2001:
The lives of some of Wales' most famous figures are set out in a new book published today. Terry Breverton's new book 100 Great Welshmen celebrates the achievements of 100 men of Welsh blood who have left their mark on history. It contains the names of four American presidents, Hollywood superstars, Christian saints and some of the political and cultural minds who have shaped the modern world. Some, like Dylan Thomas and Owain Glyndwr, immediately spring to mind, but others to make the list include great architects Frank Lloyd Wright and John Nash, and Confederate president Jefferson Davis. Below are just some of the famous names to make the list. The list is in alphabetical order.....
Part of a double-page Review from the Western Mail Magazine, June 1st 2001
'... 100 Great Welshmen is a revealing volume illustrating the great and the good with Welsh connection, either by birth or family ancestry. Admittedly all the usual suspects are included - Richard Burton, Tom Jones, Sir Geraint Evans, Gareth Edwards, Gwynfor Evans, Idris Davies, Aneurin Bevan, Jimmy Wilde and Saunders Lewis. But probably the most fascinating are the ones we either tend to forget are Welsh, or had no prior knowledge of their Celtic connection in the first place. John Adams, the first occupant of the White House; father of the American Revolution Samuel Adams; revolutionary Oliver Cromwell; cinematic pioneer D.W. Griffith; comedian Tommy Cooper, the list goes on and on. From heroes of Waterloo and computer engineers to lethal pirates and gold champions, Breverton has attempted to include them all, and that's no mean feat given our colourful heritage. Hats off to him for the painstaking research involved in every single one, a trademark which is typical of his previous work in "An A-Z of Wales and the Welsh", followed by "The Book of Welsh Saints" and "The Secret Vale of Glamorgan", all printed in Wales....'

Review from Ninnau (US) by Dr Peter Willams
'Now and again a book comes along that answers most, if not all your questions about your Welsh heritage. Who are the Welsh, who are their military heroes, political leaders, writers, poets, kings, princes, saints, historians, explorers, men of industry, famous actors, athletes, and religious leaders? T.D. Breverton, who gave us The Book of Welsh Saints and An A-Z of Wales and the Welsh, has provided the answers in his latest body of knowledge: a single volume with the informative title 100 Great Welshmen. The author includes not only those who have contributed so much to the making of Wales, but also many personalities who made their mark on American history. The single volume reference book gives biographical information on those persons of Welsh descent whom became influential in the political and industrial life of the United States, such as Presidents John Adams, John Quincy Adams, James Monroe, and Thomas Jefferson; the father of the American Revolution Samuel Adams; business tycoon J.P. Morgan, film pioneer D.W.Griffith, explorers John Evans and Meriwether Lewis and so on. The author even includes those terrors of the high seas, Black Bart, the infamous pirate, and Captain Henry Morgan. The amount of research that went into the making of this book is astounding; it seems that the author left no stone unturned in order to ferret out information concerning his subjects. He has produced a veritable gold mine of a book that you can dip into again and again. 100 Great Welshmen will make you proud of your Welsh heritage by reminding you that the little country of Wales has contributed so much to the modern world in so many different areas...'

100 GREAT WELSH WOMEN - T.D. Breverton ISBN 1 903529 042 £16.99 304pp illustrated
WELSH BOOKS COUNCIL BOOK OF THE MONTH (September 2001)
Review from Ninnau (USA), January 2002, by Dr Peter Williams
'perhaps the most prolific Welsh author today is T.D. Breverton, of Glyndwr Publishing, in the Vale of Glamorgan, South Wales. This astonishing worker has recently produced such practical reference books as An A-Z of Wales and the Welsh, The Book of Welsh Saints, The Secret Vale of Glamorgan, and 100 Great Welshmen (Vol. I of Eminent Britons). Now Terry has done it again. His latest book has finally arrived to fulfil

the massive gap in our knowledge of our enormously important, but sadly unheralded contribution of our women, not only to Welsh society and Welsh history, but to Western civilisation itself. Titled, 100 Great Welsh Women (Part II of Eminent Britons), it gives short biographies to those of the fairer sex who deserve to be added to our pantheon of Welsh heroes. Acknowledging that women have so often played subordinate roles in our male-dominant society (and Wales is no exception), Breverton's list of suitable candidates is a purely personal one, but all those included are those who have connections with Wales and who have been an inspiration for all women, everywhere. Included are queens, princesses, writers, mothers of famous men, civil rights activists, politicians, and so on to include women of every imaginable activity and status.

*This most invaluable addition to every bookshelf and library begins with the little-known Saint Almedha (5th-6th century) and ends with Jane Williams (19th century). In between, you can read of such modern notable Welsh women as singers Charlotte Church, Shirley Bassey, and Petula Clark; of world-class athletes such as Tanni Grey-Thompson; of such historical characters as Nell Gwyn, mistress of Charles II, or Saint Helena, the mother of Constantine the Great; of Catherine Zeta Jones, whose recent wedding to Michael Douglas made such a stir; and so on. This book is an **absolute must** for all those who value their Welsh heritage, and for all those who wish to see women accorded their rightful place in history...'*

Review from The Daily Mirror, November 19, 2001 by Jason Lamport

'....Kylie reckons she inherited her singing ability from Maestag-born mum Carol Jones, who emigrated to Australia aged just 10. Kylie has travelled to Wales to visit her gran - who she affectionately calls 'nain' - Welsh for grandmother. Terry's book lists the top women of all time including queens, politicians and stars of stage and screen. Charlotte Church is there for 'flying the Welsh flag' on trips to meet American presidents and the Pope. Butetown superstar Shirley Bassey and Cardiff paralympic gold medallist Tanni Grey-Thomspon also make the book...'

Review from South Wales Echo, November 17, 2001 by Mark Stead

Welsh Girl Power Through The Ages

It's not often you see Charlotte Church and Catrin Glyndwr - daughter of one of Wales' favourite sons, Owain - in the same list. Or Shirley Bassey and Tanni Grey-Thompson rubbing shoulders with Elizabeth Tudor, who ranks among England's greatest monarchs, and Gwenllian. But that's exactly where you'll find them in a new book celebrating Wales' most fascinating females. Author and publisher Terry Breverton, who estimates he has written over a million words in two years - launches his latest work, 100 Great Welsh Women, next week. The result of another extensive trawl through time, it celebrates the achievements of Welsh women through the ages. Terry, from St Athan, lectures at UWIC, but most of his recent spare time has been spent penning a string of books - An A-Z of Wales and the Welsh, The Secret Vale of Glamorgan, The Book of Welsh Saints and 100 Great Welshmen have all hit bookshelves in the last two years. And he hopes his labours of love will help bring the pride back into Welsh history. 'All my books have been about the culture and heritage of Wales, because it is not taught in schools and politicians are not interested in it', he says. 'If we don't know our history, how are we supposed to attract tourists? When I came back here to live five years ago, I couldn't find anything to show my children what being Welsh means, so I decided if nobody else was going to do it, I would do it myself. I find the Welsh attitude to history very disappointing. Nobody seems interested in it, and I believe that's because we have been put down for so long, we believe and have accepted we are second-class citizens. We've even allowed our greatest hero - King Arthur - to be hijacked by the West Country.

Terry believes the tales of Welsh heroes and heroines needs to be told to a wider audience, and hopes his books will recover some lost ground. 'We've had Braveheart - why can't the same thing be done about the lives of Owain Glyndwr and Owain Llawgoch?' he asks. The achievements of the women profiled in Terry's latest book stretch from the first century to the present day. 'Some of the women in the book were born outside Wales but considered themselves Welsh,' Terry explains. 'My criteria were that all of them must have done something for Wales and felt something for Wales. 'When I was researching 100 Great Welshmen, I kept coming across the achievements of these Welsh women, so that's how the book started.'

The journey through time starts with Wales' greatest saints, many of whom were women, and continues through the stories of Elizabeth Tudor, Gwenllian, Boadicea, Petula Clark, Laura Ashley, Shirley Bassey, Mary Quant, Sian Phillips, George Eliot, Elizabeth David, Delia Smith and modern-day icons such as Tanni Grey-Thompson and Catherine Zeta-Jones. 'Tanni is such an interesting character, but she kept telling me she wasn't good enough to be included,' laughs Terry. The book also lifts the lid on some hidden stories - such as the Welsh

woman who was the mother of the first Bishop of Rome, and the Pembrokeshire lady who was the unacknowledged Queen of England.
'I've tried to do them all justice and, to some extent, to set the record straight,' says Terry. 'Wales has a great tradition of female equality dating back well before the laws drawn up in the 10th century. Females have never been considered inferior to males, and Welsh people have always looked up to their mothers as much as their fathers.'
Hard work or not, Terry has no intention of resting on his laurels as far as books are concerned. 'Next up are a Welsh Almanac and a book on Welsh pirates,' he says. 'After all, the world's most successful pirate, Black Bart Roberts, was from Pembrokeshire, the world's most cunning pirate, Hywel Davies, was Welsh, and so was the world's most famous buccaneers, Captain henry Morgan, after whom the rum is named. I have always wanted to find out more about these people, and there should be societies devoted to them, but instead it seems we ignore everything about the past... the book is launched at Oriel Bookshop, Cardiff, with a poetry reading from Ruth Bidgood and music from singer-songwriter and actress Amy Wadge....

THE BOOK OF WELSH SAINTS - T.D. Breverton ISBN 1-903529-018 £24.99 hardback, 606 pages, illustrated (September 2000)
Review from 'Cambria', January 2001:
'Another work from the prolific pen of Terry Breverton who is blazing a trail in producing bodies of knowledge about Welsh heritage and history. The Book of Welsh Saints is **an enormous work of research and will provide a welcome and ready book of reference** to the men and women who in Tad Deiniol's words "created Wales". The much bandied term "The Dark Ages" may well have meant just that east of the Severn, but to us this period is the Age of Saints. And there are hundreds of them - over 900 in fact - monks, scholars, warriors, missionaries. Breverton places Arthur firmly in the context of Welsh history and shows how the seminal folk legends of European romance and literature originate in Wales. We see Wales at the very heart and very root of Western Christian civilisation, a pre-eminent position...
e-mail from Dr Rowan Williams, Archbishop of Canterbury:
...the book is a really extraordinary achievement: a compilation of tradition, topography and literary detective work that can have few rivals. I have enjoyed browsing it enormously, and have picked up all sorts of new lines to follow up...'
Meic Stephens, in 'The Western Mail Magazine', April 7th, 2001
An even more impressive work is Terry Breverton's Book of Welsh Saints, which lists over 900 saints - those holy men who lived as ascetics and hermits in the first centuries after Christ and to whom, so often, miracles were attributed. These men were the first representatives of Rome in Celtic Britain and their names and places of worship still reverberate throughout our history and dot the landscape, reminding ourselves of a civilisation which went into the making of the Welsh landscape. There are informative notes on Saint Cewydd (the Welsh equivalent of St Swithin), Patrick (who became the patron saint of Ireland), and many another saint remembered only because there is a village called Llan, followed by his name. (I am reminded that the awful, corrupted name Llantwit seems to be named after a saint called Twit - surely its time the people of that splendid village rose up and demanded the correct form Illtud). The book was written with one eye on the potential tourist market, because it argues in favour of celebrating the saints' days in villages the length of Wales....'
Review from Ninnau (US) by Dr Peter Williams
'Did you know that Wales had a St Elvis?...According to local tradition, St David was baptised by his cousin St Elvis at a church near Solva, in Pembrokeshire, where St Elvis Parish is now the smallest in Britain. Within the parish is also St Elvis farm, St Elvis Holy Well, St Elvis Cromlech (prehistoric tomb). Off the coast at Solva are St Elvis Rocks. St Elvis is only one of the hundred of Welsh saints of the 5th and 6th century, a time when the light of Christianity shone brightly in Wales when it had been extinguished over all of Europe, a time when England was still pagan. It was a time when Christianity itself was in danger of disappearing, the survival of the Church in Wales creating a bastion from which Ireland was first converted, and from the Irish missionaries, the rest of Britain and Europe.
Over 100 Welsh saints are associated with the leader Arthur, long before the legends had taken hold in France. It was a time when the stories of Arthur and Guinevere, of the Holy Grail, Tristan and Isolde, The Fisher King, the Black Knight, the Green Knight and all of the great and famous knights associated with Camelot and Avalon

came into being, and all originated in Wales. Wales certainly seems to have not only the oldest surviving language in Europe, but also the oldest Christian heritage; for the first millennium, it was accepted by Rome as "the cradle of the Western Church".
The unique historical importance of Wales has for too long been neglected until now...the book lists over 900 saints, gives not only their history but the historical background of each saint, their feast-days and feast Weeks, and the religious events associated with them. The book is a veritable goldmine of information. Its appendices give the derivation of Welsh place-names, the location of Roman sites in Wales, a discussion of the language problem, and even an essay on the state of parliamentary representation in Wales. The book is a must for anyone interested in the history of the Church in Wales, indeed for anyone interested in learning the glorious heritage bequeathed to them from the time when Wales was the only Christian country in the world.'

THE DRAGON ENTERTAINS - 100 Welsh Stars - Alan Roderick ISBN 1-903529-026 £12.99 paperback, illustrated 230 pages (May 2000)
The Dragon Entertains is a reference book with a difference - a highly readable, informative account of the lives of One Hundred Welsh Stars. Within its pages the reader will find 100 concise mini-biographies, word pictures detailing all the relevant, basic facts of the entertainer's career. For a small country, on the western fringe of Europe, a nation of only 3,000,000 people, Wales' contribution to the world of entertainment is immense. Actors and actresses, playwrights and directors, singers and musicians, composers and comedians - Wales has produced them all. And what other nation of comparable size can boast four Oscar winners? The first Welsh film star, the Welsh influence on the James Bond movies, Monty Python, Dr Who, The Goon Show, the Beatles films and the original Angry Young man can all be found in the pages of Alan Roderick's new book. Stars of Broadway and the West End stage, the Silver Screen, television, radio, the worlds of opera and contemporary rock music - The Dragon Entertains has them all. Welsh-speaking and non-Welsh-speaking, North Wales and South Wales - Welsh showbiz life in all its many facets can be found here.
Review by Meic Stephens, The Western Mail Magazine, January 2001
Lastly, another book published by Wales books, The Dragon Entertains (£12.99) by Alan Roderick, a highly-readable reference work listing 100 of the most famous Welsh stars of stage, screen and radio, from The Alarm to the TV comedian, Ronnie Williams. The list is a roll-call of the theatrical talent that Wales has produced over the last century: Ivor Novello, Tommy Cooper, Donald Houston, Donald Peers, Emlyn Williams from among the dead. And Tom Jones, Anthony Hopkins, Bryn Terfel, the Super Furry Animals, Harry Secombe, Kenneth Griffiths, Victor Spinetti and Max Boyce among the gloriously alive and still performing. It also includes fascinating information about the Welsh connections of stars like Glen Ford, Bob Hope, Rolf Harris, Griff Rhys Jones and Petula Clarki.
This is the book to reach for the next time someone tells you that Wales has not nurtured any great talent in the world of entertainment and showbiz.

THE SECRET VALE OF GLAMORGAN - T.D. Breverton ISBN 1-903529-00X £13.99 paperback, illustrated 230 pages (June 2000)
In between what may be the oldest university in Europe, and a cradle of early Christianity, Llanilltud Fawr (Llantwit Major), and another shining monastic light from the Dark Ages, the Welsh *Age of Saints*, lies the village of Sain Tathan. From the introduction of this millennium history, we read:
'We tend to think of where we live as unremarkable, compared to the strangeness of the new. However, the village of St Tathan and the hamlets of Flemingstone, Gileston, Eglwys Brewys and West and East Aberthaw are not only attractive, and set in wonderful countryside, but have a history almost unique in such a small area. We have buzzards, kingfishers and partridge, the Heritage Coast, two deserted villages, four mediaeval churches, three conservation areas, traces of rebellion by the great Welsh heroes Llywelyn Bren and Owain Glyndwr, Roman remains, the great antiquary Iolo Morganwg who reintroduced the Eisteddfod to Wales, mediaeval wells, four sixth century saints, an astronomer consulted by Sir Isaac Newton, a Rebecca Rioter, the remains of a thriving port, wreckers, ghosts, smugglers, West Indies slave-ships, hymn-writers, a thatched 14th century pub and no less than four castles. In the 1980's even a Humpback Whale visited...
Review by Meic Stephens, in 'The Western Mail Magazine', April 7th, 2001

Terry Breverton belongs t that rare breed of Welshmen who stake their livelihood on trying to publish books in which they passionately believe. His imprint Glyndwr Publishing/Wales Books has already made its mark on the Welsh publishing scene by bringing out substantial and handsomely produced books on Welsh subjects, particularly local history. He was born in the Vale of Glamorgan, to which he has returned after many years as a management consultant in Britain and overseas. He is the author of several useful books such as An A-Z of Wales and the Welsh and One Hundred Great Welshmen. What drives him as a publisher is the belief that the Welsh people have been deprived of their own history. He aims to provide the information that will make them proud of their country. If that means he has to lose some money, he thinks it's well worth it. Among his most recent books is The Secret Vale of Glamorgan (Glyndwr, £13.99) which shows a local man's pride in the history and culture of his native patch, combined with a historian's delight in tracing the past and relating it to the present. For anyone born or living in the Vale, this book should be essential reading. There are chapters on Cowbridge, St Athan, Gileston, Aberthaw, Flemingston, and all the places in between, together with a wealth of information about the area's most famous son, the wayward genius Iolo Morganwg.

A RHONDDA BOY - Ivor Howells - ISBN 1-903529 050 £6.99 paperback 144 pages, 33 illustrations (November 2001) A charming evocation of his childhood in Porth, Rhondda, and summer holidays in Ferryside, by the 93 year-old former headmaster of Porth and Tonypandy Secondary Schools, edited and researched by his former colleague Owen Vernon Jones.

AN A-Z OF WALES AND THE WELSH - T.D. Breverton ISBN 0- 715407-341 £14.99 paperback 296 pages April 2000 (available from Christopher Davies Publishing and the Welsh Books Council)
Review from 'Ninnau' (US)
'This A-Z has many surprising as well as predictable entries and is clearly the result of a passionate interest in post-devolution Wales combined with impeccable research... an important addition to the Welsh reference bookshelf'
Review from 'Cambria', January 2001
'Hwyl and Hiraeth, heritage and history, people and places, myths and imagination all come together in Terry Breverton's comprehensive anthology and compendium of Welshness. He starts by asking the question "What is Wales?" and then goes on to show us. The book is, as Breverton says, a sort of "Hitchhiker's Guide to the Galaxy" that is Wales and declares modestly that his background is more modest than academic. We have just what's needed in this unashamedly proud-to-be-Welsh work. Everythin from "Assassination" (Owain Llawgoch) to "Zulu Wars" (Rorke's Drift) is covered with few stones unturned (sadly Tom Ellis, one of the greatest of our political heroes, fails to get a mention). **A massive treasure chest of facts and figures covering thousands of years of history, which no collector of books on Wales can overlook.***'*
Review from the 'South Wales Echo'
'The author wants the world to know what Wales has to offer... alongside the Cool Cymru actors and pop stars, there is a wealth of information on more traditional Welsh culture, history, legend, art, literature and so on...'
Review from New Welsh Review
'This book is great fun....'

GLYN DWR'S WAR - The Campaigns of the Last Prince of Wales - G.J. Brough Isbn 1903529069 illustrated 240 pages £13.99 (May 2002)
Western Mail Books Review July 20th, 2002
NATURAL-BORN LEADER
Dean Powell finds the legacy of Owain Glyndwr lives on in a new history charting the seven years of the patriot's glorious war of independence.
Six centuries have failed to diminish the incredibly powerful emotions encountered by so many Welsh people when confronted with the name of Owain Glyndwr. There is something almost hopelessly romantic about the national hero in his attempt to achieve full and lasting independence for the homeland.
We remain fascinated by his fiercely sustained rebellion, achieved with no standing army, and few resources against possibly the greatest military force in the world at that time.
For more than any other he was the greatest leader in the history of Wales, who succeeded in eliciting spontaneous and passionate loyalty by uniting and leading the Welsh to break the English shackles.

In a fascinating new publication, Cardiff-born Gideon Brough courageously attempts to piece together Owain's outstanding military triumphs. A massive undertaking indeed for a 30-year-old, first-time author, but one which Brough, who himself boasts an impressive military background, has tackled with immense confidence and success.

"Glyn Dwr's War - the Campaigns of the Last Prince of Wales" (Wales Books, £13.99) tells the enthralling story of a rebellion ignited by greed and injustice, and the emergence of the bards' "mab darogan", the son of prophecy, who would reclaim Welsh independence lost in 1282 with the murder of Llywelyn ap Gruffudd.

It is the latest in a series of books published by Terry Breverton, whose ongoing mission is to enhance the image of Wales by ensuring that its inhabitants are aware of its immensely rich historical background - his passion for Wales and Welshness cannot be doubted.

The account examines the turbulent events and pressures that provoked Owain into violence against the kings of England, and its aftermath when laws were changed. No more could an Englishman be convicted in Wales on the evidence of a Welshman, bards were not allowed to have gatherings and the Welsh were barred from holding office under the Crown.

The book chronicles the development of the war between the Welsh and Anglo-Norman crown, demonstrating the sensational military successes and political accomplishments of his dynamic leadership.

For seven glorious years Owain rampages through Wales in a bloody battle of independence, using ordinary workers with equal passion for their homeland in a series of hugely successful surprise attacks. Until then, most uprisings were usually brief and no war had lasted as long, let alone one so enduring and fierce. Though offered a pardon by Henry, he refused to accept it. Owain ap Gruffudd Fychan (and we won't argue whether he was later Glyndwr or Glyn Dwr) was born in 1359, long after the successful invasion of Wales by Edward I. As the years passed, the Marcher Lords laid claim to lands that belonged by right to the Welsh, increasing the hatred for the English oppressors.

When in 1400 the de Gray family quarrelled with Owain he launched his campaign with an attack on de Gray's castle at Ruthin. Stimulated by his heroic deeds, his following multiplied and similar attacks were to follow at Flint, Rhuddlan and Conwy. At Bangor he set fire to the Cathedral because the Bishop supported Henry IV, then besieged the castle at Caernarfon.

At the height of the rebellion his forces captured the castles at Harlech and Aberystwyth. His vision for Wales included establishing local parliaments at Machynlleth, Dolgellau and Harlech, along with universities in the north and south.

As a statesman he sought to build alliances with France, Spain and Scotland, but by 1405 the fortunes were turning. Four years later, and Harlech was reclaimed. His wife was captured and held in the Tower of London, but the elusive Owain was never found. Five full English invasions had failed to defeat him and yet, in 1417 when his rebellion was eventually crushed, Owain refused to surrender, but instead vanished for ever. Not for him the brutal public death of Braveheart, nor a grave to desecrate - only an immortal legacy of hope and freedom.

CAMBRIA MAGAZINE REVIEW - SUMMER 2002

I don't think we can ever have enough books about the Great Liberation War and our greatest hero. When every schoolchild knows the story backwards, the dates of the battles, and the main events and personalities, then, perhaps, I would suggest that it was time to move on to Llywelyn Fawr or Gruffudd ap Cynan or the story of Rebecca, but the Great War is a very good starting-point for gaining a necessary appreciation of our history.

This book will be a welcome adjunct to the study of the great Owain, set out as it is in chronological detail with boxes, footnotes and maps complementary to the text. Mr Brough sets out to do what many historians fail to do, and that is to place the struggle of 1400-1416 within the context of the broader panoply of Welsh history, rather than seeing it as a sort of sideshow of the English imperial pageant or, worse still, as some have attempted to do, a mere element of the feuding squabbles between Anglo-Norman barons.

The Great Liberation War is THE defining moment of our nation's history. Had it not been for Owain Glyndwr and the men and women who stood at his side against over-whelming odds, there would be no Welsh nation today. You will find all the details here.

THE WELSH ALMANAC - T.D. Breverton ISBN 1903529107 320 pages illustrated £16.99
WELSH BOOKS COUNCIL BOOK OF THE MONTH (July 2002)
DEAN POWELL, WESTERN MAIL BOOKS REVIEW, JULY 27TH, 2002-09-21

Terry Breverton's ongoing series of Welsh history books continue to enthuse as my library steadily increases with his work. And the latest, The Welsh Almanac (Glyndwr Publishing, £16.99) is one of the most enjoyable to date. In fact, I'll go so far as to say it's a must for anyone with a drop of Welsh blood in them. Continuing his solo mission to make Wales' proud history more accessible or for that matter readable, in comparison to the huge dusty tomes hidden in darkened libraries, The Welsh Almanac is yet another success.

Filled with fascinating facts and figures, Breverton explains that the rationale behind the publication is two-fold. On the surface it is for welsh people to remember their loved ones' birthdays, anniversaries, important dates and events.

There is also an A-Z section annexed, so that addresses and telephone numbers can be entered. But on the other hand it is to record information about famous Welsh people and events upon each of these days. For each day there is also a quotation, usually from a Welsh source, tying in with people and events of the day.

Hoping that readers will be enthused to find out more about Wales from these entries, the genesis of the book was the author's The Book of Welsh Saints, when Breverton revealed the 900 saints from the Dark Ages that are universally neglected.

As Breverton explained, "We have records of our saints' days, only because their feasts were kept until the 19th century in the places still named after them. Their llannau were sparks of Christianity and learning in a pagan world, but the Welsh contribution to the survival of Christianity has never been properly addressed."

But the saints are just a fraction of his latest publication, with references to colliery explosions and Petula Clark, Freddie Welsh and Kitchener Davies, the Battle of Crecy and rugby triumphs. A tremendous undertaking and a very worthwhile and absolutely fascinating addition to the library of Welsh history.

The Welsh Almanac - Review by Meic Stephens, The Western Mail magazine 28th September 2002
'Although most of the books I read are works of fiction or of the creative imagination, I also enjoy ones that deal with facts and the more ordinary world in which we all live. Terry Breverton's 'The Welsh Almanac' (Wales Books, £16.99) takes the form of a hefty desk diary in which for each day he gives the events that took place on it. Some days are pretty much without incident, but on September 28th, for example, quite a bit happened that merits a note.

On this day in 1400, Henry IV led his army of 13,000 into Wales, slaughtering and pillaging as he went. On this day in 1842 was born W. J. Parry, leader of the North Wales Quarrymen's Union during the Penrhyn Strike and, as it happens, the great-great-great-grandfather of one of my grand-daughters. On the same day in 1898 Thomas Gee, publisher, died ... and so on.

Every day has space for the reader's own notes and a few apt quotations to add interest to the page. So this is a Book of Days in which people can record important dates in their personal histories and see them in the context of Welsh history. It's useful for jotting down birthdays and anniversaries, especially those one tends to forget, and will take its place on the shelf with other works of reference.

THE PATH TO INEXPERIENCE - T. D. Breverton ISBN 1903529077 160pp 2002 illustrated £10.99 (March 2002)

Terry Breverton is known as a tireless recorder of Welsh achievements in many fields. In this poetry collection, he allows us a glimpse of the tumultuous feelings that drive him. A tortured energy rushes through this book. There is bitter anger, a keen sense of injustice, national pride, compassion, fear of loss. The images whirl. He jokes and parodies, he gets drunk on words, and there are quieter moments too. Sometimes he gives us a long "found poem' like his 'inventory' of statistics about the sufferings of the miners of South Wales, where the plainly stated facts are the agonised poem; or his 'final list of endangered species' with their evocative and often musical names. It is good to know that out of this turmoil have come - and are still coming - books so positive in their celebration of Wales, its people, history, religion and arts.' (Ruth Bidgood, the leading Welsh poet) Magnificent, compassionate and moving. 'Chalice' will surely help Aberfan to always stay in our memories.(Derek Smith, Mabon)

DAVID THOMAS - FROM WALES TO PENNSYLVANIA - Dr Peter N. Williams ISBN 1903529085 104 pages illustrated £8.99 (March 2002)
In this completely revised and updated version of his *David Thomas: Man of Iron*, Dr Peter Williams takes us back to the days of mass emigration to the United states. The terrible conditions at home, which sparked the Chartist riots, are described, to put into context the reasons for this difficult transatlantic flight. Through Dr Thomas's correspondence with Wales, Dr Williams shows the Welshman's immense contribution to the industrialisation and economic growth of America.

FORTHCOMING TITLES
Spring 2003 *The Glamorgan Seascape Pathways* ISBN 1903529115 - T.D. Breverton
Spring 2003 *The Princesses of Wales* ISBN 190352914X - Deborah Fisher
Autumn 2003 - *The Castles of Wales Volume I - Glamorgan* ISBN 1903529123 - Lise Hull
Autumn 2003 - *The Journals of Llewellin Penrose - Seaman* ISBN 1903529131 - T.D. Breverton
Spring 2004 - *Another 100 Great Welshmen* - T.D. Breverton
Winter 2004 - *Wales and the Welsh - the New A-Z* - T.D. Breverton
2004 - *Madoc and America- the Evidence*
2004 - *Owain Llawgoch - the History of a Legend*
2004 - *The Quilt of Dreams*
2005 - *True Brits - the History of the British Peoples*

WALES BOOKS AND GLYNDŴR PUBLISHING ARE NON-PROFIT-MAKING ENTERPRISES DEDICATED TO PUBLISHING BOOKS UPON WALES, ITS HERITAGE, CULTURE AND HISTORY. Our (non-subsidised) books are all produced in Wales, and are available via the Welsh Books Council, direct from the publisher, from walesbooks.com or from 'good' book shops. Although it is difficult to get shelf-space for books on Wales and the Welsh, any of our books can be ordered at your local bookshop. Our publications all have a two-fold purpose - to tell the world about Wales and encourage tourism, and to tell the Welsh people what they have never been taught in schools, colleges and universities. The Welsh legacy has been deliberately suppressed for hundreds of years, and publication policy is to open up the truth about their past to the Welsh people. Without culture, a nation cannot exist. Without a knowledge of its culture, a nation will quickly die - there is nothing to hold it together.